LEGISLATIVE HISTORY OF AMERICAN IMMIGRATION POLICY, 1798–1965

Published for
THE BALCH INSTITUTE FOR ETHNIC STUDIES

Legislative History of American Immigration Policy 1798–1965

E. P. HUTCHINSON

upp

University of Pennsylvania Press
Philadelphia

Printed in the United States of America

Library of Congress Cataloging in Publication Data

Hutchinson, Edward Prince, 1906–
Legislative history of American immigration policy, 1798–1965.

Includes bibliographical references and index.
1. Emigration and immigration law--United States.
I. Balch Institute for Ethnic Studies. II. Title.
KF4805, 8 1981 342.73'082 80–54048
ISBN 0–8122–7796–1 AACR1

Second printing, 1986

Contents

Preface

The legislative history was planned during my employment with the Immigration and Naturalization Service (INS) in the early 1940s. Some notes were assembled then, and active collection of material began several years later upon transfer to the University of Pennsylvania. Since that time congressional action on immigration has been followed from session to session of Congress, and search made through the journals of Congress and other documents to trace out the history of earlier legislative action on immigration.

Immigration law is one of our largest and most complex bodies of legislation, perhaps exceeded only by the tax code; and it sets an important element of national policy. The present work is designed to make this area of policy formation more accessible by providing both a reference source and an aid to research on immigration policy development. Inevitably it will be found too detailed for some users, too brief for others. For the former a moderately detailed index is provided. For the latter users there are footnote references to the original sources: that is, to the journals of Congress, committee reports, and the immigration laws themselves. It is hoped, however, that the present work will both facilitate and encourage going to the original sources rather than being used as a substitute, especially since the account of legislative action given here is necessarily abbreviated in the case of major bills. Debate on such bills may occupy Congress for many days, with extensive materials inserted on the record, amendment after amendment proposed and voted on in turn, and the whole taking up scores of pages in the *Congressional Record.* Similarly the provisions of bills and acts in some cases can be stated only briefly. With the emphasis here on policy rather than on the detailed letter of the law, it may be noted only that "certain subversives" are to be excluded or "certain displaced persons" admitted, whereas the bill or act in question defines the excludable or admissible classes and the conditions for such action at great length. There are also some incidental rewards of a sort to the persevering reader of the journals of Congress. The reported debate on hard-fought immigration bills records the complex parliamentary battles that have shaped our immigration policy and, incidentally, includes some of the best as well as the worst of congressional eloquence.

Another condensation in the account given here is that in the case of those bills that did not progress beyond referral to committee, not all bills and their sponsors are individually mentioned. Notes were taken on all bills identifiable as related to immigration, but especially in sessions of Congress that received scores of immigration bills, those bills not acted on are sometimes reported as a group. Thus in the account of the first session of the 69th Congress it is noted that thirty bills were for amendment of the section of the 1924 Act that defined the nonquota classes. Such abbreviation in the reporting of bills and their sponsors was also indicated by the growth of the House practice of introducing duplicate bills and the Senate practice of multiple sponsorship. To take an admittedly extreme example, the so-called administration bill in the 88th Congress, the forerunner of the 1965 Act, was introduced in the form of separate bills by some twenty-nine members of the House, and the single Senate counterpart was sponsored by thirty-five Senators. In this case only the principal sponsors in House and Senate are given. All cosponsors are routinely mentioned, however, if few in number.

Subject headings in the index for the most part follow the pattern of the 1953 edition of the INS *Laws Applicable to Immigration and Nationality*, but with some modification to meet the needs of the general or nontechnically oriented reader. For example, "illegal alien" has been preferred as a collective term for the various categories of aliens present in the United States in violation of the immigration laws, because of the term's currently wider acceptance than the official terminology of "undocumented alien" or "out-of-status alien." Terms found in early legislation but no longer currently used are included in the index, cross-referenced with terms now in usage. Thus the terms "imbecile" and "idiot" in legislation of many years ago are cross-referenced from the current and more inclusive entry, "mental defect." Cross-indexing is also used for the alternative designations of acts, which in general usage may be known variously by date of enactment, title of the act, or some popular name. Thus the Act of June 27, 1952 is officially designated the Immigration and Nationality Act, but is quite commonly referred to as the McCarran-Walter Act. In such case, all alternatives are listed in the index but with page references consolidated under the official or semiofficial title (such as "Immigration Act of 1924"). Otherwise, page references are regularly given under the listing of an act according to its date of enactment.

Regarding bibliography, the principal official sources are listed in a section entitled Bibliographical Notes and References immediately following the concluding chapter. In occasional footnote references the Immigration Commission, established by the 1907 Act and popularly known at the time as the Dillingham Commission, has been referred to as the Immigration Commission of 1911, from the date of its final report to Congress, to distinguish it unmistakably from other congressional inquiries concerning immigration. The congressional document number of the Commission report volume referred to is not uniformly included in the footnote references but can be found in the Bibliographical Notes.

Lastly, in acknowledgment, I am indebted to the Van Pelt and Biddle Law libraries of the University of Pennsylvania for use of their fine collections of the congressional materials that are the principal sources for this work. Particular thanks are due to the University of Pennsylvania Press and to the Balch Institute for Ethnic Studies for support making publication possible. I am also grateful to Charles Price of the Australian National University, Robert Cross, now at the University of Virginia, and Dennis Clark of the Fels Fund for their patient reading of and advice on a long manuscript. And much is due to a succession of faithful research assistants. First of all was Dow Drukker, who over a period of years followed congressional action on immigration, obtained copies of bills and committee reports, and helped trace the history of earlier bills in Congress. Arthur Johnson checked the early chapters of the manuscript against the sources, while Barbara Logue did the same for the later chapters and the biographical notes in the index of names.

I should not close without recording my lasting regard for the people of the Immigration and Naturalization Service as I knew them many years ago; and I may owe to them something of my continuing interest in the work of the Service. First of all was the inspirational Commissioner Earl Harrison; also to be remembered are Henry Hazard, Glen Kendall, Helen Eckerson, Jerre Mangione, Marian Schibsby, Charles Gordon, Edwina Avery, Ernest Rubin, Herman Branse, Elizabeth Hart, and many others who gave their best efforts and loyalty to what has been a sometimes undervalued but always essential national service.

I

Congressional Action

1798–1965

1 Introduction

The immigration law and policy of the United States have been built up by a long series of acts of Congress, from the first and short-lived Act of June 25, 1798 (1 Stat. 570) to the present time.[1] Over this long span of years immigration law has been accumulated, provision after provision adopted by Congress, amendment after amendment added to earlier laws, and new legislation passed until the whole has grown into a complex legal structure for the regulation of immigration.[2] Our national immigration policy as formulated in law is thus the product of long growth and development over a period of more than a century and a half, in an ongoing process that may be expected to continue.

There is another aspect of immigration policy formation to be noted in addition to its long-time development. The immigration bill that becomes a law is the end product and survivor in a legislative process whereby many bills are introduced in Congress but few are enacted.[3] Furthermore, a bill may be partly or entirely rewritten in committee and amended during floor debate in House and Senate, so that an act as passed may differ considerably from the original bill. The enacted bill, therefore, is the product of what may have been a long and involved process of revision, as well as the rare survivor among the many bills that died in committee or otherwise failed of passage. To trace the development of immigration policy, one might examine only the new legislation from each session of Congress, but to do no more than that would be to overlook the greater part of the total legislative effort through which laws and policy are developed. With this in mind, the immediately following chapters of Part I give a chronological account, session by session, of

[1]International treaties, presidential proclamations, and executive orders may also relate to immigration, but they remain within the framework of policy set by law, and are not dealt with here.

[2]Concerning the extent of the accumulated body of immigration law and decisions under that law, see chapter 9, footnotes 1 and 2.

[3]For example, the 86th Congress (1959 and 1960) received 125 or more public bills and resolutions related to refugees, aliens, and immigration, of which 8 were reported out of committee and 3 passed.

congressional action on immigration bills, whether they were eventually passed or not. Part II traces the development over time of certain lines or elements of immigration policy that run through the bills enacted into law.[4]

The Legislative Process

Before proceeding to an account of congressional action on immigration, however, it may be well to review the path followed by a bill through Congress under present procedure.[5] A bill concerning immigration introduced in the House of Representatives is as a rule referred to the House Committee on the Judiciary,[6] which then assigns the bill to its standing Subcommittee on Immigration, Citizenship and International Law (formerly the Subcommittee on Immigration and Nationality). A Senate bill follows a similar path, to the Senate Committee on the Judiciary and then to its Subcommittee on Immigration and Naturalization. Action on the great majority of bills ends with assignment to committee. Unless the committee chooses to act on it, a bill remains dormant throughout the term of a Congress[7] and then expires automatically with the end of the Congress. For a bill to proceed further, it must first be approved by the subcommittee, which may accept the bill as written or may amend or rewrite it. The subcommittee then refers the approved bill back to the full Committee on the Judiciary, which in turn may reject it, accept it as it stands, or amend it. If not rejected within committee, the bill is duly reported back to the House or Senate, as the case may be, accompanied by a committee report that may range from a one-sentence statement that the committee has considered the bill and recommends that it do pass (or, rarely, that it not be passed) to a lengthy document

[4]The emphasis here is more policy-oriented than technically legal. For authoritative guides to current immigration law, see Frank L. Auerbach, *Immigration Laws of the United States.* (Indianapolis: Bobbs-Merrill, 1955 and later editions); Charles Gordon and Harry N. Rosenfield, *Immigration Law and Procedure* (Albany, N.Y.: Banks & Co., 1959 and later editions); and Jack Wasserman, *Immigration Law and Procedure* (Philadelphia: Joint Committee on Continuing Legal Education, 1961 and later editions).

[5]For a more detailed description of the legislative process, see Malcolm E. Jewell and Samuel C. Patterson, *The Legislative Process in the United States* (New York: Random House, 1966); or Charles J. Zinn, *How Our Laws Are Made,* H. Doc. 156, 86th Cong. 1st sess., March 20, 1959.

[6]Exceptions are in such cases as when a bill concerns members of the armed forces, where referral may be to the Committee on the Armed Services, or deals with farm labor and may be referred to the Committee on Agriculture.

[7]An exception is that either house of Congress may call up a bill being held in committee, but this is rarely done.

that gives the text of the bill, a section-by-section analysis of it, supporting statements from other sources, and the committee's reasons for its adoption. Divergent opinion within the committee is sometimes presented in an attached minority report.

A bill reported back to the House or Senate may be passed over (that is, not considered) or, if brought up for consideration, may be accepted or rejected as it stands in the committee draft or debated and amended, with each proposed amendment being voted on. If the bill is passed, it then goes to the other house of Congress, House bills to the Senate and vice versa, where it again goes through the same steps of referral to committee and subcommittee, still subject to rejection or amendment at each step. If amendment has taken place so that the House and Senate have passed differing drafts of a bill,[8] the originating house of Congress may either vote to accept the other's amendments or vote to disagree. In the latter case a conference committee of House and Senate is appointed to arrive at a compromise draft and report it back to both houses. If and when a draft acceptable to both House and Senate is arrived at, the bill is sent to the President, and there faces a final risk of rejection by veto. A two-thirds vote of approval by both House and Senate is required to override a presidential veto.

It should be added that the process of revision or amendment of a law does not end with its enactment. The great majority of bills related to immigration that are introduced in Congress are to amend earlier legislation, in particular the basic immigration act at that time, now the Immigration and Nationality Act of 1952, also known as the McCarran-Walter Act. In the history of federal legislation on immigration only a few basic or comprehensive acts have been passed, in 1882, 1891, 1903, 1907, 1917, and finally 1952. Each has been subjected to repeated amendment after it was passed, with words and phrases struck out, new wording added, sections deleted, and others added from year to year until the act as a whole is superseded by a new comprehensive immigration act. Consequently, immigration law is not static but is continually changing to meet old problems under the law or to adjust to new situations. The fundamental lines of policy controlling immigration, however, are relatively stable; such major changes of policy as the abandonment of the national origins quota system in 1965 occur only at long intervals.

It can be seen that a bill faces a long and tortuous gantlet from its introduction to eventual presidential approval, and it is not surprising

[8]On occasion the Senate receives a House bill, or vice versa, strikes out the entire bill after the enacting clause, and substitutes a different bill of its own, but without change of bill number.

that few progress all the way to final approval. Regardless of whether a bill fails to get out of committee or progresses further toward enactment, however, it is a part of the total congressional thought and action on immigration. Because this total record, and not only the enactments, is to be dealt with in later chapters, the sources and materials that have been used are described more particularly here.

Sources

For the bills not reported out of committee, which are in the great majority, the *Congressional Record* and its predecessors give only the subject classification of the bill, its number and title, the name of its introducer, and the committee to which it is assigned. There is much variation in the way bills are entitled; some titles tell little or nothing of the content of the bill whereas others clearly state the bill's purpose or provisions.[9] In any event, the titles are worth examining for what information they give on the direction of congressional interest at a given time, for negative evidence of what kinds of bills failed to get out of committee, and for evidence of the political and regional sponsorship of certain kinds of legislative proposals.

Some types of bill lend themselves to concise description more readily than do others. Most readily described are bills designed to accomplish a single purpose, such as to postpone the expiration date of a given provision, to grant nonquota status to a certain class of immigrants, and so on. At the other extreme is the so-called omnibus bill that would make a number of changes in immigration law. And from time to time there are major bills that present a whole revised immigration code that may run to hundreds of sections and several hundred pages. Obviously, the titles of the more complex bills cannot be descriptive except in a very broad sense.

Much more useful than the titles of bills not acted on are the full texts of the bills themselves, if copies are available. Unfortunately such copies

[9]The variability of the amount of information given by bill titles is illustrated by the following examples from the 75th Congress, 1st session (1937):

H.R. 11, Arends (Ill.). To raise the American standard of living, to relieve unemployment, to raise additional revenue, to provide for the registration of aliens, and for other purposes.

H.R. 2553, Whelchel (Ga.). For the restriction of immigration.

H.R. 2697, Phillips (Conn.). Concerning the deportation of aliens.

H.R. 3798, Kvale (Minn.). To amend sections 11 and 12 of the Immigration Act of 1924, as amended.

H.R. 8265, Pace (Ga.). To deny admittance to all immigrants, and to deport all aliens.

are not widely distributed or generally preserved. A personal collection of immigration bills for recent Congresses, from the 81st through the 89th (1949–1966), has been used, but for earlier Congresses it has not been feasible to examine more than a few of the thousands that have been introduced.[10]

There is more information on bills that have been reported out of committee. As noted above, the report accompanying these bills may be brief and uninformative. Generally, however, the report presents the committee's reasons for supporting the bill, the text of the bill is often given, committee amendments if any are noted, and there is often a section-by-section analysis of the bill to explain and support its provisions. In such cases the committee's opinion on policy matters is generally quite evident, or at least the majority opinion is if no minority report is attached. Whatever discussion or deliberation there may have been in committee does not appear in the report, and this lack is one of the principal limitations to our knowledge of how policy is formed.[11]

Still more information is provided when a bill is brought to debate and amendment on the floor of the House or Senate. Minor or routine bills may pass with little discussion, it is true, but immigration bills often arouse strong differences of opinion and stir up lengthy debate in Congress, and the process of discussion and voting section by section and amendment by amendment reveals in detail congressional thought on immigration.

Finally, there is the bill that passes one house of Congress and goes to the other, where it may again go through committee and be reported out, debated, and amended. By the time a bill has been dealt with in both House and Senate, it has accumulated a considerable history of legislative action, and the committee reports, together with the account of debate and amendment in the *Congressional Record,* provide extensive material on the development of immigration law and policy.

The materials described above are the sources for the legislative history of American immigration policy presented in the chapters that follow. These materials, to summarize, are the lists of House and Senate bills in the *Congressional Record* and its predecessor publications, the report of congressional debate and action given in the same source, and the separately published House and Senate committee reports on individual

[10]A collection of all congressional bills since the 1850s is maintained in the Library of Congress.

[11]To quote Jewell and Patterson, *Legislative Process,* p. 461, "There are serious gaps in our knowledge about Congress and about the legislative history of bills, because these committee decisions are made in secret." (Open committee sessions were not held until a later date.)

bills. In addition, use has been made of the texts of selected bills not acted on, plus the texts of bills reported out of committee, usually to be found in the committee reports or reproduced in the *Congressional Record,* and enacted bills printed in the *U.S. Statutes at Large* or in one of the various compilations of immigration law. Together these materials provide an extensive record of congressional action on immigration.

Notes on Procedure

Some selection has been exercised in the choice of material to be used in this study. Included are all bills directly concerned with immigration and related matters, such as quotas, preference classes, and excludability. Also included are bills concerning aliens in the United States in matters related to immigration, principally those having to do with deportation, but also occasional bills of interest as indications of attitudes toward immigrants and aliens.[12]

Most bills on nationality, including naturalization, have been excluded in spite of the interrelations between nationality and immigration law, for nationality in itself is too large a subject to be included within the present study. Bills that touch on both immigration and nationality have been included, so far as they relate to immigration. Occasional exceptions to the exclusion of nationality bills are made where there are direct implications for immigration: for example, in the case of the former racial eligibility to citizenship that was a condition of admission for permanent residence. Passing reference is also made at some points to nationality bills that throw light on prevailing attitudes toward aliens.

Some bills relating to immigration deal with procedural and administrative matters within the Service, such as the establishment of border stations or payment of Service officers. Because such bills do not affect immigration policy, they have been omitted if identifiable by title or otherwise. (A title such as "To amend the Immigration Act of 1917," for example, tells little of the contents of the bill unless it specifies what section or sections are to be amended.)

By far the largest group of bills to be eliminated is private immigration bills, which probably far outnumber the public bills on immigration.[13] Introduced for the benefit of a designated alien or aliens, the private bill is designed to adjust immigration status, suspend deporta-

[12]Included here would be such matters as permission for aliens to purchase public lands, eligibility for enlistment in the armed forces, right to purchase and operate a radio station, and eligibility or noneligibility for certain kinds of employment.

[13]See the discussion of the role of private bills in chapter 20.

tion, or otherwise prevent undue hardship to aliens who would suffer from strict application of the immigration and deportation laws. The device of the private bill as a means of aiding hardship cases and giving a degree of flexibility to immigration law represents an element of immigration policy; but the individual bills are not in any sense policy-forming, and therefore are not relevant to the present inquiry.

There is a problem in identifying the private bills, for public and private bills are listed together in the *Congressional Record* without distinction. The private bill can be identified readily if a beneficiary is named in the title, if the text of the bill is available for examination, or if the bill is reported out of committee. Otherwise, identification can be made only by the title. Fortunately, the titles of private bills use the formula, "For the relief of ——" and name the beneficiary or, if there are several, use a collective phrase such as "certain aliens" or "certain Cuban refugees." A bill so entitled is probably, though not invariably, a private bill. An occasional exception is the public bill for the relief of an unspecified class of aliens or immigrants, such as orphans adopted abroad or escapees from Communist countries.

The Organization of the Material

The following account of the development of immigration policy in Congress is divided into two parts that deal with different aspects of the material. Part I describes action on immigration in Congress and deals with Congresses and sessions in chronological order from the 5th Congress of 1797–1799 to the first session of the 89th Congress in 1965. The treatment within each session is not chronological by order in which bills are introduced, reported out, and debated, however, but is by topic dealt with in that session of Congress, such as protection of passengers, visas for displaced persons, and deportation.

For each Congress and session, Part I gives an account of the distribution according to the subject of the bills introduced, in order to show the directions of congressional interest. Of the bills not acted on, only a selected few are separately mentioned to illustrate the different types of proposals or to show the range of ideas for legislation. This selection of only a few examples has become especially necessary with the increased number of bills introduced in Congress in recent decades. More attention is given to the bills that are acted on, the amount of attention depending on the importance of a bill for immigration policy. For major policy-formulating bills, whether or not they were eventually enacted, the legislative history is traced through committee, House or Senate debate, and amendment.

Part II is concerned only with the immigration laws passed by Congress, and it traces the development of the major elements of immigration policy. One chapter describes the requirement, repeated in law after law since 1798, that all immigrants be manifested or listed on arrival, the manifest to include certain items of information about each immigrant. Other chapters trace the development of the criteria for exclusion, numerical limitation by immigration quotas, the introduction of preference classes, and other elements of immigration law and policy.

There is necessarily some overlapping between Parts I and II, but this is not considerable for the two represent different approaches to the material. Cross-references from one part to the other are used to minimize such overlapping as far as possible. And on the positive side, it is believed that each part contributes to the understanding of the other—the history of action in Congress describes the legislative situation out of which the immigration law and policy arose; and the summary of the elements of immigration policy presents the end product of the legislative process in the form of law and policy, whose continuity and development may not have emerged as clearly from the more detailed account of congressional action.

2 First Legislation, 1798–1860

With many other and more urgent matters calling for action, the Congress of the new nation did not at first turn its attention to the interrelated problems of immigration, naturalization, and alien minorities that the preceding colonial governments had faced earlier.[1] A first cautious step that avoided an appearance of intrusion by the federal authority in an area previously under the control of each colony was a resolution in Congress on September 16, 1788 to recommend to the several states that they "pass proper laws for preventing the transportation of convicted malefactors from foreign countries into the United States."[2] Although an expression of national concern, the resolution was also a tacit recognition of state jurisdiction over immigration; almost thirty years was to pass before Congress ventured to legislate on that subject.

It was over naturalization that Congress first exercised authority, for here the need for federal legislation had become evident.[3] The states had adopted various terms for naturalization, and as was pointed out during debate in the House of Representatives, a national rule for naturalization was needed "in order to prevent particular states receiving citizens, and forcing them upon others who would not have received them."[4] By the Act of March 26, 1790 (1 Stat. 103), entitled "An act to establish an uniform rule of naturalization," the residence requirement for naturalization was set at two years.[5] Five years later, feeling that it had set the terms of naturalization too low, Congress passed a new naturalization act, the Act of January 29, 1795 (1 Stat. 414). This repealed the 1790 Act, raised the residence requirement to five years, and required a declaration of intention to seek citizenship at least three years before naturalization.

[1]Concerning the immigration policies of the American colonies, see chapter 10.

[2]*Journals of Congress*, 13:105–6.

[3]And the Constitution, adopted in 1789, specifically gave Congress the power to regulate naturalization in article 1, section 8, clause 4, which stated that "Congress shall have Power . . . to establish an uniform Rule of Naturalization."

[4]Roger Sherman (Conn.), *Annals of Congress*, 1:1110.

[5]For a resumé of debate on the bill, see Roy L. Garis, *Immigration Restriction* (New York: Macmillan, 1928), pp. 28–29.

5th Congress (1797–1799)

Several years later, during the administration of John Adams, a strong antialien sentiment found expression in the 5th Congress (1797–1799). Various reasons for this political phenomenon have been suggested: concern during the unsettled period of the French Revolution and Napoleonic wars in Europe, strained relations with France approaching undeclared war, and distrust of alien minorities. It has been suggested also that partisan politics played a part in the antialien movement in Congress, the Federalists then in power being well aware that their Jeffersonian opponents attracted the support of many immigrants.[6] Whatever the motivations, three significant pieces of antialien legislation were passed in 1798 during the second session of the 5th Congress. These were the Naturalization Act, the Aliens Act, and the Alien Enemy Act.

There was already some intimation of the temper of the 5th Congress in the short first session, from May 15 to July 10, 1797. During debate in the House on July 1, on a revenue-raising measure to impose a stamp tax on various documents, a levy of twenty dollars on naturalization papers was first proposed, which was then reduced to ten dollars, and, when this was rejected, to five dollars. This amendment carried in the House with 56 votes in favor, and the bill as a whole was carried by a vote of 46 to 42.[7] Four days later the measure passed the Senate by the heavier margin of 20 to 7. Meanwhile Representative Brooks of New York had expressed the opinion that the naturalization laws permitted too rapid acquisition of citizenship, and he presented the following resolution in the House:

> Resolved, That a committee be appointed to prepare and report a bill to amend the act establishing an uniform rule of naturalization.

The resolution was tabled without further action.

The attempt to raise the requirements for citizenship was resumed in the second session. In the House on April 17, 1798, Coit of Connecticut asserted the need for change in the naturalization law and proposed a resolution to instruct the Committee for the Protection of Commerce and Defence of the Country to inquire and report whether the nationalization act should be suspended or amended.[8] After discussion, the resolution was unanimously adopted on April 19. The committee reported back on May 1 with a resolution calling for a lengthening of the required period of residence, a registry of all aliens residing in the nation, and a

[6]U.S. Immigration Commission of 1911, Reports, *Immigration Legislation*, vol. 39, S. Doc. 758, 61st Cong., 3rd sess., p. 6.

[7]*Annals of Congress*, 7:421.

[8]Ibid., 8:1427.

law for apprehending or removing enemy alien males aged fourteen and over in time of war.[9] The proposals were debated during the two following days, when it was made known that the committee favored a residence period of at least ten years; from elsewhere it was proposed that citizenship be obtainable only by native birth.[10] In the same spirit, Otis of Massachusetts offered a motion to deny "any office of honor, trust, or profit under the United States" to the alien born not yet a citizen. The committee resolution was adopted by the House with amendment and was referred back to the committee, which reported out a naturalization bill on May 15. This bill was debated in the House on May 21, when a 14-year residence period was moved by Sewall of Massachusetts and carried by the close vote of 41 to 40. After further debate and amendment the bill was passed on May 22 and sent to the Senate.[11] There it was referred to a committee consisting of Senators Bingham, Stockton, and Tazewell, reported out with amendment, accepted as amended by the Senate, on June 11, and by the House to become the Naturalization Act of 1798.[12]

The Aliens Act originated in the Senate with a motion by Hillhouse of Connecticut on April 25, 1798:

> That a committee be appointed to consider whether any, and what, provision ought to be made by law, for removing from the territory of the United States such aliens born, not entitled by the Constitution and laws thereof to the rights of citizenship, as may be dangerous to its peace and safety; and providing for returns to be made of all aliens that shall be landed from any vessel which shall arrive in any of the ports of the United States; and that permits be granted to such as shall be suffered to reside therein; and to report by bill or otherwise.

The motion was adopted the following day with a minor change of wording, and a committee appointed consisting of Senators Livermore of New Hampshire, Sedgwick of Massachusetts, Hillhouse of Connecticut, Laurance of New York, and Read of South Carolina. A bill in conformity with the motion was reported out by the committee on May 4, and was debated at length in the Senate. Section 7 of the bill contained the manifesting requirement called for by the motion, the first of a long series of provi-

[9]Ibid., p. 1566. [10]Ibid., p. 1567.

[11]At that time Bayard (Del.) moved suspension of the naturalization act for a limited time, but this was ruled not in order. Ibid., p. 1784.

[12]The Naturalization Act of June 18, 1798 (1 Stat. 566) supplemented and amended the Act of January 29, 1795 (1 Stat. 414), which had repealed the original Naturalization Act of March 26, 1890 (1 Stat. 103).

sions in American immigration law for the collection of information about arriving aliens,[13] and it was accepted almost unanimously.

Sections 8 and 9 proved more controversial. The Marshall amendment of section 8 read as follows:

> it shall be lawful for the President of the United States, whenever he may deem it necessary for the public safety, to have removed out of the territory thereof any alien who may or shall be imprisoned, under this act, for speaking, writing, or printing, contrary to the provisions thereof, any thing herein to the contrary notwithstanding.

This section was rejected by a vote of 8 to 14.[14] And the Livermore motion to expunge the entire section was also rejected, by a vote of 10 to 13. By the same balance of votes, the Senate then rejected the Mason motion to expunge section 9, which read as follows:

> That it shall be lawful for the President of the United States to send or remove, out of the territory thereof, all such aliens as he shall judge dangerous to the peace and safety of the United States, or shall have reasonable grounds to suspect are concerned in any treasonable or secret machinations against the Government thereof. . . .

Another amendment of the section was also rejected.

In the following days the severity of the bill was softened by a series of amendments to exempt aliens who came with the purpose of becoming citizens and who had made declaration of intention, to declare that nothing in the act should contravene any treaty (passed after a tie vote broken by the Vice President), and to exempt foreign merchants.[15] Recommitted, reported back with amendment, and further amended from the committee draft, the bill was finally passed by the Senate on June 8 by a vote of 16 to 7 and was entitled "An act concerning aliens."

The bill moved more readily through the House. Received from the Senate on June 8, it was debated for several days, during the course of which Gallatin of Pennsylvania argued that the power to remove aliens belongs to the states, not to the federal government. Debate continued, becoming heated at times, but the bill was passed with amendment on June 21, by a vote of 46 to 40. The Senate accepted the House amendments, and with presidential approval the bill became the Aliens Act of June 25, 1798 (1 Stat. 570).

In its final form, the bill was considerably changed and softened in its provisions, was reduced to six sections, and was limited to a term of

[13]For further detail, see chapter 18.

[14]*Annals of Congress,* pp. 565–66.

[15]Ibid., pp. 567, 568, 569.

only two years. The first section gave the President power to order the deportation of "all such aliens as he shall judge dangerous to the peace and safety of the United States, or shall have reasonable grounds to suspect are concerned in any treasonable or secret machinations against the government thereof." The wording was substantially that of section 9 of the original bill. A proviso was attached, however, to provide for a presidential license to permit an accused alien to remain if able to prove to the President's satisfaction that this would present no danger to the United States. The President was also empowered by the proviso to require a bond for good behavior if he saw fit.

Section 2 reinforced the preceding section by empowering the President to cause the arrest of aliens and the deportation of imprisoned aliens if "the public safety requires a speedy removal." The third section contained the manifesting requirement as in the original bill. The two following sections dealt with enforcement and with the right of the alien to his property even if he was deported; and the final section set the term of the bill at two years.

Although of brief duration, the act is of some note in the history of American immigration legislation for its direct antialien character and for its initiation of two lasting elements of policy: deportation and manifesting.

The Alien Enemy Act was initiated by a resolution in the House on May 8 that referred the question of aliens to a select committee on commerce and defense and charged the committee to prepare a bill on the subject. The resolution read in part:

> That provision be made, by law, for the apprehending, securing, or removing, as the case may require, of all aliens, being males, of the age of fourteen years and upwards, who shall continue to reside, or shall arrive within the United States, being natives, citizens, or subjects, of any country between which and the United States there shall exist a state of declared war. . . .

A bill embodying the substance of the resolution was reported to the House on May 18 by Sewall of Massachusetts. Debated and somewhat amended, it passed to a third reading, was recommitted, and reported out again on June 8. After further debate it was passed with an affirmative vote of 52 on June 26. In the Senate it was passed with amendment and then returned to the House, which agreed to the Senate amendments. With presidential approval it became the Alien Enemy Act of July 6, 1798 (1 Stat. 577).

The first of the three sections of the act provided that in case of declared war or invasion the President shall have the power to restrain or remove as he sees fit alien enemy males of fourteen years and upwards, but with due protection of their property rights as stipulated by treaty. Sections 2 and 3 dealt with enforcement by court and marshal.

The third session of the 5th Congress saw no further legislation on immigration, naturalization, or aliens, but these matters were still much in mind, for the acts of the preceding session had stirred up a vigorous reaction. Numerous petitions and memorials to Congress protested against the recent legislation affecting aliens. Included were petitions from several counties in New York and Pennsylvania, one county each in Virginia and New Jersey, and another from natives of Ireland who were resident in the United States.

Congress under Federalist leadership reacted defensively to the protests. A committee was set up to receive the petitions, which previously had been considered by the House sitting as Committee of the Whole.[16] The committee reported back on February 21, 1799, defending the constitutionality of the legislation, and offered three resolutions asserting the inexpediency of repealing the laws in question.[17] Several days later Congress took up the committee's lengthy report and passed a resolution that it was inexpedient to repeal the "Act concerning aliens." Passage of the resolution was by the narrow margin of 52 to 48.[18]

6th Congress (1799–1801)

The Federalists, who had pushed through the antialien legislation in the 5th Congress, continued to hold a House majority in the 6th Congress and were even more firmly in control of the Senate, but signs of declining Federalist strength began to appear. The important states of New York and Pennsylvania sent Republican and antiadministration delegations to the new Congress, and Federalist support was also waning in other states. The Alien and Sedition Acts had proved to be very unpopular, and although President Adams had been reluctant to enforce the acts, Congress received "sundry petitions and remonstrances" asking for repeal of the offending legislation.[19] A committee was appointed to receive the petitions, but no further action was taken. The Alien and Sedition Acts were about to expire, and some Federalist effort was made at extension, but they were finally allowed to lapse. Motions were introduced in the House to consider amendment of the Naturalization Act, but without further action being taken; and the Alien Enemy Act remained undisturbed.

[16]Ibid., 9:2884.
[17]Ibid., p. 2955.
[18]Ibid., p. 3002.
[19]Ibid., 10:257.

7th Congress (1801–1803)

During the years of the 7th Congress external affairs did little to reduce apprehensions of foreign influence. Especially disturbing was Spain's selling of Louisiana to France, followed by the closing of New Orleans to foreign commodities, which created much stir and indignation. The political composition of Congress had changed, however, for Jefferson became President and his Republicans, that is members of the Democratic Republican party, gained a majority in both houses of Congress; and with the change in controlling party came some relaxation of suspicion and severity toward immigrant minorities. The altered viewpoint found eloquent expression in Jefferson's inaugural address on December 8, 1801:

> I cannot omit recommending a revisal of the laws on the subject of naturalization. Considering the ordinary chances of human life, a denial of citizenship, under a residence of fourteen years, is a denial to a great proportion of those who ask it, and controls a policy pursued, from their first settlement, by many of these States, and still believed of consequence to their prosperity. And shall we refuse to the unhappy fugitives from distress that hospitality which the savages of the wilderness extended to our fathers arriving in this land? Shall oppressed humanity find no asylum in this globe?[20]

Petitions against the Naturalization Act continued to come to Congress. On December 15, 1801, that body accepted a resolution that the naturalization laws should be revised and appointed a committee to look into the matter.[21] A bill was duly reported out by the committee, amended and recommitted several times, and finally passed by the House on March 10, 1802 by a vote of 59 to 27. In the Senate the bill went through a similarly lengthy process of repeated amendment in and out of committee until it was finally passed on the third of April. Agreement on the bill was finally reached by the two houses; the residence period for naturalization was reduced to five years, and the bill became the Naturalization Act of April 14, 1802 (2 Stat. 153).

The following years, through the two terms each of Jefferson, Madison, and Monroe, were busy and troublous times for the young nation in both its internal and external affairs—the Louisiana Purchase, expeditions against the Barbary pirates, the Burr conspiracy, abolition of the international slave trade and continuing problems of slavery, rising friction with Britain at sea and the War of 1812, the Seminole War and the annexation of Florida, and much else. Preoccupied with other affairs or

[20] Ibid., 11:16.

[21] Ibid., p. 326.

generally satisfied with the status quo, Congress gave little attention to immigration and its related questions except for occasional reconsideration of the Naturalization Act. Petitions protesting against the terms of that act are noted in the proceedings of the 7th (1801–1803) and 8th (1803–1805) Congresses. In the first session of the latter Congress, an act was passed to supplement the existing naturalization act by exempting aliens who entered the United States between 1798 and 1802 from that part of the act requiring a declaration of intention some years before naturalization.[22] Several years later, in the second session of the 10th Congress (1807–1809), a House committee was appointed to consider further legislation on naturalization. The Committee reported back a bill on December 17, 1808,[23] but the bill did not go further.

12th Congress (1811–1813)

The onset of the War of 1812 drew renewed attention to questions of aliens and their acquisition of citizenship. On June 30, 1812 the House Committee of Foreign Relations of the 12th Congress, first session, introduced a bill to amend the Alien Enemy Act of 1798, to repeal the proviso that allowed alien enemies not actually engaged in hostilities such time as they needed for the recovery, disposal, and removal of their goods, as stipulated by treaty between the United States and the hostile nation. The bill re-enacted the further proviso that when no treaty exists, the time allowed is to be set by the President according to the dictates of humanity.[24] The bill was passed by the House on July 2 and forwarded to the Senate, where it was passed with amendment the next day. The House concurred in the Senate amendment.[25]

Meanwhile, on June 27 a House committee was appointed on motion of Lacock (Pa.) to consider amending the naturalization laws. The committee bill was introduced two days later and amended by the House. The bill was to permit naturalization of alien enemies under certain conditions; but the amendment introduced the proviso that no alien enemy is to be naturalized unless application is made within six months of the passage of the act. Passed by the House as amended on July 2, it was accepted by the Senate two days later but then received a pocket veto by President Madison.

In his message of November 6, 1812 to the second session of the 12th Congress, Madison stated he had not signed the Naturalization Act

[22]Ibid., 13:939, 1195.

[23]Ibid., 19:864.

[24]Ibid., 24:1568.

[25]Ibid., p. 1582.

amendment because he believed it was "liable to abuse by aliens having no real purpose of effectuating a naturalization." He continued,

> I also recommend that provision be now made in favor of aliens entitled to the contemplated benefit, under such regulations as will prevent advantage being taken of it for improper purposes.

On receipt of the above presidential message, the House appointed a select committee to prepare legislation to meet Madison's objections to the earlier bill. On November 18 Lacock (Pa.), who had previously taken the initiative for amendment of the Naturalization Act, reported a new bill on behalf of the committee. The bill, as drafted by the committee, would permit alien enemy residents of the United States to obtain citizenship in spite of war with Britain, provided that the aliens made application and declaration of intention within nine months after passage of the act.[26] The bill was recommitted for amendment, which was rejected by the House; the House then struck out the second section of the bill that deprived of citizenship and its privileges any citizen who departs and remains outside the country for two years or more.[27] In this amended form the bill was passed by the House on February 23, 1813[28] and transmitted to the Senate. Amended in committee and passed by the Senate on the last day of the 12th Congress, March 3, 1813,[29] the bill died without time for the House to act on the Senate amendment.

13th Congress (1813–1815)

In the first session of the 13th Congress, the Senate considered and passed a bill substantially the same as that of the preceding session. Containing the same provision that alien enemies might be admitted to citizenship if they made declaration within nine months after passage of the act, the bill also specified that nothing contained therein should prevent the arrest and removal of an alien enemy if it was called for. Tabled, reconsidered, recommitted, and reported out with amendment in the House, the bill finally passed after the defeat of a further attempt at amendment.[30] Referred back to the Senate for approval of the House amendment, the bill again met with difficulty for, although the Senate approved the House amendment, it added a new amendment of its own. The House then rejected the Senate amendment, the Senate receded

[26]Ibid., 25:153

[27]Ibid., p. 1075.

[28]Ibid., p. 1110.

[29]Ibid., pp. 120–21.

[30]Ibid., 26:469.

from the amendment, and the bill was at last enacted after its tortuous passage through Congress.[31]

15th Congress (1817–1819)

The 14th Congress, the last Congress of Madison's two terms in office, passed without new legislative action touching on immigration. The 15th Congress (1817–1819) ushered in a new administration with the inauguration of Monroe as President; and Congress showed considerable change of composition from the preceding session, with many new faces in the lower house and many prominent members of the old House now in the Senate. The Seminole War was under way, the annexation of Florida was being considered, and other problems demanded attention, but attention was also called to the subject of immigration by a marked rise in the number of alien arrivals from Europe, estimated at as many as a thousand a week.

It is in the period of the 15th Congress that a different direction of concern with respect to immigration becomes evident. Hitherto, to judge by its legislation, Congress had looked at immigration and the alien within our midst with concern tending toward suspicion, some fear of subversion, and doubts about alien conformity with American institutions. And citizenship was treated as a privilege to be granted with reservation. In this respect, Congress may have been more cautious than the country at large; but with the 15th Congress there came indications of a perhaps grudging concern for the health and welfare of the arriving alien.

It was the immigrants themselves who took the initiative in asking Congress for aid. In the preceding session, land had been granted on favorable terms to a group of immigrants from France. Early in the new Congress, on January 6, 1818, certain immigrants from Switzerland petitioned to be granted lands on equally favorable terms.[32] A week later the House Committee on Public Lands reported unfavorably on the petition, and the House accepted the committee recommendation.[33] This rejection did not deter other similar requests, for meanwhile petitions from three Irish emigrant societies came to the House.[34] One of the petitions, from the New York Emigrant Society, prayed that a tract of ten townships in Illinois Territory be put in the hands of trustees to be set aside and sold to Irish emigrants on easier credit terms than now available. Similar petitions came from sundry Irish in Pittsburgh and its vicinity, and from

[31] Ibid., p. 73.
[32] Ibid, 31:566.
[33] Ibid., p. 710.
[34] Ibid., p. 893.

the Hibernian Society of Baltimore. All three petitions were referred to the House Committee on Public Lands, which as before reported unfavorably. The committee report was debated on February 27, at which time the House voted 83 to 71 to accept the committee's adverse recommendation.[35] At about the same time the Senate received similar petitions from the New York Irish Emigrant Association, the Hibernian Society of Baltimore, and the Philadelphia Irish Emigrant Association. No action by the Senate on these petitions is noted.

An eventually more productive step was taken late in the first session of the 15th Congress when McLane (Del.) from the House Committee on Commerce and Manufactures introduced a bill for the regulation of passenger vessels.[36] Carried over to the next session, the bill was taken up in the House on December 16, 1818. Supporters of the bill stated it was for the protection of passengers, to assure sufficient food and greater security on voyages. In urging the need for such legislation, it was reported that during the preceding year 1,000 out of 5,000 persons who had sailed from Antwerp died on the voyage. Other cases were cited of especially high mortality on certain vessels and of survivors who suffered from want of food and water.[37]

The bill was promptly passed by the House, on December 17, and on its transmittal to the Senate was referred to the Committee on Commerce and Manufactures. Amended in the Senate before passage and then reamended in the House, the bill was finally put in a form acceptable to both houses and became the Act of March 2, 1819, entitled "An act regulating passenger-ships and vessels."

The first section of the new act set a limit of two passengers for every five tons of vessel burden,[38] crew excepted, applicable to all vessels conveying passengers to the United States, whether of American or foreign ownership. A second provision applicable only to vessels departing from the United States bound for Europe, required

> well secured under deck, at least sixty gallons of water, one hundred pounds of salted provisions, one gallon of vinegar, and one hundred pounds of wholesome ship bread, for each and every passenger on

[35]Ibid., p. 1053. Representatives speaking in favor of the petitioners were several from New York and others from Kentucky and Pennsylvania. Opposing speakers were from Louisiana, North Carolina, Mississippi, Georgia, and Virginia.

[36]Ibid., p. 1222.

[37]Ibid., 33:414.

[38]This was the contemporary British standard of passenger capacity. For a summary of the British passenger acts from 1809 onward, see U.S. Immigration Commission of 1911, Report, *Immigration Legislation,* 39:342–45.

board such ship or vessel, over and above such other provisions, stores, and live stock, as may be put on board by such master or passenger for their use, or that of the crew of such ship or vessel; and in like proportion for a shorter or longer voyage.

The third requirement set by the act was the delivery of "a list or manifest of all the passengers taken on board," which was to give the name and other specified information about each passenger (section 4). Various penalties were prescribed for violation of each of the requirements.

The accomplishments of the 1819 act were summarized in the report of the Immigration Commission of 1911:

> (1) It protected passengers on ships leaving this country for Europe, but not those leaving Europe for this country, from danger of death by starvation; (2) it restricted somewhat the number of passengers on all vessels, either coming or going; (3) it laid the foundation of the data which have since been collected with regard to immigration into the United States.[39]

The uninterrupted series of immigration data for the United States does in fact start with the 1819 Act. And from the viewpoint of policy the act is notable as the first federal assumption of authority for regulation of the conditions of immigration.[40] Direct federal regulation of immigration itself, however, was not to come until much later.

18th Congress (1823–1825)

The remaining years of Monroe's administration were active and troubled,[41] both in and out of Congress; but with the exception of a new naturalization act they were largely uneventful in relation to immigration. In his message of December 2, 1823 on the opening of the 18th Congress, in what was to be a stormy and contentious session that produced little legislation, Monroe did refer to immigration in the following comment on the returns from the 1820 census:

> At the first epoch, our population did not exceed three millions. By the last census, it amounted to about ten millions, and, what is more

[39]Ibid., p. 342.

[40]The regulations concerned all passengers, of course, but actually set minimum standards for steerage accommodations and thus affected immigrant travel in particular.

[41]These years saw a period of financial distress, with serious trouble for the Bank of the United States, problems related to slavery, the United States effort to support Britain's suppression of the slave trade, the Missouri Compromise, heightened controversy over the tariff, the Florida purchase, the enunciation of the Monroe Doctrine, reapportionment of Congress, and so on.

extraordinary, it is almost altogether native; for the immigration from other countries has been inconsiderable.[42]

Revision of the laws on naturalization was being considered. Early in the new session the House instructed its Committee on the Judiciary to look into the question of revision;[43] and in the first months of 1824 the House received petitions for legislation to facilitate naturalization from alien groups in New York, New Jersey, Louisiana, and Savannah, Georgia. Soon thereafter the House discharged the Committee on the Judiciary from its inquiry into naturalization and consideration of the petitions and appointed a select committee for that purpose.[44]

In the Senate, Holmes of Maine, on behalf of a committee to which a petition on naturalization had been referred, introduced a bill to amend the naturalization act.[45] Moving with delays, the bill was finally passed by the Senate on May 22, and sent immediately to the House, where it was passed without amendment on May 26. Approved at once by President Monroe, it became the Act of May 26, 1824. Its effect was to facilitate somewhat the naturalization of certain aliens who had entered the United States as minors, to set a two-year instead of a three-year interval between declaration of intention and admission to citizenship, and to simplify the validation of certificates of citizenship and of the declaration.

On March 8 the House in a threatening move instructed the Committee on the Judiciary to consider whether employment in departments of the government should be restricted to citizens.[46]

19th Congress (1825–1827) and 20th Congress (1827–1829)

The two Congresses of the John Quincy Adams administration, the 19th and the 20th, took little action related to immigration except for amendment of the naturalization laws. In the earlier of these two Congresses the administration had only a very slender majority in the House, and the Senate was controlled by the opposition. The executive therefore had little influence on Congress, and little was accomplished in the way of new legislation. This political situation did not improve in the 20th Congress, which became increasingly hostile to the President. During the session there was heated controversy on the tariff; but in spite of other issues a

[42]*Annals of Congress,* 41:23. [43]Ibid., p. 812.

[44]Ibid., p. 1627.

[45]Introduced February 4, 1824. Ibid., p. 204. On motion of Senator Holmes the bill was limited to "free white persons."

[46]Ibid., p. 1757.

revision of the naturalization laws was passed by Congress. Late in the first session of the 20th Congress (December 3, 1827 to May 26, 1828), the House took up a bill, reported out of the Committee on the Judiciary, to amend the naturalization laws.[47] The *Register of Debates in Congress* gives incomplete information about action on this bill, but it was passed, signed, and became the Naturalization Act of May 24, 1828 (4 Stat. 310). Repealing parts of previous acts, the law waived the requirement for a declaration of intention preceding naturalization for free white aliens who had resided in the United States between April 14, 1802 and June 18, 1812, conditional on proof of continuous residence since the latter date and certain other requirements.

The two Congresses of Jackson's first term of office, the 21st (1829–1831) and the 22nd (1831–1833) contributed nothing noteworthy to the development of immigration or naturalization policy. The administration was firmly in control of Congress; this control was unharmed by the reapportionment of the 23rd Congress, which gave less weight to the southern and eastern states and more to the newer states to the west.

23rd Congress (1833–1835)

The first session of the 23rd Congress met a distressing problem that was to reappear all too frequently in the years ahead: the problem of refugees. In the House on April 22, 1834 Cambreleng (N.Y.) presented a memorial expressing sympathy for Polish exiles,[48] a cause that especially appealed to American sentiments. On May 9 the Senate took up a bill to grant a township of lands to 235 exiles from Poland. An amendment was moved and accepted to require one settler per 500 acres, in place of the requirement of one for every 300 acres. Other amendments were proposed and rejected, including one to specify that the land be in Missouri. In objection it was stated that the Poles preferred not to be in slave territory.[49] The bill passed the Senate on May 12 by a vote of 25 to 14 and was forwarded to the House;[50] on passage there it became the Act of June 30, 1834 (4 Stat. 743). In final form it was a grant of thirty-six sections of land in Illinois and Michigan, with the proviso that the Polish exiles were to inhabit and cultivate the land and that payment would be at the minimum price, then $1.25 per acre. The Senate had contemplated an outright gift

[47] *Register of Debates in Congress,* 4, pt. 2:2555.
[48] Ibid., 10, pt. 3:3748.
[49] Ibid., pt. 2:1721.
[50] Ibid., pt. 2:1724.

of the land, but the House objected that this would discriminate against native purchasers of public lands.[51]

In the second session of the 23d Congress, on February 14, 1835, the Senate took up the question of revising the previous session's aid to the Polish exiles. The Senate favored adding a requirement of actual habitation on and cultivation of the land; and the House added an amendment requiring a ten-year residence. Poindexter of Mississippi spoke in favor of more generous terms, to allow the Poles to mortgage their land to acquire tools and other necessities. The bill was then tabled, and no further action on it is recorded.

24th Congress (1835–1837)

The final Congress of the Jacksonian period, the 24th Congress came at a time of greater dissension and difficulty. Monetary crisis was approaching, with distress among the poor and riots in protest. New political movements appeared: the Whig party formed in opposition to Jacksonian democracy, abolitionists became active, and the slavery issue became more and more inflammatory. And an influx of immigrants, especially from Ireland, was followed by a rise of ethnic and religious prejudice that found extreme expression in the anti-immigrant and anti-Catholic Native American movement.

The first session of the 24th Congress was presented with an immigration problem new to the federal government but one with which the colonies and individual states had struggled long and unsuccessfully.[52] On May 2, 1836 Senator Davis (Mass.) presented to the Senate a resolution adopted by the Massachusetts legislature:

> Resolved, That it is expedient to instruct our Senators and request our Representatives in Congress to use their endeavors to obtain the passage of a law to prevent the introduction of foreign paupers into this country, and to favor any other measures which Congress may be disposed to adopt to effect this object.[53]

The resolution called forth lengthy and indignant descriptions of the burden of relief of immigrant paupers and of the systematic shipping of

[51]U.S. Congress, Senate, *The Immigration and Naturalization System of the United States*, Report of the Committee on the Judiciary pursuant to S. Res. 137, 81st Cong., 2nd sess., S. Rept. 1515, p. 46.

[52]See the summary of colonial and state attempts to regulate immigration in chapter 10.

[53]*Register of Debates in Congress*, 12, pt. 2:1378.

British poor to the United States. The resolution was referred to the Committee on Commerce, which was to investigate and report. On July 4, 1836, the next to the last day of the session, the Senate passed the following resolution:

> That the Secretary of the Treasury be directed to cause to be collected and laid before the Senate, at its next session, all such facts and information as can be obtained through the custom houses, or from any other sources, respecting the deportation of paupers from Great Britain and other places, ascertaining, as nearly as possible, to what countries such persons are sent, where landed, and what provision, if any, is made for their future support.

On another matter, the House Committee on Public Lands had earlier reported a bill to amend the Act of June 30, 1834 granting land to certain Polish exiles. On consideration by the House, objection was raised and no further action was taken on the bill.[54]

The second session of the 24th Congress opened on December 5, 1836. Two days later the Senate received a report from the Secretary of the Treasury, entitled "Relative to Deportation of Paupers from Great Britain, etc., in obedience to the resolution of the Senate of the 4th of July 1836."[55] Circulars had been sent to consuls and commercial agents in Europe asking for information. Their reports, presented in the document from the Secretary of the Treasury, were from various German cities and states, Rotterdam, and a number of places in the British Isles. For the most part they denied or had no information of the assisted emigration of paupers. The London report cited a poor law amendment act of August 4, 1834 authorizing the poor law commissioners to raise money for emigration passage for the poor, but with the stipulation that emigration must be to a British colony. The stipulation might be waived for those having friends in the United States, but out of 5,141 such cases in the past year, only 191 had gone to the United States.

Another sign of the times was receipt in Congress of a petition from Sullivan County, New York, protesting against Catholic immigration. The petition was referred to the Committee on the Judiciary, after discussion in which it was commented that Congress could not well refuse admission but that it might consider revision of the conditions for naturalization.[56]

The Democratic party elected Van Buren to follow Jackson, but was weakened during his administration by bank failures and severe financial

[54]Ibid., p. 4103.

[55]S. Doc. 5 (24-II).

[56]*Register of Debates in Congress,* 13, pt. 1:533.

crisis. Antialien feeling was running high, probably increased by the hard times, and in Congress it took the form of attacks on pauper immigration and attempts to make naturalization more difficult.

25th Congress (1837–1839)

The brief and early first session of the 25th Congress took up no immigration matters. In the second session Congress received several petitions and memorials for stricter control of immigration and naturalization. One such petition made to the House on January 15, 1838, by the Native American Association of Washington, asked for the repeal of the act providing for the naturalization of aliens, or modification of the act in the best interests of native citizens. Protection by law from any future influx of foreign convicts and paupers was also requested. The petition was referred to the Committee on the Judiciary.[57] On February 19 a parallel resolution was presented in the House by Lincoln of Massachusetts, to instruct the Committee on the Judiciary to consider lengthening the residence period for naturalization and prohibiting the entry of vagrants and paupers. With this was included the further recommendation that masters and owners of vessels bringing in such persons be held liable for their relief if left destitute on landing.[58] At this time several states, notably New York, Maryland, and Massachusetts, had introduced or were soon to introduce head taxes or bonding for protection against relief costs for immigrants.

On March 19 Russell of New York, who was taking an active part in House action on immigration, introduced a resolution directing the Secretary of State to supply certain information on immigration and the arrival of foreign paupers.[59] The following resolution in further pursuit of the subject was introduced by Russell on April 30:

> Resolved, That the President of the United States be requested to communicate to this House copies of all correspondence and communications which have passed between this and any foreign

[57] *Congressional Globe,* 25th Cong., 2nd sess., p. 100.

[58] Ibid., p. 187.

[59] Ibid., p. 242. The resolution was as follows: "That the Secretary of State be directed to report to this House a statement of the number of emigrants from foreign countries, which have arrived within the United States, annually, during the last ten years; the places at which they have arrived; the countries from whence they came; the expense of their transportation hither; by whom defrayed; and their circumstances and condition generally, as far forth as may be in his power; with such other information relating to the introduction into the United States of foreign paupers, by the authority of foreign Governments, as he may possess."

> Government, and the officers and agents thereof, relating to the introduction of foreign paupers into the United States; also, what steps, if any, have been taken to prevent the introduction of such paupers into the United States.[60]

A reply in the form of a message from the President transmitting reports from the Secretary of State and the Secretary of the Treasury was received on May 15. Covering much the same ground as Senate Document 5 of the preceding Congress, the new report contained certain additional material of a nature to stir up congressional suspicions of immigration. The American consul in Jamaica, for example, reported the existence of a law requiring all foreign vessels under 100 tons to take a pauper or other unwanted person on board, for transportation away from the island. For larger vessels the requirement was one such person per 100 tons burden. The rate of payment was set at $10 per person, and the fine for noncompliance was £100 or $300. Included in the report was a copy of a note of protest to the British Secretary for Foreign Affairs, Palmerston, and his reply stating that the act in question would expire on December 31, 1831 and that the Governor of Jamaica was under instructions to accept no similar act in the future. Various consuls in Britain and Germany reported general knowledge or hearsay information, but no official confirmation, that paupers and in some cases criminals were deported or given passage money as a means of getting rid of them.[61]

On July 2, 1838 the House received two bills and an accompanying report from the select committee to which it had referred the various petitions asking for drastic changes in the immigration and naturalization laws.[62] The committee, conducting the first congressional investigation of immigration, had addressed a series of questions to the mayors of the principal coastal cities and, strangely, to the Native American organizations in New York City and Washington, D.C., the questions designed to elicit information on problems created by immigrants. Replies were received from the two nativist organizations and from the mayors of Boston and New York, the two cities where nativist sentiment was especially strong at the time. The replies were incorporated into the committee report,[63] which described the burden of relief for the alien poor and other problems, and indicated the committee's conviction that foreign nations

[60] Ibid., p. 342.

[61] H. Exec. Doc. 370 (25-II).

[62] *Congressional Globe,* 25th Cong., 2nd sess., p. 489. The seven-member committee was made up of two Representatives from Massachusetts (Lincoln, Reed), two from New York (Hoffman, Russell), and one each from Ohio (Hamer), South Carolina (Rhett), and Virginia (Garland). See also S. Doc. 758 (61-III), U. S. Immigration Commission of 1911, Report, *Immigration Legislation*, 39:11.

[63] H. Rept. 1040 (25-II).

were sending their paupers to the United States. Of the two bills, H.R. 873 and H.R. 874, the first concerned the introduction of foreign paupers into the United States, the second was for revision of the naturalization laws. According to a description, the immigration bill

> provided that any master taking on board his vessel, with the intention of transporting to the United States, any alien passenger who was an idiot, lunatic, maniac, or one afflicted with any incurable disease, or anyone convicted of an infamous crime, should be fined $1,000 or be imprisoned for not less than one year nor more than three. It was further provided that the master should forfeit $1,000 for each alien brought in who had not the ability to maintain himself.[64]

The session ended a week later, with no action taken on either bill.

Several additional matters related to immigration had been brought up in the session, but without going on to new legislation. One was a resolution adopted by the Senate on January 25, 1838 for expeditious naturalization of aliens who had served a full term of enlistment in the army;[65] another was a bill passed by the Senate and reported out by the House Committee on the Judiciary, for the better protection of passengers on board "vessels impelled in whole or in part by steam."[66] This is the earliest reference to steam vessels, as far as has been found, in congressional work on the passenger acts.[67]

The third session of the 25th Congress, from December 3, 1838 to March 3, 1839, touched on various topics related to immigration but again without final action being taken. In the Senate the troublesome grant of land to the Polish exiles in 1834 came up again. On January 14, 1839 Senator Young of Illinois gave an unfavorable report on the results of the grant in his state. Now four years later, none of the Poles were residing on the lands, which had pre-empted some eighteen miles of choice riverfront property, to the detriment of other settlers and in conflict with certain lands reserved for Indians. It was Senator Young's contention that the rights of the Poles should be considered lapsed, and he recommended that a report on the subject be referred to the Committee on Public Lands. The Senate agreed to the recommendation.[68]

[64]U.S. Immigration Commission of 1911, *Immigration Legislation,* p. 12 vol 39.

[65]*Congressional Globe,* 25th Cong., 2nd sess., p. 136.

[66]Ibid., p. 313.

[67]Eventually passed as the Act of July 7, 1838 (5 Stat. 304). Many other acts for the regulation of steamships were to follow, but because they refer to passengers in general and not specifically to immigrants, they have not been included here.

[68]*Congressional Globe,* 25th Cong., 3rd sess., p. 120.

Early in February the House was reminded by Russell of New York that in the preceding session it had received a bill to prevent the immigration of foreign paupers, and Russell attempted unsuccessfully to have the bill made the special order of business and acted on.[69] Several days later the House received a petition from several thousand citizens of Louisiana, for repeal of the naturalization acts and for protection from "the indiscriminate influx of foreign emigrants." The petition was ordered printed and referred to the Committee of the Whole on the state of the Union.[70]

And finally, near the end of the session and of the 25th Congress, Senator Ruggles (Me.) reported a bill from the Committee on Commerce to provide for the better security of passengers on board vessels propelled in whole or in part by steam,[71] the second such bill to be introduced; but it died with the end of the session.

26th Congress (1839–1841)

The only action relating to immigration in the first session of the 26th Congress was to take up the steamship bill reintroduced by the persistent Senator Ruggles. It did not deal specifically with immigration, but it did have implications for immigration, because its principal provision was to repeal the limitation of two passengers per five tons of vessel in the case of steam vessels running to certain ports.

In the second session of the 26th Congress a House bill was introduced by Hand of New York to establish a new rule of naturalization and to repeal all prior acts. The bill was referred to committee and then brought up but not acted on.

27th Congress (1841–1843) and 28th Congress (1843–1845)

The early first session of the 27th Congress received its opening message from Tyler, who had succeeded to the presidency after Harrison's few weeks in office. In dissent from the antialien position of the Native American movement, President Tyler may have represented majority opinion when, after referring to the vast resources of unoccupied or underpopulated land, he continued;

[69]Ibid., p. 168. Russell was, of course, one of the cosponsors, if not a coauthor, of the bill.

[70]Ibid., p. 178.

[71]Ibid., p. 216.

> We hold out to the peoples of other countries an invitation to come and settle among us as members of our rapidly growing family.

No action of significance for immigration was taken during the three sessions of the 27th Congress.

Again on the opening of the 28th Congress, on December 5, 1843, President Tyler's message contained a favorable reference to the immigrant. There he spoke of the tide of migration into the new states and territories, made up not only of the native born but also of

> emigrants from all parts of the civilized world, who come among us to partake of the blessings of our free institutions, and to aid by their labor to swell the current of our wealth and power.[72]

The latter part of the first session of the 28th Congress was marked by a wave of memorials and petitions for revision of the naturalization laws, all received between the end of May and the middle of June 1844. And nearly all were from Philadelphia, then a center of nativist sentiment and the site of violent anti-Catholic rioting. The petitions followed a uniform pattern of deploring the facility of naturalization and urging that the residence requirement be increased to twenty-one years. The petitions evidently did not accord with congressional thinking on the subject, for Senators Buchanan and Sturgeon of Pennsylvania and others who transmitted the petitions took care to express their personal disapproval. One or another member of Congress was disposed to move for amendment of the naturalization laws, but no further action was taken during the session.

The second session of the 28th Congress was opened on December 3, 1844, with a message from President Tyler, in which he reemphasized his conviction that immigration was in the national interest:

> In view of the vast wilderness yet to be reclaimed, we may well invite the lover of freedom, of every land, to take up his abode among us.

Congressional attention to matters related to immigration was concentrated on two problems, the immigration of undesirables, such as paupers and convicts, and revision of the naturalization laws with a new emphasis on the elimination of certain abuses.

Several more Pennsylvania petitions for change of the naturalization laws were presented to the House and Senate early in the second session.[73] On December 16, 1844 Johnson of Louisiana presented the following resolution to the Senate:

[72]Ibid., 28th Cong., 1st sess., p. 9.
[73]Ibid., 28th Cong., 2nd sess., pp. 18, 37.

> That the Committee of the Judiciary be instructed to inquire into the expediency of modifying the naturalization laws of the United States so as to extend the time allowed to enable foreigners to become citizens; to require greater guards against frauds in the steps taken in procuring naturalization papers; and to prevent, as far as practicable, fraud and violence at elections, and to prohibit the introduction of foreign convicts into the United States.[74]

The resolution was discussed at some length in the Senate, concern was expressed about naturalization frauds and illegal voting by aliens, and the resolution was adopted. This action was reinforced on December 18, when the Senate adopted the Barrow (La.) resolution with the following further instructions for the same committee:

> That the Judiciary Committee be instructed to inquire whether naturalization papers have been granted to foreigners by any federal or state courts, in violation of the provisions of the laws of Congress . . . [and]
>
> That the said Committee be instructed to inquire into the expediency of a law empowering the district courts of the United States to cancel and declare null all naturalization papers which may be found, upon judicial investigation, to have been granted in violation or fraud of the laws of Congress.[75]

Several days later, Morris of Pennsylvania offered in the House a resolution that proposed a means of controlling naturalization abuses:

> That the Committee on the Judiciary be instructed to inquire into the expediency of amending the naturalization laws, so that the name of every emigrant [meaning emigrant from abroad to the United States] shall be registered at the custom-house, a certificate of which registration shall be indispensable proof of the term of residence necessary to naturalization; and also further to amend the law, so that the right of suffrage shall not be granted until two years after naturalization; and to inquire what other amendments are necessary to the naturalization laws for the prevention of the frauds now practiced upon them; and for the preservation of the purity of the elective franchise.[76]

In the following month the House evidenced some impatience and brusquely refused leave to introduce a bill on naturalization, but received such a bill on the last day of January 1845 and advanced it to its second reading.[77]

Meanwhile the Senate made progress on a naturalization bill. On

[74]Ibid., p. 32.

[75]Ibid., p. 43.

[76]Ibid., p. 64.

[77]Ibid., pp. 150, 224.

January 27, 1845 Senator Berrien (Ga.) on behalf of the Committee on the Judiciary introduced a bill to amend the naturalization laws and pointed out that the bill did not alter the residence requirement from the prevailing five years, with one year in the state of residence.[78] The bill, S. 99, proposed a new means of checking naturalization frauds, the procedure proposed by Morris in the House a month earlier. This was contained in the first section of the bill, which reads in part as follows:

> Sec. 1. That it shall be the duty of the collectors of customs throughout the United States to receive the reports of aliens arriving in the United States, in the manner hereinafter prescribed, and for that purpose to provide and have ready a book of record, wherein they shall, on the application of any alien, being a free white person, cause a registry to be made of the name, age, personal description, including height, complexion, color of the hair and eyes, and figure, whether stout or slender, birthplace, former occupation, residence and allegiance, place of emigration from a foreign country, and intended place of residence in the United States, and the time and place of arrival and vessel in which he or she came to the United States, of the said alien, and of the members of his or her family.[79]

It was provided further in the bill that the alien was to be given a certificate of registry, that his declaration of intention could not be made until at least three years after the date of registry, and that a further period of at least two years must elapse before naturalization could take place.

Congressional attention also turned toward the problem of checking the immigration of certain classes of aliens regarded as undesirable. Early in the second session and on the initiative of Senator Johnson (La.), the following resolution of inquiry was adopted:

> That the Secretary of State be directed to communicate to the Senate such information as may be in possession of the Department of State, as to the practice of foreign governments in transporting their criminals and paupers into the United States; and that he also communicate copies of such instructions, if any, as may have been given by the government of the United States to its consuls and other agents in foreign governments upon this subject, and copies of such reports, if any, as may have been received from such consuls and agents in relation thereto.[80]

Several days later Senator Berrien (Ga.) offered another resolution of similar purpose, also addressed to the Secretary of State.[81] On January

[78] Ibid., p. 195.

[79] S. Doc. 173 (28-II), March 3, 1845.

[80] *Congressional Globe*, p. 48.

[81] Ibid., p. 62.

16, 1845 the Secretary of State replied that he had no additional information beyond that submitted earlier in House Document 350 of the 25th Congress, 2nd session.[82]

In the House, meanwhile, a resolution by Fish of New York was adopted, directing the Committee on the Judiciary

> to inquire and report to the House, whether any, and if any what further legislation is necessary to prevent the introduction into this country of foreign paupers or criminals.[83]

Finally, on the last day of the session and of the 28th Congress, the Committee on the Judiciary presented a lengthy report on the problems of immigrant paupers and criminals as revealed by committee hearings in New York, Philadelphia, Baltimore, and New Orleans.[84] The testimony so obtained was incorporated into the report and gave strong evidence of the seriousness of the problem.

29th Congress (1845–1847)

Other more pressing issues[85] demanded congressional attention, but the 29th Congress found time to deal with nativist efforts to alter the naturalization laws and also to undertake new passenger legislation. On December 17, 1845, soon after the opening of the session, the House received a resolution from the Massachusetts legislature. The resolution asserted the need for an immediate review of the naturalization laws, and continued that

> while a liberal and just policy shall be adopted towards such foreigners as are or may come among us, the rights and privileges of our countrymen shall be kept inviolate, and the ballot-box permanently guarded against every improper influence.[86]

The resolution stirred up a lengthy discussion in the House, which continued on through a second day, was interrupted for a time, and then resumed for two more days at the end of the month.[87] Adding fuel to the verbal exchange was the extension of the discussion to include comment on the Native American party, members of which were present in the

[82]Ibid., p. 144.

[83]Ibid., p. 209.

[84]S. Doc. 173 (28-II).

[85]The term of the 29th Congress saw the annexation of Texas, the consequent outbreak of war with Mexico, a dispute with Britain over the Oregon boundary, and continued and growing tension over the slavery issue.

[86]*Congressional Globe*, 29th Cong., 1st sess., p. 67.

[87]Ibid., pp. 67, 77, 105, 113.

House. The Massachusetts resolution was finally referred to the Committee on the Judiciary, which reported back on February 10, 1846:

> That no alteration of the naturalization laws is necessary for the preservation of the rights, interests, and morals of the people, or from the guarding of the ballot-box against every improper influence.[88]

This firm rejection ended discussion of the naturalization question for the time.

The second session saw a revival of concern for the protection of passengers; and while immigrants as such were not specifically singled out, it was well understood that the great majority of passengers from Europe were immigrants. On February 1, 1847 Rathbun (N.Y.), on behalf of the Committee on the Judiciary, reported out a bill to regulate the carrying of passengers in merchant vessels. Reciting the evils of overcrowding on shipboard and the diseased condition of immigrants arriving in New York, he explained that the purpose of the bill was to ensure healthful conditions of travel.[89] This purpose was especially appropriate at the time, for this was the period of the potato famine in Ireland and the wave of famine victims coming into the United States. Strong opposition was voiced by Levin (Pa.), who believed the bill was a plot to facilitate the importation of voters from abroad in order to weaken the Native American party. He moved to retitle the bill, "A bill to afford additional facilities to the paupers and criminals of Europe to emigrate to the United States," and the *Congressional Globe* report of the debate notes tersely that he spoke at length —in vain, also, for the House proceeded to pass the bill the same day without further delay. The bill was reported out promptly with amendment by the Senate Committee on Commerce, which pointed out in its report on the bill that the 1819 Act was not proving to be effective in protecting the health of passengers. In the past three months there had been 200 deaths among passengers on vessels coming to New York, and many others arrived in such poor condition that they had to be hospitalized at once. A weakness of the 1819 Act's limitation of the number of passengers on the basis of tonnage was that it did not prevent the master from filling up the vessel with cargo and leaving too little space for the passengers. The House draft of the bill required ten square feet of clear deck space per passenger. The Senate committee proposed raising this to fourteen.[90] Another committee revision concerned children. The House

[88]Ibid., p. 353.

[89]Ibid., 29th Cong., 2nd sess., p. 304.

[90]Twenty square feet if the vessel is to pass within the tropics, thirty feet of orlop deck space.

bill would count two children under fourteen years as the equivalent of one passenger in the allowance of space; the Senate committee reduced the age to eight years and under. The committee also had considered requiring a physician on board vessels with a certain number of passengers, but finally decided against the requirement.[91]

The Senate accepted the committee amendments and passed the bill on February 18, 1847. On the same day a petition from the Irish Emigrant Society of New York was read in support of the provisions of the bill. The House accepted the Senate revisions, and the bill became the Act of February 22, 1847 (9 Stat. 127).

On the following day Senator Davis of Massachusetts introduced a bill to amend the just-adopted act. This bill was passed on the same day by the Senate, amended, and passed in the House, and the amendment was accepted by the Senate. As the Act of March 2, 1847, the new act repealed section 4 of the February 22 Act, which provided that two children eight years of age and under should be counted as one passenger in the allowance of space.[92]

One other action related to immigration in the second session of the 29th Congress was the introduction by Seaman of New York of a House bill to prevent the importation of paupers and criminals. It was referred to the Committee on the Judiciary and went no further.

30th Congress (1847–1849)

Immigration remained a minor issue in relation to other problems in the 30th Congress,[93] but there was continuing attention to regulation of the conditions of passenger travel. At least four bills of that nature were introduced in the House.[94] First to be passed was the Act of January 31, 1848 (9 Stat. 210) to exempt "Vessels employed by the American Colonization Society in transporting Colored Emigrants from the United States to the Coast of Africa" from the limiting provisions of the passenger acts of February 22 and March 2, 1847.

On March 6 the House received a bill from its Committee on Commerce to provide for the better ventilation of passenger vessels.[95] Passed

[91] Ibid., p. 446.

[92] Ibid., pp. 479, 503, 527.

[93] In this second Congress of Polk's presidency, Congress was especially occupied on other than routine business by the ending of the Mexican War and by the ominously rising slavery issue. The composition of the House was considerably changed by the recent elections; among its new members was Abraham Lincoln, a Represntative from Illinois belonging to the Whig minority.

[94] *Congressional Globe*, 30th Cong., 1st sess., pp. 237, 264, 398, 433.

[95] Ibid., p. 433.

by the House, the bill went to the Senate, where it was amended and passed, and became the Act of May 17, 1848 (9 Stat. 220). A lengthy act in ten sections, it applied to all vessels with capacity for fifty or more passengers other than cabin passengers and employed in transporting such passengers between Europe and the United States. Besides ventilation standards, detailed standards for cooking facilities, food and water supplies, and sanitation were set by the act.

In the second session of the 30th Congress, Ashmun (Mass.) offered a resolution for the taking of security that certain arriving passengers would not become public charges,[96] but the House would not accept it. And on the last day of the Congress, March 3, 1849, a bill was hastily passed by both houses to amend the passenger acts. This Act of March 3, 1849 (9 Stat. 399) extended the application of the previous passenger acts to the Pacific, simplified the food requirements to the general formula of "a sufficient supply of good and wholesome food," and eliminated the higher space requirement for vessels passing through or into the tropics.

31st Congress (1849–1851)

Events during the term of the 31st Congress in part drew attention to the question of immigration, and in part raised other and more acute problems. Immigrants were arriving in unprecedented numbers, and the character of the immigration was such as to inflame nativist and anti-Catholic prejudices. It was at this time that a new nativist movement arose, the so-called Know Nothing movement, which drew support from the earlier patriotic society, the Order of United Americans. It was in this same period, however, that gold was discovered in California, to give a westward impulse to population movement and popular attention; and the slavery issue increasingly submerged all other issues in and out of Congress. Secessionist sentiment was beginning to grow in the South, party feeling ran high in a closely divided Congress, and a sectional division in Congress became more and more apparent.

Various proposals for new immigration legislation were made, but in the conflicting currents in Congress they received too little support to lead to changes in immigration or naturalization policy. Early in the first session Levin of Pennsylvania, who had made clear his nativist feelings

[96]Ibid., 30th Cong., 2nd sess., p. 483. The wording of the resolution was: "That the Committee on the Judiciary inquire into the expediency of providing a law for taking of proper security, on the arrival of alien passengers in the United States, who are diseased, impotent, or paupers, or likely to become paupers, that such alien passengers shall not become a public charge."

several years earlier, introduced in the House "A bill for the protection of the ballot-box by an extension of the naturalization law to twenty-one years and capitation tax."[97] The head tax on immigrants and bonding procedures in several states (for example, a New York act of 1829 and a Massachusetts act of 1837), had been declared unconstitutional the year before, in 1849. The Ashmun bill of the preceding session and the Levin bill can be regarded as attempts to replace with federal legislation some of the measures formerly imposed by the states. Of somewhat similar intent and presumably broader support was a bill reported out by the House Committee on the Judiciary on March 28, 1850 to impose a tax on alien passengers, the stated intention being to use the proceeds for eleemosynary purposes.[98]

Several other bills related in one way or another to immigration were reported out of committee during the session but did not go on to final action. The House Committee on the Judiciary reported out a bill to amend the naturalization laws.[99] The Senate and House Committees on Commerce considered and reported out several bills for the better protection of passengers on steam vessels.

There is still less to be reported for the second session of the 31st Congress, from December 2, 1850 to March 3, 1851. The House refused to consider an amendment to the naturalization laws, and the Senate took up a bill for the protection of passengers on steam vessels but without further action.[100]

32nd Congress (1851–1853) and 33rd Congress (1853–1855)

Several events during the term of the 32nd Congress were of eventual or immediate influence on immigration legislation. Most significant in the long run was an influx of Chinese immigrants into California in 1852, but the legislative reaction to this movement was not to come until later. A sequence of steamship disasters called for additional regulation of this new technology. Bills for the amendment of the passenger acts, including the one dealing with ventilation, and another for the protection of passengers on steam vessels appeared in both House and Senate,[101] but revision of the passenger acts was to wait until the next Congress.

Congressional attention to immigration in the first session of the

[97]Ibid., 31st Cong., 1st sess., p. 219. [98]Ibid., p. 612.

[99]Ibid., p. 345.

[100]Ibid., 31st Cong., 2nd sess., pp. 24, 26, 547.

[101]Ibid., 32nd Cong., 1st sess., pp. 121, 666, 1755, 1813, 2425.

33rd Congress was largely directed toward the health of the immigrants. At the opening of Congress Senator Hamilton Fish (N.Y.) presented a resolution calling for the appointment of a select committee

> to consider the causes and the extent of the sickness and mortality prevailing on board of emigrant ships on the voyage to this country; and whether any, and what, further legislation is needed for the better protection of the health and lives of passengers on board of such vessels.[102]

The resolution was adopted by the Senate and the select committee was appointed, with Fish as a member. In early February the House received a joint resolution of the New York legislature concerning the security of emigrant passengers, and recommending amendment of existing laws.[103] Several months later, on May 4, 1854, the Senate received a message from President Pierce urging the need for legislation such as was contemplated in the Fish resolution.[104] Several days before the end of the session, Senator Fish submitted a report on behalf of the select committee, Senate Report 386, to accompany the committee bill S. 489.[105] The report was based on answers to a series of questions sent by the committee to doctors, merchants, and others acquainted with health problems of the arriving immigrants. The principal or most serious diseases, according to this information, were typhus or ship fever, cholera, and smallpox.

The bill for better protection of life and health on passenger vessels was presented to the Senate in the second session, on January 19, 1855, and then referred to the Committee on Commerce. That committee promptly asked that the health bill be withdrawn and in its place offered a bill "to regulate the carriage of passengers in steamships and other vessels," a conventional passenger act dealing with the number of passengers allowable and their accommodation.[106] Steamship bills meanwhile were being considered in the House, with a resolution of support from ship owners and others.[107] The outcome of this activity was the Act of March 3, 1855 (10 Stat. 715), a long act in nineteen sections that repealed the preceding passenger acts and combined their provisions in a codified form.[108]

[102]Ibid., 33rd Cong., 1st sess., p. 1. [103]Ibid., p. 326.

[104]Ibid., p. 1082. [105]Ibid., p. 2077.

[106]Ibid., 33rd Cong., 2nd sess., pp. 319, 696, 741.

[107]Ibid., pp. 21, 814, 904.

[108]The act set the passenger allowance at one for every two tons of vessel, children under one year excepted and two children between one and eight years counted as one passenger; deck space per passenger was prescribed according to what deck and the amount of head room; and other specifications covered the construction of berths, hospital facilities, ventilation, cooking equipment, food supplies in considerable detail ("ten pounds of salt

The second session also saw bills for amendment of the naturalization acts introduced in both House and Senate.[109] The ensuing Act of February 10, 1855 gave derivative citizenship to foreign-born children and wives of American citizens.

The House considered several bills for the regulation of the carriage of passengers on steam vessels. Principal attention, however, as far as immigration was concerned, was given to the immigration of paupers and others regarded as undesirable. The House Committee on Commerce had received a resolution asking for an inquiry into the expediency of legislation to prevent the immigration of blind, insane, or disabled persons; and on January 2, 1855 the committee reported out a bill entitled "To prevent the introduction into the United States of foreign criminals, paupers, idiots, lunatics, and insane, and blind persons."[110]

On January 25 Senator Cooper (Pa.) offered a resolution requesting the Secretaries of State and Treasury to furnish whatever information they had on the transportation of foreign convicts and paupers into the United States; the resolution also instructed the Committee on the Judiciary to consider what laws were needed to prevent such immigration. The ensuing debate included a long speech by Cooper in support of his resolution, and speakers alleged that there was a European practice of sending outcasts to the United States.[111]

In the Senate a few weeks later Jones of Tennessee submitted a resolution that questioned the authority of the federal government over immigration:

> That Congress has no power to pass any law regulating or controlling immigration into any of the States or Territories of this Union. But that the power to prescribe such rules and regulations touching this subject as may be deemed necessary to the safety and happiness of the people, belongs to the States respectively, or the people: And that each State may determine for itself the evils resulting from the great influx of criminal and pauper immigration to this country, and apply such remedy as their wisdom may suggest, or their safety demand.[112]

---

beef, free of bones" per passenger), sanitation, and much else. The manifesting requirement was retained from the 1819 act. And various penalties were set for violations, plus payment to the collector of customs of "the sum of ten dollars for each and every passenger above the age of eight years who shall have died on the voyage, by natural disease" (section 14). And section 16 made every vessel of the American Colonization Society and other societies sending colored emigrants to Africa subject to all the requirements of the act.

[109] Ibid., pp. 24, 447.

[110] Ibid., pp. 158, 166–67.

[111] Ibid., p. 389.

[112] Ibid., p. 783.

This was clearly a declaration of state rights, with reference to the special case of immigration; and state rights feeling was running high at the time. The Senate nevertheless passed the bill to prevent the immigration of foreign criminals, paupers, and others, and it was referred when transmitted to the House to the Committee on Commerce. On the last day of the second session and of the 33rd Congress, Wentworth (Mass.) of the Committee on Commerce succeeded in bringing the bill with amendments before the House. It was first rejected 45 to 48 but without a quorum, reconsidered, and tabled by a quorum vote of 68 to 53.[113]

34th Congress (1855–1857)

The members of the 34th Congress had many things to consider besides the problems of immigration, with the overriding slavery issue and a state of civil war in Kansas; and shifting party lines marked the rise of the Republican party and a strong Know Nothing movement. Perhaps through the nativist influence of the latter, the first session did in fact give considerable attention to the range of matters related to immigration—naturalization, protection of passengers, and the undesirable classes of immigrants—but also to a new and emerging problem.

Both the Senate and the House considered naturalization bills but did not pass them. The Adams (Miss.) bill in the Senate called for a continuous residence period of twenty-one years, would allow aliens of twelve-months' residence full rights to hold real estate, and required the ship owner or master landing an alien to provide a certificate that the alien was of good character and had never been convicted of a crime or been a pauper. The bill was reported out by the Committee on the Judiciary with a recommendation against its passage. In the discussion that followed, Adams made a long supporting speech, but no further action was taken on the bill.[114] In the House, Whitney (N.Y.) introduced a bill to establish a uniform rule of naturalization and repeal all previous acts. The Committee on the Judiciary, which received the bill, reported out a substitute with the same purpose.[115]

Initiative for the introduction of bills to protect passengers in steam and sailing vessels was taken by Senators Sumner (Mass.) and Hamlin (Me.) in the Senate, and Representatives Washburne (Ill.) and Valk (N.Y.) in the House, but no new legislation was enacted. And efforts to prevent

[113]Ibid., pp. 1180, 1187.
[114]Ibid., 34th Cong., 1st sess., pp. 350, 979, 1409.
[115]Ibid., p. 1692.

the immigration of undesirable classes of aliens were continued from the preceding Congress. In the House, Smith of Alabama introduced a bill forbidding the introduction of foreign paupers, criminals, lunatics, the insane, and the blind. Referred to the Committee on Foreign Affairs, it was reported out with an accompanying document, House Report 359.[116] This lengthy report deplored the increase of crime and poverty, and stated

> That this increase is traceable to the immense influx of foreigners within the last ten years past, no one who examines the subject can deny.

The report also gave as a fact that "A policy has long prevailed on the continent of Europe to transport paupers and criminals to this country." A number of consular and other reports were included; and both federal and state legislation was recommended.

The new problem to be considered in this session of Congress was presented on April 7, 1856, when a resolution offered by Marshall (Ky.) was adopted by the House. The resolution read as follows:

> That the Committee on Foreign Relations inquire into the expediency of declaring the engagement of American ships in the Chinese Coolie trade to be illegal, and a cause of forfeiture to their captors of the ships engaged therein; and that they report by bill or otherwise.[117]

A related resolution of inquiry was offered to the House on the same day by Pringle (N.Y.):

> That the President of the United States be requested to communicate what information he may possess in regard to citizens of the United States being engaged in the slave trade, or in the transportation in American ships, of coolies from China to Cuba and other countries.[118]

Later in the month, Benjamin (La.) introduced a Senate resolution asking the Secretary of State for information on the coolie trade.[119] House Executive Document 105 was received in reply to the Pringle inquiry and Senate Executive Document 99 in reply to the Benjamin inquiry. Both were lengthy collections of miscellaneous letters and consular reports of various incidents and observations involving Chinese passengers.

Nothing of note concerning immigration was brought up in the remainder of the 34th Congress.

[116]Ibid., pp. 568, 2188.
[117]Ibid., p. 833.
[118]Ibid.
[119]Ibid., p. 1012.

35th Congress (1857–1859)

The first session of the 35th Congress, at the beginning of the Buchanan administration, did not deal directly with immigration questions, but it did receive a number of bills on the somewhat related topic of protection of passengers on steam vessels. The House received four bills on the subject, introduced by members from Louisiana, California, New York, and Illinois, the last being the persistent Representative Washburne, who evidently was devoting himself especially to steamship legislation.[120] The Senate meanwhile received three such bills, introduced by members from Louisiana, New York, and California.[121] During debate, a list was given of thirty-five steamers lost since 1851, with a tabulation of the dollar losses. One or another of the bills came out of committee, but Congress appeared impatient when they were brought up and preferred to get on to other matters.

President Buchanan's message on the opening of the second session was a recital of problems—trouble in Kansas, the Mormons, relations with China and Britain, more troubles in Cuba, the post office deficit, the transcontinental railroad project, and slave running—but no reference was made to immigration. Action related to the latter was confined to a naturalization bill adversely reported by the House Committee on the Judiciary and another attempt by Washburne to get consideration of a steamship bill.[122]

36th Congress (1859–1861)

The 36th Congress, though on the eve of the Civil War, nevertheless managed to carry on a certain amount of normal legislative business and to give some attention to immigration matters.

In the House, Washburne, undiscouraged by earlier rebuffs, continued to press for passage of a bill to protect passengers on steamships, and finally, with the support of Taylor (La.), succeeded in getting a bill through the House (H.R. 114). It was blocked in the Senate by the Committee on Commerce, which asked to defer the bill until the next session because there was too little time to examine it.

The subject of the coolie trade was still alive in the minds of certain Congressmen. On February 10, 1860 the House accepted the following resolution introduced by Morse (Me.):

[120]Ibid., 35th Cong., 1st sess., pp. 183, 326, 346, 1608.
[121]Ibid., pp. 698, 919, 1771.
[122]Ibid., 35th Cong., 2nd sess., pp. 197, 611, 656.

> That the Committee on Commerce be directed to inquire into the expediency of prohibiting by law all American vessels from engaging in the cooly trade, or from transporting apprentices, so called, to the West Indies, or other parts of the world.[123]

The committee prepared such a bill, and Eliot (Mass.) on behalf of the committee made repeated attempts to report out the bill, on March 29, April 2, and April 5, but it was not until April 16 that he got permission from the House.[124] There was apparent opposition to the bill, which was to prohibit participation in the coolie trade by American citizens and American vessels.

Although he failed to get further consideration of his bill on the coolie trade, Eliot persisted, and on May 2 introduced the following resolution in the House:

> That the President of the United States be requested to communicate to the House of Representatives any information recently received respecting the Chinese cooly trade, which has not heretofore been communicated to Congress.[125]

Objection being raised, the resolution was not accepted at the time but was adopted later, on May 21.[126] House Executive Document 88 was received in reply, supplementing the two documents received by Congress in 1856.

In spite of the troubled situation during the term of the 36th Congress, time and support could be found for legislation against another of the reputed perils of the transatlantic voyage. On December 21, 1859 Senator Bayard of Delaware introduced a bill to amend the Passenger Act of March 3, 1855, for the purpose of protecting female passengers from seduction by ship personnel.[127] The bill was supported by a memorial from the Commissioners of Emigration of the State of New York. Referred to the Committee on the Judiciary, the bill was reported out on January 4, 1860 and passed by the Senate on March 14.[128] Two days later, however, the bill was recommitted, in view of a similar and prior bill already passed by the House. The House acted on the same New York memorial, and its bill for the protection of female passengers was introduced by Cochrane of New York on February 15, 1860. Referred to the Committee on Commerce, it was passed by the House on March 6.[129] The

[123]Ibid., 36th Cong., 1st sess., p. 728.

[124]Ibid., pp. 1557, 1735.

[125]Ibid., p. 1931.

[126]Ibid., p. 2216.

[127]Ibid., p. 198. Reference was made to a similar bill apparently presented to Congress about two years before, but a report of the earlier bill has not been found.

[128]Ibid., pp. 322, 1147. A description of the bill S. 3 is given on the latter page.

[129]Ibid., pp. 795, 1013. The bill is H.R. 19.

bill next went to the Senate Committee on Commerce and the Committee on the Judiciary; then it was reported back to the Senate with two slight amendments suggested. The Senate passed the bill with the committee amendments; when the House agreed to the amendments, the bill was signed by President Buchanan on March 26, 1860. Nothing further related to immigration was undertaken in the second and final session of the 36th Congress.

Comment

The history of American immigration policy does not divide itself naturally into distinctly marked periods, for immigration legislation has tended to proceed by amendment and accumulation, and new acts as a rule repeat the wording and substance of preceding laws. As in much else, however, the Civil War marks a divide between what went before and what came after; and the end of the last prewar Congress is a convenient point to stop and look back at the development of federal immigration legislation up to this time.

During the period under review Congress moved only slowly and cautiously, one might say almost reluctantly, into an area of policy where traditionally the individual colonies and then the states had exercised authority. This was perhaps not merely because of tradition or a lack of constitutional grounds for federal action; it may also have been influenced by the strong and rising state rights sentiment that resisted any encroachment on the part of federal authority. With regard to naturalization, both the Constitution and the realities of the problem justified "an uniform rule"; but the rights and the need were less clear in other matters. Nevertheless, the trend of legal thought was leading to an expansion of the federal authority over immigration, for the courts were striking down state attempts at regulation and control of immigration.

Naturalization legislation has been described on the preceding pages only for the indications it gives of congressional attitudes toward the immigrant after arrival. A second major area of congressional action, and one that relates more closely to immigration policy, is the series of passenger acts, also referred to as the steerage legislation. Here the need for uniform national legislation regulating the conditions of travel for the protection of travelers was evident. And although it was not directly an exercise of regulation or control over immigration, it contained aspects of immigration policy; there was no doubt a considerable element of humanitarian concern for the welfare of the passengers, but doubtless also an element of national self-interest in protecting the health of the future residents and citizens who constituted the majority of the passengers. The passenger acts could also have been used to restrict immigration by limiting the carrying capacity of vessels and raising the cost of the transatlantic passage through requirements for better food and accommodations on the voyage. No evidence has been found that the acts were designed to serve a restrictive purpose. They were generally in line with the contemporary British regulations, and American ship owners were quick to protest any measures that would put them at a competitive disadvantage.

The complaints about the coming of foreign paupers, criminals, and other undesirables, long familiar to the colonial and state governments, were repeatedly heard in Congress. Proposals to prevent such immigration and to require certain financial guarantees against relief costs were also received, but Congress was not yet ready to take action. To do so would have been to assume authority for the regulation of immigration, and a final decision on state versus federal jurisdiction over immigration had not yet been made.

Much of the outcry over the immigration of paupers and criminals, and the alleged practice of European governments of shipping such outcasts to the United States, came from nativist sources in and outside of Congress; and it received some substantiation from reports made by government officials and the inquiries of congressional committees. Congress had passed severe antialien laws in 1798, a time of heightened suspicion and fear of certain European nations and of aliens in the United States, when the Federalist party controlling Congress felt such legislation to be to its political advantage. The strong popular reaction against the antialien acts and the defeat of the Federalists by Jefferson's party gave evidence that the colonial-period view of immigration as being in the national interest had not altogether disappeared; as a result, a more favorable congressional attitude toward immigration and the alien prevailed for a time. In notable contrast, Congress became markedly resistant to pressures from active nativist organizations in the 1830s through the 1850s. Although the Native American party, the Order of United Americans, and the Know Nothings never approached a majority in Congress, their nativist arguments were of a sort to have a wider appeal; but the Democratic and Whig parties did not adopt nativist principles, and Congress was presumably representative of the nation as a whole in rejecting antialien legislation.

By the eve of the Civil War, certain issues had been raised: the problem of undesirable classes of immigrants, state versus federal jurisdiction over immigration, and the Chinese coolie trade. But these would have to wait till later to be dealt with by Congress.

3 The Beginning of Federal Control, 1861–1883

As might be expected, congressional attention to immigration problems declined during the Civil War years, but it did not disappear entirely. The matters brought up in Congress were much the same as before, except that there was a temporary swing toward a policy of encouraging immigration. The Know Nothing party and the nativist issue were both swept away in the rush of events leading up to the conflict, and the pressure of wartime demands for manpower led to a greater appreciation of immigration.

37th Congress (1861–1863)

Only two items need to be noted in the brief first session of the 37th Congress, from July 4 to August 6, 1861. On July 13 the House asked President Lincoln for information on the coolie trade.[1] And shortly before the end of the session, Arnold of Illinois introduced a bill to facilitate naturalization of aliens after service in the armed forces and honorable discharge.[2]

In the second session two steamship bills were introduced in the Senate; one was adversely reported and the other was passed and sent to the House.[3] However, the most attention was given to a bill to suppress the coolie trade. Eliot (Mass.), whose efforts had been frustrated in the preceding Congress, introduced his coolie trade bill at the opening of the second session, and it was reported back with amendments from the Committee on Commerce on January 15, 1862.[4] It passed the House on the same day. In the Senate it went to the Committee on Commerce and

[1]*Congressional Globe*, 37th Cong., 1st sess., p. 117.

[2]Ibid., p. 366.

[3]Ibid., 37th Cong., 2nd sess., pp. 736, 1296, 3134, 3368. The bills are S. 195 and S. 382.

[4]Ibid., pp. 16, 350, 352. The bill is H.R. 109.

was reported back with an amendment. The original bill contained the qualifying phrase, "against their will and without their consent." The Senate committee proposed to drop this phrase, or in other words to prohibit the coolie trade entirely.[5] The proposed amendment was accepted by the Senate, and then by the House; President Lincoln signed the bill on February 19, 1862.[6]

The only action to be noted in the third session of the 37th Congress was the introduction from the House Committee on Agriculture of a bill to establish a Bureau of Emigration (that is, emigration from Europe).[7]

38th Congress (1863–1865)

Lincoln's message of December 8, 1863, on the opening of the 38th Congress, contained the following passage recommending encouragement of immigration:

> I again submit to your consideration the expediency of establishing a system for the encouragement of immigration. Although this source of national wealth and strength is again flowing with greater freedom than for several years before the insurrection occurred, there is still a great deficiency of laborers in every field of industry, especially in agriculture and our mines, as well as of iron and coal, as of the precious metals. While the demand for labor is thus increased here, tens of thousands of persons, destitute of remunerative occupation, are thronging our foreign consulates, and offering to emigrate to the United States, if essential, but very cheap, assistance can be afforded them.[8]

A week later, on the motion of Washburne (Ill.), the House set up a select committee to consider the above portion of the message. The committee, appointed on December 16, consisted of Washburne (Ill.), Grinnell (Iowa), Law (Ind.), Baldwin (Mass.), and Rollins (Mo.).[9]

The Senate independently took up a bill for the encouragement of immigration and passed it to a second reading on February 18, 1864. This Senate bill called for the appointment of a Commissioner of Immigration to begin at a salary of $2500 per annum and to be provided with two clerks. His duties would be to collect information on the climate and

[5]Ibid., p. 555.

[6]12 Stat. 340. Also passed in this session was the Homestead Act of May 20, 1862 (12 Stat. 392), which extended the same privileges to persons who had filed their declaration of intention.

[7]*Congressional Globe,* 37th Cong., 3rd sess., p. 1029.

[8]Ibid., 38th Cong., 1st sess., Appendix, pp. 1–2.

[9]Ibid., pp. 35, 37.

resources of the United States and to disseminate the information throughout Europe, the cost of printing not to exceed $20,000 per annum. The bill also provided that an emigrant office be set up in New York, under a superintendent, to make contracts with railroads for tickets for immigrants. And the President was authorized to appoint a similar commissioner for New Orleans. The bill (S. 125) was passed by the Senate on March 2,[10] transmitted to the House, and there referred to the select committee on March 15.

The House select committee asserted its independence by reporting out its own bill (H.R. 411) for the encouragement of immigration, instead of the Senate bill, and the House promptly passed its committee's bill.[11] The Senate committee amended and reported the House bill out, whereupon the Senate struck out the House bill and, reinserting its own bill previously set aside by the House select committee, passed the so-amended H.R. 411. With both House and Senate standing firm, the bill went to conference and a compromise bill was approved, signed by the President, and became the Act of July 4, 1864.[12] The act provided for a Commissioner of Immigration to be appointed by the President and under the authority of the Secretary of State, and authorized immigrant labor contracts whereby would-be immigrants might pledge their wages to pay for transportation, but with the stipulation that the wage contract was not to exceed one year's duration. It was specifically stated that the contract in no sense involved a condition of slavery or involuntary servitude. The office and duties of the New York Superintendent of Immigration were retained from the original bill.[13]

There was another legislative accomplishment during the session. After persistent effort over a number of years, Washburne of Illinois finally succeeded in getting through Congress a bill (H.R. 510) for the further regulation of the carriage of passengers on steamships. It was signed by President Lincoln the same day as H.R. 411, the immigration bill.[14] The only other business of the session to be noted was a House bill to exclude traitors and alien enemies from the courts and the public lands. Reported out of the Committee on the Judiciary, the bill was not taken up by the House but referred back to the committee.[15]

The second session of the 38th Congress was opened with a message

[10]Ibid., pp. 719, 865, 896. [11]Ibid., pp. 1673, 1764, 1793.

[12]Ibid., pp. 2510, 3292, 3368, 3495, 3546.

[13]For further details of this bill, including later developments, see U.S. Immigration Commission of 1911, Reports, Abstract, vol. 2:565–66.

[14]*Congressional Globe,* 38th Cong., 1st sess., pp. 2771, 2836, 2866, 3455, 3483, 3491, 3547.

[15]Ibid., pp. 843, 2774.

in which President Lincoln commented on the experience with the act for the encouragement of immigration and voiced his belief in the value of immigration to the nation:

> The act passed at the last session for the encouragement of emigration has, so far as was possible, been put into operation. It seems to need amendment which will enable the officers of the Government to prevent the practice of frauds against the immigrants while on their way, and on their arrival in the ports, so as to secure them here a free choice of avocations and places of settlement. A liberal disposition toward this great national policy is manifested by most of the European states, and ought to be reciprocated on our part by giving the immigrants effective national protection. I regard our emigrants as one of the principal replenishing streams which are appointed by Providence to repair the ravages of internal war, and its waste of national strength and wealth.[16]

Lincoln was also careful to point out that military service would not be required of the immigrants.

The only other actions to be noted in the second session of the 38th Congress are two bills of identical title (S. 403 and H.R. 746) to amend the steamship act of 1855 and the immigration encouragement act of 1864. The former was reported out by the Senate Committee on Finance; the latter passed the House and later was reported out by the Senate Committee on Agriculture, but neither progressed further.[17]

39th Congress (1865–1867)

The 39th Congress carried on where the preceding session had left off and received new bills to replace some that had expired with the end of the 38th Congress. In the House, Washburne reintroduced a bill (H.R. 481) to amend the 1864 act encouraging immigration and the passenger act of 1855. The bill was amended by the House to reduce from fourteen to twelve the age of segregation of male passengers not occupying berths with their wives, and it was passed in that form. The Senate Committee on Commerce recommended such extensive amendments that they amounted to a substitute bill and proposed the repeal of the 1864 act because of the labor contracts it permitted. After lengthy debate the bill was laid on the table.[18]

Another type of encouragement to immigration was proposed in a

[16]Ibid., 38th Cong., 2nd sess., Appendix, p. 2.

[17]Ibid., 38th Cong., 2nd sess., pp. 547, 653, 1070, 1125.

[18]Ibid., 39th Cong., 1st sess., pp. 1893, 2246, 2314, 4040.

bill introduced in the House by Ferry of Michigan. It would grant lands in order to promote European settlement of the upper peninsula of Michigan. The bill was referred to the Committee on Public Lands and remained there.[19]

Several steamship bills were introduced during the session, and one (H.R. 477) was passed.[20] A bill to amend the naturalization acts was introduced in the House by Raymond (N.Y.).[21] And, finally, there was a revival of concern about alien criminals. On March 15, 1866 the Senate Committee on Foreign Relations presented a joint resolution in protest against the pardoning by foreign governments of persons convicted of "infamous offenses" on condition that they emigrate to the United States. Evidence of such practice in Switzerland, Great Britain, Germany, and Newfoundland was mentioned. The resolution (S. Res. 45) read in part:

> The Congress of the United States protests against such acts as unfriendly and inconsistent with the comity of nations and hereby requests the President of the United States to cause a copy of this protest to be communicated to the representatives of the United States in foreign countries, with instructions to present it to the Governments where they are accredited respectively, and to insist that no such acts shall, under any circumstances, be repeated.[22]

The resolution was passed by the Senate after some debate, went to the House Committee on Foreign Affairs, was passed by the House, and then was signed by President Johnson on April 17.

The second session of the 39th Congress saw some further attention to the protection of passengers on steamships, a coolie trade resolution, and a bill concerning convicts. The latter followed up the resolution of the preceding session by prohibiting the transportation to the United States of persons convicted of or charged with crime. Introduced in the House by Raymond (N.Y.) on February 8, 1867, it went to the Committee on the Judiciary where it remained.[23] The following coolie trade resolution was presented to the Senate on January 16, 1867 by the Committee on Foreign Relations:

> Whereas the traffic in laborers transported from China and other eastern countries, known as the coolie trade, is odious to the people of the United States as inhuman and immoral; and whereas it is abhorrent to the spirit of modern international law and policy, which have substantially extirpated the African slave trade, to permit the

[19]Ibid., p. 919.
[20]Ibid., pp. 482, 1147, 1876, 1893, 2623, 2957, 3072, 3100, 3681, 3950.
[21]Ibid., p. 135.
[22]Ibid., pp. 1407, 1493.
[23]Ibid., 39th Cong., 2nd sess., p. 1097.

> establishment in its place of a mode of enslaving men different from the former in little else than the employment of fraud instead of force to make its victims captive: Therefore,
>
> Be it resolved, that it is the duty of this Government to give effect to the moral sentiment of the nation through all its agencies for the purpose of preventing the further introduction of coolies into this hemisphere or the adjacent islands.[24]

Because of its skillful linking of the coolie trade and the slavery issue, the resolution was adopted by the Senate without reported debate.

A bill (S. 475) to deal with a postwar problem and unrelated to previous congressional concerns was introduced on December 17, 1866 by Senator Sumner of Massachusetts. This bill was designed to prevent and punish false and fraudulent representations to induce emigration to a foreign country and apparently was aimed at attempts to get free colored people to emigrate under conditions resembling the coolie trade.[25] The bill was reported out by the Committee on Foreign Relations and debated in the Senate, but it did not progress further.

40th Congress (1867–1869)

Little action related to immigration or aliens was taken in the first session of the 40th Congress. A resolution (S. Res. 30) to amend a passenger act was adopted,[26] and Senator Sumner (Mass.) introduced a bill to remove the phrases limiting naturalization to free white persons. After procedural wrangle it was referred to the Committee on the Judiciary, in spite of its author's wish for immediate action.[27]

In contrast to the preceding session, the second session of the 40th Congress saw a considerable activity concerning immigration, naturalization, and related matters. No less than five bills on naturalization were presented to Congress,[28] and seven bills together with two House resolutions dealt with the protection of passengers.[29]

The coolie trade and oriental immigration in general were also considered. Senator Sumner of Massachusetts presented a bill (S. 644) from the Committee on Foreign Relations to extend the existing acts against the coolie trade to include Japanese workers. The bill was promptly

[24] Ibid., p. 483.

[25] Ibid., p. 143.

[26] Ibid., 40th Cong., 1st sess., p. 107.

[27] Ibid., p. 728.

[28] S. 593, and H.R. 615, 616, 1274, and 1429.

[29] The bills were S. 247, H.R. 858, 999, 1022, 1100, 1146, and 1372. The resolutions were introduced by Chanler (N.Y.) and Cole (Calif.). H.R. 1100, introduced by O'Neill (Pa.) from the Committee on Commerce, was considered by the House on several days and passed, but it progressed no further.

accepted by the Senate.[30] And Johnson of California offered the following challenging resolution of inquiry to the House on December 12, 1867:

> That the Judiciary Committee of the House be hereby directed to inquire whether the Congress can by legislation prevent the immigration and importation of Chinese and Mongolians into our country, and to report by bill or otherwise.[31]

Objection being raised, the resolution was not accepted. A few weeks later, on January 29, Johnson reoffered his resolution, rephrased and expanded after the word *Chinese* to read:

> and other inferior races to our country; and also whether the civil rights act and the proposed amendments to the Constitution of the United States confer the rights of citizenship, including the right of suffrage, upon Chinese as well as all other males born in the United States over the age of twenty-one years.[32]

Objection to the resolution was raised by Pile (Mo.), who said it was a "burlesque on common sense."

Now that the wartime manpower problems had receded, opinion on the policy of encouraging immigration became more divided. Proposals for the amendment of the 1864 act were made in both houses of Congress, following President Lincoln's recommendation on the opening of the second session of the 38th Congress, but the House and the Senate failed to come to agreement in spite of several attempts. Meanwhile the labor contract provision of the 1864 act and resentment at the alleged sending of foreign criminals led to more questioning of the policy of encouragement; and the 1864 act was quietly repealed by section 4 of the consular and diplomatic appropriation act of March 30, 1868 (15 Stat. 56). In spite of this action, however, various bills to provide aid and encouragement to immigrants continued to be presented to Congress. On June 1, 1868, Donnelly (Minn.) entered a bill (H.R. 1139) to establish agencies, under the direction of the Secretary of State, for the promotion of emigration to the United States in Great Britain, Germany, Sweden, and Norway. On the same day Flanders (Washington Territory) entered a bill (H.R. 1145) to establish unpaid immigration agencies in Liverpool, Glasgow, and Dublin. And on July 3 Cullom (Ill.) introduced a bill (H.R. 1355) for the encouragement of immigration. The Committee on Foreign Affairs reported it out as a substitute for the Donnelly bill, but it was recommitted.[33]

[30] *Congressional Globe,* 40th Cong., 2nd sess., pp. 4362, 4452.
[31] Ibid., p. 163.
[32] Ibid., p. 837.
[33] Ibid., pp. 2750, 3732.

The committee report to accompany H.R. 1355, House Report 76, presented a statement of the case for encouragement and the means to be used. Noting that bills in Congress proposed agencies abroad to encourage emigration and to disseminate information about the United States, the committee stated that it found no authority for such agencies either in public law or in treaties. And the committee considered further that such agencies might create difficulties with other nations. At the same time, the committee was cognizant of the value of immigration:

> Our nation owes much of its importance in wealth and power among the nations of the earth to the people of foreign birth who have come to our shores since the foundation of the government.

Furthermore, the report continued, people are needed to fill up the vacant lands and to help carry the burden of debt left by the war. The committee's recommendation embodied in H.R. 1355 was to give consuls responsibility to disseminate such information as may be deemed proper and as may "tend to induce persons of capital, industry, or skill, to emigrate to this country."

The third session of the 40th Congress, in the usual second period of early December to early March, was also quite active in matters related in one way or another to immigration. President Johnson's message on the opening of the session dealt with other and more pressing affairs: fiscal matters, the resumption of specie payment, the purchase of Alaska, foreign affairs, and recommendation of the direct election of President and Vice President instead of election through the electoral college.

Sumner's coolie trade bill from the preceding session (S. 644) was passed by the House on February 4, 1869 and approved by the President on February 9.[34] The Senate labored at length over a steamship bill (S. 247), also from the preceding session, finally passed and sent it to the House, but then recalled it.[35] The House had its own passenger bill (H.R. 1554) but took no action on it.

Congress also received a number of naturalization bills during this session, seven in the Senate and four in the House, none of which was passed.[36] Certain of the bills and additional resolutions proposed liberalization of the conditions of naturalization. For example, an amendment offered to a naturalization bill (S. 654) by Stewart (Nev.) provided:

[34]Ibid., 40th Cong., 3rd sess., pp. 886, 1164.

[35]Ibid., pp. 1071, 1503, 1645, 1648.

[36]The Senate bills were S. 139, 651, 653, 654, 676, 683, and 931. The House bills were H.R. 1474, 1585, 1886, and 1898.

> That all white persons of foreign birth, not convicted of crime, and who have not participated in insurrection or rebellion against the United States, and who now are or who shall hereafter become permanent residents in the United States and elect to be citizens thereof, are hereby declared naturalized citizens, and entitled to all the rights and privileges of other citizens of the United States.[37]

A resolution in the House by McKee (Ky.) stated that

> Whereas experience has demonstrated that the naturalization laws of the United States are not such as to advance and promote the best interests of the nation . . .

the Committee on the Judiciary should consider repealing all naturalization acts, giving citizenship simply on an oath to support the Constitution, and eliminating any residence period.[38]

Another House resolution, by Ross of Illinois, called on the Committee on the Judiciary to consider giving foreigners who intended to take up permanent residence their citizenship after one year of residence.[39] And a third House resolution, this one by Schenck (Ohio), stated the following purpose:

> That the Committee on the Judiciary be instructed to inquire what amendments to the laws relating to naturalization are needed to give greater security and purity to elections.

It then went on to various questions of naturalization procedure.[40]

41st Congress (1869–1871)

The 41st Congress, the first of Grant's presidency, began with a short special session from March 4 to April 22, 1869. Naturalization continued to receive particular attention, with one bill to amend the naturalization laws introduced in the Senate (S. 189) and six in the House (H.R. 121, 152, 154, 185, 231, and 423). The House also had a continuing concern about alleged naturalization frauds, and took action against such frauds in the form of a resolution presented by Ward (N.Y.). The resolution instructed the Committee on the Judiciary to prepare and present a bill to restrict the power of naturalization to such courts as are least susceptible to political influence, to discover and revoke fraudulent naturalization papers, and to reduce illegal voting.[41]

Several Senate and House bills were introduced for the protection

[37]Ibid., p. 1164.
[38]Ibid., p. 11.
[39]Ibid., p. 751.
[40]Ibid., p. 10.
[41]Ibid., 41st Cong., 1st sess., p. 59.

of passengers at sea, on steamships, and on arrival in the United States; two of these bills were designed to prevent the collection of illegal taxes from immigrants under the guise of state authority.[42] And Johnson of California continued to pursue his own particular mission by offering the following resolution:

> That in passing the resolution for the fifteenth amendment to the Constitution of the United States this House never intended that Chinese or Mongolians should become voters.[43]

The House voted 42 to 106 against introduction of the resolution.

The activity on immigration matters displayed by the 41st Congress in its first session continued into the second session. President Grant gave an unusual amount of attention to immigration-related problems in his opening message of December 6, 1869, pointing out no less than three such problems for congressional attention. A first was abuse of the naturalization laws by aliens who came merely to get naturalized, with no intention of taking up permanent residence, but returned home immediately to use their American citizenship to evade military service and taxes. Instructions had been sent already to diplomatic and consular officers abroad to examine all claims from naturalized citizens for protection. A second matter touched on in the message was that an invitation had been sent to a number of European nations to empower their Washington representatives to enter into a convention for the protection of emigrant passengers, looking toward uniform regulations on food, medical care, ventilation, and so on. In addition, the message continued,

> I advise such legislation as will forever preclude the enslavement of the Chinese upon our soil under the name of coolies, and also prevent American vessels from engaging in the transportation of coolies.[44]

A Senate bill (S. 80) from the preceding session, to punish the collection of illegal taxes from passengers, was reported out but not acted on. And the House received a new bill (H.R. 1614) for the same purpose from Hale of Maine.[45] Various bills were introduced for the protection of passengers. The Senate received a bill (S. 884) from Conkling (N.Y.) to incorporate the International Society of the United States for the Promotion and Protection of Immigration. The House was presented with a bill of the same title (H.R. 2034) from Sawyer (Wis.);[46] and incorporation was

[42]The bills include S. 46, 80, H.R. 34, 43, 97, 216, and 417.

[43]Ibid., p. 202.

[44]Ibid., 41st Cong., 2nd sess., p. 7.

[45]Ibid., p. 2235.

[46]Ibid., pp. 3207, 3494.

also sought for a National Irish Immigration Association (H.R. 1147 by Judd of Illinois). None of the latter three bills came out of committee.

Several bills to amend or replace the naturalization laws died in committee (S. 189 and 557, H.R. 437, 488, 544, and 1070). Another bill (H.R. 1399) was discussed during several days but not passed. Finally a naturalization bill was enacted after long consideration, H.R. 2201 by Davis of New York, to amend the naturalization laws and punish crimes against them. The House debated the bill and resisted repeated efforts to block it, refused a motion to reject, voted down two motions for adjournment, and then passed the bill by a vote of 130 to 47 on June 13, 1870.[47] Referred in the Senate to the Committee on the Judiciary, the bill was reported back by the committee with amendment that was actually a much longer substitute bill for the original House draft.[48] The intent of the bill, however, remained unchanged, for the Senate committee draft merely set forth in greater detail a system of checks and controls on the naturalization process and the penalties for fraudulent practices. On these points there was a considerable measure of agreement, except for the one partisan complaint that the bill was supported by the Republican majority as a means of making naturalization more difficult and thereby reducing the accession of Democrat votes.[49] But in spite of the otherwise general acceptance of the purpose of the bill, heated debate continued in the Senate for a number of days. Debate revolved around a succession of attempts to add amendments liberalizing the naturalization laws by extending them to apply to all aliens, irrespective of origin or color.

Through a series of days of sometimes impassioned oratory and involved parliamentary procedure, Sumner (Mass.), with repeated efforts,[50] renewed his earlier attempts in the 40th Congress to amend the bill by adding a provision to strike out the word "white" wherever it occurred in the naturalization laws, "so that in naturalization there shall be no distinction of race or color." Williams of Oregon followed with a proposed amendment in the form of an addition to the Sumner amendment:

> But this act shall not be construed to authorize the naturalization of persons born in the Chinese empire.

This amendment to the amendment called forth long and emotional statements of the undesirable qualities of the Chinese and the menace of Chinese immigration.

[47]Ibid., p. 4366.

[48]Ibid., pp. 4569, 4834.

[49]Ibid., p. 4837.

[50]Ibid., pp. 5121, 5124, 5177.

On the final defeat of the Sumner amendment by a vote of 12 to 26, after a complex series of parliamentary maneuvers,[51] Trumbull (Ill.) proposed an amendment to read:

> That the naturalization laws are hereby extended to aliens of African nativity, and to persons of African descent, and to persons born in the Chinese empire.

This was defeated by an even greater margin, 9 to 31. One liberalizing amendment had been accepted, however—an amendment by Warner (Ala.), which stated:

> That the naturalization laws are hereby extended to aliens of African nativity and to persons of African descent.

This amendment was accepted by a narrow margin, to become the seventh and final section of the bill. In this form the bill was passed by the Senate on July 4, 1870, by a vote of 33 to 8, accepted by the House, and signed by President Grant on July 14, 1870.[52]

Notable in the second session of the 41st Congress was the rising tide of concern over Chinese immigration, which, as noted above, stimulated much of the debate on the naturalization bill. On the very first day of the session, Senator Williams of Oregon introduced a bill (S. 279) to regulate the immigration of Chinese. It would prohibit the encouragement of such immigration, void contracts to provide employment to such immigrants, and prohibit the importation of any Chinese women unaccompanied by husband or father; and if they were so accompanied, documentary proof of the relation must be provided. The Senate discussed the bill, then referred it to the Committee on Commerce.[53]

Early the next month Johnson (Calif.) presented a joint resolution (H. Res. 102) in the House, declaring that states had the right to protect

[51]Ibid., p. 5176. The Senate action on the liberalizing amendments was, in somewhat fuller detail, as follows: Sumner offered his amendment during debate on July 2 (p. 5121), Williams followed with his amendment of the amendment, but then withdrew it. The Sumner amendment was rejected 22 to 23 (p. 5123), and the Senate then voted 17 to 33 to throw out the committee draft and thus returned to the House bill. Sumner promptly reoffered his amendment (p. 5124), which was accepted, 27 to 22, whereupon Williams again proposed his amendment. Returning to the bill on July 4, the Senate reconsidered and rejected the Sumner amendment, 14 to 30 (p. 5176), and then accepted the Warner amendment by the slender margin of 21 to 20. Up to this point the Senate had been sitting as the Committee of the Whole, so it then had to pass on its action. This afforded Sumner an opportunity to present his amendment again, to be defeated 12 to 26 (p. 5177). The Trumbull amendment was next proposed and defeated, 9 to 31, and the Senate finally voted on and passed the bill.

[52]Ibid., pp. 4569, 5177, 5607.

[53]Ibid., pp. 3, 299.

themselves against nuisance and that Chinese immigration should be discouraged. The resolution provided that a state suffering injury from filthy habits, degrading vices, or customs practiced by Chinese residents may, if these practices produce a nuisance, protect themselves by state legislation, notwithstanding treaties between the United States and China. The resolution also declared that the free immigration and importation of Chinese laborers and debased and abandoned females is not for the best interests of the country and, therefore, should not be encouraged but rather should be checked by all lawful means. The resolution was read and then referred to committee.[54] When the resolution was brought up about two weeks later, Johnson made a long supporting statement in which he warned that regardless of national laws the Chinese would not be allowed to vote in California. The House took no further action.

On June 6, 1870 Sargent (Calif.) introduced a bill (H.R. 2168) to prohibit servile contracts.[55] On July 9 resolutions were offered in both Senate and House on the coolie trade. In the Senate, Stewart (Nev.) called on the President for strict enforcement of the Act of February 19, 1862 prohibiting the coolie trade. There being objection to the resolution as worded, it was restated and accepted in the form of a request to the President to inform the Senate if coolies are being imported in violation of the act.[56] In the House, Cake (Pa.) offered a resolution that condemned the coolie trade as involving a form of slavery and called for an investigation of the trade to seek the exclusion of such bondmen,

> for the protection of those who voluntarily seek our shores in quest of free homes, and who will, as speedily as practicable, adopt the manners, habits and costumes [*sic*] of our people.[57]

Finally, on July 11, Mungen (Ohio) presented a resolution to the House calling for the appointment of a committee of two senators and five representatives,

> to inquire into the danger threatening our country from Chinese immigration, and to report proper means for guarding against or averting the same . . . [and] . . . whether total exclusion of the Chinese . . . excepting as travelers and merchants, will be best for the laboring and producing classes.[58]

Although no legislation came out of these efforts, pressure for some action on Chinese immigration evidently was rising.

[54]Ibid., p. 338.
[55]Ibid., p. 4112.
[56]Ibid., p. 5394.
[57]Ibid., p. 5412.
[58]Ibid., p. 5439.

In its third session the 41st Congress considered several passenger or steamship bills and passed one,[59] which was approved by the President on February 28, 1871. A bill (S. 1106) to amend the Naturalization Act of 1870 was introduced in the Senate, and the House received a multipurpose bill (H.R. 2974) to encourage immigration, regulate the carriage of immigrants on steamships, and provide better protection on arrival.[60]

The Chinese question was not entirely overlooked. On January 7, 1871 the House heard a long anti-Chinese address by Mungen (Ohio).[61] And in February the Senate received a bill (S. 279) to regulate the immigration of Chinese. Reported out, it was indefinitely postponed, and the committee was discharged of further responsibility for the bill.[62]

One other action was significant in the light of later developments. That was the introduction by Senator Wilson (Mass.) of a bill to make the importation of immigrants under labor contracts unlawful.[63]

42nd Congress (1871–1873)

The 42nd Congress received a small but diversified number of immigration bills during the short first session, of which none went beyond referral to committee. There were several passenger or steamship bills,[64] one to supplement the acts prohibiting the coolie trade,[65] and a bill to regulate labor contracts made with immigrants.[66]

Also, there was still some sentiment in favor of encouraging immigration, though a minority sentiment, because two bills to that effect appeared. In the Senate, Nye (Nev.) introduced a bill to aid a steamship company to open a direct line to southern Europe and to promote immigration into the southern states.[67] And in the House, Coburn (Ind.) presented a bill to encourage immigration and to regulate the carriage of passengers.[68]

It was also in this session that the House received the *Special Report on Immigration,*[69] House Executive Document 1, by Edward Young, Chief of the Treasury Department's Bureau of Statistics. The report of several hundred pages contained a brief introduction in which Young estimated

[59]H.R. 2212 substituted for S. 716.

[60]Ibid., 41st Cong., 3rd sess., pp. 50, 996, 1814.

[61]Ibid., p. 351. The report of the speech occupied nearly nine pages in the *Congressional Globe.*

[62]Ibid., p. 1630.

[63]S. 563, ibid., p. 58.

[64]S. 189, 316, H.R. 18; ibid., 42nd Cong., 1st sess., pp. 54, 90, 729.

[65]H.R. 382, ibid., p. 598.

[66]H.R. 107, ibid., p. 78.

[67]S. 111, ibid., p. 22.

[68]H.R. 81, ibid., p. 77.

[69]Also published separately by the Government Printing Office in 1872.

the capital value of an average immigrant at $800, presented statistics of immigration including occupational data, but was largely made up of information for each state and territory that might be helpful to prospective settlers interested in knowing of land prices, quality of soil, access to markets, labor demand, and so on.

The principal concern related to immigration in the second session of the 42nd Congress was for the protection of the immigrants from the various fraudulent practices that had multiplied as the volume of immigration increased. The problem was called to the attention of Congress in President Grant's message of December 4, 1871 on the opening of the session. In his words,

> The number of immigrants, ignorant of our laws, habits, etc., coming into our country annually, has become so great, and the impositions practiced upon them so numerous and flagrant, that I suggest congressional action for their protection.

Presidential interest in the subject was again expressed in a special message on immigration, sent to Congress on May 14, 1872.[70] The message recommended legislation to assure the health and comfort of the immigrants on shipboard and protection on land from "the knaves who are ever ready to despoil them."

Meanwhile the Senate Committee on Commerce had been directed to look into the subject and had received a resolution from the Pennsylvania legislature asking for further legislation to protect the immigrants. On March 7, 1872 the committee submitted a resolution empowering it to make the following more comprehensive inquiry:

> That the Committee on Commerce be authorized and directed to make thorough inquiry into the subject of immigration and the reception and treatment of immigrants on shipboard and after their arrival in this country. . . .[71]

The committee also wished to look into health conditions and quarantine. The resolution was amended in the Senate to make it clear that it applied to immigrants while in transit within the United States, but was further modified to limit its application to the ports of Philadelphia, New York, and Baltimore. Later in the month a steamship bill was discussed and much amended in the House and passed. It was further discussed, amended, and passed in the Senate; but in the end the Senate refused to consider the conference report on the bill and it died there.[72]

[70] *Congressional Globe,* 42nd Cong., 2nd sess., p. 3431.
[71] Ibid., p. 1490.
[72] H.R. 2116, ibid., pp. 1961, 2168, 3579, etc.

Three bills for the indicated purpose of promoting immigration were introduced in the House.[73] One of them (H.R. 1925) was evidently aimed also at replacing state by federal control of immigration, for it would prohibit state head taxes and impose a federal head tax of $1.50. Objection to the bill came especially from Wood of New York, and after some debate further action on the bill was blocked, not to be resumed until the next session.

Several other topics received attention in the form of bills during the session. One concerned naturalization and the punishment of crimes against the naturalization laws.[74] Another was to punish the illegal collection of taxes on passengers, presumably taxes levied by state and local authorities.[75] And still others dealt with coolie labor and the manifesting of passengers.

A bill to prohibit contracts for servile labor and to amend and enforce the laws against the coolie trade (S. 1058) came from Senator Casserly of California, pursuant to a memorial from the California legislature. In the House, Representative Coghlan from the same state was author of another bill of similar intent, and he presented his views at considerable length.[76] Also in the House, Townsend (N.Y.) presented a bill (H.R. 2186) to amend the passenger act of 1855 by repealing section 13 concerning manifesting and to enact that every collector of customs receiving manifests should make return of them to the Secretary of the Treasury in accordance with his instructions. The Secretary would then have the responsibility to publish reports of the information so obtained. The bill passed the House, was reported out by a Senate committee, but was not acted on; and it was again passed over by the Senate in the third and final session.[77]

The third session of the 42nd Congress did little more on immigration than discuss without acting on several bills from the preceding session. The steamship bill (H.R. 2116) of the second session was brought up in the Senate but then passed over.[78] A bill to promote immigration, by Senator Chandler of Michigan was referred to committee, with no further action; and the House again took up a bill (H.R. 1925) for the promotion of immigration that had been introduced in the second session.

[73]H.R. 1006 and 1925 by Conger (Mich.), 1744 by Shellabarger (Ohio); ibid., pp. 395, 1213, 1581.

[74]S. 484, by Kellogg (La.); ibid., p. 405.

[75]H.R. 1924 by Sawyer (Wis.); ibid., p. 1581.

[76]Ibid., pp. 1737, 2909.

[77]Ibid., 42nd Cong., 2nd sess., p. 2077; 42nd Cong., 3rd sess., p. 126.

[78]Ibid., p. 73.

The provisions of this bill included the appointment of a Commissioner of Immigration at a salary of $5000 per annum, a head tax of $1.50 for each adult immigrant steerage passenger, and questioning of immigrants on arrival to find if they had complaints of their treatment on the voyage. The bill went further into matters of adequate meals; space limitations on the number of passengers; segregation of single males, families, and single females; ventilation; and cooking facilities. Dangerous cargo was prohibited on vessels with fifty or more passengers, and information to be recorded on the manifest was specified. A New York representative, Cox, presented a memorial to the House, a protest against the bill from the Commissioners of Emigration of New York State. They opposed federal control of immigration as contemplated in H.R. 1925 and S. 1245 and argued that it would be harmful to end the long-established New York system of immigrant protection. The bill was discussed at length in the House but not brought to a vote.[79]

43rd Congress (1873–1875)

After a short special session of the Senate, the 43rd Congress convened on December 1, 1873, at which time it received President Grant's message to the new Congress. In the message he returned to a topic mentioned in his communication to the second session of the 41st Congress four years before, the practice of certain naturalized citizens of residing permanently abroad where they claimed the protection of the United States for themselves and their children. The need, he stated, was for legislation on expatriation. Congress, however, chose to turn its attention to several other aspects of immigration during the first session: to the coolie trade problem, to the encouragement of immigration and the protection of immigrants, and to the older problem of convict immigration.

The House received two bills on the coolie trade, one from Myers of Pennsylvania to supplement earlier acts, and one from Page of California to prohibit the employment of coolie labor. Neither bill got out of committee during the session.[80]

Three House bills were designated for the promotion of immigration and the protection of immigrants.[81] Two House bills were to protect passengers of foreign birth against forcible constraint or involuntary servitude,[82] of which one was passed by the House. There were three

[79]Ibid., pp. 422, 447.

[80]*Congressional Record,* 2:200, 207.

[81]H.R. 149, 165, and 192; ibid., pp. 66, 67, 68.

[82]H.R. 1208, 3581; ibid., pp. 589, 4443.

steamship bills, of which one was in the Senate;[83] and a Senate bill was designated as being for the better protection of immigrants.[84] Finally, a double-purpose bill was introduced by Conger (Mich.) for the better protection of immigrants and the prevention of the importation of criminals.[85] None of the bills got out of committee, with the single exception noted above.

The mention of criminals in the Conger bill, presented on May 27, 1874, followed some earlier House attention to the subject. On May 9 the House adopted the Cox (N.Y.) resolution of inquiry:

> Resolved, That the President of the United States be respectfully requested to communicate to this House any correspondence between the State Department and other governments as to the landing of foreign convicts on our shores; and what legislation, if any, in his judgment is necessary to prevent such outrages.[86]

On May 19 the House received the reply to its resolution, in the form of a *Report of the Secretary of State as to the Landing of Foreign Convicts* (House Executive Document 253). The report gave the text of all official diplomatic correspondence since March 4, 1869 on the subject. Various rumors were reported by the consuls, including the statement of a consul in Switzerland that there was reason to believe one canton made a practice of sending its paupers to the United States at public expense. And mention was made of isolated cases of transportation of convicts, involving Great Britain, Cuba, Greece, several German states, Italy, and Switzerland.

The second session of the 43rd Congress received a diverse group of immigration bills and passed only one of them, but that one marked a turning point in American immigration legislation. At the opening of the session, Grant's message mentioned the problems of naturalization frauds and Chinese immigration. Two naturalization bills were offered during the session, one each in the Senate and House, with the noncommittal title of "concerning naturalization."[87] A representative from California presented a bill to exclude Chinese from naturalization, which received an adverse report from the House Committee on Foreign Affairs.[88] The Senate took up a bill from the preceding session for the protection of immigrants.[89] It provided for the appointment by the Secretary of the Treasury of not more than five immigration agents to super-

[83]S. 605, H.R. 1191, 1364; ibid., pp. 589, 765, 2211.

[84]S. 808; ibid., p. 3828.

[85]H.R. 3512; ibid., p. 4305.

[86]Ibid., p. 3727.

[87]S. 1122, H.R. 4318; ibid., 3:411, 434.

[88]H.R. 4146; ibid., pp. 224, 1561.

[89]S. 808; ibid., p. 600.

vise the execution of the laws and protect immigrants from fraud; and it would amend the 1855 Act by extending its application to all vessels, foreign and domestic, bringing fifty or more steerage passengers to the United States. The bill was postponed and never acted on. In addition there were several other bills to provide one or another sort of protection to immigrants.[90]

None of these bills went beyond committee or came to a vote, but on another aspect of immigration the session produced a significant piece of legislation. Grant's message of December 7, 1874 had stated strongly the need for legislation to curb the twin evils of Chinese immigration: the coolie trade and the importation of women for prostitution. In the words of the message,

> the great proportion of the Chinese immigrants who come to our shores do not come voluntarily . . . [and] In a worse form does this apply to Chinese women. Hardly a perceptible percentage of them perform any honorable labor, but they are brought for shameful purposes, to the disgrace of the communities where settled and to the great demoralization of the youth of these localities. If this evil practice can be legislated against, it will be my pleasure as well as duty to enforce any regulation to secure so desirable an end.[91]

On February 10, 1875 Myers of Pennsylvania introduced a bill (H.R. 4679) in the House to supplement the act (unspecified) in relation to immigration and to carry out the recommendations in Grant's message of the preceding December 7 for legislation to prohibit the importation of Chinese women for immoral purposes. The bill was referred to the Committee on Foreign Affairs, which on the 18th reported out another bill (H.R. 4747) of similar purpose. The latter bill was brought up in the House on February 22 and passed the same day. The Senate passed the bill on March 3, and with prompt signing by the President it became the Immigration Act of March 3, 1875 (18 Stat. 477).[92]

The act, in five sections, provided first that consular officers, before delivering the required permit or certificate to masters of vessels enrolled or licensed in and bound for the United States, must ascertain whether any immigrant on board had entered into a contract or agreement for a term of service in the United States for "lewd or immoral purposes." The second section prohibited the bringing of any Oriental persons "without their free and voluntary consent." The third section prohibited the importation of women "for the purposes of prostitution." The next section declared the contracting to supply coolie labor a felony; and the long final

[90]S. 971, 1188, H.R. 1588, 3895; ibid., pp. 2, 32, 37, 680.

[91]Ibid., pp. 3–4.

[92]Ibid., pp. 1113, 1454, 1599, 2161.

section was chiefly notable for its designation of certain excludable classes of aliens: (1) "persons who are undergoing a sentence for conviction in their own country of felonious crimes, other than political or growing out of or the result of political offenses, or whose sentence has been remitted on condition of their emigration," and (2), in reaffirmation of section 3, women "imported for the purposes of prostitution." Penalties for violation were provided in each section.

The Immigration Act of 1875 marks the beginning of direct federal regulation of immigration. It was only a limited beginning, under the immediate pressure of concern and moral indignation at the alleged importation of Chinese prostitutes and European criminals, but it began an extension of federal authority that soon was to be developed much further. Apart from the immediate and emotional issues at the moment, the time was ripe for this exercise of federal authority. For one thing, the old state rights issue was in disrepute. And the courts, up to the Supreme Court, had progressively declared unconstitutional and struck down the efforts of the states to protect themselves against unwanted immigration and the financial burdens it brought. Almost by default the regulation of immigration was falling to the federal government, and the representatives of the states that had formerly opposed federal intervention were now asking for it.[93]

Another aspect of the 1875 Act is of particular significance in the history of American immigration policy. This is the first designation, in sections 3 and 5, of certain classes of aliens as excludable. From this beginning, exclusion was to develop into a major instrument of immigration policy.

44th Congress (1875–1877)

President Grant's message on the opening of the 44th Congress called their attention to the problem of fraudulent naturalizations, as had his message of one year before to the preceding Congress. The new Congress did indeed give considerable attention to immigration, but followed its own concerns and priorities. Several naturalization bills were introduced and one was passed, though not fulfilling the President's recommendations. The encouragement and protection of immigrants received its share of attention; concern was expressed about the immigration of undesirable aliens but without new legislation; and further regulation of immigration and amendment of the immigration laws was proposed. But

[93]For a summary of court decisions ending state legislation on immigration, see U.S. Immigration Commission of 1911, Report, *Immigration Legislation,* vol. 39:24–27.

outranking all other concerns was the problem of Chinese immigration.

The House received at least four naturalization bills during the session, of which only one, introduced by Dunnell of Minnesota, was reported out of committee. Relating to the declaration of intention, it was passed without amendment by the House, and then by the Senate, and signed by President Grant on February 1, 1876.[94]

Concern for the well-being of the immigrant found expression in several bills. A House bill and a Senate bill had the related double objectives of promoting immigration and protecting immigrants.[95] Another House bill had the twin objectives of protecting immigrants and preventing the entry of criminals.[96] And in the Senate, Sargent of California introduced a bill of the same title as one he had introduced a year before in the second session of the preceding Congress, to protect persons of foreign birth against forcible constraint or involuntary servitude, evidently concerning the coolie trade. It was reported out with amendment by the Senate Committee on the Judiciary but progressed no further.[97]

One of the bills referred to above concerned the exclusion of criminals. Covering a broader range of undesirable aliens was a resolution offered in the Senate by Edmunds (Vt.). It was to instruct the Committee on Commerce to consider what legislation was needed to protect the nation

> against the evils of pauperism, crime, and other injuries to the morals and good order of society, and with a view to lending all lawful aid to the States in the exercise of their sanitary and policy jurisdiction.[98]

The resolution was not accepted at the time but laid over.

During the session the House received three bills to regulate immigration or to amend or supplement the immigration laws.[99] One of these (H.R. 2812), introduced by Piper of California, was referred to the Committee on the Judiciary, which reported out a substitute bill (H.R. 3688) to amend section 5 of the Immigration Act of 1875, in reinforcement of the exclusion provisions:

> When any two citizens shall file with the collector of any port of the United States an affidavit stating that they have reason to believe that on board any vessel or vessels arriving at said port there are persons prohibited from landing by this act, it shall be the duty of said

[94]H.R. 626; *Congressional Record,* 4: 300, 470. The other naturalization bills were H.R. 145, 428, and 999.

[95]The bills were S. 695 by Harvey (Kans.), and H.R. 4051 by Conger (Mich.); ibid., pp. 2176, 5030.

[96]H.R. 304 by Conger (Mich.); ibid., p. 243.

[97]S. 71; ibid., pp. 194, 5015.

[98]Ibid., p. 2866.

[99]H.R. 2812, 3688, 3853; ibid., pp. 1885, 3814, 4432.

> collector to make or cause to be made the inspection provided for in this act.[100]

Passed by the House, the bill was not acted on by the Senate.

Throughout the session, both branches of Congress received a series of bills and resolutions from their California members calling for measures against Chinese immigration. On January 6, 1876 Piper (Calif.) in the House presented a joint resolution asking for modification of existing treaties with the Chinese empire. It read as follows:

> Whereas the large immigration to the Pacific States and Territories of the United States of Mongolians, who are by nature, disposition, and habits incapable of assimilating with our laws and customs, tends to establish a foreign colony in the Republic, and directly brings American free labor in competition with that which is semi-servile. . . . That the President be, and is hereby, requested to use all means he may deem expedient to have the existing treaties of the Government of the United States with the government of the Chinese Empire so modified as to prevent any further immigration of the subjects of that empire to the United States.[101]

The resolution was referred to the Committee on Foreign Affairs. On January 18, Luttrell, also of California, introduced a House bill (H.R. 1303) to prevent the naturalization of Chinese and Mongolians. No action was taken on it.[102] In early February the Senate received a resolution of the California legislature calling for revision of treaties with China. A Senate committee was appointed to investigate Chinese immigration.[103] This was followed up on April 20 by a resolution introduced by Senator Sargent of California that the President enter into negotiations looking toward treaty revision to permit restrictions on Chinese immigration. The resolution was discussed at length and amended to provide for a committee of three Senators to investigate the Chinese problem on the West Coast and to report at the next session. On further consideration, the committee was made a joint committee with the House.[104] Several weeks later, Sargent submitted another resolution concerning the evils resulting from the influx of Chinese and calling on the Committee on Commerce to report a bill providing adequate restriction. The resolution was agreed to by the Senate.[105]

A week later, on May 15, Sargent introduced a bill of his own to restrict Chinese immigration (S. 829).[106] On the same day in the House,

[100] Ibid., p. 3744.
[101] Ibid., p. 300.
[102] Ibid., p. 477.
[103] Ibid., p. 901.
[104] Ibid., p. 2639.
[105] Ibid., p. 3026.
[106] Ibid., p. 3084.

Page introduced a resolution requesting the President to submit to the Chinese government an additional article to the existing treaty to the effect that the United States reserves the right "to regulate, restrict or prevent the immigration or importation of Chinese subjects into the United States except for commercial pursuits." It was referred to the Committee on Commerce. On the following day Piper introduced a House bill (H.R. 3468) for the same purpose as the Sargent bill in the Senate; and on June 12 he introduced a joint resolution in the House worded essentially the same as the Page resolution of May 15.[107] It was accepted by the House and forwarded to the Committee on Commerce. No further action with respect to Chinese immigration was taken during the remainder of the session.

The Chinese problem was still much in mind in the second session of the 44th Congress, but it brought no new legislation. The problem was referred to in Grant's message of December 5, 1876 on the opening of the session. On the coolie trade it was his advice to Congress to prepare

> such legislation as will forever preclude the enslavement of the Chinese upon our soil under the name of coolies, and also prevent American vessels from engaging in the transportation of coolies to any country.

With regard to Chinese immigration, the message stated that the majority of Chinese laborers came under contract, the women in a worse form, and legislation against these evils would be welcome. Further on in the message, following reference to Mormon polygamy in Utah, the President added,

> I invite the attention of Congress to another, though perhaps no less an evil, the importation of Chinese women, but few of whom are brought to our shores to pursue honorable or useful occupations.

On February 28, 1877 the House received the report of the special joint committee on Chinese immigration that had been set up in the preceding session. The committee had taken extensive testimony on the West Coast, and though they found some difference of opinion there, they believed there was evidence that the coming of the Chinese checked white migration to the area. They also reported evidence that the Chinese did not come to stay or to become citizens. Beyond this, there was a collection of accusations against the morals and sanitary habits of the Chinese—"They are cruel and indifferent to their sick"—and much else. The committee's recommendation was modification of the treaty with

[107]Ibid., pp. 3120, 3763.

China to permit restraint of "the great influx of Asiatics into this country."[108] No action was taken on the committee's recommendation at the time.

The only other matter related to immigration was the reporting out of a bill from the preceding session, the Cox bill for the regulation of immigration (H.R. 3853), with amendment. It was not acted on further.

45th Congress (1877–1879)

The extra and early first session of the 45th Congress received a scattered few bills on immigration, none of which progressed beyond referral to committee. In the House Conger (Mich.) introduced a bill of the same title as one he had presented in the preceding Congress, for the better protection of immigrants and to prevent the importation of criminals.[109] He also introduced a bill to promote immigration and to protect immigrants on their passage.[110] Page (Calif.) was author of a bill in the House to prohibit the immigration of subjects of China;[111] and several other bills concerned naturalization and passenger ships.

The second session of the 45th Congress convened at the usual opening date of early December. A few bills for the promotion and regulation of immigration were introduced, but the great preoccupation in the field of immigration was with the Chinese problem. No new legislation, however, came out of the session.

Three bills for the regulation of immigration were introduced, by Potter and Eickhoff of New York in the House, and by Sargent of California in the Senate.[112] Accompanying his bill, Potter presented a memorial from the commissioners of emigration of the State of New York. And the Senate received a bill from Davis (Ill.) to promote immigration and protect the immigrants.[113] All four of the above bills were referred to the Committee on Commerce and remained there.

At least five bills to regulate or restrict Chinese immigration were introduced early in the session. Several days after the opening, Shelley (Ala.) presented a House bill to regulate Chinese immigration, and its counterpart was introduced later in the Senate by Sargent (Calif.).[114] Three bills with the stated purpose of restricting Chinese immigration were introduced, one by Sargent in the Senate and the others by Wren

[108]Ibid., 5:2004.

[109]H.R. 640; ibid., 6:191

[110]H.R. 637; ibid.

[111]H.R. 727; ibid., p. 195.

[112]S. 1281, H.R. 3704, 4708; ibid., 7:3559, 1460, 3207, respectively.

[113]S. 514; ibid., p. 327.

[114]H.R. 1924, S. 477; ibid., pp. 68, 251.

(Nev.) and Davis (Calif.) in the House.[115] Luttrell (Calif.) entered two House bills, one to prohibit the employment of Chinese or Mongolians upon any public works, the other to deny naturalization to the same peoples.[116] Meanwhile two joint resolutions had been introduced by representatives from California, one by Luttrell concerning Chinese immigration and modification of the Burlingame treaty with China, the other by Eickhoff concerning the immigration of coolie labor.[117]

On January 28, 1878 the House received a memorial from the California senate appealing for congressional action on the Chinese problem and referred the memorial to the Committee on Education and Labor. On February 25 Willis, on behalf of the committee, reported out a joint resolution on Chinese immigration,[118] together with an accompanying report. The resolution was recommitted; the report that accompanied it, House Report 240, summarized the arguments against the Chinese—that they degrade labor, have undesirable personal habits, and do not assimilate—and the points in their favor. Especially because of unassimilability the committee concluded that their immigration should be restricted or prohibited, and advised discussions to that end with China and Great Britain (Hong Kong being the principal port of emigration).

Soon after in the Senate Sargent of California introduced a joint resolution, S. Res. 20, related to Chinese immigration. Presumably an authoritative statement of California views, this resolution read that,

> Whereas it appears that the great majority of Chinese immigrants are unwilling to conform to our institutions, to become permanent citizens of our country, and to accept the rights and assume the responsibilities of citizenship; and
>
> Whereas they have indicated no capacity to assimilate with our people, Therefore
>
> Resolved, etc., That the President of the United States be requested to open correspondence immediately with the governments of China and Great Britain with a view of securing a change or abrogation of all stipulations in existing treaties which permit the unlimited immigration of Chinese to the United States.[119]

Sargent followed up his resolution with a lengthy supporting statement in which he dwelt on the dangers of large immigration, the evils of

[115]S. 409, H.R. 2423, 2485; ibid., pp. 81, 318, 383.

[116]H.R. 2143, 2144; ibid., p. 271.

[117]H. Res. 72 and 74; ibid., pp. 98, 310. The Burlingame treaty of July 28, 1868 included sections stating the right of international migration. It also assured to Chinese subjects "most favored nations" treatment with respect to privileges, immunities, travel, and residence; but naturalization was denied.

[118]H. Res. 123; ibid., p. 1311.

[119]Ibid., p. 1446, 1544.

prostitution, undesirable conditions in Chinese areas of San Francisco, secret tribunals among the Chinese, their undependability under oath, the harm to American labor, and so on.[120] After further discussion on March 7, the resolution was sent to the Senate Committee on Foreign Relations on April 11. One month later, on May 7, the committee reported out a substitute, a concurrent resolution in place of Sargent's joint resolution. The brief new resolution was phrased in restrained and diplomatic form to urge that the existing treaty with China might wisely be modified to serve the best interests of both nations, and the President was respectfully invited to give the matter his attention.[121] The Senate on May 25 adopted its committee's resolution, and the House concurred on June 17 at the urging of Page, one of its members from California.[122] This ended action on the Chinese question for the session, which closed soon after.

President Hayes's message on the opening of the third session of the 45th Congress the following December did not call for legislation on Chinese immigration, but that subject monopolized the attention of Congress to the exclusion of other aspects of immigration.

Congress continued to show some resistance to the demands of its West Coast members. On January 7, 1879 a memorial was received from the Oregon legislature, the gist of which was that the importation of coolie slaves and laborers was a violation of treaty stipulations, for it was not voluntary immigration, that it was injurious to the laboring classes in the West, and that there was a heavy and harmful outflow of specie to China. Modification of the treaty with that country was urged. The memorial went to the Senate Committee on Foreign Relations, which a month later reported back asking to be discharged from further consideration of the memorial. The Senate agreed to the committee request. Meanwhile the same committee had received on January 24 a bill by Grover of Oregon to restrict Chinese immigration; and at the time of reporting on the Oregon memorial, the committee recommended indefinite postponement of the Grover bill.[123]

The House, in contrast, was more disposed to consider new legislation. On January 14, 1879 the House Committee on Education and Labor reported back with amendment the Wren (Nev.) bill, from the preceding session, to restrict Chinese immigration. At the same time the committee asked that the bill be recommitted for further consideration, which was done. Brought up again on January 28, the bill provided for limitation of

[120] Ibid., pp. 1544, 2439.

[121] Ibid., p. 3226.

[122] Ibid., p. 4782.

[123] Ibid., 8:361, 699, 1072. The Grover bill was S. 1697.

the number of Chinese passengers taken on board American vessels for passage to the United States, required separate manifesting of Chinese passengers, and set penalties for violation. In its accompanying report, the committee reasoned that the existing treaty with China did not prevent regulation of immigration and restriction was needed for the protection of American society and American labor.[124] The bill was discussed at length in the House, remarks were extended, and various materials were inserted in the *Congressional Record* (including Bret Harte's poem "Plain Language from Truthful James" and a petition from citizens of California). The bill was then taken up section by section and passed by a vote of 155 to 72 on January 28. The Senate Committee on Foreign Relations reported out the bill on February 7, and, consistently with its other action of that day on the Chinese question, asked to be discharged from further responsibility. The Senate took up the bill on February 12, and the protracted debate continued to the fifteenth, with Sargent of California one of the principal proponents. A number of amendments were proposed, of which the Senate adopted eight, including the exemption of Chinese officials from the terms of the bill and a call on the President to notify the Chinese government of abrogation of a portion of the treaty. In this amended form, the bill passed the Senate by a vote of 39 to 27, was accepted by the House,[125] and then was vetoed by President Hayes. His reasons were principally two: that constitutionally it is not Congress but the President who has the right to abrogate a treaty, with the advice and consent of the Senate; and, second, that since the Chinese government would probably accept some modification of the treaty, it was preferable to proceed by diplomatic negotiation rather than by unilateral action.[126]

46th Congress (1879–1881)

The 46th Congress met in an early first session from March 18 to July 1, 1879. Except for the Chinese question, there was almost no action on immigration.[127] In the House, Goode of Virginia entered a bill to restrict Chinese immigration.[128] In the Senate, a bill restricting employment of Chinese was introduced by Slater of Oregon. One section provided that

[124]Ibid., pp. 447, 791, 793.

[125]Ibid., 8:1072, 1235, 1264, 1299, 1383, 1400, 1796.

[126]Ibid., p. 2275.

[127]The only other bill was for the regulation of passenger travel by sea, S. 1824, ibid., 9:4228.

[128]H.R. 335; ibid., p. 614.

> it shall not be lawful for any citizen or subject of the Chinese Empire, then resident or thereafter becoming resident of the United States, to engage in, carry on, or work at any manufacturing or mechanical business, or to own or lease, carry on, or work any mine, or to own or lease any real estate for any purpose other than that of lawful commerce and for places of residence, or to conduct any farm, garden, vineyard, or orchard for agricultural, horticultural, or other like purpose, or to own, have, or keep any herd of cattle, horses, sheep, goats, or swine for the purpose of making profit by the increase, product, or use thereof, or to keep any hotel or restaurant for public entertainment, excepting for the use and accommodation of the citizens and subjects of China, or to work or engage to work as mechanic, artisan, laborer, waiter, servant, cook, clerk, or messenger, or in any other capacity, or at any other kind of labor, skilled or unskilled, except for and in the employ of citizens and subjects of China lawfully engaged in commerce in the United States or travelling or residing therein.[129]

The bill would also make unlawful the employment of Chinese in such capacity by any person or corporation. Slater defended his bill in a lengthy speech, but without further debate. Both the Goode and Slater bills were referred to committee and remained there.

In the second session of the 46th Congress, the Chinese question was still prominent and the western members continued their efforts to get restrictive legislation, but the issue no longer absorbed attention to the exclusion of other immigration matters.

The message from President Hayes at the opening of the second session on December 1, 1879 stated that discussions had been held with the government of Switzerland about pauper and convict emigration. And the President was pleased to report that the government of China had indicated willingness to consider problems of migration and to cooperate in such measures "as may tend to prevent injurious consequences to the United States."

On the second day of the session, the House received a petition from the New York commissioners of emigration asking for legislation to protect immigrants.[130] A bill for that purpose and to promote immigration was introduced later in the House by Barber of Illinois.[131] The House also received two bills to regulate the carriage of passengers by sea.[132] One bill was reported out but went no further.

Somewhat more action was taken on a bill introduced by Cox of New

[129]S. 622; ibid., pp. 1507, 2258.

[130]Ibid., 10:19.

[131]H.R. 3890; ibid., p. 529.

[132]H.R. 4984 and 5705; ibid., pp. 1389, 2243.

York at the beginning of the session. The bill for the regulation of immigration went to the House Committee on Foreign Affairs, was reported back, recommitted, and then reported out again with amendments and an accompanying committee report.[133]

The bill was debated on April 22, 1880,[134] and the discussion on the floor of the House plus the committee's report gave not only the terms of the bill but also some of the thinking behind it. The bill itself was said to be the same as an earlier bill introduced in the 44th Congress and reported out by the committee in January 1877 (probably H.R. 3853, also by Cox, 44th Cong., 2nd sess.). The need for the legislation proposed was felt to have been created by a recent Supreme Court decision. This was presumably the decision of March 20, 1876, in which the Supreme Court declared unconstitutional the state laws imposing head taxes and gave its opinion that under the Constitution power over immigration lies in the hands of the federal government.

Requirements set by the bill included a listing of the name, place of birth, last legal residence, age, and occupation of each immigrant, and a separate reporting of all paupers, convicts, lunatics, idiots, deaf and dumb, blind, maimed, and infirm persons, and all immigrants unable to support themselves. Landing was prohibited for those who had been inmates of lunatic asylums or poorhouses within the past six months, and they, together with those found on inspection to be unable to support themselves, were to be returned to the port of embarcation at the expense of the owners of the ship that brought them. Also prohibited was the immigration of persons pardoned for a crime on condition of emigration. The bill was debated at length but not voted on, and it was not brought up again during the session.

Strong pressure for restriction of Chinese immigration continued. On December 17, 1879 the House received a report of a vote in California to find the wishes of the people of that state regarding Chinese immigration.[135] The vote was 883 in favor, and 154,638 opposed. In January 1880 two bills for the restriction of Chinese immigration were introduced by Representatives Page and Davis of California.[136] And on March 10 the House Committee on Education and Labor reported out a bill, H.R. 5058, for the restriction of Chinese immigration, as a substitute for the Goode bill of the same purpose (H.R. 335) from the first session of the 46th Congress.[137] The brief accompanying report explained that the committee amendments were to change the effective date of the bill from

[133] H.R. 2408; ibid., pp. 15, 45; and H. Rept. 1, December 9, 1879 (46-II).
[134] Ibid., pp. 2662–72.
[135] Ibid., 10:151; H. Rept. 572.
[136] Ibid., pp. 221, 286.
[137] Ibid., p. 1436.

1879 to July 1, 1880 and to eliminate part of one section, in which form the bill was identical with one reported out by the committee in the 45th Congress.[138]

Still other reports on the Chinese question came to the House during the session. Early in the session, on December 10, 1879, the select committee "relative to the causes of the general depression in labor and business; and as to Chinese immigration" presented a long report of its labors, a compilation of testimony taken at hearings in San Francisco, New York, and other cities.[139] On March 19, 1880 the committee issued its final report.[140] With respect to the Chinese question, which drew nearly all of the committee's attention, the committee was of the opinion that the people of California had just cause for complaint and that it is impossible for the Chinese and American citizens ever to meet on common ground or occupy the same social level.[141] The solution in the judgment of the committee was annullment of the treaties with China that permitted the immigration. In an accompanying minority report, two members of the committee, Sherwin (Ill.) and Martin (N.C.), expressed doubt whether the depression of business and labor in California was due to the presence of the Chinese; but they nevertheless agreed with the majority that the immigration should be checked. And in a more extended dissent, another committee member, Cowgill (Ind.), questioned whether the committee's conclusions were justified by the biased sort of testimony received, and further asserted that the majority's attention to the Chinese was not consistent with the purpose of the committee.

In a final report, on April 12, the House received a message from the President transmitting a report of the Secretary of State on the progress of negotiations with the government of China concerning the emigration of its subjects to the United States.[142] The session concluded on June 16, 1880 without legislation on the Chinese question, in continued hope that the problem might be solved by the treaty negotiations in progress.

Before the opening of the third session of the 46th Congress a new treaty was concluded with China, on November 17, 1880. In the section relating to immigration, the government of China recognized the right of the United States to "regulate, limit, or suspend such coming or residence, but may not absolutely prohibit it," provided the coming or residence of Chinese laborers was considered to endanger the interests

[138] H. Rept. 519. The number of the earlier bill was not given.

[139] H. Misc. Doc. 5, 465 pages in length.

[140] H. Rept. 572 (46-II).

[141] Ibid., p. 25.

[142] *Congressional Record,* 10:2326.

or good order of the United States or any locality therein. It was stipulated in the same section, however, that the controls on immigration be reasonable and that they apply only to laborers.

In his message to the third session of the 46th Congress, President Hayes touched on varied matters such as reform of the civil service, rights of colored citizens, suppression of polygamy in Utah, the blessings of prosperity at home and good relations abroad, the project of an interoceanic canal at the Isthmus of Panama, together with the usual fiscal and budgetary matters. There was little reference to immigration.

In the House Cox of New York introduced a resolution on the opening day, asking the President for information on correspondence and treaties with China regarding immigration and commerce between the two nations. The resolution went to the Committee on Foreign Affairs for their consideration.[143] And the Governor of Nevada submitted the results of a ballot similar to that taken in California. Out of 18,397 votes cast, "a very full vote," 17,259 were opposed to Chinese immigration and 955 refrained from giving an opinion.[144]

The only other action touching on immigration was a resolution introduced by Kernan (N.Y.), and agreed to in the Senate, to request the President to communicate any correspondence since 1869 between the Secretary of State and agents of the United States abroad concerning the sending of criminals, paupers, or insane persons to this country.[145]

47th Congress (1881–1883)

In his message on the opening of the 47th Congress, the new President Chester A. Arthur made two recommendations concerning immigration legislation. One was for attention to the supervision and transitory care of immigrants at ports of landing, since the financial burden now fell on the states and they had been denied relief through head taxes. The second recommendation, perhaps made with shrewd appreciation of the temper of Congress, was to be considerate of the interests and susceptibilities of the Chinese government in any modification of the immigration laws.

The unusually long first session (from December 5, 1881 to August 8, 1882, instead of the customary three-month session) saw an unprecedented flood of immigration bills, which fell into two or three broad groups somewhat along the lines indicated by the presidential message, regulation of immigration, care of immigrants, and Chinese immigration.

[143]Ibid., 11:11.
[144]Ibid., p. 709.
[145]Ibid., p. 775.

In retrospect, the session was one of the most productive, with the enactment of three major acts concerning immigration.

With the advances in shipbuilding and the rapid increase in size of the steamship, the earlier passenger or steerage acts of 1854, 1848, and earlier were becoming obsolete, and need was felt for a modernization of the regulation of passenger travel and accommodations. On January 9, 1882 a House bill was introduced by Deuster (Wis.) to regulate the carriage of passengers by sea. It was reported out favorably by the Committee on Commerce at the end of the month, and was brought up in the House on April 18.[146] In an improvement on earlier legislation, the carrying capacity of vessels was specified in terms of cubic feet of space, rather than tonnage of vessel or square feet of deck space. Passenger quarters were limited to the main deck and the next deck below, and minimum space on those decks was set at 100 or more cubic feet per passenger, with children under one not counted and those aged one to eight counted as one-half person. Other specifications dealt with height between decks, the segregation of the unmarried, ventilation, food on board, supply of water, hospital facilities, and the availability of a physician. The bill passed the House without difficulty on April 18, was favorably reported in the Senate, and was passed there after little debate on June 19. On July 1 it was vetoed by President Arthur. In his veto message he acknowledged the good purpose of the act but enumerated certain objections. The limitation of passenger accommodations to two decks was undesirable, for among other reasons the new steamships had added a spar deck above the main deck, and the terms of the present bill would impose a heavy loss. The requirement of seven feet of clear height in passenger decks, too, would penalize the smaller vessels; and the requirement of a complete list of all passengers before clearance for sailing was also undesirable.[147] The veto was sustained, whereupon Congress set to work on a new bill to meet the presidential objections.[148]

Promptly after the veto message, Deuster (Wis.), author of the vetoed bill, introduced a new House bill of the same title, modified in

[146]H.R. 2744; ibid., 13:296, 739, 3012; accompanied by H. Rept. 121. In the Senate another bill of the same title, S. 1100, was introduced by Conger (Mich.) on February 3, 1882.

[147]Ibid., pp. 5572–73. The final objection applied to section 12 requiring that, before a vessel is cleared, "the master of such vessel shall furnish to the collector of customs . . . a correct list of all passengers who have been, or are intended to be, taken on board the vessel, and the said list shall specify the age, sex, and nationality of each passenger."

[148]Meanwhile Davis (Ill.) on February 20 had introduced H.R. 4571 to promote immigration and for the protection of immigrants, but it did not get out of the Committee on Commerce; ibid., p. 1302.

view of the objections stated in the veto message, and it was further changed in the Committee on Commerce to which it was referred. Passengers were allowed on three decks, the main deck and the two immediately below, with 100 cubic feet of space per passenger on the two upper decks and 120 on the lowest deck. Committee amendment set the food allowance per passenger as "equal in value to one and a half navy rations of the United States, and of fresh water not less than four quarts per day shall be furnished each of such passengers." And three meals per day were to be served. In this form the bill was passed in the House on July 22, 1882, it was passed by the Senate without debate on July 29, and it was approved by the President on August 4.[149]

A second task that Congress set itself during this productive session was the regulation of immigration beyond the first steps taken in the 1875 Act. Numerous petitions were coming to Congress from the states, now deprived of head tax revenue, asking for legislation to protect them from the burden of indigent and unwanted immigrants. A dozen or more such petitions came from New York, including one from the legislature asking for protection from the care and expense occasioned by the importation of criminals, paupers, and lunatics,[150] and several petitions came from other states.

The New York members of Congress took the initiative in introducing bills for the regulation of immigration, one in the Senate (S. 2074) by Miller and two in the House (H.R. 5115, 5669) by Van Voorhis.[151] On June 19, 1882 the House Committee on Commerce reported out its own bill to regulate immigration (H.R. 6596). A first provision of the bill was a head tax of fifty cents on each alien coming by vessel, the money so obtained to be administered by the Treasury Department as an immigrant fund to defray the expenses of regulating immigration and caring for immigrants in the United States. The expenditure at a given port, however, was not to exceed the sum collected there. The second section authorized the boarding of vessels and examination of passengers, and

> if on such examination there shall be found among such passengers any convict, lunatic, idiot, or any person unable to take care of himself or herself without becoming a public charge, or any persons who, from any attending circumstances, are likely to become a public charge, . . . such persons shall not be permitted to land, but shall be returned in such vessel to the countries from whence they came at the expense of the owners of said vessel.[152]

[149]H.R. 6722; ibid., pp. 5752, 6367, 6904. The accompanying report was H.Rept. 1699.
[150]Ibid., p. 1368.
[151]Ibid., pp. 5205, 1840, 2678.
[152]Ibid., p. 5105, 1506.

Section 4 read:

> That all foreign paupers, convicts, or accused persons of other than political offenses, or persons suffering from mental alienation, in the United States who are a public charge on their arrival in this country shall be sent back by the United States to the nations to which they belong and from whence they came.[153]

Such return passages were to be paid for out of the immigrant fund.

The House passed the bill by the overwhelming vote of 110 to 16. Forwarded to the Senate, it was recalled by the House for revision and correction. In its revised and renumbered form (now H.R. 6677) the bill omitted the phrase "or any persons who, from any attending circumstances, are likely to become a public charge" from section 2; the return of those excluded at the expense of the owner of the vessel was also omitted. And section 4 was revised to read:

> That all foreign convicts, except those convicted of political offenses, upon arrival shall be sent back to the nations to which they belong and from whence they came.

In this revised form, the bill passed the House again, was reported without amendment in the Senate, considered, and passed without debate by the Senate on July 29, and was signed by President Arthur to become the Immigration Act of August 3, 1882 (22 Stat. 214).[154]

The principal addition made by this 1882 Act to the still small but growing body of American immigration policy was the expansion of the excludable classes from the two designated in the 1875 Act, the convict and immoral classes, to four with the addition of mental defectives (lunatic, idiot) and those unable to take care of themselves without becoming public charges. Perhaps quite as significant was what Congress chose to delete from the original draft of the bill. Amendment in committee removed two major features of the bill as originally written, the excludability of those considered likely to become a public charge, and the deportability of certain classes if they became public charges on arrival. Except for the brief term of the 1798 Aliens Act, deportability had not existed in American immigration law. (See, however, the Chinese Exclusion Act of 1882, below.)

The third immigration problem to be attacked during the first session of the 47th Congress was that of the Chinese. Pressure for legislative action had not relaxed on the West Coast, and the encouraging progress of diplomatic negotiations led to a flood of proposals from without and

[153]Ibid., p. 1506.

[154]Ibid., pp. 5415, 6282, 6627, 6904.

within Congress. On the order of twenty-five petititions on the subject came to the 47th Congress during its first session, not just from California but also from citizens of Alabama, Indiana, Iowa, Maryland, Massachusetts, Minnesota, Missouri, New York, Ohio, Pennsylvania, West Virginia, and Wisconsin. Various civic groups were also represented among the petitioners: the San Francisco Board of Trade, the San Francisco Immigration Association, the Methodist Church, the New York Board of Trade, the New York Union League Club, and the Milwaukee Trades Assembly. Varying in their terms, the petitions were nevertheless uniform in appealing for restrictions on the admission of Chinese.

There was a corresponding multiplication of bills in Congress for the restriction of Chinese immigration, at least four in the Senate and eight in the House.[155] Titles of the bills varied: some were "to execute certain treaty stipulations relating to Chinese," one was for "the protection of labor in the United States," and two were more explicitly entitled "to regulate, limit, and suspend the immigration of Chinese"; but all had the same intent of checking the inflow from China.

Work in the Senate started on a bill introduced by Miller of California (S. 71) on the opening day of Congress, December 5, 1881. Referred to the Committee on Foreign Relations, it was reported back with a new text substituted on January 26, 1882 and debated at great length in the Senate on February 28 and on into several days of March.[156] As reported by the committee, the bill would suspend the immigration of Chinese laborers, including skilled laborers, for twenty years. During debate mention was made of the 1880 Democratic party convention plank of no Chinese immigration except for travel, education, and foreign commerce. The Republican party in the same year called only for a restriction of such immigration. The Senate finally passed the bill on March 9 by a vote of 29 to 15. After more lengthy debate, the House passed the bill by the wide margin of 167 to 66 on March 23. On April 4 President Arthur vetoed the bill as a repudiation of treaty obligations and contrary to good foreign policy. The veto was upheld by the Senate, whose vote of 29 to 21 for the bill fell short of the required majority.[157]

On April 6, two days after the veto, the House received no fewer than three bills providing shorter periods of suspension, to satisfy the presidential objections; and on April 10 McLane of Maryland introduced a

[155]S. 21, 71, 1648, 1655 by Senators Grover (Oreg.), Miller (Calif.), Miller and Farley (Calif.); H.R. 49, 52, 2116, 3285, 5667, 5668, and 5669 by Representatives Page (Calif.), Page and Berry (Calif.), Willis (Ky.), Page, Willis, and Van Voorhis (N.Y.), respectively. The House Committee on Education and Labor also introduced its own bill, H.R. 3540.

[156]*Congressional Record,* 13:5, 630, 1480–88, 1515–23, 1545–49, etc.

[157]Ibid., pp. 2551, 2607, 2617.

resolution for the abrogation of the offending articles 5 and 6 of the Burlingame treaty.[158] The House Committee on Education and Labor had earlier worked on its own Chinese immigration bill (H.R. 3540), through recommittal and amendment, but at last had substituted the Senate bill S. 71.[159] Following the veto of the latter, the committee took up a recently submitted bill from Page of California (H.R. 5667) but then substituted a new bill (H.R. 5804) for it on April 12.[160] The latter was in most respects like the vetoed bill, but provided a suspension period of ten rather than twenty years. Passed by the House, 201 to 37 after debate, it went to the Senate, where a number of amendments were attached. In its final form, section 12 of the bill provided for the deportation of "any Chinese person found unlawfully within the United States," and section 14 stated that "hereafter no State court or court of the United States shall admit Chinese to citizenship." It was then passed by a vote of 32 to 15 on April 28.[161] The House accepted the Senate amendments, and President Arthur gave approval on May 6, 1882 (22 Stat. 58).

Immigration matters settled down to a stage of comparative quiet after the legislative accomplishments of the 47th Congress in its first session. In his message of December 4, 1882 on the opening of the second session, President Arthur was pleased to report that

> the immigration of paupers and criminals from certain cantons of Switzerland has ceased and is no longer sanctioned by the authorities.

A question of interpretation had arisen in connection with the Chinese exclusion act:

> The recent legislation restricting immigration of laborers from China has given rise to the question whether Chinese proceeding to or from another country may lawfully pass through our own.

Legislative attention was called for here, but the direction for it to take was indicated, for

> Construing the act of May 6, 1882, in connection with the treaty of November 17, 1880, the restriction would seem to be limited to Chinese immigrants coming to the United States as laborers, and would not forbid a mere transit of our territory.

During the session, two bills were introduced to amend the Immigration Act of 1882, and one to amend the naturalization laws.[162] And a new

[158] H. Res. 187; ibid., p. 2735.
[159] Ibid., pp. 645, 737, 1899.
[160] Ibid., p. 2810.
[161] Ibid., pp. 2967–74, 3412.
[162] S. 2391, H.R. 7438, 7618; ibid., 14:1374, 1734, 2941.

concern suddenly appeared, on the danger of immigrants bringing infectious disease. Fifteen or more petitions to Congress asked that the sanitary inspection of immigrants be continued. Among the petitions there were several from Illinois, including one from the state legislature, others from citizens of Iowa, Kentucky, Michigan, Ohio, West Virginia, and Wisconsin, together with petitions from boards of health in Iowa, Michigan, Dayton, and Pittsburgh. In the Senate a bill to provide for the sanitary inspection of immigrants was introduced by Conger of Michigan, and the House received a bill of the same title from Rich, also of Michigan.[163] No bills were passed by either the House or the Senate during the session.

Comment

The 47th Congress and the two major immigration bills it enacted in 1882 mark the end of the indecision between state and federal jurisdiction over immigration. During the two decades from the beginning of the Civil War, the federal government moved slowly and almost reluctantly to assume responsibility over immigration, but the logic of the problems, just as in the case of naturalization, called for a uniform national system, rather than local regulation; the state rights issue had died with the outcome of the war, and the Constitution as interpreted by the courts provided grounds for ruling against state immigration laws.

Under the temporary stimulus of wartime manpower shortages, national policy had swung toward encouragement of immigration, but this soon changed with the end of the war and the rising tide of immigration that brought more and more immigrants across the Atlantic. As state controls were successively declared unconstitutional, Congress began to face problems the states and seaport cities had confronted earlier, the problems of poor relief and of immigrants who were undesirable for reasons other than dependency, the latter compounded by the suspicion that other nations were dumping their least-wanted citizens in the United States. Special problems also arose from time to time, such as the Chinese coolie trade with its repugnant resemblance to the slave trade, the exploitation and victimization of immigrants at sea and after arrival, and finally the violent anti-Chinese reaction to Oriental immigration on the West Coast.

Congress had proceeded slowly, step by step, in extending its authority in the areas of immigration, first with the passenger acts or steer-

[163] S. 2284, H.R. 7121; ibid., pp. 548, 530.

age legislation that was continued from prewar days and that most clearly called for treatment on a national basis; second, with the coolie acts that dealt with a problem where federal action was most appropriate; third, with the Immigration Act of 1875, which was aimed primarily against two unwanted classes of aliens and also reinforced the coolie trade acts; and, finally, with the Immigration Act of 1882 that broadened the control exercised over immigration by Congress.

In this gradual assumption of responsibility for the regulation and control of immigration, Congress had employed the customary devices of prohibiting and penalizing, but several new instruments of immigration policy came to be added. One such instrument was the exclusion of certain designated undesirable classes, as was done in the 1875 and 1882 acts; another was deportation, so far applicable only to Chinese as provided in the Chinese Exclusion Act of 1882. Also added in the Immigration Act of 1882, but only to a limited degree, was a tax levy, a device long used by the states. As applied, its purpose was evidently to produce revenue, but it was a readily available instrument for later restrictive use.

In justice it should be recognized that even after the brief period of encouragement, congressional concern with immigration was not exclusively regulatory and restrictive. Much congressional thought and legislative effort went into attempts to ensure the welfare of the migrants at sea and to protect them from abuses after arrival. Congress, too, in its legislation against the convict class of aliens was always careful to exempt those whose crime or conviction was of a political nature.

4 The Development of the Regulatory System, 1883–1913

With the acts of 1875 and 1882, Congress had at last made a commitment to the principle of federal regulation and responsibility for immigration. From that time through the following decades, the basic problems were to remain much the same as before, only magnified by the rising volume of immigration. The legislative response to these long familiar but newly expanded problems was essentially within the already established framework, through act after act, to expand and reinforce the regulatory system and to strengthen its enforcement.

48th Congress (1883–1885)

The first session of the 48th Congress directed its attention to a wide range of immigration problems. In his annual message on December 4, 1883, President Arthur pointed out two matters needing congressional action. One was the persistent and troublesome question of pauper emigration from Great Britain. Paupers from that country had been sent back, it was stated, and assurances had been received from the British government that it was taking precautions to prevent such emigration. Numbers of such cases were still arriving, however, and their coming also by way of Canada showed the need for revision of the laws on the subject.

The second matter touched on in the message was experience under the Chinese exclusion act of the year before. On this point, the President stated,

> There is good reason to believe that the law restricting the immigration of Chinese has been violated, intentionally or otherwise, by the officials of China upon whom is devolved the duty of certifying that the immigrants belong to the excepted classes.

The Chinese immigration problem was evidently still far from a satisfactory solution, for Congress received well over a hundred petitions on the subject during the course of the first session. It was notable, too, that now it was no longer the far western states, but midwestern states such as Illinois, Ohio, and Kansas, that sent the most petitions.[1]

In the Senate, Miller of California promptly entered a bill to amend the Chinese Exclusion Act of 1882. It was reported out of committee with amendment, but then passed over by the Senate in favor of a House bill of the same purpose.[2] The House bill, introduced by Henley of California, had been drawn up by the delegations from Oregon, California, Nevada, and the Territories of Arizona and Washington, and therefore was presumably a reliable reflection of western views. It was reported out by the Committee on Foreign Relations with an attached report and was brought up in the House on May 3, 1884.[3]

A first objective of the bill was to make clear that reference to Chinese laborers in the 1882 Act applied to all Chinese, whether or not they were subjects of China, for courts had held that the 1882 Act did not apply to Chinese from places other than China. A second purpose of the bill was to meet the "manifold evasions" of the act; and the committee report referred to "the notorious capabilities of the lower classes of Chinese for perjury." The exemption of merchants and travelers from the exclusion provisions had provided a loophole, which the bill was designed to close by requiring evidence of bona fide exempt status. A minority report attached to the committee report raised various objections to the bill, including the one that the bill would have effects beyond the laborer class.

The bill was debated at length in the House, with arguments presented both for and against. A few amendments were accepted, for the most part with the recommendation of the committee, and it was finally passed by the one-sided vote of 184 to 13, but with a large number (125) of abstentions. On July 3 it passed the Senate almost without debate, by a vote of 43 to 12 with 21 abstentions, and was signed by the President to become the Act of July 5, 1884 (23 Stat. 115).

The first session of the 48th Congress received a second flood of petitions, less numerous than those on Chinese immigration, but representing a rapidly rising if not entirely new concern over the effects of heavy immigration on native labor. Principally, this concern took the form of attack on so-called contract labor. Distaste for the labor contract with immigrants had appeared earlier, it will be remembered, for the reason given for the repeal in 1868 of the 1864 act encouraging immigra-

[1]The distribution of the petitions by state was as follows: Alabama, California, Connecticut (2), Illinois (21), Indiana (5), Iowa (10), Kansas (15), Kentucky, Maine, Maryland (3), Michigan (12), Minnesota (2), Missouri (6), Nebraska (2), New Jersey (9), New York (11), Ohio (20), Pennsylvania (9), Tennessee (2), Texas (3), West Virginia (4), and Wisconsin.

[2]S. 791; *Congressional Record*, 15:154.

[3]H.R. 1798, with H. Rept. 614; ibid., pp. 240, 3752.

tion was that it provided for such contracts. But now contract labor became a leading issue and, one may suspect, a rallying point for anti-immigration forces.

Well over fifty petitions against contract labor came to the 48th Congress during its first session, from groups of citizens in thirteen states, together with others from several state legislatures, labor organizations, and the Chicago Board of Trade.[4] Predictably, the petitions were accompanied by a series of bills, variously titled, against contract labor. On January 8, 1884 the House received from Foran (Ohio) a bill to prohibit the importation and migration of foreigners and aliens under contract or agreement to perform labor. On January 14 a similar bill, to protect American workers from the effects of importation of foreign labor under the contract-labor system, was introduced in the House by Ferrell (N.J.). And on April 14 the Senate received a bill to protect American laborers, from George (Miss.).[5] The Foran bill made the most progress, being reported out by the Committee on Labor, brought up in the House on June 19, 1884, and passed after amendment by a vote of 102 to 17. In the Senate it was reported out and debated, but no final action was taken.

Two later House bills of essentially the same title were introduced, evidently aimed at contract labor without mentioning it by name; one was introduced by Caldwell of Tennessee, the other by Bagley of New York. As stated in the titles, the purpose of the bills was "to prohibit the business of importing pauper laborers, lazzaroni, and beggars . . . and hiring out the same."[6] Neither progressed beyond referral to committee.

Several other topics received less attention during the session. On January 17, 1884 the Senate received a resolution adopted by the American Public Health Association pointing to "the large number and undue proportion, according to population, of insane, criminals, and paupers among our foreign-born population," and stating the urgent need for laws to exclude such undesirables. The resolution was referred to a Select Committee on Epidemic Diseases.[7] In the House a resolution was submitted by Guenther (Wis.) calling for a commission on immigration.[8] Three bills to amend the Immigration Act of 1882 were introduced in the House.[9] The House also received H.R. 6179 to regulate the carriage of

[4]The distribution by state of the petitions from citizens was Illinois (3), Indiana (3), Iowa (3), Massachusetts (2), Michigan (10), Missouri (2), New Jersey (3), New York (5), Ohio (11), Pennsylvania (10), South Carolina, West Virginia, and Wisconsin (1 each).

[5]H.R. 2550, 3313, S. 2042; ibid., pp. 283, 390, 2919.

[6]H.R. 5602, 7460; ibid., pp. 1567, 5798.

[7]Ibid., pp. 460, 476.

[8]H. Res. 62; ibid., p. 120.

[9]H.R. 685, 1032, 2992; ibid., pp. 81, 99, 297.

passengers by sea and two bills, H.R. 1629 and 6402, to amend the naturalization laws. In addition, both the Senate and the House received a bill to forbid the purchase of land by aliens. These were S. 2154 by Plumb of Kansas, to prevent the acquisition of real property by aliens, and H.R. 5266 by Oates of Alabama, to prohibit aliens and foreigners from acquiring title to or owning lands within the United States. These were not acted on until the next session.

The one other action concerning immigration during the session was initiated by the Senate in amendment of a House bill for the aid of the American merchant marine. This bill was H.R. 2228, introduced by Dingley of Maine, and entitled "A bill to remove certain burdens on the American merchant marine and encourage the American foreign carrying trade." Heavily amended in the Senate, the Dingley bill received a number of new sections. One Senate provision was that until the head tax of fifty cents levied by the Act of August 3, 1882 (22 Stat. 214) on every alien passenger arriving by steam or sailing vessel should be made applicable to aliens coming by land, "passengers coming by vessels employed exclusively in the trade between the ports of the United States and the ports of the Dominion of Canada or the ports of Mexico" should not be subject to the head tax. Passed as part of the amended bill in the Senate and retained in the conference report, this exemption from head tax became effective as section 22 of the Act of June 26, 1884 (23 Stat. 58).

President Arthur's message to the second session of the 48th Congress mentioned the need for clarification of the Chinese exclusion and of the naturalization laws. With regard to immigration, the session dealt with bills carried over from the preceding session, for the most part, but enacted one important piece of legislation. The Foran contract labor bill (H.R. 2550) after repeated attempts was brought up in the Senate and debated for several days. After amendment, it was passed by the Senate on February 18, 1885, the House accepted the amendment, and with presidential approval it became the Alien Contract Labor Act of February 26, 1885 (23 Stat. 332), the first of the contract labor laws.[10]

Stated in comprehensive terms, the first section of the new act provided that

> it shall be unlawful for any person, company, partnership, or corporation, in any manner whatsoever, to prepay the transportation, or in any way assist or encourage the importation or migration of any alien or aliens, any foreigner or foreigners, into the United States, its Territories, or the District of Columbia, under contract or agree-

[10]For further account of this act, see U.S. Immigration Commission of 1911, Report, *Immigration Legislation*, 39:33–34.

> ment, parol or special, express or implied, made previous to the importation or migration of such alien or aliens, foreigner or foreigners, to perform labor or service of any kind in the United States, its Territories, or the District of Columbia.

The second section voided all contracts or agreements for employment if made prior to immigration. The next two sections provided penalties for violation, including a fine of five hundred dollars on the master of any vessel who knowingly brings a contract laborer into the country. The fifth section exempted from the terms of the act (1) foreigners temporarily in the United States and engaging other foreigners as secretaries, servants, or domestics; (2) skilled laborers, provided such laborers cannot be obtained in the United States; (3) professional actors, artists, lecturers, or singers, or persons employed strictly as personal or domestic servants; and (4) assistance by a resident of a member of his family or a personal friend to come for the purpose of settlement.

Two other bills carried over from the first session, S. 2154 by Plumb (Kans.) and H.R. 5266 by Oates (Ala.), prohibiting land purchase by aliens, were reported out of committee but were not acted on further.

A new bill was introduced in the House to explain certain provisions in the Chinese Exclusion Act of 1884, but it did not get out of committee.[11]

49th Congress (1885–1887)

Immigration and related matters touched on in President Cleveland's message to the incoming 49th Congress included certain hardships under the Chinese exclusion act, mob violence against Chinese in the West, deficiencies in the naturalization laws, and a recommendation that Mormons wishing to immigrate be excluded.

After a year or two of comparative quiet, Chinese immigration again became a subject of active agitation. Citizens of eighteen states sent petitions to Congress, Knights of Labor who heretofore had concerned themselves with the contract labor issue now sent petitions from nine states, and additional petitions came from other sources. Three bills of identical title or intent, to change treaties with China and to exclude all Chinese except diplomatic and consular representatives, were entered in the Senate and House.[12] A bill to amend the Chinese immigration laws was entered in both House and Senate by Fair from Nevada (S. 1991) and

[11]H.R. 7519; *Congressional Record,* 16:56.

[12]S. 1483 and H.R. 5565, 5567, by Mitchell (Oreg.), Henley (Calif.), and Felton (Calif.), respectively.

Morrow from California (H.R. 171). The former (S. 1991), was amended and passed by the Senate. Its purpose was to make clear that the term *Chinese laborer* applied to all Chinese regardless of place of origin. One other bill (H.R. 5824), to prohibit Chinese immigration altogether, was introduced in the House by Voorhies (Wash.). In marked contrast were a Senate bill (S. 2225) and a House Resolution (H. Res. 147) "to indemnify Chinese for the outrages at Rock Springs, Wyoming." The former passed the Senate but went no further. Meanwhile, Congress received two reports, in the form of executive documents (H. Exec. Doc. 102, S. Exec. Doc. 118), concerning the treaty rights of Chinese subjects, and another (S. Exec. Doc. 103) on the fraudulent importation of Chinese.

The drive to prohibit land purchases by aliens or to restrict their holding of land, which had appeared in the preceding session, increased sharply in the 49th Congress. Plumb of Kansas and Oates of Alabama, authors of the Senate and House bills in the 48th Congress, reintroduced their bills in the 49th (S. 188 and H.R. 3183). Four additional House bills of similar purpose were also presented, these being H.R. 467, 1415, 1479, and 3280 by Owen (Ind.), Laird (Nebr.), McAdoo (N.J.), and Payson (Ill.), respectively. The terms of these bills varied, from prohibition of purchase of real property by aliens to prohibition of ownership of public lands or lands in the territories; but there was a common purpose to limit alien rights with respect to land. Some legislative progress was made on two of the bills, one passed by the House and one by the Senate,[13] the House bill then being amended and passed by the Senate.

Several other immigration matters received attention during the session. Two bills (H.R. 4587 and H.R. 7662) to amend the immigration laws were introduced by Muller (N.Y.) and Felton (Calif.) but not acted on. A bill to supplement the passenger acts (H.R. 5286) was introduced by Davis (Mass.) in the House. On April 26, 1886 the House received a resolution from McComas of Maryland calling for an investigation of disputes between bituminous coal miners and mine owners in Pennsylvania, to inquire into the causes and in particular whether the trouble had resulted from violations of the immigration laws.[14] One other bill was to amend the contract labor law (H.R. 9232, introduced by O'Neill of Missouri). It was passed by the House and went to the Senate, where it was not acted on until the next session.

President Cleveland, in his message of December 6, 1886 to the second session of the 49th Congress, made the following plea for better treatment of the Chinese:

[13]S. 188 and H.R. 3280; ibid., 17:4575, 5108, 7830–32.

[14]*Congressional Record,* 17:3839.

> In opening our vast domains to alien elements, the purpose of our law-givers was to invite assimilation, and not to provide an arena for endless antagonisms. The paramount duty of maintaining public order and defending the interests of our own people, may require the adoption of measures of restriction, but they should not tolerate the oppression of individuals of a special race.

He held out hope of cooperation from the Chinese government in "an effective limitation of Chinese immigration"; and he mentioned the need for new legislation on naturalization.

Sympathy in Congress for the Chinese was indicated by two bills to indemnify them for the Rock Springs mob action; and a number of petitions asked for steps to prevent such persecution of this minority group. A bill (H.R. 11129) was introduced by Morrow (Calif.) to amend the Chinese Exclusion Act of 1882, but was not acted on.

Two bills were enacted during the session, the first being an amendment of the contract labor law. On February 7, 1887 the Senate passed the O'Neill bill it had received from the House during the preceding session. The bill added three major new sections to the 1885 Act, which, though sweeping in its prohibition of labor contracts, had not proved enforceable in practice. The new sections charged the Secretary of the Treasury with enforcement of the act, gave him power to establish needful rules and regulations, and provided that prohibited persons were to be sent back on arrival. With presidential approval, the bill became the Contract Labor Law of February 23, 1887 (24 Stat. 414).

The other bill to become law was the Payson bill on alien land holding (H.R. 3280), which had been passed by both houses of Congress in the first session. The Senate had amended the bill while passing it, and the House did not concur in the amendments. A conference committee was appointed and reported a compromise bill in four sections. The first section read as follows:

> That it shall be unlawful for any person or persons not citizens of the United States, or who have not lawfully declared their intention to become such citizens, or for any corporation not created by or under the laws of the United States or of some State or Territory of the United States, to hereafter acquire, hold, or own real estate so hereafter acquired, or any interest therein, in any of the Territories of the United States or in the District of Columbia, except such as may be acquired by inheritance or in good faith in the ordinary course of justice in the collection of debts heretofore created: Provided, that the prohibition of this section shall not apply to cases in which the right to hold or dispose of lands in the United States is secured by existing treaties to the citizens or subjects of foreign countries.

The following sections forbade any corporation of 20 percent or more alien ownership to thereafter acquire, or to hold real estate thereafter acquired, in any of the Territories or the District of Columbia, limited land holdings of corporations in the Territories to 5000 acres excepting railroads and canal and turnpike companies, and held forfeit to the United States any land holdings in violation of the act. The conference report was accepted, and President Cleveland gave his signature on March 3, 1887, the closing day of the Congress, to the act, entitled "An act to restrict the ownership of real estate in the Territories to American citizens" (24 Stat. 476).

Concerning the regulation of immigration, the House received a bill introduced by Muller (N.Y.) to amend the immigration laws (H.R. 10542) and an executive document giving consular reports on immigration (H. Exec. Doc. 157).

50th Congress (1887–1889)

The first session of the 50th Congress, which convened on December 5, 1887, was one of great legislative activity in the immigration field, in this respect reflecting the rising popular concern as the volume of immigration rose higher and higher. A great number of bills were introduced in Congress, of which all but a few fell into one of three groups: Chinese immigration, restrictions on the rights of resident aliens, and the regulation of immigration in general.

In all, the session saw nine bills to prohibit Chinese immigration,[15] one to terminate treaty stipulations with China,[16] one to enforce restrictions on Chinese immigration (S. 1797), one to amend the existing act (S. 2186), and two to execute a treaty prohibiting Chinese immigration (S. 2854, H.R. 9613). There were, in addition, several resolutions on the subject, a number of petitions were received, and there were two presidential messages during the session.

Only two bills received active attention, one originating in the Senate and one in the House. On July 11, 1888 the Senate Committee on Foreign Relations introduced a bill to prohibit the coming of Chinese laborers (S. 3304). Consideration of the bill occupied parts of three or more days in the Senate, the time taken up largely by long statements on the subject, with little actual debate. The bill was passed by the Senate on August 8 without debate and without a recorded count of votes. The House had an identical bill (H.R. 9534) but tabled it and transmitted the Senate bill to the Committee on Foreign Affairs. This committee re-

[15]S. 582, 3304, 3579, H.R. 4448, 5659, 5679, 9534, 10605, 11336.
[16]H.R. 1217; in addition, S. 582 called for abrogation of the treaty.

ported out an amended bill to repeal not only the 1884 Act, as in the Senate draft, but also the underlying 1882 Act, on execution of the pending treaty with China. The House accepted the committee's amendment, and passed the bill on August 20. The Senate agreed to the amendment, and the bill was signed by the President to become the Chinese Exclusion Act of September 13, 1888 (25 Stat. 476).

On the assumption that the pending treaty would be adopted, the bill imposed a twenty-year suspension of all Chinese immigration, with the exception of officials, teachers, students, merchants, and travelers, set certain conditions for the departure and return of resident Chinese, set certain penalties for violations, and provided for imprisonment and deportation of those unlawfully present in the United States. When the Chinese government did not ratify the treaty, however, the suspension provisions of the act were held to be void.

Congress moved rapidly to pass another act. On September 3, 1888, Scott of Pennsylvania entered a bill in the House to supplement the 1882 act (H.R. 11336). A short bill, it was introduced, debated, and passed by the House, and then it was taken up by the Senate all on the same day. In the Senate it was debated immediately, without being referred to committee, and discussed further on September 4 and 5. On the latter day, the Senate voted 32 to 0 for the bill, but lacked a quorum. Considered further on September 6, the favorable vote rose to 37 to 0, again lacking a quorum. Again on the seventh it was considered and a motion to refer the bill to committee was made in view of doubt whether the Chinese had really rejected the treaty, but the motion was rejected, and the bill was finally passed by the quorum vote of 37 to 3. It was approved by President Cleveland on October 1, 1888 (25 Stat. 504).

The principal features of the act were to make unlawful the return of any Chinese laborer resident who departed from the United States, to stop the issuance of certificates of identity under sections four and five of the 1882 act, and to declare void any such certificates already issued. The certificates of identity were in fact reentry permits for Chinese residents leaving the United States and intending to return.

A presidential message of October 1, 1888 accompanied the approval of the bill, and it gave a report on the drafting of the proposed treaty with China. The Senate had confirmed the treaty on May 7, with two amendments. Word had been received that the Chinese government objected to signing the treaty unless the period of suspension was shortened and reentry was permitted. The Chinese government had also proposed a third change whereby reentry permits for departing Chinese alleging property in the United States should be issued by a Chinese consul instead of a United States official. These proposals were apparently considered unacceptable by the United States government.

The series of antialien bills, designed to put certain restrictions on the rights of alien residents, was long and varied. Several were to restrict the purchase and ownership of land, or to exclude aliens from benefit under the homestead laws.[17] Others were to exclude aliens from certain types of work.[18] Several bills of another sort were introduced, to correct difficulties that had arisen under the March 3, 1887 act against alien purchase and ownership of land. On December 20, 1887 the Senate Committee on Foreign Relations introduced a bill (S. 1029) to permit acquisition of property in the District of Columbia for the use of any foreign government. It was passed readily by the Senate but was not acted on by the House, which had its own bill on the subject. The House bill, by Belmont of New York (H.R. 4756), would exempt the District of Columbia from the 1887 Act. The House committee receiving the bill amended it to read that the District of Columbia was exempted "so far as related to the ownership of legations, or the ownership of residences by representatives of foreign governments, or attaches thereof." In this form, the bill was passed by the House on February 27, by the Senate on March 1, and signed by President Cleveland.

The 1887 Act had also led to difficulties regarding mining property. In the Senate Stewart of Nevada, a state particularly involved, introduced a bill (S. 1176) to authorize the sale to aliens of certain mineral lands. It provided exemption from the 1887 Act of mineral lands in the Territories, provided they had been acquired under the mineral land laws. After recommittal and prolonged debate the bill was passed by the Senate on April 10, 1888, by a vote of 31 to 13, with 32 not voting. The House Committee on Public Lands recommended amendment to forbid alien ownership of coal and iron resources in the territories,[19] but the bill was not brought up in the House during the session because of objections.

The regulation or restriction of immigration was also an active issue at the time. Congress received fifty-two petitions concerning restriction, all or nearly all of which presumably favored it. Pennsylvania was the source of the largest number of the petitions, fifteen in all. Eight bills entitled "To regulate immigration" were introduced in the Senate and House;[20] and the author of one, in an accompanying statement, explained

[17]H.R. 3422, Laird (Nebr.), "To prevent the acquisition of property by aliens," etc.; H.R. 4916, Oates (Ala.), "To prohibit aliens from acquiring title to or owning lands"; H.R. 6094, Oates (Ala.), "To prevent aliens from pre-empting or entering homesteads," etc.; and H.R. 7425, Jackson (Pa.), "To amend the homestead laws to prevent aliens acquiring title to public lands," etc.

[18]H.R. 5643, 8724, and 11503, "To prohibit employment of aliens on public works"; H.R. 4279, Gallinger (N.H.), "For the protection of the public service"; H.R. 6121, Chipman (Mich.), "To prevent aliens from engaging in certain businesses."

[19]H. Rept. 3014 (50-I).

[20]S. 141, 369, 553, 745, 1285, H.R. 1504, 1541, 3416, the authors of which represented Vermont, Illinois, Michigan, Texas, Maine, and Missouri.

that he would exclude various "delinquent, dependent and dangerous classes."[21] To this he added the constructive suggestion that exclusion be by means of thorough investigation abroad rather than at the port of entry. One bill was to amend the immigration laws (H.R. 1223, by Felton of California), one was to restrict the immigration of foreigners into the United States (H.R. 10322, by Oates of Alabama), and a final bill of the group had the ambitious objectives "To prohibit objectionable foreign immigration, encourage desirable immigration, defend American institutions, and protect American labor" (S. 578, by Mitchell of Oregon).

At the same time the House initiated certain inquiries into current problems of immigration. On January 9, 1888 Oates of Alabama, who had taken an active part in legislation on the subject, introduced the following resolution in the House:

> That the Judiciary Committee be, and they are hereby, instructed to inquire into and report to this House during the present session of Congress, by bill or otherwise, what further legislation may be necessary to limit and restrict the number of foreigners who are annually immigrating to the United States, and to secure better protection to the people of this country against the evils arising from indiscriminate admission to domicile and citizenship of paupers, criminals, outlaws, and turbulent persons from other countries.

On July 30 McAdoo of New Jersey introduced House Resolution 209 calling for information from our consuls in foreign countries relative to migration to the United States and providing for an investigation of alleged infractions of existing laws. Most significant, however, from a later perspective was a third proposal, a report on July 12, from the Committee on Military Affairs, presented by Ford of Michigan:

> Whereas it is charged by prominent journals that the laws prohibiting the importation of contract laborers, convicts, paupers and other classes are being extensively evaded, owing to the lack of machinery to enforce the provisions of said laws: Therefore,
>
> Be it resolved, that the Speaker shall appoint a select committee of five.

The resolution was adopted by the House, and Ford was appointed chairman, with Oates of Alabama, Spinola of New York, Guenther of Wisconsin, and Morrow of California as the other members of the committee.

Several bills on other matters appeared during the session. A supplement to the passenger acts was offered (H.R. 1525, by Davis of Massachusetts), and a bill "to provide for the removal of dangerous aliens from the

[21]Senator Palmer of Michigan, introducing S. 553; *Congressional Record*, 19:655.

territory of the United States" (H.R. 1291, by Adams of Illinois). Neither was reported out of committee. Congress did, however, authorize the "return" of contract laborers illegally landed in the United States. Contained in a deficiency appropriation bill[22] was a section dealing with the Treasury Department that included amendment of the Contract Labor Act of February 23, 1887 to authorize the Secretary of the Treasury

> in case he shall be satisfied that an immigrant has been allowed to land contrary to the prohibition of that law, to cause such immigrant within the period of one year after landing or entry, to be taken into custody and returned to the country from whence he came, at the expense of the owner of the importing vessel, or, if he entered from an adjoining country, at the expense of the person previously contracting for the services.

This was supplemented by amendment of the Contract Labor Act of February 26, 1885 to provide for payment of up to one-half of the above penalty to an informer "who furnishes original information that the law has been violated" (Act of October 19, 1888, 25 Stat. 566).

President Cleveland's message to the second session of the 50th Congress called for revision of the naturalization laws to correct certain abuses, and it referred to the unratified treaty with China. The Senate received a report (S. Rept. 2690), dated February 27, 1889 from the Committee on Mines and Mining, of a survey made by state or territory and mine by mine. The conclusion of the inquiry was that the people of the territories did not object to the investment of foreign funds in mines, but rather welcomed it and desired repeal of the alien land law provisions affecting mineral lands.

Three bills on immigration were introduced in the House during the session and none in the Senate. Cox of New York proposed an amendment of the 1885 contract labor act (H.R. 11685), and Oates of Alabama presented a bill to regulate immigration (H.R. 11633). Both were referred to committee and then tabled. The third bill and an accompanying report were from the Select Committee on Investigation of Foreign Immigration, appointed in the preceding session and known as the Ford committee.[23]

The committee had inquired particularly into the importation of members of the excludable classes, especially contract laborers, convicts, and paupers. Thus the committee's report was a comprehensive survey

[22]H.R. 10896, enacted as the Act of October 19, 1888 (25 Stat. 566).

[23]H.R. 12291, accompanied by H. Rept. 3792, dated January 19, 1889. According to U.S. Immigration Commission of 1911, Report, *Immigration Legislation,* 39:37, testimony received by the committee was presented in H. Misc. Doc. 572.

of the problems of regulation and enforcement. As regards paupers, it seemed obvious to the committee that

> it was almost impossible to properly inspect the large number of persons who arrive daily during the immigrant season with the facilities afforded . . .

and the committee members found evidence of assisted emigration of paupers. There was also evidence of assisted or encouraged emigration of convicts; and the contract labor law had proved to be easily evaded and hard to enforce. The committee also noted that on the Canadian border there was "no inspection whatever," and that large numbers of excludables came by the land route.

Immigrants in the past had been of great aid to the United States, the report continued, but it was doubtful if present-day immigrants were of the same quality as their predecessors. The time had come, therefore, to select out the desirables from the undesirables. Especially undesirable were the anarchists; they were being driven out of Germany and Britain, and

> This class of persons, in the judgment of the committee, ought to be rigidly excluded from entering the country.

The so-called birds of passage, too, were undesirable if for no other reason than their low standard of living. In summary,

> the committee believe that the time has come when immigration should be more effectively regulated, that persons who immigrate to the United States should at least be composed of those who in good faith desire to become citizens and are worthy to be such.

The committee's bill (H.R. 12291) would have increased the excludable classes by adding polygamists, anarchists, and persons afflicted with a loathsome or dangerous contagious disease. It also reaffirmed the contract labor laws and provided for the deportation within two years of arrival of aliens who had entered unlawfully, deportation to be at the expense of the transportation company that brought them. In spite of the committee's inquiry and recommendations, their bill was not acted on by the House. At the request of Chairman Ford, the bill was recommitted, and did not reappear.

51st Congress (1889–1891)

President Harrison's message of December 3, 1889 on the opening of the 51st Congress was the usual survey of foreign relations, departmental activities, and fiscal matters, but it included brief mention of the difficulty of enforcing the Chinese exclusion laws. The session itself saw a number of immigration bills introduced; they were divided into the regulation of immigration, restrictions on resident aliens, the contract labor problem, and the long-continuing and ever troublesome issue of Chinese immigration.

The session received six bills for the regulation of immigration (S. 543, 2633, H.R. 58, 411, 990, 3909), offered by Senators and Representatives from Maine, New Hampshire, Alabama, Maryland, and Pennsylvania. In addition, Mitchell of Oregon reintroduced the multipurpose bill he had presented in the first session of the 50th Congress (S. 453), and a House bill of the same title came from Stahlnecker of New York (H.R. 8294). Owen of Indiana introduced a bill in the House (H.R. 5614) with the more limited objectives of prohibiting objectionable foreign immigration and encouraging desirable immigration.

None of the above bills proceeded further than assignment to committee, but more progress was made by both House and Senate in moving toward further preparation for action on immigration. At the beginning of the session, the Senate had established a standing Committee on Immigration and the House a Select Committee on Immigration and Naturalization. On January 15, 1890 Chandler of New Hampshire presented a resolution authorizing the new Senate Committee on Immigration to investigate the working of the immigration laws, especially of the Act of August 3, 1882. This he followed a week later with a concurrent resolution to make the proposed investigation a joint inquiry by the newly established Senate and House committees. The resolution was referred to the Senate Committee on Audit and Control of the Contingent Expenses but, pressing for more immediate action, Chandler reintroduced his resolution on the following day and it was agreed to by the Senate. It was brought up in the House on January 28, 1890, and after some delay was accepted there with amendment on March 10. The Senate agreed to the amended resolution two days later. Several reports were issued by the joint committee during the two sessions of the 51st Congress; and two bills were sponsored in the second session.

Strong efforts to restrict or deny certain opportunities to aliens continued. A bill introduced by the Committee on Naval Affairs was to prevent enlistment of aliens in the Navy. As the accompanying report stated, the number of American sailors had decreased with the decline of the merchant marine, and there were now many aliens in the Navy. It was hoped that the bill (H.R. 568, accompanied by H. Rept. 1255) would promote the naval apprenticeship system. Another bill, H.R. 4549, by DeHaven of California, provided that public lands should be sold only to citizens; still another, S. 3311, by Daniel of Virginia, provided that citizens should be given preference in employment on public works and in the execution of contracts for work. Nothing came of these bills. Still more drastic in the limitations it would have imposed on aliens was a bill introduced by Oates of Alabama (H.R. 63) to prohibit aliens from acquiring title to or owning lands in the United States. It was reported back by the Committee on the Judiciary on June 9, 1890 with amendment and with an accompanying report (H. Rept. 2388). In this report it was stated as a principle that a government has power to exclude aliens entirely, and consequently the lesser power of defining the property rights of aliens. Proceeding further with its argument, the committee reported its information that certain members of the European nobility owned approximately 21 million acres of land in the United States, and there were doubtless many other alien land holdings. This absentee ownership was undesirable. In addition there were large foreign holdings of land bonds and other securities whose foreclosure might put additional great amounts of land in foreign hands. The bill, aimed against absentee ownership, would forbid all aliens to take title to lands except by leaseholds not exceeding five years' duration. The committee amendment would allow land ownership to those who came with the intention of becoming citizens but would declare forfeit lands whose alien owners did not become citizens within ten years. There was no further action on the bill beyond this point until the next session of the 51st Congress.

Two bills were designed to amend the earlier alien land act of 1886. A Senate bill (S. 69) by Dolph (Oreg.) was adversely reported and indefinitely postponed. The other, a House bill (H.R. 4654) by Smith (Ariz.), was to permit the investment of foreign capital in mining. Amended by the Committee on Mines and Mining, it was reported out with an accompanying committee report (H. Rept. 1140), which argued that foreign capital in mining is not detrimental and provides employment for workers, and that the mining area held by foreigners is small. The committee's approval of the bill was not shared by the House. Debate proceeded on August 19 and 20, 1890, during which time the sentiment of at least one member was expressed by the words "America for Americans." The bill was then tabled by a vote of 50 to 27.[24]

Evidence of dissatisfaction with the operation of the contract labor laws appeared during the first session of the 51st Congress. The House approved a resolution of inquiry directed to the Attorney General asking for information on suits and prosecutions to enforce the laws. And five bills for the amendment of those laws were entered during the session.[25] Most progress was made with the House bill introduced by Wade (Mo.).

[24]*Congressional Record,* 21:8877–81.

[25]S. 3123, Evarts (N.Y.), S. 3406, Blair (N.H.), H.R. 5405, Shively (Ind.), H.R. 9632, Wade (Mo.), and H.R. 10215, O'Neil (Mass.).

It was reported out by the Committee on Labor in the form of a substitute bill (H.R. 9632, with H. Rept. 2997), amended and passed in the House, and then reported back and debated in the Senate on September 25, 26, and 27, 1890; however, the session ended soon after without passage of the bill. All the other bills remained in committee to the end of the session.

Agitation against the Chinese continued, but in somewhat diminished magnitude. During the session Congress received six petitions to prohibit Chinese immigration and one protesting against exclusion. Resolutions of inquiry on the subject were introduced in the Senate, and several bills were introduced. Senator Mitchell of Oregon introduced a bill "To absolutely prohibit the coming of Chinese persons, whether subjects of the Chinese Empire" or not (S. 1942), and a bill of the same title was sponsored by Morrow of California in the House (H.R. 5357). Other bills were to supplement the exclusion act of October 1, 1888 and to prohibit Chinese immigration (S. 1315, by Mitchell of Oregon, and H.R. 4548, by Clunie of California). The House Committee on Foreign Affairs, which received the House bills, substituted its own bill to exclude all Chinese persons (H.R. 11656) and accompanied it with a report (H. Rept. 2915), but no further action was taken.

The second session of the 51st Congress gave little or no attention to the Chinese question. A number of petitions, fourteen in all, asking for the prohibition of Chinese immigration were presented to Congress, but no new bills on the subject were introduced or taken up from the first session.

Congress gave the most attention, as far as immigration was concerned, to regulation, and this corresponded to the direction of outside opinion as indicated by petitions. During the session there were at least 116 petitions on immigration, of which Pennsylvania contributed the most (48), followed by Ohio (16), and Massachusetts (13).

In the Senate the bill sponsored by the joint committee set up in the preceding session was S. 5035, entitled, "In amendment of the various acts relative to immigration and the importation of aliens under contract or agreement to perform labor." Introduced on February 9, 1891, it was accompanied by a report (S. Rept. 2165) that set forth the terms of the bill and the committee's thinking on the subject. The first section of the bill designated the excluded classes: idiots, insane persons, paupers or persons likely to become public charges, persons suffering from a loathsome or dangerous contagious disease, persons convicted of a felony or other infamous crime or misdemeanor involving moral turpitude, polygamists, persons whose tickets or passages are paid for with the money of another, or who are assisted by others to come, unless it is affirmatively and satisfactorily shown that they do not belong to one of the excluded classes, or to the contract labor class.

Following sections prohibited the encouragement of immigration by advertisements, exempted professors, ministers, and members of recognized professions from the contract labor laws, and required the manifesting of alien passengers. The Senate postponed the bill indefinitely in favor of a bill it received from the House.

The House meanwhile had been considering several bills for the regulation of immigration. On the first day of the second session a bill for this purpose was introduced by Lodge of Massachusetts,[26] who in the coming years was to take a prominent part in matters of immigration. The bill went to the Committee on Immigration and Naturalization, where it ended. Two days later Owen of Indiana introduced a bill of the same title, which went to the same committee (H.R. 12298). As a substitute, the committee on January 15, 1891 reported out its own bill (H.R. 13175, H. Rept. 3472), the counterpart of the Senate-House joint committee bill already introduced in the Senate. Like the Senate bill, it would have added to the excludable classes persons likely to become public charges, persons suffering from a loathsome or dangerous contagious disease, polygamists, and assisted immigrants. The accompanying report, which with included testimony and statistical tables was about 1,100 pages in length, cited testimony showing that it was difficult to detect contract labor cases on inspection because they were "coached" before arrival. The committee believed, however, that it might be more feasible to detect violations after entry, and it made the important recommendation that the period of deportability for contract labor cases be extended to five years after arrival. With regard to the problem of entries through Canada, it was estimated that some 50,000 immigrants had come by way of Canada in the past six months, thereby avoiding inspection.

Meanwhile, other immigration bills were being prepared and presented. On February 14, 1891 the Committee on the Judiciary reported out the Oates bill (H.R. 58) from the first session. The accompanying report (H. Rept. 3808) described the need for legislative action, stating that of an estimated 500,000 immigrants per annum, more than one-fifth are undesirable, and adding that

> At least 50 per cent of the criminals, insane, and paupers of our largest cities belong to this class and are of foreign birth.

The bill itself went somewhat beyond the joint committee bill, especially in increasing the head tax and providing for consular inspection abroad.

On February 12, 1891 the House received another immigration bill (H.R. 13586), from Owen of Indiana, of the same title as the preceding

[26]H. R. 12209. As far as has been found, this was Lodge's first immigration bill.

House bill from the joint committee,[27] and evidently a modification of this bill and of the joint committee's other bill in the Senate. It was reported out by the House Committee on Immigration and Naturalization on February 14, 1891, the same day as the judiciary committee's bill, and was accompanied by a committee report (H. Rept. 3807). Debate in the House began on February 16 and continued on the nineteenth, at which time an amendment was accepted to exclude state immigration agencies from the prohibition on advertisement to promote immigration.[28] Inserted in the record during the debate was the text of a recent article by Lodge of Massachusetts in the *North American Review* of January 1891, in which he recommended the exclusion of illiterates.[29] This appears to be the first presentation in Congress of a proposal that was to be a subject of contention through many later Congresses. Another amendment was to qualify the exclusion of assisted immigrants in the first section of the bill by adding the statement that it does not prevent residents of the United States from sending for a relative or friend if not of an excluded class.[30] Debate was resumed on February 23, at which time the House accepted the Dickinson amendment, a proviso

> That nothing in this act shall be construed to apply to or exclude a person convicted of a political offense, notwithstanding said political offense may be designated as a "felony, crime, infamous crime, or misdemeanor, involving moral turpitude" by the laws of the land whence he came or by the court convicting.[31]

Two days later, the House passed the bill by a vote of 125 to 48.[32] After committee approval, the Senate passed the bill almost without debate and without amendment on February 27. It was approved by President Harrison, to become the Immigration Act of March 3, 1891 (26 Stat. 1084).

The act was designed to supplement and reinforce both the Immigration Act of 1882 and the Contract Labor Act of 1885. It made the additions to the excludable classes that had been introduced by the joint committee into its Senate and House bills—persons likely to become public charges, persons suffering from a loathsome or dangerous contagious disease, polygamists, and assisted immigrants—and forbade the encouragement of immigration by means of advertisement, state activities excepted. The act also amended section five of the Contract Labor Act of 1885 by adding to the classes exempt from the contract labor laws ministers of any religious denomination, persons belonging to any recog-

[27]H.R. 13175: In amendment of the various acts relative to immigration and the importation of aliens under contract or agreement to perform labor.

[28]*Congressional Record,* 22:2954.

[29]Ibid., pp. 2956–58.

[30]Ibid., p. 2958.

[31]Ibid., p. 3181.

[32]Ibid., p. 3245.

nized profession, and professors for colleges or seminaries. However, it removed the exemption of relatives and personal friends, and provided for the deportation within one year of arrival of aliens who enter in violation of law or who become public charges within one year of arrival.

The new immigration act was the real accomplishment of the second session of the 51st Congress. Of secondary importance was some further attention given to the question of land ownership by aliens. Early in the second session, on December 19, 1890, the House Committee on the Judiciary reported out a bill from the first session, the Oates bill (H.R. 63) but in an amended form that was essentially a substitute bill. The accompanying report (H. Rept. 3323) expressed concern over the large investments by wealthy foreigners in lands and property in the United States and pointed to the undesirability of absentee ownership. The original Oates bill was to prevent future purchase of land by aliens and allow only five-year leaseholds; but the committee draft would allow aliens to purchase land at mortgage sales and to hold it for up to five years. Vandever of California introduced a bill to prevent unnaturalized persons from acquiring title to public lands (H.R. 13533); and the Missouri legislature presented a resolution in endorsement of a bill to prevent alien land ownership. No related action was taken, however.

52nd Congress (1891–1893)

Immigration was touched on in President Harrison's message to the 52nd Congress only in his mentioning of the fear that excludable Chinese were entering by way of Canada. The first session itself was very active on immigration matters; the principal issues were the Chinese question and immigration regulation, and there was lesser activity concerning contract labor and restrictions of the rights or privileges of aliens.

During the session Congress received over fifty petitions in favor of prohibiting Chinese immigration, but there were also sixteen petitions against a bill to prohibit the immigration. Congress itself felt some urgency to come to a decision on the Chinese question, for the ten-year suspension provided for in the Act of May 6, 1882 was about to expire. A number of bills were introduced to meet the approaching deadline. At least eight were to prohibit Chinese immigration, including two substitute bills from the House committees on Foreign Affairs and on Immigration and Naturalization.[33] The titles of the bills varied, but for the most part they were "To absolutely prohibit" and they applied to all Chinese

[33]S. 719, Mitchell (Oreg.), S. 2109, Sherman (Ohio), H.R. 37, Geary (Calif.), H.R. 65, Cutting (Calif.), H.R. 3934, Loud (Calif.), H.R. 4575, Stump (Md.), H.R. 5809, Committee on Immigration and Naturalization, and H.R. 6185, Committee on Foreign Affairs.

whether subjects of the Chinese Empire or not. Another six bills were to amend the 1882 exclusion act, of which five presumably were to extend the exclusion period.[34] Two additional bills were to continue the restriction of Chinese immigration (S. 540, introduced by Dolph of Oregon, and H.R. 5550, by Wilson of Washington). And a final bill, with a different title but the same purpose, was to suspend the coming of Chinese laborers (S. 84, by Cullom of Illinois).

In the Senate the Dolph bill, S. 540, to continue in force the various acts restricting Chinese immigration, was reported with amendment by the Senate Committee on Foreign Relations, debated, amended, and passed. Transmitted to the House, it was referred first to one committee and then to another, but it went no further.

In the House the Committee on Foreign Affairs reported out a bill, H.R. 6185, as a substitute for several other bills of like subject. It was debated and passed by the House, and it then went to the Senate Committee on Foreign Relations. On April 13, 1892 Senator Dolph, acting for the committee, reported back the bill with favorable recommendation, but also, as he noted, with amendment.[35] The amendment, he explained, was to substitute the bill that had already passed the Senate in place of the House bill. The Senate bill so substituted was Dolph's own S. 540, then in the hands of a House committee and not to their liking. With lengthy debate and amendment, the bill in its substitute form was passed by the Senate. The House, predictably, did not concur, but finally accepted the conference report, a compromise between the Senate and House drafts of the bill; and it was signed by President Harrison to become the Chinese Exclusion Act of May 5, 1892 (27 Stat. 25), also known as the Geary law.

The bill extended the excluding acts for another ten years, required all Chinese laborers to obtain a certificate of residence within one year, and provided certain penalties including deportation for failure to apply for the certificate. Section 6, in prescribing how Chinese might establish that they had been unable to procure a certificate, included the galling requirement of "at least one credible white witness."

A second major concern during the first session of the 52nd Congress was with the control of immigration. During the session Congress received a flood of petitions calling almost unanimously for restriction of

[34]S. 65, Stewart (Nev.), S. 630, Felton (Calif.), S. 3360, Dolph (Oreg.), H.R. 56, McKenna (Calif.), H.R. 4606, Dungan (Ohio). The sixth, H.R. 9396, Andrew (Mass.), had the now surprising purpose of amending the Chinese exclusion act so as to permit persons of African descent to become witnesses in a court of law.

[35]*Congressional Record*, 23:3236.

immigration. The only petitions noted that did not call for restriction asked for the exclusion of paupers and criminals, for the requirement of consular inspection abroad, and for admission of "only persons friendly to our institutions." From a sample of about half, it is estimated that the petitions approached 550 in number, representing twenty-three or more states. Labor organizations were particularly active as petitioners, and they included local chapters of the Order of United American Mechanics, the junior branches of the Order, chapters of the American Defense Association, brotherhoods, unions, labor congresses and councils, as well as churches, granges, and many groups of people identified as citizens of a given state or county.[36]

The legislative reaction in Congress was the submission of ten or more bills calling variously for the regulation of immigration, amendment of the immigration laws, or consular certificates of inspection.[37] The only bill acted on, introduced by the Senate Committee on Immigration, was to facilitate the enforcement of the immigration and contract labor laws (S. 3240, with S. Rept. 787, June 6, 1892). This was intended as a preliminary or stopgap measure in anticipation of further legislation and was designed to minimize the number of departures from abroad of inadmissible immigrants. Consular certificates were proposed for this purpose; and a further requirement to be introduced by the bill was that steamship companies prepare identifying lists of passengers in advance and deliver them to the immigrant inspectors on arrival. The accompanying report explained that the regular manifest or passenger list is taken by the customs officers, so that no descriptive list is available to the immigrant inspectors. The latter, therefore, were having to make out lists from the information given them by the immigrants as they left a vessel. The bill was passed by the Senate with minor amendments on July 27, but progressed no further until the next session.

The Senate evidently had felt the need for further information regarding the regulation of immigration, for there were two resolutions to that effect. One, a concurrent resolution of February 15, 1892, authorized

[36]A sampling of the labor group petitioners includes the Knights of Labor of Pocatello, Idaho, Illinois State Federation of Labor, Cigar Makers Union of Quincy, Illinois, Typographical Union, Illinois, Brotherhood of Carmen in Illinois and Pennsylvania, Musicians National League, United Brotherhood of Joiners and Carpenters, Trades and Labor Congress of Dubuque, Iowa, Trade and Labor Council of Zanesville, Ohio, and the Council of American Mechanics of Des Moines, Iowa.

[37]The bills are S. 134, Chandler (N.H.), S. 357, Peffer (Kans.), S. 2543, Washburn (Minn.), S. 2753, Quay (Pa.), S. 3240, Committee on Immigration, H.R. 12, Oates (Ala.), H.R. 32, Geary (Calif.), H.R. 401, Stone (Pa.), H.R. 575, Lodge (Mass.), and H.R. 8904, Stump (Md.).

the Senate and House immigration committees to investigate the working of the immigration and contract labor laws. The other, on July 16, called on the Senate immigration committee to look into the working of the immigration, contract labor, and naturalization laws.

Generally the problem of enforcement of the contract labor laws was considered along with that of the immigration laws, but several bills concerned solely with amendment of the contract labor laws were introduced (H.R. 100, by Shively [Ind.], and H.R. 552, by Cummings [N.Y.]). And there were both Senate and House resolutions to investigate contract labor.

There continued to be question of what rights and opportunities should be granted or denied to aliens. Two petitions to Congress opposed the employment of aliens on American vessels, and one objected to licensing of aliens as officers on such vessels. A House bill would have restricted the right of aliens to hold lands in the United States (H.R. 5147, Oates, of Alabama); another would allow only citizens to acquire public land (H.R. 45, Bowers, of California). With regard to employment, one bill was to prohibit employment of aliens in the civil service (S. 770, Gallinger, N.H.), another to prevent aliens from engaging in certain businesses (H.R. 204, Chipman of Michigan), and most drastic was a bill to prohibit aliens holding "offices or places of profit, honor, or trust under the Government of the United States" (H.R. 47, Bowers, of California).

On the other hand, there was sentiment for some relaxation of the earlier land law so far as mining property was concerned. Four bills for amendment of the earlier law or for authorization of the sale of mineral lands to aliens were introduced,[38] but they were not acted on.

The only other activity related to immigration during the session was the introduction of several bills to amend the passenger acts, to enlarge the ship room and increase the comfort of immigrants.[39]

President Harrison's message to the second session of the 52nd Congress spoke of a twenty-day quarantine on all vessels bringing immigrants from foreign ports, and that this measure, introduced because of an outbreak of cholera abroad, would be continued. In this connection, he pointed to the need for more restriction of immigration, in view of health hazards in addition to political, moral, and other considerations. Mention was also made of apologies and indemnity to the Italian government because of the lynching of Italians in New Orleans.

[38] S. 57, Stewart (Nev.), H.R. 2781, Smith (Ariz.), H.R. 6070, Joseph (N. Mex.), H.R. 7202, Taylor (Ohio).

[39] S. 1127, Chandler (N.H.), S. 3050, Frye (Me.), H.R. 5988, Stump (Md.).

Activity on immigration during the session centered largely on regulation. Various bills to regulate or to suspend immigration were introduced, and a bill to reinforce the immigration and contract labor laws was passed.

The bills fell into two groups: those to regulate immigration and those to suspend immigration for a certain period. The threat of cholera had been deeply alarming, and several bills provided variously for the strengthening of the quarantine service and the suspension of immigration under certain circumstances.[40] The House Committee on Immigration and Naturalization introduced its own bill, H.R. 9999, in substitute for one of the bills referred to it (H.R. 9980), and in the accompanying report (H. Rept. 2197), on December 22, 1892, gave the opinion that the danger of cholera in the coming spring and summer would disappear, so that a complete suspension of immigration was not called for. The bill, as a precaution, however, provided standby powers to suspend immigration from any port, totally or partially, if control measures failed. In the Senate a bill by Chandler of New Hampshire called for a one-year suspension of immigration. An inquiry was addressed to the Secretary of State on January 6, 1893 regarding the effect of such a suspension on treaty relations with other nations. The President transmitted the opinion of the Secretary of State that absolute suspension for one year was not contrary to treaty stipulations.[41] The committee then reported back the bill with amendment, but both it and the House bill were dropped in favor of another bill reported out by the House Committee on Interstate and Foreign Commerce on January 9, 1893.[42] This bill, entirely rewritten in committee, took care of the quarantine question in section 7, which provided

> That whenever it shall be shown to the satisfaction of the President that by reason of the existence of cholera or other infectious or contagious diseases in a foreign country there is serious danger of the introduction of the same into the United States . . . the President shall have power to prohibit, in whole or in part, the introduction of persons and property from such countries or places as he shall designate and for such period of time as he may deem necessary.

Passed by the House and then by the Senate with this section intact, the bill in retitled and somewhat amended form became the Act of February 15, 1893 (27 Stat. 452).

[40] S. 3570, Gallinger (N.H.), H.R. 9899 and H.R. 9957, Brosius (Pa.), H.R. 9980, Stump (Md.).

[41] S. Exec. Doc. 25, January 6, 1893.

[42] H.R. 9757, Rayner (Md.), with H. Rept. 2210.

The Senate and the House both received two bills to regulate immigration or to establish additional regulations, but without taking action on them.[43] The House, however, took up a bill from the first session, to facilitate the enforcement of the immigration and contract labor laws (S. 3240). As reported out on January 7, 1893 with amendment by the Select Committee on Immigration and Naturalization, the bill added the following to the excludable classes:

> All persons physically capable and over sixteen years of age who can not read and write with reasonable facility their own language, except that an aged person not so able to read and write who is the parent or grandparent of an admissible immigrant may accompany or be sent for by such immigrant.
>
> Persons blind or crippled, or otherwise physically imperfect, so that they are wholly or partially disabled from manual labor, unless it is affirmatively and satisfactorily shown on special inquiry that such persons are sure of an abundant support and not likely to become a public charge.
>
> Persons belonging to any society or organization which sanctions or justifies the unlawful destruction of life or property.

Accompanying the bill was the select committee's report (H. Rept. 2206, January 7, 1893), with the committee's recommendation that section 6 of the bill be amended by addition of the above three excludable classes, of which the first and third, illiterates and anarchists, would be additions to the excludable classes. Recommitted on February 21, 1893, the bill was reported out after revision and accompanied by a new report (H. Rept. 2542). So amended, it passed the House on March 3, close to the end of the session, by a vote of 93 to 31, was agreed to by the Senate, and signed by the President to become the Immigration Act of March 3, 1893 (27 Stat. 569).

The act had been very much softened in the final amendment. The new excludable classes proposed in the earlier draft were gone, and the bill confined itself to requirements for furnishing manifests to the immigration inspectors, the information to be so supplied, special inquiry in case of doubt about the admissibility of an immigrant, and certain lesser changes in control procedures. It brought no new developments of immigration policy but rather was a reinforcement of existing laws.

Other immigration-related bills during the second session of the 52nd Congress included one to restrict the employment of aliens (H.R. 9750, by Chipman of Michigan). With regard to Chinese immigration, the

[43] S. 3663, Chandler (N.H.), S. 3786, Committee on Immigration, H.R. 9804, Beltzhoover (Pa.), H.R. 10486, Greenleaf (N.Y.).

House received a bill to repeal a portion of the 1892 exclusion act (H.R. 10334, by Andrew of Massachusetts), and the Senate took up and passed a bill (S. 3360) from the first session to amend the same act.

53rd Congress (1893–1895)

During its first session the 53rd Congress gave considerable attention to certain problems of Chinese immigration that had not been altogether solved by the recently and hastily passed Act of 1892; and more limited attention was given to the regulation of immigration and restrictions on aliens.

The enforcement of the Chinese exclusion laws was considered unsatisfactory, and there were both Senate and House resolutions of inquiry into the enforcement of the laws. Two bills of identical title were introduced by Dolph (Oreg.) in the Senate and Loud (Calif.) in the House, to make an appropriation to enable the Secretary of the Treasury to enforce the Chinese exclusion acts (S. 745, H.R. 3248). A Senate bill by Hoar of Massachusetts and a House bill by Hitt of Illinois were "To cause the laws relating to Chinese aliens lawfully in the United States to conform to existing treaties, and to suspend the further coming of other Chinese laborers" (S. 885, H.R. 2631). A bill by Baker of New Hampshire would have repealed sections 2 to 9 of the exclusion act, which dealt largely with measures for enforcement of the act (H.R. 1900). Neither this nor the preceding bills related to Chinese immigration was acted on.

A difficulty had arisen under the 1892 Act requirement of certificates of residence for Chinese laborers. Numbers of the Chinese had failed to obtain the certificates within the prescribed period of one year, on advice that the requirement would be found unconstitutional. When it was upheld by the Supreme Court, legislative action was set in motion to extend the registration period by six months. A bill was introduced in the House by Everett of Massachusetts, but the Committee on Foreign Affairs chose to report out a substitute.[44] After lengthy debate that continued over a number of days, the committee bill was amended and passed by the House,[45] received briefer discussion in the Senate and was passed without amendment, signed by the President, and became the Act of November 3, 1893 (28 Stat. 7).

Besides extending the registration period by six months, the act changed the wording of the requirement of a supporting witness from

[44]H.R. 1973, Everett (Mass.); the committee substitute was H.R. 3687, accompanied by H. Rept. 70, October 4, 1893.

[45]*Congressional Record,* 28:2567. The vote was an overwhelming 178 to 1.

"one credible white witness" to "one credible witness other than Chinese." It also specified that the term *laborer* as used in the exclusion act should be interpreted to include both unskilled and skilled laborers, including miners, fishermen, launderers, and others.

Three Representatives and one Senator introduced bills concerning restrictions on aliens, their purpose being identical with those of bills introduced by the same members in the 52nd Congress.[46] None went beyond committee. The three bills for the regulation of immigration that were introduced during the first session likewise remained in committee.[47] No action was taken on a bill (H.R. 3206) by Geary of California to suspend immigration.

Although not passing new legislation to regulate immigration, Congress continued to seek current information on regulation and enforcement. The President transmitted a report to Congress on regulations for enforcement of the Chinese exclusion laws;[48] and on March 27, 1893 Chandler (N.H.) submitted a resolution that the Committee on Immigration of the Senate be authorized to make inquiry into the condition and character of the alien immigrants coming to the United States for employment in mining, to inquire into the enforcement of the contract labor laws, to see whether immigration laws are economically enforced, and to look into the workings of the immigration law of 1893 and prior acts. The resolution was passed in substantially this form at a later date, April 5, 1893.

The second session of the 53rd Congress opened on December 4, 1893. The message from President Cleveland at the time mentioned opposition on the part of the Chinese to the so-called Geary law requiring registration of Chinese laborers. In another connection, concerning the treatment of American citizens by the government of Turkey, he stated the general principle that "The right to exclude any or all classes of aliens is an attribute of sovereignty." The message also included statistics supplied by the Superintendent of Immigration.

During the session that followed, Congress gave most attention to the regulation of immigration. Actually, it would appear that the popular demand at the time was for restriction of immigration, for Congress received over a hundred petitions for restriction during the session. Several bills to amend the immigration laws were introduced.[49] Two

[46]S. 729, Gallinger (N.H.), H.R. 15, Bowers (Calif.), H.R. 361, Joseph (N.Mex.), H.R. 3651, Smith (Ariz.).

[47]S. 396, Chandler (N.H.), H.R. 243, Stone (Pa.), H.R. 3473, Curtis (Kans.).

[48]S. Exec. Doc. 31 (53-I).

[49]S. 1164, Peffer (Kans.), S. 2282, Chandler (N.H.), H.R. 5593, Walker (Mass.).

others were for the declared purpose of protecting American labor and restricting immigration (H.R. 5107 and 7604, Lockwood [N.Y.]), and one bill called directly for the restriction of immigration (H.R. 7784, Meicklejohn [Nebr.]).

The only immigration bill acted on by the House during the second session was introduced on January 17, 1894 by W. A. Stone of Pennsylvania and bore the descriptive title "Providing for the inspection of immigrants by United States consuls" (H.R. 5246). Referred first to the Committee on Immigration and Naturalization and then to the Committee on the Judiciary, it was reported out with amendment by the latter committee on February 12. In the accompanying report, House Report 416 (53-II), the committee explained that the purpose of the bill was to prevent paupers and criminals from being admitted as immigrants. Data on the number of such persons in the United States were said to indicate that

> with a foreign population of 14.77 per cent, more than half of our white penitentiary convicts and more than half of the white inmates of our poorhouses, are foreigners.

The earlier acts of 1891 and 1893, the report continued, were inadequate to keep out such immigrants; and investigation by consuls abroad should be more reliable for identification of excludables than the unsupported statements of immigrants on arrival. In conclusion, it was said, "The bill does not add to the excluded list, but seems only a better method of enforcing existing law."

The Stone bill was brought up in the House on July 20, 1894.[50] Discussion at that time brought out that no alien would be admitted without a certificate of consular inspection, to show that an investigation had been made and that the alien did not belong to an excluded class. The House accepted the committee's amendments, and the bill was passed without debate or record vote. Its course from then on, however, was much less smooth. The Senate did not think well of consular inspection, and the Senate Committee on Immigration, to which the bill was referred, struck it out and substituted an alien anarchist bill then being considered in the Senate (see S. 2314 below).

Reported out in the Senate on August 2, the amended or really substitute bill was accompanied by a report that explained the committee action.[51] Supporting opinions from the Secretaries of State and Treasury were cited. The former estimated that even with a tenfold increase of staff the consular offices abroad would not be able to discharge the duties that

[50] *Congressional Record,* 26:7756.

[51] S. Misc. Doc. 253 (53-II).

would be placed on them by the Stone bill. The Secretary of the Treasury approved in principle the apparent purpose of the bill to restrict immigration and to inspect abroad, but cited the report of a commission that had looked into consular inspection earlier. The conclusion had been that such inspection was not feasible and that it was preferable to put responsibility for refusing excludables on the transportation companies as was done in the 1893 act. Further objections were that to set up a system of inspection of citizens of other nations might lead to international complications, that the duties to be given to the consuls were unrecognized in international law, and that in any case there were too few consuls. In conclusion the Senate committee urged that the system employed under the 1893 act be kept.

The provisions of the substitute bill recommended by the Senate committee were as follows, by section: (1) that no alien anarchist shall be admitted, but political refugees are not to be excluded; (2) that accused anarchists are to be tried by a board of special inquiry, with deportation on conviction; (3) that if the presiding judge, at a trial where an alien is convicted of a crime or misdemeanor, certifies that the alien in question is an anarchist, he is to be taken before a commissioner of immigration, who shall order his deportation; and if the alien returns, he is to be imprisoned for up to four years; (4) that the Secretary of the Treasury is to appoint immigrant inspectors at designated ports of embarcation, who may inspect passengers and strike the names of those found excludable off the manifest and forbid transportation to the United States; and (5) that a declaration of intention to become a citizen is no bar to action under this act.[52]

The amended bill was debated in the Senate on August 4 and 6, and was passed on the latter day after rejection of an amendment to raise the head tax to ten dollars.[53] A compromise with the House was requested. As reported later, the House conferees did not want their draft killed, and they wanted the principle of consular inspection to go over to the next session. The understanding that was reportedly reached was for the House bill to remain in conference in the Senate, and the House conferees would concur in the Senate's alien anarchist bill when it was passed by the Senate.[54]

Several alien anarchists bills were introduced during the session, one in the House by Geissenhainer (N.J.) to amend the immigration and contract labor laws, including the exclusion and deportation of anarchists (H.R. 7897), and one in the Senate by Chandler (N.H.) for the exclusion

[52]*Congressional Record,* 26:8215–16. [53]Ibid., p. 8240.
[54]Ibid., p. 8557.

and deportation of anarchists (S. 2282). Neither was acted on, but on August 15, 1894 the Senate Committee on Immigration reported out a bill (S. 2314) of the same title as the Chandler bill and with the same provisions as the Senate committee's substitute for the Stone bill (see above).

The Senate substitute bill was not well received in the House Judiciary Committee, even though it incorporated the principle of inspection abroad with the substitution of a treasury official for a consul as inspector. The committee reported out the bill to the House and enumerated its doubts about the bill in the accompanying House Report 1460 (53-II). According to the committee, the term *anarchist* is loosely stated and undefined, deportation on the verdict of a jury is questionable in principle, the alien may have been given undue right of appeal, and there are other questionable features. Consideration of the bill was objected to in the House,[55] and it went no further. The Senate-House confrontation over the regulation of immigration had thus blocked any new legislation on consular inspection or alien anarchists during the term of the 53rd Congress. The only changes of law to affect immigration during this Congress were an increase of the head tax from fifty cents to one dollar and certain administrative changes made in the appropriations acts of August 18, 1894 and March 2, 1895 (28 Stat. 390, 391, and 780).

During the second session, Congress received a number of petitions to prohibit Chinese immigration, and one bill to that effect was introduced but not acted on (S. 2309, White [Calif.]). A few other bills related to immigration were introduced but proceeded no further. These included one to amend the contract labor laws (H.R. 6625), one to prohibit alien land ownership (H.R. 7846), one to prohibit their enlistment as sailors or marines (S. 2246), and one to forbid their voting in any national or state election (S. 1165).

The third session of the 53rd Congress, extending the usual term from early December 1894 to early March 1895, received a number of petitions but spent little time on immigration matters. The presidential message reported that a treaty with China was signed on March 17, 1894, ratified by the Senate on August 13, and awaited ratification by China.[56] About fifty petitions called for a constitutional amendment to make it unlawful to grant the franchise to aliens. Two House resolutions for this purpose were referred to the Committee on the Judiciary. As many or

[55]Ibid., p. 8627.

[56]The treaty was concluded on December 8, 1894. It extended the exclusion of Chinese laborers for another ten years, repealed the exclusion act of 1888, required registration, and provided for the return to the United States of visitors to China, provided they left near relatives or a certain amount of property in the United States.

more petitions called for consular inspection, but no action in that direction was to be taken until the next Congress.

54th Congress (1895–1897)

The President's annual message on the opening of the 54th Congress referred to the padrone system as "this growing evil" and suggested that Congress should try to find legislation to check it. Congressional attention to immigration during the session was directed toward the problem of health controls, limitations on the rights of aliens, labor questions and contract labor in particular, but above all the regulation of immigration. Heavy and rising immigration, stirrings of nativistic sentiments as represented by the American Protective Association and other such groups, and dissatisfaction with the existing regulatory legislation and enforcement all led to growing pressures in and out of Congress for more strict control and selection of immigrants.

With regard to health controls, which received the least attention, bills of identical title, "To provide for medical inspection of emigrants at the port of debarcation," were introduced in Senate and House by members from Ohio (S. 3127, Sherman, and H.R. 8777, Burton).

On the subject of alien disabilities, the House received two resolutions for amendment of the Constitution to prohibit alien suffrage, one of which carried an additional prohibition on the holding of public office by aliens.[57] Neither went past the Committee on the Judiciary. Two bills were introduced to prevent the holding of public office by aliens, and they also stayed in committee (H.R. 187, Bowers [Calif.], and H.R. 6752, Corliss [Mich.]). Another was to prohibit alien enlistment in the armed forces (S. 1368, Allen [Nebr.]). It was adversely reported by the Senate Military Affairs Committee and indefinitely postponed.

Several bills for the regulation of immigration included some attention to contract labor, but the emphasis as indicated by the subjects of proposed legislation had shifted to the protection of American labor from immigrant competition. The tone of these bills is well illustrated by the following statement of their objectives:

> H.R. 28, Johnson (Calif.): To protect the American laborer from unfair competition and to prevent foreign laborers from coming to the United States.
>
> H.R. 273, Barham (Calif.): To prohibit immigration of all skilled and unskilled foreign manual labor.

[57]H. Res. 44, 59 (54-I).

H.R. 4440, Mahany (N.Y.): To protect American labor, and enforcement of the law of domicile and the restriction of immigration to such a degree as will serve that end.

H.R. 7415, Corliss (Mich.): To protect American labor and to establish additional regulations concerning immigration.

H.R. 8474, Mahany (N.Y.): Same title as H.R. 4440.

The Corliss bill was reported back favorably and with amendment by the Committee on Immigration and Naturalization. The brief report from the committee made unfavorable mention of the "bird of passage" immigrant, who comes with no intention of taking up permanent residence; and it referred also to the need for inspection of aliens coming by way of foreign contiguous territory.[58] The second Mahany bill was also reported favorably by the committee. The attached report merely stated that the committee recommended its passage, with amendment.[59] Neither bill was brought up for action in the House.

The main drive in the immigration field, as already noted, was for further and more effective regulation but, one may infer, with an underlying motive in many cases for restriction. A review of legislative proposals during the first session of the 54th Congress shows the adoption on January 9, 1896 of a Senate resolution by Chandler (N.H.):

> That the Committee on Immigration be directed to inquire whether or not any legislation is necessary to prevent the introduction into the United States of aliens imprisoned in penal colonies of European nations established in their American possessions.

There were also some fourteen bills for the regulation of immigration or the amendment of the immigration laws.[60] Only three of the fourteen went beyond committee and need be noted here, these being the Stone bill and the two from committees.

The House bill submitted by W. A. Stone of Pennsylvania (H.R. 58), providing for consular inspection, appears to be the same as his bill of the same purpose in the 53rd Congress (H.R. 5246[53-II]). The accompanying report, House Report 1082 (54-I) likewise contained material from the report on the earlier bill and pointed in the same way to the disproportionate representation of the foreign-born population in pris-

[58]H. Rept. 1597 (54-I) [59]H. Rept. 1589 (54-I).

[60]S. 209 and 210, Chandler (N.H.); S. 301, Lodge (Mass.); S. 1685, Peffer (Kans.); S. 2147, Committee on Immigration; H.R. 9, McCall (Mass.); H.R. 15, Walker (Mass.); H.R. 58, Stone (Pa.); H.R. 166, 168, Morse (Mass.); H.R. 3354, Curtis (Kans.); H.R. 4327, Graff (Ill.); H.R. 4455, Corliss (Mich.); and H.R. 7864, Committee on Immigration and Naturalization.

ons, penitentiaries, charitable institutions, and poorhouses. To the committee this proved that

> of the immigrants coming here during the past few years too many are deficient in morals and are incapable, physically, of self-support.

Consular inspection abroad was strongly recommended; and the bill was said to be self-enforcing, for any alien without a certificate of consular inspection would be automatically inadmissible. In spite of the strong committee support, the bill was not acted on in the House, which turned its attention to another immigration bill, reported out the same day by the committee, that took an approach to regulation other than by consular inspection (see H.R. 7864 below).

The effort to introduce an educational or literacy test of immigrants as a solution for the problem of regulating immigration gathered strength in the 54th Congress. At the opening of Congress, two bills providing for a literacy test were introduced, one in the Senate by Lodge, now a Senator from Massachusetts (S. 301), the other in the House by McCall from the same state (H.R. 9). Neither was approved by the Senate and House committees, but substitutes incorporating a literacy test were reported out. Debate on the Senate committee's bill (S. 2147) began on March 16, 1896, and in later perspective it is especially notable for the detailed statement of the argument for the literacy test as a means of selection, given by Lodge speaking for the committee. The bill would amend the first section of the 1891 Act to add the following to the inadmissible classes:

> All persons over 14 years of age who can not read and write the language of their native country or some other language, except that an aged person not so able to read and write who is the parent or grandparent of an admissible immigrant may accompany or be sent for by such immigrant.[61]

Also prescribed was the nature of the text to be used in the test: printed passages from the Constitution, five lines in length, and in the language of the immigrant. Rejected aliens were to be sent back at the expense of the steamship or railroad company.

Lodge gave an account of three methods considered by the committee for the purpose of excluding a maximum number of undesirables and a minimum number of desirable immigrants. The methods were the capitation tax, consular inspection, and the literacy test. The first of these was considered to be undiscriminating. The second was rejected because

[61] *Congressional Record,* 28:2817.

of practical difficulties in its application, for it would be a burden on the consular service and might arouse objections from foreign governments. The literacy test, in contrast, would be a discriminating test, bearing most heavily on Italians, Russians, Poles, Hungarians, Greeks, and Asiatics, only lightly on the English-speaking peoples, Germans, Scandinavians, and French.

According to committee information, Lodge continued, the poor congregate in cities, and

> The committee's report proves that illiteracy runs parallel with the slum population, with criminals, paupers, and juvenile delinquents of foreign birth or parentage [and] It also appears . . . that the immigrants who would be shut out by the illiteracy test are those who bring least money to the country and come most quickly upon private or public charity for support.[62]

Lodge then went on to discuss at length the quality of citizenry and the racial composition of the population, with reference to the danger of

> changing the quality of our race and citizenship through the wholesale infusion of races whose traditions and inheritances, whose thoughts and whose beliefs are wholly alien to ours.[63]

The bill was discussed further on May 14, at which time Gibson of Maryland presented a rebuttal to Lodge. Much of the nation is undeveloped, he pointed out, and "immigration is as essential now to our development as it ever was." The present laws are adequate for the purpose; and the literacy test would exclude the manual laborers whose strength is needed, but would let in "the communist and socialist, and loud-mouthed and filthy anarchists . . . because they are able to read." Many statistics and quotations were included in the lengthy prepared rebuttal. The committee report on the bill, Senate Report 290 (54-I), asserted:

> There can be no doubt that there is a general and very earnest desire among the people of the United States to restrict, by proper measures, foreign immigration.

The bill, however, was not brought to a vote in the Senate, which meanwhile was about to receive a literacy test bill approaching passage in the House.

On April 2, 1896 the House Committee on Immigration and Naturalization reported out its substitute for the McCall bill.[64] It provided that

[62]Ibid. [63]Ibid., p. 2820.
[64]H.R. 7864, with H. Rept. 1079 (54-I).

three months after passage the following class of aliens would be excluded:

> All male persons between 16 and 60 years of age who can not both read and write the English language or some other language.[65]

Exemption from the literacy requirement would be given to parents of persons then living in or thereafter admitted to the United States. The committee report explained further that in the original draft the literacy test requirement applied to both male and female immigrants, but in view of a shortage of white female servants the committee had decided to restrict the requirement to males only. The report also stated that the proposed test would not greatly affect immigration from Great Britain, Germany, Scandinavia, or other parts of northern Europe, but would "considerably restrict" immigration from southern Europe.

The bill was brought up in the House on May 19, at which time a number of amendments and substitutes were offered, including one by Johnson of California to prohibit the admission of foreign-born laborers, whether skilled or unskilled, after August 1, 1896. On the following day the Corliss amendment was accepted by a vote of 121 to 45. This amendment added four more sections to the bill to make it unlawful for an alien to enter the United States to work while maintaining his home in another country or to enter the country except where immigrant inspection is maintained, subjects of Canada and other American countries excepted. As amended, the bill passed the House on May 20, 1896 by a vote of 195 to 26. In the Senate it was reported out by Lodge for the immigration committee on May 23, and brought up on several days; but it was not acted on and was finally put on the Senate calendar as unfinished business to go over to the next session. The first session of the 54th Congress thus ended without passage of the literacy test, which more and more was coming to be regarded as the solution by both those who wanted more selective admissions and those who wanted restriction of the number admitted.

The Republican party platform for the presidential election of 1896 strongly endorsed the literacy test, in these terms:

> For the protection of the quality of our American citizenship, and of the wages of our workingmen, against the fatal competition of low-priced labor, we demand that the immigration laws be thoroughly enforced, and so extended as to exclude from entrance to the United States those who can neither read nor write.[66]

[65]*Congressional Record,* 28:5417.

[66]Ibid., 29:1936.

Although of the opposing party, the outgoing President Cleveland indicated concern about the literacy question in his message on the opening of the second session of the 54th Congress, on December 7, 1896. There he gave data showing, among other things, that the percentage of illiteracy among immigrants over fourteen years of age had risen from 20.37 percent in the preceding year to 28.63 in the current year. Other evidence of concern about the general effects of immigration, without specific mention of literacy, was the following resolution introduced by Senator Lodge of Massachusetts:

> Authorizing and directing the Commissioner of Labor to institute an investigation for the purpose of ascertaining the effect of foreign immigration upon the social, moral, economic, and industrial conditions of the country.[67]

Following the pattern set by the first session, the second session gave little attention to anything but regulation in the immigration field. No bills on Chinese immigration were introduced, and the only bill related to immigration but not concerned with regulation was one to prevent the employment of migratory aliens on government work (H.R. 9487, by Mahany [N.Y.]).

The Senate took up the unfinished business of the House immigration bill (H.R. 7864) on the second day after the opening of the session. The Senate committee, which had reported out the bill, recommended striking out the literacy test provision in the first section, together with all of the following sections, and to rephrase the passage on a literacy test excludable class as follows:

> All persons over 14 years of age who can not read and write the language of their native country or some other language, except that an aged person not so able to read and write who is the parent or grandparent of an admissible immigrant may accompany or be sent for by such immigrant.

As before, the test itself was to consist of five printed lines from the Constitution.

Consideration of the bill continued on December 10, at which time a commission report of October 7, 1895 was quoted in favor of a literacy test as follows:

> There is no doubt that the introduction of the literacy test would greatly facilitate the solution of the immigration problem, and do

[67]S. Res. 193, January 21, 1897; ibid., p. 1005.

> more than any one thing to lessen the present popular aversion to immigration.[68]

The committee revision or substitution was then accepted by the Senate.[69] A week later, when consideration of the bill was resumed, the Senate amended the excluding passage to read:

> All persons over 14 years of age who cannot read and write the language of their native country or some other language, but an admissible immigrant over such age of 14 years, may bring in with him or send for his wife or parent or grandparent or minor child or grandchild, notwithstanding the inability of such relative to read and write as aforesaid.

Further amendment raised the age from fourteen to sixteen, but a motion to raise it to twenty-one was defeated.

Among other amendments offered during discussion in the Senate was one to exempt persons arriving from Cuba from the literacy test "during the continuance of the present disorders there," and provided they had been inhabitants of the island. It was accepted, 47 to 6. A motion to raise the head tax to ten dollars on immigrants not coming in American vessels was tabled, as was a motion that the test be on ability to read the Ten Commandments and the Constitution. The bill as amended was passed by the Senate on December 17, 1896, by vote of 52 to 10, with 27 not voting.[70]

The bill then went to conference between House and Senate. The conference report, which presented a completely rewritten bill, recommended that the Senate recede from its amendment of the literacy test passage and accept the following revised statement of the excludable class:

> All persons physically capable and over 16 years of age who can not read and write the English language or the language of their native or resident country; but a person who is not so able to read and write who is over 50 years of age and is the parent or grandparent of a qualified immigrant over 21 years of age and capable of supporting such parent or grandparent may accompany such immigrant, or such a parent or grandparent may be sent for and come to join the family of a child or grandchild over 21 years of age similarly qualified and capable.[71]

Section 2 of the conference draft provided that the test material was to consist of printed slips with twenty or twenty-five words from the Consti-

[68]Ibid., 29:69.

[69]Ibid., p. 71.

[70]Ibid., p. 247.

[71]Ibid., p. 1125.

tution. Sections 4, 5, and 6 of the bill, from the Corliss amendment, would be stricken out and replaced with three new sections to prohibit employment on public works of male aliens who had not declared their intention to become citizens, to prohibit such aliens from coming regularly to the United States for employment and then departing from time to time, and to set forth terms of enforcement of the above restrictions. Section 7 would permit entry of aliens to teach new arts or industries; section 8 would be added to incorporate the Senate exemption of Cubans from the literacy test. And a final section 9 provided that aliens entering in violation of the act may be taken into custody and upon special inquiry "shall be dealt with as provided by law for alien immigrants upon their first arrival."

The House discussed the conference report on January 27, 1897 and accepted the rewritten bill by a close vote of 131 to 117, with 107 not voting. The Senate took up the conference report on February 2 and 4, at which time it accepted the Lodge motion not to concur in the conference recommendations.

The bill was then returned to conference and a second report produced. This report amended the first section of the bill to read "the English language or some other language," and added at the end of the literacy test statement, "and a wife or minor child not so able to read and write may accompany or be sent for and come to join the husband or parent similarly qualified and capable." The nature of the test and other parts of the bill remained substantially as before, but section 9 was dropped. On February 9 the House agreed to the second conference report by the strong majority of 217 to 36, with 125 not voting, and it was narrowly accepted by the Senate, 34 to 31, with 25 not voting. On March 2 the bill was vetoed by President Cleveland, who in his veto message questioned literacy as a basis for selection, expressed disagreement with the restrictive attitude toward immigration, and called un-American the forbidding of an alien to come for temporary employment. The House passed the bill over the President's veto by a strong margin, as in its previous vote on the bill, but the Senate took no action and the bill died.

55th Congress (1897–1899)

The 55th Congress opened in an early session on March 15, 1897, now with a Republican President who could be counted on not to veto a literacy test bill. In his inaugural address of a few days before, on March 4, President McKinley had testified to his support of the Republican platform declaration on the literacy test, saying that

> Our naturalization and immigration laws should be further improved to the constant promotion of a safer, a better, and a higher citizenship. A grave peril to the Republic would be a citizenship too ignorant to understand or too vicious to appreciate the great value and beneficence of our institutions and laws, and against all who come here to make war upon them our gates must be promptly and tightly closed.

To this he added that illiteracy among citizens must be reduced.

During the session there were an estimated 350 or more petitions to Congress for the restriction of immigration. About half were from citizens of Pennsylvania, smaller numbers from Massachusetts, New Jersey, West Virginia, Virginia, and other states. A few of the petitions were identified as coming from labor organizations. On the first day of the new Congress, Lodge introduced a bill (S. 112) to amend the immigration laws, actually a new literacy test bill. Referred to the Senate Committee on Immigration, it was reported back promptly, with an accompanying report that began with the statement,

> There can be no doubt that there is a general and very earnest desire among the people of the United States to restrict, by proper measures, foreign immigration.[72]

Data on illiteracy among immigrants were assembled in the report. The bill was passed over in the Senate and not taken up until the next session.

Five other bills to amend the immigration laws were introduced during the session, one with specific reference also to alien anarchists, and several of them appear to have been more concerned with restriction than with regulation of immigration.[73] One other bill was to levy a tax on immigrants (H.R. 3903, Ridgley [Kans.]).

On other matters, Congress received several reports on violations of the laws restricting Chinese immigration, but no bills on the subject were proposed. In continuation of attempts in previous sessions of Congress, a bill to prohibit enlistment of aliens in the armed forces was entered (S. 24, Allen [Nebr.]) and one to provide for medical inspection of immigrants at ports of debarcation (H.R. 2401, Burton [Ohio]). The only immigration bill to get out of committee during the session, however, was the Lodge bill mentioned above.

Except for the introduction of a House resolution for a Constitutional amendment to prohibit alien suffrage (H. Res. 124) and two bills

[72]S. Rept. 13, March 25, 1897 (55-I).

[73]S. 1051, Chandler (N.H.); H.R. 1, McCall (Mass.); H.R. 70, Danford (Ohio); H.R. 74, Corliss (Mich.); and H.R. 3863, W. A. Stone (Pa.).

relating to Chinese,[74] the second session of the 55th Congress occupied itself entirely with matters of regulation in the immigration field. One petition on immigration was received, this from the German Society of Philadelphia, against further restrictions on immigration. Bartholdt (Mo.) introduced a House resolution to create a commission for the study of immigration, but the resolution remained in committee.

Five bills calling variously for the regulation of immigration or for amendment of the immigration laws were presented,[75] of which two specifically concerned the insane. None of the new bills were acted on, but two literacy test bills were brought forward from the preceding session for further consideration. These were the McCall bill (H.R. 1) in the House and the Lodge bill (S. 112) in the Senate.

The McCall bill was reported out on December 17, 1897 with a committee report stating,

> The accompanying bill represents the idea of those who are of opinion that restriction of immigration along the line of illiteracy is the only practicable means of meeting the very urgent and general demand in some portions of the country for a bill that will give at least some measure of relief.[76]

No further action on the bill was taken by the House.

The Lodge bill, after several postponements, was brought up in the Senate on December 13, 1897. Its literacy test exclusion provisions were those of the second conference report of the preceding Congress, and the Corliss amendment was removed. Debate in the Senate continued over a number of days from December 13, 1897 to January 17, 1898, with long statements for and against the test. On the latter day Lodge presented a letter from the American Federation of Labor, adopted at its Nashville convention in 1897, that included a request for "a reasonable law to restrict undesirable immigration, such law to be based upon an educational qualification."

On the same day an important amendment, proposed by Spooner of Wisconsin, was adopted by a vote of 42 to 22. It changed the first sentence of the bill to read "All persons physically capable and over 16 years of age who can not read or write," in place of the former "read and write." A motion by Caffery (La.) to raise the specified age from 16 to 21 was rejected. The bill was then passed by the Senate, 45 to 28, with 16

[74] H.R. 5182, Smith (Ill.): To permit naturalization of Americanized Chinese; and H.R. 10829, Committee on Foreign Affairs: To amend the Act of November 3, 1893.

[75] S. 2779, Kyle (S.D.); S. 4521, Fairbanks (Ind.); H.R. 7742, Corliss (Mich.); H.R. 8869, Robbins (Pa.); H.R. 10342, Danford (Ohio).

[76] H. Rept. 69 (55-II).

not voting. No action on the bill was taken by the House until the next session.

The third session of the 55th Congress, of normal length from December 5, 1898 to March 3, 1899, had very little time for immigration matters. The presidential message was largely occupied with Cuba and the American involvement there, but the need for amendment of the contract labor laws was briefly noted.

The House on December 14 refused to take up the Senate's literacy test bill from the preceding session by a vote of 101 to 104, with 150 not choosing to vote.[77] Only one new bill on immigration, concerned with the Chinese, was introduced (H.R. 12150, McIntire [Md.]). It was to repeal certain acts relating to Chinese immigration, and it remained in committee.

In looking back to the 55th Congress it is surprising that such legislation was not passed, in view of the strong sentiment that had built up in and out of Congress for restrictive legislation and a favorably disposed resident of the White House. The war in Cuba intervened to distract attention from domestic problems, it is true; but congressional support for the literacy test and restrictive legislation may have been weakened also by another influence—that was the then rather common procedure of setting up an investigating commission before considering legislation. During the second session of the 55th Congress, a bill (H.R. 4073, Grosvenor [Ohio]) had been introduced in the House to authorize the appointment of a "nonpartisan commission" with the broad mandate "to collate information and to consider and recommend legislation to meet the problems presented by labor, agriculture, and capital." Reported back with amendment (in H. Rept. 353), the bill was debated, amended, and passed by the House, and then sent to the Senate, where it was substituted for a Senate bill of similar purpose (S. 2253, Perkins [Calif.]), passed, and signed to become the Act of June 18, 1898.

As set forth in the first section of the Act, the commission so established was to be known as the Industrial Commission and to consist of five members chosen from the Senate, five from the House, and nine other persons chosen by the President "with the advice and consent of the Senate" and to "fairly represent the different industries and employments." The second section spelled out the directives for the Commission, stating "that it shall be the duty of this commission to investigate questions pertaining to immigration, to labor, to agriculture, to manufacturing, and to business, and to report to Congress and to suggest such legislation as it may deem best upon those subjects."[78] Proceeding with

[77] *Congressional Record,* 32:196.

[78] Ibid., 31:4988.

extensive hearings and collection of information, the commission prepared a massive report in nineteen volumes that was not completed and presented to Congress until several years later in the first session of the 57th Congress. Included in the report was to be an extensive body of testimony concerning immigration matters and a series of recommendations concerning immigration legislation.[79]

56th Congress (1899–1901)

President McKinley's message to the opening session of the 56th Congress deplored outbreaks of mob violence against foreigners and recommended legislation then in Congress for their protection. The session itself made little contribution to the development of immigration law, for only a few bills were proposed, of which only two were reported out of committee, and these were passed over.[80]

In accordance with the President's recommendation, House and Senate bills were introduced to provide punishment for the violation of the treaty rights of aliens (S. 1580, Davis [Minn.]; H.R. 5070, Hitt [Ill.]). Chinese immigration was dealt with in two bills, one to regulate the coming of Chinese persons and the other to repeal certain of the acts affecting the Chinese (S. 1998, Proctor [Vt.]; H.R. 11280, Baker [Md.]).

A few proposals were made concerning the regulation of immigration, most of them reintroduced from previous sessions. Bartholdt (Mo.) reoffered his resolution to create a commission to examine the subject of immigration (H.J. Res. 87 [57-I]), Fairbanks (Ind.) tried again for amendment of the immigration laws relative to the insane (S. 1490), and Lodge (Mass.) reintroduced what was presumably his literacy test bill (S. 233). The last of these was reported back with amendment but then passed over by the Senate. Two members of Congress, concerned at the lack of inspection at the land borders, proposed the designation of ports of entry for aliens along boundary lines between the United States and foreign contiguous territory, these being S. 4780 by Fairbanks (Ind.) and H.R. 11715 by Kahn (Calif.).

The second session of the 56th Congress opened with a lengthy message from President McKinley concerning the Boxer uprising in China, insurrection in the Philippines, and, nearer home, the lynching of

[79]For the Commission's recommendations with regard to immigration legislation, see below, p. 128.

[80]Not included here are two bills, S. 2011 and H.R. 5297, to amend the Act of March 2, 1897 concerning the holding of real estate by aliens in the District of Columbia, the latter being passed by the House. There was also a new contract labor act of April 30, 1900.

five Italians in Tallulah, Louisiana. The need for amendment of the contract labor laws was again mentioned.

Perhaps the distant disturbances in China, but more particularly the continuing and considerable evasions of the Chinese exclusion acts at home, led to renewed efforts in Congress to deal with the Chinese problem. Four bills were introduced during the session, two of them to regulate the coming of Chinese persons, one to supplement the exclusion acts, and one to prohibit and regulate the coming of Chinese.[81] Of those four, a House bill for the regulation of Chinese immigration, by Jenkins of Wisconsin, was reported back with minor amendment by the Committee on Foreign Affairs on January 25, 1901. The purpose, as explained by the accompanying report (H. Rept. 2503 [56-II]), was to make certain changes in existing law in order to facilitate the enforcement of the controls and to combat the smuggling in of Chinese. It was discussed in the House on February 1, amended, and passed. In the Senate it was not reported out by the Committee on Foreign Relations.

More progress was made on another House bill, for the purpose of supplementing the Chinese exclusion act.[82] Directed toward the continuing problem of clandestine and illegal entry of Chinese, the bill provided for the hearing of cases of Chinese charged with illegal entry by United States commissioners. The bill was supported by the Attorney General. It was passed without debate by the House, and by the Senate on the last day of the Congress, March 2, 1901, and was signed into law as the Act of March 3, 1901 (31 Stat. 1093). The final section of the bill provided that it was to take effect immediately.

The only other immigration bills of the session were two of identical title, to amend the immigration laws relative to the insane, idiotic, and epileptic (S. 5598, H.R. 13605). The Senate bill, introduced by Lodge, stayed in committee. The House bill, by O'Grady of New York, was reported out with amendment and accompanied by House Report 2751 (56-II). As explained in the latter, the purpose was more effective exclusion. Existing law excluded only those who were members of the excludable classes at time of entry. The O'Grady bill would exclude those who had been confined in an institution for the insane, idiotic, or epileptic before arrival in the United States, and would extend the deportability period from one year to two years after landing. Further, the existing law for deportation required the showing that insanity arose from causes existing prior to entry, whereas the present bill would require deporta-

[81]S. 5625, Proctor (Vt.); H.R. 13197, Jenkins (Wis.); H.R. 12665, Ray (N.Y.); and H.R. 13301, Kahn (Cal.).

[82]H.R. 12665, Ray (N.Y.), with H. Rept. 2156 (56-II).

tion within two years after entry unless it could be shown that insanity arose from causes arising after entry. The burden of proof was thus reversed, now falling on the alien. Regarding admission, the bill called for a certificate of mental health from a qualified physician, plus a certification from a consular officer that he is "a qualified physician of experience"; and the manifest form would be changed to include a question of whether the alien was ever insane or confined in an institution for the insane. The House did not act on the bill.

57th Congress (1901–1903)

Theodore Roosevelt, succeeding to the presidency on McKinley's assassination, exceeded his predecessors in the emphasis he gave to immigration. In his annual message of December 3, 1901 at the beginning of the 57th Congress, he dwelt on the menace of trusts or "great corporations," but in connection with remarks on the assassination he went on to say,

> I earnestly recommend to the Congress that in the exercise of its wise discretion it should take into consideration the coming to this country of anarchists or persons professing principles hostile to all government. . . . They and those like them should be kept out of this country; and if found here they should be promptly deported to the country whence they came.[83]

Later in the message he stated his convictions on immigration and outlined what he considered a proper immigration policy:

> Our present immigration laws are unsatisfactory. We need every honest and efficient immigrant fitted to become an American citizen; every immigrant who comes here to stay, who brings here a strong body, a stout heart, a good head, and a resolute purpose to do his duty well in every way and to bring up his children as law-abiding and God-fearing members of the community. But there should be a comprehensive law enacted with the object of making a threefold improvement over our present system. First, we should aim to exclude absolutely not only all persons who are known to be believers in anarchistic principles or members of anarchistic societies, but also all persons who are of a low moral tendency or of unsavory reputation. This means that we should require a more thorough system of inspection abroad and a more rigid system of examination at our immigration ports, the former being especially necessary.
>
> The second object of a proper immigration law ought to be to secure by a careful and not merely perfunctory educational test some

[83] *Congressional Record,* 35:82.

> intelligent capacity to appreciate American institutions and act sanely as American citizens. This would not keep out all anarchists, for many of them belong to the intelligent criminal class. But it would do what is also in point, that is, tend to decrease the sum of ignorance, so potent in producing the envy, suspicion, malignant passion, and the hatred of order, out of which anarchistic sentiment inevitably springs. Finally, all persons should be excluded who are below a certain standard of economic fitness to enter our industrial field as competitors with American labor. There should be proper proof of personal capacity to earn an American living and enough money to insure a decent start under American conditions. This would stop the influx of cheap labor, and the resulting competition which gives rise to so much of bitterness in American industrial life.[84]

Two days after the presidential message, on December 5, 1901, the 57th Congress received Volume XV (H. Doc. 184 [57-I]) of the Industrial Commission report, presented to Congress by the Commission chairman, Albert Clarke. This volume contained the collected testimony and information on immigration, in all some 840 pages of material. The Commission's recommendations regarding immigration, together with the draft of a bill in thirty-five sections embodying the Commission's views on codification and revision of the immigration laws, followed in the nineteenth and final volume (H. Doc. 380) of the Commission's report. The recommendations, eighteen in all, included an increase of the head tax from one dollar to three dollars, establishment of effective inspection on the land borders, a change of wording in the immigration laws that would extend immigrant inspection to cabin class passengers, exclusion and deportation of anarchists, continuation and strengthening of the Chinese exclusion and contract labor laws, extension of the period of deportability to five years after entry, and penalties on steamship companies that bring aliens having a loathsome or contagious disease.

Two members of the Commission, including the chairman, registered their support for an educational test for would-be immigrants. And nine members stated their disagreement with the proviso that the Chinese exclusion acts be carefully adjusted in order not "to seriously interfere with commerce with China."

The accompanying draft of a codifying immigration bill incorporated the Commission's recommendations. Other points than those noted above are that proceeds from the head tax in excess of costs of inspection were to be put into an immigrant fund; the exclusion of aliens with a criminal record was modified by the proviso, following but not identical

[84]Ibid., p. 84.

in wording with that in the preceding Immigration Act of 1891, that the exclusion does not apply to political offenses not involving moral turpitude; and the contract labor provisions were qualified by the proviso that "skilled labor may be imported if labor of like kind unemployed cannot be found in the country." With regard to excludable classes, the Commission's bill mainly followed the wording of the Immigration Act of 1891 but supplemented the earlier list of excludables with "anarchists or persons who advocate the overthrow of all government or of all forms of law or the assassination of public officials," "prostitutes and persons who procure or attempt to bring in prostitutes or women for the purpose of prostitution"; and the definition of persons to be excluded as contract laborers was also expanded. Generally, however, the Commission in its recommendations and draft bill incorporated ideas regarding the regulation of immigration that had come up frequently in Congress, except for the omission of an educational or literacy test.

The session thus begun proved to be one of great activity in immigration legislation, concentrated in two areas. First, the presidential message stimulated an outpouring of bills for the regulation of immigration; and second, the approaching expiration of the ten-year suspension of Chinese immigration by the 1892 Act led to a heavy flow of legislative proposals together with a few memorials and petitions on Chinese immigration. Classified by title, the latter bills fell into one of two or three types. The majority called for continuation or extension of the exclusion laws. One of these, by Mitchell of Oregon, went further than others by calling for a twenty-year extension of the exclusion acts and a twenty-year prohibition of the coming of Chinese, Japanese, and natives of the Philippines archipelago (S. 638). Other bills were "to prohibit the coming of Chinese persons and persons of Chinese descent." The most sweeping of this type was introduced in the House by Kern of Illinois (H.R. 6525),

> To prohibit the coming of all natives of the Chinese Empire and of all persons of Chinese extraction into the United States and Territories thereof, and also into Porto Rico, the Philippine Islands, and all of the other colonial possessions of the United States, without reference to time limitation.

One other bill simply called for amendment of the Chinese Exclusion Act of 1892; but whatever the title, the common purpose was to continue exclusion of the Chinese.

Only two of the bills were brought up for consideration, one in the Senate and one in the House. The Senate bill (S. 2960, Mitchell [Oreg.]), to prohibit the coming into the country and to regulate the residence of Chinese persons and persons of Chinese descent in the United States, was reported out with amendment (S. Rept. 776 [57-I]), debated over a number of days, amended, and passed by the Senate. However, the House did not choose to consider it. The House bill[85] was identical with the Senate bill except for one section dealing with Chinese coming to participate in a fair or exposition. The minority report on the bill opened with the assertion that "The question of Chinese exclusion is largely a racial question and largely a labor question." Since it is the Pacific Coast people who have had the most experience with the Chinese, the report continued, they are "better fitted to know what legislation is necessary." And that being the committee's opinion, the committee bill is "substantially the bill desired by our Pacific coast citizens and by the laborers of the whole country."

The House bill was amended and passed by the House, reported back with amendment by the Senate Committee on Immigration, amended further, and passed by the Senate. A first conference report being rejected by both House and Senate, the bill went to a second conference report, which was accepted, and with presidential signature the bill became the Chinese Exclusion Act of April 29, 1902 (32 Stat. 176).

Less drastic than in the original draft or as passed by the House, the act extended the existing exclusion acts until such time as a new treaty with China was negotiated and extended the application of the exclusion acts to insular territory of the United States, including the requirement of a certificate of residence, except in Hawaii.

The second large group of bills related to immigration in the first session of the 57th Congress included nineteen bills dealing in one way or another with the regulation of immigration. Eight were designated as regulatory in purpose, although several might more properly be called restrictive. Seven bills were stated to be for the amendment of the immigration laws, including one relative to the mentally handicapped and one by Lodge with the noncommittal title of an amending bill, which was very possibly the literacy test bill he had offered several times before under the same title. Three bills were for the exclusion and deportation of alien anarchists, of which one also contained a literacy test provision. One or two concerned contract labor.

Only one bill was acted on, that being a House bill for the regulation of immigration, introduced by Shattuc of Ohio. Reported out on March 18, 1902, it was designed to codify the immigration acts from that of March 3, 1875 onwards.[86] The first section increased the head tax from

[85]H.R. 13031, Committee on Foreign Affairs, with H. Rept. 1231 (57-I), and part 2, the minority report.

[86]H.R. 12199, with H. Rept. 982 (57-I). Shattuc was then chairman of the House Committee on Immigration and Naturalization. This was known as the Industrial Commission bill.

one dollar to one dollar and a half, and the tax was extended to those coming over the land borders. The second section added the following to the excludable classes:

1. epileptics, persons who have been insane within five years previous, persons who have had two or more attacks of insanity at any time previously;
2. anarchists, or persons who believe in or advocate the overthrow by force or violence of all governments, or of all forms of law, or the assassination of public officials;
3. prostitutes and persons who procure or attempt to bring in prostitutes or women for the purpose of prostitution.

The third was added to round out the 1875 Act, which made the importation of such aliens a felony punishable with fine and imprisonment but did not provide for exclusion at time of entry. Also added to the second section was a proviso that the contract labor laws do not apply to the importation of skilled labor if labor of like kind unemployed cannot be found in the country. Section 2 of the bill is seen to follow the recommendations of the Industrial Commission closely in the matter of excludable classes, except for differences in number 1, above.

Section 10 introduced a new humane provision for the return of an alien accompanying a rejected alien who is helpless because of physical inability or infancy. Sections 12, 13, and 14 were reenactments of the first three sections of the 1893 Act and the first part of section 8 of the 1891 Act concerning manifests, but with amendment to permit the oath or affirmation of masters and physicians of vessels to be made before an immigration officer at the port of arrival instead of before a United States consul at the port of departure. This change was called for because cabin passengers booked by inland agents often arrived only just as the vessel was about to sail, making it virtually impossible to comply with the former requirement.

Section 21 proposed an important change in deportation law by extending the period of deportability of an alien unlawfully in the United States to five years after arrival. The committee amendments to the bill were minor, apparently matters of wording only.

The bill was brought up for discussion in the House on May 21, 1902. An attempt was made by Underwood of Alabama to insert a literacy test applicable to persons over fifteen years of age and physically capable of reading. Discussion was resumed on the twenty-second, at which time the increased head tax was accepted, but its collection was limited to immigrants only.[87] Shattuc (Ohio) of the Committee on Immigration and

[87] *Congressional Record,* 35:5818.

Naturalization proposed an amendment declaring that an alien who enters except at a designated port of entry shall be adjudged to have entered unlawfully and be deported. The amendment was accepted, 54 to 13.[88]

The Underwood literacy test amendment was voted on and inserted in the bill, by a vote of 86 to 7.[89] Corliss (Mich.) then proposed the addition of a section embodying the so-called Corliss amendment attached to a House bill in the 54th Congress six years before. It would prohibit a male alien who has not in good faith declared his intention to become a citizen from being employed on any public works in the United States or to come regularly for the purpose of engaging in labor and then returning from time to time to a foreign country. A "bird of passage" measure, it was not incorporated into the bill. Consideration of the bill was continued on May 27, at which time it was discussed at length and passed.[90]

A month later the bill was reported out in the Senate, with a committee report attached (S. Rept. 2119, June 27, 1902 [57-I]). The committee recommended that the head tax be doubled to three dollars, citizens of Mexico, Cuba, and Canada excepted. Further action in the Senate was postponed to the second session.

President Roosevelt in his annual message to the second session of the 57th Congress limited himself to the following mention of immigration:

> I again call your attention to the need of passing a proper immigration law, covering the points outlined in my Message to you at the first session of the present Congress; substantially such a bill has already passed the House.

With this presidential endorsement, the House bill from the preceding session (H.R. 12199) was promptly taken up by the Senate. On December 8, 1902 the Senate accepted its committee's amendment raising the head tax to three dollars but changed the applicability of the tax from passengers to alien immigrants. On the following day the McCumber (N.D.) amendment to add "professional beggars" to the excluded classes in section 2 was accepted.

The Penrose (Pa.) amendment substituting a new section 21 was next adopted.[91] It provided that any alien coming into the United States in violation of law, or an alien becoming a public charge "from causes

[88]Ibid., pp. 5824, 5832.

[89]Ibid., p. 5833.

[90]Ibid., p. 6014.

[91]Ibid., 36:136. In the final draft of the bill, this became section 20, and the following section set a three-year period of deportability for aliens in the United States in violation of the act.

existing prior to landing" shall be deported at any time within two years after arrival, and that

> Any alien who becomes a public charge by reason of lunacy, idiocy, or epilepsy within two years after arrival will be presumed to have become such from causes existing prior to landing unless the contrary be affirmatively shown.

Consideration of the bill in the Senate continued on February 27, 1903, at which time the Dryden (N.J.) amendment to drop the head tax from three to two dollars was accepted. Also accepted was a motion by Clay (Ga.) to strike out the portion of the Penrose amendment dealing with deportation of public charges because of lunacy and so on.[92] Further provisions against alien anarchists were also adopted. The bill passed the Senate the following day. Because the House disagreed with the Senate amendments and the Senate insisted on its amendments, a conference committee was appointed. The principal changes recommended in the conference report were to strike out the literacy test inserted by the House and drop the Senate amendment restricting the head tax to alien immigrants rather than all alien passengers. With approval by both Senate and House and presidential signature, the bill became the Immigration Act of March 3, 1903 (32 Stat. 1213).

A long codification of immigration law in thirty-nine sections, the act reaffirmed the contract labor law and the prior immigration laws, made the several additions to the excludable classes noted above, repeated the manifesting requirements, levied a head tax of two dollars on every arriving alien passenger, with the exceptions noted, set the two-year period of deportability according to the first part of the Penrose amendment, and contained strengthened sections against alien anarchists as added by the Senate.[93]

Little else related to immigration occurred during the second session of the 57th Congress. An amendment (S. 7130) to the Chinese Exclusion Act of 1888 was proposed by Senator Dillingham of Vermont, who was to take an active part in immigration legislation during the years to come; a bill (H.R. 16877) to prevent aliens drawing pensions was introduced by Russell (Tex.); and Bartholdt of Missouri patiently reintroduced a resolution (H. J. Res. 251) to create a commission to examine the subject of immigration.

[92]Ibid., p. 2750.

[93]Section 34 of the act is a surprisingly unrelated rider, "That no intoxicating liquors of any character shall be sold within the limits of the Capitol building of the United States."

58th Congress (1903–1905)

After the efforts of the preceding Congress, the early and short first session of the 58th was uneventful regarding immigration. Four bills to regulate immigration or amend the immigration laws were introduced.[94] Two others concerned the right of aliens to hold real estate in the District of Columbia, and one bill, which should have been superfluous but perhaps was not, was to punish lynching of aliens (H.R. 2872, Crumpacker [Ind.]). A final bill (H.R. 5221, Robinson [Ind.]), an intimation of things to come, was to prohibit the immigration of Japanese and persons of Japanese descent. None of these went beyond committee.

With his message of December 7, 1903 to the second session of the 58th Congress, President Roosevelt returned to his earlier theme of the need for congressional attention to immigration, implying that the recently passed 1903 Act left some problems unsolved. To quote:

> We can not have too much immigration of the right kind, and we should have none at all of the wrong kind. The need is to devise some system by which undesirable immigrants shall be kept out entirely, while desirable immigrants are properly distributed throughout the country. At present some districts which need immigrants have none; and in others, where the population is already congested, immigrants come in such numbers as to depress the conditions of life for those already there.[95]

The majority of new legislative proposals were for the regulation of immigration, but a scattering of other topics was represented. The Senate received a bill (S. 5317) from Dillingham (Vt.) to provide for medical inspection at the port of departure, which was reported out by the Committee on Immigration. The accompanying report pointed out that the existing law has medical inspection at the port of arrival, which does not meet the danger that healthy immigrants may contract a disease on shipboard. The bill was not acted on. Another bill (H.R. 11443, Gardner [Mass.]) was to amend earlier legislation in order to extend head tax exemption to citizens of Newfoundland entering the United States. Favorably reported in both House and Senate (H. Rept. 1233, S. Rept. 2619), the bill was passed and signed as the Act of March 22, 1904 (33 Stat. 144).

Three bills called for amendment of the Chinese exclusion acts.[96] A fourth bill was to prohibit employment on vessels of American registry of Chinese persons not admissible, evidently to meet the problem of

[94] S. 15, Lodge (Mass.); S. 902, Perkins (Calif.); S. 1376, Lodge (Mass.); H.R. 832, Watson (Ind.).

[95] *Congressional Record,* 38:3.

[96] S. 5343, Patterson (Colo.); H.R. 14619, Livernash (Calif.); H.R. 15167, Hitt (Ill.).

deserting seamen (H.R. 12230, Livernash [Calif.]). None of the above bills relating to the Chinese progressed out of committee, but a section reinforcing the Chinese exclusion laws was included in a deficiency appropriation bill (H.R. 15054) that became the Act of April 27, 1904 (33 Stat. 428). Section 5 of this act "reenacted, extended, and continued, without modification, limitation, or condition" the exclusion laws but (1) explicitly added that such laws applied to the island territory under the jurisdiction of the United States, (2) prohibited the migration of alien Chinese laborers from such island territory to the mainland, whether or not they were residents of the island territory at the time of its annexation, (3) similarly prohibited the migration of such alien Chinese laborers from one island territory to another except within the same group of islands, and (4) specified that islands under the jurisdiction of any state or the District of Alaska should be regarded for the purpose of this act as part of the mainland.

The session also saw three bills to establish a laboratory for the study of criminal, pauper, and defective classes (S. 2951, H.R. 10011, 13984). Bills of the same purpose had appeared in earlier sessions of Congress and were to reappear later. Although the proposals were not concerned specifically with aliens, they nevertheless concerned classes with which aliens had been identified prominently in the public discussion of immigration policy.

Following the presidential invitation for further action, eleven bills and three resolutions were introduced to amend the 1903 Act. Another was for amendment of the 1875 Act, and two other bills called for the exclusion of certain aliens and for limiting of immigration.

The only one of the above proposals acted on was a Senate resolution by Lodge, a measure to change the wording of the 1903 Act to accord with the transfer of the Bureau of Immigration from the Treasury Department to the Department of Commerce and Labor. It was passed by both houses of Congress and signed by the President.

The message with which President Roosevelt opened the third session of the 58th Congress, on December 6, 1904, took a more decisive position on the need to keep out undesirable migrants, especially for the protection of the laboring class:

> the citizenship of this country should not be debased. It is vital that we should keep high the standard of well-being among our wage-workers, and therefore we should not admit masses of men whose standards of living and whose personal customs and habits are such that they tend to lower the level of the American wage-worker.[97]

[97]*Congressional Record,* 39:17.

There was little immediate legislative reaction, however. Two bills from the first session were reactivated, both concerning alien ownership of real estate in the District of Columbia, and one was passed (S. 1258, H.R. 4513). An amendment to the 1888 Chinese Exclusion Act was proposed (S. 6531, Dillingham [Vt.]). There were two new bills to amend the 1903 Act (S. 7025, Dillingham [Vt.]; H.R. 15967, Littlefield [Me.]), and one with the general title of regulating the immigration of aliens (H.R. 16800, Connell [Pa.]). None got out of committee.

59th Congress (1905–1907)

The next annual message from President Roosevelt, at the beginning of the 59th Congress, was even more emphatic and dwelt at greater length on the need for more effective protection from unwanted immigration and for other legislative changes. Noting the heavy volume of immigration, which was rising to record heights almost every year, he suggested that for better distribution there might be limitation of immigration to New York but not to the South, and efforts should be made to get immigrants to the land rather than to the cities. It would be well to allow only natives of Canada and Mexico to enter over the land borders. The immigration laws should be strengthened, and designed to keep out all who would not make good citizens and, most important from a later viewpoint, admission should be based not on creed or nationality but on individual quality. And severe limitation of the allowable passenger capacity of vessels was recommended. Further,

> There should be an increase in the stringency of the laws to keep out insane, idiotic, epileptic and pauper immigrants. But this is by no means enough. Not merely the anarchist, but every man of anarchistic tendencies, all violent and disorderly people, all people of bad character, the incompetent, the lazy, the vicious, and physically unfit, defective, or degenerate should be kept out.[98]

In this renewed plea for decisive congressional action, President Roosevelt was at last successful, for the 59th Congress responded with a burst of legislative activity related to immigration. Most attention was directed toward the regulation of immigration in accordance with the presidential recommendations, but there were also several bills dealing with Chinese immigration; and in a quite different direction there was congressional support for barring aliens from the fishing industry in Alaska.

[98]Ibid., 40:101.

To consider these lesser concerns first, two House bills called for the suspension or prohibition of Chinese laborer immigration: H.R. 12973, by Foster (Vt.) and H.R. 18022, by Denby (Mich.). A rare opposite viewpoint, however, was represented by a memorial from the Georgia legislature that called for repeal of the Chinese exclusion acts. And there were three bills to prohibit aliens from fishing in the waters of Alaska: S. 267, by Fulton (Oreg.), and H.R. 472, 10850, by Cushman (Wash.). The two House bills were referred to the Committee on Territories, which took no action. The Senate bill went to the Committee on Foreign Relations, was reported back with amendment (S. Rept. 785 [59-I]), and passed by the Senate. In the House it was reported out (H. Rept. 2485) and passed with new amendment, but on Senate disagreement it went to a conference committee whose compromise draft (H. Rept. 4770, June 5, 1906) was accepted and with presidential signature became the Act of June 14, 1906 (34 Stat. 263). In substance, this act made it unlawful for aliens to engage in fishing in Alaskan waters unless they had declared their intention of becoming citizens (that is, first papers) and were bona fide residents. Companies or organizations not organized and authorized under the laws of the United States were similarly prohibited, but exception was made of fishing with rod, spear, or gaff; and those entitled to carry on fishing were entitled to employ alien laborers.

Relevant to policy and planning for the regulation of immigration were four bills to establish a laboratory for the study of the criminal, pauper, and defective classes. The bills were not reported out, nor did Bartholdt's renewed proposal to create a commission to inquire into the subject of immigration have any more success than in previous Congresses (H. J. Res. 161 [59-I]).

At least thirty bills concerned with immigration regulation in one way or another were introduced during the session. Of these fourteen were to amend the 1903 Act, several specifying in the title what section or sections were to be amended. Four bills were to amend the immigration laws without further specification, but most probably concerned the 1903 Act. Six were for the stated purpose of regulating the immigration of aliens, whereas others were to limit immigration or to exclude undesirable aliens. One bill was to promote a better distribution of immigrants, following a presidential recommendation (H.R. 11020, Gardner [Mass.]). Two were to enable the President to call an international conference to secure agreement on the regulation of immigration to the United States (H.R. 6018, Bonynge [Colo.]; H.R. 8987, Wiley [N.J.]). And a final proposal was to prohibit the coming of both Japanese and Korean laborers (H.R. 3160, McKinlay, [Calif.]). Of all these immigration bills introduced during the session, only two or three were acted on, a House bill and a later substitute for it to regulate immigration, and a Senate bill to amend the 1903 Act (H.R. 17941, replaced by H.R. 18673, and S. 4403).

On April 9, 1906 Gardner of Massachusetts, acting for the House Committee on Immigration and Naturalization, introduced a bill (H.R. 17941) prepared by the committee as a substitute for the nineteen or so immigration bills it had received. Accompanying it was a committee report, with dissenting minority report attached.[99] No further action was taken, for the bill was withdrawn, to be replaced by another bill substantially the same and accompanied by the same majority and minority reports.[100]

The latter bill retained unchanged ten of the thirty-nine sections of the 1903 Act, and others were changed or omitted. Following are the principal changes proposed, by section:

Sec. 1. Changes the head tax from two to five dollars, the returns to be used for bureaus of information.

Sec. 2. Adds to the excluded classes imbeciles, consumptives, feeble-minded persons, those who have at any time been insane, and under certain conditions persons of poor physique.

Sec. 3. Revises and strengthens the prostitute provisions.

Sec. 11. Permits exclusion of an alien accompanying a helpless alien.

Sec. 12. Provides for a manifesting of departures of aliens.

Sec. 20. Extends the deportability period to three years after entry in certain cases.

Sec. 35 (new). Designates ports of entry on the Canadian border.

Sec. 38 (new). Provides an educational or literacy test, according to the report embodying the recommendation in President Roosevelt's message of December 3, 1901. The wording was as follows:

> That no alien over sixteen years of age physically capable of reading shall be admitted to the United States until he has proved to the satisfaction of the proper inspection officers that he can read English or some other tongue.

The method of testing was to be prescribed by the Secretary of Commerce and Labor. An attached proviso is that an immigrant may bring in or send for his wife or mother, affianced wife, or father if over fifty-five years of age, "if they are otherwise admissible, whether they are able to read or not." Aliens from Canada, Newfoundland, Cuba, and Mexico were exempt, provided they had resided there for at least three years. Also exempt from the educational test were aliens entering the outlying

[99]H. Rept. 3021, parts 1 and 2 (59-I).

[100]H.R. 18673, with H. Rept. 3635, parts 1 and 2 (59-I).

possessions of the United States, but not if they later sought to enter the continental United States.

Sec. 39 (new). Adds the following financial test for admissibility:

> That every male alien over sixteen years of age shall be deemed likely to become a public charge unless he shows . . . that he has in his physical possession at the time of his inspection money to the equivalent of twenty-five dollars . . . or that the head of his family entering with him so holds that amount on his account.

The requirement was for fifteen dollars for every female alien and every alien under sixteen, but fifty dollars in the possession of a head of a family would exempt female members of the family and males under eighteen.

Sec. 40 (new). Provides for bureaus of information.

Reasons for the terms of the act, as explained in the committee report were, among others, that the higher head tax would decrease the number of immigrants while also tending to exclude some undesirables. And the literacy test section was stated to be in accordance with the President's recommendation.

The objections presented in the minority report, the same as those on the preceding bill, were that it "makes no proper and adequate provision for the proper execution of the contract labor law," the increase of the head tax is "absolutely unjustified," obviously intended to keep out southern Italians, Hungarians, Poles, and Slovaks. But in fact it will penalize the Germans, Scandinavians, English, and others who come with large families. And the literacy test is likewise unjustified, evidently designed to restrict immigration.

Meanwhile the Senate had been working on its own bill, very much like the House bill. On February 14, 1906 Dillingham (Vt.) introduced a bill to amend the 1903 Act, which was reported back on March 29 (S. 4403, with S. Rept. 2186). Like the bill in the House, it raised the head tax from two to five dollars, required the manifesting of departing aliens, and provided in section 40 for a division of information, but it did not contain a literacy test. Other changes in immigration law to be made by the bill included exemption from the head tax (section 1) of

> duly accredited officials of foreign governments who shall enter the United States from time to time from foreign contiguous territory upon the business of the government to which they are accredited.

Additions to the excludable classes in section 2 were imbeciles, feebleminded persons, epileptics, and

> persons not comprehended within any of the foregoing excluded classes who are found to be and are certified by the examining surgeon as being mentally or physically defective, such mental or

physical defect being of a nature which may affect the ability of such alien to earn a living.

And to the existing exclusion of persons who have been convicted of a felony were added those who admit to having committed a felony. Other additions were

> persons who admit their belief in the practice of polygamy; . . . or women or girls coming into the United States for the purpose of prostitution or for any other immoral purpose; persons who have been induced to migrate to this country in consequence of offers, solicitations, promises, or agreements, oral, written, or printed, express or implied, to perform labor of any kind, skilled or unskilled, in this country; . . . all children under seventeen years of age unaccompanied by their parents, unless coming to join parents already in this country who are able to support them.

On May 22, 1906 the Senate agreed to the increase of the head tax to five dollars.[101] A literacy test amendment was proposed, to be replaced by a reworded statement supplied by Lodge (Mass.), to exclude

> All persons over sixteen years of age and physically capable of reading who can not read the English language or some other language; but an admissible immigrant or a person now in or hereafter admitted to this country may bring in or send for his wife, his children under eighteen years of age, and his parents or grandparents over fifty years of age, if they are otherwise admissible, whether they are so able to read or not.[102]

The Lodge substitute was then agreed to by the Senate. Various other amendments were rejected, including ones for the removal of the five-year limit on excludability for a prior attack of insanity, exemption of agricultural laborers from the contract labor acts, and elimination of the first proviso regarding contract labor.[103] The bill was passed by the Senate and sent to the House.

The House Committee on Immigration and Naturalization reported out the Senate bill on May 29 with the recommendation to strike out the entire bill and substitute the quite similar House bill[104] (H.R. 18673), whose features have been noted above. The committee report was accompanied by a minority report restating the objections previously made to the earlier House bills (H.R. 17941, 18673). The bill was then recom-

[101] *Congressional Record,* 40:7230. [102] Ibid., p. 7298.

[103] Ibid., pp. 7299, 7300. The first proviso permitted importation of skilled labor if labor of like kind unemployed cannot be found in the country.

[104] H. Rept. 4558, parts 1 and 2, May 29, 1906 (59-I).

mitted, to be reported out again on June 11 with a new committee report attached.[105] The report gave further justification for the higher head tax, saying that it

> was adopted largely owing to the belief that it will tend to decrease the number of aliens and tend to exclude the less desirable.[106]

The report also noted that the first draft of the bill had exempted aliens entering island territory from the head tax.

Debate on the bill continued in the House on June 25, 1906, at which time Underwood of Alabama spoke in favor of the literacy test, which he considered to be a good measure of the quality of an immigrant. Further advantages of the test, he asserted, were that it would help maintain the same racial composition of the population.[107] Furthermore,

> the educational test will not only separate the ignorant, vicious, and the lazy from the intelligent and industrious classes that are coming to this country, but to a large extend it will eliminate the lower classes of immigration from the countries that are not of Teutonic and Celtic origin, and to some degree will solve the problem of the assimilation of the dissimilar races.

An amendment was proposed by Littauer (N.Y.) to add the word "solely" to the provision concerning political and religious refugees, which would then read:

> That an immigrant who proves that he is seeking admission to this country solely to avoid prosecution or punishment on religious or political grounds, for an offense of a political character, or prosecution involving danger of imprisonment or danger to life and limb on account of religious belief, shall not be deported because of want of means or the probability of his being unable to earn a livelihood.[108]

The amendment first appeared to be lost, for on division of the House the count was aye 66, no 79; but tellers were called for and the motion was carried, 92 to 69.[109] Another amendment was accepted to reduce the head tax from five to two dollars. Grosvenor (Ohio) made a motion to eliminate the literacy test and substitute a section providing for an immigration commission to study the question. The motion carried, 128 to 116.[110] Then, as amended, the substitute bill was passed by the House.

[105]H. Rept. 4912, June 11, 1906 (59-I).

[106]Ibid., p. 19.

[107]*Congressional Record,* 40:9155.

[108]Ibid., p. 9164.

[109]Ibid., p. 9166. The Denby motion to exempt religious refugees from the literacy test was adopted at the same time.

[110]Ibid., p. 9195.

The Senate disagreeing, a conference committee was appointed to report the next session of Congress.

The second session of the 59th Congress convened on December 3, 1906. Reference to immigration matters in the annual message from President Roosevelt on the following day was limited to the general statement that we must treat all nations fairly and do the same with immigrants. And an act specifically permitting the naturalization of Japanese was recommended by the President.

The conference committee report (H. Rept. 7607 [59-II]) appeared on February 13, 1907. The conference decision, in effect, was to strike out the House draft and to write a new bill. The Senate conferees accepted omission of the literacy test, the House conferees gave up the Littauer amendment on refugees, the head tax was set at four dollars, and the Senate agreed to the appointment of an investigating commission. Two new features of the conference bill were added in conference. One was a change in minimum deck space per passenger; the other was a proviso that the President may refuse entry to the citizen of any country if satisfied that the alien was given a passport to another country or to a possession of the United States but with the purpose in fact of gaining entry to the continental United States.[111] With the agreement of the House and Senate and the signature of President Roosevelt, the conference draft became the Immigration Act of February 20, 1907 (34 Stat. 898).

A major codifying act incorporating and consolidating earlier legislation, the new immigration act extended to forty-four sections. The head tax money of four dollars per alien entering the United States was to constitute an "immigrant fund," to be used to defray the expenses of regulating immigration and certain legal enforcement expenses. Exemption from the tax was granted to aliens from Canada, Newfoundland, Cuba, and Mexico who had an uninterrupted residence there of at least one year. The excludable classes were added to, and the exclusion of subversive and immoral classes and contract laborers was reaffirmed. The manifesting requirements were also reaffirmed, and the manifesting of departing aliens added. Section 39 created a commission for the study of immigration, to consist of three Senators, three Representatives, and

[111]This proviso, at the end of section 1 of the conference bill that became the 1907 Act, was soon used by President Roosevelt to deal with the problem of Japanese immigration at the executive level. In a proclamation on March 14, 1907, based on the authority given in the proviso, he excluded Japanese and Korean laborers, whether skilled or unskilled, whose passports were for travel to Canada, Mexico, or Hawaii. This exclusion was reinforced by an understanding with the Japanese government that it would continue to discourage the migration of its subjects to the United States.

three presidential appointees. On February 22 the congressional members of the commission were appointed: Dillingham (Vt.), Lodge (Mass.), and Latimer[112] (S.C.) from the Senate, Howell (N.J.), Bennet (N.Y.), and Burnett (Ala.) from the House. The presidential appointees were Charles P. Neill, Jeremiah W. Jenks, and William R. Wheeler. The commission was known as the Dillingham Commission after its chairman.

Other legislative activity on immigration was limited during the session. Denby of Michigan introduced H.R. 24646 to amend the 1903 Act, and H.R. 25785 by Russell of Texas was to deny pensions to aliens. No action was taken on them.

60th Congress (1907–1909)

The first session of the 60th Congress, for once without recommendations on immigration from the White House, turned its attention to a variety of immigration matters remaining after the 1907 Act, principally for the further regulation of immigration and amendment of the newly passed act. The House again received a bill to punish the lynching of aliens, H.R. 7592; and House and Senate bills H.R. 16733 and S. 3066 were to establish a laboratory for the study of certain problem classes. A passenger act, S. 5083, passed by both houses of Congress but not signed into law until the second session, was to make space requirements more uniform with the British Board of Trade regulations recently set by act of Parliament in 1906.

Six bills of varying titles proposed amendment of the immigration laws.[113] Two others concerned the regulation of immigration to Hawaii, these being S. 2643 by Clark of Wyoming and H.R. 10568 by Hepburn of Iowa. A bill to exclude undesirables was H.R. 9177 by Burnett (Ala.). Two bills concerned racial groups, one being by Hayes of California (H.R. 246) for regulation of the entry of Chinese, Japanese, and others, and the other by French of Idaho (H.R. 18790) to prohibit laborer immigration of Japanese and Koreans. The only bills to be reported out were H.R. 10568 by Hepburn of Iowa relating to immigration into Hawaii, and H.R. 13079 by Bennet of New York to amend the immigration act.

The Hepburn bill (H.R. 10568) was reported out, on January 11, 1908, with an accompanying report from the committee (H. Rept. 90

[112]Senator McLaurin of Mississippi was originally appointed but was unable to accept at the time, and so Latimer of South Carolina was appointed in his place. On the death of the latter on February 20, 1908, Senator McLaurin succeeded him, but he died a year later, on December 22, 1909. His successor was Senator Percy of Mississippi.

[113]S. 2246, H.R. 367, 6167, 7628, 11326, and 13079.

[60-I]). The background of the bill, as explained in the report, was that prior to the 1907 Act the government of Hawaii had actively imported several thousand Portuguese laborers, paying their transportation and other costs. This had been considered desirable, to replace Oriental with white labor. The Hepburn bill was to permit such importation. The House committee had reported it out with an amendment consisting of a new section 3 to specify that nothing shall be construed to permit the admission of an alien excludable under the 1907 Act. The bill was debated in the House on April 22, 1908 and defeated, 19 to 186. The main argument against the bill was that it abrogated the contract labor laws for Hawaii.

The second House bill to come out of committee was the Bennet (N.Y.) bill to amend section 21 of the immigration act, concerned with deportation.[114] The proposed amendment consisted of adding the following proviso to section 21:

> Provided further, That any alien who is now under sentence because of conviction in this country of a felony, or who may be hereafter convicted of a felony, shall, at the expiration of his sentence, be taken into custody and returned to the country whence he came in the manner provided by section 20 of this act.[115]

The House debated and rejected the bill on March 2.[116] One of the most telling arguments of the opponents was that the definition of felony varies widely from state to state and includes minor crimes in some of them. The bill was brought up again in the second session of the 60th Congress, with an amendment to meet this objection that would limit deportation to felony cases in which the sentence is one year or more; but the House took no action.

President Roosevelt continued to refrain from comment on immigration in his message to the second session of the 60th Congress, and the Congress itself made only scattered proposals for new legislation. The laboratory bill appeared again; and as noted above, no action was taken on the deportation of felony cases provided by the bill from the preceding session. A Senate bill concerning the inspection of immigrants remained in committee, but the House did accept a resolution requesting the Secretary of Commerce and Labor to provide certain information about aliens in the United States (H. Res. 556, Gardner [Mass.]).

Another matter to receive attention during the session was the manifesting of certain aliens departing by vessel. The Act of February 20, 1907

[114]H.R. 13079, with H. Rept. 957, February 15, 1908 (60-I).
[115]*Congressional Record*, 42:2752. [116]Ibid., pp. 2752–58.

(34 Stat. 898) had reaffirmed the requirement for manifesting of aliens arriving by water and had added a like requirement with regard to departing aliens.[117] A bill introduced by Senator Crane of Massachusetts (S. 7785) called for suspension of this requirement in the case of vessels bound for Canada or Mexico. Reported favorably and with amendment in the committees concerned (S. Rept. 714; H. Rept. 1893), the bill was passed by both Senate and House, and signed into law as the Act of March 4, 1909 (35 Stat. 1060). It provided that until the provisions of section 12 of the 1907 Act concerning the manifesting of departing aliens should be made applicable to passengers going from the United States to Canada by land,

> said provisions shall not apply to passengers going by vessels employed exclusively in the trade between the ports of the United States and the Dominion of Canada and the Republic of Mexico.

61st Congress (1909–1911)

The early first session of the 61st Congress ran from March 15 to August 5, 1909. Immigration was at a high tide, exceeding a million in some years, and Congress began again to receive petitions and memorials to restrict immigration. On April 20, for example, there were resolutions from the Ohio legislature asking for "more stringent immigration laws."[118] On the following day, identical resolutions were received from the Pennsylvania House of Representatives. On April 26 a resolution came from the General Assembly of Virginia, "to oppose in every possible manner the influx into Virginia of immigrants from southern Europe," and the resolution contained reference to "Anglo-Saxon supremacy."[119] On the same day Senator Overman of North Carolina proposed an amendment to a tariff bill to raise the head tax to ten dollars. He saw the higher tax as both a source of revenue and a means to a better class of immigrants.[120] On June 1 a petition from the American Cotton Manufacturers Association favored a twelve-dollar head tax. On June 26 a petition from the Central Labor Council of Seattle urged the head tax be increased from four to ten dollars. And finally on July 29 a petition

[117]Section 12 of the 1907 Act read in part as follows: "that it shall further be the duty of the master or commanding officer of every vessel taking alien passengers out of the United States, from any port thereof, to file before departure therefrom with the collector of customs of such port a complete list of all such alien passengers taken on board. Such list shall contain the name, age, sex, nationality, residence in the United States, occupation, and the time of last arrival of every such alien in the United States."

[118]*Congressional Record,* 44:1400.

[119]Ibid., p. 1526.

[120]Ibid., p. 1524.

from the Winona, Alabama, Council, Junior Order of United American Mechanics asked for protection from immigration from southern Europe and for exclusion of anarchists.[121]

The number of new immigration bills was small, however. Bennet (N.Y.) again proposed amendment of section 21 of the immigration act, concerning deportation for felony (H.R. 1022). Amendment of the immigration laws was proposed by Austin (Tenn.) without further specification (H.R. 12255), and a bill concerning the inspection of immigrants was introduced by McCumber (N.D.) in the Senate (S. 122). The only other legislative proposal of the session to be noted was the reintroduction by Hayes (Calif.) of his bill of the preceding Congress to regulate the entry and residence of Chinese, Japanese, and others (H.R. 2215).

The second session of the 61st Congress, meeting at the usual time for the opening session in early December 1909, received the first annual message of President Taft. He mentioned immigration only in connection with the need for legislation against the importation of prostitutes. Congress itself, however, had no lack of ideas for needed changes of law and introduced a large number and variety of immigration bills.

Dolliver (Iowa) in the Senate and Sterling (Ill.) in the House persistently reintroduced their bills for a laboratory to study certain problem classes (S. 5806, H.R. 17172). Russell (Tex.) in the House reoffered his bill that would discontinue payment of pensions to aliens (H.R. 13888). Dillingham (Vt.) in the Senate and Howell (N.J.) in the House introduced bills of identical title to provide for United States surgeons, immigrant inspectors, and matrons on immigrant-carrying vessels (S. 4667, H.R. 17262).

In all, about thirty bills and one or more resolutions for the regulation of immigration in some form were introduced during the session. Ten of these were to amend the 1907 Act in general,[122] and six others were to amend section 21 of the act, concerning the deportation of alien criminals. Heretofore, the alien criminals had been excluded and deported for crimes committed prior to entry, but one of the new bills, H.R. 20166, from the Committee on Immigration and Naturalization, would add aliens convicted of crimes in the United States to the deportable classes. Two bills called for the further regulation of immigration; two were to amend the immigration laws, of which one bill concerned aliens

[121] Ibid., p. 4627.

[122] One of the amending bills, H.R. 15431, is of interest for being, apparently, the first immigration bill from Representative Sabath of Illinois, who was to have an interest in immigration throughout his long term in the House, which ended in 1952 with the 82nd Congress. His was the longest period of service in the history of the House.

coming in violation of law; and two were for the further exclusion of undesirables. One of the latter was S. 4514 by Overman of North Carolina, a multipurpose bill to further exclude undesirable immigrants, regulate the residence of aliens, and repress the white slave trade.

There was an evident concern to adjust the immigration laws to avoid the separation of families, a concern that was to be a continuing element of policy. Three bills and one resolution to that effect were introduced during the session.[123] The bill introduced by Bennet (N.Y.) for the House Committee on Immigration and Naturalization was representative of the others. It would permit the admission of a wife or a child under sixteen who if coming alone would be deportable because of physical defect or other cause that gave liability of becoming a public charge.[124] Two bills were to set the head tax on immigrants (H.R. 21588 and 22843). Another bill was to require immigrants to come in vessels of American registry, this being S. 8813 by Gore of Oklahoma. And a final bill was to prohibit the transportation in interstate or foreign commerce of women for immoral purposes (H.R. 12315 by Mann of Illinois). The Mann bill, together with another House bill, H.R. 15816, were the only ones to be passed during the session.

The bill proposed by Mann of Illinois to prohibit the importation or interstate transportation of women for immoral purposes was reported out by the Committee on Interstate and Foreign Commerce on December 21, 1909 (H. Rept. 47 [61-II]). With it was a report, "White Slave Traffic," that explained the bill and gave a history of earlier federal legislation on the subject. Passed readily by both House and Senate, the bill was signed by President Taft and was known as the White Slave Traffic Act of June 25, 1910 (36 Stat. 825), or more popularly as the Mann Act.

The other bill to be passed was introduced later but was acted on more promptly. Introduced in the House by the Committee on Immigration and Naturalization to amend the 1907 Act,[125] its purpose was the exclusion and deportation of immoral aliens engaged in prostitution or similar offenses; the exclusion, deportation, and punishment of procurers; and the punishment of persons engaged in interstate traffic in prostitutes. It amended sections 2 and 3 of the 1907 Act, adding to the excluded classes in section 2, "persons who are supported by or receive in whole or in part the proceeds of prostitution." Section 3 was expanded to deal more fully with the punishment and deportation of aliens profiting

[123]H.R. 21325, Sabath (Ill.); H.R. 24550, O'Connell (Mass.); H.R. 24695, Bennet (N.Y.); and H. Concurrent Res. 29, Sulzer (N.Y.).

[124]H.R. 24695, with H. Rept. 1064, April 19, 1910 (61-II).

[125]H.R. 15816, with H. Rept. 44 (61-II).

by the proceeds of prostitution. In the same section the 1907 wording, "any alien woman or girl," was shortened to "any alien," and the former three-year period of deportability was changed to an unlimited period. Passing the House without amendment, the bill received only minor amendments in the Senate.[126] The House accepted the Senate amendments,[127] and the bill was signed by President Taft to become the Act of March 26, 1910 (36 Stat. 263).

The third session of the 61st Congress, from December 1910 to March 1911, showed much reduced legislative activity on immigration. President Taft's message of December 6 referred to the desirability of wider distribution of immigrants, especially in the West and South. A few memorials and petitions favored the literacy test and further restriction.

The two summary volumes with the recommendations of the Dillingham Commission were presented to the 61st Congress at the opening of the third session, on December 5, 1910.[128] Some of the detailed reports had appeared during the preceding session, and the others appeared soon after in the third session. The recommendations were presented in the first volume and included the following points:

1. Other matters being already covered by present law, new legislation should look especially to the economic well-being of our people.
2. The expansion of industry should not be promoted by means that imperil the wage level and conditions of employment.
3. There should be a five-year period of deportability of aliens convicted of serious crimes committed after entry, and a three-year period of deportability for those who become public charges.
4. The immigration laws should be made applicable to alien seamen.
5. The Chinese exclusion policy should be continued, and the present mode of regulation of Japanese and Korean immigration should stand.
6. Because committee investigation shows a surplus of unskilled labor, legislative means of further restriction of the admission of unskilled aliens is desirable.
7. Of several means of restriction considered by the Commission, the reading and writing test was favored by the majority.[129]

Only about half a dozen immigration bills were received, a bill from the preceding session to amend the immigration act was reported back,

[126] S. Rept. 187 (61-II).

[127] H. Rept. 783, March 17, 1910 (61-II).

[128] S. Doc. 747, vols. 1 and 2 (61-III).

[129] U. S. Immigration Commission of 1911, Report, 1: 45–48. The one dissent to the recommendation of the educational test was by Representative Bennet of New York.

and a joint resolution on deportation was proposed. The bills dealt with such varied subjects as further exclusion of undesirable immigrants, alien seamen and stowaways, criminal aliens, and amendment of the immigration laws. None came up for discussion in the House or Senate.

62nd Congress (1911–1913)

The 62nd Congress met in an early first session from April 4 to August 22, 1911. No new immigration legislation got out of committee, but a few bills were introduced, for the most part dealing with matters of regulation. The massive forty-two-volume report of the Immigration Commission had appeared, published as Senate documents of the 61st Congress, second or third session, but its influence on legislation was somewhat slower in developing.

It can be noted that the subject of racial exclusion began to appear again, and again the initiative came from the West Coast. A House resolution was proposed by Raker of California to ask the President for copies of correspondence relating to Japanese immigration. And a bill for comprehensive regulation of Oriental immigration was introduced by Hayes, also of California, under the title,

> To regulate the coming into and the residence within the United States of Chinese, Japanese, Koreans, Tartars, Malays, Afghans, East Indians, Lascars, Hindoos, and persons of Chinese, Japanese, Korean, Tartar, Malayan, Afghan, East Indian, Lascar, Hindoo, or other Mongolian extraction. (H.R. 4677)

It was appropriately referred to the Committee on Foreign Affairs rather than to the immigration committee.

A dozen immigration bills were introduced in all, some of the same authorship and title as ones that had failed to receive attention in earlier Congresses. Five called for amendment of the immigration laws, especially the 1907 Act. Three were for the regulation of immigration without further specification, and another three were specifically concerned with the exclusion of undesirable aliens. A final bill, a reoffering of one from the preceding Congress, was to require immigrants to come in vessels of American registry. None was acted on.

The second session of the 62nd Congress, meeting on December 4, 1911, occupied itself with two immigration matters, regulation and Oriental immigration. Two bills of identical title and introduced by members from Washington proposed further regulation of the admission of Chinese persons and those of Chinese descent: S. 4951, by Jones (Wash.), and H.R. 17478, by Humphrey (Wash.). Another bill of wider scope was to regulate the admission of Japanese, Hindus, Turks, Koreans, Malays, East Indians, Abyssinians, and Afghans, together with all persons of those descents (H.R. 14126, Roberts [Nev.]). A fourth bill was to amend one of the Chinese exclusion acts (H.R. 20683, Smith [Tex.]). None of the four received committee approval.

About twenty bills, variously titled, were concerned with the regulation of immigration in one manner or another. One related to the separation of families, two were on alien seamen and stowaways, one would give the Secretary of Commerce and Labor authority to suspend the immigration laws in certain cases, two concerned the exclusion of undesirables, seven called for amendment of the 1907 Act,[130] and others were for the amendment of unspecified immigration laws. Only four were reported out of committee, including one carried over from the preceding session.

On February 6, 1912 a House bill to amend section 9 of the 1907 Act was introduced by Kindred of New York and was later reported out.[131] It proposed amendment of the section to include insane persons among the excluded classes of aliens against whose transportation to the United States a penalty was imposed, and it raised the penalty from $100 to $200 for each violation. The bill was considered in the House on August 5, at which time an effort was made to add a literacy test clause, but the action was blocked. It was brought up again on August 19, but consideration was blocked and no further action on the bill was taken until the third session of the 62nd Congress.

A bill by Burnett of Alabama, concerning alien seamen and stowaways, was reported out of committee.[132] The occasion for the bill was a recent Supreme Court decision in the so-called Taylor case (207 U.S. 120) that alien seamen leaving their ships were not amenable to provisions of immigration law. The number of desertions since this decision had become considerable, and need was felt for a law to cover such cases. Although reported out, the bill was not considered by the House.

A third bill to be reported out was also by Burnett of Alabama, and its stated purpose was to further restrict immigration (H.R. 22527, with H. Rept. 559 [62-II]). A literacy test bill, it proposed to add the following to the excluded classes:

> All aliens over sixteen years of age, physically capable of reading, who can not read the English language, or the language or dialect of some other country, including Hebrew or Yiddish.

[130]One of these, H.R. 22588, represents the first appearance in immigration legislation of James M. Curley, Representative from Massachusetts, who was to have a long political career in his home state.

[131]H.R. 19544, Kindred (N.Y.), with H. Rept. 590 (62-II), April 23, 1912.

[132]H.R. 21489, with H. Rept. 426 (62-II).

It included a proviso similar to ones attached to its predecessors that an admissible alien or alien resident can bring in his father or grandfather who is over fifty-five years of age, his wife, mother or grandmother, or his unmarried or widowed daughter regardless of their literacy. A second proviso exempted refugees from religious persecution from the literacy requirement. No further action was taken on the bill.

The Senate meanwhile had taken up a Dillingham bill from the first session, which was reported out January 18, 1912 (S. 3175, with S. Rept. 208 [62-II]). For the further regulation of immigration and residence of aliens, the bill was mainly a revision and codification of existing law, including the Chinese exclusion acts. As Lodge explained, acting for the committee, a new feature of the bill was to bring alien seamen and stowaways under immigration law. The original bill as introduced by Dillingham had contained a literacy test provision, but that was dropped by the committee, which thought the test should be considered separately, on its own merits and without prejudice to other features of the bill (S. Rept. 208 [62-II]). Briefly recommitted and reported out again with some revision, it came to discussion in the Senate on February 15. Various committee amendments were agreed to.[133] Overman (N.C.) moved that the head tax be raised from four to ten dollars, an increase he had proposed in a bill introduced several years earlier. His motion was not acted on at the time.

Consideration of the bill was resumed on March 18, at which time a literacy test amendment was offered. Further discussion occurred on April 17, when Dillingham stated that the bill embodied the recommendations of the Immigration Commission as set forth in the first volume of their report. He spoke further of the heavy immigration in recent years as having aroused the country to a realization of the problem. In this connection, he cited the first volume of the report of the Commission, of which he was chairman, which stated that the objective of most workers from southern and eastern Europe was to earn as much as possible, to live as cheaply as possible, and to save as much as possible. It was noted further that the bill provided for a consolidation of the Chinese exclusion acts but no change in their substance. And the bill proposed that something similar to the certificate of admission given to the Chinese for identification might be given to all immigrants.[134]

Also in accordance with the Immigration Commission's views was the provision of a deportability period of five years after entry for crimes involving moral turpitude, and of three years after entry for persons

[133] *Congressional Record,* 48:2080–84. [134] Ibid., pp. 4906–17.

becoming public charges *for any reason.* Deportability in the latter case would therefore no longer be limited to instances in which the cause existed prior to entry.[135]

Debate continued on April 18 and 19,[136] and on the latter day amendments were voted on. The Smith (S.C.) amendment was accepted. It added to the proviso in section 3 of the 1907 Act so that it read

> Provided: That skilled labor, if otherwise admissible, may be imported if labor of like kind unemployed can not be found in this country.[137]

The words "if otherwise admissible" were added by the amendment. In section 3, again, a committee amendment was changed to exempt aliens seeking admission in order to escape religious persecution from the literacy test that the Senate had voted to retain in the bill, contrary to the committee recommendation.[138]

Watson (W.Va.) then moved to amend the Overman (N.C.) amendment raising the head tax to ten dollars. The Watson amendment of the amendment would have raised the head tax still further, to twenty-four dollars, but it was rejected. The Overman increase was likewise rejected, by a vote of 32 to 26.[139] Watson then tried again, proposing an increase to seven dollars, and again met rejection; but later in the same day Gallinger (N.H.) was successful with an amendment to raise the tax to five dollars.[140]

A variety of other amendments was proposed with varying success. Root of New York offered an amendment to section 20 of the 1907 Act, concerning deportations at the expense of the transportation company, to add

> Any alien who shall take advantage of his residence in the United States to conspire with others for the violent overthrow of a foreign government recognized by the United States.[141]

It was accepted, as was an amendment by Williams (Miss.) to make excludable persons who have had one or more attacks of insanity.[142] After this success, Williams offered another addition to section 3, to exclude persons of African descent, whether from Africa or the West Indies, excepting Puerto Rico. This bill was rejected, 28 to 25, with 42 not voting,

[135]Ibid., p. 4916.
[136]Ibid., pp. 4966–76, 5017–33.
[137]Ibid., pp. 5017, 5028.
[138]Ibid., p. 5020.
[139]Ibid., p. 5023.
[140]Ibid., pp. 5028, 5032.
[141]Ibid., p. 5027.
[142]Ibid., p. 5028. The original bill proposed excludability for two or more attacks of insanity.

offered again, and rejected the second time.[143] The amended bill was passed by the Senate on April 19, 1912.

The House committee reported out the bill with amendment on June 7, accompanied by House Report 851 (62-II). The committee amendment was to strike out the entire bill and substitute its own Burnett bill (H.R. 22527), which has been described above. It was a brief literacy test bill, in four sections, instead of the long codifying Senate bill of about forty sections. There was heated debate in the House on introduction of the bill, to be resumed later.[144] With the end of the session approaching, further discussion of the bill in the House was put over to the next session.

The third session of the 62nd Congress convened on December 2, 1912. During the three-month session, Congress received petitions and memorials for and against the literacy test, for and against the Dillingham bill, S. 3175, pending in the House, for the so-called Asiatic exclusion act, and concerning the immigration of Russian Jews. The main business of the session regarding immigration was the Dillingham bill.

Discussion of the bill occupied the House on December 14, 17, and 18,[145] under limitation of time allowed for debate. The bill was supported as a check on immigration and a means of protecting the wage level and the standard of living; and the endorsement of the American Federation of Labor was cited. President Roosevelt, in his first message to Congress in 1901, was quoted as saying, in favor of the literacy test provision, that an objective of "a proper immigration law ought to be to secure a careful . . . educational test." On this point, the Dillingham or Senate draft would require the reading of not less than twenty nor more than twenty-five words of the Constitution; the Burnett or House substitute prescribed thirty to forty words in ordinary use printed in plain type in some language or dialect familiar to the immigrant and selected by himself.

At this point Raker of California sought to modify the literacy test requirement for Asiatics, by adding the following to the excludable classes:

> All aliens, natives of any part of Asia or the islands adjacent to Asia or in Asiatic seas and the descendants of such natives, who can not read in some European language.[146]

The amendment was rejected. Bartholdt (Mo.) then proposed limitation of the literacy test to male aliens, which was not accepted.[147] Other

[143]Ibid., p. 5029.
[144]Ibid., pp. 7834, 11882–90.
[145]Ibid., 49:650–91, 794–823, 861–66.
[146]Ibid., p. 804.
[147]Ibid., p. 806.

proposed amendments of the literacy test were also rejected, including the Madden (Ill.) amendment to exempt religious and political refugees, and other amendments to make it both a reading and a writing test.

On December 18, 1912 the House accepted the substitute and amendments to the Senate bill, in spite of determined opposition and after rejection of many more amending proposals. The vote was 179 to 52. The Senate disagreeing and the House insisting on its amendments, the bill went to conference. The conference report on January 16, 1913[148] incorporated the greater part of the original Senate bill, thirty-eight of the thirty-nine sections. The House conferees agreed to increase the head tax to five dollars, to exclude aliens not eligible to citizenship,[149] to deport aliens becoming criminals within three years after entry, and to a few lesser points. The literacy test was to become effective four months after passage of the act, with exemption of certain close relatives of admitted aliens. The conference report being accepted by the House but rejected by the Senate, a second conference report was required, and then a third, for certain minor changes. Agreement was finally reached, but the bill was vetoed by President Taft. In his veto message of February 14, 1913, he conceded there was much merit in the bill, but he could not accept it because of the literacy test. The Senate voted to override the veto, 72 to 18, but the House failed to do so by a slight margin of 213 votes to override, 114 against. This ended temporarily what had been a continuing and determined congressional drive for restriction through the literacy test.

Little else affecting immigration occurred during the last session of the 62nd Congress. The Kindred bill (H.R. 19544) from the second session, to add insane persons to the list of excluded persons in section

[148]Ibid., p. 1645.

[149]The original Dillingham bill added to the excludable classes "persons who are not eligible to become citizens of the United States by naturalization." During the preceding session the Senate Committee on Immigration had recommended addition of the qualifying phrase, "unless otherwise provided for by treaties, conventions, or by agreements as to passports" (*Congressional Record,* 48:2081). In the conference report accepted by both House and Senate, H. Rept. 1340, January 17, 1913 (*Congressional Record,* 49:1675), the statement of the excludable class was greatly expanded to read, "persons who can not become eligible, under existing law, to become citizens of the United States by naturalization, unless otherwise provided for by existing agreements as to passports, or by treaties, conventions, or agreements that may hereafter be entered into. The provision next foregoing, however, shall not apply to persons of the following status or occupations: Government officers, ministers or religious teachers, missionaries, lawyers, physicians, chemists, engineers, teachers, students, authors, editors, journalists, merchants, bankers and travellers for curiosity or pleasure, nor to their legal wives or their children under 16 years of age who shall accompany them or who subsequently may apply for admission to the United States."

9 of the 1907 Act and impose a penalty for their transportation to the United States, was passed by the House. It raised the penalty to $200, to be assessed against steamship companies but not against railroads.[150] In the Senate it was referred to a committee but was not acted on further.

Comment

At the close of the 62nd Congress in 1913 is a convenient point to stop and look back in summary at the course of American immigration legislation over the preceding three decades. The 62nd was the last peacetime Congress before the outbreak of the First World War in Europe, and 1913 was almost at the end of the great wave of transatlantic migration that culminated in the prewar decade.

During the years from 1883 to 1913 Congress faced and wrestled with several special and urgent immigration problems, those of Chinese immigration and of contract labor in particular. The broad and continuing problem, however, was that of devising an effective and enforceable system for the regulation of immigration. From the beginnings made in the 1875 and 1882 acts, Congress went on constructing a series of codifying and comprehensive acts, the Immigration Acts of March 3, 1891, March 3, 1903, and February 20, 1907, in addition to lesser pieces of legislation.

Comparing this series of acts, we can see the development of more and more excludable classes; reinforcement through deportation provisions that extended longer and longer after entry; greater and greater elaboration of the wording of the laws in an attempt to cover every conceivable case and aspect of the labor contract, the immoral classes, the anarchist or subversive classes, and others; provision after provision for penalties; attempts to put the burdens of advance screening and responsibility on the steamship companies; steps to close the open land borders; and much more to the same purpose.

An unhappy fact that must have been more or less apparent to Congress or to its interested committees was that the regulatory system was not working, or at least not working efficiently or adequately. Every legal loophole could be closed by new legislation, but some parts of the body of immigration law simply were not enforceable. There was notorious evasion of the Chinese exclusion laws, the provisions against anarchists and other subversive classes grew longer and longer on the statute books but could not be really effective, and the contract labor laws

[150]Ibid., pp. 1573–79.

reaffirmed and elaborated in act after act were not enforceable. Meanwhile the tide of immigration during these years was rising higher and higher to numbers that were alarming to many, quite apart from any misgivings about undesirable classes within the migrant stream and its changed composition by country of origin.

It is not surprising, under these circumstances of combined feelings of urgency and frustration, that Congress and its members should look for solutions, including ones more drastic than the prevailing system of regulation. In this situation it is instructive to see in what direction Congress moved; but quite as significant is what Congress chose not to do. The review that has been given in this chapter of legislative proposals over three decades shows that Congress received a wide range of bills but few were accepted. The pressure for continued exclusion of the Chinese and of contract labor was indeed too strong to resist, but Congress did resist and reject the many proposals for discriminatory antialien measures, to prohibit purchase and ownership of real estate, to deny public employment, to forbid enlistment in the armed forces, to require passage on American vessels, to end pension rights, to impose a heavy head tax on aliens, and so on.

There was a tendency on the part of Congress to proceed cautiously and deliberately by making an investigation before proceeding to consider major new legislation. There were uncounted proposals for studies and inquiries into immigration during the period, and several that were accepted had influence on the course of legislation. The Ford Committee of 1888 prepared an extensive report and made suggestions for the regulation of immigration but failed to get action on its bill. The joint Senate and House study committee of two years later, however, led to the Immigration Act of 1891. And the Dillingham Commission, whose massive report appeared in 1911, strongly influenced legislation for some years, perhaps less through the report itself than through the personal influence and prestige of its members, especially Dillingham and Lodge in the Senate and Burnett in the House, who played dominant roles in congressional work on immigration.

Finally, two separate but related elements of immigration policy can be seen taking shape, although still rudimentary and tentative compared to their later development. One was the protection of the domestic labor force from immigrant competition. It could be argued that this policy had much earlier roots, for nativist reactions both unorganized and organized presumably are stimulated in part at least by such considerations. Dislike of alien labor contracts had appeared earlier, but the contract labor act of 1884 can be regarded as a first protectionist step for the labor market. This was reinforced by later attempts to outlaw solicitation and advertisement for labor abroad, as well as by more and more explicit protectionist statements such as that in President Roosevelt's message of December 5, 1904 to the 58th Congress, in which he stated that it was vital to protect "the standard of well-being among our wage-workers." Labor organizations were then less active and influential politically than they were to become later, but their memorials to Congress urged the same viewpoint.

The other trend of thought, in Congress and perhaps even more strongly outside Congress, was toward restriction of the number of immigrants admitted. It is impossible to say at what point more and more rigorous selection and regulation became restriction, but during the period under review the call for restriction became more and more explicit. Petitions to Congress called for it, and the term came to be used more frequently by supporters of various measures in Congress. The head tax increases and the literacy test were both recommended for their selective effects, but there were undertones of restrictive intent, especially in the latter. The head tax, starting at fifty cents, went to a dollar in 1894, was doubled to two dollars in 1903, and was doubled again in the 1907 Act. Congress had, however, rejected proposals to raise it to ten, twelve, and even twenty-four dollars.

The long continued and determined drive to introduce a literacy or educational test was one of the features of the prewar decades, during which it was almost continuously before Congress in one bill or another. Beginning, as near as its discussion in Congress can be traced, with a proposal by Lodge of Massachusetts in 1891, it appeared in an 1893 bill and again in 1896, was defeated by Cleveland's veto in 1897, was soon revived, failed of inclusion in the 1903 Act through House-Senate disagreement, failed again of inclusion in the 1907 Act by a last minute substitution of a provision for the appointment of an immigration commission to study the subject, and was again defeated by the Taft veto of the Dillingham bill in 1913. Many advantages were claimed for the literacy test by its proponents, with reduction of the volume of immigration among them.

A darker side of the discussion of this and other immigration measures during the period in question was what now would be considered strongly racist and ethnocentric sentiments. It was a time when beliefs about race and ethnic superiority or inferiority were common, and these beliefs come out strongly in the discussion of immigration questions. Chinese exclusion met little or no opposition, the Japanese case was handled with more diplomacy for the time at least, but Congress had refrained from considering certain bills outlawing all Oriental and Asiatic immigration. However, the eligibility for citizenship through naturalization had been included in the Dillingham bill of 1913 as a condition for admission as an immigrant, and it would have barred immigration for many peoples had it not been for the Taft veto because of the literacy test in the same bill. Debate on the head tax and more particularly on the literacy test had brought out that these measures had the great advantage in some eyes of operating selectively to repress immigration from southern and eastern Europe but not immigration from northern and western Europe.

The years after 1913 were to bring new immigration problems and intensify some of the old problems, and Congress would have to search for new solutions while continuing and further developing the established system of regulation.

5 From Regulation to Restriction, 1913–1929

The history of American immigration policy during the years immediately following 1913 shows a combination of continuity and change, with maintenance and supplementing of the established system of regulation together with a search for new measures to meet certain continuing old problems and emerging new ones. The search had been going on in Congress for some time, in the Immigration Commission and its predecessors as well as in the immigration committees of Senate and House, but now developments after 1913 were to give new urgency to the search.

63rd Congress (1913–1915)

The early and extra first session of the 63rd Congress convened on April 7, 1913 and continued to the first day of December. During this long session only a moderate number of immigration bills were introduced, and none was acted on further.

Hayes (Calif.) reoffered a bill of the same title as one he had presented two years before to the preceding Congress, to regulate the coming and residence of a number of Asiatic peoples.[1] Two bills called for a laboratory in the District of Columbia to study various classes of undesirables, and a number of bills directly concerned immigration. Six or more of them were to regulate the immigration of aliens, and a similar number were to amend the Act of 1907. Two bills called for the restriction of undesirable immigration, among other things (S. 50, Overman [N.C.]; H.R. 1958, Roddenberry [Ga.]), and another was for the deportation of aliens temporarily or permanently residing in the United States (S. 2979, Smith [Mich.]).

The second session of the 63rd Congress opened immediately on the close of the first session and continued until October 24, 1914. A variety of bills touching on immigration were introduced. Two called for a bu-

[1]H.R. 2870. See H.R. 4677 (62-I).

reau to study certain problem classes, two were for the exclusion of Hindu laborers (S. 5050, Smith [S.C.]; H.R. 14627, Church [Calif.]), and two more would impose restrictions on resident aliens. One of these was to prevent the employment of aliens on public works (H.R. 15113, Smith [Tex.]), the other to make it unlawful for any alien to have, keep, or bear firearms (H.R. 18520, Kindel [Colo.]).

The regulation of immigration was the subject of two bills: H.R. 9999, Johnson (Wash.) and H.R. 10249, Hayes (Calif.); another was to exclude certain persons from readmission, and it had further reference to the expatriation of certain citizens (H.R. 18220, Harrison [Miss.]). At the time there was unfavorable reaction to the return of naturalized citizens as well as aliens to Europe for military service on the outbreak of war there. Gillett of Massachusetts introduced a House bill indicating concern that undue immigration would affect the wage level and have other harmful effects.[2]

None of the bills introduced during the session was acted on, but a bill introduced by Burnett (Ala.) from the first session was reported out on December 15, 1913.[3] It was to regulate the immigration and residence of aliens in the United States. A general immigration bill, it resembled the Dillingham bill vetoed by President Taft in the preceding February. It added to the excludable classes those "who advocate or teach the unlawful destruction of property," an additional anarchist provision, also excluded aliens over sixteen years of age unable to pass a literacy test, exempted certain close relatives and religious refugees from the test, and raised the head tax to five dollars.

The bill was recommitted and reported out again with amendment on December 16, with a new report and two additional dissenting opinions attached.[4] Johnson of Washington during House debate on the bill stated that he would approve a literacy test only if it followed the Commission's recommendation of exclusion of aliens unable to read and write; and he also favored a percentage limitation of immigration in addition. Debate proceeded from January 30 to February 4, 1914. Various committee amendments were accepted. A Sabath (Ill.) amendment to exempt aliens of five or more years residence from the literacy test on reentry from a visit abroad was defeated, but a later amendment to the same effect by Stafford (Wis.) was accepted by the close vote of 132 to 130.

[2]H.R. 11314, "To prevent the disturbance by undue immigration of the scale of wages and of the social and economic conditions of the population of the United States, and to prevent the evasion of the immigration, naturalization, and sanitary laws and regulations."

[3]H.R. 6060, Burnett (Ala.), with H. Rept. 140 (63-II).

[4]H. Rept. 149 (63-II).

Many other amendments were offered but were mostly rejected. Among others, there was a motion by Hayes (Calif.) to strike out the clause excluding aliens on the basis of ineligibility to citizenship by naturalization and to substitute the direct exclusion of

> Hindoos and all persons of the Mongolian or yellow race, the Malay or brown race, the African or black race.[5]

The racial issue so raised led, as it had before, to some emotional debate. (In the words of one Senator, "God Almighty Himself hates the hybrid.") The Hayes amendment was defeated on the following day, February 3, 1914, by a vote of 54 to 203. It was on that day that Platt of New York offered what was presumably a tongue-in-cheek proviso to be attached to the section dealing with exclusions:

> That nothing in this act shall exclude anybody who can prove that his grandfather could read.

Whether or not the House was amused, the *Congressional Record* only tells us that the amendment was rejected.[6] On the same day the House accepted a committee-sponsored amendment to strike out the words excluding "persons who have been insane within five years."[7] On the following day, February 4, a committee amendment to extend the deportability of anarchists from three to five years after entry was also approved. A motion to recommit being defeated, the bill was then passed by the House, 253 to 126.

The Burnett bill was reported out in the Senate on March 19 with a committee report that characterized the bill as follows:

> All laws heretofore enacted on this subject have been of a selective rather than restrictive character. None of the existing selective features have been omitted in preparing this act; on the contrary, they have been strengthened.[8]

The report also stated that

> The bill contains one provision intended directly to restrict immigration, although said provision is also, incidentally and to a certain extent, selective in its operation.[9]

The latter was, of course, a reference to the literacy test.

Several amendments were introduced by the Senate committee. These included raising the head tax from five to six dollars, except that

[5] *Congressional Record,* 51:2781.
[6] Ibid., pp. 2829-30.
[7] Ibid., p. 2830.
[8] S. Rept. 355 (63-II), p. 1.
[9] Ibid., p. 2.

an alien accompanied by wife and children would pay only four dollars for each person. Added to the excluded classes in section 3 were "persons of constitutional psychopathic personality" and "persons with chronic alcoholism." Another change was to remove the word "mental" from the clause excluding those defectives whose defect might affect their ability to earn a living. As was stated, it was preferred to exclude mental defectives for that reason in itself, and not for likelihood of becoming a public charge.

In section 19 a proviso was added that in the case of a sexually immoral female alien whose exclusion or deportation is prescribed by the act, marriage to a citizen does not invest her with United States citizenship.

Senate action on the bill and committee amendments were deferred to the next session.

The third session of the 63rd Congress convened on December 7, 1914. The Burnett bill was taken up two days later, and Senate debate continued on December 10, 15, 16, 18, 19, 21, 30, and 31, ending on January 2, 1915 after exceptionally long consideration and a large number of proposals for amendment. The more significant action was as follows.

The committee amendment to raise the head tax to six dollars was agreed to.[10] On December 10 there was extended discussion of a new term that had been introduced, *constitutional psychopathic inferiority,* which was said to be taken from the "American Society of Medicine."[11] Later the amendments to add the excludable classes of constitutional psychopathic inferiority and chronic alcoholism were referred back to committee.

The Senate accepted the amendment to remove the word *mental* from the statement of defects interfering with ability to earn a living[12] but rejected a committee amendment that would have broadened the excludable class of criminals from persons convicted of or admitting to having committed a felony or other crime involving moral turpitude to include those "who at the time of seeking admission to the United States are legally charged with a felony." Most other committee amendments, however, were accepted.

Amendments from the floor were considered on December 16 and succeeding days. An amendment by Nelson (Minn.) to exempt children under sixteen and accompanying a parent from the head tax was accepted.[13] Several amendments to grant exemption from the literacy test were then considered, for the House bill gave such exemption to religious refugees only. Thomas (Colo.) offered an amendment to extend

[10] *Congressional Record,* 52:47.

[11] Ibid., p. 82.

[12] Ibid., p. 83.

[13] Ibid., p. 256.

exemption to victims of political persecution as well,[14] and O'Gorman (N.Y.) later proposed the addition of racial refugees.[15] On December 31 the Senate voted on whether to exempt aliens coming to escape "religious, political, or racial persecution," and rejected the motion, 26 to 34.[16] Thomas and O'Gorman attempted to modify the motion to make it acceptable but were defeated again by essentially the same margin.[17]

Reed of Missouri offered a series of amendments resembling those proposed by Hayes in the House, of which the first was to exclude all aliens not of the Caucasian race.[18] This being rejected, he then proposed exclusion of "all members of the African or black race." It was accepted by the slender margin of 29 to 25, with the large number of 42 not voting. After this success he moved for exclusion of Turks and East Indians, but without approval.[19] A later amendment of his was accepted, however, to change an excluding phrase from those who "admit their belief in the practice of polygamy" to "believe in, advocate, or practice polygamy."[20]

After long debate and many motions for amendment, the Senate finally passed the bill on January 2, 1915 by a vote of 50 to 7, with 39 abstaining. In the following conference committee the House conferees agreed to increase the head tax to six dollars and to deny to aliens of the immoral class the acquisition of citizenship through marriage to a citizen. The Senate conferees on their part receded from the exclusion of members of the African race. These concessions were in vain, however, for the bill after passage by House and Senate was vetoed by President Wilson. His principal reasons were the literacy test and the denial of political asylum. The House failed by a few votes to override the veto, by a vote of 261 to 136, which made this the third successful veto of a literacy bill.

Otherwise the third session of the 63rd Congress gave little thought to immigration. Three bills were introduced to regulate the entrance of Chinese aliens, one to prohibit the coming of Asiatic laborers. Bartholdt (Mo.) proposed a measure for the better protection of aliens and for the enforcement of their treaty rights. All stayed in committee.

64th Congress (1915–1917)

The first session of the 64th Congress lasted for nine months, from December 1915 to September 1916. The presidential message at the opening of the Congress spoke of the problem of disloyalty on the part

[14]Ibid., p. 261.
[15]Ibid., p. 342.
[16]Ibid., p. 787.
[17]Ibid., p. 788.
[18]Ibid., p. 803.
[19]Ibid., pp. 805, 807.
[20]Ibid., p. 812.

of naturalized citizens, but there was nothing directly on immigration. A scattering of bills introduced during the session dealt with matters other than the regulation of immigration which constituted the chief focus of congressional attention.

There was one bill to forbid the employment of aliens and naturalized citizens in certain cases (H.R. 12045, Clark [Fla.]). Four bills were to regulate the entrance of Chinese, and Hayes of California again offered his bill that would regulate the admission and residence of a number of Asiatic peoples, from Chinese and Japanese to Lascars, Hindus, and others. Two bills were to prohibit the entrance of Asiatic and Hindu laborers (H.R. 363, Raker [Calif.]; H.R. 9926, Church [Calif.]). Four bills called for the establishment of an agency to study the criminal, pauper, and defective classes.

The drive for further regulation of immigration was not checked by the veto of the Burnett bill in the preceding session. Ten bills entitled "To regulate the immigration and residence of aliens" or some variant were introduced, two of them from Burnett. Another bill was for amendment of section 36 of the 1907 Act,[21] and two bills were to exclude certain returnees and others who had engaged in foreign wars (H.R. 275, Harrison [Miss.]; H.R. 396, Vinson [Ga.]).

The only bill to be acted on was a Burnett bill (H.R. 10384) of the same title as the one vetoed in the preceding Congress. Reported out on January 31, 1916 with a covering report (H. Rept. 95 [64-I]), it was in part a codification of existing immigration law like its predecessor, but with a few differences. The proposed head tax was raised to eight dollars, double the prevailing amount, and a new feature was exemption from the tax of children under sixteen accompanying a parent. Also, the tax exemption of aliens who had resided at least one year in Canada, Newfoundland, Cuba, or Mexico was to be abolished.

The report included discussion of constitutional psychopathic inferiority, which was added to the grounds for exclusion. The term was said to have a well-defined meaning among alienists, one of whom had defined it as "a congenital defect in the emotional or volitional fields of mental activity which results in inability to make proper adjustment to the environments."[22] Also added to the excludable classes were vagrants, stowaways, persons suffering from tuberculosis in any form, those who advocate or teach the unlawful destruction of property or are affiliated with or

[21] H.R. 6049, Humphrey (Wash.). Section 36 provided that an alien who enters except at a seaport or at a designated place is considered to have entered illegally and is to be deported.

[22] H. Rept. 95 (64-I), p. 2.

members of organizations that do so, and persons deported from the United States who seek to return within one year unless with prior consent.

The usual formula for the literacy test was adopted, with exemption of certain close relatives, and the prescribed test was to consist of thirty to forty words in ordinary use. Exemption from the test was granted to persons fleeing from religious persecution.

The bill was debated at length in the House on five days, from March 24 to March 30, 1916,[23] during which time a number of amendments came to vote. Bell of Georgia moved that the head tax be raised to ten dollars, and Bennet of New York moved that it be reduced to six dollars from the eight set in the bill. Both were defeated.[24] Sabath (Ill.) proposed striking out the literacy test and, when that was rejected, tried for exemption of political refugees from the test. That proposal also met rejection.[25] Other unsuccessful proposals for amendment were introduced by Siegel (N.Y.) to remove the constitutional psychopathic inferiority clause, and by Bennet (N.Y.), to do away with exclusion for ineligibility to citizenship.[26]

Numerous other amendments were proposed but were quickly defeated unless approved by the committee. Sabath of Illinois moved amendment in section 19 of the proviso directing deportation of any alien sentenced to imprisonment of one year or more on conviction of a crime involving moral turpitude within five years after entry. His motion was to remove the five-year limit on deportability after a second such offense, and it was accepted by a vote of 53 to 11.[27] A motion by Sabath to reduce the period of deportability for the first such offense from five to three years was defeated.[28] On the same day, March 30, 1916, the House accepted a committee amendment to provide deportation without time limit for

> any alien who was convicted or who admits the commission prior to entry of a felony or other crime or misdemeanor involving moral turpitude.[29]

The bill so amended was then passed by the House, 307 to 87.[30]

The Senate committee report on the Burnett bill (S. Rept. 352 [64-I]) stated it was in most respects identical with Burnett's preceding bill, H.R. 6060 in the 63rd Congress. The literacy test provision had been somewhat reworded but without substantial change, and the exemption from excludability of persons guilty of political offenses had been broadened, to meet one part of President Wilson's reasons for veto.

[23]*Congressional Record,* 53:4768–816, 4841–85, 4932–62, 5023–52, and 5164–95.
[24]Ibid., p. 4861.
[25]Ibid., pp. 4932, 4933.
[26]Ibid., pp. 4937, 4953, 4954.
[27]Ibid., pp. 5167, 5168.
[28]Ibid., p. 5169.
[29]Ibid., pp. 5171, 5172.
[30]Ibid., p. 5194.

The report also enumerated the grounds for exclusion that the bill would add to those in the existing law. These were:

1. constitutional psychopathic inferiority,
2. chronic alcoholism,
3. vagrancy,
4. tuberculosis in any form,
5. advocating or teaching unlawful destruction of property,
6. return within one year after deportation, unless with prior consent, and,
7. ineligibility to citizenship through naturalization.

The Senate committee made some technical amendments, and the bill was then brought up in the Senate on August 17, 1916 and debated on that day and the twenty-first.[31] A notable point was brought up during the course of debate by Dillingham (Vt.), chairman of the Immigration Commission that had reported several years before, who mentioned having introduced a bill to restrict immigration to the fixed percentage of the foreign born from each country given in the most recent census of the United States. This was one of the alternative modes of restriction considered by the Immigration Commission, which had decided in favor of the literacy test; and in his remarks Dillingham stated that he did not want to urge the percentage plan for he thought the literacy test was in fact more feasible.[32]

The Senate committee amendments were quickly accepted. One of these was to strike out the House-approved excluding clause:

> Hindus and persons who can not become eligible, under existing law, to become citizens of the United States by naturalization.

For this clause the exclusion of persons from an Asiatic barred zone defined by latitude and longitude would be substituted.[33] The barred zone amendment was adopted without debate and without a record vote. With the session ending soon after, Senate discussion of the bill was carried over to the next session.

The second session of the 64th Congress convened on December 4, 1916 and sat for the customary three months. The Burnett bill was debated in the Senate on consecutive days from the eleventh to the fourteenth. Reed (Mo.) offered a series of amendments to exempt "persons of the white race" from the exclusion of natives of Africa and certain Asiatic nations, and additionally to exclude "all persons, except white persons, from the West Indies and the Cape Verde and Azores Islands."

[31] Ibid., 53:12763–77, 12923–30.
[32] Ibid., p. 12773.
[33] Ibid., p. 12926.

All his amendments were rejected.[34] Accepted, however, was an amendment by McCumber (N.D.) that was originally to deny exemption from the literacy test of religious refugees but was revised by Sterling (S.D.) to give such exemption to aliens coming to escape religious persecution if the persecution included denial of sufficient education to meet the literacy test.[35] And on December 14 the Senate passed the amended bill by the strong majority of 64 to 7, with 25 abstaining.

The first conference report was accepted by the Senate, but not by the House. Both accepted the second conference report. It dropped two Senate amendments, to exclude aliens coming with the intention of staying only for a time and also those who had returned to Europe for military service. The Senate barred zone provision was accepted instead of the House exclusion of Hindus and those ineligible for citizenship. President Wilson then vetoed the bill, his second veto of a literacy test bill, commenting that

> Tests of quality and of purpose can not be objected to on principle, but tests of opportunity surely may be.

Congress quickly overrode the veto, the House by 287 to 106, the Senate by 62 to 19, and the bill was passed as the Immigration Act of February 5, 1917 (39 Stat. 874).

The provisions of the bill have already been described, but it is worth noting in review that it represents a turning point in American immigration policy, a definite move from regulation to attempted restriction through the final passage of the literacy test. Congress, or at least an active segment of Congress, had been trying to pass such a test for approximately twenty-five years, and had at last succeeded in spite of many blocks in Congress and four presidential vetoes.

Not less significant in its way, but with much less opposition at the time, was the Asiatic barred zone provision, an unmistakable declaration of a white immigration policy. Further indication of the strongly restrictionist and antialien temper of Congress at the time was the raising of the head tax to eight dollars and the addition of several new classes to a considerably expanded list of excludables.

Not much further legislative activity regarding immigration occurred during the rest of the session. Concern about the treatment of aliens was indicated in a bill to punish conspiracy "to injure, oppress, threaten, or intimidate any alien in the exercise of any right under any treaty" (H.R. 20784, Rogers [Mass.]) and a House joint resolution for a constitutional amendment to prohibit states making or enforcing laws discriminatory to aliens (H. J. Res. 386, Husted [N.Y.]). And one bill called for repeal of

[34]Ibid., 54:207, 208.

[35]Ibid., pp. 266, 270.

the literacy test (H.R. 20759, Bennet [N.Y.]). Of the opposite character was a bill to require the registry of aliens (H.R. 20936, Edmonds [Pa.]), and one to limit the net immigration of aliens during a fiscal year to 200,000 (H.R. 20756, Gardner [Mass.]), the latter being an early move toward a numerical ceiling on immigration. None of the above bills was reported out of committee.

65th Congress (1917–1919)

The first session of the 65th Congress, convened in April 1917 soon after the close of the last session of the 64th Congress, received a number of war-related bills concerning enemy aliens, naturalization of those enlisting in the armed services, and penalties for evasion of military service. Uncertainty about the loyalty of aliens in wartime was reflected in bills to prevent the employment of aliens or even of naturalized citizens in certain types of work and to compel the registration of all aliens (H.R. 6026, Clark [Fla.]; H.R. 4959, Taylor [Colo.]). Two bills (H.R. 5369 and 5667) for the deportation of certain aliens were introduced in the House by Burnett (Ala.).

The second of these bills by Burnett, a modification of the first, was reported out by the House committee, with an accompanying report (H. Rept. 127, August 4, 1917 [65-I]). The first section of the bill permanently debarred aliens who were natives or subjects of countries then at war with Germany and its allies from ever becoming citizens of the United States if they claimed exemption from compulsory military service, and required their deportation at the first opportunity. The second section gave the President power to draft any alien to perform mental and physical labor on farms, in manufacturing establishments, and in other enterprises as he deemed necessary. The third section excluded aliens subject to military service in countries at war with Germany and its allies. As a wartime measure, it was to remain in force only for the duration of the war.

An impression of the prevailing wartime climate of opinion is given by the language of the report. It stated, for example, that

> From all over the country comes the cry of the rank injustice of forcing American citizens into the war, while alien slackers are here in vast numbers enjoying the peaceful privileges of our country and immunity from fighting for the very integrity of their own countries.[36]

The bill received some debate in the House, but no further action was taken until the next session of Congress.

[36] H. Rept. 127, August 4, 1917, p. 2.

Other bills introduced during the session dealt with a variety of topics. On the subject of migration from Asia, one bill was for the further regulation of Chinese immigration (H.R. 1675, Burnett [Ala.]), another to prohibit the coming of Asiatic laborers (H.R. 243, Raker [Calif.]). Two representatives from New York submitted bills for the repeal of the literacy test (H.R. 85, Hulbert; H.R. 3810, Riordan). And another by Burnett was to repeal the ninth proviso of section 3 of the 1917 Act, which gave the Commissioner General of Immigration authority over the admission and return of otherwise inadmissible aliens applying for temporary admission (H.R. 4852). Of quite different purpose was a Senate bill proposed by Pomerene of Ohio for the promotion of Americanization through education (S. 621). None of these bills was acted on during the session.

The second session of the 65th Congress, from early December 1917 to late November 1918, was occupied with wartime measures and received no more than a scattering of bills and resolutions related to immigration.

The Burnett bill to set certain wartime restraints on aliens from countries at war with Germany and its allies, introduced during the preceding session, was debated at length in the House, amended, and passed. It went to the Senate Committee on Immigration, which failed to report it out.

Several of the other bills received during the session were sponsored by Burnett. One was for the regulation of immigration, another to exclude and expel aliens who are members of the anarchistic and similar classes (H.R. 11280, 12309). Meanwhile a bill of the same title as the latter was introduced in the Senate (S. 4632, Hardwick [Ga.]). Burnett soon after presented a revised bill on the same subject, which was reported out, debated at length, and then passed by the House (H.R. 12402, with H. Rept. 645 [65-II]). After extensive debate it was also passed by the Senate, and signed by President Wilson. The Act of October 16, 1918 (40 Stat. 1012) amended sections 3 and 19 of the 1917 Act, to clarify the wording of the designation of anarchists as excludable, remove any time limit on their deportability, and make the return of such deported aliens a felony.

Wartime labor shortages can be seen to have reversed the previous attitude toward Chinese labor. Congress received a resolution from the Pasadena Board of Trade in favor of the importation of Chinese laborers under suitable restrictions, and both Senate and House received resolutions to direct their committees on agriculture to look into the importation of Chinese farmers during the continuance of the war.[37] And a

[37] S. Res. 160, H. Res. 234 (65-II).

House joint resolution, to authorize the readmission of certain aliens who had been conscripted or had volunteered for service in the military forces of the United States or cobelligerent forces, was passed by both House and Senate (H. J. Res. 255 [65-II]). It was signed by the President to become the Act of October 19, 1918 (40 Stat. 1014).

The third session of the 65th Congress, from December 2, 1918 to March 4, 1919, received certain war-related bills such as for the denial of citizenship to "alien slackers." One bill was for the deportation of alien enemies (S. 5176, King [Utah]), and six were to expel and exclude certain undesirable aliens. An additional three to expel and exclude were directed against "aliens who, to escape military service, have withdrawn their declaration of intention to become citizens." Other bills were to prohibit the payment of pensions to alien enemies and to provide for the registration and Americanization of all aliens.

The most notable feature of the bills introduced during the session was an evidently rising sentiment for prohibiting immigration. A Senate bill and four in the House called for a four-year prohibition of immigration;[38] an additional House bill would have suspended immigration without specification of term (H.R. 13325, Lufkin [Mass.]). All of the House bills for the four-year suspension were introduced by Burnett (Ala.).

The fourth of Burnett's bills, H.R. 15302, was reported out without amendment (with H. Rept. 1015 [65-III]). As set forth in the committee's report, it would prohibit immigration for four years from its date of passage, but would exempt aliens with lawfully acquired domiciles in the United States, certain relatives of legally admitted aliens, aliens fleeing from religious persecution, skilled labor under the fourth proviso,[39] and aliens admitted under the House joint resolution of the preceding session.[40] Another element of the bill was revision of sections 31 to 36 inclusive of the 1917 Act, for the purpose of facilitating the administrative control of alien seamen.

The accompanying report was informative in setting forth reasons for the suspension of immigration: the prevailing unemployment at the close of the war, the problem of reemployment of returning soldiers, and fear that the rate of immigration was exceeding the powers of assimilation. Particular mention was made of the prospect of huge numbers of immigrants once wartime dislocations of travel were over. A minority

[38]S. 5572, Hardwick (Ga.); H.R. 13669, 14163, 14774, 15302, Burnett (Ala.).

[39]The fourth proviso of section 3 of the 1917 Act provided that with the approval of the Secretary of Labor, "skilled labor, if otherwise admissible, may be imported if labor of like kind unemployed can not be found in this country."

[40]H. J. Res. 255 (65-II), to admit certain aliens who have been conscripted or have volunteered for service with the military forces of the United States or cobelligerent forces.

report by two members of the House committee registered their dissent from the proposal to suspend immigration.

66th Congress (1919–1921)

The first session of the 66th Congress received a number of bills that were a legislative aftermath of the recent war, including a number to deny naturalization to aliens who had evaded military service and others concerned with former alien enemies. Raker of California reintroduced his bill to prohibit the coming of Asiatic laborers (H.R. 1106). Other legislative proposals related to immigration fell into four groups: to regulate immigration, to suspend or prohibit immigration, to deport certain undesirable aliens, and to deal with aliens resident in the United States. Only one of the bills became law during the session.

Several of the bills concerned with one or another aspect of the regulation of immigration were to amend the 1917 Act, one being to repeal the literacy test provision in section 3 of the act. One called simply for limitation of immigration. The only bill to be acted on, by Rogers (Mass.), concerned the extension of passport control (H.R. 9782), and empowered the President to make additional rules and regulations if he believed

> the public safety requires that restrictions and prohibitions in addition to those provided otherwise than by this act be imposed upon entry of aliens.

Conceived as a stopgap measure, it was to expire one year after passage. Approved by the House almost unanimously (315 to 1), on October 16, 1919, it was then passed by the Senate on October 22 without debate but with removal, at the Senate committee's recommendation, of the one-year limit on duration. Conference between House and Senate set the terminal date of the bill at March 4, 1921, and after approval by both houses of Congress the bill became law without presidential signature.

Fear of heavy postwar immigration and sentiment in favor of at least a temporary suspension of immigration was evidenced by some of the bills presented to Congress. One such called for a suspension of immigration for a period of three years, two for a four-year suspension, and one proposed five years.[41] Another would prohibit immigration from Germany, Austria-Hungary, Bulgaria, Turkey, and their possessions for a period of fifty years, and immigration from other countries for twenty

[41]H.R. 5645, Aswell (La.); H.R. 61, Lufkin (Mass.); H.R. 1107, Raker (Calif.); S. 1472, Harrison (Miss.).

years (S. 2096, Myers [Mont.]). Two bills (H.R. 563 and 8572) of quite similar title by Johnson of Washington were for the multiple purposes

> To provide for the protection of the citizens of the United States by the temporary suspension of immigration; for the deportation of additional classes of aliens; for the registration of aliens . . . [etc.].

The majority of the bills concerned with resident aliens were to restrict their rights and opportunities in some manner, or otherwise revealed an antialien intent. Two called for punishment of aliens for conspiracy against the government, the bills from Smith of Arizona (S. 69) and Aswell of Louisiana (H.R. 5642). Another Aswell bill was nervously designed to punish aliens for placing or throwing bombs or explosives (H.R. 5643). Others were to bar aliens from the civil service and from acquiring unappropriated public lands (H.R. 9974, 10066, both by Newton of Minnesota). More constructive were bills to regulate the education and naturalization of aliens (S. 3233 and 3396 by McKellar of Tennessee), and to promote Americanization by providing for cooperation with several states in the education of non-English-speaking persons (H.R. 10710 by Vestal of Indiana). And Rogers (Mass.) reintroduced his bill from the 64th Congress to punish conspiracy to injure, oppress, threaten, or intimidate any alien in the exercise of any right under any treaty.[42]

Another expression of prevailing thought was the number of bills for the deportation of certain classes of aliens, often designated as "undesirable," and no doubt often aimed at former alien enemies. Three such bills appeared in the Senate and eight or more in the House.[43]

The only one of the deportation bills reported out of committee was by Johnson of Washington, for the deportation of certain undesirable aliens and to deny readmission to those so deported (H.R. 6750, with H. Rept. 143 [66-I]). As explained in the committee's report, it concerned alien enemies presently interned as dangerous but not actually convicted of a crime, plus alien enemies convicted of violation of various wartime acts. It was passed by the House after debate, referred to the Senate, and reported out (S. Rept. 283 [66-I]) but not acted on during the session.

[42]H.R. 2313. The earlier bill of the same title was H.R. 20784 (64-II).

[43]S. 28, King (Utah); S. 159, Jones (Wash.); S. 2430, Spencer (Mo.); H.R. 1240, Kleczka (Wis.); H.R. 1347, Raker (Calif.); H.R. 5644, Aswell (La.); H.R. 6514, Johnson (Wash.); H.R. 6557, Mays (Utah); H.R. 6750, Johnson (Wash.); H.R. 9623, Raker (Calif.); and H.R. 9975, Newton (Minn.). Most sweeping in its objectives was the last of these, "To protect the Government of the United States of America and its national emblem; to prevent the teaching or advocacy of crime, sabotage, or other unlawful methods of terrorism; to deport certain aliens; and for other purposes."

In the second session of the 66th Congress the Johnson deportation bill was taken up and promptly passed, and with presidential signature it became the Act of May 10, 1920 for the Deportation of Certain Specified Aliens (41 Stat. 593). It was subsequently repealed in 1952 by the McCarran-Walter Act.

Other deportation bills were introduced during the session but remained in committee. Three of them were designated as providing for the exclusion, deportation, and expulsion of certain aliens.[44] Another was for the deportation of aliens convicted of importing narcotics (H.R. 14283 by Miller of Washington), and two were for the deportation of aliens convicted a second time for illegal traffic in narcotics (S. 4337, Jones [Wash.]; H.R. 13980, Johnson [Wash.]).

Various other directions of concern about alien residents of the United States were indicated by several measures proposed during the session. One was for the protection of aliens and for the enforcement of their treaty rights (H.R. 13946, Temple [Pa.]). Vestal (Ind.) introduced a bill of the same title as the one he presented in the preceding session, for the promotion of Americanization and other purposes (H.R. 14059); and another with identical title was debated in the Senate at considerable length, passed, and transmitted to the House Committee on Education, where it remained (S. 3315, Kenyon [Iowa]). Imposing restrictions on aliens was a proposal to prohibit certain persons engaging in business in the District of Columbia or in the territories (H.R. 11086, Clark [Fla.]). And a bill to define and punish "criminal syndicalism" carried with it provision for the deportation of implicated aliens (H.R. 10736, Kelley [Mich.]). None of these bills was reported out of committee.

The further regulation of immigration was the purpose of half a dozen bills proposed during the second session of the 66th Congress, four of which were for the amendment of the 1917 Act, in most cases dealing with the third section (exclusions) of that act.[45] Two of these bills were acted on and passed. One, S. 3566 by Calder (N.Y.), amended section 3 of the 1917 Act by adding the proviso:

> That an alien who can not read may, if otherwise admissible, be admitted if, within five years after this Act becomes law, a citizen of the United States who has served in the military or naval forces of the United States during the war with the Imperial German Government requests that such alien be admitted and with the approval of

[44]H.R. 11092 and 11193, Johnson (Wash.); H.R. 11205, Raker (Calif.).

[45]S. 3566, Calder (N.Y.); H.R. 10837, Nicholls (S.C.); H.R. 11224, Johnson (Wash.); H.R. 11396, Lea (Calif.); H.R. 11492, 14135, Siegel (N.Y.).

> the Secretary of Labor, marries such alien at a United States immigration station.[46]

Passed by the Senate, favorably reported by the House committee (H. Rept. 575 [66-II]), and then passed by the House, it received presidential signature and became the Act of June 5, 1920 (41 Stat. 981). By its terms, it expired five years later.

The other bill to be acted on, from Johnson of Washington, was to amend the Act of October 16, 1918 for the exclusion and expulsion of anarchists and similar classes (H.R. 11224, with H. Rept. 504 [66-II]). Reported favorably on December 16, 1919, it passed the House, was reported favorably in the Senate (S. Rept. 648, June 1, 1920 [66-II]) and passed with some changes of wording that the House accepted, and became the Act of June 5, 1920 (41 Stat. 1008) for the Exclusion and Expulsion of Alien Members of the Anarchistic and Similar Classes. It amended the first section of the 1918 act and specified the exclusion of aliens who (1) are anarchists; (2) advise, advocate, or teach, or are affiliated with organizations that so oppose all organized government; (3) personally or as members of organizations promote the overthrow of government or law, the assaulting or killing of public officers, attacks on property, or sabotage; (4) are associated in any way with publications advocating the foregoing; or (5) are members of organizations concerned with such publications.

The third session of the 66th Congress was for the customary three-month term, from December 1920 to March 1921. Aside from a Senate joint resolution to permit Chinese to register, a bill concerning Americanization of aliens, and two to set up an immigration board,[47] the immigration bills introduced during the session were for the suspension or limitation of immigration or for its regulation. Of these, one called for a five-year suspension (S. 4671, Overman [N.C.]), one for a two-year suspension (H.R. 14461, Johnson [Wash.]), and two others for a temporary suspension of immigration (S. 4528, King [Utah]; H.R. 14671, Box [Tex.]). Others were for the purpose of limiting or further regulating immigration (S. 4627, Dillingham [Vt.]; H.R. 15601, Johnson [Wash.]).

The only bill of the group to be acted on (H.R. 14461) was introduced by Johnson (Wash.); it was entitled "To limit the immigration of aliens into the United States," but in fact it provided for a two-year suspension with some exceptions. An abridgment of an earlier Johnson bill (H.R. 12320, introduced February 4, 1920 [66-II]), it would permit

[46] *Congressional Record,* 59:1362.

[47] S. J. Res. 232, Wadsworth (N.Y.); H.R. 15129, Welty (Ohio); S. 4594, Sterling (S.D.); H.R. 15164, Vaile (Colo.).

entry of immediate blood relatives and exempt them from the literacy test, and it would allow temporary admissions but with deportability at any time for those found to have entered in violation of the act or to have stayed longer than permitted. In justification of the proposed suspension of immigration, it was pointed out that immigration was increasing in volume, that a large percentage of the immigrants were Jews, that numbers were without funds, and that they were settling in cities. Steamship agents were quoted as saying that 10 million would come in one year if there were ships enough to carry them.

The bill was debated in the House on several days from December 9 to 13, 1920. On the last day the Mann amendment to limit the suspension period to fourteen months was accepted;[48] and the Siegel amendment extended exemption from the literacy test to brothers and sisters. The bill so amended was accepted by the House on December 13, by a vote of 296 to 42.

The Senate committee recommended the substitution of another bill, to set a quota limit on immigration for the period April 1, 1921 to June 30, 1922.[49] The terms of the quota limitation as set by section 2 of the Senate draft provided

> That the number of aliens of any nationality who may be admitted . . . shall be limited to 5 per centum of the number of foreign born persons of such nationality resident in the United States as determined by the United States census.

For this purpose, the 1910 census was to be used. Exemption from the quota limitation was specified for temporary visitors, native-born or naturalized citizens of Western Hemisphere countries, members of certain learned or professional classes, and domestic servants. Estimates set the quota as so determined at about 337,000 for northwestern Europe and 255,000 for other countries. On this point it was stated that the need was not to exclude all immigrants, but to check immigration from southern and eastern Europe, from which the greater part of current immigration was coming. Included in the Senate bill was the discretionary proviso that in individual cases the Secretary of Labor might admit additional aliens in excess of quota when he considered it justifiable as a measure of humanity.

Debate began in the Senate on February 17, 1921 and continued for a second day. On the latter day, Senator Thomas pointed to the danger of admitting naturalized citizens of Western Hemisphere countries free

[48] *Congressional Record,* 60:192; reconsidered and reaccepted, p. 285.
[49] S. Rept. 789, February 15, 1921 (66-III).

of quota, for "citizen factories" might be set up. The danger of immigration of persons with typhus fever was also mentioned. A number of amendments were offered, especially by Harrison (Miss.) and Smith (S.C.). The former's amendment of the House bill, to strike out section 4 that granted free admission to certain close relatives of citizens and aliens applying for citizenship, was rejected.[50] Also rejected was his proposal to base the quota of a country on the number of naturalized citizens in 1910.[51] The Senate then accepted two amendments by Smith, one to remove the discretionary power of the Secretary of Labor to admit aliens above quota, and another to give preference under quota to "wives and children of citizens and of aliens now in the country who have applied for citizenship."[52] This was a first step toward the later much developed system of preferences under quota.

Another attempt by Harrison was to change the quota formula from 5 percent to 1 percent of the 1910 base figure. This was rejected, whereupon he proposed that it be 3 percent, which was accepted by the Senate.[53] The amended bill was passed, 61 to 2, with 33 not voting.

The conference report (H. Rept. 1351 [66-III]) accepted the Senate plan to limit immigration during the fifteen-month period of April 1, 1921 to June 30, 1922 to 3 percent of the number of natives of the given country enumerated in the 1910 census, the quota number so obtained to be the limit for any fiscal year. Native-born and naturalized citizens of Western Hemisphere countries were exempted, admissions in any one month were not to exceed 20 percent of the annual quota, and as far as possible preference was to be given to wives and minor children of naturalized citizens and of aliens who had applied for naturalization. The conference report was agreed to by both House and Senate, and the bill was forwarded to the President on February 28, 1921, four days before the end of the 66th Congress. It received a pocket veto from President Wilson.

67th Congress (1921–1923)

The first session of the 67th Congress convened immediately at the end of the preceding Congress, on March 4, 1921, and continued on to late November of that year. The regulation, or more precisely, the limitation of immigration was a major order of business during the session, but with a scattering of bills on other aspects of immigration.

[50]*Congressional Record,* 60:3443, 3456.
[51]Ibid., p. 3457.
[52]Ibid., p. 3458.
[53]Ibid., pp. 3456, 3457.

Bills relating to alien residents of the United States were mostly concerned with their protection and assistance. Johnson of Washington, whose earlier legislative proposals do not appear to be those of a supporter of immigration, introduced a bill (H.R. 9238) with the benevolent purposes:

> To provide for the guidance and protection, the better economic distribution and the better adjustment of the foreign-born residents of the United States . . . and to create a bureau of citizenship in the Department of Labor.

Other proposed measures concerned the education and naturalization of aliens, enforcement of their treaty rights (S. 322, McKellar [Tenn.]; S. 1943, Kellogg [Minn.]), and the punishment of "conspiracy to injure, oppress, threaten, or intimidate any alien in the exercise of any rights under any treaty" (H.R. 2286, Rogers [Mass.]). Clark of Florida, on the other hand, reentered his bill to prohibit certain aliens from engaging in business in the District of Columbia and the territories (H.R. 5628).

Three deportation bills were introduced, at least two of which concerned aliens who had evaded military service.[54] One of these bills had the second purpose of suspending all immigration until January 1, 1930, a period of eight years or more.

Outright suspension of immigration was contained in several proposals. Raker (Calif.) again urged that the coming of Asiatic laborers be prohibited (H.R. 4580), two bills were for the temporary suspension of immigration (S. 569, King [Utah]; H.R. 4386, Raker [Calif.]), and one would prohibit immigration for a period of four years (H.R. 4133, Wilson [La.]). These were in addition to the deportation bill noted above that would stop all immigration until 1930.

Various approaches to the regulation of immigration were represented by legislative proposals during the first session of the 67th Congress. A bill from an earlier Congress was introduced again to establish an immigration board.[55] A House and a Senate bill were for the exclusion of certain alien immigrants (S. 570, King [Utah]; H.R. 6201, Leatherwood [Utah]). Amendment of the section of the 1917 Act providing for exclusions was proposed (H.R. 2171, Lea [Calif.]). Registration of aliens at the port of entry was to be required by another bill (H.R. 6427, Rosenbloom [W. Va.]); and still another called for inspection at the port of embarcation of aliens desiring to emigrate to the United States (H.R. 7542, Kelly [Pa.]). Late in the session a bill to provide for more thorough regulation

[54]S. 135, Spencer (Mo.); H.R. 2469, Crisp (Ga.); H.R. 5939, Raker (Calif.).

[55]S. 1253, Sterling (S.D.), apparently the same as his S. 4594 (66-III).

of immigration through the passport visa system was introduced (H.R. 7804, Johnson [Wash.]).

In addition to these bills on various topics, there were four to limit the immigration of aliens,[56] three of which were submitted by the leading members of Congress in matters of immigration, Dillingham of Vermont in the Senate and Johnson of Washington in the House. The congressional drive for limitation centered on one of these bills, offered in the House by Johnson and along the lines of his bill vetoed in the preceding Congress (H.R. 4075, with H. Rept. 4 [67-I]).

Reported out by the House committee on April 19, 1921, the central provision of the Johnson bill, like that of its predecessor, was a quota limit on immigration, computed at 3 percent of

> the number of foreign-born persons of such nationality resident in the United States as determined by the United States census of 1910.

Exempted from the limitation were the following:

1. government officials and their families, servants, attendants, and employees;
2. aliens in continuous transit through the United States;
3. aliens residing in the United States and returning from a temporary visit abroad;
4. aliens lawfully admitted to the United States who go through foreign territory in transit from one part of the United States to another;
5. aliens visiting the United States temporarily;
6. aliens who have resided continuously, for at least one year, immediately preceding their admission, in a Western Hemisphere country.

A committee addition to the excepted classes was

> aliens who shall prove to the satisfaction of the proper immigration officer or of the Secretary of Labor that they are seeking admission to the United States to avoid religious persecution.

Nationality for the purpose of the bill was to depend on country of birth, which is to say, nativity. And not over 20 percent of the quota was to be allowed to enter in any one month.

Two provisos in the bill further modified the operation of the quota system. One proviso was that professional actors, artists, lecturers, singers, nurses, ministers of any religious denomination, professors for colleges or seminaries, aliens belonging to any recognized learned profession, or aliens employed as domestic servants were to be admitted regardless of

[56] S. 87, Dillingham (Vt.); H.R. 2 and 4075, Johnson (Wash.); H.R. 4589, Focht (Pa.).

quota, but to be charged to the quota if that had not yet been filled. Another proviso was that

> in the enforcement of this act preference shall be given so far as possible to the parents and minor children of aliens now in the United States and who have applied for naturalization.

The bill was taken up in the House under a rule limiting debate to four hours, to forestall what might have been determined opposition and delaying tactics. An amendment added the word "solely" to the committee modification concerning religious persecution, and that clause of the bill was then reworded to read

> that they are actually subjects of religious persecution in the country of their last permanent residence and are seeking admission to the United States solely to avoid the suffering and hardship involved in such persecution.[57]

Various other amendments were then considered. An attempt by Siegel (N.Y.) to change the quota base year from 1910 to 1920 was defeated,[58] as was a proposal to reduce the quota from 3 to 1 percent of the base number.[59] Nonquota status was granted to aliens under eighteen years of age who are the children of citizens of the United States, but was refused to political refugees.[60] The amended bill was then passed by the House, on April 22, 1921, and forwarded to the Senate.

The Senate committee, just as it had done with the Johnson bill passed by the House in the preceding Congress several months before, substituted a new bill of its own, which, however, was close in essentials to the House draft.[61] It set a quota of 3 percent of the number of foreign born of a given nationality shown in the 1910 census, with exemption granted to government officials, aliens in continuous transit, temporary visitors, aliens who have resided continuously in a Western Hemisphere country for one year prior to entry into the United States, and certain other exemptions, but with deletion of the House exemptions, especially those added by amendment from the floor of the House.

The Senate then voted down a series of proposals for amendment, these being to reduce the quota to 1 percent, to require immigrants to come in United States vessels, to stop immigration for two years, and to give nonquota status to religious and political refugees. Accepted later, however, was an amendment to require at least half of all immigrants to come in American flag vessels.[62] The bill was then passed by the Senate,

[57] *Congressional Record,* 61:544.
[58] Ibid., p. 559.
[59] Ibid., pp. 559, 572.
[60] Ibid., pp. 579, 588.
[61] S. Rept. 17, on H.R. 4075 (67-I).
[62] *Congressional Record,* 61:967.

78 to 1, with 17 abstaining. This was even stronger than the Senate support of the similar bill of three months before in the 66th Congress, when thirty-three senators had refrained from voting.

The conference between House and Senate delegates recommended elimination of two exemptions from quota limitation: the House exemption of aliens returning from a temporary visit abroad and the exemption of religious refugees. As the report said with no exaggeration, "The elimination of the provisions mentioned above makes H.R. 4075 more rigid in its restrictive effect than when it left the House." The conference report being accepted by both Senate and House, the bill went to President Harding, was signed, and became the Act of May 19, 1921 (42 Stat. 5).

The new immigration law, the first quota act, set the annual quota for each nationality group at 3 percent of the number of foreign-born persons of that national origin enumerated in the 1910 census, excepting the Asiatic barred zone, and "treating as separate countries the colonies or dependencies for which separate enumeration was made in the United States census of 1910."[63] The quota limitation, however, did not apply to eight designated classes of aliens:

1. government officials and their households;
2. aliens in transit through the United States;
3. lawfully admitted aliens going through foreign contiguous territory en route to another part of the United States;
4. alien visitors for business or pleasure;
5. aliens whose immigration is regulated by immigration treaty;
6. aliens who have resided continuously for at least one year in a Western Hemisphere country; and
7. aliens under eighteen, who are children of citizens.[64]

In addition, three provisos concerning quotas were included. The first limited the number admitted in any one month to 20 percent of the annual quota. A second proviso, following the lines of a proviso in the original House bill, specified that aliens returning from a temporary visit abroad, certain professional classes as designated in the original bill, and domestic servants were to be admitted regardless of quota limit but to be charged to the appropriate quota if it was unfilled. The third proviso granted preference "so far as possible" to wives, parents, brothers, sisters, children under eighteen, and fiancées of citizens, resident aliens who had made application for citizenship, and aliens eligible for citizenship who had served in the armed forces between April 6, 1917 and November

[63]Section 2(b) of the act.

[64]Section 2(a).

11, 1918 and received honorable discharge.[65] The act was to take effect fifteen days after enactment and to continue in force until June 30, 1922.[66]

During the long second session of the 67th Congress, from early December 1921 to late September the following year, particular emphasis was given to the further regulation of immigration, but with some attention to other related matters. Relating to resident aliens were proposals for their registration and for amendment of the Constitution to exclude aliens in the apportionment of representation in Congress (S. 3403, Shortridge [Calif.]; H. J. Res. 235, Larsen [Ga.]). Several bills concerned deportation; one provided for penalty for "aliens who participate in riotous gatherings," and two called for deportation of aliens convicted of unlawful possession of or traffic in drugs or narcotics.[67] Johnson of Washington introduced two bills for the deportation of certain undesirable aliens (H.R. 11058 and 11118), the second of which concerned aliens who violate national or state laws on prohibition and on the registration of processors of opium products. This bill was reported back in House Report 867 (67-II), debated, and passed by the House. It was not acted on in the Senate. Johnson also introduced a resolution to authorize the Secretary of Labor to stay the deportation of certain aliens in cases of extreme hardship (H. J. Res. 237 [67-II]). With the one exception noted above, none of these bills was reported out of committee.

The principal legislative activity on immigration during the second session of the 67th Congress concerned the regulation of immigration, either in the form of proposals for new legislation or of amendments to the 1921 Act. From Johnson (Wash.), chairman of the House Committee on Immigration and Naturalization, came a bill to suspend immigration for a period of three years (H.R. 9458). Four bills in the House called for the further limitation of immigration,[68] and no fewer than six were to amend the 1921 Act.[69] Two bills by Cable of Ohio (H.R. 10623 and 11604) continued the effort to require immigrants to come in vessels of the United States. Others concerned such various topics as the establish-

[65]Section 2(d).

[66]Soon after its passage and before the end of the session, bills were quickly introduced to repeal and to amend the act (H.R. 7826, Perlman of N.Y.; H.R. 8511, Cable of Ohio; H.R. 8525, Raker of California).

[67]H.R. 12344, Edmonds (Pa.); S. 3120, McNary (Oreg.); H.R. 10075, McArthur (Oreg.).

[68]H.R. 10314, Focht (Pa.); H.R. 12169, 12237, Johnson (Wash.); H.R. 12193, Raker (Calif.).

[69]S. 2866, Dillingham (Vt.); H.R. 9385, 11604, Cable (Ohio); H.R. 11730, Steenerson (Minn.); H.R. 12119, Ellis (Mo.); H. J. Res. 273, Johnson (Wash.).

ment of an immigration board, proposed by King of Utah and Vaile of Colorado (S. 2882, H.R. 9880), and the extension of special immigration privileges to alien veterans.[70] Several bills were designed to mitigate difficulties or hardships following the 1921 Quota Act. S. 2988 by Robinson of Arkansas was to make permanent the admission of excess-quota aliens who had been allowed to land temporarily, and H.R. 12470 by McPherson of Missouri was to authorize the Secretary of Labor to grant permanent admission to aliens temporarily admitted since 1914 who were minors at the time of their admission. A House Joint Resolution (H. J. Res. 279) by Johnson (Wash.) was to grant permanent admission to certain aliens admitted temporarily under bond and in excess of quota. Reported out (H. Rept. 776), it concerned aliens so admitted prior to March 1, 1922, "if otherwise admissible, and if not subject to deportation for other causes"; and it provided for the return of the bond. The committee report on the resolution stated that 2,453 aliens qualified for such relief, changed the cut-off date from March 1 to March 7, and favored the bill for what the committee felt were humanitarian reasons. The resolution was passed by the House, 243 to 91, but the Senate took no action until the fourth session (see below).

Another matter calling for prompt attention was the approaching expiration of the 1921 Quota Act, section 5 of which limited the duration of the act to June 30, 1922. On February 14, 1922, Johnson (Wash.), chairman of the House committee, introduced House Joint Resolution 268, that the operation of the 1921 Act be extended to June 30, 1923, inclusive. It was reported back promptly in House Report 710 (67-II), on February 17, without amendment by the Committee on Immigration and Naturalization but with a dissenting minority report that enumerated objections to the quota system. During brief debate on February 20, Johnson defended the resolution and pointed out the great reduction of immigration effected in the first months of the operation of the 3 percent quota law. Opposition was voiced by Sabath (Ill.) and others.[71] The resolution was passed the same day, 280 to 36, with 113 not voting. In the Senate the resolution was favorably reported on April 5, but with amendment to extend the life of the act an additional year, to June 30, 1924. Debate in the Senate extended over April 14 and 15, with Senator Colt, chairman of the Committee on Immigration, supporting the resolution and in his remarks pointing to the allegedly more permanent character of immigration from the favored areas of northern and western Europe. Reference was made to the report of a special agent, Lillian

[70]H.R. 12461, Brennan (Mich.); S. J. Res. 233, McCormick (Ill.).

[71]*Congressional Record,* 62:2798–806.

Russell Moore—better known by her maiden name, Lillian Russell, as a singer and actress—appointed by President Harding to make an investigation of the immigration problem in Europe. Her qualifications for the assignment were not mentioned during the course of the debate in the Senate, but a passage from her report quoted there indicated a strongly restrictionist attitude:

> The higher civilizations of past ages, history teaches us, succumbed to such foreign invasions as now threaten us.

The report recommended a five-year suspension of immigration.[72]

The Senate accepted the Sterling (S.D.) amendment to change section 2(a), subdivision 7 of the 1921 Act to increase the period of continuous residence in a Western Hemisphere country required for quota exemption from one to five years, and to change section 3 of the act to inflict a fine of $200 on a transportation company for each alien inadmissible under the 1921 Act brought to the United States.[73] Two proposed amendments by Harris (Ga.) were then rejected, these being to suspend immigration for five years as recommended in the Moore report, but with exemption of certain classes of aliens, and to require immigrating aliens to come in vessels of the United States.[74]

The bill so amended was passed by the Senate, the House disagreed with the Senate amendments, and a conference report was then prepared. The conference draft extended the 1921 Act for two years, to June 30, 1924, accepted the five-year residence in a Western Hemisphere country but with some change of wording, and added a new section 6 providing for a $200 fine for each alien inadmissible under the act who was brought to the United States. The latter section was revised by the House with some rewording and with provision for remission of the fine on a showing that inadmissibility was not known to the transportation company and could not have been discovered with reasonable diligence. With approval by President Harding, the resolution became the Act of May 11, 1922 (42 Stat. 540).

The brief third session of the 67th Congress, opening in late November of 1922, took no action on immigration. It was followed by the fourth session, which ran for the normal duration, from December 1922 to March 1923, and dealt with various aspects of migration. Resolutions from the first session were considered in both House and Senate to relieve shortage of labor in Hawaii,[75] but no action was taken. Several

[72]Ibid., pp. 5558, 5562.

[73]Ibid., pp. 5565, 5566.

[74]Ibid., pp. 5566, 5567.

[75]H. J. Res. 171, Kalanianaole (delegate from Hawaii); S. J. Res. 82, Dillingham (Vt.).

House bills were for the purpose of registration or enrollment of aliens: H.R. 13417 by Rainey (Ala.) and H.R. 14430 by Vaile (Colo.). Sentiment in favor of a further reduction of immigration was indicated by a bill to prohibit immigration: H.R. 13713 by Sanders of Texas; and four or more bills for its further limitation.[76] Another was specifically to limit the immigration of aliens ineligible to citizenship: H.R. 14285 by Miller (Wash.). Four proposals were for amendment of the 1921 Act,[77] and a further bill would permit the admission of certain aliens in excess of quota but charge them to the quota for the next fiscal year, that ending June 30, 1924: H.J. Res. 416 by Johnson (Wash.). And there was a proposal to repeal the literacy test, by Perlman of New York: H.R. 13661.

During the session the Senate finally took up the Johnson resolution, H. J. Res. 279, from the second session to permit certain aliens temporarily admitted under bond and in excess of quota to remain in the United States. Passed by the Senate without amendment, it was signed by President Harding, and constituted the Act of December 27, 1922 (42 Stat. 1065).

One other matter related to immigration received congressional attention at this time: the plight of Armenian refugees from Turkish territory. Four bills and one resolution for their relief were introduced.[78] Only one, that introduced by Keyes of New Hampshire, was acted on further. Reported out with amendment on January 9, 1923 by the Senate committee,[79] the bill as originally written provided that any resident of the United States who is a citizen or an alien having made declaration of intention to obtain citizenship, may petition for admission of wife or close relative by blood. The Senate committee amendment was in fact to strike out the entire bill and substitute a new bill in thirteen sections entitled "The Near East Refugee Act of 1923." It was applicable to Armenians who had become refugees since August 1, 1914, and it was passed by the Senate without further amendment.[80]

The House committee reported out the bill with amendment[81] that consisted of striking out the entire bill as passed by the Senate and substituting a new bill. Entitled "The Immigration Act of 1923," this was a long general bill in many sections. It contained a new basic formula for

[76]H.R. 13234, Rainey (Ala.); H.R. 13628, Box (Tex.); H.R. 13930, Vaile (Colo.); H.R. 14273, Johnson (Wash.).

[77]S. 4222, Reed (Pa.); S. 4303, Colt (R.I.); S. 4403, Harrison (Miss.); H. J. Res. 464, Johnson (Wash.).

[78]S. 4092, Keyes (N.H.); S. 4298, Williams (Miss.); H.R. 13269, 13830, White (Kans.); S. J. Res. 252, Walsh (Mass.).

[79]S. Rept. 1010 (67-IV).

[80]*Congressional Record,* 64:3036.

[81]H. Rept. 1621, February 15, 1923 (67-IV).

determining the quota of a country to be 2 percent of the number of foreign-born residents from that country in the United States at the census of 1890. With a minimum quota of 400 for each country, the total possible quota immigration under the 1921 Act stood at 387,803. The new formula would reduce the number to 186,437.

A prominent feature of the bill was the series of nonquota classes, that is, those admissible without being charged to the quota, which were enumerated in section 4:

1. an immigrant who is the husband, wife, father, mother, unmarried minor child, unmarried minor brother or sister, or unmarried minor niece or nephew of a citizen;

2. an immigrant who is the husband, wife, or unmarried minor child of an alien who has been *(a)* permanently admitted to the United States, *(b)* has resided in the United States at least two years, and *(c)* has filed declaration of intention at least one year previously;

3. an alien returning from a temporary visit abroad, provided the alien has been legally admitted previously;

4. an immigrant who has resided continuously at least five years in a Western Hemisphere country;

5. an immigrant who for at least two years has been and seeks admission to carry on his vocation of minister, professor of a college or seminary, or member of any recognized learned profession;

6. an immigrant who is a skilled laborer, if labor of like kind unemployed cannot be found in the United States;

7. the wife or minor child of an immigrant admissible under items 5 and 6 above, if accompanying or coming to join him;

8. a bona fide student over sixteen years of age seeking to enter for study at an accredited educational institution; and

9. a veteran who served between April 6, 1917 and November 11, 1918 and was not dishonorably discharged.

The bill was not considered by the House, and it expired with the end of the session.

68th Congress (1923–1925)

Sentiment for revision of the immigration laws ran high during the first session of the 68th Congress, at which time great numbers of memorials, petitions, and letters concerning immigration policy were received by Congress, suspension of all immigration was called for by a number of bills introduced during the session, and many others sought to limit immigration.

Perlman of New York reintroduced his bill from the preceding session (H.R. 625) to repeal the literacy test, but his was a lone effort, and the tide of opinion was running strongly in the opposite direction.

The creation of a commission on immigration policy was proposed by Kelly (Pa.) (H.R. 9775), but the great majority of the new bills offered during the session proceeded directly to urge modifications of immigration policy. Six bills called for a suspension of immigration, one being for a five-year suspension, two for a six-year suspension, and one for a suspension of ten years.[82] An additional bill (H.R. 113, Raker [Calif.]) was to prohibit the coming of Asiatic laborers.

A total of fifteen bills during the session were designed to make certain additional classes of aliens subject to deportation. Of these, at least one concerned those who had been convicted under the prohibition act. Others provided deportation for conviction of unlawful possession of or traffic in drugs or narcotics, evasion of military service by withdrawal of declaration of intention, failure to register at port of entry or otherwise qualify for citizenship, participation in riotous gatherings, or membership in the communistic or similar classes.[83]

Another and smaller group of bills dealt with resident aliens in other respects than deportability. Two that were introduced by Cable of Ohio provided for the arrest and punishment of aliens who enter the country unlawfully (H.R. 3245 and 4083). McKellar of Tennessee was author of a bill (S. 430) regarding the education and naturalization of aliens and their children. Rogers of Massachusetts reintroduced the bill he had proposed in the preceding Congress to punish conspiracy against aliens (H.R. 550); and a bill of somewhat similar purpose, for the better protection of aliens and for enforcement of their treaty rights, came from Moores of Indiana (H.R. 7081).

The majority of the immigration bills presented to the first session of the 68th Congress were for the regulation of immigration in one fashion or another, including amendment of the 1921 or earlier acts, and the further limitation of the number of immigrants to be admitted. Tinkham of Massachusetts, in the first immigration bill of his long career in Congress, proposed the registration of certain nonresident aliens at port of entry (H.R. 6872), and Dickstein of New York began his long association with immigration legislation during this session with a bill to amend the Act of 1917 (H.R. 4502). Other bills were to create an immigration

[82]H.R. 3197, Steagall (Ala.); H.R. 3932, Watkins (Oreg.); H.R. 4466, Romjue (Mo.); H.R. 6067, Wilson (Miss.); H.R. 8439, Parks (Ark.); S. J. Res. 50, Harris (Ga.).

[83]S. 296, 297, 298, Spencer (Mo.); S. 2591, McNary (Oreg.); H.R. 102, 109, 5322, Raker (Calif.); H.R. 188, Johnson (Wash.); H.R. 691, Rosenbloom (W.Va.); H.R. 2856, Watkins (Oreg.); H.R. 4090, Lineberger (Calif.); H.R. 4152, Taylor (Colo.); H.R. 5079, Edmonds (Pa.); H.R. 5418, Cable (Ohio); H.R. 6867, Holaday (Ill.).

board, to amend the acts of 1906 and 1917, to facilitate the immigration of alien veterans and their families, to provide for inspection of immigrant aliens at the port of embarcation for the issuance of certificates of immigration, to ensure the use of the English language by those admitted, and to provide safeguards for those admitted legally and penalties for those who entered by fraud.[84] Other bills were introduced to promote the entry of certain relatives of citizens of the United States.[85]

The Quota Act of 1921 was the subject of eight or more bills and resolutions, one to repeal the act (H.R. 622, Perlman [N.Y.]), several to extend its operation, some to liberalize, and others to strengthen the act.[86]

A considerable group of other bills proposed to limit[87] or to limit and select immigration;[88] and among them were all but one of the bills to be reported out and considered by Congress during the session (see H. J. Res. 283, below). With the 1921 Quota Act as extended about to expire on June 30, 1924, both House and Senate began working on new bills to replace it: the Johnson bill (H.R. 6540) in the House and the Reed bill (S. 2576) in the Senate. The House committee, reporting out the Johnson bill on February 9, 1924, in House Report 176 (68-I), emphasized the urgent need for new legislation. Impending immigration was said to be large, and already would have risen to between 1.5 million and 2 million, annually, except for the 1921 Act. It was the Committee's opinion also that the literacy test and other selective provisions in the 1917 Act would be powerless to check the influx. With this prospect in view, the Johnson bill with committee approval would reduce the quota for each country to 2 percent plus 200 immigrants and shift the base year from 1910 back to 1890, provide for an examination of prospective immigrants overseas, and put the burden of proof of admissibility on the would-be immigrants. Under the bill, nonquota status was more limited

[84]S. 2082, Sterling (S.D.); S. 2451, Wadsworth (N.Y.); H.R. 83, McClintic (Okla.); H.R. 455, Clancy (Mich.); H.R. 2900, Kelly (Pa.); H.R. 3239, Vestal (Ind.); H.R. 4089, Lineberger (Calif.); H.R. 5628, Fredericks (Calif.).

[85]S. 1497, Copeland (N.Y.); H.R. 3844, Hill (Md.); H.R. 5713, Doyle (Ill.).

[86]H.R. 83, McClintic (Okla.); H.R. 2696, Graham (Ill.); H.R. 4127, Lindsay (N.Y.); H.R. 6247, 7178, Cable (Ohio); H. J. Res. 96, Sabath (Ill.); H. J. Res. 233, Dickstein (N.Y.). The Lindsay bill was to exempt from quota the wives, parents, children, brothers and sisters, together with their accompanying spouses and children, of citizens who served in the armed forces during the recent war.

[87]S. 2576, Reed (Pa.); H.R. 5, Raker (Calif.); H.R. 539, Phillips (Pa.); H.R. 561, Sabath (Ill.); H.R. 4098, Box (Tex.); H.R. 5320, McReynolds (Tenn.); H.R. 6540, 7995, Johnson (Wash.).

[88]S. 35, Lodge (Mass.); S. 2365, Watson (Ind.); H.R. 101, Johnson (Wash.); H.R. 7684, Aswell (La.); H.R. 7919, Kunz (Ill.).

than under the 1921 Act, being granted to wives, children under eighteen, and parents over fifty-five of citizens; aliens of ten years continuous residence in a Western Hemisphere country prior to admission to the United States; ministers and professors; skilled laborers if labor of like kind unemployed was not to be found in the United States; and the wives or unmarried children under eighteen of the two preceding classes. Excluded would be "persons ineligible to citizenship" unless admissible as a nonquota immigrant, wife, or child under eighteen of an admissible immigrant, or in a nonimmigrant class, that is, admitted on a temporary basis. The bill in this form, as reported out by the committee, was debated in the House but then tabled in favor of a revised bill, also by Johnson, for the limitation of immigration.

The new bill (H.R. 7995, with H. Rept. 350) was reported out by the House committee on March 24, 1924. It retained the 1917 Act as the basic immigration act, but replaced the 1921 quota formula by setting national quotas at 2 percent of the 1890 population of the given country of birth. It also followed the preceding Johnson bill in providing the same nonquota classes, reducing the number of such exempt classes in comparison with the 1921 Act, and placing the burden of proof of admissibility on the alien.

The bill raised a most serious issue regarding the Japanese, who would be excluded on the grounds of ineligibility to citizenship, in violation of the long-standing Gentlemen's Agreement between Japan and the United States. Secretary of State Hughes, in reference to the preceding bill of like nature, had recommended that the exclusion of ineligibles be eliminated and that Japan be given a quota. It was his further opinion that to go back to 1890 might offend Italy, Romania, and certain other countries; and the new bill had been revised in part by the committee in order to meet these considerations.[89]

There was lengthy debate in the House, after which consideration of amendments began on April 11 as the bill was taken up section by section.[90] A first amendment was offered by Rogers (Mass.), to limit immigration to 200,000 in any fiscal year after July 1, 1926, the quota of each nation to be based on a new formula, a national origins formula. As set forth in the proposed amendment, the Secretaries of Commerce and Labor were to be instructed

[89]The committee, however, approved the exclusion of persons ineligible to citizenship, in its report intimating that the Gentlemen's Agreement was an infringement of congressional powers and had failed to prevent the coming of large numbers of Japanese laborers; and resolutions from the American Federation of Labor and the National Grange in support of the committee action were noted.

[90]*Congressional Record,* 65:6110.

> to make an estimate showing, as nearly as may be, the several national origins of the persons who in 1920 composed the whole population of continental United States, excepting the descendants of such persons as were involuntary immigrants.[91]

The quota of a country was to bear the same ratio to 200,000 as persons of that national origin were to the population of 1920. The amendment was discussed but not voted on. On the following day Rogers again offered a national origins quota amendment, at which time he disclaimed authorship and referred to a similar amendment to the immigration bill then in the Senate.[92] Opposed by Johnson, the amendment was rejected.[93]

The House then considered and accepted the important section 10 of the bill, providing a quota of 2 percent of the 1890 base population, with a minimum quota of 100, and with a limit of one-tenth of the annual quota in any one month. Section 12 was then accepted in its turn with the provision for exclusion of persons ineligible to citizenship,[94] but with exception of the nonquota classes enumerated in section 4,[95] the wives and unmarried children under eighteen of admissible aliens, and nonimmigrants as defined in section 3 of the bill.[96] In this form the section effected exclusion of the Japanese.[97]

Section 23, acted on in its turn, introduced a significant new element, the previously mentioned burden of proof clause. In the committee draft, this read:

> In any proceeding under the immigration laws the burden of proving the right of any alien to enter or remain in the United States shall, as between him and the United States, be upon such alien.[98]

During the consideration of this section the Begg substitute wording was proposed, as follows:

[91]Ibid., p. 6111.

[92]Ibid., p. 6226.

[93]Ibid., pp. 6227–29.

[94]Ibid., pp. 6247, 6251.

[95]Spouse, unmarried child under eighteen, parent over fifty-five of citizen; returning resident alien; alien with ten years' continuous residence in a Western Hemisphere country, together with his wife and unmarried children under eighteen; professors or ministers; skilled laborer if labor of like kind unemployed cannot be found in the United States; wives and unmarried children under eighteen of the two preceding classes; and bona fide students.

[96]Government officials, alien visitors, aliens in transit, aliens going from one part of the United States to another through foreign territory, bona fide seamen, and spouses of citizens.

[97]*Congressional Record,* 65:6252.

[98]The committee substituted the word *alien* for *individual* in section 23.

> Whenever any alien attempts to enter the United States the burden of proof shall be upon such alien to establish that he is not subject to exclusion under any provision of the immigration laws; and in any deportation proceeding against any alien the burden of proof shall be upon such alien to show that he entered the United States lawfully, and the time, place, and manner of such entry into the United States, but in presenting such proof he shall be entitled to the production of his immigration certificate, if any, or other documents concerning such entry in the custody of the Department of Labor.[99]

The amendment was accepted, 140 to 131, and the entire bill was then passed by the House on April 12, by a vote of 323 to 71.

The Senate committee, on receipt of the House bill, chose to substitute for it the Reed bill (S. 2576) on which the Senate was then working. The latter bill had been introduced by Senator Reed of Pennsylvania, who in discussion of the bill on April 3 stated that his draft was taken in part from the Johnson bill then in the House.[100] As introduced, the Reed bill followed the previous formula of a 2 percent quota but retained 1910 as the base year rather than going back to 1890. There was sentiment in the Senate, however, in favor of the national origins quota plan as already introduced in the House, for during discussion of the bill on the following day, April 4, Lodge of Massachusetts spoke of an amendment to be offered by Reed to provide a national origins quota based on the population of 1920. It was Lodge's judgment that

> If such a basis is adopted, there can be no question then of discrimination, because it will treat all races alike on the basis of their actual proportion of the existing population.[101]

Doubtless he was thinking of the problem of Japanese immigration; and discussion of the effect of the bill on Japanese immigration took a prominent place in Senate debate on the bill on April 7, 8, and 9. On the last day Reed explained his national origins proposal, and emphasized its advantage of giving no basis for an accusation of discrimination against any one race or national group.[102] He also noted the exclusion of the Negro population from the base population used in the computation of quotas.[103]

Inserted into the record at this point was a comparison of the number of quota immigrants admissible under different formulas. The 1921 Act (3 percent of 1910) allowed 357,801 per annum. The Johnson bill in the House (2 percent of 1890), with a minimum of 100, gave 161,990.

[99] Ibid., p. 6256.
[100] Ibid., p. 5467.
[101] Ibid., p. 5568.
[102] Ibid., pp. 5942–3.
[103] Ibid., p. 5944.

The present Senate bill (2 percent of 1910), with the same minimum, would allow 240,459; and the national origins proposal was put at 200,000.[104]

It was the issue of Japanese exclusion that remained uppermost. On April 14 it was mentioned in the course of Senate debate on the bill[105] that the House had already adopted Japanese exclusion—actually, two days before, on the twelfth. Shortly after the Senate was told that the Japanese ambassador had spoken of "grave consequences."[106] With little or no delay the Senate proceeded, on the same day, to reject an amendment proposed by the committee that would have avoided outright exclusion of Japanese by adding the following clause to section 3 of the bill in order to establish a seventh class of aliens who were exempt from the category of immigrants:

> (7) An alien entitled to enter the United States under the provision of a treaty or an agreement relating solely to immigration.[107]

Rejection was by the overwhelming majority of 76 to 2, and it left the Japanese subject to whatever action might be taken with respect to national quotas.[108]

Shortly thereafter, Reed (Pa.) offered his national origins amendment, after the pattern of the corresponding Rogers amendment in the House, but with the provision of a lower limit on quota immigration of 150,000 rather than the 200,000 of the House version. The quota formula was stated as follows in Reed's amendment:

> After July 1, 1926, the annual quota of each nationality shall bear the same ratio to said maximum total number of immigrants as the number of inhabitants of the United States having that national origin shall bear to the total number of inhabitants other than the descendants of involuntary immigrants.[109]

The amendment was not voted on in this form but redrafted and brought up several days later.

On the following day, April 15, the Senate adopted another Reed amendment, that no alien ineligible for citizenship shall be admitted

[104]Ibid., p. 5962. The comparison gave the distribution of quotas by country. The striking feature of the national origins quotas was that over 60 percent, 182,221, went to one country, Great Britain and Ireland. Actually, the Rogers amendment in the House set a limit of 200,000, not 300,000.

[105]Ibid., p. 6302. [106]Ibid., p. 6309.

[107]The other six nonimmigrant classes were (1) government officials, (2) temporary visitors, (3) aliens in continuous transit, (4) admitted aliens going through foreign territory, (5) bona fide seamen, (6) aliens returning from a temporary visit abroad.

[108]*Congressional Record,* 65:6315. [109]Ibid., p. 6316.

unless he is (1) a nonimmigrant, (2) a minister or professor, (3) a student over eighteen, or (4) the wife or unmarried child under eighteen of an admissible immigrant.[110] This was similar to the House bill and would effectually exclude the Japanese except as noted. The vote on this amendment was not recorded at the time, but was reported on the following day as 71 to 4, with 21 not voting.[111]

The redrafted national origins amendment was brought up on April 16. It now read

> After July 1, 1927, the maximum total number of immigrants that shall be admitted into the United States in each fiscal year shall, unless the Congress shall in the interim provide otherwise, be 150,000, and the annual quota of each nationality shall bear the same ratio to said maximum total number of immigrants as the number of inhabitants of the United States having that national origin shall bear to the whole number of inhabitants other than the descendants of involuntary immigrants.[112]

The Senate accepted the new draft with little debate and without record vote.

Encouraged by the adoption of the national origins limitation on immigration, the restrictionists in the Senate pressed for other amendments to reduce immigration. The Harris (Ga.) amendment to suspend immigration for five years followed on the Reed amendment, but was defeated, 16 to 46. But on the next day, April 17, an amendment proposed by Willis of Ohio to reduce the quota from 2 percent to 1 percent was accepted, by vote of 55 to 25.[113] A national minimum quota of 100 under the 1 percent quota was then set.[114] This was followed by the Harrison amendment, accepted by a 47 to 32 vote, to change the base year from 1910 back to 1890. Thereupon the Harris amendment was reconsidered and the quota raised back to 2 percent, but on the 1890 base population; and another amendment was accepted to give preference to "skilled farmers and experienced farm laborers" when a shortage of such workers was demonstrated.[115] On April 18 the Senate voted to substitute the bill as so amended for the House bill, H.R. 7995, and then approved the whole bill, 62 to 6, with 28 abstaining.[116] Before the final vote, Reed summarized the major differences between the Senate and House bills, which were that the House gave nonquota status to certain relatives of citizens and to certain categories of skilled labor and

[110]Ibid., p. 6377.

[111]Ibid., p. 6460.

[112]Ibid., p. 6471.

[113]Ibid., p. 6538.

[114]Ibid., p. 6540.

[115]Ibid., p. 6620.

[116]Ibid., pp. 6645–49.

the Senate gave preference to some classes of aliens but did not grant nonquota status.

The conference report[117] presented a revised bill, described as "in effect the original House bill, considerably tightened as to its restrictive features." The Senate conferees accepted the nonquota features of the House bill but reduced them by limiting the nonquota status of residents of adjacent territory to those born there, and limiting the "relatives" clause to wives and children of American citizens. The nonquota status of skilled labor was eliminated. And the Senate device of preference classes under the quota appeared in the form of preference for fathers and mothers of citizens and for bona fide farmers with their wives and children up to 50 percent of national quotas of 300 or more. The House managers of the bill accepted the nonquota provisions after some rewriting, with the quota formula to be in the House form of 2 percent of the 1890 population during the next three years and then to change to the national origins basis on and after July 1, 1927. Thereafter quota immigration was to be set at 150,000 per annum, but with the minimum quota of any nationality at 100. The conference draft of the bill added an amendment to the clause excluding ineligibles, section 13 (c), which postponed its operation for eight months beyond the time set in the House draft. This made its effective date March 1, 1925, in order to give time to adjust diplomatic relations for abrogation of the present agreement and to give a temporary quota of 80 to Japan from July 1, 1924 to March 1, 1925, not counting students, ministers, and teachers who might enter with nonquota status.

Objection being raised, the bill went to a second conference, which made its report on May 12, in House Report 716 (68-I). The conference committee had amended section 13 in accordance with a House vote to strike out the proviso in section 13(c) that had been inserted in the first conference report. This was the proviso that postponed the effective date of Japanese exclusion to March 1, 1925. The subsection now read

> No alien ineligible to citizenship shall be admitted to the United States unless such alien (1) is admissible as a nonquota immigrant under the provisions of subdivision (b), (d), or (e) of section 4, or (2) is the wife, or the unmarried child under 18 years of age, of an immigrant admissible under such subdivision (d), and is accompanying or following to join him, or (3) is not an immigrant as defined in section 3.[118]

[117]H. Rept. 688, May 8, 1924 (68-I).

[118]Section 4(b) concerned aliens returning from a temporary visit abroad, 4(d) ministers and professors, and 4(e) students.

The second conference report was accepted by both House and Senate, and received presidential signature. The Act of May 26, 1924 (43 Stat. 153) was known as the Immigration Act of 1924. A long act in thirty-two sections, it provided for issuance of immigration visas by consular officers abroad, defined the immigrant and nonimmigrant, quota and nonquota classes, set forth the procedure and supporting evidence for the issuance of visas, provided for reentry permits, set the quota formula for the interim period and for the national origins quotas effective July 1, 1927, and dealt with deportation and numerous other matters relating to the administration of the act. The formulation of the major provisions of the act has been described above, but to set forth their final form they can be summarized as follows:

1. National quotas: two percent of the 1890 population of that nationality, with a minimum of 100 (section 11[a]); after July 1, 1927 to bear the same ratio to 150,000 as the population of that national origin to the 1920 population of the United States.[119]

2. Nonquota immigrants: unmarried children under eighteen years of age and wives of citizens,[120] returning temporary visitors abroad, natives of Western Hemisphere countries with their families, ministers and professors with their families, bona fide students at least fifteen years of age, and women, formerly citizens, who lost citizenship through marriage to aliens but were no longer so married (section 4).

3. Quota preference: up to 50 percent of the quota of each country to unmarried children under twenty-one, parents, and spouses of a citizen aged twenty-one or over; also preference in countries with quotas of 300 or more to a quota immigrant aged twenty-one or over who is skilled in agriculture, together with his wife and dependent children under age sixteen (section 6).[121]

Also passed during the first session of the 68th Congress was a relief act to permit certain aliens arriving in excess of quota to remain in the United States. Introduced as House Joint Resolution 283, it was favorably

[119]To be excluded from the 1920 base population of the United States were immigrants from Western Hemisphere countries and their descendants, aliens ineligible for citizenship and their descendants, descendants of slave immigrants, and descendants of American aborigines (sec. 11d).

[120]Changed to under age twenty-one for children by the Act of May 29, 1928 (45 Stat. 1009); and husbands of citizens by marriage prior to June 1, 1928 were added by the Act of July 11, 1932 (47 Stat. 656).

[121]Amendment by the Act of May 29, 1928 (45 Stat. 1009) gave preference in the allocation of any remaining quota visas for a given country to unmarried children under age twenty-one and wives of alien residents lawfully admitted for permanent residence.

reported in the House, in House Report 995 (68-I), and was debated and passed in a form that was estimated to provide relief for approximately 13,000 aliens. This figure was reduced to somewhat under 10,000 by a rewritten draft prepared in the Senate committee, accepted by the Senate, and then by the House to become the Act of June 7, 1924 (43 Stat. 669). As passed, the act provided that if otherwise admissible and not subject to deportation for other causes, aliens previously admitted in excess of quota and charged to the quota of a later month would be allowed to remain, as would other aliens whose admission was put in question by a recent court decision or who had been admitted temporarily under bond in relief of extreme hardship.

After its efforts with immigration legislation during the first session, the 68th Congress in its second session received relatively few bills on the subject, and only one was acted on in the House. Johnson of the House committee introduced a bill to amend the 1917 Act, and eight others were for the amendment of the 1924 Act.[122] Two bills were to provide for registration or certificates of identification of alien residents, and another was for the punishment of deported aliens who return.[123]

The only bill to be acted on was a deportation bill (H.R. 11796), introduced in the House by Holaday of Illinois on January 21, 1925 and reported back on January 27. One provision of the bill was for amendment of section 18 of the 1917 Act, whereby deportation was prescribed for an alien brought in in violation of law, unless the Secretary of Labor considers that deportation is not practicable or proper. The Holaday bill would amend the section to make deportation mandatory unless the alien in question is diseased and in a hospital, or if deportation would cause undue hardship prior to hospitalization, or if the testimony of the alien is needed. The bill further listed fourteen classes of deportables[124] and

[122]One of them, H.R. 10409, was the first immigration bill introduced by a Representative from New York, Fiorello LaGuardia.

[123]H.R. 10469, Aswell (La.); H.R. 10606, Hayden (Ariz.); H.R. 11887, Johnson (Wash.).

[124]The deportable classes, briefly described, were aliens who (1) at time of entry were excludable, (2) entered at an undesignated place or by fraud, (3) remained longer than the terms of admission, (4) became a public charge from causes not shown to have arisen after entry, (5) suffer from mental defect, constitutional psychopathic inferiority, or chronic alcoholism, (6) are convicted and sentenced to imprisonment for one year or more, (7) are sentenced on different convictions to a total of eighteen months of imprisonment or more, (8) are convicted of violation of the Prohibition Act to a cumulative total of one year or more, (9) were convicted of or admit commission prior to entry of a crime involving moral turpitude, (10) are convicted under the white slave act or narcotics acts, (11) are of an immoral class as defined by law, (12) conceal an alien liable to deportation, (13) assist an alien to enter unlawfully, (14) are employed on a coastwise vessel without having been admitted for permanent residence.

put no time limit on deportability. The House passed the bill on February 10, 1925 by vote of 213 to 39, but it was not acted on by the Senate committee.

69th Congress (1925–1927)

The first session of the 69th Congress, convening on December 7, 1925, received the greatest flood of immigration bills yet faced by any session of Congress, but took only limited action. The principal topics of these proposals for new legislation were amendment of the 1917 and 1924 acts, including repeal of the national origins quota system, the regulation of aliens in the United States, the admission of certain relatives, special provisions for alien veterans, Western Hemisphere immigration, and deportation.

Five bills called for amendment of the 1917 Act, of which two concerned sections 24 and 26, dealing with administrative aspects of the act—the appointment and classes of immigrant inspectors and certain facilities at immigrant stations. Fifty-nine or more bills were introduced to amend the 1924 Act, twenty-three of which were introduced in the Senate and the rest in the House. Fully half, thirty to be exact, were designated for the amendment of section 4 defining the nonquota classes. A number of the bills to amend section 4 were from Senator Copeland of New York. The only one of his proposals to be acted on was in the form of a joint resolution (S. J. Res. 82) to amend section 4(a) concerning nonquota classes, to make it read

> (a) an immigrant who is the unmarried child under eighteen years of age, or the wife, or the husband, of a citizen of the United States who resides therein at the time of the filing of a petition under section 9.

Introduced on March 26, 1926, the resolution was reported back without amendment on June 9 and passed by the Senate on July 1.[125] Because the session ended two days later, the resolution was not acted on in the House until the second session of the 69th Congress. It was then reported out by the House committee (H. Rept. 1965 [69-II]), with amendment including revision of section 4(c) concerning Western Hemisphere nonquota status. The amended resolution was debated in the House on March 2, 1927,[126] amended, and passed, but it died in conference.

Another bill for amendment of section 4 of the 1924 Act to be dealt with in Congress was H.R. 6238 from Bacon of New York. It was to add the following subsection to the list of nonquota classes:

[125] *Congressional Record,* 67:12535–36.

[126] Ibid., 68:5435–40.

(f) A woman who was a citizen of the United States by birth and who prior to September 22, 1922, lost her citizenship by reason of her marriage to an alien.

Reported back without amendment,[127] it was passed by the House on April 5, 1926, transmitted to the Senate, and there reported back with amendment on April 14, then brought up for debate on April 29[128] but not acted on further until the second session. In that session, it came up again for debate on December 14, 1926 and was amended with the Wadsworth amendment that added a new subsection (g) to give nonquota status also to the wife or unmarried child under eighteen years of an alien legally admitted prior to July 1, 1924 and who had declared his intention to become a citizen, but with the proviso that those so applying for nonquota status have a valid unexpired nonquota immigration visa and that the number of persons so admitted shall not exceed 35,000. So amended, the bill was passed by the Senate[129] but failed of approval by the House.

There were bills for amendment of other sections of the 1924 Act —four bills called for repeal of the national origins quota system,[130] and the remaining twenty bills were simply designated as being for amendment of the 1924 Act.

Several bills gave attention to the resident alien population of the United States. Two called for the registration of such aliens (H.R. 102 and 5583, Aswell [La.]). One bill concerned the education and naturalization of aliens (S. 680, McKellar [Tenn.]), and another was to legalize the residence of certain aliens in the United States (H.R. 8194, Sosnowski [Mich.]). Others were for regulation of the employment of aliens by the federal government and the better protection of aliens together with enforcement of their treaty rights (S. 4024, Blease [S.C.]; H.R. 7573, Weller [N.Y.]). Johnson of Washington was the author of a House resolution proposing an amendment of the Constitution to declare that persons born in the United States of ineligible alien parentage shall not be eligible to citizenship (H. J. Res. 23).

Six bills sought to facilitate the admission of relatives of American citizens. Two of these were for the admission of the wives of citizens without reference to date of marriage, condition of quota, or other provisions of the immigration laws (S. 983, Copeland [N.Y.]; H.R. 5820, Doyle [Ill.]). Another two would admit certain alien wives and children of

[127]H. Rept. 659, March 25, 1926 (69-I).

[128]*Congressional Record,* 67:8423.

[129]Ibid., 68:427.

[130]S. J. Res. 114, Copeland (N.Y.); H.R. 12520, 12567, Sabath (Ill.); H. J. Res. 250, Douglass (Mass.).

American citizens as nonquota immigrants (S. 2358, King [Utah]; H.R. 6544, Dyer [Mo.]); and one was to exempt from quota the husbands, parents, and children under eighteen years of age of citizens, and the wives of declarants (H.R. 3757, Dickstein [N.Y.]). These were not acted on, but action was taken on a bill amending section 4 of the 1924 Act to provide for the admission of the wife and children under eighteen of alien ministers and professors who entered the United States before July 1, 1924 (H.R. 10661, Dickstein [N.Y.]). Reported out in House Report 650 (69-I), it was passed by the House, amended in the Senate on motion by Reed of Pennsylvania to limit the application of the bill to relatives arriving before July 1, 1927,[131] passed by the Senate, approved in its amended form by the House, and then signed by the President as the Act of July 3, 1926 (44 Stat. 812).

Eight bills concerning alien veterans were introduced during the first session of the 69th Congress. Five of them dealt with the immigration and naturalization of such aliens.[132] Another, by Fish of New York, was to give nonquota status for veterans of the World War together with their wives and unmarried children (H.R. 9973), and two from Wadsworth of New York and Tilson of Connecticut were to authorize the Shipping Board to give a preference rate to alien veterans and their families (S. 4419, H.R. 12659). Of the latter, the Senate bill by Wadsworth of New York was passed by both Senate and House, and signed into law by the President.

Action was also taken on the Bacon bill to facilitate the immigration and naturalization of alien veterans. Reported back in the House (H. Rept. 382 [69-I]), it was passed there, then reported with amendment (S. Rept. 566 [69-I]) and passed in the Senate. With House agreement to the amendment and presidential signature, the bill became the Act of May 26, 1926 (44 Stat. 654). It gave nonquota status to any alien who served in the armed forces after April 5, 1917 and before November 12, 1918, who was honorably discharged, not ineligible to citizenship, and not a member of certain excludable classes.[133] Nonquota status was also extended to the veteran's unmarried children under eighteen, wife or husband if accompanying or following within six months. Other sections of the act limited its application to veterans applying within one year after enactment, and exempted the veteran from deportation on becoming a public charge.

It was especially to deportation that Congress gave attention during

[131]*Congressional Record,* 67:12535.

[132]S. 2608, Reed (Pa.); H.R. 7968, Johnson (S.D.); H.R. 9761, Bacon (N.Y.); H.R. 10603, 11208, Tilson (Conn.).

[133]The excludable classes were persons afflicted with a loathsome or dangerous contagious disease excepting tuberculosis, polygamists, of an immoral class, contract laborers, previously deported, or convicted of a crime.

the session, and nine bills dealing variously with the subject plus one substitute bill were introduced. Bills by Hayden of Arizona and Taylor of Colorado provided for the punishment of deported aliens who return (H.R. 3748, 6523). One dealt with the deportation of certain alien seamen,[134] and six were to provide for the deportation of certain aliens.[135] Of these, the second of two bills introduced by Holaday of Illinois was reported out without amendment, but with a minority report by Sabath, also of Illinois (H. Rept. 991 [69-I], parts 1 and 2). The bill was later withdrawn and a substitute of the same title and purpose was introduced, H.R. 12444.

The substituted bill, "practically identical" with the preceding bill was reported out with majority and minority reports (H. Rept. 1348 [69-I], parts 1 and 2), themselves practically identical with the preceding reports. The principal change was that the substitute bill eliminated certain provisions regarding alien seamen that the minority at least felt would weaken deportation powers with regard to seamen. The majority rebuttal was that the problem of alien seamen would be dealt with in another bill; and the bill itself provided for repeal of section 34 of the 1917 Act that had put a three-year limit on the deportability of alien seamen for unlawful entry. This would put the alien seamen on the same basis as other aliens who entered illegally.

The bill, to be called the Deportation Act of 1926 if passed, was chiefly designed to extend and revise the deportation provisions of section 19 of the 1917 Act. Numerous changes in detail were proposed, but the principal changes noted below show the direction of thinking of the committee with regard to deportation:

1. Removal of the existing limitations on deportation for illegal entry to within three years of such entry and to entry by water only.

2. Deportation at any time after entry, subject to certain conditions, of a temporarily admitted alien who stays longer than authorized (supplement to a similar provision in section 14 of the Act of October 16, 1924).

3. Increase from five to seven years after entry of the period within which an alien, by becoming a public charge or being found to have mental defect or chronic alcoholism, "from causes not affirmatively shown to have arisen subsequent of entry," becomes deportable at any time after entry.[136]

4. Definition of a criminal offense that gives deportability in terms

[134] S. 3574, King (Utah), passed in the second session but not acted on in the House.

[135] H.R. 344, 11250, Johnson (Wash.); H.R. 3774, 11489, Holaday (Ill.); H.R. 11054, Manlove (Mo.); H.R. 11945, Sabath (Ill.).

[136] Deportability for such cause was limited to within five years after entry, under section 19 of the 1917 Act.

of length of sentence only, one year or more, and elimination of the further condition that the offense involve moral turpitude.

5. Increase from five to ten years after entry of the time within which the commission of designated offenses renders an alien deportable.

6. A new deportable class of aliens who are habitual criminals, defined as having cumulative sentences totaling eighteen or more months of imprisonment for offenses committed after the enactment of the bill and within ten years of entry.

7. Some expansion and strengthening of the deportation provisions against the immoral and narcotics classes of aliens.

8. Deportation at any time after entry of an alien who willfully conceals or otherwise aids an alien liable to deportation, or who willfully aids an alien to enter unlawfully.

An appended minority report by Sabath of Illinois argued that the 1917 and 1924 acts were adequate and that the problem was one of enforcement. He noted further that the new bill did not reach some undesirable classes such as professional gamblers and that it was too harsh on others such as public charges.

Debated in the House on June 7, 1926, the bill was defended in particular by Johnson of Washington, who argued that stronger deportation laws were needed to reinforce the immigration laws. Passed by the House, 138 to 28,[137] the bill went to the Senate, where no further action was taken.

A few other bills on various topics were introduced during the first session of the 69th Congress. These included a resolution authorizing the President to use the Army, Navy, and militia to suppress the smuggling in of alcohol, narcotics, and aliens (H. J. Res. 5, Blanton [Tex.]), a bill to permit the coming of aliens in excess of quota when the quota for the preceding year had not been exhausted (H.R. 190, Lindsay [N.Y.]), and three bills to establish a Border Patrol for better law enforcement (S. 3411, Jones [Wash.]; H.R. 8837, 9731, Hudson [Mich.]). There was a bill to create a commission on immigration policy (H.R. 3875, Kelly [Pa.]), and another that proposed to extend the 1924 Act to set quotas for Western Hemisphere countries (H.R. 6741, Box [Tex.]). Finally, two bills were to exempt from quota provisions the Spanish citizens resident in Puerto Rico at the time of the American occupation (H.R. 5838, 11204, Davila, delegate from Puerto Rico). One of the latter was reported out by the House Committee on Immigration and Naturalization (H. Rept. 927 [69-I]), passed by the House and Senate,

[137] *Congressional Record,* 67:10870.

and signed by the President. This was the Act of May 26, 1926 (44 Stat. 657).

The second session of the 69th Congress convened on December 6, 1926 and adjourned at the customary time of March 4, 1927, during which term only moderate numbers of immigration bills were introduced. Further congressional action was limited to consideration of three bills from the preceding session as already noted above, and the passage of an act to postpone the introduction of the national origins quota system.

Most numerous were the bills for amendment of the 1924 Quota Act, eighteen in all. Various sections of the 1924 Act were designated for amendment, most frequently section 6, which dealt with preference under quota, and section 11 for the allocation of quotas. Among the measures concerning quotas were resolutions by Johnson of California and Jacobstein of New York (S. J. Res. 152, H. J. Res. 337). Quota-related bills were to admit all persons having duly visaed passports prior to July 1, 1924, to exempt certain relatives of citizens and declarants from the quota, and to do the same for certain alien veterans and their families.[138] A House bill by Harrison of Virginia was to permit persons engaged in agriculture to enter in excess of quota (H.R. 17036), and one by Johnson of Washington was to provide for the reduction of immigration quotas (H.R. 17407).

On February 1, 1927 the Senate took up the joint resolution to amend sections 11(b) and 11(e) of the 1924 Act in order to postpone the effective date of the national origin quotas by one year to July 1, 1928. It was passed without record vote.[139] Of interest with regard to the authorship of the national origin basis for quotas was a remark made by Senator Reed of Pennsylvania during Senate Immigration Committee hearings on December 22, 1926:

> The idea, whether a good one or a bad one, I think, originated with myself. Trevor had never heard the suggestion.[140]

Other bills introduced during the session but not acted on were one to define certain aliens as undesirable and deportable (H.R. 15535, Miller [Wash.]), another for the deportation of an alien who fails to maintain his

[138]H.R. 13468, 13469, and 13470, Dickstein (N.Y.); H.R. 15548, Dyer (Mo.).

[139]*Congressional Record,* 68:2682. This was the Act of March 4, 1927 (44 Stat. 1455).

[140]Ibid., p. 2668. The Trevor referred to is John B. Trevor, whose paper, "Preliminary Study of Immigration Problems," was inserted in the *Congressional Record* of April 3, 1924, pp. 5469–71, by Senator Reed. In the paper Trevor urged that quotas be based on "racial analysis of the population of the United States," included a table showing the estimated national origin composition of the population, and stated that the computation was based on Reed's amendment of H.R. 6540 (68-I).

wife or minor children living abroad (H.R. 17035, Dickstein [N.Y.]), three to provide for the registration of certain classes of aliens (H.R. 16115, 16648, Holaday [Ill.]; H.R. 16767, Brand [Ga.]), and a resolution by Johnson to create a commission to study the immigration and naturalization laws (H. J. Res. 342). The only legislative accomplishment of the session relating to immigration remained the postponement of the national origins quotas by one year.

70th Congress (1927–1929)

As in the preceding Congress, the 70th Congress in its first session received a heavy load of proposals for new legislation on immigration. As before, the greatest number of the bills introduced during the session were for amendment of the 1924 Quota Act, but it was on the development of a deportation bill that Congress labored especially.

Before these areas of particular legislative activity are described, there are several other groups of immigration or immigration-related bills to be noted. A variety of bills concerned resident aliens. There were two bills to legalize the entry of certain classes of resident aliens, one of which specified that they be eligible to citizenship (S. 3630, Wheeler [Mont.]; H.R. 12237, Bloom [N.Y.]). One bill provided for the registration of aliens (H.R. 5473, Aswell [La.]); another concerned the reentry of aliens who had gone abroad for a temporary visit (H.R. 13785, Sabath [Ill.]). Senate bills dealt with the naturalization and education of aliens and their children (S. 845, McKellar [Tenn.]), and with the voting of those who had become naturalized (S. 783, Blease [S.C.]). A resolution was introduced in the House proposing amendment of the Constitution to exclude aliens in the counting of population for the apportionment of representation in Congress (H. J. Res. 102, Stalker [N.Y.]); and there was a Senate bill to regulate the employment of aliens by the government.[141]

The admission of relatives of citizens and declarants was dealt with by another group of measures, ten or more in number. Two were designed to give nonquota status to alien wives and children of citizens (S. 2271, King [Utah]; H.R. 6974, Dyer [Mo.]). Another bill (H.R. 6998, Dickstein [N.Y.]) added parents and husbands, and a fourth extended the same benefit to wives and children under eighteen of declarants (H.R.

[141]S. 780, Blease (S.C.). At the same time Senator Blease introduced a bill requiring separate accommodations for white and colored passengers on street cars in the District of Columbia and a bill prohibiting intermarriage between certain races.

7000, Dickstein). Two concerned the relatives of citizens and lawfully admitted aliens.[142] Three joint resolutions permit admission "within the quota" of certain relatives of declarants who had been admitted to the United States prior to July 1, 1924.[143] A joint resolution from Senator Copeland of New York was designed to grant preference in the issuance of immigration visas to the wives and minor children of declarants. This last measure, the only one to be acted on among the bills concerning relatives, was reported out with amendment by the Senate committee (S. Rept. 245 [70-I]), debated, amended further, and passed by the Senate. In the House it was reported with amendment by the committee (H. Rept. 1539 [70-I]), amended further, and then passed. The Senate disagreeing, the revised bill went to conference. With the conference report accepted (H. Rept. 1918 [70-I]) and with presidential signature, the bill became the Act of May 29, 1928 (45 Stat. 1009).

The act established a new nonquota class by adding the following subsection to section 4 of the 1924 Act:

> (f) A woman who was a citizen of the United States and who prior to September 22, 1922, lost her citizenship by reason of her marriage to an alien, but at the time of her application for an immigration visa is unmarried.

Section 6 of the 1924 Act was also amended to revise the preference categories to give one-half of the quota of each nationality to (A) parents or the husbands by marriage occurring after May 31, 1928 of citizens aged twenty-one and over; and (B) for countries with quotas of 300 or more, immigrants skilled in agriculture, with their wives and dependent children under eighteen. Preference in the remaining quota plus any unused balance under the first preference was then to be given to the unmarried children under twenty-one and the wives of lawfully admitted alien residents. Any unused balance would go to other quota immigrants.

Seven bills to facilitate the immigration of alien veterans and their families were also introduced. One was to permit citizen veterans of the World War to bring in wives who had committed petty offenses during legal infancy (H.R. 13514, Tilson [Conn.]). Another would grant nonquota status to the widows of veterans of the World War killed in action (H.R. 12876, Rogers [Mass.]). A Senate resolution was to give nonquota status to children under twenty-one of gold star mothers (S. J. Res. 81,

[142]H.R. 12626, 12816, Jenkins (Ohio). The latter bill was reported out (H. Rept. 1317) and discussed but not acted on.

[143]S. J. Res. 122, Walsh (Mass.); H. J. Res. 233, 234, MacGregor (N.Y.).

Copeland [N.Y.]). Other bills variously proposed to aid the immigration of alien veterans and their families.[144]

Western Hemisphere immigration also received a share of attention. Two of the bills introduced for the amendment of the 1924 Act would have extended the quota system to include Western Hemisphere countries, one by applying quota limits to the immigration from all countries except those barred by the 1924 Act (H.R. 10995, Allgood [Ala.]) and the other by specifically applying quotas to Mexico, Cuba, Canada, and the countries of continental America and adjacent islands (H.R. 6465, Box [Tex.]). Another bill concerned Puerto Rican immigration (H.R. 10956, Davila [P.R.]). There was a bill to subject certain immigrants born in the Western Hemisphere to quotas (S. 1437, Harris [Ga.]), and there were Senate and House bills to exempt American Indians born in Canada from the 1924 Act (S. 716, King [Utah]; H.R. 11351, MacGregor [N.Y.]). The Senate bill was amended and passed in both the Senate and the House and signed to become the Act of April 2 1928 (45 Stat. 401). It provided that the 1924 Act was not to be construed to limit the right of American Indians to cross the border, but with the proviso that the right does not extend to members of Indian tribes by adoption.

Topics of lesser concern were represented by two bills for the admission of Chinese wives of certain American citizens (S. 3442, Walsh [Mass.]; H.R. 12034, Houston [Hawaii]) and one related to the enforcement of the contract labor provisions in the 1917 Act (H. J. Res. 312, Johnson [Wash.]).

A number of bills concerned the regulation of immigration in one manner or another. There were bills for the issuance of certificates of arrival to immigrants (H.R. 12768, MacGregor [N.Y.]), for the keeping of records of arrival of certain immigrants (H.R. 13714, Sabath [Ill.]; H.R. 13793, Schneider [Wis.]), and for the recording of certain information about immigrants (H.R. 9828, Brand [Ga.]). Blanton of Texas again brought forward a resolution authorizing the President to use the Army, Navy, and militia to prevent the smuggling in of alcohol, narcotics, and aliens (H. J. Res. 6), and another representative from Texas proposed a bill to increase the Border Patrol for better enforcement of the immigration laws (H.R. 11982, Hudspeth [Tex.]). Representatives from New York introduced bills to permit certain aliens to come to the United States when the quotas for their countries for the preceding year had not been exhausted, or if they were in possession of visaed passports prior to July 1, 1924 (H.R. 6672, Lindsay [N.Y.]; H.R. 6999, Dickstein [N.Y.]). John-

[144]H.R. 385, Dyer (Mo.); H.R. 8273, Schafer (Wis.); H.R. 11403, Bacon (N.Y.); H.R. 13066, Tilson (Conn.).

son of Washington introduced bills to provide for the seizure and forfeiture of vehicles used in violation of the immigration laws and to authorize the refund of visa fees in certain cases.[145] And several other bills concerned amendment of the immigration laws without specification of the particular sections in question (S. 3019, Watson [Ind.]; H.R. 13756, Langley [Ky.]).

Amendment of the 1917 Act was called for by five bills that mainly or entirely dealt with administrative sections of the act. It was the 1924 Act, however, that was the principal target for amendment by over forty bills and three or four resolutions, plus an additional three measures dealing specifically with the national origins quotas. As previously noted, two or three bills would subject Western Hemisphere immigration to quota limitation. The various bills dealt with many sections of the act, but most frequently designated for amendment were sections 4, 6, and 11, dealing respectively with nonquota status, quota preference, and the quota formula. Johnson (Wash.) introduced a bill to reduce immigration quotas (H.R. 166). More drastic were two bills to suspend all immigration until January 1, 1935, to deport aliens who withdrew their declarations of intention in order to avoid military service and those illegally in the country, to punish those who violate the immigration laws, and to permit emergency farm and ranch labor to come from Canada and Mexico on a temporary basis (H.R. 30, 8827, Blanton [Tex.]). Two other bills were to abolish the not yet introduced national origins quota provisions of the 1924 Act (S. 2920, Walsh [Mass.]; H.R. 11271, Goodwin [Minn.]). A joint resolution in the Senate (S. J. Res. 113, Johnson [Calif.]) called for a postponement of the national origins quotas by one year. Introduced on March 14, 1928,[146] the resolution was passed by the Senate, reported out in the House (H. Rept. 1027[70-I]), passed,[147] and signed to become the Act of March 31, 1928 (45 Stat. 400). The introduction of the national origins quotas was thereby postponed to July 1, 1929, the reasons given for the postponement being that the computation of the new quotas was "indefinite and uncertain" and that the experts working on the quotas wanted more time.

One further bill for amendment of the 1924 Act received a measure of attention, this being a bill by Senator Reed of Pennsylvania. Reported out with amendment, the committee report described the bill as being

> to remove the requirement that persons permitted to enter the United States for the purpose of teaching shall have been actively

[145]H.R. 169, 12407. The latter was reported out of committee (H. Rept. 1061), debated, amended, and passed by the House but not acted on in the Senate.

[146]*Congressional Record,* 69:4669.

[147]Ibid., p. 5579.

engaged as teachers for two years immediately preceding their application for admission.[148]

It had been found that the existing act prevented admission of those who had been doing special research work. The Senate committee amendment added the requirement that the institution of learning receiving the teacher agree to report to the Secretary of Labor the termination of employment of the teacher. On further recommendation of the committee, the original bill was also amended to limit it to colleges and other institutions approved by the Secretary of Labor. So amended the bill was passed by the Senate,[149] but made no progress in the House.

Deportation was the other topic of congressional concern, and seven bills were introduced to provide variously for the deportation of certain aliens,[150] certain alien seamen (S. 717, King [Utah]), and any alien who fails to maintain his wife or minor child living abroad.[151] A final bill of this group, by Tarver of Georgia (H.R. 5688), was to extend the provisions of the existing deportation laws and to define the manufacture and sale of intoxicants as a crime involving moral turpitude (and therefore grounds for deportation).

The only bill of this group to be acted on was the second of the two bills introduced by Johnson of Washington, H.R. 10078. Entered in the House on January 26, 1928, it went to committee and was reported back (H. Rept. 484 [70-I]). Referred to as the Deportation Act of 1928, the bill was practically identical with the deportation bill passed by the House in the 69th Congress (H.R. 12444 [69-I]). The new bill would amend section 19 of the 1917 Act to designate twelve deportable classes, just as in the preceding bill and with only certain changes in the period of liability to deportation.[152] The bill did not progress in the House, in spite of the earlier acceptance of a similar measure.

The second session of the 70th Congress, convening on December 3, 1928, was presented with a wide range of bills related to immigration, but labored especially to develop a deportation bill and to further regulate immigration.

There were a number of bills to amend the basic immigration acts

[148]S. Rept. 244 (70-I), on S. 2450.

[149]Congressional Record, 69:3428.

[150]H.R. 3, 10078, Johnson (Wash.); H.R. 5673, Sabath (Ill.); H.R. 6069, Holaday (Ill.).

[151]H.R. 6997, Dickstein (N.Y.): evidently the same bill as his H.R. 17035 in the second session of the preceding Congress.

[152]See description of H.R. 12444 in the 69th Congress. In deportable classes (2) and (3) the new bill increased the period of deportability of those entering before July 1, 1924 from three to five years after entry, decreased from seven to five years after entry the period of liability for classes (4) and (5), and for class (8) increased from eighteen months to two years the cumulative terms of imprisonment leading to deportability.

of 1917 and 1924. Two or more bills were to amend the 1917 Act.[153] Seven bills and resolutions called directly for amendment of the 1924 Act,[154] and other bills concerned the national origins quota and non-quota classes of the 1924 Act. Two of the amending bills concerned subdivisions (b) and (e), section 11 of the 1924 Act, which provided for the national origins quotas and designating the Secretaries of Labor and Commerce and the Attorney General to determine the quotas. Two resolutions were introduced in the House to postpone the introduction of the national origins quotas (H. J. Res. 402, 423, Chindblom [Ill.]). One of the resolutions was reported out (H. Rept. 2811 [70-II]) and passed by the House, but not considered in the Senate.

Also involving amendment of the 1924 Act was a Senate bill concerning Western Hemisphere immigration introduced in the first session and reported out with amendment by the Senate committee in the second session.[155] The committee amendment was to strike out the body of the bill and substitute a new section to delete "The Republic of Mexico" from the Western Hemisphere countries given nonquota status by section 4(c) of the 1924 Act. This action was apparently motivated by the problem of illegal entry from Mexico; but the action was effectively opposed by the Senators from the sugar-beet growing states and the bill was passed over.

Amendment of the 1924 Act was also contemplated in two bills by Free of California, "granting preference within the quota to certain aliens trained and skilled in a particular art, craft, technique, business, or science" (H.R. 16880, 16926). The latter of his two bills, introduced on February 6, 1929,[156] was reported back with amendment the following day (H. Rept. 2400 [70-II]), debated in the House,[157] and passed on February 15.[158] Free's original bill would have brought in skilled workers outside of quota, but the committee amended the bill by substituting quota preference in place of nonquota status. So amended, the bill changed section 6(a)(1) of the 1924 Act to add a third class eligible to share in the first 50 percent preference. The original first class (A) remained as certain specified relatives, the original second class of skilled agricultural laborers became the third class (C), and the new class was designated as follows:

[153] H.R. 15079, Houston (Hawaii); plus one or more of the deportation bills.

[154] S. 5447, Metcalf (R.I.); S. 5451, Copeland (N.Y.); S. J. Res. 192, Nye (N.D.); H.R. 14666, 14667, Dickstein (N.Y.); H.R. 15969, Free (Calif.); H. J. Res. 402, Chindblom (Ill.).

[155] S. 1437 (70-I); S. Rept. 1343 (70-II).

[156] *Congressional Record*, 70:2963.

[157] Ibid., p. 3533.

[158] Ibid., p. 3542.

(B) Quota immigrants who, being trained and skilled in a particular art, craft, technique, business, or science, are needed by bona fide employers to engage in work to perform which persons so trained and skilled can not be found unemployed in the United States, and the wives, and the dependent children under the age of twenty-one years of such immigrants.

Referred in the Senate to the Committee on Immigration, the bill made no further progress.

Miscellaneous bills dealt with manifesting requirements (H.R. 14464, Houston [Hawaii]), a commission for the study of the immigration and naturalization laws (H. J. Res. 435, Johnson [Wash.]), and the issuance of certificates of admission or arrival (S. 5093, Blease [S.C.]; S. 5892, Hayden [Ariz.]). Deportation was the subject of only three House bills, of which one was acted on. The first of the deportation bills to be introduced in the House during the second session was by Fish of New York, to amend section 19 of the 1917 Act to provide for the deportation of an alien convicted under the Harrison narcotics act and its amendments (H.R. 15272). It went to committee but was not reported out. Johnson of Washington introduced two bills for the deportation of certain aliens and for punishment of unlawful entry by aliens (H.R. 16567 and 16850). The second of his bills was reported back unamended by the committee on February 6, 1929 (H. Rept. 2397[70-II]). As explained in the accompanying report, the bill added seven new classes of deportables, with the proviso that deportation take place only if, after hearings, the Secretary of Labor decides that the alien is an undesirable resident of the United States. As defined in the bill, the seven classes were:

1. An alien who hereafter violates or conspires to violate the white slave traffic act,

2. An alien who violates or conspires to violate any statute concerning drug traffic,

3. An alien who wilfully conceals . . . any alien liable to deportation,

4. Any alien who wilfully aids or assists in any way any alien unlawfully to enter the United States,

5. An alien who enters at other than a designated place or gains entry through false representations, etc.

6. Any alien sentenced to a term of one year or more, and thereafter sentenced to another term of one year or more,

7. An alien who is convicted of any offense (committed after the enactment of this act and within ten years after entry) and sentenced to a term which added to other sentences amounts to two years or more.

The bill was not acted on further in this form by the House, but was revived later in the session as noted below.

Certain bills for the regulation of immigration appeared in the House and Senate. A House bill by Johnson (Wash.) concerned the immigration and naturalization of certain citizens of islands under the jurisdiction of the United States (H.R. 16392). Two House bills by Box (Tex.) were designed to clarify the law relating to the temporary admission of aliens (H.R. 16851 and 16927). The second of the two was reported back (H. Rept. 2401 [70-II]) with the explanation that a recent court decision had greatly broadened the interpretation of temporary admission, far beyond the intent of Congress, and that the bill was to correct this interpretation. Passed by the House, the bill was not acted on by the Senate. In the Senate a bill was entered to amend the 1924 Act with regard to the issuance of immigration visas, was reported back,[159] and passed by the Senate.[160] It was not considered by the House.

The one other regulatory bill in the Senate was to make it a felony for previously deported aliens to enter the United States and to prescribe the penalties for so entering (S. 5094, Blease [S.C.]). It was reported out with amendment on January 17, 1929 (S. Rept. 1456 [70-II]), the committee amendments being changes of wording rather than of the substance of the bill.[161] On January 23 it was passed in amended form by the Senate[162] and forwarded to the House. There it was reported out by the House committee on February 7 (H. Rept. 2418 [70-II]), debated on two successive days,[163] amended and passed. The House committee amendment was to strike out the body of the Senate bill and substitute the text of the Johnson bill just reported out by the committee (see above), to add seven classes of deportables. In the course of debate in the House, Sabath (Ill.) twice offered an amendment to reduce from ten to five years the period of deportability after entry of an alien sentenced to a total of two years or more.[164] The amendment was rejected.[165] On behalf of the committee its chairman, Johnson (Wash.), offered two amendments, both accepted. The first added an eighth deportable class consisting of aliens convicted of carrying any weapon or bomb and sentenced for a term of six months or more.[166] The second added a ninth deportable class, aliens convicted of violation of the prohibition law for which a sentence of one

[159]S. 5472, Stephens (Miss.), with S. Rept. 1841 (70-II).

[160]*Congressional Record,* 70:4718.

[161]As the committee explained in S. Rept. 1456, the 1917 and 1924 acts provided no other penalty than redeportation for the previously deported alien who returns.

[162]*Congressional Record,* 70:2092.

[163]Ibid., pp. 3542, 3614, February 15 and 16, 1929.

[164]Deportable class 7 in the Johnson bill, H.R. 16850.

[165]*Congressional Record,* 70:3549.

[166]Ibid., p. 3547, February 15, 1929.

year or more is received.[167] A number of other amendments were offered but not accepted. So amended, the bill was passed by the House and then went to conference after both Senate and House insisted on their amendments. The conference report, House Report 2802 (70-II), was accepted and the bill was signed to become the Act of March 4, 1929 (45 Stat. 1551).

The conference report recommended "That the Senate recede from its disagreement to the amendment of the House and agree to the same with an amendment." With this face-saving preface, the amendment was in fact to strike out the body of the House substitute and insert a new draft in five sections, incorporating the substance of the original Senate bill. Specifically, the conference bill contained three principal provisions regarding deportation, to make the reentry of a previously deported alien a felony punishable by fine or imprisonment or both, to make entry by an alien at other than a designated place or by fraud to be a misdemeanor punishable in the same manner, and to provide that deportation of an alien sentenced to imprisonment shall not take place until termination of the imprisonment.

Comment

The years from 1913 to 1929, spanned by the 63rd to the 70th Congresses, were a period of legislative search and development in the formulation of policy to meet the yet unsolved old problems and the emerging new problems of immigration. It was during this period that immigration law crystallized into the form it was to maintain for many years to come and in many respects still maintains. The period began on the eve of the First World War and near the end of the great wave of migration from Europe; it saw the final triumph of the long-continued campaign, both in and out of Congress, for restriction; and the 70th Congress closed only a few months before the introduction of the much postponed national origins quota system. Only shortly thereafter came the onset of the Depression, which was to bring new problems and a new chapter in American immigration history.

The principal objective of legislative work on immigration during the years in question was restriction of immigration. Within months after President Taft had vetoed a literacy test bill in early 1913, the next Congress began work on a new bill of similar content, but was checked

167Ibid., pp. 3616–17, February 16, 1929.

again by President Wilson's veto, the third successful veto of a literacy test bill. An even stronger bill, which is to say more restrictive in its provisions, was developed in the next Congress, received another veto from President Wilson, but was passed over his veto to become the Immigration Act of 1917.

Long regarded by the restrictionists as the most effective means for the selection and restriction of immigration, the literacy test in practice was found no barrier to mass immigration under the conditions of the immediate postwar period. Faced with the prospect of a new flood of immigrants as soon as transatlantic shipping could be restored in volume, Congress resorted to another mode of restriction that had been considered by the Dillingham Commission but rejected then in favor of the literacy test. This was a system of national quotas determined as a percentage of the number of immigrants from the country in question at a designated census. First considering a quota of 5 percent of the 1910 census base, Congress reduced the quota to 3 percent, passed the bill in that form in early 1921, and met a veto from President Wilson that was not overridden. With a new Congress and Chief Executive, a similar bill was promptly passed later in the same year, the Immigration Act of 1921, the original quota act that set national quotas at 3 percent of the 1910 base.

As soon as passed, the 1921 Act became the target of proposals to amend and repeal. Originally due to expire at midyear of 1922, it was extended for two more years, to June 30, 1924. With the expiration date approaching and continued fears of heavy immigration, Congress passed the 1924 Act, which reduced national quotas to 2 percent of the 1890 base population and provided that beginning on July 1, 1927 the quota limit would be 150,000, allocated on the basis of the estimated national origins distribution of the population of continental United States in 1920. Twice postponed, the national origins quotas became effective on July 1, 1929.

In thus moving toward greater and greater numerical limitation of immigration with the literacy test, the addition of a percentage quota, and then the substitution of the lower national origins quota in place of the percentage quota, Congress had brushed aside the delaying tactics of the antirestrictionists, had doubled the head tax from four to eight dollars, and had ignored the many proposals to repeal the literacy test and to repeal or raise the quota limits on immigration. But Congress had also ignored the numerous bills for the complete suspension of immigration for various periods of time.

At the same time, Congress had purposefully adjusted and modified the literacy test and quota provisions by granting various exemptions and nonquota (that is, free of quota) classes, especially for the benefit of designated relatives of citizens and resident aliens and for the benefit of veterans and their families. There was also the first development of certain modifying provisions used to increase the selectivity of quota immigration. This was the device of the quota preference classes, originally only two in number but added to later.

The 1917 Act and those that followed were designed to serve additional purposes besides restriction. The list of excludable classes of aliens was considerably extended by the 1917 Act in addition to the literacy test, and the trend of legislation was toward more exclusions. The legal ground for deportation was also expanded during the period in question, the time of deportability after entry was lengthened, and for certain classes it was proposed to set no time limit on deportability. In the years immediately preceding 1929 the House and its Committee on Immigration and Naturalization labored to perfect and pass a deportation bill greatly increasing the number of deportable classes, but in spite of repeated attempts it failed to bring the bill to enactment.

There was some attention to war-related problems such as alien enemies, resident aliens who were thought to evade military service by withdrawing their first papers, and alien veterans, but these were temporary matters rather than long-range policy. What was an area of policy formation was that of exclusion by reason of origin or race. Chinese exclusion continued from the preceding century, and from time to time Congress received bills calling for broader racial exclusions. The 1917 Act contained the Asiatic barred zone provision prohibiting the admission for permanent residence of natives of the designated area; and this was continued in the Quota Act of 1921, which gave no quota to the peoples native to the area. Asiatic exclusion was extended further by the 1924 Act that ended the Gentlemen's Agreement with Japan by abruptly making eligibility to citizenship by naturalization a condition for admission for permanent residence.

In addition to the exclusion of some races was what might be called a policy of selective restriction of certain other peoples. Congress had definite preferences among the various sources of immigration and sought an admissions formula that would permit the entry of favored national groups and restrict immigration from other sources. It had been hoped that the literacy test would operate in such a differential fashion as well as restrictively. When the test was found to be neither as effective a barrier nor as selective as hoped, Congress turned to a system of national quotas based on the number of foreign-born from each country. This favored certain countries of origin over others, as desired, and the shift of the base year from 1910 to 1890 gave an even stronger differential in admissions between favored and disfavored nations. A temporary measure, this was followed by the national origins quota formula, which was designed to preserve the status quo in the composition of the American population.

Thus, by 1929, Congress had developed a quite highly evolved legislative structure for the regulation and numerical restriction of immigration, supplemented with the selective exclusion of certain classes of aliens and provision for the deportation of aliens considered undesirable. The legislative instruments for the control of immigration were therefore ready for use during the years of depression that were to follow.

6 The Depression Decade, 1929–1939

As a result of congressional efforts during the preceding years, the United States by the late 1920s was provided with an extensive body of legislation for the regulation and restriction of immigration. The new and more restrictive national origins quota system became effective on July 1, 1929, and together with it was the elaborate structure of nonquota, quota preference, exclusion, and deportation provisions that had accumulated through the preceding series of immigration acts. Built into the system, whether purposefully or not, was some latitude of administrative discretion that gave a degree of flexibility to the immigration law. Under the conditions and pressures of the Depression period, this flexibility could be and was used for the further limitation of immigration, especially the excludability of persons liable to become a public charge, which took on a different meaning with a depression; and since the instruments for such limitation were already at hand, little or no additional legislation of a basic policy-forming character was needed to meet the specialized problems of the Depression years.

71st Congress (1929–1931)

The majority of the immigration bills introduced in the first session of the 71st Congress concerned the 1924 Act. Eighteen or more bills and resolutions were for amendment of the act, the greater number of which referred to section 11 containing the national origins quota provision. An additional five or six bills were presumably for the outright repeal of the national origins method of establishing immigration quotas. None of the above bills came out of committee.

Amendments of other acts were also proposed, including the Immigration Act of 1917 (H.R. 1216, Houston [Hawaii]) and the very recently passed Act of March 4, 1929 that made it a felony to enter in violation of law.[1] Of the latter, the Johnson bill was the only immigration legislation to be passed during the session. This bill added to section 1(a) of

[1] S. 1537, Johnson (Calif.); S. 1608, King (Utah); H.R. 2020, Mooney (Ohio).

the 1929 Act the proviso that the act does not apply to any alien arrested and deported before March 4, 1929 provided the Secretary of Labor has granted such alien permission to reapply for admission. The bill was passed by the Senate on June 18, 1929. Taking up the bill the following day, the House accepted the Box (Tex.) amendment requiring that the action by the Secretary in granting permission to apply for readmission shall have been taken prior to March 4, 1929. The Senate accepted this limiting amendment, and the bill was signed by the President to become the Act of June 24, 1929 (46 Stat. 41).

Three bills were to revise preferences under the quota, one to remove the agricultural preference (S. 1455, Metcalf [R.I.]) and substitute another, the others to grant preference to "aliens trained and skilled in a particular art, craft, technique, business, or science" (S. 311, Edge [N.J.]; H.R. 3399, Letts [Iowa]). Of the three, only the first was reported out of committee, but not until the following session.

There were three bills dealing with deportation, of which two submitted by Senator King of Utah concerned alien seamen (S. 202, 1941); the third was for deportation of aliens convicted of violation of the Harrison narcotics law (H.R. 3394, Fish [N.Y.]). No action was taken on any of these at the time, but two of the three came up in the second session.

Several bills related to resident aliens, three being to authorize the issuance of certificates of admission on arrival;[2] and one bill was to regulate the voting of naturalized aliens (S. 1279, Blease [S.C.]). All remained in committee.

Various other bills introduced during the session and not acted on were to suspend all immigration (S. 890, Black [Ala.]), to give nonquota status to certain alien wives and children of citizens (H.R. 2404, Dyer [Mo.]), to give nonquota status to certain alien veterans and their families (H.R. 2409, Dyer [Mo.]), to amend the immigration laws as applied to Puerto Rico (H.R. 1912, Davila [P.R.]), and to subject natives of Western Hemisphere countries to immigration quotas (S. 51, Harris [Ga.]).

The long second session of the 71st Congress, which began on December 2, 1929 and lasted for seven months instead of the customary three, saw considerably more legislative activity on immigration. The distribution of concerns as represented by the new bills was much the same as in the first session, however, and several bills from the earlier session were brought up for further action.

Amendment of the Quota Act of 1924 was again a leading subject of the proposals for new legislation, with eleven or more general bills introduced for that purpose, not including bills specifically dealing with revi-

[2]S. 226, Hayden (Ariz.); S. 1278, Blease (S.C.); H.R. 961, Douglas (Ariz.).

sion of the preference and nonquota class provisions. With regard to preference within the quota, a bill similar in title to two entered in the preceding session proposed an occupational preference class consisting of "certain aliens trained and skilled in a particular art, craft, technique, business, or science" (H.R. 7258, Free [Calif.]). Another was to give preference to certain alien relatives of American citizens (H.R. 8758, Sirovich [N.Y.]), and a bill relating to preference classes from the first session was reported out by the Senate committee (S. 1455, Metcalf [R.I.], with S. Rept. 322). The bill would amend the 1924 Act to remove the agricultural preference and substitute immigrants coming to "engage in executive, administrative or supervisory work" if persons to fill such positions are not to be found unemployed in the United States. Passed by the Senate, the bill was not acted on in the House.

Nonquota status was variously proposed for American-born women (H.R. 11634, Evans [Calif.]) and for wives, husbands, parents, and children of American citizens.[3] Other bills were designed to facilitate the immigration of family members.[4]

Amendment of the recent Act of March 4, 1929 was also proposed, there being no less than eight such bills. The subject of deportation itself was treated in a Senate resolution,[5] and in two bills from the first session. Of the latter, the Fish bill (H. R. 3394) to amend section 19 of the 1917 Act by adding a new deportable class of aliens convicted of violation of the Harrison narcotics law and its amendments, was reported out, debated, amended, and passed by the House on July 3, 1930. It made no progress in the Senate until the next session. The Senate for its part passed and further discussed a deportation bill from the first session (S. 202), but attention to the bill in the House was postponed to the third session of the 71st Congress.

Miscellaneous bills dealt with varied aspects of the regulation of immigration. One would have authorized the admission of all aliens having duly visaed passports prior to July 1, 1924 (H.R. 5645, Dickstein [N.Y.]). Another was to establish a border patrol and to regulate the entry of aliens (H.R. 11204, Hudson [Mich.]). After being reported back, debated, amended, and passed by the House, the bill went to the Senate Committee on Commerce and remained there. An early women's rights bill would prohibit discrimination in the naturalization and immigration laws because of sex (H.R. 9405, Cable [Ohio]). There was a bill to require

[3]S. 3788, Gould (Me.); H.R. 5646, 11190, Dickstein (N.Y.); H.R. 11634, Evans (Calif.).

[4]H.R. 5648, Dickstein (N.Y.); H.R. 10524, Dyer (Mo.); H.R. 13257, Houston (Hawaii).

[5]S. J. Res. 153, Heflin (Ala.), "Relating to the deportation of certain aliens illegally in the United States."

the recording of certain information about immigrants (H.R. 8962, Brand [Ga.]), and another to regulate the issuance of visas during the next fiscal year, 1930–1931 (H.R. 13110, Johnson [Wash.]). Except as noted, the foregoing bills were not acted on.

More important in their policy implications and as indicators of the trend of thought were several bills to reduce immigration. Three bills were to limit the number of immigrants admitted,[6] and a House resolution would authorize the President to suspend immigration for a specified period (H. J. Res. 385, Cable [Ohio]). None was reported out by the House committee.

The sentiment in favor of reduced immigration also manifested itself in a renewal of concern about Western Hemisphere immigration as evidenced by several bills to control immigration from that source. Four new House bills on that subject, together with a Senate bill from the first session, were considered. Two bills by Box of Texas were to amend the Quota Act of 1924 to make it applicable to Mexico (H.R. 12341 and 12382). And Johnson of Washington likewise submitted two bills to provide quota limitations on immigration from certain countries of the Western Hemisphere (H.R. 10289 and 10343). The second of these was reported out, with a dissenting minority report attached.[7] The terms of the bill were to set the immigration quotas for Canada, Newfoundland, Mexico, and Cuba at four times the number of American citizens departing thereto for permanent residence during the fiscal year ending June 30, 1929; and for the other Western Hemisphere countries the quota was to be equal to the number of immigrant visas issued during the same fiscal year to immigrants from that country, but with a minimum quota of 100. The intent of the bill is suggested by the quotas so determined, 67,558 for Canada, 860 for Cuba, 2900 for Mexico, and lesser numbers for other countries. No action was taken on the bill.

The Senate bill brought up from the first session (S. 51, Harris [Ga.]) would have arrived at a similar effect by means of a different formula. Reported out of committee without amendment, it was to amend section 4(c) of the 1924 Act to admit immigrants from Canada and Newfoundland free of quota limit but to establish quotas for other countries of the hemisphere. The bill was debated intermittently in the Senate between April 2 and April 25, 1930, and recommitted on the latter day. Brought up again on May 13, the bill was amended on motion of Harris (Ga.) to apply quotas only to Mexico, and was then accepted by a vote of 51 to 16. It was reported out by the House committee,[8] which added specifica-

[6]H.R. 8523, Box (Tex.); H.R. 8530, Johnson (Wash.); H.R. 8702, Bacon (N.Y.).

[7]H. Rept. 898 (71-II).

[8]H. Rept. 1594 (71-II).

tion of the procedure for setting the Mexican quota and set its effective date. The quota for Mexico was to be 1500 to 1900. In an accompanying minority report Dickstein of the committee pointed out that the Mexican quota of 1900 being included in the overall quota total of 150,000, there would be a corresponding reduction in the quotas of other countries. Whether for this or other reasons, the House took no further action on the bill.

The long-quiescent subjects of Chinese immigration and contract labor reappeared in somewhat altered contemporary form. Johnson of Washington offered a bill (H.R. 10816) to construe the contract labor provisions of the 1917 Act with reference to "instrumental musicians." The stated purpose was to protect American musicians from competition from foreigners, who were said to come in large numbers as professional artists, but to allow artists of recognized reputation to come in freely. Reported out by the committee, the bill was not acted on in the House. A Senate and two House bills were to permit the admission of Chinese wives of certain American citizens.[9] The Senate bill was reported out of committee,[10] debated, and passed, then passed by the House in lieu of one of its own bills, and signed into law as the Act of June 13, 1930 (46 Stat. 581). It amended section 13(c) of the 1924 Act by adding a fourth admissible class of aliens ineligible to citizenship, "the Chinese wife of an American citizen who was married prior to the approval of the immigration Act of 1924."

The only other bills of the session to be noted are a miscellaneous group concerning aliens within the United States. Included were two Senate bills from the preceding session that came out of committee, one to authorize the issuance of certificates of arrival to persons born in the United States who are now aliens,[11] the other to authorize the issuance of certificates of admission to duly admitted aliens.[12] The former passed the Senate but was not supported by the House committee. The latter was returned to the committee, reported out with amendment and passed, reconsidered, returned to the Senate calendar, and not acted on further.

Three resolutions called again for a constitutional amendment to exclude the counting of aliens in the apportionment of representation in Congress among the states.[13] A bill by Patman of Texas would prohibit the employment of any person who is illegally within the United States

[9] S. 2836, Bingham (Conn.); H.R. 5654, Houston (Hawaii); H.R. 12379, Dyer (Mo.).
[10] S. Rept. 556 (71-II).
[11] S. 226, Hayden (Ariz.), with S. Rept. 557.
[12] S. 1278, Blease (S.C.), with S. Rept. 444.
[13] S. J. Res. 187, Capper (Kans.); H. J. Res. 263, 356, Sparks (Kans.).

(H.R. 9443). And finally there were three bills providing variously for the registration of resident aliens (H.R. 9101, Aswell [La.]; H.R. 9147, 10207, Cable [Ohio]). Except as noted above none of these bills concerning aliens was acted on by Congress during the session.

The third session of the 71st Congress, facing the problems of a deepening depression, met on the first of December 1930. On the following day it received the annual presidential message, from President Hoover, which included the following brief recommendation concerning adjustment of immigration policy with reference to the unemployment situation:

> There is need for revision of our immigration laws upon a more limited and more selective basis, flexible to the needs of the country.
>
> Under conditions of current unemployment it is obvious that persons coming to the United States seeking work would likely become either direct or indirect public charges. As a temporary measure the officers issuing visas to immigrants have been . . . instructed to refuse visas to applicants likely to fall into this class.[14]

It can be noted that the regulatory system already possessed a considerable degree of flexibility, at least in the direction of further restriction. The "temporary measure" mentioned in the message, perhaps aided by some reduction in the number of applications for admission, brought a prompt reduction of the average number of immigrant visas issued per month from 24,000 to 7000; and for Mexico the average dropped even more drastically from 4000 to 250 per month.

With or without presidential recommendation, the national problem of unemployment was sufficient in itself for immigration to be regarded with increasing disfavor; and the immigration bills received during the third session of the 71st Congress were mainly concerned with the deportation of aliens and the suspension of further immigration. Five new deportation bills were introduced during the course of the session, and two others were brought up from the first session. Of the new bills, one provided for the arrest of aliens unlawfully present in the United States, for the deportation of undesirable aliens, and for registration to protect lawfully resident aliens (H.R. 16036, Cable [Ohio]). The other four new bills were to expedite the deportation of certain classes of aliens.[15] One of these, H.R. 17152, was reported back in the House with minority report attached (H. Rept. 2799, pts. 1 and 2), and another was reported back in the Senate and debated (S. 6172, with S. Rept. 1640). Neither came to a vote.

[14]H. Doc. 519 (71-III), pp. 9–10.

[15]S. 6116, 6172, Hayden (Ariz.); H.R. 17004, 17152, Johnson (Wash.).

Of the two deportation bills from the first session, a Senate bill, S. 202, was debated at considerable length and passed, sent to the House and reported out with amendment (H. Rept. 2922 [71-III]), but not acted on further. More successful was the Fish (N.Y.) bill (H.R. 3394) to provide for the deportation of aliens convicted of violation of the Harrison narcotics law and its amendments. Introduced in the first session and passed by the House in the second session, it was reported out with amendment by the Senate committee, amended and passed by the Senate, agreed to by the House, and signed on February 18, 1931 (46 Stat. 1171). In its amended and enacted form the act provided for the deportation of any alien, excepting an addict not a dealer or peddler of narcotics, convicted for violation or conspiracy to violate any statute of the United States or subdivision thereof, "taxing, prohibiting, or regulating the manufacture, production, compounding, transportation, sale, exchange, dispensing, giving away, importation, or exportation of opium, coca leaves, heroin, or any salt, derivative, or preparation of opium or coca leaves."[16]

Four bills and eight resolutions proposed suspension or severe restriction of immigration. Of the four bills,[17] all providing for suspension, one was for the stated purpose "To suspend immigration in aid of the unemployed," and the others were doubtless of the same intent. Four of the resolutions were to suspend immigration for a stated period, two years in two cases, five and ten years in the others.[18]

The foregoing bills and resolutions remained in committee, but a joint resolution by Free of California to further restrict immigration for a period of two years was reported out of committee with amendment.[19] It provided for a reduction of quotas by 90 percent for a period of two years but with retention of the 100 minimum. Nonquota visas to Western Hemisphere countries would be prohibited, and those countries would instead be given a quota of 10 percent of the nonquota visas issued to them in the fiscal year 1929–1930 but with a minimum of 100. Citizens of American Samoa, Guam, and the Philippine Islands who were not citizens of the United States would be treated the same as the citizens of other countries. And a final provision was for exemption from the terms of the bill of specially skilled and trained persons if persons of like qualifications were not to be found unemployed in the United States. Minority views accompanied the committee report, and there was no

[16]Marihuana added by sec. 21, Act of June 28, 1940 (54 Stat. 670).

[17]H.R. 13554, McClintic (Okla.); H.R. 14037, Cable (Ohio); H.R. 15075, Blanton (Tex.); H.R. 15614, Alman (Ala.).

[18]S. J. Res. 207, Reed (Pa.); H. J. Res. 410, 439, Johnson (Wash); H. J. Res. 427, Garber (Okla.).

[19]H. J. Res. 473, with H. Rept. 2405, January 27, 1931.

further action on the bill. A later joint resolution by the same author was to restrict immigration from the Philippine Islands to continental United States to 500 a year and from Guam and Samoa to 100 a year, for a period of two years (H. J. Res. 507, Free [Calif.]). The resolution was not acted on.

Similar to the first Free resolution was one by Jenkins of Ohio (H. J. Res. 500). It provided that only 10 percent of the quotas were to be used in the fiscal years beginning July 1, 1931 and 1932. Except for omission of the restriction of immigration from the Philippine Islands, it agreed in its provisions with the Free resolution. An additional joint resolution by Johnson of Washington was to regulate the immigration of certain peoples for a period of two years (H. J. Res. 504). Neither this nor the other resolutions above came to debate in the House or Senate, much occupied with other and more urgent matters at the time.

In addition to the principal topics of legislative attention noted above, a variety of other matters received attention in a few bills introduced during the third session. A bill for the exclusion and expulsion of alien communists was introduced and reported out but failed of further action (H.R. 16296, Bachmann [W.Va.], with H. Rept. 2797). Other proposals, none of which was reported out of committee, were to place certain restrictions on the naturalization of aliens (H. J. Res. 418, Chase [Pa.]), to authorize the use of the various armed forces to prevent the smuggling in of aliens and for other purposes (H. J. Res. 435, Blanton [Tex.]), to amend the laws relative to the admission of members of the family of a citizen (S. 6057, Copeland [N.Y.]; H.R. 16780, Cable [Ohio]), to revise section 4 of the 1924 Act dealing with nonquota classes (S. 5284, Bingham [Conn.]; H.R. 14035, Britten [Ill.]), to exclude certain aliens (H.R. 13565, Bachmann [W.Va.]), and to regulate the immigration of citizens of the Philippines to continental United States (H.R. 13535, Welch [Calif.]). Of all the various proposals, only the Fish narcotics act was passed; and although several other bills came out of committee, none was passed by either House or Senate.

72nd Congress (1931–1933)

The first session of the 72nd Congress received a large number of immigration bills, of which the principal topics were the further restriction or temporary suspension of immigration, the imposition of controls on immigrant labor, and amendment of the acts regulating immigration. Other bills concerned deportation, restraints on subversives, the admission of relatives, and various other topics.

Several bills called for the suspension of immigration, and a more numerous group of bills and resolutions was for further restriction of the numbers admitted. Three bills proposed suspending immigration,[20] of which one by Dies of Texas set a period of five years. Three other bills[21] and ten resolutions of almost identical title were for further restriction of immigration.[22] The only one of these to be reported out of committee was the bill proposed by Moore of Kentucky.[23] Resembling bills in the preceding Congress, it was to reduce quotas by 90 percent, to give Western Hemisphere countries quotas of 10 percent of the number of nonquota visas issued to that country in the fiscal year ending June 30, 1930, to set the minimum for any country at 100, and to grant nonquota status to persons of special skills, not to exceed 300 in any one year and not to exceed five family members with one applicant, provided similar workers were not to be found unemployed in the United States. Congress took no further action on this or the other proposals for limiting immigration.

In reaction to the existing unemployment problem was a revival of attention to the contract labor laws, interest in which had lapsed during the immediately preceding decades. In part the concern was with the application of the laws to certain artistic groups. Two bills in the House were to clarify the application of the contract labor laws to singers and choristers (H.R. 7613, Dickstein [N.Y.]; H.R. 8978, Dies [Tex.]). A third bill was for the same purpose with respect to actors (H.R. 8877, Dickstein). Reported out (H. Rept. 876 [72-I]), it was debated and passed by the House but made no progress in the Senate. A fourth bill of the same type concerned instrumental musicians. Reported out in the House, it passed both House and Senate,[24] and was signed to become the Act of March 17, 1932 (47 Stat. 67). A brief act in three sections, it provided that the contract labor laws are applicable to alien instrumental musicians whether coming for permanent residence or temporarily; that such aliens shall not be considered artists or professional actors under the terms of the fifth proviso of section 3 of the 1917 Act and thereby exempt from the contract labor laws unless they are recognized to be of distinguished ability and are coming to fulfill professional engagements corresponding to such ability; and that, if the alien qualifies for exemption under the above proviso, the Secretary of Labor later may prescribe such conditions, including bonding, as will ensure the alien's departure at the end of his engagement.

[20]H.R. 4514, Blanton (Tex.); H.R. 4548, Dies (Tex.); H.R. 9696, Palmisano (Md.).

[21]H.R. 8331, Rutherford (Ga.); H.R. 9548, Jeffers (Ala.); H.R. 10602, Moore (Ky.).

[22]S. J. Res. 83, Harris (Ga.); H. J. Res. 55, 190, 201, 216, Jenkins (Ohio); H. J. Res. 75, Johnson (Wash.); H. J. Res. 277, Moore (Ky.); H. J. Res. 300, 301, Dies (Tex.); H. J. Res. 306, Underwood (Ohio).

[23]H.R. 10602, with H. Rept. 1016, April 7, 1932.

[24]H.R. 8235, Johnson (Wash.), with H. Rept. 258, S. Rept. 419.

Two additional bills, introduced by Reed of Pennsylvania and Johnson of Washington, were to authorize increased expenditures for enforcement of the contract labor laws (S. 4177, H.R. 9598). One of these, proposed by Johnson, was reported out in the House, amended and passed, then passed by the Senate[25] and signed to become the Act of May 2, 1932 (47 Stat. 145). A brief act, it amended section 24 of the Immigration Act of February 5, 1917 to double the allocation for enforcement of the contract labor laws to $200,000 per annum.

Amendment of the Immigration Act of 1917 was proposed by several other bills,[26] of which one concerned the administration of deportation proceedings. Approximately twenty bills were for amendment of the 1924 Act, of which one (H.R. 6045, by Schafer of Wisconsin) was for repeal of the national origin provisions, and four were for amendment of section 4 on nonquota immigration.[27] House and Senate bills were introduced to amend the sixth exception in section 3 of the 1924 Act, which exempted an alien and immediate family from classification as immigrants if entering solely to carry on trade between the United States and a foreign state (S. 3698 and H.R. 7801 by Copeland and Dickstein of New York). The Senate bill was reported back (S. Rept. 805 [72-I]) and then indefinitely postponed, with a new House bill being considered in its place. The new bill, of the same title, was reported back by the House committee,[28] passed by the House on June 18, 1932, amended and passed by the Senate, accepted in the amended form by the House, and approved by the President as the Act of July 6, 1932 (47 Stat. 607). The purpose of the bill was to clarify the wording of section 3 of the 1924 Act, to make clear that the sixth exception granted nonimmigrant status only to merchants engaged in international trade, not to those engaged in local trade; and the application of the section was extended to the wife and minor children of such treaty merchants. The Senate amendment substituted the words "of which he is a national" in place of "from which he comes," to make the exempting clause read, "An alien entitled to enter the United States solely to carry on trade between the United States and the foreign state of which he is a national . . . and his wife, and his unmarried children under 21. . . .[29]

[25]H.R. 9598, with H. Rept. 660, S. Rept. 571.

[26]H.R. 205, Houston (Hawaii); H.R. 7804, Jenkins (Ohio); H.R. 12406, LaGuardia (N.Y.).

[27]S. 268, Harris (Ga.); S. 435, Bingham (Conn); S. 991, Tydings (Md.); H.R. 8561, McLeod (Mich.).

[28]H.R. 8766, Dickstein (N.Y.), with H. Rept. 431, Feb. 12, 1932.

[29]The *Congressional Record* lists an additional bill, H.R. 5871 by Dickstein (N.Y.), entitled "To amend the Act of March 4, 1924 making it a felony for certain aliens to enter," of the

Five bills were introduced to limit the application of section 1(a) of the Act of March 4, 1929 providing for the exclusion of previously deported aliens.[30] The only one of these to come out of committee was the second of the two House bills introduced by Dickstein of New York, which was reported out with amendment on March 30, 1932 (H. Rept. 938). The committee report noted that prior to the 1929 Act a deported alien could reapply for admission one year after deportation. In view of certain hardships arising under the 1929 Act, as when a nonimmigrant married to a citizen has overstayed his period of admission and then been deported, the Dickstein bill would give the Secretary of Labor discretionary power to authorize the readmission of an alien one year or more after deportation. The House tabled the bill, for meanwhile the substance of the Dickstein bill had been added to a naturalization bill by the Senate committee. That bill, H.R. 6477 introduced by Brunner (N.Y.), had been passed by the House on February 1, 1932 as a short bill in one section to extend the naturalization privileges granted to alien veterans of the World War (H. Rept. 272, Jan. 25, 1932). Amended and expanded to nine sections by the Senate committee, the bill received a tenth section by amendment in the Senate,[31] and was then passed with approval of all committee amendments. With the House conferees recommending acceptance of the Senate amendments, the bill was approved with revised title and signed, to become the Act of May 25, 1932 (47 Stat. 165). Section 7 of the act, corresponding to the Dickstein bill, exempted previously deported aliens from the excluding provisions of the Act of March 4, 1929, section 1(a), after expiration of one year following the date of deportation, provided the Secretary of Labor granted permission to reapply for admission.[32]

Growing concern over subversives was indicated by an increased number of bills, eight in all, for the exclusion and/or expulsion of alien Communists.[33] Only one was reported out, the last of the four such bills introduced by Dies of Texas. The bill added Communists after anarchists to the excludable and deportable classes. Committee additions were a

---

same title as a bill introduced by the same Congressman in the second session of the 71st Congress (H.R. 5647); but no immigration act of that date is found, and it is assumed that the intended amendment was of the Act of March 4, 1929 that made it a felony under certain conditions for a deported alien to reenter or attempt to reenter.

[30]S. 3714, Hastings (Del.); H.R. 210, Jenkins (Ohio); H.R. 5871 (see note 29) and 10521, Dickstein (N.Y.); H.R. 8917, Hancock (N.Y.).

[31]*Congressional Record*, 75:7905–7.

[32]The other sections of the act concerned naturalization.

[33]S. 3815, Hatfield (W.Va.); H.R. 10975, 10979, Johnson (Wash.); H.R. 11389, 11924, 11946, 12044, Dies (Tex.); H.R. 11733, Cable (Ohio).

definition of a Communist, and safeguards to protect from deportation aliens who may have become members of Communist organizations through fear, fraud, and so on. Reported out without amendment by the House committee (H. Rept. 1353), it was debated and passed by the House, reported out unamended by the Senate (S. Rept. 808), and debated there on several days but not brought to vote.

An additional four bills during the session were to provide for the deportation of certain classes of aliens other than Communists. Three of them concerned alien seamen (S. 7, King [Utah]; H.R. 4648, 12173, Schneider [Wis.]), of which the Senate bill by King was reported back, debated on a number of days, recommitted, and reported out again with amendment but not acted on further (S. Rept. 16, 677). A fourth bill was for the deportation of aliens who enter into collusive marriages with a citizen for the purpose of gaining admission to the United States (H.R. 7789, Cable [Ohio]). Another bill, avoiding the term *deportation,* was to secure the departure of certain aliens (H.R. 7793, Cable [Ohio]). Reported out and passed by the House and then the Senate (H. Rept. 622, S. Rept. 826), it received presidential approval to become the Act of July 1, 1932 (47 Stat. 524). It amended section 15 of the 1924 Act to provide that the specified classes of nonimmigrant aliens be admitted for a prescribed time and under such conditions, including bonding where deemed necessary, as would ensure departure at the expiration of the prescribed time or upon failure to maintain the status under which admitted.

The terms of admission of immigrant aliens received attention in a number of bills; most frequently concerned was the admission of relatives, but bills also dealt with admission terms for veterans, quota preference, admission of natives of the Western Hemisphere, and other matters. Three bills were to facilitate the admission of wives of American citizens.[34] Two others stated the general purpose of facilitating the reuniting of families (H.R. 9696, Palmisano [Md.]; H.R. 10747, Dickstein [N.Y.]). An additional four bills, three of which were introduced by Dickstein of New York, would give nonquota status to fathers and mothers of United States citizens, with minimum age of the parents set at fifty-five or sixty years (S. 3359, Copeland [N.Y.]; H.R. 5308, 7714, 8174, Dickstein). The third of the Dickstein bills was reported back by the House committee (H. Rept. 245) with a minority report attached,[35] debated,

[34] S. 2760, Bingham (Conn.); H.R. 304, Houston (Hawaii); H.R. 4675, Dyer (Mo.).

[35] The minority report, presented by Jenkins (Ohio), argued that the quota as it stands is sufficient to take care of fathers and mothers for all countries except Romania and Turkey, where the waiting list does not exceed several hundred and can be taken care of in about three and one-half years. And the bill, it was pointed out, would in effect permit a large increase of immigration, especially from the European countries of large past immigration.

amended, and passed by the House. Action on the bill in the Senate did not come until the second session.

Another proposal, made in several bills, was to exempt from quota limits the husbands of American citizens, that is, to give them nonquota status (S. 2656, King [Utah]; H.R. 5869, 10600, Dickstein [N.Y.]). The Senate bill of this group was reported out with amendment (S. Rept. 124), amended and passed by the Senate, and transmitted to the House. Meanwhile the House committee had reported out its own bill of the same purpose.[36] Reported without amendment, the bill would have amended section 4(a) of the 1924 Act to remove the limitation of nonquota status of husbands of citizens to marriages prior to June 1, 1928.[37] It was passed by the House on April 18, 1932 by vote of 209 to 112, amended by addition of the Johnson proviso "that the marriage shall have occurred prior to issuance of visa." In this form the bill was passed in the Senate, but the vote was rescinded and the bill repassed with amendment of the above proviso to read, "Provided that the marriage shall have occurred prior to issuance of visa and prior to July 1, 1932." The conference report of July 1, 1932 revised the proviso to make the limiting date of July 1, 1932 applicable only in the case of husbands, and wives of citizens would be accorded nonquota status without limit on the time of the marriage. Both the House and Senate accepted the conference report, the bill was signed, and it became the Act of July 11, 1932 (47 Stat. 656).

Extension of the immigration and naturalization privileges of alien veterans of the First World War was provided in a Senate and a House bill (S. 2643, Copeland [N.Y.]; H.R. 4519, Brunner [N.Y.]), neither of which was reported out of committee; and the same treatment was met by two bills for the restriction of Western Hemisphere immigration with particular reference to Central and South America (H.R. 55, Johnson [Wash.]; H.R. 8541, Crail [Calif.]), as well as one for exclusion of Filipinos (H.R. 8542, Crail [Calif.]).

Action was taken, however, to facilitate the immigration of certain natives of the Virgin Islands residing in any foreign country. Two bills for this purpose were introduced during the session, one in the House and one in the Senate (S. 4425, Reed [Pa.]; H.R. 11363, Dickstein [N.Y.]). The House bill was reported back by the committee (H. Rept. 1114) but then tabled in favor of the Senate bill, already passed and transmitted to the House. The Senate bill had been reported back (S. Rept. 641) and passed without amendment in the Senate, was promptly approved in the House,

[36]H.R. 10600, with H. Rept. 919, March 26, 1932.

[37]The bill also amended section 6(a)(1)(A) of the act to make it conform to the proposed wording of section 4(a).

amended there only by change of spelling from *Porto Rico* to *Puerto Rico*, agreed to by the Senate, and signed into law as the Act of June 28, 1932 (47 Stat. 336). It gave nonquota status to natives of the Virgin Islands residing in a foreign country, but subject to all other provisions of the Immigration Act of 1924 except for their exemption from head tax, the passport or immigration visa requirement, deportation on the ground of becoming a public charge, and exclusion under section 3 of that act if not a member of any one of six designated excludable classes[38] and if otherwise admissible.

Various bills for the further regulation of immigration included two for readjustment of quota preferences (H.R. 9550, 12354, Jenkins [Ohio]), two others to provide that "religious views or philosophical opinions against war" shall not debar otherwise qualified aliens from citizenship (H.R. 297, 298, Griffin [N.Y.]), and certain revisions in the regulation of immigration (S. 2489, King [Utah]; H.R. 7791, Cable [Ohio]). Reflecting prevailing concerns was a bill dealing with the admission of aliens likely to become public charges (H.R. 7614, Dickstein [N.Y.]); and three bills provided for review of the action of consular officers in refusing immigration visas (S. 34, King [Utah]; H.R. 8878, 11552, Dickstein [N.Y.]). One of the latter bills was reported with minority report attached, but no further action was taken (H.R. 11552, with H. Rept. 1193).

The one other considerable group of bills offered during the session related to alien residents of the United States. There were the perennial resolutions for a constitutional amendment to exclude aliens in the apportionment of representation (S. J. Res. 45, Bratton [N.M.]; H. J. Res. 97, Sparks [Kans.]). Another constitutional amendment was proposed concerning the employment of aliens (S. J. Res. 184, Ashurst [Ariz.]). A bill would have repealed laws providing that aliens who have filed their first papers for naturalization shall be accorded the same services and protection of American vessels as are given to citizens (H.R. 6710, Davis [Tenn.]). There was a bill for the punishment of aliens who enter unlawfully (H.R. 7792, Cable [Ohio]), and a resolution to place restrictions on aliens becoming citizens (H. J. Res. 325, Chase [Pa.]). And finally there were six bills proposing various forms of certificates of arrival, certificates of identity, and registration for resident aliens. None of the above bills relating to aliens progressed beyond the Senate and House committees.

The relatively few immigration bills of the second session of the

[38]Afflicted with a loathsome or dangerous contagious disease, a polygamist, a prostitute or procurer or other like immoral person, a contract laborer, previously deported, or convicted of a crime.

72nd Congress included several that reflected concerns prevalent during the Depression years as well as others on the more usual matters for the regulation of immigration. As occurs in periods of economic depression and unemployment, there were attempts to redirect immigration policy toward certain economic and especially labor market objectives. One bill would have made it illegal to employ any alien while there are American citizens who are willing and able but out of work (H.R. 13307, Crail [Calif.]). Two bills called for the restriction or suspension of immigration (H.R. 14711, 14713, Green [Fla.]), and another bill had a double purpose, one of which was to increase from three to five years the period after entry during which an alien who falls into distress and who is willing may be removed voluntarily to his homeland at government expense without deportation proceedings. The other provision in the bill was to make it possible for an alien to be so returned not to his native country only, but also to the country from which he came, or to the country of which he was a citizen (H.R. 13811, Dickstein [N.Y.]). Said to have been introduced at the request of the Department of Labor, the bill was reported back without amendment (H. Rept. 1852, Jan. 11, 1933), debated, and then passed over without further action in the House.[39]

Other bills during the session included two for amendment of the Act of March 2, 1929 (S. 5347, King [Utah]; H.R. 14457, Bacon, N.Y.]) concerning registry of aliens. Two other bills were on the perennial subject of registration and certificates of identification of aliens (H.R. 14712, Green [Fla.]; H.R. 14783, Bacon [N.Y.]); and Dickstein of New York proposed allowing lawfully admitted aliens to adjust their status without the burdensome requirement of departing to a foreign country and returning later (H.R. 13810). None of the above was acted upon beyond referral to committee.

The principal legislative activity relating to immigration during the session was Senate consideration of the bill passed by the House in the preceding session to exempt parents over sixty years of age of American citizens from quota limitation (H.R. 8174, Dickstein [N.Y.]). It was reported out by the Senate committee on February 10, 1933, amended to limit its application to parents over sixty at the time of application for an immigration visa and with its effective date advanced to the fiscal year beginning July 1, 1933. A multipurpose bill, section 2 amended section 1(a) of the Act of March 2, 1929 to read as follows:

> That (a) the registry of aliens at ports of entry required by section 1 of the Act of June 29, 1906 (34 Stat. 596), as amended, may be

[39] *Congressional Record,* 76:3576, Feb. 7, 1933.

made as to any alien not ineligible to citizenship in whose case there is no record of admission for permanent residence prior to July 1, 1924, if such alien shall make a satisfactory showing to the Commissioner General of Immigration . . . with the approval of the Secretary of Labor, that he
(1) First entered the United States prior to July 1, 1924;
(2) Has resided in the United States continuously since such entry;
(3) Is a person of good moral character; and
(4) Is not subject to deportation.

At the same time the registry fee was raised to twenty dollars, and eight dollars for those who had entered prior to June 3, 1921. Sections 3 and 4 concerned loss of derivative citizenship and acquisition of citizenship by a child born abroad to an American citizen parent. On what were presumably objections raised by the State Department, the bill was first passed over and sections 3 and 4 were then dropped, to be replaced by substitute sections concerning derivative citizenship and nationality.[40] So amended, the bill was passed by the Senate without record vote on March 3; but the 72nd Congress came to an end the following day without House action on the amended bill.

73rd Congress (1933–1934)

New immigration bills submitted during the first session of the 73rd Congress followed the pattern of the preceding Congress. There were five bills for the further restriction of immigration,[41] and an additional two called for suspension of all immigration (H.R. 109, Blanton [Tex.]; H.R. 2842, Green [Fla.]). There was a House resolution to restrict the employment of commuting aliens (H. J. Res. 120, Dingell [Mich.]), and another contained the recurrent proposal to use the armed forces to check the smuggling in of aliens and other violations of the borders (H. J. Res. 4, Blanton [Tex.]). And Dickstein of New York offered a bill identical with his H.R. 13811 of the 72nd Congress to amend section 23 of the 1917 Act to extend authority for the voluntary removal of indigent aliens not subject to deportation (H.R. 3524). It was reported out of committee on May 11, 1933 but received no further action.

Deportation was dealt with in three bills, one to set up a select committee to investigate procedures in deportation and to inquire into the extent of alien smuggling from Cuba, one to clarify the laws relating

[40] *Congressional Record,* 76:4968, February 25; and p. 5522, March 3, 1933.

[41] H.R. 133, Jenkins (Ohio); H.R. 1616, Jeffers (Ala.); H.R. 2843, Green (Fla.); H.R. 4114 and H. J. Res. 119, Dies (Tex.).

to the exclusion and deportation of aliens with criminal records, and a third to add to the deportable classes.[42]

Dickstein of New York reintroduced a bill, presumably much the same as his H.R. 8174 of the preceding Congress, to give nonquota status to the parents of citizens (H.R. 3519). It was reported out on April 25, 1933 (H. Rept. 52), amended in committee to limit its application to parents sixty years of age or over. Quota preference was given to parents under sixty years of age. Support of the bill was urged as a humanitarian measure, especially needed for countries of small quota, but no action was taken.

Amendment of the 1924 Act was proposed in several bills,[43] and two others were to clarify the position of actors, singers, and choristers under the contract labor laws (H.R. 3674, 3675, Dickstein [N.Y.]). Another was to change preferences within the quotas (H.R. 134, Jenkins [Ohio]).

Resident aliens were variously dealt with. Dickstein reintroduced bills to permit adjustment of status without required departure to a foreign country (H.R. 3518, 5629, Dickstein [N.Y.]). Several bills concerned registration or record of entry.[44] Another was to rescind certain privileges of citizens extended to aliens who had filed a declaration of intention to be naturalized (H.R. 1497, Bland [Va.]); and another was for the purpose of extending the period of time allowed certain aliens to remain in the United States (H.R. 5570, Bloom [N.Y.]). Finally, there was a reappearance of bills, like those in the 72nd Congress, to provide for review of the action of consular officers in refusing immigration visas.[45] No immigration bills were passed, however, during the session.

The second session of the 73rd Congress, which ran from early January to mid-June 1934, saw a number of immigration bills introduced and considerable committee activity, but no important additions to the body of immigration law. Of the various topics related to immigration, deportation was the one to receive most attention. The early Depression-period concern with such matters as public charges, unemployment, and immigration restriction had largely waned, and the session brought only a few bills on these matters. Several bills dealt with adjustment of status; and beyond this was a scattering of bills on the usual range of topics, such as relatives, alien veterans, Western Hemisphere immigration, and other immigration matters.

[42]H. Res. 50, Dickstein (N.Y.); H.R. 4223, Weideman (Mich.); S. 868, King (Utah).

[43]H.R. 1644, McLeod (Mich.); H.R. 1705, Rudd (N.Y.); H.R. 4352, Kvale (Minn.).

[44]H.R. 8, Bacon (N.Y.); H.R. 2841, Green (Fla.); H.R. 3522, Dickstein (N.Y.).

[45]S. 287, King (Utah); H.R. 3525, 5630, 5765, Dickstein (N.Y.).

Eight bills dealing variously with deportation were introduced during the session, and two more from the first session were reported out of committee. The latter two, one each in the Senate and the House, concerned the problem of deserting alien seamen, and were similar in their provisions for the deportation of such aliens.[46] According to the accompanying committee reports, there was a wholesale jumping of ship in the United States, averaging over thirteen thousand cases a year. Both bills were designed especially to check the coming of Chinese seamen, and the House bill with certain qualifications would not allow a vessel except in distress to enter a port of the United States with persons ineligible to citizenship on board.

The other deportation bills were especially directed against aliens of the criminal class. A Senate bill (S. 3068), jointly sponsored by Senators Copeland of New York, Vandenberg of Michigan, and Murphy of Iowa would require the deportation of aliens convicted of a felony. Four bills of identical or quite similar titles (S. 3771, Coolidge [Mass.]; H.R. 9363, Crowe [Ind.]; H.R. 9518, 9725, Dickstein [N.Y.]) were to authorize the deportation of habitual criminals, but at the same time "to guard against the separation from their families of aliens of the noncriminal classes." The second of the two such bills introduced by Dickstein of New York was reported back (H.R. 9725, with H. Rept. 1772). The purpose of the bill as described in the committee report was to strengthen the deportation provisions regarding alien criminals and to give the Secretary of Labor discretion to prevent the separation of families. It proposed making three additional classes of alien criminals subject to deportation: violators of any state narcotic law;[47] habitual criminals, defined as those who had committed two or more crimes involving moral turpitude; and aliens who aid others to enter illegally. The bill was debated, but the motion for passage was defeated.

Of all the deportation bills, most legislative progress was made on one to clarify the provisions of the immigration law relative to exclusion and deportation of certain alien criminals (H.R. 4223, Weideman [Mich.]). Said to be favored by both the Labor and Justice Departments, the bill was to amend sections 3, 14, and 19 of the 1917 Act. In section 3, dealing with the excludable classes, the existing wording, "persons who have been convicted of or admit having committed a felony or other crime or misdemeanor involving moral turpitude," was to be changed to the more comprehensive phrasing,

[46]S. 868, with S. Rept. 1439; and H.R. 3842, with H. Rept. 627.

[47]At that time only the violation of a federal narcotic law made an alien liable to deportation.

> persons who have been convicted, anywhere at any prior time, of, or admit having committed, anywhere at any prior time, a felony or other crime or misdemeanor involving moral turpitude.

The revised wording was designed to apply to certain types of cases excepted by recent court decisions.

Section 14 as it stood provided for the deportation at any time after entry of aliens found not to have been entitled to enter, but with the proviso that the Secretary of Labor might permit children under sixteen to remain. The present bill would have added the following further proviso:

> That deportation under this section shall be ordered in the case of any alien who at any time after last entry is found to have been convicted anywhere prior to last entry, or who admits the commission anywhere prior to last entry of a felony or other crime or misdemeanor involving moral turpitude.

The portion of section 19 reading

> any alien who was convicted, or who admits the commission, prior to entry, of a felony or other crime or misdemeanor involving moral turpitude . . . shall, upon the warrant of the Secretary of Labor, be taken into custody and deported.

was to be amended to

> any alien who has been convicted anywhere prior to last entry, or who admits the commission anywhere prior to last entry, of a felony. . . .

The bill was brought up in the House on February 19, 1934, debated, and passed. It was not reported out by the Senate committee.

Two other bills relating to deportation sought to mitigate the immigration laws with respect to certain cases. One was to permit the readmission of aliens previously deported by reason of insanity who had recovered and maintained their sanity for a period of more than fifteen years (H.R. 8885, Martin [Oreg.]). The other was to authorize the Secretary of Labor to continue the suspension of deportation in certain cases until July 1, 1935 (H.R. 9965, Dies [Tex.]).

Next most numerous during the session[48] were bills concerning the adjustment of status, of which there were two in the Senate and three in the House.[49] Of the Senate bills, both introduced by Coolidge of Massa-

[48]Not included here are eight or more bills concerning registry, for these pertain more to naturalization than immigration.

[49]S. 3769, 3770, Coolidge (Mass.); H.R. 8312, Dickstein (N.Y.); H.R. 9364, Schulte (Ind.); H.R. 9760, West (Tex.).

chusetts, one was to legalize the residence in the United States of certain classes of aliens without record of legal admission for permanent residence, the other to permit adjustment of status by certain aliens without requirement that they depart to a foreign country and then return. The former of the Coolidge bills was duplicated in the House by bills introduced by Schulte of Indiana and West of Texas, the latter of the Coolidge bills by one introduced by Dickstein of New York. The West bill was essentially a registry bill.[50] The Dickstein bill to permit adjustment of status from nonimmigrant to immigrant (that is, from temporary to permanent admission) was reported out by the House committee (H. Rept. 871) but not acted on further.

A few bills designed to regulate and restrict immigration, to deal with aliens who become public charges, and to limit exemptions from the contract labor laws may be thought of as various reflections of continuing Depression-period concerns regarding immigration. There was a House bill "to limit immigration from each country which, or any political subdivision of which, is in default on its governmental indebtedness to the United States or to any citizen of the United States" (H.R. 8223, McFadden [Pa.]). Another House bill, perhaps restrictive as well as selective in its intent, was to admit only aliens able to speak, read, and write the English language, and to provide schools for the further education of aliens entering the United States (H.R. 7300, Strong [Tex.]). And in a revival of earlier legislative attempts, there was a resolution for temporary restriction of the "habitual commuting" of aliens from foreign contiguous territory for skilled or unskilled work in the United States (H. J. Res. 288, Schulte [Ind.]). The resolution was reported out by the House committee with slight modification of wording and with a favorable recommendation that jobs should be reserved for citizens until economic conditions improved (H. Rept. 1236, April 12, 1934). No further action was taken in the House.

With regard to public charges, the Dickstein bill from the first session (H.R. 3524 [73-I]) was brought up in the House on February 19, 1934. To amend section 23 of the Act of February 5, 1917 (39 Stat. 874), the bill would extend authority for the removal out of the country of indigent aliens not actually subject to deportation. In the course of debate on the bill, the House accepted the Jenkins amendment to the effect that aliens so removed would be ineligible for subsequent readmission except on consent of the Secretary of State and the Secretary of Labor. The bill

[50]It provided for registration to legalize the residence of certain aliens, amending the Act of March 2, 1929 (45 Stat. 1512) by requiring ten years of continuous residence rather than continuous residence since June 3, 1921, and making some change of wording concerning nondeportability. It was reported out (H. Rept. 1827) but progressed no further.

further extended the period of such voluntary removal from three to five years after entry. As amended, it was passed by the House but not acted on in the Senate.

Two contract labor amending bills from the first session of the 73rd Congress were reported back from committee.[51] Concerning the first of these, the committee noted that the existing exemption of professional actors from the contract labor laws was being used as a loophole for entering the United States by aliens coming in for minor positions that could be as well filled by native actors. The bill accordingly was drawn up to limit such exemption to actors of "distinguished merit and ability." The second bill applied the same terms to singers and choristers.

A few other bills introduced during the session remain to be noted. One was to extend nonquota status to certain additional classes of relatives, but to limit those eligible to first preference in the issuance of immigration visas (H.R. 9365, Weideman [Mich.]). There were proposals to apply quotas to immigration from Mexico and the Philippine Islands (H.R. 8222, Schulte [Ind.]; H.R. 9281, Colden [Calif.]). Amendment of the Immigration Act of 1917, section 8, providing penalties for bringing in, harboring, or concealing illegal immigrants, was proposed in another bill (H.R. 9366, Colmer [Miss.]); and Senate and House bills concerned the admission and naturalization of alien veterans of World War I (S. 3797, Reed [Pa.]; H.R. 6912, Cannon [Wis.]). Of these, the House bill was reported out of committee with amendment (H. Rept. 1786) but did not progress further. Finally, a House bill provided a two-year extension of the temporary stay of aliens lawfully present in the United States who found themselves political or religious refugees (H.R. 8309, Bloom [N.Y.]). The bill as originally introduced specified the country of origin of the refugees to be so aided, but committee amendment deleted mention of any particular country (H. Rept. 929, March 12, 1934).

74th Congress (1935, 1936)

The first session of the 74th Congress, a long session from January 3 to August 26, 1935, received an exceptionally large number of proposals for new immigration legislation. Deportation was by far the leading subject of these proposals. Restriction or suspension of immigration was also provided in a number of the new bills; in addition there was the usual range of other concerns such as aliens in the United States, the admission of relatives, the control of subversive classes, and so on. As in the preceding Congress, however, no important additions were made to the body of immigration law.

[51]H.R. 3674, with H. Rept. 874; and H.R. 3675, with H. Rept. 902.

No fewer than twenty bills and two House resolutions dealt with deportation; these were especially directed against alien seamen, criminals, and subversives. Three bills were to provide for the deportation of certain alien seamen.[52] Only one was reported back and debated, but not brought to a vote in the House (H.R. 5380, with H. Rept. 1126). There were thirteen bills providing in various terms for the deporting of criminal aliens. Senators Copeland, Vandenberg, and Murphy combined again, as in the preceding Congress, to sponsor a bill for the deportation of aliens convicted of certain crimes (S. 22); and a bill for the same purpose was offered in the House (H.R. 8906, Smith [Va.]). Eleven multipurpose bills of somewhat varying titles but similar to several bills in the 73rd Congress were to provide for prompt deportation of alien criminals and to guard against the separation from their families of law-abiding aliens.[53] The only one of the above group to come out of committee was the first of the two Coolidge bills in the Senate (S. 2969, with S. Rept. 1156; see pp. 239–40). It was debated, not voted on at the time, but considered again in the second session.

Several other bills related to deportation in various ways. One would have authorized the Secretary of Labor to deport aliens whose presence is inimical to the public interest, another was for the deportation with some exceptions of aliens who had entered illegally, another had the general purpose of excluding and deporting certain classes of aliens, and a fourth bill in the House with the primary purpose of reducing quotas also increased the grounds for deportation.[54] A House resolution was introduced by Dies of Texas to set up a Bureau of Alien Deportation in the Department of Justice, and another House resolution, by Mrs. O'Day of New York, called for stay of deportation in hardship cases of aliens of good character until such time as Congress could consider appropriate legislation (H. J. Res. 69 and H. Res. 350). There were said to be about 2,600 cases that would be affected by the latter resolution, which was passed by the House, 201 to 119, on August 23, 1935.[55]

Finally, Dickstein of New York introduced a bill to authorize shorten-

[52]S. 379, King (Utah); H.R. 2885, Dies (Tex.); H.R. 5380, Schulte (Ind.).

[53]S. 2542, Russell (Ga.); S. 2969, 2970, Coolidge (Mass.); H.R. 5921, 8731, Dies (Tex.); H.R. 6367, Taylor (Tenn.); H.R. 6795, 8163, Kerr (N.C.); H.R. 6994, 7079, Green (Fla.); H.R. 7223, Focht (Pa.). The Russell and Focht bills had the additional purpose of further restriction of immigration. Several of the bills specifically designated habitual criminals (S. 2970, H.R. 6994, 7079, 7223). Four added "direct-action Communists" to the categories of deportable aliens (H.R. 6994, 7079, 7223, 8731). See also H.R. 7120 below, under subversives.

[54]H.R. 3989, Taylor (Tenn.); H.R. 4551, Sirovich (N.Y.); H.R. 6322, May (Ky.); H.R. 8445, Starnes (Ala.).

[55]*Congressional Record,* 79:14381.

ing or termination of the stay in the United States of certain aliens not admitted for permanent residence and the deportation of certain aliens admitted for permanent residence (H.R. 7221, with H. Rept. 1057). The bill was reported back but not acted on further until the next session.

The restriction of immigration was another subject to receive considerable attention during the session, in part no doubt an expression of long-continued restrictionist sentiment, but also, one may infer, an expression of Depression-period concern with labor market problems and especially unemployment. One such bill stated its objectives to be the protection of American labor, reduction of crime, and lessening the danger of foreign entanglements (H.R. 2792, Hoeppel [Calif.]). As unexceptionable was the stated purpose of another bill to raise the American standard of living, relieve unemployment, raise additional revenue, and so on (H.R. 9175, Arends [Ill.]). Four bills directly proposed the further restriction of immigration,[56] and there was one to suspend all immigration (H.R. 2733, Blanton [Tex.]).

Perhaps similarly motivated were several attempts to set quota limits on immigration from countries granted nonquota status under the immigration laws. One such bill would establish a quota for Mexico (H.R. 4679, Schulte [Ind.]), and there were three to impose quotas on immigration from both Mexico and the Philippine Islands (H.R. 3007, Colden [Calif.]; H.R. 6649, 6808, Kramer [Calif.]). And a joint resolution in the House (H. J. Res. 236, Schulte [Ind.]) proposed suspension of the issuance of nonquota immigration visas to natives of Mexico, suspension of the issuance of all nonpreference quota immigration visas, and giving a quota to Mexico. The resolution was reported out, withdrawn, and then reported out again (H. Rept. 1100 and 1138), but it progressed no further.

More explicit in their labor market implications were several other House bills and resolutions. Two bills of identical title were introduced by Stubbs of California to make it illegal to employ any alien while citizens able and willing to work are unemployed.[57] Two other bills continued the effort from preceding sessions of Congress to restrict "habitual commuting" of aliens from foreign contiguous territory for skilled or unskilled work in the United States.[58] One of the latter was reported out with amendment. It provided that aliens who live in foreign contiguous terri-

[56]H.R. 50, Rudd (N.Y.); H.R. 2008, Dies (Tex.); H.R. 6022, Whelchel (Ga.); H.R. 8455, Starnes (Ala.). See also Russell and Focht deportation bills above.

[57]H.R. 3048, 8602, Stubbs (Calif.). Compare H.R. 13307 (72-II).

[58]H.R. 4340, Sadowski (Mich.); H.R. 6083, Beiter (N.Y.). Compare H. J. Res. 288 (73-II).

tory and work in the United States are to be treated as immigrants, being excluded unless provided with an unexpired immigration visa or a reentry permit. The number of such aliens was estimated at 130,000. The committee expressed the opinion that aliens should be prevented from earning money in the United States for the support of themselves and families abroad "when millions of bona fide residents, both citizens and aliens . . . are unemployed."[59]

To be included in the group of bills concerned with labor conditions are a joint resolution in the Senate to amend the Constitution in order to permit restriction on the employment of aliens, and a bill in the House to clarify the application of the contract labor laws to actors (S. J. Res. 17, Ashurst [Ariz.]; H.R. 3473, Dickstein [N.Y.]). The latter was reported out of committee but not acted on thereafter.

An additional reflection of the economic problems of the time was a bill to provide for the removal at government expense of aliens in financial distress who apply for return to their native country (H.R. 3472, Dickstein [N.Y.]). Reported out on February 12, 1935 (H. Rept. 120), the bill had been amended in committee to strike out the time limitation of such removal to within three years of arrival and to authorize such removal without time limit. Another provision of the bill as it came from the committee was to amend existing law permitting removal only to the alien's native country, to permit removal also to the country from which the alien came or the country of which the alien was a citizen or subject. The committee supported its revision and the final bill by citing the prevailing burden of poor relief; but consideration of the bill was objected to in the House, and it did not come up for discussion until the next session.

The matter of subversives also received attention during the session. Several bills for the deportation of "direct-action Communists" have been noted above. An additional bill by Dies of Texas called for the exclusion and expulsion of alien Fascists and Communists. It was reported back but received no later action in the House (H.R. 7120, with H. Rept. 1023).

Various other aspects of immigration were dealt with in bills introduced during the session. Four bills were for amendment of the 1924 Act,[60] none of which came out of committee. And not all the proposals for new legislation were restrictionist or antialien in their implications. Three bills were to facilitate the entry of certain relatives of American citizens, the classes of aliens in question being wives whose marriage to

[59]H. Rept. 1276, on H.R. 4340, June 20, 1935.
[60]H.R. 2805, Kvale (Minn.); H.R. 7762, 8386, 8408, Sirovich (N.Y.).

a citizen was prior to the Quota Act of 1924, certain alien relatives to be given quota preference, and spouses entitled to a nonquota visa.[61] There was a bill by Marcantonio of New York to assure asylum to certain refugees (H.R. 8384). Two bills offered by Representatives from New York, Griffin and O'Day, provided that religious views or philosophical opinions against war should not debar otherwise qualified aliens from citizenship (H.R. 2021 and 5170). Another pair of bills was to give nonquota status to certain aliens (H.R. 4549 and 5804 by Sirovich of New York); and House and Senate bills were proposed to authorize the issuance of reentry permits in specified cases to aliens ineligible for citizenship, these being S. 3325 and H.R. 8660 by Copeland and Millard of New York. None of the above, however, was reported out by the committees.

A final group of bills dealt with aliens in the United States. Included was another and at last successful attempt by Bland of Virginia (H.R. 67) to repeal the laws giving privileges of citizenship regarding service on and protection by American vessels to aliens having their first papers (that is, having made declaration of intention to become citizens). It was identical with two bills previously passed by the House but not by the Senate, H.R. 1497 in the second session of the 73rd Congress and H.R. 6710 in the first session of the 72nd. The new bill was reported out in a third attempt by the House committee, which made only minor change of wording, used the report on the predecessor bill, and pointed out that the acts to be repealed were wartime measures no longer appropriate (H. Rept. 21, Jan. 23, 1935). The House again passed the bill, which was finally reported out in turn by the Senate committee (S. Rept. 796, May 13, 1935) to which it was referred. It was then passed by the Senate and signed, to become the Act of June 15, 1935 (49 Stat. 376), designated as being for the protection of American seamen.

Several bills were concerned with the registration of alien residents and the legalization of their presence in the United States.[62] The perennial proposal not to count aliens in apportionment of representation in Congress reappeared (H. J. Res. 4, Tarver [Ga.]); and another bill had the very original provision that any citizen who married an alien should pay a capital tax on his fortune (H.R. 8658, Cannon [Wis.]). Dickstein of New York made a proposal that was later incorporated in another bill[63] he introduced later in the session, to authorize shortening or termination of the stay in the United States of aliens admitted on a temporary basis who "engage in the promotion or dissemination of propaganda or en-

[61]H.R. 7975, King (Hawaii); H.R. 4547, 4548, Sirovich (N.Y.).

[62]S. 811, Hayden (Ariz.); H.R. 4546, Sirovich (N.Y.); H.R. 8616, Starnes (Ala.).

[63]H.R. 7221. See above under deportation bills, and also below in the second session.

gage in political activity" (H.R. 5839). Reported out on February 21, 1935 (H. Rept. 200 [74-I]), the original bill was said to embody recommendations from the Special Committee on Un-American Activities, which had been appointed pursuant to House Resolution 198 of the preceding Congress. The bill was debated in the House but was dropped in favor of the later Dickstein bill.

The second session of the 74th Congress, which convened January 3 and adjourned June 20, 1936, saw continuation of efforts to strengthen the deportation laws and a few new bills on a variety of matters related to immigration and alien residents.

Several deportation bills from the first session were brought up for consideration, of which one was the bill concerning alien seamen, debated but not brought to a vote (S. 379 [74-I], King [Utah]). Another was the Kerr bill concerning habitual criminals, also debated but not voted on (H.R. 8163 [74-I], Kerr [N.C.]). Likewise from the first session was the Senate bill by Coolidge of Massachusetts for the deportation of alien criminals and other purposes (S. 2969 [74-I]). Reported out and debated in the first session, it was brought up again in the following session for more lengthy consideration. The bill would add to the deportable classes those aliens who were (1) violators of state narcotics laws, (2) convicted of crimes involving moral turpitude whether or not sentenced, (3) engaged in smuggling in other aliens, and (4) convicted of violation of the concealed weapons law. Deportation was to be mandatory for the first of these classes of aliens, but for the other three classes deportation was to be dependent on its being judged in the public interest by decision of an interdepartmental committee. It was further provided that a deportable alien is eligible to remain if he has lived for ten years or more in the United States or if he has near relatives in the United States who are citizens or legal residents; but this relief was not to be available to "radical" cases, criminals, prostitutes, or other immoral classes of deportables. With such limitation, this provision was nevertheless estimated to aid some 2600 hardship cases.

Section 4 of the bill would permit an alien to change his status from temporary to permanent admission without the necessity of departure and return. And section 5 would permit registry of aliens, to thereby make their residence legal, if they had entered prior to July 1, 1924.[64]

In its supplemental report on the bill (S. Rept. 1156, pt. 2, Feb. 24, 1936), the Senate committee stated that the bill was designed to accom-

[64]The date for eligibility for registry had been set at July 1, 1924 by the Act of March 2, 1929 (45 Stat. 1512), and was subsequently amended to June 3, 1921 by the Act of August 7, 1939 (53 Stat. 1243).

plish two principal purposes, to permit the deportation of vicious criminals and to alleviate hardship under existing law that made mandatory the deportation of aliens convicted of a crime involving moral turpitude committed within five years after entry or with two such convictions irrespective of time after entry. The Senate debated the bill at length but took no final action.

A fourth deportation bill (H.R. 7221) from the first session to be considered in the second was the Dickstein bill to shorten or terminate the stay of certain aliens admitted temporarily and to deport certain others who had been admitted permanently. Aimed at aliens who engage in "the promotion or dissemination of propaganda instigated from a foreign source" or in political activities while in the United States, the bill was debated in the House on June 18, 1936 and passed with minor amendment by the one-sided vote of 172 to 22. It went no further than the Senate Committee on Immigration, to which it was referred.

The session also received several new bills on deportation. Members of Congress from North Carolina and Alabama introduced bills of identical title in Senate and House for the multiple purposes as stated of further reducing immigration, authorizing the exclusion of any alien whose entry is inimical to the public interest, prohibiting the separation of families by admission of aliens who leave dependents behind them, and providing for the prompt deportation of habitual criminals (S. 4011, Reynolds [N.C.]; H.R. 11172, Starnes [Ala.]). Both remained in committee, as did a bill to deport at any time after entry aliens who enter illegally and to prohibit the making of loans or giving of relief or employment to such aliens (H.R. 12083, Green [Fla.]).

New grounds for deportation were contained in two bills introduced by Dickstein of New York (H.R. 9992 and 11040), both entitled "To deport certain aliens who received preference quota or nonquota visas through fraud by contracting marriage abroad solely to expedite entry. . . ." The substance of the proposal was contained in section 3 of the second of the two bills, where it was stated, in part,

> That any alien who at any time after entering the United States is found to have received either nonquota or preference-quota visa through fraud, by contracting a marriage which, subsequent to entry into the United States, has been judicially annulled retroactively to date of marriage, shall be taken into custody and deported.

This bill was reported out on February 7, 1936 (H. Rept. 2017, on H.R. 11040). The House took no further action on it, but it was reintroduced by its author in the next Congress (H.R. 28 [75-I]).

Additionally, a multipurpose bill included deportation among its various purposes, which were to restrict immigration, prevent the purchase and possession of firearms by aliens, and provide for the deportation of criminal and certain other aliens (H.R. 12057, Whelchel [Ga.]).

Various other bills in addition to the preceding dealt with regulation or restriction of immigration. Amendment of the Quota Act of 1924 was called for by several bills, of which one at least concerned administrative provisions of the act (S. 3871, Schwellenbach [Wash.] and Bone [Wash.]; H.R. 9679, Stubbs [Calif.]). Regulation or control of immigration was the design of a bill whose stated purpose was "to protect American citizens" as well as to aid in the enforcement of the naturalization laws (H.R. 11304, Kramer [Calif.]); and another proposal was that immigration be suspended (H.R. 11741, Green [Fla.]). But in a move to liberalize the immigration laws concerning relatives, the House passed the King bill (H.R. 7975 [74-I]) from the first session to permit the entry of alien wives of American citizens if the marriage had occurred prior to the Immigration Act of 1924.[65] It was not acted on in the Senate.

A few bills dealt with alien residents of the United States. Two registration bills were introduced (H.R. 11740, Green [Fla.]; H.R. 12652, Carter [Calif.]). The Sadowski bill (H.R. 4340 [74-I]) to restrict "habitual commuting" of aliens for employment in the United States, reported out in the preceding session of the 74th Congress, was debated, amended, and passed by the House, but made no progress in the Senate. The Stubbs bill to make it "illegal to employ any alien while there are American citizens unemployed who are qualified, able, and willing to work" was reintroduced.[66] Varied disabilities to be imposed on aliens were to prevent their occupying lands within the Yakima Indian Reservation (H.R. 11370, Knute Hill [Wash.]), to prohibit expenditures for alien members of the military and naval forces (H.R. 12357, Gasque [S.C.]), and to deny them any benefits from the newly passed Social Security Act (S. 4721, Reynolds [N.C.]). Also debated and passed by the House was the Dickstein bill from the first session (H.R. 3472 [74-I]), for the voluntary removal at government expense of financially distressed aliens. The House approved the committee amendment to eliminate any duration of residence time limit on such removal; and in the course of debate it was pointed out that an alien so removed would not be eligible for reentry. Passed without record vote, the bill did not progress in the Senate.

The 74th Congress adjourned on June 20, 1936 without having passed new legislation on immigration except for the Bland Act concerning alien seamen. This very limited action was in spite of the efforts by many members of the Congress to strengthen the laws for deportation

[65]*Congressional Record,* 80:2228, Feb. 17, 1936.

[66]H.R. 12662, Stubbs (Calif.). See his H.R. 3048 (74-I), p. 236.

of aliens, together with efforts to further regulate or restrict immigration and alien employment as means of alleviating unemployment. A few measures were passed by the House, it is true, but with the one exception none succeeded in gaining Senate approval.

75th Congress (1937, 1938)

The first of the three sessions of the 75th Congress convened on January 5, 1937 and continued until August 21. The long session was characterized, as far as immigration matters were concerned, by a continued and principal concern with deportation and by persistent reintroduction by their sponsors of bills that had failed of passage in previous Congresses. Otherwise there was about the same distribution of new bills by subject as in the immediately preceding sessions.

Thirteen bills relating to deportation were introduced, of which ten remained in committee. Of the ten, four called for the deportation of alien criminals,[67] and one for the deportation of "habitual alien criminals and other undesirable aliens" (S. 1365, Reynolds [N.C.]). Two would deport "aliens inimical to the public interest" and aliens on relief (S. 1363, Reynolds [N.C.]; H.R. 4356, Starnes [Ala.]). And a Senate bill concerned stay of deportation for certain aliens.[68]

Of the three deportation bills to be reported out of committee, all in the House, two were by Dickstein of New York and one by Dies of Texas. The first of the Dickstein bills (H.R. 27), identical with his H.R. 7221 of the preceding Congress, was to authorize deportation or shortening the stay of aliens for propaganda or political activities; and the latter sections of the bill defined propaganda and unlawful political activities for the purposes of the measure. The bill was reported out early in the session (H. Rept. 67 [75-I]), on January 28, 1937, was debated, and then was recommitted, where it remained for the rest of the session.

More progress was made on the other Dickstein bill, for deportation of aliens who expedite their entry by means of fraudulent marriage (H.R. 28). Identical with a bill of the preceding Congress (H.R. 11040 [74-II]), it was reported out on January 27, 1937 (H. Rept. 65), brought up in the House on March 1 but passed over, and finally brought up again on March 17. At that time the House accepted the Jenkins amendment for

[67] H.R. 264, Smith (Va.); H.R. 1969, Taylor (Tenn.); H.R. 5573, Dies (Tex.); H.R. 7437, Jenkins (Ohio).

[68] S. 990, Copeland (N.Y.). The other deportation bills were H.R. 2532, May (Ky.) and H.R. 2697, Phillips (Conn.).

immediate deportation of an alien who fails to fulfill a promise of marriage made to procure admission to the United States. As amended, the bill was passed by the House,[69] reported without amendment by the Senate committee on April 29, 1937 (S. Rept. 426), and then passed by the Senate on May 3, 1937. With presidential approval it became the Act of May 14, 1937 (50 Stat. 164).

The Dies bill (H.R. 6391), similar to but not identical with his H.R. 5921 in the 74th Congress, was designed to strengthen the laws for the deportation of alien criminals, to authorize limited discretion in certain hardship cases, and to make several other changes in laws affecting aliens. It was reported back without amendment by the House committee (H. Rept. 618) on April 15, 1937. With regard to the deportation provisions of the bill the committee explained that under existing law an alien criminal, except in narcotics cases, can be deported only if convicted of a crime involving moral turpitude committed within five years of entry and sentenced to one year or more in jail or if there is a record of two such convictions and sentences subsequent to February 5, 1917. The first section of the Dies bill provided prompt deportation if an alien

> (1) Is hereafter convicted in the United States within five years after entry of the institution of deportation proceedings against him for a crime involving moral turpitude for which the alien is committed to an institution as a result of such conviction; or
> (2) has been convicted in the United States within five years after entry of the institution of deportation proceedings against him for the crime of possessing or carrying any firearm, even if the alien was not sentenced to imprisonment; or
> (3) has been convicted of violation of any narcotics law of any State, Territory, insular possession, or the District of Columbia; or
> (4) knowingly and for gain has encouraged anyone to enter the United States in violation of law.[70]

The second section granted limited discretion concerning deportation in the case of aliens of good character who have resided in the United States for ten years or more; who have so resided for a year or more and have a parent, spouse, or child in the United States; or, for deportable aliens who are minors, if they have a lawfully admitted or citizen brother or sister in the United States. Such relief, however, was denied to criminal, immoral, and radical classes of aliens, and it was limited to 3500 cases in the first year of operation, 1500 in subsequent years, and was to run

[69]*Congressional Record,* 81:2351.

[70]Note the resemblance to the Coolidge bill in the Senate during the preceding Congress, S. 2969 (74-I).

only four years. Other sections of the bill proposed repealing the agricultural preference in section 6(a) of the 1924 Act and extending the time period of entry for which registry was permitted by the Act of March 2, 1929 (45 Stat. 1512).

The Dies bill was brought up for debate in the House on June 10, 1937, at which time its author noted that it represented a compromise, and that going back to the Kerr-Coolidge bill and earlier, Congress had been trying for at least five or six years to arrive at a compromise bill on deportation that could command majority support.[71] Debate then proceeded at length. Numbers of amendments were offered, but all were rejected except the Bradley amendment to exempt from the terms of the act those whose "crime involving moral turpitude prior to entry relates solely to the fraudulent securing of a visa or passport."[72] The amendment being accepted, 67 to 57, and others rejected, the bill survived a motion to recommit and was passed by the House without record vote on June 10 and then transmitted to the Senate, where further action was delayed until the next session.

Deportationist and restrictionist sentiment were closely allied, and not infrequently both were expressed in the same bill. One of the bills for the deportation of alien criminals mentioned above also proposed further restriction of immigration (H.R. 1969, Taylor [Tenn.]); and the title of another bill stated its purpose in the sweeping terms, "To deny admittance into the United States to all immigrants, and to deport all aliens" (H.R. 8265, Pace [Ga.]). For the most part, it is true, the restrictionist bills were the product of a small but persistent group in Congress that reintroduced their favorite bills session after session. Included among the legislative proposals were bills of the same title in Senate and House for the further reduction of immigration, the exclusion of "any alien whose entry is inimical to the public interest," and for other purposes (S. 1365, Reynolds [N.C.]; H.R. 4356, Starnes [Ala.]). A representative from Georgia was author of two bills for the restriction of immigration, one presumably the same as a bill he offered in the 74th Congress.[73] The other, in addition to the restriction of immigration, was to prevent the purchase and possession of firearms by aliens and for the deportation of criminal aliens and others.[74] Deportation was also provided in a bill by Dies of Texas for the exclusion and expulsion of alien Fascists and Communists.[75] And reintroduced from the preceding ses-

[71]*Congressional Record,* 81:5540 et seq. [72]Ibid., p. 5570.

[73]H.R. 2553, Whelchel (Ga.). Compare his H.R. 6022 (74-I).

[74]H.R. 2543, Whelchel (Ga.); apparently the same as his H.R. 12057 (74-II).

[75]H.R. 3025, Dies (Tex.). See also his H.R. 7120 (74-I).

sion was a bill to raise the American standard of living and for other purposes, presumably restrictionist in intent.[76]

Continuing concern with unemployment, of course, contributed to efforts to restrict immigration and strengthen the deportation laws, but it also found expression in various measures to reduce immigrant competition with native labor. Three bills of the same title renewed the attempt to restrict commuting in of alien workers from contiguous territory.[77] One of the three was reported back (H. Rept. 159, on H.R. 3679), debated, amended, and passed by the House, but it made no progress in the Senate. For at least the fourth time Stubbs of California introduced a bill to make the employment of aliens illegal when there are any citizens unemployed though qualified, able, and willing to work.[78] Also to be mentioned in this connection is a bill to amend the Act of June 14, 1906 (34 Stat. 263), "An act to prevent aliens from fishing in the waters of Alaska" (H.R. 7878, Dimond [Alaska]). Two bills sought to protect Americans in the artistic professions from alien competition. The purpose of one, by Dickstein of New York, was, in its terms, "To protect the artistic and earning opportunities in the United States for American actors, vocal musicians, operatic singers, solo dancers, solo instrumentalists, and orchestral conductors" (H.R. 30). The other was to require bond to guarantee "the departure of alien actors, artists, lecturers, dancers, and singers, temporarily admitted to the United States for professional engagements, upon expiration of the time for which admitted" (H.R. 6280, Rees [Kans.]).

A few other bills may also be regarded as reflections of the national problems of the period. A renewed attempt was made to impose a quota limit on immigration from Mexico and the Philippines;[79] and another bill was designed to amend the section of the act setting the quotas (H.R. 3798, Kvale [Minn.]). Dickstein of New York again introduced his bill for the voluntary repatriation at government expense of aliens in financial distress.[80] In the form of an amendment to section 23 of the Immigration Act of February 5, 1917, the bill was reported back without amendment (H. Rept. 64, Jan. 27, 1937) and passed by the House on March 1, 1937;

[76]H.R. 11, Arends (Ill.). Compare his H.R. 9175 (74-I).

[77]S. 1803, Brown (Mich.); H.R. 1542, Sadowski (Mich.); H.R. 3679, Schulte (Ind.). For predecessor bills, see H.R. 4340, 6083 (74-I).

[78]H.R. 2541, Stubbs (Calif.). Earlier bills were H.R. 3048, 8602 (74-I); H.R. 12662 (74-II).

[79]H.R. 246, Colden (Calif.). Compare his H.R. 3007 (74-I), H.R. 9281 (73-II), and other similar bills in those sessions.

[80]H.R. 26, Dickstein (N.Y.). See also his H.R. 3472 (74-I), H.R. 3524 (73-I), and H.R.13811 (72-II).

it was reported again without amendment by the Senate committee (S. Rept. 425, April 29, 1937). The Senate then passed the bill without debate on May 3, and it was signed to become the Act of May 14, 1937 (50 Stat. 164). It modified existing law to permit the return of aliens without time limit instead of only within three years after entry, and the return was no longer limited to the alien's native country but could also be made to the country from which the alien came or of which he was a citizen or subject.

Not all of the measures introduced during the session were restrictionist or antialien in their tone. Pertaining to naturalization rather than immigration were several registration bills and a renewed bill by Mrs. O'Day of New York that "religious views or philosophical opinions against war" should not prevent the naturalization of otherwise eligible aliens (H.R. 8259). For the relief of possible hardship cases in deportation a bill was proposed to prevent the separation from their families of certain aliens convicted of crime who arrived in the United States as minors and to set a time limit on deportability for crime (S. 884, McNary [Oreg.]). Another bill sponsored by Mrs. O'Day was for the recognition in immigration law of valid foreign pardons (H.R. 3671). And a sign of the times was a group of three bills to assure asylum to refugees, referred to in one of the group as persons "subject to persecution on account of their race, religion, or political beliefs" (H.R. 5687, 7640, Celler [N.Y.]; H.R. 6245, O'Toole [N.Y.]). None of the above made headway in Congress, but somewhat more successful was a bill, identical with one passed by the House in the preceding Congress (H.R. 7975 [74-I]), to permit alien wives of American citizens whose marriage was prior to May 26, 1924 to enter the United States (H.R. 3471, King [Hawaii]). To amend section 13(c), paragraph 4 of the 1924 Act, it would permit the entry of wives not otherwise ineligible to citizenship.[81] Reported back without amendment (H. Rept. 71, Jan. 28, 1937), the bill was again passed in the House and again failed of action in the Senate.

The brief second session of the 75th Congress, from November 15 to December 21, 1937, received few immigration bills. In addition to a registry bill there were only three others, all concerned with deportation. Of the latter, one was for clarification of the Act of February 18, 1931 (46 Stat. 1171) that provided for the deportation of aliens convicted and sentenced for violation of any narcotics act (H.R. 8562, Lea [Calif.]). A Senate bill called for the prompt deportation of aliens engaged in espionage or other activities against the public interest (S. 3151, Reynolds

[81]The amending Act of June 13, 1930 had permitted the entry of Chinese wives; the King bill would extend the same privileges to all races ineligible to citizenship.

[N.C.]). The third, also aimed against subversives, provided for the cancellation of citizenship and the deportation of certain naturalized citizens advocating political doctrines "subversive of the best interests of the United States" (H.R. 8349, Weaver [N.C.]). No action was taken on any of the above beyond routine referral to committee.

The third and final session of the 75th Congress, which convened on January 3, 1938, continued the preoccupation with deportation and received only a scattered few other bills on immigration matters. The House received a resolution calling for the appointment of a committee for thorough study of the need for revision and codification of the laws on immigration, deportation, naturalization, and expatriation (H. Res. 483, Poage [Tex.]). It was referred to the Rules Committee and went no further. Of the four bills related to deportation during the session, one was for the prompt deportation of habitual criminal aliens, but with some softening provisions to prevent undue hardship or separation of families (S. 3202, Reynolds [N.C.]), another was for the deportation of aliens who advocate fealty to other governments (H.R. 10517, Voorhis [Calif.]), and a third was identical in title to one of the preceding session for cancellation of the citizenship of certain naturalized citizens advocating political doctrines considered subversive (S. 3200, Reynolds [N.C.]). None of the above came out of committee.

A fourth deportation bill dealt with in the Senate in the third session was the Dies bill (H.R. 6391) that had been passed by the House in the first session. As passed there the bill made deportable four classes of alien criminals not then subject to deportation: aliens convicted of a crime involving moral turpitude and committed to an institution, violators of concealed weapons laws, certain narcotics law violators not then deportable, and those smuggling in other aliens. The Senate committee, reporting out the bill on January 5, 1938, considered the first of the above four provisions too harsh and amended it to specify two classes of aliens deportable for crimes involving moral turpitude. These were:

1. Those convicted of crime involving moral turpitude during a period of five years antedating the act or at any time within five years prior to the deportation proceedings, but not unless the alien has been committed to an institution for six months or more without option of fine instead of imprisonment.

2. Aliens who after passage of the act are convicted more than once of crimes involving moral turpitude and who have been committed to an institution each time without option of fine in lieu of imprisonment.

Section 2 of the House draft conferred discretionary powers on the Secretary of Labor for waiver of deportation, but with certain cases excepted. The Senate committee increased the exceptions to such waiver to include the physically or mentally defective, diseased, illiterate, contract labor, and public charge classes; and it was also stipulated that the alien must be of good moral character to be eligible for the waiver of deportation.

A new section added by the Senate committee provided that lawfully admitted aliens going to Mexico, Canada, or Cuba for business or pleasure shall not be considered to make a new entry for immigration purposes on their return unless they are anarchists, criminals, or of an immoral class.

In consideration of the bill, the Senate accepted its committee's amendment of the first section[82] and other amendments, including the so-called Austin amendment of section 8 of the House draft and section 9 of the Senate draft, which was to allow hardship cases to remain in the United States, to be charged to quota, and their number to be reported to Congress.[83] The bill progressed no further, however, in spite of a letter from the Commissioner of Immigration recommending its passage;[84] it died soon after, with the end of the session and Congress on June 16, 1938.

On other matters, Senate and House bills renewed an earlier effort to amend the Act of June 14, 1906 (34 Stat. 263), entitled "An act to prevent aliens from fishing in the waters of Alaska."[85] The House bill was reported back (H. Rept. 2243, April 27, 1938) without amendment and passed by the House. Other than certain minor changes of wording, it was to amend the 1906 Act by adding a proviso to permit any bona fide resident of Alaska, who had been such for three consecutive years and during that time had engaged in fishing, to continue to do so for three years from the date of enactment of the bill, even though not a citizen. The Senate committee reported the bill out (S. Rept. 2066, June 7, 1938) with amendment to make sure there was no possible discrimination against Filipinos, adding the proviso, "That any person owing allegiance to the United States shall not be considered an alien for the purpose of this act." Passed in this form by the Senate and with House acceptance of the Senate amendment, the bill was signed by President Roosevelt (52 Stat. 1174).

Several other immigration-related bills were introduced during the session but did not go beyond referral to committee. These included a bill by Celler of New York to ensure admittance for permanent residence

[82]*Congressional Record,* 83:8289, June 7, 1938; and S. Rept. 1616 (75-III).

[83]Ibid., p. 8993, June 13, 1938. [84]Ibid., p. 8995.

[85]S. 3932, Copeland (N.Y.); H.R. 10432, Crowe (Ind.). An earlier bill of the same title was H.R. 7878 (75-I).

to certain classes of aliens (H.R. 10013), one to amend the Immigration Act of 1924 (H.R. 8998, Cannon [Wis.]), one relating to certain Filipino residents (S. 3506, Shipstead [Minn.]), and a bill by Reynolds of North Carolina, a leader in proposing antialien and anti-immigration measures, to suspend immigration for permanent residence for the period of one year (S. 3201).

Comment

The years immediately preceding 1929 had been a period of legislative activity and policy formation with regard to immigration, during which Congress adopted the policy of numerical limitation by means of national quotas and, after several postponements, instituted the national origins quota formula beginning in 1929. The decade that followed, from 1929 to 1939, was spanned by the 71st to the 75th Congresses, and it was itself an eventful decade. It began with the severe and worldwide Depression, saw the rise of Nazi power and a mounting wave of refugees from Central Europe, and ended with the onset of the Second World War.

Predictably, these major events during the decade influenced the type of immigration measures presented in Congress. In response to depression and unemployment were numerous bills to restrict immigration further and even to suspend all immigration while there were American citizens out of work, to facilitate the departure of aliens in financial distress, to check the commuting in of aliens for employment, and to restrict the admission of aliens in certain professional categories.

Perhaps most numerous were the bills to provide for the deportation of certain designated classes of aliens. Economic considerations were presumably present in the several bills for the deportation of alien public charges, but it was alien criminals who were the principal targets of the deportation bills. But these bills also give evidence of rising fears of subversive activities; and deportability was variously proposed for aliens disseminating foreign propaganda, acting as espionage agents, belonging to the Communist party, or considered inimical to the national interest.

Amendments of the Quota Act of 1924 and especially of the national origins quota system were proposed, including modification of the quota preference and nonquota classes. And there were persistent attempts to extend the quota limitations to the Western Hemisphere and the Philippines, with Mexico the leading subject of such restrictive proposals.

On the whole, however, there was notably little legislative reaction in the form of immigration bills to the domestic and international problems of the time, compared with the amount of legislative activity in preceding and following periods. The number of depression-related bills was not large, there were only a scattered few concerning subversives, and not more than several bills for the relief of refugees. Even more notable is the fact that almost none of the immigration bills introduced during the decade was enacted; and those enacted were in the nature of small adjustments and amendments to existing law rather than new formulations of policy. It was as if Congress, having labored long and hard during the preceding years and finally having brought forth an elaborate structure of law and policy for the regulation of immigration, was now disposed to consider the subject adequately cared for. In administration, the structure built by Congress had proved to be flexible enough to meet the problems of the Depression period as they were seen at the time, without need for new legislation. Also, there were other and much more pressing problems to occupy Congress's attention during the ten-year period, and immigration was no longer the major subject of policy debate it had been earlier.

7 The War Years and Their Aftermath, 1939–1953

The pendulum of legislative attention had swung away from immigration and related matters during the Depression decade, as described in the preceding chapter, but it swung back during the years that followed. The outbreak of the Second World War in 1939 reactivated the old questions of policy toward immigration and alien minorities, and there was the added matter of refugees to be considered. Pushed into the background for a time by more urgent wartime demands on congressional attention when the United States itself became involved in the conflict, these questions returned to prominence in the postwar years, just as they had toward the end of and after the First World War. And in the second as in the first postwar period, the congressional debate over immigration policy revolved around the central question of a liberal versus a restrictive policy, which lay behind and was partly screened by legislative skirmishes on many lesser issues.

76th Congress (1939–1941)

Deportation bills again outnumbered those dealing with other aspects of immigration, numbering at least eighteen during the first session of the 76th Congress. Two carried on a concern from the Depression period by making provision for the deportation of aliens subsisting on relief, under certain circumstances (S. 410, Reynolds [N.C.]; H.R. 3030, Starnes [Ala.]). Four others dealt wholly or in part with alien criminals,[1] but the majority were directed against aliens considered to be disloyal or subversive. Among the grounds for deportation provided by these bills was being held inimical to the public interest (S. 411, 1979, Reynolds [N.C.]; H.R. 3031, Starnes [Ala.]), advocating fealty to other governments (H.R.

[1]H.R. 273, Smith (Va.); H.R. 279, Taylor (Tenn.); H.R. 3029, 6724, Starnes (Ala.). H.R. 3245, Whelchel (Ga.), was primarily for the restriction of immigration, but also provided for the deportation of alien criminals.

117, Voorhis [Calif.]), advocating the making of any changes in the American form of government,[2] advocating political doctrines subversive of the best interests of the United States by a naturalized citizen,[3] being a Fascist or a Communist,[4] engaging in un-American activities (H.R. 4006, Boland [Pa.]), failing to make declaration of intention to become a citizen (H.R. 4172, Randolph [W.Va.]), and attempting to subvert members of the armed forces (H.R. 5138, Randolph [W.Va.]). And, finally, there were two bills for the prompt deportation of aliens engaging in espionage or sabotage, together with alien criminals and "other undesirable aliens" (H.R. 3029, 6724, Starnes [Ala.]).

Also touching on deportation were two House resolutions to authorize the Committee on Immigration and Nationality "to make a thorough study of need for revision and separate codification of laws relating to immigration, deportation, naturalization, and expatriation,"[5] these being reintroductions of a resolution from the third session of the preceding Congress.

Only three of the above deportation bills were reported out. The bill by Dempsey of New Mexico to amend existing law to provide for the exclusion and deportation of aliens advocating change in the American form of government was reported favorably (H. Rept. 259, on H.R. 4860, March 21, 1939) and then passed with amended title by the House. It made no progress in the Senate.

The Randolph bill, to outlaw attempts to interfere with the discipline of the armed forces and to provide a penalty of deportation for an alien, also carried the stipulation that aliens seeking to enter the United States be fingerprinted. As amended and reported out by the House committee (H. Rept. 994, on H.R. 5138), it was an entirely new bill in four titles. The first title was to protect members of the armed forces from subversive influences; the second amended section 19 of the 1917 Act by adding four new deportable classes, to consist of an alien who at any time after entry engages in any of the following activities:

1. knowingly and for gain aids or encourages another alien to gain entry or try to gain entry in violation of law;
2. "engages in espionage for a foreign government or international

[2]S. 1941, Connally (Tex.); H.R. 4860, Dempsey (N.M.). Such advocacy was also to be made ground for exclusion.

[3]H.R. 5454, Flaherty (Mass.). The bill provided for cancellation of citizenship prior to the deportation. See also S. 3200 (75-III).

[4]H.R. 4905, Dies (Tex.); also constituting ground for exclusion under the terms of the bill.

[5]H. Res. 86, 115, Schulte (Ind.). Compare H. Res. 483 (75-III).

political agency, seeking to change the character of the Government of the United States or influence its politics";

3. has been convicted of violation of a state narcotics law;

4. possesses or carries without legal authority any weapon that is an automatic or semiautomatic, or that has a silencer, or is a sawed-off shotgun.

In this form the bill reflected some concerns of the moment as well as some concerns of longer standing. It also retained the provision for registration and fingerprinting of arriving aliens. Several amendments were proposed under strict time limitation of debate, and they were for the most part rejected except for committee-sponsored amendments. The amended bill was then passed by the House.[6] It next went to the Senate Committee on the Judiciary and was reported out without amendment (S. Rept. 1154), but was not acted on further in the Senate until the third session (see below).

The remaining bill to be reported out and acted on was the second of the two Starnes (Ala.) bills for the prompt deportation of aliens engaging in espionage or sabotage, of alien criminals, and of "other undesirable aliens" (H.R. 6724). It was reported back to the House without amendment (H. Rept. 829, June 13, 1939). According to the description in the committee report, the bill would require prompt deportation of any alien who

1. has admitted in writing that he has engaged in, or been convicted of, espionage or sabotage for a foreign government since entry into the United States;

2. has at any time after entry been convicted of a violation of any narcotics law of the United States or any of its subdivisions;

3. has been lawfully committed to a public or private institution as a habitual user of narcotic drugs.

The House passed the bill without debate and sent it to the Senate. It was reported out by the Senate committee without amendment (S. Rept. 918) but did not come up for consideration by the Senate until the third session.

In addition to the deportation bills, the heightened feeling of distrust and insecurity with respect to aliens in the late 1930s found expression in proposals to limit alien rights, to increase controls in various ways, and to further restrict and regulate immigration. Senate bills called for the securing of special information with respect to aliens in the forthcoming

[6] *Congressional Record,* 4:10456, July 29, 1939.

1940 census (S. 1324, Ellender [La.]) and to prohibit the employment of aliens in the manufacture of airplanes for the government (S. 2711, McCarran [Nev.]). There were House bills to require all aliens to declare allegiance to the United States within thirty days (H.R. 5481, Brooks [La.]), to amend the Shipping Act regarding the denial of certain benefits to aliens (H.R. 5837, Kramer [Calif.]), to regulate the taking by nonresident aliens of title to or proceeds from personal property within the United States by descent or inheritance and to provide for the escheat of such property (H.R. 5871, Crawford [Mich.]), and to disclose the interest of nonresident aliens and others in securities registered on the national exchanges.[7] None of the above was reported out by the Senate or House committees to which it was referred.

Bills to require the registration of aliens were another expression of congressional concern about the alien population. Seven such bills appeared during the first session of the 76th Congress, and as noted above another bill as amended in committee provided for the registration and fingerprinting of aliens (H.R. 5138, Smith [Va.]). Registration bills were by no means new, but the earlier emphasis was on the creation of a record of lawful entry where such did not exist, in order to facilitate naturalization. Now, in the climate of distrust of aliens that then existed, registration was seen as a means or a step toward exercising tighter controls over alien minorities.

Of this group of bills, two by members of Congress from Tennessee were simply noted as being for the registration of aliens (S. 2830, Stewart; H.R. 7379, Gore). A third bill by a member from Tennessee called for both registration and fingerprinting (S. 1470, McKellar). An additional two bills indicated a further purpose with the title, "To provide for the national defense by the registration of aliens" (S. 408, Reynolds [N.C.]; H.R. 3392, Starnes [Ala.]). The remaining two bills were to require registration of all aliens employed by the federal government or any part or agency thereof (H.R. 5483, Shafer [Mich.]; H.R. 5484, Evans [N.Y.]). Only one of the registration bills above was reported out, in the Senate (S. Rept. 937, on S. 2830), where it was debated but not brought to vote.

Another type of bill that appeared with greater frequency at the time was for the suspension or further restriction of immigration. Representative Pace of Georgia reintroduced a bill he had sponsored before (H.R. 999), whose purpose, as succinctly stated in the title, was "To deny admittance into the United States to all immigrants and to deport all

[7]H.R. 6048, Boren (Okla.). Also reappearing but not inherently antialien were resolutions to exclude aliens in the apportionment of representation: S. J. Res. 54, Capper (Kans.); H. J. Res. 37, Tarver (Ga.).

aliens." Whelchel, also a representative from Georgia and long on record as being no friend of immigration, introduced a bill for its restriction (H.R. 3241). He was also author of a bill for the more diverse purposes of restricting immigration, preventing the purchase and possession of firearms by aliens, and deporting criminal and certain other aliens (H.R. 3245). Two bills by Senator Holman of Oregon were to prohibit immigration during the prevailing period of unemployment and high expenditure for unemployment relief (S. 2451 and 2840). And another pair of bills was designed to reduce immigration, exclude aliens whose entry is "inimical to the public interest," and prohibit the separation of families through the entry of aliens who leave dependents behind them (S. 407, Reynolds [N.C.]; H.R. 3033, Starnes [Ala.]). None of the above bills progressed beyond referral to committee.

The session also received the customary types of bills offered in every Congress for the regulation of immigration in certain of its aspects. Included here were two Senate bills for amendment of the Immigration Act of 1924 (S. 2361, Downey [Calif.]; S. 2968, Brown [Mich.]), two House bills to amend immigration law so as to restrict the landing of certain alien seamen (H.R. 5838, 7004, Kramer [Calif.]), and two for restriction of the habitual entrance of aliens for employment in the United States (S. 1383, Brown [Mich.]; H.R. 4496, Lesinski [Mich.]). The authors of the two latter bills were from Michigan, as had been most of the sponsors of similar bills before. A Senate bill with a distinctly restrictive flavor would have required all aliens to pass an intelligence test before admission for permanent residence (S. 2435, Smathers [N.J.]); but the same sponsor introduced a bill for the admission for permanent residence of certain aged persons "whose admission would not be contrary to the interest of the public" (S. 1029). Another bill was to provide a method whereby some aliens now in the United States might be readmitted for permanent residence (H.R. 7321, Lesinski [Mich.]). And Dickstein of New York proposed elimination of the requirement that Chinese passengers be listed on a separate ship manifest (H.R. 4823). Neither this nor the other foregoing bills came out of committee.

Somewhat more successful was a bill introduced by King of Hawaii to permit entry of alien wives of American citizens who were not otherwise eligible to citizenship and who were married prior to approval of the Immigration Act of 1924 (May 26, 1924). Similar to a bill by the same author that was passed by the House in the 74th Congress and identical to one also passed by the House in the 75th Congress, the new bill was reported out without amendment (H. Rept. 123, on H.R. 160, King [Hawaii]) and passed without debate on March 20, 1939. It went to the Senate, where nothing more was heard of it.

A final topic of legislative proposals during the first session of the

76th Congress was aid to refugees. Three such bills were introduced, all by Celler of New York, of which two were designated for assurance of asylum to refugees (H.R. 221 and 2533), and the other to assure them legal admission for permanent residence (H.R. 2722). They remained in committee to the end of the session.

Only one immigration bill is to be noted during the second session of the 76th Congress, from September 21 to November 3, 1939. It was identical in title with a bill from the preceding session, for the deportation of certain aliens who do not make declaration of intention to acquire citizenship (H.R. 7569, Ludlow [Ind.]). No action was taken on it.

The third session of the 76th Congress, which ran for a full year from January 3, 1940 to January 3, 1941, followed the pattern of the first session regarding immigration. The *Congressional Record* for the session, however, gave evidence of much increased public concern, in the form of numbers of addresses over the radio and published articles dealing with questions of immigration and alien minorities. This was clearly a reaction to the war in Europe and the growing threat of American involvement, for wars, like depressions, always have strong effects on attitudes toward immigration and the alien.

Deportation continued to rank high among immigration questions, and Congress was now more disposed than before to take action. A new deportation bill was entered in the Senate (S. 4263, Clark [Mo.]), but attention centered on several bills carried over from the first session. The Dempsey (N.Mex.) bill (H.R. 4860 [76-I]) to amend existing immigration law for exclusion and deportation of aliens advocating any change in the American form of government, which had been passed by the House in the first session, was now reported with amendment of wording by the Senate committee (S. Rept. 1684). There was debate on the bill in the Senate, but it was not brought to vote.

Another bill passed by the House and reported out in the Senate in the first session was the Starnes (Ala.) bill for the prompt deportation of aliens guilty of espionage or sabotage, together with several other classes of aliens (H.R. 6724 [76-I]). It was debated, amended in wording, and passed by the Senate; the House accepted the Senate amendments, but the bill was then vetoed by President Roosevelt.[8] Substantially the same bill, for the prompt deportation of aliens engaging in espionage or sabo-

[8]In his veto message of April 6, 1940 (*Congressional Record,* 86:4157) the President stated with respect to the bill's three principal provisions that there was already sufficient authority for the deportation of saboteurs and spies, that he approved the deportation of narcotics act violators, but that the deportation of habitual users of narcotics was not justified, for they were victims of a disease rather than criminals.

tage, alien criminals, and "other undesirable aliens," was reintroduced in the House (H.R. 9774, Poage [Tex.]). It was reported out there with amendment (H. Rept. 2327, May 28, 1940) by the House committee, which struck out the phrase "has admitted in writing that he has engaged" in espionage, and substituted the wording "is a spy or has engaged." Passed by the House as so amended, it went to the Senate where it was not acted on further.

The third deportation bill to be brought up from the first session was the now much rewritten Randolph bill (H.R. 5138 [76-I]) to outlaw interference with discipline of the armed forces, to require fingerprinting of arriving aliens, and to call for the deportation of certain classes of aliens. Amended and passed by the House, it had been reported out by the Senate committee in the first session. Recommitted in the third session, it was reported out again with amendment, the report was then withdrawn, and a substitute report was entered with amended title.[9] According to the latter report, the Senate amendment of the bill was "in the nature of a substitute," with title changed to "Prevention of Subversive Activities and Registration of Aliens." Among the purposes of the amended bill, as stated in the final report, were the following:

1. to prohibit the advocacy of insubordination, disloyalty, and so on, in the armed forces;
2. to prohibit the advocacy of the overthrow or destruction of any government in the United States by force or violence;
3. to add several new grounds for deportation;
4. to require registration and fingerprinting of aliens.

The new deportable classes under the bill were

> aliens who knowingly and for gain have assisted any other alien to enter or try to enter the United States in violation of law; aliens who have been convicted of possessing and of carrying certain firearms in violation of law, and aliens convicted of violating the provision of Title I of this bill [concerning subversive action in the armed forces].

Registration and fingerprinting of aliens entering the United States was to be required after the effective date of the act, and the same applied to all resident aliens, with the exemption of those under fourteen years of age from fingerprinting.

The bill was then debated, amended, and passed by the Senate, and on disagreement by the House to the Senate amendments it went to conference. The conference report (H. Rept. 2683, June 21, 1940) was

[9] S. Rept. 1721, followed by S. Rept. 1796, June 10, 1940.

accepted by both Senate and House, and with change of title and presidential signature the bill became the Alien Registration Act of June 28, 1940 (54 Stat. 670).

The following provisions of the bill are to be noted in particular:

> Title I, sec. 1(a). It shall be unlawful to attempt any form of subversion of the Armed Forces.
>
> Sec. 2. It shall be unlawful to advocate in any way the overthrow of the Government of the United States.
>
> Sec. 20. The following classes are made deportable:
>
> 1) Any alien who, at any time within five years after entry, shall have, knowingly and for gain, encouraged . . . any other alien to enter or try to enter the United States in violation of law.
> 2) Aliens who at any time after entry shall have on more than one occasion aided another alien to enter in violation of law.
> 3) Aliens who at any time after entry have been convicted of possessing or carrying an automatic or semiautomatic weapon.
> 4) Any alien within five years after entry who violates any provision of the Alien Registration Act of 1940.
> 5) Any alien at any time after entry who has been convicted of more than one violation of the Alien Registration Act of 1940.
>
> Sec. 30. Registry and fingerprinting required for issuance of a visa to an alien seeking to enter the United States.
>
> Sec. 31. It is the duty of every alien in the United States aged 14 and over to be registered and fingerprinted, if to remain for 30 days or longer.
>
> Sec. 32. Foreign government officials and their families are exempt from the requirement of the preceding section.

Other bills relating to aliens within the United States were in part for the relief of hardship cases and in part to limit the rights or privileges of such aliens. Of the former type was a bill, introduced by Walter of Pennsylvania, who was later to become the influential chairman of the House Committee on Immigration and Nationality, for the relief of wives of alien clergymen (H.R. 8302). And Celler of New York, later to serve for many years as chairman of the House Judiciary Committee of which the immigration committee is a subcommittee, presented a bill to record as lawfully admitted for permanent residence certain aliens who entered on visitors' visas but were in fact refugees or unable to return to their country of origin because of the war in Europe (H.R. 10702). Restrictive in character were two bills to limit the use of arms and "other implements of war" by aliens (S. 4038, Bridges [N.H.]; H.R. 9881, Hawks [Wis.]), one for the regulation of alien-controlled publications (H.R. 9977, Rich [Pa.]), and House and Senate bills for amendment of the 1924 Act in order to require aliens admitted as officials of foreign governments to maintain their status or depart (S. 4149, Russell [Ga.]; H.R. 10112, Dickstein [N.Y.]). The House bill, by Dickstein of New York, was the only one to be acted on. Reported out (H. Rept. 2645) and passed by the House, it was then passed by the Senate in lieu of its own S. 4149 and signed into law as the Act of July 1, 1940 (54 Stat. 711).

A few additional bills for the restriction or suspension of immigration were introduced during the third session, added to the half-dozen or so such bills carried over from the first session. One of the new bills asked for the suspension of immigration for permanent residence as long as hostilities continued in Europe and Asia (H.R. 7875, Seccombe [Ohio]). Another proposed to prohibit the entry of quota immigrants (H.R. 9685, Vinson [Ga.]), still another would accomplish the same purpose by prohibiting the issuance of quota visas and further restricting the admission of aliens (S. 3201, Reynolds [N.C.]). There was a Senate bill (S. 3826, Gibson [Vt.]) to restrict and control immigration for the stated purpose of "protection of American homes and industry." And a final member of this group was to limit immigration and to extend the quota system to all countries of North, Central, and South America, and the adjacent islands (S. 3730, Reynolds [N.C.]). None of these bills came out of committee.

There were a few additional bills for amendment of the immigration laws and the further regulation of immigration. Four of them were to amend section 4(d) of the 1924 Act,[10] the subsection that gave nonquota status under certain conditions to a minister of religion or a professor, together with his wife and children. Of the four bills, the second of two entered by Mrs. O'Day of New York was reported back (H. Rept. 1725, March 11, 1940) with the following explanation:

> The purpose of the bill is to place women on the same basis as men and to give them the same privileges that run to a male alien under section 4(d) of the nonquota section in connection with the vocations of minister of any religious denomination, or professor of a college, academy, seminary, or university.

No further action was taken on the bill.

Also to be noted are three bills for preventing the illegal entry of aliens (S. 4071, Lee [Okla.]; H.R. 9863, 9903, Snyder [Pa.]), one to increase the number of immigration visas available for children under the age of fourteen from certain European countries (H.R. 10150, Mrs. O'Day [N.Y.]), and a resolution to authorize the admission of a limited number of refugee children from Great Britain (H.J. Res. 580, Havenner [Calif.]).

[10] S. 3542, Lucas (Ill.); S. 3988, Pepper (Fla.); H.R. 8236, 8753, Mrs. O'Day (N.Y.).

77th Congress (1941, 1942)

The first session of the 77th Congress was another long session, from its opening on January 3, 1941 to January 2, 1942. Elected as a peacetime Congress, for the attack on Pearl Harbor was not to come until the closing weeks of the session, on December 7, 1941, the 77th Congress in its first session faced a period of mounting anxiety from war abroad and rumors of impending war at home. Relative to the larger issues of the time, immigration probably did not merit high priority, but certain concerns of the time were reflected in the immigration bills introduced in Congress, as they had been to a lesser extent in the immediately preceding sessions. Deportation bills were still numerous, as were proposals to restrict or suspend immigration, but the principal emphasis was now on controls and restrictions applied to the resident alien population.

Deportation bills, to consider them first, were at least eleven in number, and considerations of national security and the public interest at a time of external and internal threat were prominent among the new bills. Comprehensive in its terms was a bill entitled

> To direct deportation for any person who, while in the United States, is, or has been, by his words or acts, sympathetic with, associated with, or affiliated with, or sought the support of, Communists, Fascists, or Nazis in the United States or elsewhere (H.R. 1811, L. M. Ford [Calif.]).

Reintroduced from the previous Congress was a bill "to diminish un-American activities by deporting aliens guilty of them."[11] Three bills were to authorize the prompt deportation of aliens engaging in espionage or sabotage.[12] Deportation was also advocated for aliens "inimical to the public interest."[13] There were two bills for deportation of certain aliens who do not make declaration of intention to become citizens.[14] Exclusion and deportation were also proposed for aliens who advocate basic changes in the American form of government.[15] Other bills related to deportation were introduced by Senators Russell of Georgia (S. 1232) and Reynolds of North Carolina (S. 1382), the former bill being for the supervision and detention of certain deportable aliens, for a board to supervise deportable aliens, and for the relief of certain aliens from

[11]H.R. 1826, Boland (Pa.). Same title as his H.R. 4006 (76-I).

[12]H.R. 1080, Carlson (Kans.); H.R. 1436, Starnes (Ala.); H.R. 2600, Poage (Tex.). The last of these also applied to alien criminals and "other undesirable aliens."

[13]S. 1382, Reynolds (N.C.). Same title as his S. 411 (76-I).

[14]H.R. 1001, Randolph (W.Va.); H.R. 1031, Ludlow (Ind.). Compare H.R. 4172 (76-I).

[15]H.R. 1435, Starnes (Ala.). The two similar bills in the 76th Congress were directed against aliens who advocate *any* change in the American form of government.

deportation. None of the deportation bills received committee approval during the session.

Another type of bill that became more numerous in reflection of attitudes of the time proposed the suspension, restriction, or further regulation of immigration. Pace of Georgia, whose support of drastic measures has been noted before, reintroduced an earlier bill to deny admission to all immigrants and to deport all aliens (H.R. 1417), together with another to deny admission to all immigrants as long as unemployment in the United States exceeds 1 million (H.R. 3163). Similar in intent if different in means were other bills to reduce all immigration quotas to zero during the existing national emergency (H.R. 3865, Kramer [Calif.]) and to prohibit the issuance of visas to quota immigrants (S. 1384, Reynolds [N.C.]). There were House and Senate bills to authorize the refusal of visas to aliens "whose admission into the United States would endanger the public safety" (H.R. 4817, Beckworth [Tex.]; S. 913, Russell [Ga.]). The House bill, after being reported out (H. Rept. 762), was tabled in favor of the Senate bill, which meanwhile had been reported out and passed in the Senate (S. Rept. 386). Passed by the House, the bill was signed to become the Act of June 20, 1941 (55 Stat. 252). It authorized diplomatic and consular officers to refuse a visa to an alien who they had reason to believe sought to enter the United States for purposes that would endanger the public safety.

Some bills called for restriction of immigration, such as one by Whelchel of Georgia (H.R. 3108), whereas others proposed a selective restriction in the national interest. Of the latter sort were two bills introduced in the House by Allen of Louisiana. One was "To promote the national defence by limiting the entry of certain aliens" (H.R. 4873); the other was to promote both the national defense and public welfare by reducing quota immigration, excluding and deporting undesirable aliens, putting such aliens under detention, and creating a Board of Deportation Appeals and Supervision of Deportable Aliens (H.R. 4861). The former of these bills, redrafted and renumbered in committee in place of an earlier bill,[16] was reported back (H. Rept. 875, on H.R. 4873) with minority views attached. In its redrafted form it was to exclude persons interned in nations at war. The House took no further action on the bill.

Approximately a dozen bills concerning alien residents of the United States were introduced, many with predominant emphasis on security considerations. Among the stated objectives of such bills were to prohibit

[16]H.R. 4215, Allen (La.), the title of which was "To provide for the exclusion of aliens who have been imprisoned or otherwise incarcerated in the United States or in a foreign country."

the employment of aliens in the manufacture of aircraft for the government (S. 17 by McCarran of Nevada), to protect national defense industries from possible sabotage and espionage by aliens (S. 1719 by Stewart of Tennessee), to provide for the incarceration of dangerous aliens (S. 1720, also by Stewart), to restrict the use of arms and other implements of war by aliens,[17] to amend the Criminal Code to make certain activities by aliens unlawful (H.R. 1842 by L. M. Ford of California), to prohibit aliens from voting in labor organizations or acting as their officers or agents (H.R. 4406 by Woodruff of Michigan), and to provide for the control and regulation of alien-published periodicals, newspapers, and other publications.[18] Other alien bills were to record the lawful admission for permanent residence of certain aliens who desire to serve in the armed forces (H.R. 3374, Voorhis [Calif.]), to exempt certain resident aliens from military service,[19] to prevent government expenditures for aliens illegally in the United States (H.R. 3385, Peterson of Georgia), to provide for the readmission for permanent residence of certain aliens (H.R. 1097, Lesinski of Michigan), and, resubmitted, Celler's bill to give lawful admission for permanent residence to aliens who entered on visitors' permits and who are refugees from or unable to return to their home country by reason of the war in Europe.[20]

There were House and Senate bills to amend the Act of May 22, 1918 (40 Stat. 559), which gave the President certain wartime powers (S. 1598, Van Nuys [Ind.]; H.R. 4973, Bloom [N.Y.]). The House bill was reported with amendment and passed (H. Rept. 754), then passed by the Senate and signed. The Act of June 21, 1941 (55 Stat. 252), it gave the President power during a time of national emergency or war to prevent departure from or entry to the United States contrary to the public safety. Several amendments of an administrative nature were proposed for the 1917 Act (H.R. 4548 and 5870, Schulte [Ind.] and Dickstein [N.Y.]), as was amendment of the Quota Act of 1924 (S. 1013, Downey [Calif.]). None of the above received action except as noted.

Miscellaneous other bills, none of which was acted on, were to permit unlimited immigration by natives of Iceland until July 1, 1946 (S. 1781, Langer [N.D.]), to prohibit the immigration of nationals of certain countries (S. 1237, Holman [Oreg.]), to amend the Alien Registration Act (H.R. 1841, L. M. Ford [Calif.]), and to define the legality of entry of

[17]S. 1401, Bridges (N.H.). See also his S. 4038 (76-III).

[18]H.R. 1426, Rich (Pa.). See also his H.R. 9977 (76-III).

[19]S. 1397, Reynolds (N.C.). Reported out (S. Rept. 394), debated and passed by the Senate.

[20]Same title as his H.R. 10702 (76-III), and as resubmitted drafts in the first sessions of the 78th and 80th Congresses.

certain persons born in a foreign contiguous country (S. 1465 by Walsh and Lodge of Massachusetts).

King of Hawaii again presented a bill to permit alien wives of American citizens married prior to the 1924 Act to enter (H.R. 591). It was reported out (H. Rept. 28), debated, and passed by the House but did not progress in the Senate. And, finally, a novel idea was advanced by Dickstein of New York to utilize unused quotas to colonize Alaska for "national defense and as a market for surplus production" (H.R. 2791).

The long second session of the 77th Congress, a wartime session from January 5 to December 16, 1942, gave relatively little time to immigration matters and added only one immigration act to the statute books.[21] As in the preceding session, deportation received the most attention. Bills to authorize the deportation of aliens to countries allied with the United States were introduced in both Senate and House (S. 2876, Russell [Ga.]; H.R. 7746, Dickstein [N.Y.]). The House bill was reported out with amendment (H. Rept. 2640), and debated but not brought to a vote during the session. A principal feature of the bill, however, the provision for deportation to the location of a government in exile where deportation to the country of citizenship was impossible by reason of war conditions, would reappear in a later Congress.

A third bill related to deportation received more ready acceptance (H.R. 6450). Introduced by Dickstein of New York, the bill would amend section 19(c) of the Immigration Act of February 5, 1917 to alter the procedure in suspension of deportation cases. Existing law required the Attorney General to report to Congress all suspensions of six months or more, the report to be made within ten days of the beginning of the next regular session of Congress. Dickstein's bill would permit such report to be made at any time during a session of Congress, and congressional objection if any was to be made by concurrent resolution of the two houses; but if the report from the Attorney General was within less than thirty days from the end of a session, objection might be made during the next session. The bill was reported out (H. Rept. 1744, Feb. 4, 1942) with minor amendments, which the House accepted, and the bill was passed on February 16, 1942. The Senate committee amended the bill (S. Rept. 1666, Oct. 29, 1942) to read that the Attorney General's report of suspensions be submitted on the first and fifteenth of each month in which Congress is in session. The Senate accepted the committee's amendment and passed the bill without debate, the House agreed, and on presidential signature the bill became the Act of December 8, 1942 (56 Stat. 1044).

[21]Excluded here is the Act of June 20, 1942 (56 Stat. 373), which dealt with administrative matters, the classification and salary of immigrant inspectors.

Alien enemies were also the target of several legislative proposals. Senate and House bills were "To provide for taking into custody certain persons who are citizens or subjects of, or owe allegiance to, any nation or country with which the United States is at war" (S. 2293, Stewart [Tenn.]; H.R. 6699, Rankin [Miss.]). The Senate bill was reported out (S. Rept. 1496) and debated, but was not acted on further. The House bill remained in committee. A third bill concerning alien enemies would have prohibited their employment in war industries (S. 2460, Maybank [S.C.]), but no action was taken on it.

The only other immigration-related bill during the session was for the exclusion of certain aliens (S. 2789, Holman [Oreg.]), and it likewise remained in committee.

78th Congress (1943, 1944)

The presidential message on the opening of the 78th Congress dealt entirely with the war and related matters, but bills on a number of aspects of immigration were introduced during the long first session that followed, from January 6 to December 21, 1943. Prominent among the subjects of these bills were certain wartime problems and issues, in addition to more routine matters; and reappearing for the first time since the preceding decade were proposals, indicative of concern with present or prospective unemployment, to check immigration in the event that the number of unemployed exceeded a specified number.

Most important in terms of long-range policy was recognition that Chinese exclusion was inappropriate treatment of a wartime ally and was being exploited by the Japanese for propaganda purposes. Early in the session bills were introduced in both Senate and House to authorize the admission of alien Chinese wives of American citizens, regardless of excludability because of race or area of birth provided they were otherwise admissible (S. 691, Downey [Calif.]; H.R. 1607, Lesinski [Mich.]). These bills were not acted on, for a more comprehensive proposal to repeal the Chinese exclusion acts was under consideration (H.R. 3070, Magnuson [Wash.]). Reported out by the House committee on October 7, 1943 (H. Rept. 732), the bill would amend section 303 of the Nationality Act of 1940 to add to the classes eligible for naturalization "Chinese persons or persons of Chinese descent," and to assign them a quota of 105 per annum. Four days after the committee report, a minority report was presented by Bennett of Michigan, whose argument against the bill contained three main points. In the first place, he maintained, basic policies should not be changed in time of war, and the exclusion policy had stood for sixty years. Second, all other Asiatics now being excluded, it is questionable policy to discriminate in favor of the Chinese alone.

And, finally, the action proposed in the bill is only a gesture, would be of little benefit to the Chinese until the end of the war, and is of doubtful effectiveness against Japanese propaganda.

The House debated the bill on October 20 and 21, adopted a slight change of wording but rejected all other amendments, and passed the bill without a record vote on the second day of debate.[22] It was reported without amendment by the Senate committee on November 26, and debated. Various materials were inserted in the *Congressional Record* at the time, including letters from the American Federation of Labor and certain veterans' groups opposing the bill. An attempt was made, as in the House, to attach an amendment to suspend immigration in any calendar year in which unemployment is one million or more. The amendment had been ruled not germane in the House; in the Senate the amendment, by Reynolds of North Carolina, was rejected. Reynolds then presented a second amendment, a substitute for the text of the bill, to suspend all immigration during the present war. It was also rejected, and the bill was passed by the Senate on November 26, 1943.[23] Signed by the President, it became the Act of December 17, 1943 (57 Stat. 600).[24]

The first session of the 78th Congress also received several bills to add new grounds for deportation and to extend the powers of the government in deportation cases. One would authorize the holding for deportation of aliens who refuse to bear arms in defense of the United States (S. 239, Stewart [Tenn.]), another provided for the deportation of aliens who do not make declaration of intention to become citizens (H.R. 1183, Randolph [W.Va.]). A Senate bill was to amend the Immigration Act of 1917 to extend the authority to deport aliens (S. 913, Russell [Ga.]); and two deportation bills were introduced by Dickstein of New York (H.R. 1681, 2076). Both were of the same title as one of the Dickstein bills in the second session of the preceding Congress, to authorize the deportation of aliens to countries allied with the United States. The first Dickstein bill was reported out (H. Rept. 135) but went no further. The second was reported out not long after (H. Rept. 211, March 4, 1943). It was designed to meet a problem raised by a recent court decision that the wording of section 20 of the 1917 Act applies to "country" in a territorial sense and not to locus of government as in the case of a government in exile. The Dickstein bill was to provide for the deportation of aliens who because of the war could not be sent to their own country, for it authorized deportation to the location of the government in exile.

[22]*Congressional Record,* 89:8635. [23]Ibid., p. 10019.

[24]For a case study of the repeal of Chinese exclusion, see Fred W. Riggs, *Pressures on Congress* (New York: Kings Crown, 1950).

In the course of House debate on the bill, it was brought out that the purpose, or at least a main purpose, of the bill was to check "jumping ship" by Chinese and others who knew that they could not be deported to their home country. The House amended the bill to limit its application to recognized governments in exile, accepted a slight change of wording, and then passed the bill on March 23, 1943. It was reported out soon after by the Senate committee (S. Rept. 156, Apr. 6, 1943), considered by the Senate, and passed after brief discussion on April 9. Three days later there was a motion to reconsider because the bill was understood to be repugnant to the Chinese government. On July 6, substitute wording was proposed to permit deportation to a country "proximate" to the country of citizenship, or, with consent of the country of which the alien is a citizen, to any other country. Passed in that form by the Senate and the House concurring in the amendment, the bill was signed into law as the Act of July 13, 1943 (57 Stat. 553).

Several bills concerned resident aliens, in addition to those mentioned above under deportation. Two Senate bills called for incarceration for the duration of the war and for six months thereafter, one bill applicable to deportable aliens, the other to "dangerous" aliens (S. 745, Russell [Ga.]; S. 780, Stewart [Tenn.]). A House bill would have prohibited aliens from voting in labor organizations or acting as their officers or agents (H.R. 804, Woodruff [Mich.]). More liberal toward aliens was a proposal by Downey of California to permit aliens other than enemy aliens to become tenants in low-rent housing projects maintained under section 10 of the U.S. Housing Act of 1937 (S. 1322). And for the third time the undiscouraged Celler of New York entered a bill "to record the lawful admission for permanent residence of certain aliens who lawfully entered the United States upon visitors' permits and are refugees from or unable to return to their country of origin because of the emergency created by the existing war in Europe."[25] None of these alien bills received committee approval.

Attempts to link suspension of immigration with unemployment above a certain critical level have been noted above in connection with the repeal of Chinese exclusion, and bills to the same effect were also introduced. Allen of Louisiana favored the suspension of all alien immigration for the duration of the war (H.R. 3041); and he was also author of a bill to suspend the immigration of aliens after the war until such time as the number of unemployed, including American war veterans, is less

[25]H.R. 825. The preceding bills of same title are H.R. 10702 in 76-III (1940) and H.R. 1588 in 77-I (1941). Celler was later to resubmit what appears to be the same bill in the first session of the 80th Congress, in 1947.

than one million (H.R. 3631). And without reference to the stage of the war were four bills of identical title to deny admission to all immigrants as long as the number of unemployed within the United States is one million or more (S. 240, Stewart [Tenn.]; H.R. 712, Pace [Ga.]; H.R. 3566, Rankin [Miss.]; H.R. 3577, Brooks [La.]). All remained in committee.

House and Senate resolutions were introduced for the admission of refugees, the House resolution being to give temporary admission to political or religious refugees from the Axis nations (H. J. Res. 154, Dickstein [N.Y.]), and the Senate resolution to admit aliens who are religious or racial refugees (S. J. Res. 85, Barbour [N.J.]).

Only a few other bills on various topics, none of which was reported out, remain to be noted for the first session of the 78th Congress. These include a bill to repatriate native-born women residents of the United States who have hitherto lost their citizenship by marriage to an alien (H.R. 1289, D'Alesandro [Md.]), one to exclude certain aliens (S. 211, Holman [Oreg.]), and finally one relating to the legality of the entry of certain persons born in a contiguous country (S. 291, Walsh [Mass.]).

The second session of the 78th Congress, from January 10 to December 19, 1944, received only a few immigration bills, of which only two were reported out by the House committee and none was enacted. The message to Congress from President Roosevelt at the opening of the session contained no recommendations for immigration legislation; and as might be expected, war-related matters and wartime attitudes toward aliens were conspicuous among the few new bills presented during the session.

Alien veterans were the beneficiaries of two bills to facilitate their immigration.[26] One of the bills was to grant nonquota status to certain alien veterans and their wives (H.R. 4571, Kearney [N.Y.]). It was reported out (H. Rept. 1943), amended, and passed by the House but was not acted on in the Senate. The second bill, "To permit certain aliens who served honorably in the armed forces of the United States during any period of war in which the United States was engaged to enter the United States as nonquota immigrants" (H.R. 4749, Andrews [N.Y.]), remained in committee.

Nonveteran aliens were more severely treated, for there were three proposals, all by the same author, Randolph (W.Va.), to deport those who "do not diligently attempt to become citizens" (H.R. 4353); to prohibit their acting as officers or agents of corporations or business associations

[26]There were also bills to facilitate the naturalization of such veterans, but naturalization legislation is not dealt with here.

engaged in interstate commerce, or of labor organizations (H.R. 4556); and to "prohibit any Government agency from entering into any construction contract with an alien or with any corporation, partnership, or other business association any officer of which is an alien" (H.R. 5063). Two bills called for the deportation of Japanese if aliens or if their loyalty as citizens was in doubt (H.R. 4779, Mott [Oreg.]; H.R. 5276, Engle [Calif.]).

Although no action was taken at the time, three significant bills were introduced, as a logical sequel to the repeal of Chinese exclusion, to extend the privileges of immigration and naturalization to natives and descendants of natives of India (H.R. 4415 and 4636, Celler [N.Y.]; H.R. 4479, Luce [Conn.]). A parallel bill was to give the same privileges to Koreans (H.R. 4940, Farrington [Hawaii]). Other bills related to immigration during the session were to amend the wording of the 1924 Act to remove inconsistencies with the act that repealed Chinese exclusion (H.R. 5156, Dickstein [N.Y.], reported in H. Rept. 1928); to state a temporary policy on immigration (S. 1907, Thomas [Okla.]); and, an expression of the author's anti-immigration sentiments, to end all quota immigration for five years after the end of the war (H.R. 4354, Randolph [W.Va.]). Finally, there were two House resolutions with the novel proposal of establishing a "free port" for the temporary admission of political and religious refugees (H. Res. 576, Dickstein [N.Y.]; H. Res. 581, Lane [Mass.]).

79th Congress (1945, 1946)

The first session of the 79th Congress, from January 3 to December 21, 1945, saw a trend back toward a peacetime pattern with a quite considerable number of immigration bills introduced during the session and the usual concerns to regulate and restrict immigration, to protect the labor market from immigration in times of unemployment, and to impose various limitations on resident aliens. But intermingled with these peacetime concerns were certain war and postwar problems of veterans, refugees, and enemy aliens.

To consider the war-related bills first, Kearney of New York resubmitted his proposal to grant nonquota status to certain alien veterans and their wives (H.R. 433), including veterans of the Spanish-American War as well as the First and Second World Wars. It was reported out (H. Rept. 164), amended, and passed by the House,[27] but it died in the Senate. Another veterans' bill, of quite specialized application, was to permit the

[27] *Congressional Record,* 91:1715.

nonquota admission into the territory of Alaska of Finnish persons or those of Finnish descent who have served honorably in the land or naval forces of the United Nations (H.R. 2499, Case [S.D.]). An allied bill was to grant certificates of lawful entry to foreign seamen who served on American-owned vessels for a period of at least one year while the United States was at war (S. 1040, Pepper [Fla.]). And two bills were introduced to facilitate the admission of alien spouses and minor children of citizen members of the armed forces (S. 1654, Russell [Ga.]; H.R. 4857, Dickstein [N.Y.]). Of these, only the House bill was reported out (H. Rept. 1320) and passed by the House, and then by the Senate (S. Rept. 860), and signed into law as the Act of December 28, 1945 (59 Stat. 659). Under section 2 of the act, alien relatives of veterans so admitted are to be accorded nonquota status. Two House joint resolutions proposed the admission of religious and racial refugees (H. J. Res. 95 and 288, Bennet [N.Y.]); and vindictive measures would have forbidden immigration and naturalization of nationals of enemy countries for a thirty-year period (H.R. 3773, Izac [Calif.]), or naturalization of Germans for twenty-five years (H.R. 3077, McMillan [S.C.]).

Resident aliens were the subject of half a dozen or more bills, the majority of which were to impose further restrictions on aliens. Randolph of West Virginia was again active in introducing antialien legislation. He was author of two bills to prohibit any government agency from entering into any construction contract with an alien or with a corporation, partnership, or other business association any officer of which is an alien (H.R. 539, H.R. 3634; same title as his H.R. 5063 [78-II]). He again introduced a bill for the deportation of aliens who do not diligently attempt to become citizens (H.R. 546; same title as H.R. 4353 [78-II]); and he also proposed a new bill to prescribe restrictions relating to government contracts with aliens (H.R. 3900). Finally, Randolph reintroduced a bill from the preceding Congress to prohibit aliens from acting as officers or agents of various types of organizations engaged in interstate commerce or of labor organizations (H.R. 544; same title as his H.R. 4556 [78-II]). Of parallel title was a bill introduced by Bennett of Missouri which barred felons as well as aliens from the specified positions (H.R. 4165). Another antialien bill reintroduced by Woodruff (Mich.) from the preceding Congress was to prohibit aliens from voting in labor organizations or acting as their officers or agents (H.R. 354; same title as his H.R. 804 [78-I]). And Japanese aliens were singled out in a bill to provide for their deportation (H.R. 1444, Mott [Oreg.]). The House committee endorsed none of these antialien bills but did report favorably on a bill from Dickstein of New York to establish the lawful entry of certain aliens not subject to deportation who entered prior to July 1, 1924 (H.R. 4149; reported out in H.

Rept. 1286). The House passed the bill as amended in committee, but it failed of action in the Senate.

A number of bills dealt with the regulation and restriction of immigration; of these, seven were concerned with the Chinese and were introduced by Congressmen from California. Six of these seven were to permit the admission of alien Chinese wives of American citizens who are admissible except for racial and geographical restrictions in existing law (S. 412, 580, Downey [Calif.]; H.R. 3976, Havenner [Calif.]; H.R. 4109, Douglas [Calif.]; H.R. 4179, 4844, Miller [Calif.]). One of the six, H.R. 4844 introduced by Miller of California, was reported out with amended and abbreviated title (H. Rept. 1325). It was not acted on further until the second session. The remaining bill on Chinese immigration concerned the reentry of Chinese laborers and wives and children (H.R. 4531, by Patterson of California).

Bills to grant admission and naturalization to natives of India[28] and Korea,[29] like those that died at the end of the preceding Congress, were resubmitted. Of these, the second of two bills by Celler of New York for natives of India was reported back (H. Rept. 854), debated, and passed by the House but was not acted on in the Senate until the next session.

An increase of antialien and restrictionist sentiment appeared. Inserted in the *Congressional Record*[30] by Allen of Louisiana was a resumé of various resolutions passed by the American Legion at its September 1944 convention in Chicago and previous meetings. These called variously for the deportation of persons denaturalized for subversive activities, barring of enemy aliens from naturalization and government jobs during the war, deportation and permanent exclusion of aliens who refuse military service, and various other measures against aliens. Certain new bills were of a restrictionist nature. Two of this type were to amend the immigration and naturalization laws to deny admission and citizenship to aliens who had served in the armed forces of enemy nations (H.R. 3263, 3663, Gossett [Tex.]), and the second of the two bills carried the additional provision of a reduction in immigration quotas. Another would deny admission to all aliens unable to establish good moral character (H.R. 4066, Dolliver [Iowa]). Two bills were for the purpose of reducing immigration quotas (H.R. 414, Gossett [Tex.]; H.R. 1368, Fisher [Tex.]), and another would prohibit all quota immigration for a period of five years after the end of the war (H.R. 545, Randolph [W.Va.]; same title as his

[28]S. 505, Capper (Kans.); H.R. 1584, Luce (Conn.); H.R. 2256, Dirksen (Ill.); H.R. 2609, 3517, Celler (N.Y.).

[29]S. 730, Pepper (Fla.); H.R. 1586, Farrington (Hawaii); H.R. 1901, Powell (N.Y.).

[30]*Congressional Record* 91:A1836.

H.R. 4354 [78-II]). None of the above bills of restrictive intent received committee approval.

There were additionally several proposals to link restriction or suspension of immigration with unemployment, a type of bill that had appeared before. One would suspend immigration from the end of the war until such time as the number of unemployed, including war veterans, was below one million (H.R. 677, Allen [La.]). Another, without reference to the end of the war, was to suspend immigration whenever unemployment is one million or more (H.R. 748, Pace [Ga.]). And there were two bills to suspend immigration whenever unemployment is 100,000 or more (S. 1020, Stewart [Tenn.]; H.R. 3286, Rankin [Miss.]). No action on these bills was taken by the Senate or House committees.

Two bills were resubmitted from the preceding session, to repatriate native-born women residents who have lost citizenship by marriage to an alien (H.R. 384 by D'Alesandro of Maryland), and to deal with the legality of the entry of certain natives of contiguous countries (S. 258 by Walsh of Massachusetts). Neither was reported out.[31]

The second session of the 79th Congress saw the introduction of a few bills similar in range of topics to those of the first session, but new were two bills for the aid of displaced persons (H.R. 7213 and 7218, by Mrs. Woodhouse [Conn.] and Klein [N.Y.]). Both were to provide for D.P. immigration. Also war-related was a bill to grant nonquota status as immigrants to certain veterans of the Polish army (H.R. 6120 by Sadowski of Michigan), and a multipurpose bill to exclude aliens who had served in the armed forces of enemy nations and aliens considered dangerous.[32] Surprisingly, in view of its seemingly extreme character, the bill was reported out (H. Rept. 2351) and passed by the House, but died in the Senate committee. Also reported out by the House committee was a bill from the first session for the exclusion of former enemy aliens (H. Rept. 2041, on H.R. 3663, Gossett [Tex.]). Another bill which was war-related but of a quite different character was a proposal by Mrs. Luce of Connecticut to authorize the admission as nonquota immigrants of certain orphan

[31]Among naturalization bills in the first session of the 79th Congress were four to make natives of India eligible for naturalization, two for Koreans, and one for Filipinos. Eligibility for naturalization would have conferred automatic admissibility under quota in these cases.

[32]H.R. 6869, Gossett (Tex.). The full title is "To amend the immigration and naturalization laws to deny admission to the United States of certain aliens who have served in the armed forces of countries at war with the United States, also members of certain parties and organizations, and to deny naturalization to such persons, and to deny admission to the United States of persons who the Attorney General knows or has reason to believe seek to enter the United States for the purpose of engaging in activities which will endanger the public safety of the United States."

children now interned within the American zone of occupation in Europe (H. J. Res. 363).

Two bills were to facilitate the admission of alien fiancées or fiancés of members of the armed forces (S. 2122, Russell [Ga.]; H.R. 6279, Lesinski [Mich.]). The Senate bill was reported out (S. Rept. 1441) and passed. The House committee then reported it out (H. Rept. 2108) in lieu of the House bill but with extensive amendments, which for the most part dealt with administration but made the substantive change of adding a section requiring bonding of the aliens to be admitted. With Senate agreement to the amendments and presidential signature, the bill was enacted as the Act of June 29, 1946 (60 Stat. 339). Admission provided under the act was to be as a nonimmigrant temporary visitor for three months, on the conditions that the alien be admissible, that the nonpreference portion of the appropriate quota is already exhausted, and that there is a presumption of bona fide intent of marriage to a veteran. The bond was to be sufficient to cover costs of deportation and to be cancelled upon marriage or departure of the alien.

Within the customary peacetime pattern were the various bills to deport, to regulate and restrict immigration, and to amend the basic immigration acts. Senate and House bills were to amend the 1917 Act concerning the deportation of "undesirable aliens" (S. 2120, Thomas [Utah]; H.R. 5454, Eberharter [Pa.]). Five other bills were to amend one or another section of the 1917 Act, in particular the sections dealing with suspension of deportation, boards of special inquiry to determine admissibility, and the excludable classes.[33] Another bill, unspecified as to purpose in its title, was to amend the 1924 Quota Act (H.R. 5429, Miller [Calif.]).

Three bills considered during the session related to racial restrictions on immigration and naturalization. One to remove all such restrictions did not come out of committee (H.R. 7128, Farrington [Hawaii]). A second was to give nonquota status to the Chinese wives of American citizens (H.R. 4844, Miller [Calif.]). It had been introduced and reported out in the first session of the 79th Congress (H. Rept. 1325 [79-I]) with an amended title. It was passed by the House in the second session, approved by the Senate committee (S. Rept. 1927), and progressed to become the Act of August 9, 1946 (60 Stat. 975).

The third of the three bills, also from the first session, was to authorize the admission of persons of races indigenous to India and to make them racially eligible for naturalization (H.R. 3517, Celler [N.Y.]). It had

[33]S. 1825, Russell (Ga.); H.R. 5927, Gossett (Tex.); H.R. 6505, Judd (Minn.); H.R. 6996, Hedrick (W.Va.); H.R. 7060, Klein (N.Y.). Several of these were designed particularly to check the entry of stowaways.

been reported out, debated, and passed by the House in the first session. In the second session it was accepted by the Senate committee without amendment (S. Rept. 1440), passed, and then reconsidered. On reconsideration the Senate added the Ball (Minn.) amendment to extend the bill to include "Filipino persons or persons of Filipino descent" as well as peoples of India.[34] With House agreement and presidential signature the bill became law as the Act of July 2, 1946 (60 Stat. 416).

The only other bill to be noted for the second session was one to suspend immigration for five years (S. 1758, Maybank [S.C.]). It was not acted on by the Senate committee.

80th Congress (1947–1948)

The 80th, the first postwar Congress, saw a great increase in legislative activity related to immigration. Most numerous were bills concerned with alien veterans, displaced persons, and Asiatics; but there were also numbers of legislative proposals dealing with the common topics that receive attention at every session of Congress.

The bills related to alien veterans were designed to serve a wide range of purposes. One would have given nonquota status on immigration to certain alien veterans and their wives (H.R. 251, Kearney [N.Y.]). Another was to give quota exemption to persons who had served in the armed forces of allied governments during World War II (H.R. 3445, Bloom [N.Y.]). There was a bill to limit the grounds for deportation in the case of certain classes of honorably discharged alien veterans (H.R. 1756, Lynch [N.Y.]). And both Senate and House received bills to permit the naturalization, regardless of race, of the parents of servicemen killed during World War II (S. 1300, Downey [Calif.]; H.R. 3555, Gossett [Tex.]). The House bill was reported out and passed but progressed no further (H. Rept. 595, June 17, 1947). None of the other veterans' bills was reported out.[35]

Related to the above is a group of five bills concerning the admission of Polish veterans and nationals. Two were to provide for the admission of certain persons who had served in the Polish army (H.R. 3373, Clason [Mass.]; H.R. 3620, MacKinnon [Minn.]). One was for the admission as nonquota immigrants of such Polish veterans (H.R. 466, Sadowski

[34]Eligibility to naturalization, as previously noted, also conferred eligibility to immigration under quota. Prior to the Act of July 2, 1946, a proviso under section 303 of the 1940 Act specified the eligibility to naturalization of native-born Filipinos who have served honorably in the armed forces of the United States.

[35]Omitted here are certain bills of a specialized wartime and postwar character concerning residence of veterans, etc.

[Mich.]), and another would have admitted as nonquota immigrants certain displaced Polish citizens who have rendered service to the United States army (H.R. 4665, Pfeifer [N.Y.]). And stated in more general terms was a Senate bill to permit certain Polish nationals to enter for permanent residence (S. 643, Baldwin [Conn.]). None of these Polish bills was reported out by the Senate or House committees.

There were at least fourteen bills to provide variously for the aid of displaced person immigrants. Three bills were to authorize the admission of displaced persons,[36] two made the same provision but set a time limit on the effective period of the provision,[37] and three were for the admission of both displaced persons and refugees.[38] There was a bill to authorize the admission of 250,000 displaced persons and refugees (H.R. 37, Celler [N.Y.]), one to make available the unused immigration quotas for all nationalities to displaced persons and refugees (H.R. 1230, Celler [N.Y.]), and two to grant nonquota immigration status to certain displaced persons under fourteen years of age and orphaned as a result of World War II (S. 830 and H.R. 2446, by Ives and Javits of New York). And two bills of very similar titles were to authorize the United States during an emergency period to assist in the resettlement of certain displaced persons up to the total of unused quotas during the war years.[39] None of the displaced person bills progressed during this term of Congress.

Another large group of legislative proposals in the first session of the 80th Congress concerned various Asiatic peoples, for the giving of eligibility to naturalization and immigration to the Chinese during the war as well as to Filipinos and Indians later stimulated attempts to get similar treatment for other Asiatics.

One bill concerned people from India, to permit all those residing in the United States to be naturalized (S. 207, Langer [N.D.]). Two bills concerned certain Chinese, one relating to the entry of Chinese laborers and Chinese wives and children, the other concerning the status of lawful wives and children of Chinese treaty merchants.[40] There were two bills

[36]H.R. 464, Sabath (Ill.); H.R. 732, Lesinski (Mich.); H.R. 1251, Klein (N.Y.).

[37]S. 1563, Ferguson (Mich.) and eight other sponsors; H.R. 4123, Clason (Mass.).

[38]H.R. 38, Celler (N.Y.); H.R. 1249, 1250, Klein (N.Y.).

[39]H.R. 2910, Stratton (Ill.); H.R. 4240, Chelf (Ky.). The full title of the Stratton bill was "To authorize the United States during an emergency period to undertake its fair share in the resettlement of displaced persons in Germany, Austria, and Italy including relatives of citizens or members of our armed forces by permitting their admission into the United States in a number equivalent to a part of the total quota numbers unused during the war years." The Chelf bill was limited in application to those then in D.P. camps in the American zones in Germany and Austria.

[40]H.R. 1100, Havenner (Calif.); S. 1137, Downey (Calif.) and Magnuson (Wash.).

to authorize the admission of persons of races indigenous to Siam and to make them racially eligible for naturalization (S. 958, Magnuson [Wash.]; H.R. 2978, Jackson [Wash.]). Four bills were introduced to give the same treatment to Koreans.[41] And finally certain Japanese were subjects of a bill to confer eligibility for naturalization on Japanese persons and persons of Japanese descent who are residing in the United States and whose sons died while serving in the armed forces of the United States during World War II (H.R. 3305, Gossett [Tex.]).

In addition to these piecemeal attacks on racial restrictions on naturalization and immigration were several bills of more general purpose. Such was a bill by Judd of Minnesota to grant the privilege of naturalization to all immigrants having a legal right to permanent residence in the United States and to grant all Asiatic and Pacific peoples equal treatment with peoples from China and India under immigration law (H.R. 4824). Additionally there were three bills to remove all racial restrictions on naturalization and to grant naturalization rights to all regardless of race, color, or national origin (S. 602, Langer [N.D.]; H.R. 857, Farrington [Hawaii]; H.R. 4473, Celler [N.Y.]). None of the above fourteen bills was acted on during the session.

There was a postwar residue of a few bills relating to subversives and former alien enemies, but with some softening of attitude toward the latter at least. One of the bills was to strengthen the immigration laws for the exclusion of persons "who may be coming here for the purpose of engaging in activities which will endanger the public safety" (H.R. 1878, Gossett [Tex.]), and two others were to revoke naturalization and to deport persons discharged from government service because of disloyalty.[42]

The exclusion of aliens who have borne arms against the United States and certain other aliens considered dangerous to the public safety was provided in a House bill, a resubmission of one that passed the House but not the Senate in the second session of the preceding Con-

[41]S. 152, Pepper (Fla.); H.R. 860, 2932, Farrington (Hawaii); H.R. 1437, Celler (N.Y.).

[42]H.R. 2745, 3015, Chelf (Ky). The title of the former was "To revoke acquired citizenship of all former aliens and to deport those residents and any alien residents who for sufficient reason or just cause shall have been duly purged, released, or otherwise properly discharged from any United States Government position, as a result of their disloyalty, subversive activities, or sympathies against the United States of America, by amending subsection (a) of sec. 19 of the Immigration Act of February 5, 1917, as amended." The latter read "To revoke the naturalization of persons who have been discharged from the U.S. Government service in compliance with Executive Order No. 9885; to deport such persons; and to deport aliens concerning whom the Attorney General knows or has reason to believe their presence may endanger the public safety or welfare of the country."

gress (H.R. 1116, Gossett [Tex.]; see his H.R. 6869 [79-II]). With regard to enemy aliens already in the United States, Langer of North Dakota introduced bills for the relief of those under detention and to provide for full and fair hearings before deportation or removal of those under internment (S. 1690 and 1709). And a proposal was made for suspension of a subsection of the Nationality Act of 1940 (328b, Title I) concerning a registry of aliens for whom there is no record of admission for permanent residence (S. 1920, Baldwin [Conn.]).

More routine matters that were the subject of legislative proposals during the session were the regulation and restriction of immigration, the admission of relatives, the immigration quotas, and numerous other topics. Two bills were to suspend immigration for a term, in one case for five years and in the other for ten years after the termination of the war (S. 271, McKellar [Tenn.]; H.R. 1117, Gossett [Tex.]). Proposed revisions of or exceptions to the existing regulation of immigration were proposals to grant the unused portion of the German immigration quota to the countries recently conquered and occupied by German armed forces (S. 962, McMahon of Connecticut), to admit certain adopted children of American citizens free of quota (H.R. 1629, Sadowski [Mich.]; S. 1764, Knowland [Calif.]), to admit an additional number of Italians above the quota limit (H.R. 3568, Keogh of New York), and to stop the issuance of immigration visas to the natives of certain countries (H.R. 4555, Jenkins [Ohio]). There was also a bill for declaration of a temporary immigration policy (S. 213, Thomas of Oklahoma). None of the above was acted on during the session.

Special treatment of certain classes of relatives was also considered. A Senate bill was to extend the time within which alien fiancées and fiancés of members of the armed forces may be admitted (S. 1264, Revercomb [W.Va.]). The bill was not acted on in the Senate for meanwhile a bill of the same purpose had been introduced and reported out in the House.[43] It passed the House, was reported favorably in the Senate (S. Rept. 354), was passed, and was signed by the President to become the Act of June 28, 1947 (61 Stat. 190). It extended by six months the authority conferred on the Attorney General by the Act of June 29, 1946 (60 Stat. 339) to admit alien fiancées and fiancés of veterans as temporary visitors pending marriage, from the original terminating date of July 1, 1947 to December 31, 1947.

Another House bill was to amend the Act of December 28, 1945 (59 Stat. 659) concerning the admission of alien spouses and alien minor children of members of the armed forces (H.R. 3149, Fellows [Me.]). It

[43]H.R. 3398, Fellows (Me.), with H. Rept. 479.

was reported out by the House committee with amendment, passed by the House, reported favorably by the Senate committee (H. Rept. 478; S. Rept. 501), and signed to become the Act of July 22, 1947 (61 Stat. 401). Its amendment of the earlier act was to add a sixth section reading as follows:

> Sec. 6. The alien spouse of an American citizen by a marriage occurring before thirty days after the enactment of this Act, shall not be considered as inadmissible because of race, if otherwise admissible under this Act.

Several of the bills presented in this session of Congress involved labor market considerations. One, of a familiar type, would have stopped immigration as long as the number of unemployed in the United States is one million or more (S. 820, Stewart [Tenn.]); another would have stopped immigration whenever the number of unemployed reaches or exceeds 100 [*sic*] (H.R. 138, Pace [Ga.]). More constructive were other bills to facilitate the admission of foreign workers for agricultural employment (H.R. 4348, Anderson [Calif.]) and to authorize the recruitment of qualified workers needed in the United States and to reduce the burden of supplying relief in Germany, Austria, and Italy (H.R. 4723, Case [S.D.]).

A group of bills dealt with the administrative matters of suspension of deportation and adjustment of status. One was a Senate bill to amend subsections 19c and 19d of the 1917 Act, the sections defining the Attorney General's powers for the suspension of deportation in certain cases (S. 1065, Langer [N.D.]). No progress was made by the bill, but a somewhat related bill for amendment of subsection 19c of the 1917 Act and subsection 338a of the 1940 Nationality Act was introduced and reported out in the House (H.R. 1975, Gossett [Tex.], with H. Rept. 86). Its purpose was to give the Attorney General authority to cancel a suspension of deportation order and to reinstate deportability, and also to cancel naturalization. It was amended and passed by the House but not taken up by the Senate until the second session.

A second bill dealing with suspension of deportation was also received by the House, reported out, passed, and taken up by the Senate in the next session.[44] It provided for extension of the Attorney General's authority to adjust the status of deportable aliens and for charging of the adjusted cases to the national quota, but not to exceed half of the quota of a given country. And the second section stated that no private bill or resolution for relief is to be introduced for an alien unless the Attorney

[44]H.R. 3566, Fellows (Me.), with H. Rept. 647, June 24, 1947.

General reports that all remedies under existing law have been exhausted.

Grounds for deportation were the subject of only two bills during the session, one concerned with the deportation of undesirable aliens (H.R. 1115, Eberharter [Pa.]), the other to provide for the deportation of certain aliens eligible to citizenship who do not take action to become citizens (H.R. 4189, Smith [Wis.]).

There were several proposals for revision of immigration quotas, in addition to those noted above. One was to make available to European countries with small quotas the unused portion of the quotas of other European nations (H.R. 36, Celler [N.Y.]). The other was to make the unused portions of quotas during the wartime years, 1940 to 1946, available for issuance during the next ten years (S. 1152, McMahon [Conn.]). And there was a bill to provide for preference under the quota (H.R. 3255, Herter [Mass.]).

Only a few other immigration bills remain to be noted for this active first session of the 80th Congress. Three bills made what in retrospect appears the unfeasible suggestion that a fence be built along the length of the Mexican border.[45] The sponsors were from the border states of Texas and Arizona.

A Senate bill called for amendment of section 12 of the 1917 Act, the section prescribing the manifesting of arriving aliens (S. 1463, Holland [Fla.]). Reported with amendment by the Senate committee,[46] the bill was amended and passed by the Senate, and later became the Act of July 30, 1947 (61 Stat. 630). The amendment of the 1917 Act deleted the lengthy list of information to be included on the manifest form and substituted the formula: "such information as the Commissioner of Immigration and Naturalization, with the approval of the Attorney General, shall by regulation prescribe as necessary for the identification of the persons transported and for the enforcement of the immigration laws."

Finally, a Senate resolution called for an investigation of the immigration system (S. Res. 137, Revercomb [W.Va.] and McCarran [Nev.]). After review and amendment by two committees (S. Rept. 503) it was debated over several days, amended, and passed by the Senate.[47]

The second session of the 80th Congress, another long session like the first, ran for eleven months from its opening on January 6, 1948. It

[45] H.R. 1454, Thomason (Tex.); H.R. 1460, Harless (Ariz.); H.R. 1471, Murdock (Ariz.).

[46] S. Rept. 596. The amendment was to strike out all after the enacting clause and insert new wording. It was accepted without debate by the House and retained in the enacted draft of the bill.

[47] *Congressional Record,* 93:10352.

continued the legislative activity of the first session with regard to immigration, in which it carried on the first session's range of concerns and brought several bills from the earlier session to enactment.

The largest group of new bills and the principal legislative accomplishment of the session concerned displaced persons. Rather early in the new session the Senate received a bill introduced by Wiley of Wisconsin from the Committee on the Judiciary to authorize for a limited time the admission of certain European displaced persons (D.P.s) for permanent residence (S. 2242, March 2, 1948), and the House received a first and later a second bill of similar title from Fellows of Maine, probably introduced on behalf of the House Committee on Immigration and Nationality of which he was the chairman (H.R. 6163, 6396, April 7 and 29, 1948). The second of these bills was reported out (H. Rept. 1854, May 4, 1948), with a critical statement by Celler of New York attached.[48] The bill authorized the issuance of 200,000 quota immigration visas over a two-year period to go to displaced persons (D.P.s) in the west zones of Germany and Austria, provided for corresponding reduction of national quotas, facilitated admission as nonquota immigrants of unmarried minor children who were orphans in the D.P. category, authorized the Attorney General to adjust the status of up to 15,000 D.P.s previously admitted on a temporary basis to the United States but to charge them to the quotas also, although not in excess of one-half of each annual quota, and set priorities for admission on the basis of skills and relation to residents and citizens of the United States. As set in section 5a of the House bill, first priority was to aliens "qualified as farm laborers, physicians, dentists, medical nurses, household, construction, clothing and garment workers; or aliens possessing educational, scientific, or technological qualifications"; second priority went to "aliens who are the blood relatives of citizens or lawfully admitted alien residents of the United States, such relationship in either case being within the third degree of consanguinity computed according to the rules of the common law"; and third priority went to all other aliens classifiable as displaced persons. The House added to the bill by accepting the Stefan (Nebr.) amendment to add 2000 recent political refugees from Czechoslovakia, and the following Walter (Pa.) amendment to increase the visa allocation to 202,000.[49] The House

[48]Points made by Celler were that it was a compromise bill, less generous than the Stratton bill from the first session (H.R. 2910) that would have admitted 400,000 D.P.s over a four-year period, but not as restrictive as the Senate bill (S. 2242) that would admit only 100,000 in a two-year period and had provisions favoring certain national groups. He also objected to the proposal of charging the 200,000 admissible under the bill to the quotas, especially those of countries with small quotas that might be filled up for years.

[49]*Congressional Record,* 94:7885.

then passed the bill on June 11, 1948 by a vote of 289 to 91, with 49 not voting.

Meanwhile, the Senate committee had reported out (S. Rept. 950) and passed the Wiley bill, which differed from the House bill by providing for only 100,000 D.P.s to be admitted over a two-year period and giving priority to those in D.P. camps and centers prior to January 1, 1948 and those with "special circumstances." The admissions were to be "in addition to persons admissible as immigrants under other laws of the United States."

The Senate passed the bill on June 2, 1948, before the House had passed its bill. The House then received the Senate bill, struck out all after the enacting clause, substituted its own bill that had been passed by this time, and then passed the Senate bill as amended. As the Senate did not accept the new draft, the bill went to conference, and a compromise version containing elements of both Senate and House drafts was prepared (H. Rept. 2410). Accepted by both houses of Congress and signed, the bill became the Displaced Persons Act of June 25, 1948 (62 Stat. 1009). In its final form, the Act provided

1. That during the two years following passage, not in excess of 202,000 immigrant visas may be issued without regard to quota limitations, not less than 40 percent of the visas to be issued to eligible displaced persons whose homeland has been de facto annexed by a foreign power and not more than 2,000 to consist of Czechoslovaks otherwise admissible for permanent residence (sec. 3a).

2. That the visas so issued be charged to the national quota, but not more than one-half of any annual quota; and that special nonquota visas up to the number of 3000 may be issued to "eligible displaced orphans" (sec. 3b).

3. That the Attorney General is authorized to adjust the status of certain displaced persons residing in the United States to that of permanent residence, but not to exceed 15,000, and to be charged to the alien's national quota up to one-half of the quota of any year (sec. 4).

4. Preferences set by the Act for the issuance of visas were as follows (sec. 6):

> *First.* Eligible displaced persons who have been previously engaged in agricultural pursuits and who will be employed in the United States in agricultural pursuits: *Provided,* That not less than 30 per centum of the visas issued pursuant to this Act shall be made available exclusively to such persons; and *Provided further,* That the wife, and unmarried dependent child or children under twenty-one years of age, of such persons may, in accordance with the regulations of the Commission, be deemed to be of that class of persons who have

been previously engaged in agricultural pursuits and who will be employed in the United States in agricultural pursuits.

Second. Eligible displaced persons who are household, construction, clothing, and garment workers, and other workers needed in the locality in the United States in which such persons propose to reside; or eligible displaced persons possessing special educational, scientific, technological or professional qualifications.

Third. Eligible displaced persons who are the blood relatives of citizens or lawfully admitted alien residents of the United States, such relationship in either case being within the third degree of consanguinity computed according to the rules of the common law.

5. Priority within the above preferences was further specified in section 7 of the Act as follows:

> first to eligible displaced persons who during World War II bore arms against the enemies of the United States and are unable or unwilling to return to the countries of which they are nationals because of persecution or fear of persecution on account of race, religion or political opinions and second, to eligible displaced persons who, on January 1, 1948, were located in displaced persons centers, but in exceptional cases visas may be issued to those eligible displaced persons located outside of displaced persons camps and centers upon a showing, in accordance with the regulations of the Commission, of special circumstances which would justify such issuance.

6. From June 30, 1948 until July 1, 1950, one-half of the German and Austrian quotas were to be available exclusively to "persons of German ethnic origin who were born in Poland, Czechoslovakia, Hungary, Romania or Yugoslavia and who, on the effective date of this Act reside in Germany or Austria" (sec.12).

The other displaced persons bills of the second session can be noted briefly. There were two bills, resembling ones of the first session, to authorize during the emergency period the admission of displaced persons and expellees by the United States to undertake its "fair share in the resettlement,"[50] there was a bill by Langer of North Dakota for the admission of displaced persons "without regard to race or nationality" (S. 2493), and Celler of New York would admit certain displaced persons from Shanghai for permanent residence (H.R. 6760). And finally, after passage of the Displaced Persons Act, there were at least eight bills for its

[50]H.R. 6094, Youngblood (Mich.); H.R. 6640, Kersten (Wis.). H.R. 5501, Lewis (Ohio) also concerned displaced persons.

amendment in various respects.[51] None of them came out of committee.

The second session of the 80th Congress also received various veterans bills. Three of these concerned the admission of alien spouses and minor children of citizen veterans,[52] one proposed by Havenner of California admitting aliens who had served in the armed forces or the merchant marine in World War II (H.R. 5780). Two called for admission of veterans of the Polish army,[53] and three proposed extending the opportunity for admission of alien fiancées or fiancés of veterans.[54] The Forand bill was the only one of all these veterans bills to progress in this session of Congress. Passed by both House and Senate, it became the Act of March 24, 1948 (62 Stat. 84). It amended the Act of June 29, 1946 (60 Stat. 339) by extending its effective date by one year, to December 31, 1948 and removing a limiting proviso.[55]

In addition to those concerned with present or prospective relatives of veterans was a group of bills to facilitate the admission of certain alien relatives of citizens. Four were to grant nonquota status to adopted children of citizens,[56] two were to facilitate the admission of alien parents of citizens,[57] and another was for amendment of the 1924 Act to facilitate the admission of alien husbands of citizens (H.R. 5137, Lesinski [Mich.]). It was reported with amendment in the House (H. Rept. 1574) and passed, reported in the Senate (S. Rept. 1206) and also passed, there to become the Act of May 19, 1948 (62 Stat. 241). It gave nonquota status to the husbands of citizens if the marriage was prior to January 1, 1948,[58] and inclusion in the first-preference category if marriage was on or after January 1, 1948.

Another topic of legislative interest was the granting of rights of

[51] S. 2901, McGrath (R.I.) and Hatch (N.Mex.); S. 2902, Smith (N.J.) and six others; S. 2913, Johnson (Colo.); H.R. 7034, Case (N.J.); H.R. 7050, Walter (Pa.); H.R. 7058, Celler (N.Y.); H.R. 7077, Holifield (Calif.); H.R. 7114, Keating (N.Y.).

[52] S. 2356, Young (N.D.) and Magnuson (Wash.); H.R. 5691, Lemke (N.D.); H.R. 5955, Farrington (Hawaii).

[53] H.R. 6639, Kersten (Wis.); H.R. 7010, McMahon (N.Y.); these in addition to the five similar bills of the first session.

[54] S. 1962, Gurney (S.D.); H.R. 4838, Forand (R.I.); H.R. 4839, Gross (Pa.).

[55] The second provision in section 1 of the Act, which limited its application to instances in which the nonpreference portion of the applicable quota was exhausted.

[56] S. 2336, Johnson (Colo.); H.R. 6191, Foote (Conn); H.R. 7073, Multer (N.Y.); H.R. 7121, Keating (N.Y.). The Johnson bill was to redefine the word "child" as used in the 1924 Act so as to include children by adoption provided adoption occurred before July 1, 1949; the Foote bill applied only to children under twenty-one years of age.

[57] H.R. 4982, McGarvey (Pa.); H.R. 7121, Keating (N.Y.). The Keating bill was to grant nonquota status to adopted children as well.

[58] The previous limiting date of marriage was July 1, 1932, set by the Act of July 11, 1932 (47 Stat. 656).

immigration and naturalization to Asiatic and Pacific peoples. Bills by Langer (N.D.) and Judd (Minn.) were for the benefit of peoples of races indigenous to Indochina (S. 2668, H.R. 6809), and another pair of bills was for Indonesians (S. 2057, Langer [N.D.]; H.R. 5593, Celler [N.Y.]). There was a another Langer bill to give immigration quotas and full rights of immigration and naturalization to Asiatics and Pacific peoples generally (S. 2569), and one by Jackson of California (H.R. 5499) to permit certain citizens of the Philippines but not of races indigenous there to qualify for naturalization without certificates of arrival or declarations of intention, that is, first papers. And, finally, the only bill in this group to make progress was an additional Jackson bill proposing to make natives of Siam eligible for immigration and naturalization (H.R. 5310). It was reported out and passed the House, then reported out in the Senate (H. Rept. 1432, S. Rept. 1341), but did not come to a vote.

Except for several bills that proposed various amendments to the Quota Act of 1924[59] and failed of committee approval, the remaining bills of the session dealt in various ways with aliens within the United States. Lodge of Massachusetts introduced a bill to authorize the enlistment of aliens in the Regular Army (S. 2016), and three related to the issuance of reentry permits to certain aliens.[60] One of these, introduced by Farrington of Hawaii, was completely reworded in committee and then reported out (H. Rept. 1934, May 11, 1948) and passed by the House; it was also passed by the Senate, in lieu of its own bill on the subject. As the Act of June 3, 1948 (62 Stat. 335), it allowed qualified aliens lawfully admitted between July 1, 1924 and July 5, 1932, inclusive, to be provided on departure from the country with a reentry permit assuring them of readmission.

House bills by Gossett of Texas and Fellows of Maine concerned with adjustment of status and suspension of deportation which were passed by the House in the first session were brought up in the Senate in the second session (H.R. 1975, 3566). The first of the two, by Gossett of Texas, was to give the Attorney General authority to cancel a suspension of deportation order and to reinstate deportability. It was reported out in the Senate in the second session (S. Rept. 1201) and then recommitted. The other bill, by Fellows of Maine, was in the House draft to extend the authority of the Attorney General to adjust the status of deportable aliens and to charge such cases to the appropriate immigra-

[59]S. 2355, Young (N.D.), and Magnuson (Wash.); S. 2639, Wherry (Nebr.); H.R. 5034, Johnson (Calif.). The Wherry bill had the purpose, as stated in its title, of providing for a minimum diet in occupied Germany as well as amending the 1924 Act.

[60]S. 2349, Baldwin (Conn.); H.R. 5922, Farrington (Hawaii); H.R. 5929, Mitchell (Ind.).

tion quota. As amended and reported out by the Senate committee (S. Rept. 1204), the House bill was struck out and a new bill substituted, which created two new classes of aliens eligible for suspension of deportation, and changed the confirmation procedure to require affirmative congressional action before deportation proceedings could be cancelled. When the House disagreed with the drastic change, the bill went to conference. In its report (H. Rept. 2369) the conference committee recommended that the House recede from its disagreement with the Senate amendments after some change of wording in the Senate draft. The change of wording concerned the procedure for congressional approval or rejection of the Attorney General's recommendations for the suspension of deportation. The new wording read, in part, "If prior to the close of the session of the Congress next following the session at which a case is reported, the Congress does not pass such a concurrent resolution [i.e., in favor of the recommended suspension of deportation], the Attorney General shall thereupon deport such alien in the manner provided by law." Approved as recommended by both House and Senate, the bill was enacted as the Act of July 1, 1948 (62 Stat. 1206). Conditions for suspension set by the bill were that the alien shall have proved good moral character for the preceding five years, and that the Attorney General finds that (a) "deportation would result in serious economic detriment" to a citizen or legally resident and closely related alien, or (b) the alien "has resided continuously in the United States for seven years or more." As an alternative to suspension of deportation, the Attorney General might permit the deportable alien to depart voluntarily at his own expense and to any country of his choice in lieu of deportation. The advantage to the alien of such voluntary departure is the possibility of readmission at some later time.

Another bill from the first session was the antisubversive bill (H.R. 1878, Gossett [Tex.]) entitled "To amend the immigration laws to deny admission of persons who may be coming here for the purpose of engaging in activities which will endanger the public safety." Reported out and passed in both House and Senate (H. Rept. 1286, S. Rept. 1199), this became the Act of May 25, 1948 (62 Stat. 268). Its purpose fully stated by its title, it amended the Act of October 16, 1918 (40 Stat. 1012) for the exclusion and expulsion of anarchists and similar classes and gave the Attorney General essentially the same powers to exclude as the Secretary of State has through the refusal of immigration visas.

Several other bills introduced during the second session of the 80th Congress but not acted on were to authorize the temporary admission of agricultural workers as students from countries currently receiving assistance under the Economic Cooperation Act of 1948 (H.R. 6245, Mrs. St. George [N.Y.]), to facilitate the deportation of aliens and provide for their supervision and detention until deportation can be effected (H.R.

6333, Hobbs [Ala.]), and to amend the subsection of the Nationality Act of 1940 dealing with the registry of aliens (H.R. 4848, Mitchell [Ind.]; H.R. 4870, Farrington [Hawaii]).

81st Congress (1949–1951)

The 81st Congress saw a continuing and increasing flood of immigration and immigration-related bills, among which the wartime or postwar issues of veterans' rights, fiancées, and displaced persons were still numerous, although in diminishing proportion. Concerning veterans were bills to facilitate their admission or to grant nonquota status to them and their spouses,[61] to facilitate the admission of their alien spouses and minor children (S. 1858, McCarran [Nev.]; H.R. 2183, Hays [Ohio]), and to permit the admission of such close relatives in spite of racial ineligibility (H.R. 4577, Chelf [Ky.]; H.R. 4578, Farrington [Hawaii]). There was additionally a proposal (H.R. 256 by Lynch of New York) to limit the grounds for exclusion in the case of certain classes of honorably discharged alien veterans.[62]

Further veterans' legislation was proposed in the form of nine or more bills to extend the expiration date of the so-called War Brides Act of December 28, 1945 and the GI Fiancées Act of June 29, 1946 by one year to December 31, 1949.[63] A House resolution by Walter of Pennsylvania called for completion of the processing of all pending fiancée cases of which there were estimated to be about 1000, but without extension of the Fiancées Act (H. J. Res. 160, Walter [Pa.]). The resolution set the conditions that the visa be granted before January 1, 1949 and that entry be made before July 1 of the same year. Approved by the House committee (H. Rept. 150, Feb. 21, 1949), the bill was passed by the House on March 3, 1949. The Senate committee reported it out (S. Rept. 210, April 4, 1949) with amendment of the cut-off date for granting of the visa from January 1 to April 1, 1949; and in consideration of the bill the Senate accepted a second amendment, proposed by Langer of North Dakota, to change the final date for entry from July 1, 1949 to "within five months after the effective date of this act," and passed the bill on April 11. With House acceptance of the amendments, the bill was signed into law as the Act of April 21, 1949 (63 Stat. 56).

Twenty-five or more bills for amendment of the Displaced Persons

[61]H.R. 433, Kearney (N.Y.); H.R. 2205, Murphy (N.Y.); H.R. 2865, Havenner (Calif.).

[62]Not included here are bills concerning the naturalization of relatives of veterans.

[63]S. 657, Langer (N.D.); S. 1005, Pepper (Fla.); S. 1055, Wiley (Wis.); H.R. 171, Farrington (Hawaii); H.R. 999, Multer (N.Y.); H.R. 1899, Forand (R.I.); H.R. 2150, Rodino (N.J.); H.R. 2557, Lynch (N.Y.); H.R. 2668, Smathers (Fla.).

Act of 1948 were introduced during the session. Some of the bills had several sponsors, and many were companion bills of similar wording or substance, most commonly to broaden the definition of an eligible displaced person, provide for the admission of 400,000, and set two preference classes based on occupation and blood relationship. Individual bills, however, ranged from 202,000 to 502,000 admissions, several would have ended the charging of the admissions against national quotas, and one was for the admission of Russian refugees residing in China (S. 666, Knowland [Calif.]). Two bills were to amend the Act of 1948 to include within the immigration quotas for Germany and Austria ethnic Germans born in the Soviet Union (S. 1060, Ecton [Mont.]; S. 1226, Langer [N.D.]). And another proposed amendment of the Act would have authorized the admission of 500 displaced doctors and 1000 displaced nurses and provided them with employment in government hopitals (H.R. 2018, Case [S.D.]). What was presumably a negative reaction to this group of bills came from Langer of North Dakota in the form of a resolution in the Senate for investigation of lobbying for the D.P. legislation (S. Res. 186).

The only bill of this group to come out of committee was one of the two introduced by Celler of New York (H.R. 4567, with H. Rept. 581, May 16, 1949). The principal purposes of the bill as described in the committee report were to (1) change the cut-off date on eligibility of prospective displaced person immigrants from December 22, 1945 to January 1, 1949, (2) eliminate the 40 percent preference for persons from annexed countries and the 30 percent preference for agricultural workers, (3) increase by 2000 the number of nonquota visas for displaced orphans, (4) provide immigration visas not to exceed 339,000 over the next three years (from 205,000 in the existing act), (5) provide for the corresponding reduction of quotas, and (6) change the cut-off date for the adjustment of status of D.P.s already in the United States from April 1, 1948 to April 1, 1949. The bill was debated and passed in the House, reported out in the Senate without recommendation for or against, debated at considerable length in the Senate, and then recommitted. It was later taken up in the second session (see below).

A number of bills continued to be introduced to broaden the eligibility of Asiatic peoples for immigration and naturalization. Five bills were to grant immigration quotas and the privilege of naturalization to Asian and Pacific peoples.[64] Of these, only the Judd bill was reported out with amendment (H. Rept. 65, Feb. 10, 1949), debated, and passed by the House; but it died in the Senate. The provisions of the bill, however, are

[64] S. 1860, Kilgore (W.Va.), and Langer (N.D.); H.R. 90, Miller (Calif.); H.R. 199, Judd (Minn.); H.R. 1214, Farrington (Hawaii); H.R. 1444, Yates (Ill.).

of more lasting significance, for they foreshadow later legislative developments. The purposes of the bill as stated in the committee report were to (1) remove all racial restrictions on the naturalization of immigrants having a legal right to permanent residence in the United States,

> [2] make immigration quotas available to Asian and Pacific peoples in accordance with the national origins provisions of the 1924 Immigration Act, under specific provision that persons indigenous to an Asia-Pacific triangle described therein shall be charged to the quota for the quota area to which they are by ancestry indigenous, wherever born,[65]

(3) give quota status to the alien spouse and unmarried children of a citizen if chargeable to a quota area with a quota of fewer than 200,[66] (4) reserve up to 75 percent of the quota of Asia-Pacific triangle areas for persons born there, (5) change the quota formula to one-sixth of one percent of the number of inhabitants of the United States in 1920 born in the area, and (6) limit to 100 the number of immigrants from a colony chargeable to the annual quota of the governing country. It was pointed out in an additional comment that several peoples of the Asia-Pacific triangle area, namely Chinese, Indians, and Filipinos, had already been made eligible by earlier legislation.

Other bills were proposed to make specific Asian peoples admissible for permanent residence and eligible for naturalization, of which two bills were for Siamese (S. 467, Magnuson [Wash.]; H.R. 1221, Jackson [Wash.]), four for Koreans,[67] and three for Indonesians and others.[68] With regard to Chinese, three bills were to declare that the lawful wives and children of treaty merchants admitted under section 6 of the Act of May 6, 1882, repealed on December 17, 1943, are to be considered to have been admitted for permanent residence.[69] Eligibility for naturalization would thereby be established.

Several non-Asiatic peoples were also singled out for more favorable

[65]This is an early use of the term "Asia-Pacific triangle," and the term was used several times in the report. The formal designation of the triangle was to come later in the 1952 Act.

[66]Section 4a of the 1924 Act as amended gave nonquota status to alien husbands married prior to January 1, 1948, wives, and unmarried children of citizens. The intent of the bill in doing away with such nonquota status in the case of areas of less than 200 quota was to affect Asia-Pacific triangle areas, none of which had quotas that large. First preference to such relatives was to be given instead.

[67]S. 554, Pepper (Fla.); S. 761, Langer (N.D.); S. 853, Magnuson (Wash.); H.R. 374, Celler (N.Y.).

[68]H.R. 308, Walter (Pa.); H.R. 342, Celler (N.Y.); H.R. 1234, Klein (N.Y.).

[69]S. 206, Downey (Calif.) and Magnuson (Wash.); H.R. 1834, 3381, Havenner (Calif.).

treatment. There were six bills to give Italy a larger quota,[70] two to grant nonquota status to certain Poles who had served in the Polish army or rendered service to the American army (H.R. 298, Sadowski [Mich.]; H.R. 1728, J. L. Pfeifer [N.Y.]), two for establishing an immigration quota for Israel (S. 887, Magnuson [Wash.]; H.R. 1910, Keating [N.Y.]), and one to increase the Greek quota, S. 1193 introduced by Miller of Idaho and Wagner of New York.

Another considerable group of bills concerned facilitating the admission of relatives of citizens other than veterans by the granting of nonquota status. Relatives so favored were alien parents (H.R. 438, Keating [N.Y.]; H.R. 3261, Coffey [Pa.]), husbands of certain female ministers and professors admitted to the United States (H.R. 5917 by Wm. Pfeiffer of New York), certain unmarried dependent grandchildren (H.R. 2139 by Dollinger of New York), stepchildren (H.R. 3628 by Davis of Wisconsin), and adopted children. The last-named were most frequently dealt with, being the subject of at least six bills including several of those above concerned with other relatives as well.[71]

A second class of children for whom special treatment was proposed was that of war orphans, to whom five bills would give nonquota status.[72] In several of them a maximum age of sixteen years was set, and one specified a limit of 25,000 to be so admitted.

Domestic labor market or labor policy considerations appeared in another group of bills. Four were designed to facilitate the entry of certain agricultural workers,[73] and two others brought up the perennial subject of admitting alien sheepherders in relief of the sheep-raising industry.[74] Two bills were to authorize the admission of aliens possessing special skills. Of these the Walter bill, H.R. 3001, was designated as the "Foreign Skilled Personnel Admission Act," proposed the creation of a Foreign Skilled Personnel Board to oversee operations under the act and provided for up to 3,200 special nonquota visas annually for foreign specialists and their families. The other bill concerning special skills was S. 1842 by McMahon (Conn.). Resubmitted from the preceding session

[70]H.R. 455, Keogh (N.Y.); H.R. 964, Poulson (Calif.); H.R. 1428, Sadlak (Conn.); H.R. 1550, Lodge (Conn.); H.R. 1928, Fulton (Pa.); H.R. 2194, McGrath (N.Y.).

[71]S. 917, McMahon (Conn.); H.R. 438, Keating (N.Y.); H.R. 550, Sadowski (Mich.); H.R. 3483, Denton (Ind.); H.R. 3628, Davis (Wis.); H.R. 5394, Fulton (Pa.).

[72]S. 669, Ives (N.Y.); S. 1653, Tydings (Md.); S. 2577, Humphrey (Minn.); H.R. 1836, Javits (N.Y.); H.R. 2881, Tollefson (Wash.).

[73]S. 272, Anderson (N.M.); H.R. 5672, Patten (Ariz.); H.R. 5820, Fernandez (N.M.); H.R. 5828, Phillips (Calif.).

[74]S. 1165, McCarran (Nev.); H.R. 5698, Baring (Nev.). The McCarran bill was reported out, S. Rept. 590, but its consideration was objected to in the Senate.

was a proposal for the temporary admission as agricultural workers of students from countries receiving assistance under the Economic Cooperation Act of 1948, in H.R. 925 and H. J. Res. 149 by Mrs. St. George of New York. And a bill which appeared to be concerned with labor market conditions but which was restrictive in purpose was the resubmitted bill by Pace of Georgia to stop all immigration whenever unemployment in the United States exceeds 100 (H.R. 889).

A small and diverse group of bills concerned deportable aliens. Bills introduced by Rodino of New Jersey dealt with the employment of deportable aliens and barred them from certain social security benefits (H.R. 5653 and 5793). Three bills were to facilitate the deportation of aliens and to provide for supervision and detention of them pending deportation,[75] evidently in reaction to the Gerhart Eisler case in which a suspected Communist agent had evaded the authorities by secret departure on a Polish vessel. One of the three bills was reported out with amendment and with dissenting opinions attached (H. Rept. 1192, on H.R. 10). Among other provisions, the bill stated more clearly to what places an alien may be deported and denied to any court the jurisdiction to release under bond any alien detained under deportation proceedings. Minority views from committee members Celler and Gorski stated that the bill was too severe, that it would create detention camps where aliens might be held at administrative discretion, that it was first offered in the 76th Congress some ten years before and was now in its fifth edition, and that legislation should not be hurriedly passed in emotional reaction to the Eisler case. The bill was not brought up in the House.

Somewhat more progress was made in the House on remedial legislation to correct a difficulty that had arisen with regard to the procedure for congressional review of the Attorney General's recommendations for the suspension of deportation. Probably on behalf of the House committee, Walter of Pennsylvania introduced a bill for change of the existing procedure, and it was reported out without amendment by the committee (H.R. 3875, with H. Rept. 362 of March 31, 1949). As described in the committee report, the procedure from 1940 onward had been for suspension of deportation to take place on the Attorney General's recommendation unless within a specified time Congress passed a concurrent resolution of disapproval. But with the Act of July 1, 1948 (62 Stat. 1206) "affirmative congressional action in each individual case is required before the suspension of deportation could become final." Experience of the past months, the report continued, had shown this procedure unworkable, a burden with the thousands of cases to be considered by the

[75] S. 1985, Lucas (Ill.); S. 1987, Cain (Wash.); H.R. 10, Hobbs (Ala.).

congressional committees. The House committee's recommendation, embodied in the present bill, was to go back to the procedure provided in the original House version of the bill that became the 1948 Act, H.R. 3566 in the 80th Congress, which was rewritten in the Senate to what was substantially the enacted form of the bill. In the original House draft and in the current Walter bill, the right to object is retained by Congress, and if within a specified period "either of the two Houses passes a resolution stating in substance that it does not favor the suspension of such deportation, the Attorney General shall thereupon deport such alien in the manner provided by law." The House passed the Walter bill, but the bill did not progress in the Senate.

Other bills dealt with various routine subjects related to the regulation of immigration. Several legislative proposals were designed to provide tighter control on the entrance of stowaways.[76] Several were to legislate against the smuggling in of aliens (S. 954, McCarran [Nev.]; H.R. 2165, Celler [N.Y.]) and to tighten safeguards against subversive aliens by stronger provisions for their exclusion and expulsion.[77] And perhaps related in purpose to the latter was a bill to terminate the issuance of immigration visas to natives of Soviet Russia and Soviet-dominated nations (H.R. 197, Jenkins [Ohio]).

With regard to the quotas, there was a bill to authorize the President to allocate to any country any unused portion of its annual quotas since June 30, 1929 or a portion of the current quota of any other country deemed unlikely to be used (H.R. 2195, McGrath [N.Y.]). And two identical bills, in the Senate and House, were to establish five preference classes of quota immigrants (S. 967, Ferguson [Mich.]; H.R. 946, Herter [Mass.]), as follows:

1. First preference of not more than 10 percent of a nation's quota to "qualified immigrants . . . highly beneficial to the national welfare . . . from the standpoint of public security; and aliens whose services are urgently needed . . . because of the highly skilled, technical, or scientific education, training, experience, or ability of the aliens. . . ."

2. Second preference of not more than 50 percent to immigrants who are parents of citizens at least twenty-one years of age or husbands of citizens at least eighteen years of age.

3. Third preference of the next 20 percent to immigrants who are the wives or unmarried children under twenty-one years of age of lawfully admitted alien residents.

4. Fourth preference of the next 10 percent to brothers, sisters,

[76]S. 953, McCarran (Nev.); H.R. 1956, Celler (N.Y.); H.R. 2027, Klein (N.Y.).

[77]S. 1694, 1832, McCarran (Nev.); S. 2311, Mundt (S.D.), Ferguson (Mich.), Johnston (S.C.); H.R. 4870, Walter (Pa.).

unmarried children over twenty-one years of age, or the orphan nephews or nieces under twenty-one years of age of citizens able and willing to support such immigrants.

5. Nonpreference class of the remaining 10 percent plus the unused portion of the preference classes, available to qualified immigrants not eligible for preference.

None of the foregoing bills except as noted was reported out by the Senate and House committees.[78]

The second session of the 81st Congress lasted a full year, from January 3, 1950 to January 2, 1951, but it dealt with only a moderate number of immigration bills, some of which were carried over from the first session. The principal legislative activity related to immigration during the session was for amendment of the Displaced Persons Act of 1948. Two new bills for amendment were introduced (S. 2889, Langer [N.D.]; H.R. 9647, Walter [Pa.]) but not acted on, and the Walter bill passed by the House in the first session was reported out with amendment by the Senate committee (S. Rept. 1237 of Jan. 25, 1950 on H.R. 4567). In the preceding session that committee had reported out the bill with a one-line statement of no recommendation, either favorable or unfavorable. The Senate had then wrestled inconclusively with the bill over many days and returned it to the committee. Early in the new session, on January 25, 1950, the Senate committee again reported out the bill, evidently after extensive work on it in the light of the foregoing Senate debate, for the committee presented a considerably rewritten bill that introduced new provisions and deleted or modified parts of the House bill. Again there was long Senate debate, but the much-amended bill was passed, and on House disagreement with the Senate revisions went to a conference committee. The conference committee labored further in redrafting to compose Senate and House differences, and finally presented its recommendations on June 2 (H. Rept. 2187, presented by Walter [Pa.]). With House and Senate acceptance and presidential signature it became the Act of June 16, 1950 (64 Stat. 219).

A long and involved act, it amended and rewrote many sections of the Displaced Persons Act of 1948. Some of the principal changes made by the Act were to

1. Add a new provision (section 2f) for the issuance of not to exceed 5000 nonquota immigrant visas for war orphans under ten years of age.[79]

[78]Not included here are several bills to give eligibility to naturalization, which would automatically confer admissibility for permanent residence.

[79]Changed from the Senate-originated provision of 20,000 visas and an age limit of sixteen.

2. Enlarge the definition of eligible displaced persons to include refugees from Yugoslav occupation of Venezia Giulia, not to exceed 2000 in number (section 2g).[80]

3. Increase the number of immigrant visas available for eligible displaced persons, including orphans, from 202,000 to 341,000, but limited to three years from July 1, 1948.[81]

4. Add three new specially designated refugee classes (section 3b), these being European refugees in China not to exceed 4000 in number, Polish army veterans residing in the British Isles limited to 18,000, and Greek refugees from Nazi and Communist attack limited to 7500. To the latter were added, not to exceed 2500, residents and nationals of Greece eligible for first or second preference and who had applied to an American consular officer in Greece prior to June 30, 1951.

5. Eliminate the 40 percent preference for persons from annexed countries (section 3a) and the 30 percent first preference for agricultural workers and their families (section 6a); and combine the former second preference for "household, construction, clothing, and garment workers" and "persons possessing special educational, scientific, technological or professional qualifications" (section 6b) with agricultural workers to form a new first-preference class.[82]

6. Amend section 7 of the 1948 Act, concerned with priority in the issuance of visas within the foregoing preference classes to eliminate the second priority to persons who on January 1, 1948 were in displaced persons camps and centers; and in the first-priority class to retain only those persons who have borne arms against the enemies of the United States in World War II, and to eliminate inclusion of those who "are unable or unwilling to return to the countries of which they are nationals because of persecution or fear of persecution on account of race, religion, or political opinions."

Another subject of high legislative priority during the second session of the 81st Congress was protection of the nation from subversive activities, this at a time of strong anti-Communist feeling further heightened by the conflict in Korea. For the most part, congressional efforts were for the prevention of subversion and the preservation of internal security, but certain of the measures proposed and adopted included the exclusion of suspect aliens.

[80]Reduced from the original Senate allocation of 5000.

[81]Extended to December 31, 1951 by amendment in the Act of June 28, 1951 (65 Stat. 96).

[82]The third preference class of the 1948 Act, consisting of blood relatives of citizens and lawfully admitted aliens, was retained and became the new second preference class.

Carried over from the first session were several bills dealing with subversives. A Senate bill (S. 2311, Mundt [S.D.], and others [81-I]) was for the purpose of protection against un-American and subversive activities. It was reported out by the Senate committee with minor amendment (S. Rept. 1358) and with the explanation that it was to outlaw conspiracy to establish a totalitarian dictatorship under foreign control, to require regulation of Communist organizations, to restrict the travel of American Communists, and deny them government employment. Minority views in dissent were attached to the committee report. Objection was raised when the bill was brought up in the Senate, and it was postponed indefinitely.

More progress was made by another Senate bill from the first session, the author of which was the influential Senator McCarran of Nevada (S. 1832 [81-I]). As reported out by the Senate committee in the second session (S. Rept. 2230, Aug. 2, 1950), it had been amended to what was a substitute bill. As thus amended it provided for the exclusion and expulsion of subversive classes of aliens, which were specified in very considerable detail, and called on the Attorney General to publish an annual or more frequent list of subversive organizations in the Federal Register. Passed by the Senate, the bill went to the House, where it did not progress further.

Although not adopted by Congress, the unsuccessful Mundt, McCarran, and other bills from the first session were not without influence on later legislation, for the congressional committees in both House and Senate were laboring to produce antisubversive or more particularly anti-Communist measures. Parts of bills already in the committees' hands were incorporated in what was to become the Internal Security Act of 1950.

In the House a new bill for the control of Communists and related classes was introduced from the Un-American Activities Committee,[83] to require registration and to place various disabilities on individuals and organizations regarded as subversive. It was passed by the House with only brief debate on August 29, 1950 by a one-sided vote.[84] The Senate meanwhile was working on its own bill (S. 4037, McCarran [Nev.]), entitled "For the protection of the internal security of the United States," and introduced by McCarran of Nevada, chairman of the Judiciary Commit-

[83]H.R. 9490, Wood (Ga.), with H. Rept. 2980, Aug. 22, 1950.

[84]One dissenting vote was from Marcantonio of New York, who had recently introduced a bill to repeal the Act of October 16, 1918 for the exclusion and expulsion of anarchists, etc. (H.R. 8346). During the debate Celler of New York had spoken against the bill, referring to "anti-Communist hysteria" and the emotional reaction to the Korean War, but he refrained from voting against the bill.

tee. The new McCarran bill incorporated parts of earlier Senate bills, including a section that rewrote the Act of October 16, 1918 to set more stringent terms for the exclusion of Communists and related classes, which came from the McCarran bill of the preceding session (S. 1832 [81-I]). Reported out (S. Rept. 2369, Aug. 17, 1950) with a minority report attached as was the Mundt bill from the first session, the bill was debated at length on September 12 and somewhat amended by the Senate. The Senate then took up the just-passed House bill and amended it by substituting the body of the Senate's McCarran bill just acted on. The House objecting to this drastic revision, the bill went to conference and was reported back in a form that retained the features of the Senate bill (H. Rept. 3112, Sept. 19, 1950). Accepted by both House and Senate, the conference draft was vetoed by President Truman, passed over the veto, and became the Internal Security Act of September 23, 1950 (64 Stat. 987).

A lengthy act in many sections, the new measure included strong anti-Communist provisions from the Mundt and other bills and the McCarran bill's revision of the October 16, 1918 Act that gave a much expanded definition of the subversive classes to be excluded.[85]

Veterans legislation was represented by a bill for the admission of alien spouses and minor children of citizens who are members of the Armed Forces (H.R. 9216, Judd [Minn.]); and the McCarran bill of the same title was brought up from the first session (S. 1858 [81-I]). The latter, designed to remove racial limitations on the admissibility of alien wives and minor children of servicemen, was reported out (S. Rept. 1878, June 26, 1950) with amendment by the Senate committee, the amendment being to limit its application to marriages contracted earlier than ninety days after the effective date of the bill if enacted. Passed by the Senate, the bill was approved by the House committee with amendment of the limiting time to six months instead of ninety days after the effective date (H. Rept. 2768, Aug. 1, 1950). Approved as amended, the bill became the Act of August 19, 1950 (64 Stat. 464).

Another successful effort to reduce restrictions based on race was in the field of naturalization law, with passage of the Act of August 1, 1950 (64 Stat. 384) that among other provisions removed the racial bar for

[85]The excluded classes, in brief, were aliens whose entry would be prejudicial to the interests and security of the United States, who are anarchists, who advocate opposition to organized government, who are or have been members or affiliates of the Communist party or are associated with world communism, who advocate in any way the overthrow of organized government, or who engage in or are associated with publication and distribution of subversive writings.

Guamanians. Close to success in the same direction, but eventually failing of enactment, was a bill introduced by Walter of Pennsylvania to remove the racial restriction on naturalization for all aliens legally present in the United States for permanent residence (H.R. 9780). It was favorably reported by the House committee (H. Rept. 3140, Nov. 30, 1950), which estimated it would apply to 84,658 aliens of Japanese descent, 3139 of Korean descent, and 145 Polynesians and "other Asians" then residing in the United States. The House passed the bill, which was quite promptly reported out without amendment by the Senate committee (S. Rept. 2636, Dec. 14, 1950), but was then objected to and not brought up for vote. Concerned in another way with Asiatics were two bills to permit Chinese students to remain for a period of three years (S. 3298, Magnuson [Wash.]; H.R. 8080, Mitchell [Wash.]). Both bills stayed in committee to the end of the 81st Congress.

Dealing with admissions for other classes of aliens were three bills to authorize additional Italian immigration above the annual quota to the amount of the cumulative unused Italian quotas for the seven fiscal years including the World War II period, from June 30, 1939 to July 1, 1946.[86] Other bills were to grant nonquota status to adopted children (H.R. 7712, Multer [N.Y.]; H.R. 7872, Rodino [N.J.]) and the fathers and mothers of citizens.[87] None of the above received committee approval.

The idea of reallocation of unused quota numbers, noted above in the case of Italian immigration, also appeared in two identical bills introduced in the Senate on July 20, 1950 by Humphrey of Minnesota and three colleagues, and in the House on the following September 22 by Celler of New York. The proposal was to limit the immigration visas issued in any one quarter for a given nationality to 25 percent of the annual quota, to assign all quota visas unused in a given quarter to a visa pool, and to make the pooled visas available to any nationality at any time during the two years following. The pooled visas were to be assigned according to a series of four preferences: (1) a national need preference of not more than 25 percent of the visas to be used exclusively for aliens determined by the Attorney General to fill occupational needs in the United States; (2) a family reunion preference of not over 25 percent to be used exclusively to care for pending applications on the part of spouses, parents, children, and siblings of persons already admitted to the United States; (3) a persecutee preference of up to 25

[86]S. 3759, Ives (N.Y.); H.R. 8046, Clemente (N.Y.); H.R. 8496, Barrett (Pa.).

[87]H.R. 8209, Klein (N.Y.); H.R. 8656, Addonizio (N.J.); H.R. 8768, Rodino (N.J.); H.R. 8849, Tauriello (N.Y.).

percent available exclusively to "persons . . . who have been persecuted abroad on religious or racial grounds or because of their adherence to democratic beliefs or because of their opposition to totalitarianism or dictatorship, or who face the danger of such persecution"; and (4) non-preference cases, to receive all remaining visas "in the order of their registration."[88]

Several bills for the admission of special classes of workers were brought up from the first session. One was to facilitate the admission of certain agricultural workers (S. 272, Anderson [N.Mex.][81-I]). The Senate committee inserted several amendments before reporting it out (S. Rept. 1474, April 10, 1950), to change it from a permanent to a temporary measure, limit the period of admission to six months and limit renewals to not over another six months, and give the Attorney General authority to pass on the admissibility of all aliens as a safeguard against the entry of subversives. The bill was brought up for discussion in the Senate but did not come to vote.

A second labor market bill brought up from the first session was the Walter (Pa.) bill to authorize the admission of certain aliens with special skills (H.R. 3001 [81-I]). It was debated and passed by the House but made no progress in the Senate. And a third carryover from the first session was the McCarran bill (S. 1165 [81-I]) for the admission of up to 250 sheepherders, which had been passed by the Senate previously. The House committee reported out the bill with minor amendment (H. Rept. 2268, June 15, 1950), it was passed, and became the Act of June 30, 1950 (64 Stat. 306). Each sheepherder admitted under the bill was to be charged to the present or future quotas of the appropriate country, but not in excess of half of any annual quota.

A not-yet-solved problem of this period was how to effect deportation when circumstances abroad made it impossible, under existing procedures, to deport an alien to his homeland. Several bills designed to meet the problem had appeared in the preceding session, and another was introduced by Celler of New York (H.R. 9447). The House chose, however, to act on and pass one of the bills from the first session (H.R. 10, Hobbs [Ala.] [81-I]). The Senate committee struck out the House draft and wrote a new bill (S. Rept. 2239, Aug. 3, 1950) of which the principal features were (1) wider authority to the Attorney General to determine the country to which an alien may be deported; (2) specified procedure for the control of aliens illegally in the United States, and the provision of criminal penalties for violations; (3) criminal penalties also for aliens in the criminal, subversive, and immoral classes who fail to

[88]S. 3950, Humphrey (Minn.) and three others; H.R. 9736, Celler (N.Y.).

depart as ordered; and (4) forbidding of the release of a deportable alien before his case is determined, except on court order from three federal judges. When brought up in the Senate its consideration was indefinitely postponed.

Another bill to enlarge the Attorney General's powers in a different type of deportation proceedings from the first session was to give the Attorney General the authority to cancel suspension of deportation proceedings, to reinstate deportability, and to cancel naturalization (H.R. 4684, Celler [N.Y.][81-I]). The bill was approved by the House committee (H. Rept. 1549, Jan. 27, 1950) and then by the House as a whole, but made no progress in the Senate.

The only other bills to be noted for the second session, none of which received committee support, are two providing that no arriving alien shall be excluded without a hearing (S. 3448, Langer [N.D.]; H.R. 7476, Roosevelt [N.Y.]), and one to record the lawful admission for permanent residence of certain aliens lacking such record (S. 3843, Kem [Mo.]), the effect of which would be to facilitate naturalization.

82nd Congress (1951, 1952)

The 82nd Congress saw a shifting of the distribution of immigration concerns as evidenced by the new bills that were introduced, with dwindling attention to the special problems from the preceding decade, such as displaced persons and veterans legislation, and relatively greater attention to routine and continuing matters, such as the regulation of immigration, quota and nonquota admissions, and amendment of the basic immigration acts. Important new legislation was to come out of this reconsideration of immigration law and procedure.

Legislation for the admission of alien veterans and their immediate families was the subject of three bills in the first session.[89] Of these, the Kearney bill in the House was to give nonquota status to alien veterans of the Spanish-American War and both world wars, together with the veterans' wives and unmarried minor children. It was not reported out by the committee. More progress was made by Senate and House bills to extend by six months the recently passed Act of August 19, 1950 (64 Stat. 464) that waived racial restrictions on the admission of alien spouses and minor children of citizen veterans. The Senate bill, introduced by McCarran of Nevada, chairman of the Senate committee, was reported out (S. Rept. 56, Jan. 29, 1951) but then was postponed and the House bill was acted on instead. The House bill, from Walter of Pennsylvania, chairman

[89]S. 552, McCarran (Nev.); H.R. 100, Kearney (N.Y.); H.R. 1090, Walter (Pa.).

of the House committee, was reported out by his committee (H. Rept. 117, Feb. 12, 1951), passed by the House and then by the Senate in lieu of the McCarran bill. Signed by the President, it became the Act of March 19, 1951 (65 Stat. 5).

Amendment of the Displaced Persons Act of 1948 was the subject of two House bills and two House resolutions,[90] primarily for the purpose of extending the Act, provisions of which were due to expire on June 30, 1951. The only one of the group to be acted on was the first of the two Walter bills. It was reported out without amendment by the House committee (H. Rept. 325, April 16, 1951) and passed. The Senate committee reported favorably on it, with amendment (S. Rept. 412, June 11, 1951), and it was approved by the Senate and enacted as the Act of June 28, 1951 (65 Stat. 96). It did not increase the number of immigrant visas to be issued under the bill but extended the time allowed for admission by six months, to December 31, 1951, for eligible displaced persons and by one year, to June 30, 1952, for eligible displaced orphans. And for the former group, selection or processing of the case must have begun on or before July 31, 1951.

Of general application was a Senate bill to abolish all discrimination on the basis of race and sex in the immigration laws,[91] not limited to special cases as in the veterans bills above. A multipurpose bill, the Senate bill also provided for the pooling of all unused quota visas to be assigned without reference to national origins and according to a fourfold preference structure of family reunion, national need, persecutee, and nonpreference classes of 25 percent each,[92] and to give nonquota status to parents of citizens, certain orphans under eighteen years of age, and alien members and former members of the Armed Forces together with their immediate families.

The subject of unused quotas was also brought up in a House bill (H.R. 2242, McGrath [N.Y.]) to authorize the President at his discretion to allocate to immigrants of any nationality any part of the quotas for that nationality unused since June 30, 1931, or any part of the current quotas of any other nationality that the President finds will not be needed.

In addition to the just noted Senate bill for abolition of racial barriers to immigration and naturalization were several bills for the aid of specific classes. Judd of Minnesota reintroduced a bill to grant the naturalization

[90] H.R. 3576, 5057, Walter (Pa.); H. J. Res. 105, Machrowicz (Mich.); H. J. Res. 184, Multer (N.Y.).

[91] S. 2343, Lehman (N.Y.), Humphrey (Minn.), and thirteen other Senators.

[92] This is the same preference structure as appeared in two Senate bills of the second session of the 81st Congress, S. 272, Anderson (N.Mex.), and S. 3950, Humphrey (Minn.) and others.

privilege to all immigrants having a legal right to permanent residence and to give immigration quotas to Asian and Pacific peoples (H.R. 199). A companion bill came from Miller of California (H.R. 246). And as in the second session of the preceding Congress, there were two bills to allow Chinese students to remain for a period of up to three years (S. 748, Magnuson [Wash.]; H.R. 3171, Klein [N.Y.]).

Other groups were singled out for favorable treatment. Increase of the Greek quota was proposed (H.R. 3359, Fulton [Pa.]), and there were eight bills to do the same for Italy.[93] Of these, two were to grant additional immigration visas to the amount of unused quotas over past years (S. 663 and H.R. 3357), and one was to make an outright allocation of 50,000 (H.R. 5648). Opposite in purpose was a reintroduced bill from the 81st Congress to deny immigration visas to natives of Soviet Russia and its satellite countries (H.R. 92, Jenkins [Ohio]).

Legislation in favor of the admission of various classes of relatives was proposed, in addition to the veterans bills already noted. Included here were two bills for the admission of children adopted by citizens (H.R. 491, Keating [N.Y.]; H.R. 1374, Multer [N.Y.]), one for alien spouses and minor children of citizens (H.R. 1015, Farrington [Hawaii]), and one to give preference under quota to brothers and sisters of citizens (H.R. 4625, Addonizio [N.J.]).

Other legislative proposals dealt with the admission of certain needed classes of workers. Two concerned the admission of aliens possessing special skills (S. 1265, Lodge [Mass.]; H.R. 402, Walter [Pa.]). These were entitled "Foreign Skilled Personnel Admission Act," and they appear to be the same as a Walter bill of the preceding Congress (H.R. 3001 [81-I]) which was described earlier. There was also a bill for the admission of agricultural workers who are natives of the Western Hemisphere whenever the Secretary of Labor determines that the supply of domestic labor for agriculture is inadequate (S. 225, Anderson [N. Mex.]). Admissions under the bill were to be for six months only, subject to a renewal period of the same length, with exemption from head tax and literacy test but required to be identified by photograph and fingerprints. Wyoming Senator Hunt introduced a bill, S. 1217, to provide, under suitable safeguards, additional quota immigrant visas to aliens willing to accept employment as sheepherders, and amending the Sheepherders Act of June 30, 1950 (64 Stat. 306) to increase the numerical limitation on such admissions in section 3 of the act from 250 to 550. And the

[93] S. 663, Ives (N.Y.); H.R. 9, Anfuso (N.Y.); H.R. 267, Poulson (Calif.); H.R. 370, Sadlak (Conn.); H.R. 2314, Donovan (N.Y.); H.R. 3357, Fulton (Pa.); H.R. 5648, Celler (N.Y.); H.R. 5825, Clemente (N.Y.).

author of the above act, McCarran of Nevada, introduced an amending bill, S. 1696, to extend the cut-off date for admissions under the act by six months, from June 30, 1951 to December 31, 1951. The Senate committee promptly reported out its chairman's bill (S. Rept. 449, June 20, 1951), which was duly passed by the Senate. The House committee also acted promptly (H. Rept. 686, July 10, 1951) but to strike out the entire bill after the enacting clause and to insert a new draft. The original purpose of the bill, to extend the life of the 1950 Act by six months, was kept, however, and it was made clear that no increase in the number of sheepherders to be admitted was contemplated. The bill was then recommitted, and the 1950 Act expired because of time limitation.

Resident aliens were the concern of several bills, of which one was to record the lawful admission for permanent residence of certain aliens (H.R. 4614, by Bolling of Missouri), and two others were to give the Attorney General authority to amend the record of certain aliens who were admitted only temporarily, under the ninth proviso of section 3 of the 1917 Immigration Act, because of affiliations other than Communist (H.R. 2339, Walter [Pa.]; H.R. 2467, Rodino [N.J.]). They also instructed the Attorney General to interpret the provisions of the Act of October 16, 1918 (the Act for the Exclusion and Expulsion of Anarchists, etc.) referring to persons as members of or affiliated with Communist organizations to include only membership or affiliation that was voluntary, excluding cases where the person in question was under fourteen years of age, where membership was required by law, or where it was for the purpose of obtaining employment, food rations, or other necessities. Of the two identical bills, the Walter bill was reported out (H. Rept. 118, Feb. 12, 1951) with an amendment changing the age from fourteen to sixteen. So amended, it passed the House and then the Senate and was signed to become the Act of March 28, 1951 (65 Stat. 28).

For the protection of the arriving alien, Langer of North Dakota again introduced a bill to ensure that none would be excluded without a hearing (S. 149). And there were two deportation bills, one to provide deportation as the penalty for aliens convicted of indictable crimes within ten years of admission (H.R. 3204, Taylor [N.Y.]), the other providing similar penalty for aliens who have violated federal marihuana [*sic*] laws (H.R. 3908, Boggs [La.]).

A problem that grew in prominence and became a matter of increasing concern at the time was that of illegal entry, especially from Mexico, known as the "wetback" problem. The Mexican government had protested the draining off of its labor supply and had urged tighter border control. And efforts to put pressure on the employers of wetback labor north of the border had been ineffective. Section 8 of the Immigration Act of 1917 made it a misdemeanor punishable by fine to bring in or harbor in any way an alien not duly admitted by an immigration officer, and the Act of June 25, 1948 (62 Stat. 683) had made it a felony; however, a recent Supreme Court decision had held that there was no enforceable law against harboring an illegal immigrant. The 82nd Congress reacted to the Court decision in the first session with at least six bills for amendment or clarification of section 8 of the 1917 Act;[94] but action on them was postponed until the second session. Generally, the bills reaffirmed and strengthened the provisions in section 8 making the bringing in or harboring of an illegal immigrant a felony and setting a penalty.[95]

Amendments of other sections of the 1917 Act were proposed, in one case of section 33 to forbid the paying off or discharge of an alien seaman in the United States unless with consent of the Attorney General and to provide penalty for violation (H.R. 4548, Celler [N.Y.]). And two bills were for amendment of section 19 of the same act, concerning authorization of the Attorney General to permit voluntary departure of a deportable alien or to suspend deportation proceedings.[96]

Amendment of the Quota Act of 1924 was also proposed by several members of Congress at this time. Suggestions for the reallocation of unused quota numbers have been noted above. Another proposal was for an altered preference structure within the national origins quotas (S. 123, Ferguson [Mich.]), consisting of a first preference of 10 percent to qualified immigrants who would be beneficial to the national security or who were needed because of "the highly skilled, technical, or scientific education, training, experience, or ability of the aliens"; a second preference of 50 percent to parents of adult citizen children and to husbands of citizens at least eighteen years of age; a third preference of 20 percent to wives and minor children of lawfully admitted alien residents; a fourth preference of 10 percent to siblings, unmarried children over twenty-one years of age, and orphan nephews and nieces of citizens; and the remaining 10 percent plus any unused visas from the preference classes to nonpreference cases. A final bill for amendment of the 1924 Act was to remove the age limitation on nonquota and preference status for the unmarried children of citizens and resident aliens (H.R. 3833, Martin [Mass.]).

Apart from amendment of individual acts, there was feeling in Congress that a thorough revision and codification of the immigration laws

[94]S. 1391, Ellender (La.); S. 1661, O'Conor (Md.) and four others; S. 1851, Kilgore (W.Va.); H.R. 2793, 4854, Celler (N.Y.); H.R. 4845, Walter (Pa.).

[95]See below under the second session of the 82nd Congress for description of the Kilgore bill, the only one to be acted on.

[96]S. 1662, O'Conor (Md.) and four others; H.R. 2258, Celler (N.Y.).

was needed following the many years of amendment of the basic acts of 1917 and 1924; and this view was also being strongly urged by individuals and organizations outside of Congress. During the first session of the 82nd Congress there were five bills of identical title, "To revise the laws relating to immigration, naturalization, and nationality,"[97] and more significant than the number of these bills was their sponsorship, for they were introduced by McCarran of Nevada, chairman of the Senate committee, Celler of New York, chairman of the House Judiciary Committee which has the subcommittee on Immigration and Nationality, and Walter of Pennsylvania, chairman of the latter committee. House and Senate bills included in this group were lengthy codifying bills that ran to over 150 sections and nearly 280 pages. Action on them was deferred to the second session.

The second session of the 82nd Congress, from January 3 to July 7, 1952, labored principally with two legislative problems taken up in the first session and carried on to completion in the second: the illegal entry of aliens, especially the so-called wetbacks from Mexico, and the need for revision and codification of the whole patchwork body of immigration law.

Early in the new session the Senate committee reported out (S. Rept. 1145, Feb. 4, 1952) the Kilgore bill from the first session, S. 1851, whose stated purpose was "to assist in preventing aliens from entering or remaining illegally." The committee had exercised its prerogative and struck out the entire bill and in its place written a new draft of section 8 of the 1917 Act. The substance was to make it a felony to bring in, transport within the United States if in furtherance of an illegal entry, willfully conceal, or willfully induce an alien unlawfully to enter or reside in the United States. Penalty was set at a fine not to exceed $2000, or imprisonment not to exceed five years, or both, "for each alien in respect to whom any violation . . . occurs." But the force of the measure was weakened by the proviso that "the usual and normal practices incident to employment shall not be deemed to constitute harboring."

During discussion of the bill in the Senate on the day after it was reported out, Kilgore of West Virginia, author or ex-author of the bill, stated in answer to questions that the draft of the bill as amended had been approved by the Department of Agriculture and representatives of agricultural organizations and that it applied to the illegal employment of aliens in the cities as well as upon farms.

Passed by the Senate, the bill was approved by the House committee

[97] S. 716, 2055, McCarran (Nev.); H.R. 2379, 5678, Walter (Pa.); H.R. 2816, Celler (N.Y.).

without amendment (H. Rept. 1377, Feb. 19, 1952) but it was attacked in the course of debate in the House with the accusation that the Senate amendments of the original bill had "removed all its teeth" and left it too weak to meet the problem of illegal immigration. The direction of ensuing House amendments was to widen authority for making arrests for violation and to make other changes in enforcement procedure. After passage by the House, the bill went to a conference committee, which was unable to fully reconcile the Senate and House positions and therefore recommended that the powers of immigration officials remain as provided in earlier acts (H. Rept. 1505, March 11, 1952). With agreement by both houses of Congress and presidential signature, the bill became the Act of March 20, 1952 (66 Stat. 26). Its amendment of section 8 of the 1917 Act remained essentially as described above for the original bill. It also amended an earlier act defining powers of the Border Patrol (Act of Aug. 7, 1946, 60 Stat. 865), to give to the officers of the Immigration and Naturalization Service authority to have access to private lands, but not dwellings, within twenty-five miles of an external boundary "for the purpose of patrolling the border to prevent the illegal entry of aliens."

A parallel and newly entered bill in the second session was to amend section 10 of the 1917 Act in order "to strengthen the internal security of the United States" (H.R. 6775, Celler [N.Y.]). Section 10 dealt with the obligation of certain transportation officials to prevent the unauthorized entry of aliens. The bill remained in committee.

The other and principal subject of legislative activity concerned revision of the immigration and nationality laws. Several new bills to this effect were introduced during the second session, principally a Senate bill from McCarran of Nevada on behalf of the Senate committee of which he was chairman (S. 2550, with S. Rept. 1137, Jan. 29, 1952); and there were several other bills of similar purpose.[98] The McCarran bill, reported out in place of another McCarran bill of the first session (S. 2055 [82-I]), was to repeal all immigration and naturalization law and to enact a revised code. The principal features of this massive bill of approximately 300 pages were stated to be a new preference system for selection within the quotas, an end to race and sex discrimination in immigration law, more rigorous screening of security risks, strengthened exclusion and deportation procedures, and greater safeguards in naturalization and denaturalization procedures against subversives and other undesirables. The new preference system consisted of four classes, with a first preference of 50 percent to aliens with high qualifications, a second preference of 30 percent plus any unused portion of the first and third classes to parents

[98]S. 2842, Humphrey (Minn.) and twelve others; H.R. 7032, Roosevelt (N.Y.).

of citizens of at least twenty-one years of age, a third preference of 20 percent plus any unused portion of classes one and two to spouses and children of aliens lawfully admitted for permanent residence, and a fourth class to receive any remaining unused portion of a national quota in the allocation of which preference of not more than 25 percent of the total was to go to brothers, sisters, sons, and daughters of citizens.

The committee report was accompanied by a dissenting minority report signed by Senate Judiciary members Kefauver, Magnuson, Kilgore, and Langer. The principal points of criticism were that the bill injected new racial discriminations (this was presumably in reference to the racial rather than national origins basis for Asia-Pacific triangle peoples), introduced new and vague requirements for admission, and by stringent screening would impede the coming of refugees from totalitarian regimes.

Not long after this, a group of liberal Senators headed by Humphrey of Minnesota and Lehman of New York introduced a substitute bill which was a duplicate of the McCarran bill except for revision of several key sections to remove the racial basis for certain Asian quotas, to provide for pooling of unused quota numbers, to change the base year for the computation of quotas from 1920 to 1950, to add new nonquota classes, to moderate the exclusion and deportation provisions, and otherwise to liberalize various provisions of the immigration and naturalization laws. McCarran reacted vigorously, by classifying the substitute bill as the product of "a certain radical group . . . dedicated to the destruction of our protective immigration system," and he pointed out that the substitute would give nonquota status to an estimated 800,000 Orientals born in Western Hemisphere countries, would permit an increase of quota immigration by 85,000 annually because of the change to a 1950 base year, would destroy the national origins quota system, and much else.[99] Predictably, the Humphrey–Lehman bill was not reported out by McCarran's committee, and its sponsors had to turn their efforts to amendment of the committee bill.

Meanwhile, the House was working on its own immigration and naturalization bill, a Walter bill from the first session (H.R. 5678 [82-I]) that was a counterpart of the McCarran bill in the Senate. It was reported out by the House committee early in the second session,[100] where it had been considerably reworked. According to the committee report, the

[99] *Congressional Record,* 98:5623–24, May 21, 1952. The Humphrey–Lehman bill was H.R. 2842.

[100] H. Rept. 1356, Feb. 14, 1952. This is a voluminous report in 328 pages that includes detailed comparison of the bill with existing law, section by section.

principal changes in immigration law that would be effected by the bill were an elimination of racial barriers to immigration and naturalization, elimination of sex discrimination in immigration law, and broader grounds for the exclusion and deportation of criminal aliens. The same was being said of the McCarran bill in the Senate. One of the committee amendments was to rewrite section 274 of the bill to incorporate the wording of the recently enacted Kilgore bill, the Act of March 20, 1952 (66 Stat. 26), which amended section 8 of the 1917 Act.

The Walter bill was brought up in the House on April 23, 1952, at which time Walter himself was the floor manager of the bill and opened debate with an explanatory statement. He then offered a number of committee-sponsored amendments of a clerical nature together with several technical or administrative amendments, all duly accepted. Celler of New York then rose to offer several amendments, which were to carry forward unused quota numbers, to give a special quota of 100 to aliens of at least half ancestry attributable to Asia-Pacific triangle countries, and to charge aliens coming from a colony or dependency to the quota of the governing country. Walter argued against these amendments and all were rejected; but on his recommendation an amendment was accepted to repeal the Act of March 20, 1952, the just-passed Wetback Act, since its provisions were incorporated in a section of the present bill. Numerous other amendments were proposed, including two by Javits of New York to restore nonquota status to professors and to change the base year for the computation of national immigration quotas, as had been proposed in the Humphrey-Lehman bill, from 1920 to 1940,[101] and three were also proposed by Meader of Michigan to restore the right of review by any court of competent jurisdiction of the Attorney General's decisions on detention, release on bond, parole, and deportability of aliens. All were opposed by Walter and were defeated. Numerous other amendments were offered and the voting pattern persisted, with a solid majority supporting the committee bill and voting down all amendments unless accepted by Walter as representative of the committee. After efforts at amendment and recommittal were defeated, the bill was passed by the House on April 25, 1952 by vote of 206 to 68.[102]

The Walter bill was received by the Senate and placed on its calendar on April 28, then brought up for consideration on May 1, at which time

[101]Walter obtained rejection of these amendments by arguing that professors, if needed, would be taken care of adequately by the first preference, and that to change to a 1940 [*sic*] base would reduce quotas for recent allies and increase them for former enemy nations.

[102]*Congressional Record*, 98:4444.

objection was raised and consideration was postponed while the Senate labored on its own bill. Consideration of that bill began on May 9 with lengthy debate, largely on procedural matters, and resumed on May 15. McCarran as author and floor manager of the bill described principal features of the bill and noted that they were much the same as those of the recently passed House bill. Opposition to the bill was led by Lehman of New York and Humphrey of Minnesota, the leading sponsors of the substitute bill introduced earlier, who strongly condemned the McCarran bill as anti-immigration and antialien.

Senate debate on the bill continued over a number of days. On request, McCarran as sponsor and floor manager of the bill set forth the principal points of difference between his and the Walter bill, which included the following:

1. some differences in grounds for deportation, although both bills strengthen the provisions concerning deportation;
2. somewhat less strict provisions concerning suspension of deportation in the House bill;
3. provision in the House bill but not in the Senate bill for a joint congressional committee for continuing study of the administration of the act.

After attempts to return the bill to committee were decisively defeated, the opponents of the bill offered a long amendment to strike out all after the enacting clause and to insert a new draft incorporating substantially the same provisions as had been defeated in proposed amendments in the House.[103] After arguments on both sides, the amendment was defeated two days later by a vote of 27 to 51, with 18 not voting. Subsequently, a number of amendments making technical changes in the bill were accepted, as was a McCarran amendment to incorporate the provisions of the wetback bill (Act of March 20, 1952) as had been done in the House. Numerous other amendments were proposed and rejected.

Without bringing the amended bill to a vote, the Senate proceeded to consideration of the House bill. McCarran immediately moved an amendment of the House bill to strike out all after the enacting clause and to insert the Senate bill as amended. This action was agreed to, the House bill so amended was passed by the Senate, and the original Senate bill was indefinitely postponed.

Failing House agreement to the substitution, a conference committee was appointed to reconcile the relatively minor differences in the Senate and House drafts, under the leadership of McCarran for the

[103]Ibid., p. 5427, May 19, 1952.

Senate and Walter for the House. The conference report (H. Rept. 2096, June 9, 1952) consisted of a revised draft of the bill in approximately 125 pages of small print accompanied by a three-page statement by the managers of the bill, which presented the common position of the Senate and House conferees and noted about a dozen points on which the conference draft was unlike one or the other of the two drafts. Among these points were acceptance of the House position to make the quota charge in such a way as to facilitate the entry of persons of Oriental stock who are the children of certain aliens residing in the United States, to accept the Senate exemption of certain relatives of citizens from the literacy requirement, to drop the requirement of preexamination for certain adjustment of status cases, as was favored by both Senate and House, but with some modification of the provision by the conference committee, and to accept the House version of exclusion of aliens with criminal records as referring to actually imposed sentences in excess of an aggregate five years. The conference report was agreed to by both houses of Congress and the bill was sent on June 16 to President Truman, who was known to favor a much more liberalized immigration policy.

The forthcoming veto message (H. Doc. 520) on June 25, 1952 expressed approval of some aspects of the bill, especially its needed codification of immigration and naturalization law, its removal of the racial barriers to naturalization, and the nonquota or preference status given to alien husbands of citizens and residents. But, the message continued, the objectionable features of the bill were greater, for it continued the national origins quota system, was all too restrictive of immigration, discriminated against Asian peoples in applying a racial rather than a national origins criterion for quota allocation, and was of greater severity in admissions and deportations.

The House took up the vetoed bill the next day, with Walter leading the debate. He strongly condemned the veto message for what he called its display of ignorance of the actual provisions of the bill, and spoke of the message as the product of the President's ghost writers. The House quickly voted to override the veto by well over the required two-thirds majority, the vote being 278 to 112 with 40 abstentions. McCarran led the discussion in the Senate the next day and began his statement by reading an attack on the bill published the day before in the *Daily Worker,* which he referred to as the Communist voice of America. The Senate also voted to override the veto, by the narrower margin of 57 to 26, with 13 not voting, and so the bill was passed over the veto. Popularly known as the McCarran-Walter Act, the Act of June 27, 1952 (66 Stat. 163) codified and repealed earlier legislation to become the basic immigration and naturalization act.

Of the many changes made by the new act, the following are particularly concerned with various elements of immigration policy.

1. Change of the formula for computation of the annual quota of any country to one-sixth of 1 percent of the number of persons of that national origin in the United States in 1920 as computed for the 1924 Act.[104] The minimum quota remained 100; and there was an increase of only a few hundred in the total allowable immigration (section 201a).

2. Removal of racial barriers to naturalization, and thereby to immigration (section 311).[105]

3. Provision of quotas for independent, self-governing, and UN trustee areas within the Asia-Pacific triangle, plus a special quota of 100 for the triangle area as a whole; but requirement that immigrants one-half or more of whose ancestry is attributable to Asia-Pacific triangle peoples be charged to a triangle area quota or to the special quota, whether or not they were born in the Asia-Pacific triangle (section 202b).[106]

4. Charging of an immigrant from a colony or dependent area to the quota of the governing country but not to exceed 100 in number;[107] except if of one-half or more Asia-Pacific triangle ancestry the immigrant is to be allocated as in the preceding paragraph (section 202c).

5. The nonquota classes changed to include children and spouses of citizens without regard to age of children or date of the marriage,[108] to exclude professors of educational institutions, and to include aliens, with families, who have been employed for fifteen or more years by the United States government abroad (section 101a 27).

6. Revision of the quota preference structure, from the 1924 Act's 50 percent first preference for parents of adult citizens, husbands of citizens, and immigrants skilled in agriculture, and the former second preference of the same amount plus unused visas for the minor children and wives of resident aliens; to the 1952 Act's four preference classes as contained in the original McCarran bill. This was a 50 percent first prefer-

[104]The preceding national origins formula was "a number which bears the same ratio to 150,000 as the number of inhabitants in continental United States in 1920 having that national origin . . . bears to the number of inhabitants in continental United States in 1920."

[105]Section 311 provides that naturalization shall not be denied or abridged because of race, sex, or marriage.

[106]Previously this allocation according to place of ancestry rather than place of birth applied only to persons of Chinese and Indian ancestry.

[107]Previously there was no limit in the access of colonial peoples to the quota for the governing country (sec. 12(b) of the 1924 Quota Act).

[108]Previously nonquota status was limited to children under twenty-one, spouses of marriages prior to issuance of the visa, and husbands in marriages prior to Jan. 1, 1948.

ence for immigrants with high qualifications, a 30 percent second preference plus unused visas for parents of adult citizens, a 20 percent third preference plus unused visas for spouses and children of lawfully admitted aliens, and any remaining unused visas for other qualified immigrants but with a 25 percent[109] preference within this fourth class to certain close relatives of citizens (section 203a).

7. Revision and expansion of grounds for exclusion, as follows, omitting certain changes of wording or detail (section 212a):

a. leprosy designated specifically as grounds for exclusion;[110]

b. exemption from excludability for crime involving moral turpitude if committed under eighteen years of age and more than five years previously;

c. exclusion of aliens convicted of two or more offenses, other than purely political offenses and whether or not involving moral turpitude, if the actually imposed sentences to confinement were five years or more in total;

d. exclusion of aliens who are narcotic drug addicts or have been convicted of violation of antinarcotics laws or are believed to have been illicit traffickers in drugs;

e. exclusion of aliens seeking entry to perform skilled or unskilled labor, if the Secretary of Labor certifies that there is an adequate supply of such labor or that such entry would have an adverse effect on wages or working conditions;

f. exclusion of aliens who have used fraud or misrepresentation in seeking entry documents.

There was, in addition, extensive rephrasing in order to strengthen certain excluding provisions, in particular those regarding immoral, subversive, and narcotics classes.

8. General revision and tightening of deportation provisions (section 241), in particular:

a. deportability for entry at other than designated place, formerly limited to three years after entry, no longer so limited;

b. deportation provided for institutionalization at public expense because of mental disease, defect, or deficiency made grounds for deportation if within five years after entry, unless the alien can show that such condition did not exist at the time of admission.

9. Abolition of the head tax of eight dollars for every alien admitted, children under sixteen excepted, but increase of the fee for verification

[109]Changed to 50 percent by section 3, Act of September 22, 1959 (73 Stat. 644).

[110]Leprosy had in fact been grounds for exclusion since 1891 under the broader class of a loathsome or dangerous contagious disease.

and issuance of an immigrant visa from ten dollars to twenty-five dollars, plus generally increased fees for other papers.

In addition to those enumerated above were numerous lesser changes relating to procedure and administration for the various provisions of the act. Generally, the bill reflected the continuing concerns of the congressional majority, concerns that had been present in earlier sessions, related to the problems and tensions of the postwar and "Cold War" period, with particular emphasis on fears of subversive activities, the conviction that large numbers of aliens were entering illegally, and a feeling of a need for more rigorous procedures for screening of immigrants and expulsion of undesirable and illegal alien residents.

The one other immigration bill to be enacted during the second session of the 82nd Congress was another sheepherder bill, introduced by the influential and persistent friend of the sheep-raising industry, Senator McCarran of Nevada (S. 2549). Its purpose was to provide relief for that industry by making special immigrant visas available to alien sheepherders, not to exceed 500 in number and to be kept within the quota framework by being charged to present and future quotas. Reported out and then passed without amendment by both Senate and House,[111] it became the Act of April 9, 1952 (66 Stat. 50).

The session saw a revival or increase of concern over the refugee problem in Europe, stimulated by a message from President Truman on March 24, 1952 "relative to authorizing 300,000 additional immigrants to alleviate the problems created by Communist tyranny in Western Europe" (H. Doc. 400). The message pointed to the overcrowding in western Europe, aggravated by refugeee movements, and asked Congress to authorize an additional 300,000 immigrants over the three-year period with special reference to Greek and Dutch nationals, Italians from Italy and Trieste, Germans and others of German ethnic origin, and religious or political refugees from Communist Europe. Several bills incorporating the President's recommendations and apportioning the 300,000 special nonquota immigrant visas[112] were introduced but not acted on during the session.[113]

Other bills introduced during the session but not acted on were two to provide an additional 5000 special nonquota visas for displaced person orphans under ten years of age, with a terminal date for issuance set at July 1, 1953 (S. 2406, Ives [N.Y.]; H.R. 5995, Javits [N.Y.]), two bills to

[111] S. Rept. 1151, Feb. 4, 1952; H. Rept. 1636, March 25, 1952.

[112] Including 117,000 each to German ethnic persons and Italian nationals, 22,500 each to Greek and Dutch nationals, and 21,000 to refugees in Turkey and the above countries.

[113] S. 3109, Hendrickson (N.J.); H.R. 7376, Celler (N.Y.); H.R. 7895, Ross (N.Y.).

amend the immigration laws to eliminate race and sex discrimination, to reallocate unused quotas, and for other purposes,[114] and three bills to admit 50,000 immigrants from Italy.[115]

Comment

The period covered by this chapter, 1939 through 1952, was disturbed by a succession of happenings that all had their impact on attitudes toward immigration: the lingering aftereffects of the Depression, the outbreak of World War II in Europe and the eventual involvement of the United States, the postwar period with its attendant problems, the Cold War tensions, and the conflict in Korea. The most apparent consequences for immigration policy were an increased disfavor, if only temporary, of aliens and immigration generally in Congress and very possibly in the country as a whole, a growth of pressure to do away with racial discrimination in the immigration and nationality laws, and strong sentiment for aid to victims of the war and its aftereffects. In addition, various subsidiary and lesser influences on immigration policy can be noted.

Misgivings about the economic and especially the labor market impact of immigration probably still lingered after the worst years of unemployment were past, and soon there were added wartime anxieties about enemy aliens, divided loyalties, and "fifth-column" saboteurs. After the war came new fears of radical and subversive alien ideologies. The principal legislative fruits of these concerns were, first, the Alien Registration Act of June 28, 1940, which not only required the registration of all aliens aged fourteen and over but also required fingerprinting of immigrants and resident aliens, outlawed various activities as subversive, and added five new classes to the already lengthy list of grounds for deportation; second, various acts that further defined and broadened the powers of the Attorney General for exclusion and deportation; third, the postwar Internal Security Act of September 23, 1950[116] that was directed against subversive activities; and finally the Immigration and Nationality Act of June 27, 1952, the McCarran-Walter Act, which broadened the definition of subversive classes of aliens subject to exclusion and deportation and also expanded and strengthened provisions for the exclusion and deportation of other classes of aliens.

[114]H.R. 6034, Celler (N.Y.); H.R. 6299, Roosevelt (N.Y.); same title as the Lehman bill, S. 2343, of the first session.

[115]H.R. 5939, Addonizio (N.J.); H.R. 5969, Rodino (N.J.); H.R. 7123, Heller (N.Y.).

[116]This act is not strictly an immigration act, and has not been dealt with in this chapter.

Although strongly criticized at the time and subsequently for its severity and for certain other features, the 1952 Act can best be judged against the background of the legislative proposals that preceded and accompanied it. These, as described on preceding pages, included some bills for liberalization of the immigration laws but also many others that were severely restrictive or even isolationist, and still others that sought to impose strict controls and disabilities on resident aliens. If the Senate and House committees that developed the 1952 Act were swayed by the restrictive temper of the period, they nevertheless chose a middle course corresponding with the majority position of Congress, and they did resist and reject the more extreme proposals that arose out of wartime emotions and fears of alien ideologies.

Other legislative accomplishments of the period were less controversial and more progressive from a later perspective. Wartime pressures not only produced the antialien reaction noted above but also stimulated successful attack on racial discrimination in the immigration and nationality laws. Selective elimination of the racial barriers, first for the wartime allies, the Chinese, and then for other Asian peoples, led to efforts to do away with all racial limitations in the immigration and nationality laws. This objective was finally accomplished in the 1952 Act, which removed racial ineligibility for naturalization and immigration and gave quotas to all Asian and Pacific areas. The effect was incomplete, however, because of the small quotas allowed under the national origins quota formula and the requirement that immigrants of Asian or Pacific ancestry be charged to quotas on a racial rather than birthplace basis. Complete elimination of these remnants of racial limitations had to wait until the next decade.

A second selective relaxation and liberalization of the immigration laws was in aid of certain hardship cases resulting from the war. There were many bills and several acts to facilitate the admission of refugees, war orphans, and displaced persons, the principal measure of this sort being the Displaced Persons Act of June 25, 1948 which as later amended provided for the admission of well over 300,000 eligible aliens in addition to those who could gain entry through the normal procedures.

Several less prominent but nevertheless important themes can be observed in the many bills introduced in Congress and those enacted. One was to facilitate the admission of close relatives of citizens and, in some cases, relatives of resident aliens by means of the granting of nonquota status or preference under quota. Included here were children adopted or to be adopted by citizens. And there were numerous proposals and acts for the ready admission of alien fiancées, wives, and children of veterans, whether such alien relatives were racially eligible or not. Major pieces of legislation in this area were the so-called War Brides Act of December 28, 1945 and the GI Fiancées Act of June 29, 1946.

Wartime labor shortages led to programs for the temporary admission of agricultural and other workers,[117] and labor shortages in the sheep-raising industry led to repeated acts to gain admission for alien sheepherders. There was a disposition also to favor the admission of aliens possessing special qualifications, and such aliens were given highest preference in the 1952 Act.

On the other hand there were concerns about an overabundance of aliens who had entered illegally—in particular the so-called wetbacks from Mexico, but also aliens who might be coming for subversive purposes. Numerous measures were proposed and some passed to cope with stowaways on vessels and airplanes, deserting seamen, and illegal border crossers. The powers of the Border Patrol were enlarged, the wetback bill passed and later incorporated in the 1952 Act, and greater enforceability was sought through an attempt to put legal responsibility on those who transported or harbored illegal immigrants. The problem of effective enforcement cannot be said to have been solved then or since.[118]

The principal legislative accomplishment on immigration during the period was, of course, the 1952 Act. It was a codification and revision of immigration and nationality law, repealing earlier acts, and it embodied the majority opinion in Congress at the time. It also became the focus of persistent efforts at revision and relaxation of the immigration laws over the following years into the next decade.

[117]The measures providing for such temporary admissions, not included in this chapter, were principally the Act of April 29, 1943 for the admission of agricultural workers from the Western Hemisphere, the Act of February 14, 1944 on the supply and distribution of farm labor, the Acts of April 28, 1947 and July 3, 1948, and the Agricultural Act of October 31, 1949.

[118]The measures relating to stowaways did not concern aliens as such and have not been included in this account of immigration legislation. They were the Acts of June 11, 1940 (54 Stat. 306), March 4, 1944 (58 Stat. 111), and April 4, 1944 (58 Stat. 188). The Act of August 7, 1946 (60 Stat. 865) extended the powers of the Border Patrol.

8 After the McCarran–Walter Act, 1953–1965

In the years immediately following the McCarran-Walter Act of 1952, there was some carryover of the old business of the postwar refugee problem, together with a return to the normal peacetime concerns with immigration policy and the various problems associated with resident aliens; but the new act was itself the central bone of contention and was to remain so for many years. During the war and the immediate postwar years the pendulum of attitudes on immigration had swung in the direction of tightened control and regulation, under the leadership of the two strong chairmen of the Senate and House committees. Thereafter, the principal battle on immigration policy was to revolve around defense and attack of the McCarran-Walter Act, with the trend of the times toward progressive liberalization of immigration policy.

83rd Congress (1953, 1954)

The 83rd Congress, convened on January 3, 1953 for its first session that was to last seven months, was greeted with a renewed presidential attack on the McCarran-Walter Act of the preceding session and on the immigration policy it represented. Unwilling to concede defeat after Congress overrode his veto of the bill on June 27, 1952, President Truman on September 4 (Exec. Order 10392) had appointed a presidential Commission on Immigration and Naturalization "to study and evaluate the immigration and naturalization policies of the United States" and to recommend "such legislative, administrative, or other action as in its opinion may be desirable in the interest of the economy, security, and responsibilities of this country."[1] Directed to report on January 1, 1953,

[1]The Commission members were Philip B. Perlman, chairman, formerly Solicitor General of the United States; Earl G. Harrison, vice chairman, formerly Commissioner of Immigration and Naturalization; Thomas G. Finucane, chairman of the Board of Immigration Appeals; Adrian S. Fisher, legal adviser to the State Department; Rev. Thaddeus F. Gullixson, president of the Lutheran Theological Seminary of St. Paul; Msgr. John

just before the opening of the 83rd Congress and only a few days after the effective date of most provisions of the McCarran-Walter Act (Dec. 24, 1952), the Commission worked rapidly to conduct hearings in eleven cities throughout the country and received oral and written testimony from over 600 individuals, some of whom testified as representatives of governmental or private organizations. The weight of testimony as reported by the Commission was heavily against the principles of the new act, and the Commission's report, *Whom We Shall Welcome,* supported and amplified the criticisms made by the President in his veto message.

The broad recommendations presented by the Commission were abolition of the national origins quota system, an overall ceiling on quota immigration of around 250,000 per annum, and the allocation of immigration visas within the quota on the basis of need or hardship of individual migrants, overpopulation in the sending nations, and the needs of the United States.[2] Spelled out in more detail were the recommendations for five preference classes, designated as Right of Asylum, Reunion of Families, Needs in the United States, Special Needs in the Free World, and General Immigration.[3] The last of these, it was emphasized, should be without regard to national origin, race, color, or creed, and the granting of the visas should be in the order of application, on a "first-come, first-served" basis. Among other questions considered by the Commission were the appropriate agency for the administration of the immigration laws and the judicial review of administrative decisions. In the former matter the Commission's recommendation was for a new and independent agency in place of the existing division of functions between the Department of Justice and the State Department. With regard to judicial review, the Commission was generally approving of the existing procedures but did recommend provision for judicial review in case of denial of bail to aliens under deportation proceedings.[4]

The Congress as a whole and its immigration committees in particular were no more influenced by the presidential commission's report than by the presidential veto message. The new act, it is true, still received active congressional attention, for it was the subject of by far the largest group of immigration bills, some forty or more introduced during the session. Five at least were for repeal or replacement of the act, but the majority were only to amend the act in various respects. Among the varied purposes of these amending bills were to assign unused quota numbers

---

O'Grady, secretary of the National Conference of Catholic Charities; and Clarence E. Pickett of the American Friends Service Committee.

[2] *Whom We Shall Welcome,* p. 13.

[3] Ibid., pp. 118–22, 264.

[4] Ibid., p. 171.

to countries of oversubscribed quotas, to extend certain privileges to alien veterans of ninety days or more service in Korea, to remove the time limit within which a court may make recommendation to the Attorney General against the deportation of a convicted alien, and to authorize the Attorney General to grant voluntary departure to certain Mexican aliens.

Incorporating some of the presidential commission's recommendations and in the pattern of the "liberal" bills offered as alternatives to the McCarran-Walter bill of the preceding session was one of the bills (S. 2585) for repeal of the 1952 Act. It was introduced in the Senate by Lehman of New York, and its seven cosponsors, of whom the future President Kennedy was one, included some of the sponsors of the Humphrey-Lehman bill of the preceding Congress. A wholly new immigration and nationality code offered as a substitute for the McCarran-Walter Act, its stated purpose was

> to establish and provide for the administration of an immigration and naturalization policy which will give faithful and positive expression to the basic human values to which American political institutions are dedicated; promote entry of desirable immigrants on a basis responsive to national need and international responsibility; protect this country from infiltration by those who would destroy or impair its political institutions and, more specifically—to provide for immigration eligibility without regard to national origin, race, color, or creed; to foster the reuniting of families; to serve the needs of the domestic economy; to provide a haven for the persecuted and oppressed; to further the aims of American foreign policy.

Among the features of the Lehman bill was an immigration quota of one-sixth of 1 percent of the population of the United States at the most recent census, to be distributed without regard to race, color, national origin, or religion, according to the following preferences:

1. Family Unification Preference of 25 to 35 percent;
2. Occupational Preference of 5 to 10 percent;
3. Asylum Preference of 15 to 25 percent;
4. National Interest Preference of 20 to 25 percent;
5. Newcomer Group of not less than 20 percent.

Another feature was provision of an emergency immigration program to admit 300,000 emergency immigration visa refugees over a three-year period, with allocation somewhat as in the Refugee Relief Act of 1953.

No action was taken on this or any of the other bills for amendment or replacement of the McCarran-Walter Act. The coalition that had passed the act over President Truman's veto in the 82nd Congress was still firmly in control of the House and Senate committees, and presumably still held a safe majority in both houses of Congress. Certain of the presidential commission's recommendations, however, were to reappear in bills persistently offered year after year by those who found the McCarran-Walter Act objectionable, and finally found congressional endorsement a dozen years later in the Act of 1965 that gave a new direction to American immigration policy.

If resistant to presidential pressures for change of immigration policy, Congress was more disposed to heed urging from the same source for aid to refugees. The problem of refugees in Europe was in fact the principal subject of legislative activity related to immigration during the first session of the 83rd Congress. The many bills that were introduced in this connection followed the pattern of the recommendations in the Truman message to the preceding Congress, although with some variation in designation of the refugee groups to be aided and the numbers to be admitted. Several set a ceiling of 240,000 nonquota immigrant visas to be allocated to refugees, designating "certain escapees, German expellees, and nationals of Italy, Greece, and the Netherlands" as the beneficiaries.[5] Other bills were to grant the same number of admissions over a two-year period, for the purpose of "relieving the current immigration and refugee problem,"[6] and another added Polish war veterans while keeping the same total (H.R. 5825, Dingell [Mich.]). Two bills offered by Graham of Pennsylvania provided 217,000 and 247,000 admissions (H.R. 6397 and 6481), three proposed to admit 300,000,[7] three set a total of 328,000,[8] and the highest would admit 380,000 expellees, refugees, and orphans (H.R. 4842, Carrigg [Pa.]).

Only two of the above were acted on, one each in the Senate and House. The Senate bill by Watkins of Utah and a number of other sponsors was reported out (S. Rept. 629, on S. 1917) after amendment in committee. The original bill provided for the admission of 240,000 refugees in two years. The committee felt the staff and facilities to process the refugees at this rate were lacking, and they amended the bill to provide 215,000 special nonquota visas over a three-year period. The prescribed allocation was 97,000 to certain escapees and German expellees, 13,000 to escapees in NATO countries or Turkey or Trieste, 66,000 to refugees of Italian ethnic origin in Italy or Trieste, 17,500 to refugees

[5]S. 1917, Watkins (Utah) and seventeen others; H.R. 4925, Bosch (N.Y.).

[6]S. 1746, Ferguson (Mich.), Ives (N.Y.), and Hendrickson (N.J.); H.R. 4935, Javits (N.Y.); H.R. 5583, Multer (N.Y.).

[7]S. 1379, Hendrickson (N.J.); H.R. 337, Rodino (N.J.); H.R. 1707, Addonizio (N.J.).

[8]S. 1186, Langer (N.D.); H.R. 3845, Rodino (N.J.); H.R. 2076, Celler (N.Y.).

of Greek ethnic origin in Greece, 17,500 to refugees of Dutch ethnic origin in the Netherlands, and 4,000 to certain orphans. In addition there was an allowance of up to 5,000 adjustments of status of refugees already in the United States. There was debate on the bill in the Senate on July 29, 1953,[9] at which time the Senate considered the Jenner amendment to empower the President to suspend or stop the issuance of visas to displaced persons if he finds that other receiving nations are unduly delaying their admissions. The amendment was rejected, as was the Ives amendment to broaden the bill to include Italian nationals. Jenner then offered the following amendment:

> Every alien over the age of fifty admitted to the United States under this act shall at the time of entry renounce or waive all rights to old-age assistance or relief under the Social Security Act . . . until such time as such alien shall have become a citizen.

It was rejected. Seemingly ready then to vote on its bill, the Senate learned that the House had just passed the Graham refugee bill. The House bill was then brought up for consideration in the Senate, which indefinitely postponed its own bill.

The House committee had reported out the second of the two Graham bills,[10] after some amendment of wording. The bill authorized the issuance of up to 240,000 special immigrant visas, including 4,000 to orphans under ten years of age, and the visas were to be issued prior to January 1, 1957. The Attorney General was authorized to adjust the status of certain aliens admitted on a temporary basis, in addition to the refugee admissions under the bill; there were safeguards against admission of security risks; and the annual quota limits were waived as were the Asia-Pacific triangle restrictions. The designated beneficiaries of the bill were German expellees, refugees of German ethnic origin from Soviet-occupied areas, Italian and Dutch nationals, and certain other groups including European refugees in the Far East.

Walter and six others appended a minority report to point out that the bill would superimpose 240,000 immigrants on the regular quota and nonquota immigration and so destroy the national origins principle, and that it would be impossible to screen the refugees fully, especially those from behind the iron curtain and without papers.

The bill was debated at length in the House. Some feared that Communists could come in with the refugees, and others urged that the United States should do its share along with the other nations who were

[9] *Congressional Record,* 99:10235 et seq.

[10] H. Rept. 974, July 27, 1953; on H.R. 6481.

accepting refugees. A move to postpone action was defeated, and the bill was supported as being an important element in American foreign policy.[11] A number of amendments were offered, especially by Walter, but with little success. Several Judd (Minn.) amendments were accepted, however: one to open the act to Asians and especially Chinese and European refugees in Asia, another to provide up to 2,000 visas for Japanese refugees and a like number for Palestinian refugees. After amendment, the bill was finally passed by the House, 221 to 185 with 25 not voting.

The Senate, having laid aside its own bill, amended and passed the House bill by vote of 63 to 30, and the bill then went to conference. With acceptance of the conference report (H. Rept. 1069, July 31, 1953) by both houses of Congress and presidential signature, the bill was enacted as the Act of August 7, 1953 (67 Stat. 400), also known as the Refugee Relief Act of 1953.

The conference draft as enacted provided 205,000 special nonquota visas for eligible refugees and their spouses and unmarried children under twenty-one years of age, including stepchildren and adopted children. The visas were to be apportioned as specified to fourteen classes of eligibles, of which the largest were 55,000 for German expellees residing in West Germany, West Berlin, and Austria, 45,000 to refugees of Italian ethnic origin, and 35,000 to escapees in West Germany, West Berlin, and Austria. There were in addition 4,000 nonquota visas provided for eligible orphans under ten years of age and adopted or to be adopted by citizens.

A smaller group of bills and resolutions, eight in all, concerned the admission of adopted children or those to be adopted. Various upper age limits for the children so admitted were proposed, from under six years of age in some bills to eighteen years of age in others. Included in the group were two resolutions by Walter of Pennsylvania (H. J. Res. 212 and 228) to admit 500 children under six years of age, adopted by citizens serving abroad in the Armed Forces or government employees abroad. The second of the two resolutions was reported out in the House and passed, and then reported out with amendment in the Senate.[12] The Senate committee changed the upper age limit from six to ten years and specified nonquota status. In this form the bill was passed as the Act of July 29, 1953, with a terminal date of December 31, 1954.

[11]The debate brought out a lot of old-fashioned oratory, partly in extensions of remarks for the record or for the benefit of constituents back home. The Emma Lazarus verses on the base of the Statue of Liberty were quoted at least three times during the debate, the names of servicemen killed in Korea were recited, and much else was put on the record.

[12]H. Rept. 294, April 20, 1953; S. Rept. 605, July 21, 1953.

In addition to the foregoing principal immigration concerns of this session were scattered bills on various topics of immigration policy. Three were to gain admission for additional numbers of Italian immigrants,[13] one of which was to admit 50,000, one to admit 100,000, and the third was to give Italy an annual immigration quota of 300,000.[14] Labor market policy was also represented by a House bill from Javits of New York to authorize the admission of immigrants having skills beneficial to the United States (H.R. 454), and a Senate bill to expedite the admission of certain German and Austrian scientists.[15] There was a Senate resolution from Ives of New York to make all unused quota numbers for the years 1950 to 1952 inclusive available to the President for assignment at his discretion to any quota area (S. J. Res. 66). And a House bill by Multer of New York would make sure that aliens in quota waiting lists prior to January 1, 1944 would not lose priority on such lists under the 1952 Act (H.R. 4459). Other proposals were for admission of certain Korean orphans (H.R. 6411, Walter [Pa.]), to permit the admission of alien spouses of servicemen if the marriage was with the consent of the proper military authorities even though the spouse belonged to an excludable class (H.R. 3701, LeCompte [Iowa]), to authorize the employment in government service of alien veterans (H.R. 4221, Mrs. Rogers [Mass.]), and to provide for the deportation of aliens and the loss of citizenship and deportation of naturalized citizens, if convicted of subversive activities (H.R. 3207, Sutton [Tenn.]). None of the above came out of committee.

The second session of the 83rd Congress, from January 6 to December 2, 1954, saw fewer immigration bills introduced and only little new legislation in that area. The principal topics of contemporary concern as indicated by the new bills were generally the same as in the preceding session, with emphasis on revision of the 1952 Act, amendment of the more recently passed Refugee Relief Act of 1953, and a few bills on the status of resident aliens, on the checking of illegal immigration, and several other topics.

With regard to the 1952 Act, there were two lengthy bills to repeal and replace it (H.R. 7654, Friedel [Md.]; H.R. 8499, Williams [N.J.]), which on inspection appear to be House counterparts of the Lehman bill in the Senate the preceding session. A Senate bill and seven House bills which appear to be identical were for revision of the 1952 Act, to provide

[13] H.R. 361, Addonizio (N.J.); H.R. 3654, Fino (N.Y.); H.R. 5450, Heller (N.Y.).

[14] At that time the Italian quota was 5,677 and the total quota for all countries was 154,277 per annum.

[15] S. 378, Sparkman (Ala.). Two resolutions, H. J. Res. 307 and 308, for the admission of certain scientists were probably private bills.

among other things more rigorous screening out and exclusion of aliens representing what were referred to as totalitarian ideologies, and to establish the right of an alien to seek judicial review of exclusion and deportation orders.[16]

There were several proposals for change of the quotas set by the 1952 Act, one by Judd of Minnesota to give a quota of 100 to the Ryukyu Island area under American administration (H.R. 10194), and two to make the unused quota numbers of one year available to oversubscribed areas the next year (H.R. 10012, O'Neill [Mass.]; H.R. 10239, Donohue [Mass.]).

There were eight bills to amend the Refugee Relief Act of 1953 in various respects. Three of them were to facilitate the admission of former members of the Polish armed forces residing in the British Isles.[17] One was for readjustment of the number of special immigrant visas allocated to refugees of Italian origin, by transfer of the visas from one category to another but without increase of the total number (H.R. 7197, Morano [Conn.]); and the remaining four were for various other amendments of the act.[18] Of these latter, the House committee reported out the second of the two Graham (Pa.) bills, which was to make the visas allocated to Italian, Greek, and Dutch refugees available to the preference groups according to the current demand for visas and to assure adjustment of status to temporarily admitted aliens who cannot return to their homeland because of fear of persecution on racial, religious, or political grounds.[19] Passed by the House, the Graham bill was amended and reported out by the Senate committee (S. Rept. 2045, Aug. 2, 1954). The committee amendment was to add a fourth section to the bill requiring that refugees in Italy, Greece, and the Netherlands admitted under the seventh section of the 1953 Act and who are qualified for preference as relatives of citizens or residents of the United States, in second, third, and fourth preferences, under the 1952 Act must present satisfactory evidence to a responsible consular officer "that the alien in question will have suitable employment and housing, without displacing any other person therefrom, after arrival in the United States." With acceptance of this amendment by the House, the bill became the Act of August 31, 1954 (68 Stat. 1044).

With regard to immigrant admission, there was a renewed proposal to admit 50,000 from Italy (H.R. 10013, O'Neill [Mass.]), and another

[16]S. 3292, Ives (N.Y.), Hendrickson (N.J.) and Saltonstall (Mass.); H.R. 8802 to 8807 inclusive by Javits (N.Y.), Cretella (Conn.), Fino (N.Y.), Frelinghuysen (N.J.), Morano (Conn.), and Scott (Pa.); and H.R. 10272, Curtis (Mass.).

[17]H.R. 9407, Burdick (N.D.); H.R. 9428, Donovan (N.Y.); H.R. 9536, Philbin (Mass.).

[18]S. 3005, Watkins (Utah); H.R. 7475, 8193, Graham (Pa.); H.R. 10227, Celler (N.Y.).

[19]H. Rept. 1323, March 8, 1954, on H.R. 8193. In the wording of the bill, the visas provided by the Act were to be "available bilaterally" within each of the three ethnic groups.

sheepherder bill from McCarran of Nevada (S. 2862). Providing for the issuance of not over 385 special nonquota immigrant visas to skilled and otherwise admissible alien sheepherders if no unused quota numbers are available, limited to one year from date of passage, the bill was routinely accepted by both Senate and House,[20] and became the Act of September 3, 1954 (68 Stat. 1145).

A prominent theme running through the legislative proposals in the second session of the 83rd Congress was protection of the nation against alien subversion and especially Communism.[21] The principal legislative expression of this concern was the Communist Control Act of 1954 (68 Stat. 775), which condemned the Communist party of the United States as authoritarian, "an instrumentality of a conspiracy to overthrow the Government." The session received a number of other bills against Communism, and for the loss of citizenship by persons convicted of subversive activities.[22] A bill entitled "To promote the national security" was to provide up to a thousand special nonquota visas for defecting Communist officials (H.R. 8000, Hillings [Calif.]); and to strengthen enforcement powers was a proposal for expatriation of any national who refuses to return to testify as a witness before a federal court, grand jury of a federal court, or a committee of Congress (S. 3230, McCarran [Nev.]).

Congress also continued to wrestle with the unsolved and perhaps unsolvable problem of illegal immigration. Two pairs of identical bills were introduced in the House and Senate. The first, entitled the "Illegal Employment of Aliens Act of 1954" (S. 3660, Watkins [Utah]; H.R. 9731, Graham [Pa.]), noted that the illegal immigration of hundreds of thousands of aliens each year "is seriously affecting our domestic working conditions, health, and crime rate, and constitutes a serious threat to our internal security and safety," and that this illegal immigration is in large part induced and encouraged by persons who knowingly employ such aliens. The bill declared illegal the employment of such immigrants by any person or organization knowingly or having reasonable grounds to believe that the alien in question had entered illegally within the past three years. The Senate bill was acted on by the committee (S. Rept. 2451, Aug. 11, 1954), which amended it by adding two new subsections to make unlawful the acceptance for membership by a labor union of aliens known to have entered illegally, primarily to seek employment,

[20] S. Rept. 1600, June 16, 1954; H. Rept. 2662, Aug. 16, 1954.

[21] The President's State of the Union message of January 7, 1954 stated that the subversive nature of the Communist party had been demonstrated and asked for legislation to denaturalize persons convicted of conspiring against the government.

[22] Including, among others, S. 2757, Ferguson (Mich.) and Mrs. Smith (Me.); H.R. 7265, Feighan (Ohio); H.R. 7325, Reed (Ill.).

within three years of entry. The other pair of bills, entitled the "Illegal Transportation of Aliens Act of 1954" (S. 3661, Watkins [Utah]; H.R. 9732, Graham [Pa.]), provided for "the seizure and forfeiture of any vessel or vehicle used in the transportation of any alien known by the owner thereof to have entered the United States illegally within three years thereof." The Senate committee reported out the bill with the comment that over a million illegal entrants had been apprehended within the past year. The committee reported the bill favorably, with amendment of wording and extension of the period of liability from three to five years. The Senate did not take further action.[23]

84th Congress (1955, 1956)

In immigration matters the first session of the 84th Congress, from January 5 to August 2, 1955, directed its attention in particular to amendment of the McCarran-Walter Act of 1952, to revision of the quota system as established in the 1924 Act and reaffirmed in the 1952 Act, and to amendment of the Refugee Relief Act of 1953.

There were three bills for the outright repeal of the 1952 Act, of which two called for a return to the prior acts regulating immigration and repealed in 1952.[24] Exclusive of those dealing with the quota system alone, there were approximately thirty-eight bills for variously amending the 1952 Act. Included among them was a Senate bill[25] that among other provisions would have restored nonquota status to professors whose services were needed by an institution of higher education, make some revision in the preference classes and the allocation of immigrants to quota areas, set up a pool of unused quota numbers to be assigned to certain stipulated preference classes including victims of persecution abroad and aliens in friendly nations suffering from "over-concentration of population." Another was a reintroduction of the Lehman bill of the preceding Congress, this time with thirteen sponsors of the substitute for the McCarran-Walter Act.[26] In the House an equally lengthy bill was introduced by Celler of New York (H.R. 636). None of these was reported out by the Senate or House committees.

[23]Two measures passed during the second session of the 83rd Congress and not dealt with above are the Act of September 3, 1954 (68 Stat. 1146) for the expatriation of persons convicted of engaging in a conspiracy to overthrow or levy war against the government, and another act of the same date (68 Stat. 1232), which among other things corrected the wording of sections 242d and 340a of the 1952 Act.

[24]H.R. 663, Fine (N.Y.); H.R. 3097, Dollinger (N.Y.); H.R. 3445, Klein (N.Y.).

[25]S. 1315, Humphrey (Minn.), Douglas (Ill.), Kennedy (Mass.), McNamara (Mich.).

[26]S. 1206, Lehman (N.Y.), Kennedy (Mass.), and eleven others.

The bills specifically for change of the quota system proposed a variety of changes. Four were to make the unused quota numbers of one year available to oversubscribed areas the following year.[27] Another was to make the same reallocation, also change from 1920 to 1950 the base year for the computation of quotas, and to grant quotas to nations of the Asia-Pacific triangle in the same way as for other nations (H.R. 5003 by Mrs. Kelly of New York). Multer of New York again tried to provide for the carrying forward of priority on old quota waiting lists to the new lists under the 1952 Act.[28] And two bills by Judd of Minnesota were to revise the section of the 1952 Act that prescribed the method of quota determination, and to establish as a separate quota area any territory over which the United States has jurisdiction by treaty (H.R. 534 and 5135).

Amendment of the Refugee Relief Act of 1953 was the object of approximately twenty bills introduced during the session,[29] of which two, by Donovan of New York and Philbin of Massachusetts (H.R. 3105 and 4377), were for the benefit of Polish veterans in the British Isles, and two by Saltonstall and Mrs. Rogers of Massachusetts (S. 2248 and H.R. 7675) for Armenians. The other bills, with considerable duplication among themselves, contained a variety of proposed amendments, including liberalization of the provisions of the 1953 Act,[30] the reallocation of unused special visas for refugees (H.R. 4357, Anfuso [N.Y.], and others), and the requirement of assurance that a refugee if admitted would not displace a resident of the United States from employment or housing. No further action was taken on any of the above.

A few bills on other subjects appeared during the session. Concern-

[27]H.R. 358, Donohue (Mass.); H.R. 466, O'Neill (Mass.); H.R. 772, Johnson (Calif.); H.R. 4387, Philbin (Mass.).

[28]H.R. 2640; compare his H.R. 4459 (83-I).

[29]The influx of bills was stimulated by a May 27, 1955 special message to Congress from President Eisenhower (H. Doc. 173) recommending certain changes in the Refugee Relief Act of 1953. Stating that over 30,000 visas have been issued and nearly 85,000 applicants are in various stages of processing, the message made certain recommendations of needed amendments. These included:

1. reassignment of unused visas, for growing prosperity in Europe has reduced the number of applicants in some classes;

2. broadening the definition of eligible refugee to include those already "firmly resettled," who may be among the most diligent and competent;

3. inclusion of "escapees" and "expellees" even if not refugees in the terms of the Act;

4. relaxation of the term "refugee" to include those still in their homeland but victims of some disaster;

5. granting of permanent residence to meritorious aliens already in the United States even without record of lawful entry for temporary residence;

6. discretionary waiver of the requirement for documents.

[30]S. 2149, Langer (N.D.); H.R. 6594, Cretella (Conn.); H.R. 6733, Scott (Pa.).

ing veterans were two bills to authorize the Attorney General to suspend deportation and to admit for permanent residence certain aliens who have served honorably in the Armed Forces (S. 846, Lehman [N.Y.]; H.R. 752, Celler [N.Y.]) and another to exempt certain alien spouses of servicemen from exclusion because of tuberculosis in any form, leprosy, or other dangerous contagious disease (H.R. 380, LeCompte [Iowa]). There was a bill to grant nonquota status to children under sixteen years of age coming to be adopted by a citizen or an alien admitted for permanent residence (H.R. 7539, Multer [N.Y.]). The perennial subject of sheepherders came up in a bill to extend the authorization contained in the Act of September 3, 1954 (H.R. 7616, Hagen [Calif.]); and Walter of Pennsylvania proposed an amendment of the same act to facilitate the admission of wives and minor children of Basque sheepherders (H.R. 6888). The latter was reported out (H. Rept. 1362), amended by the committee with the addition, among other things, of the unrelated provision that escapees from Communist-controlled countries temporarily in Spain may qualify for visas under the Refugee Relief Act of 1953. The so-amended bill was passed by the House but did not progress in the Senate until the second session. Watkins of Utah again introduced drafts of an Illegal Employment of Aliens Act and an Illegal Transportation of Aliens Act.[31]

Several other bills dealt with administrative or procedural matters. One was to authorize the Attorney General at his discretion to allow an alien born in Mexico and under deportation proceedings to depart voluntarily if able to establish good moral character over the preceding five years, if the Attorney General finds deportation would result in hardship to the alien or his citizen or lawfully resident alien spouse, parent, or child (H.R. 4927, Holifield [Calif.]). Another was to direct the Attorney General, in the case of aliens departing to readjust their status, to reestablish preexamination procedures to determine in advance their eligibility for readmission for permanent residence (H.R. 315, Yates [Ill.]). Another bill advocated a more direct approach to the same matter by amendment of the 1952 Act to permit certain aliens to adjust their status from temporary to permanent admission without leaving the country and being readmitted (H.R. 7568, Reuss [Wis.]).

The second session of the 84th Congress opened on January 3, and continued to July 27, 1956. Early in the session Congress received a special message from President Eisenhower concerning the immigration and nationality laws (H. Doc. 329, Feb. 8, 1956). With approval of the Secretary of State, the Attorney General, and the Commissioner of Immi-

[31]S. 1151, Watkins (Utah) and five others; S. 1152, Watkins and five others. See his S. 3660, 3661 (83-II).

gration and Naturalization, recommendations were made for changes in four aspects of immigration policy as represented in the 1952 Act: the quota system, the use of private bills in hardship cases, some restrictions and procedures deemed unnecessary, and judicial review of deportation cases. With regard to the quota system, the recommendations were for change of the computational base year from 1920 to 1950, and thereby increase of the annual immigration quota from 154,657 to approximately 220,000; formation of a pool of 5,000 visas per annum to be assigned without regard for national origin to aliens with special skills and qualifications; and the reallocation of unused quota numbers also without regard to national origin, but within the four regions of Europe, Africa, Asia, and the Pacific area. Regarding private bills, it was stated that they numbered 4,797 in the 83rd Congress and 3,059 in the first session of the 84th. The recommendation was that this burden be lifted from the congressional committees by giving the Attorney General limited discretionary power in matters of admissions and deportations of aliens who have close relatives in the country or who are veterans or functionaries of religious organizations. On various procedural matters the message urged among other things that the fingerprinting requirement for arriving aliens be waived in the case of temporary admissions and that procedures be simplified for aliens in transit and those arriving from the outlying possessions of Alaska and Hawaii. And, on the fourth topic, it was reported that the Attorney General was preparing a legislative proposal to prevent abuse of the legal process by the tactics of repeated appeals in deportation cases.

The legislative response to the presidential message was to come principally in the next Congress, but various bills were introduced for amendment or replacement of the McCarran-Walter Act of 1952. Four identical or quite similar bills were entire immigration and nationality codes of over 200 pages and in many sections, which were to be substituted for the existing act.[32] Four other bills, in accord with the presidential recommendation, were to regulate the judicial review of deportation and exclusion orders.[33] Thirteen others were to amend various sections of the 1952 Act, in particular the sections on the determination of the national quotas (sec. 201 and 202) concerning which there were five bills; and an additional three amending bills[34] were to provide that

[32]H.R. 7999, Williams (N.J.); H.R. 8392, Rodino (N.J.); H.R. 8531, Addonizio (N.J.); H.R. 9617, Reuss (Wis.).

[33]S. 3169, Watkins (Utah); H.R. 9182, Keating (N.Y.); H.R. 9223, Scott (Pa.); H.R. 9242, Lane (Mass.).

[34]S. 2906, Lehman (N.Y.) and others; H.R. 8341, Dingell (Mich.); H.R. 8380, Machrowicz (Mich.).

after the fiscal year ending June 30, 1955 no more deductions were to be made from the immigration quotas of any quota areas pursuant to the Displaced Persons Act of 1948.[35]

The principal legislative effort of the second session regarding immigration, however, was in follow-up of the presidential message of the first session calling for certain changes in the Refugee Relief Act of 1953. No less than twenty-eight Senate and House bills and resolutions for amendment of the act were introduced during the session, of which nine were contributed by Senator Langer of North Dakota and eight by Representative Shelley of California. Among the proposed amendments were to extend the time allowed for the issuance of visas, to increase the number of visas issuable for certain classes, especially orphans, to facilitate the admission of refugees from the Far East, to relax certain requirements for eligibility and for assurances against becoming a public charge. Of special note are four bills that would authorize the admission of up to 1,000 refugees afflicted with tuberculosis, together with their immediate families, on the condition that assurance is given to the satisfaction of the Attorney General and of the Surgeon General of the Public Health Service that the alien in question will not become a public charge or endanger the public health.[36]

A few other bills for various purposes were also introduced during the session. Four were to give the Attorney General the authority to approve the admission, in spite of technical excludability, of aliens who have served honorably in the Armed Forces in a time of war or national emergency; who are the spouse, parent, brother, sister, or child of a citizen or alien lawfully admitted for permanent residence; or who are ministers or priests of a recognized religious denomination.[37] Several ethnic groups were to be admitted in greater numbers under certain bills, of which one by Macdonald (Mass.) was to grant additional visas under the Refugee Relief Act to persons of Armenian origin (H.R. 11151), one by Capehart (Ind.) to do the same for certain Greeks (S. 4088), and one to give natives of Malta unlimited access to the large immigration quota for Great Britain (H.R. 9335 by Mrs. Griffiths of

[35]The presidential recommendations were followed up by Secretary of State John Foster Dulles, who told the Senate Judiciary Subcommittee that the prevailing system of national origins quotas was damaging to foreign relations and inconsistent with the principles of the Constitution. As understated by the New York *Times*, "The subcommittee did not receive Mr. Dulles' testimony with any special warmth."

[36]S. 3572, Langer (N.D.); H.R. 10511, 10878, Dingell (Mich.); H.R. 11595, Barrett (Pa.).

[37]S. 3167, Watkins (Utah); H.R. 9180, Keating (N.Y.); H.R. 9221, Scott (Pa.); H.R. 9243, Lane (Mass.).

Michigan). And finally there were efforts to facilitate the entry of needed laborers and their families. One such bill was for the relief of the spongefishing industry by making special nonquota visas available to skilled spongedivers (H.R. 12022, Cramer [Fla.]). The other was the Walter bill for the admission of wives and minor children of Basque sheepherders, passed by the House in the first session and now reported out with amendment by the Senate committee (S. Rept. 2226, June 13, 1956, on H.R. 6888[84-I]). The committee amendment was to strike out the House bill and write a new bill to provide up to an additional 350 special nonquota immigrant visas for urgently needed sheepherders, to facilitate the entry of wives and minor children of previously admitted sheepherders provided marriage had been prior to July 1, 1955, and to waive the deportation of certain aliens admitted under the Displaced Persons Act in cases where deportability was because of misrepresentation by the alien of his nationality or birthplace and the misrepresentation was for the purpose of avoiding repatriation to a Communist-controlled country. The amended bill was passed after some debate by the Senate on the last day of the 84th Congress, July 27, 1956, and therefore died without opportunity for House action on the Senate substitute. The session thus ended without addition to the body of immigration law and policy.

85th Congress (1957, 1958)

The first session of the 85th Congress began on the customary opening date of January 3 and continued to August 30, 1957. By far the leading immigration business of the session was amendment of the 1952 Act, in accordance with the presidential message of the year before. At least sixty-five bills specifically for that purpose were introduced, a number of them counterpart bills; and they ranged from single-purpose to omnibus bills for extensive revision of the act.

Among the specific purposes of some of the bills were to provide for the admission of escapees who have fled from persecution in Communist or Communist-dominated countries,[38] to facilitate the entry through granting of nonquota status to certain orphans adopted by citizens (S. 681 by Potter of Michigan), to extend the nonquota status granted alien parents of citizens to include the minor children of such parents (S. 561 by O'Mahoney of Wyoming), and to give the Attorney General authority

[38] S. 1554, Javits, Ives (N.Y.); S. 2023, Case (N.J.) and five others; H.R. 6536, Farbstein (N.Y.); H.R. 4505, Cretella (Conn.); H.R. 5026, Lane (Mass.).

to permit aliens born in Mexico to depart voluntarily instead of being deported if certain conditions of eligibility are met.[39] Other proposals were to revise the system for determination of the quotas,[40] and to grant quota numbers unused in one year to Italy and other oversubscribed areas the following year.[41] And as in the preceding Congress there were several bills to amend the 1952 Act to limit judicial review of deportation and exclusion orders,[42] introduced by the same sponsors as the earlier such proposals.

The more comprehensive omnibus bills were numerous and varied in purpose, from extensive revision to repeal and replacement of the 1952 Act. Of the latter type and representative of a number of the new bills was one from Celler of New York, long-time chairman of the House Judiciary Committee.[43] A lengthy bill, it was a whole new and condensed code of immigration and nationality law; and it began with a declaration of purpose following that of several earlier bills introduced by the "liberal" members of the Senate and House. The declaration stated the objective of the bill as an immigration law

> which will give faithful and positive expression to the basic human values to which American political institutions are dedicated; promote entry of desirable immigrants on a basis responsive to national need and international responsibility; protect this country from infiltration by those who would destroy or impair its political institutions.

It then stated the more specific objectives of no discrimination with regard to national origin, race, color, or creed; uniting of families; serving the domestic economy; providing a haven for the oppressed; and furthering the aims of American foreign policy. Among the features of the bill was a quota ceiling of 250,000 per annum, a preference structure of five classes as in certain earlier bills,[44] with presidential authority for allocation of visas to the five classes within the limits set by the bill. Another

[39]H.R. 2869, Holifield (Calif.); same as his H.R. 4927 (84-I).

[40]S. 346, Watkins (Utah); H.R. 298, Lane (Mass.); H.R. 508, Keating (N.Y.); H.R. 1247, Scott (Pa.). Bills for the same purpose were introduced by the same Congressmen in the second session of the 84th Congress.

[41]H.R. 861, Philbin (Mass.); H.R. 1106, Donohue (Mass.); H.R. 2027, O'Neill (Mass.); H.R. 5003, Barrett (Pa.).

[42]S. 345, Watkins (Utah); H.R. 507, Keating (N.Y.); H.R. 1258, Scott (Pa.).

[43]H.R. 3364, introduced early in the session, on January 22, 1957.

[44]The preference classes were designated Family Unification, Occupational, Refugee Asylum, National Interest, and Resettlement classes, not to exceed 50 percent to the first, 20 percent to the others.

feature was provision of flexibility by giving authority to the President during a declared national emergency to reduce or postpone the issuance of visas from year to year to any of the preference classes. The nonquota classes established under the bill included alien parents as well as spouses and children of citizens; and nonquota status was to be reinstated for professors in educational institutions. No action was taken on this or the other parallel bills in the House.

A Senate bill from Watkins of Utah and fourteen other Senators contained a number of amendments of the 1952 Act (S. 1006), notably setting the annual quota at one-seventh of 1 percent of the 1950 population; allotment to each quota area of the same quota as previously but then allocation of the remaining quota numbers to the separate quota areas in proportion to actual immigration from those areas in the fiscal years 1925 to 1955 inclusive; grouping of quota areas into four regions (Europe, Asia, Africa, and Oceania), and forming a pool for each region of quota numbers unused at the end of a fiscal year, which would be available during the following fiscal year to any alien born in the respective region without regard to country of birth; authorization for the Attorney General to suspend deportation proceedings, adjust the status, and charge to the appropriate quota an alien with a record of honorable service in the Armed Forces during a time of war or national emergency or who is a close relative of a citizen, or a minister or priest of a recognized denomination, if such action is deemed not contrary to the national interest, safety, or security; reaffirmation of the registration and fingerprinting requirement for aliens; and giving to district courts jurisdiction to review deportation orders provided the alien in question has exhausted all possibilities for administrative review and is still within the United States.

Of the numerous bills for the amendment of the 1952 Act, including the above Watkins bill, the only one to progress was a Senate bill introduced by Kennedy of Massachusetts and eight cosponsors.[45] A revision of another Kennedy bill introduced earlier in the session,[46] this bill incorporated a number of provisions to facilitate the admission of certain

[45]S. 2792; followed by S. Rept. 1057, August 20, 1957. The other sponsors were Senators Humphrey (Minn.), Pastore (R.I.), Lausche (Ohio), Neuberger (Oreg.), Clark (Pa.), Jackson (Wash.), Watkins (Utah), and Dirksen (Ill.), all Democrats except the last two. Kefauver (Ky.) later joined in sponsorship of the bill.

[46]S. 2410, Kennedy (Mass.), Pastore (R.I.), Lausche (Ohio), and Humphrey (Minn.). The revision consisted principally of the removal of provisions for reallocation of unused quota numbers to certain classes of refugees and for the adjustment of status of parolees who were then predominantly Hungarian refugees.

adopted children and to relax various sections of the 1952 Act with respect to the admission of refugees and the adjustment of status.[47] Reported out very late in the session, on August 20, 1957, the bill had been amended in committee. The amendments were small technical changes except for a reworded section 15 concerning the reallocation of unused nonquota immigrant visas authorized under the Refugee Relief Act of 1953. Passed as amended by the Senate, by vote of 65 to 4 the next day, it was hastily taken up by the House on August 28 under suspension of the rules, without committee report but with the support of Celler of New York, chairman of the Judiciary Committee, who also presented a letter urging passage of the bill from subcommittee chairman Walter, who was absent because of hospitalization. Without time for formal report on the bill, the House committee nevertheless presented the bill with amendments to make a few technical changes, to clarify wording, and to bring it closer to a somewhat similar Walter bill (H.R. 8123, Walter [Pa.]); but the amendments were carefully kept within limits the Senate would presumably accept. The House passed the bill as amended by a vote of 295 to 58, with 79 not voting. Accepted by the Senate and signed by President Eisenhower,[48] it became the Act of September 11, 1957 (71 Stat. 639).

The act, an omnibus measure in sixteen sections, did not differ greatly from the original Kennedy bill. Amending the Immigration and Nationality Act of 1952 and other acts, its first and second sections facilitated the admission of stepchildren whether legitimate or not provided they were under eighteen years of age at the time of the marriage of the stepparent, illegitimate children, and children adopted for at least two years if under fourteen years of age at the time of adoption. Section 3 conferred first preference status on spouse and children of first preference immigrants if following to join the immigrant. Section 4 set an age

[47]The bill was introduced after several days of public hearings by the Senate subcommittee, during which amendment of the 1952 Act was opposed by the Junior Order of American Mechanics, the Daughters of the American Revolution, and several other organizations; and it was favored by representatives of a number of religious and voluntary organizations such as the National Council of Churches, the National Lutheran Council, the Union of American Hebrew Congregations, the AFL-CIO, and the Anti-Defamation League of B'nai B'rith. Later House hearings heard opposition from the American Legion and Veterans of Foreign Wars.

[48]On signing, the President expressed disappointment that not all inequities in the 1952 Act were removed by the new act and mentioned in particular that it left 1920 as the quota base and did not provide for the permanent admission of the Hungarian refugees. The principal sponsor of the bill, Kennedy of Massachusetts, stated that much still remained to be done and promised to work for further adjustment of immigration policy.

limit of fourteen for the adoption of orphans to qualify for nonquota status and further defined what orphans were eligible under the act. Sections 5 through 7 gave the Attorney General authority to admit certain aliens formerly excludable, in particular close relatives of citizens and lawfully admitted immigrants who have committed certain crimes or are members of immoral classes, who are afflicted with tuberculosis, or who have gained entry through misrepresentation because of fear of persecution in their place of origin. Waiving of the requirement of fingerprinting of nonimmigrants was authorized (sec. 8). Other sections provided for the adjustment of status of several classes of aliens already present in the United States. Section 10 amended the Displaced Persons Act of 1948 and other acts to end the mortgaging of quotas.[49] Other provisions were for the granting of nonquota status to aliens with special skills or close relatives in the United States, if their petitions for admission were approved before July 1, 1957, and reallocation as specified of unused nonquota visas authorized by the Refugee Relief Act of 1953.

Other major legislative concerns during the first session of the 85th Congress, as witnessed by the subjects of the bills introduced, were refugee problems and the admission of adopted children and war orphans. The bills themselves were generally in the form of amendments of the 1952 Act and the Refugee Relief Act of 1953. In addition to those already mentioned were approximately a dozen bills to facilitate the admission of one or another category of refugees. Several were specifically for the admission of Hungarian refugees or, as they were then termed, escapees (H.R. 4907, 4909, Dingell [Mich.]). Certain of these and other bills were to serve several purposes, in particular with regard to refugees, children, and orphans.[50] All of the above refugee and escapee bills remained in committee to the end of the session.

In addition to those already mentioned were fourteen or more bills to facilitate the admission of various categories of children, especially adoptees and refugee orphans. Approximately half of the bills concerned nonquota status for adopted children.[51] Several were to amend the 1953 Act to provide additional visas for the admission of refugee orphans.[52] Others related to the preference or nonquota status of children of certain

[49]It was reported at the time that the quota for Poland was mortgaged to the year 2000, that for Latvia to the year 2274, and to intermediate dates for several other countries. H. Doc. 400(82-II), p. 6.

[50]Additional bills of this type were S. 2222, Kennedy (Mass.); H.R. 7904, Keating (N.Y.); H.R. 8926, Dennison (Ohio); H.R. 8981, O'Hara (Ill.).

[51]S. 681, Potter (Mich.); H.R. 4008, 8123, Walter (Pa.); H.R. 8358, Dellay (N.J.); H.R. 8426, Santangelo (N.Y.); H.R. 8830, Macdonald (Mass.).

[52]S. 772, Ives and Javits (N.Y.); S. 866, Neuberger and Morse (Oreg.); H.R. 3783, Porter (Oreg.); H.R. 4189, Burns (Hawaii); H.R. 4198, Dawson (Utah).

aliens admitted for permanent residence.[53] Only one of this group of bills was reported out, a House bill by Walter of Pennsylvania (H. Rept. 1199, on H.R. 8123), which was tabled when the House took up the Kennedy bill instead.

In smaller numbers, other bills of the session dealt with a wide range of topics, including increased admissions for certain national-origin groups. Two such bills proposed additional visas to be made available to Greeks;[54] another would provide admission for 50,000 from Italy (H.R. 1969, O'Neill [Mass.]). There was one for the benefit of refugees from Armenia (S. 1888, Saltonstall [Mass.]), and one to give natives of Malta unlimited access to the large British quota (H.R. 666, Mrs. Griffiths [Mich.]).

With regard to the quotas, in addition to the already mentioned bills for the reassignment of unused quota numbers was a House bill to set up a selective immigration board and to provide for the allocation of unused quota numbers (H.R. 8454, Feighan [Ohio]). There were two renewed attempts to ensure to aliens on old waiting lists equal priority on new lists (H.R. 844, 2476, Multer [N.Y.]); and Judd of Minnesota resubmitted a bill to give quotas to territory under American jurisdiction (H.R. 244; see his H.R. 5135 [84-I]).

Other miscellaneous bills were to liberalize and to extend the Refugee Relief Act of 1953 for two more years (H.R. 1253, Scott [Pa.]; H.R. 3866, Shelley [Calif.]), to amend that act in order to reassign unused visas and to permit the admission of aliens afflicted with tuberculosis under certain conditions (H.R. 547, Barrett [Pa.]), to remove epilepsy as a cause for exclusion (S. 1247, Wiley [Wis.]), to grant nonquota status for a two-year period to the unmarried children of certain former members of the Philippine Scouts (H.R. 7311, Shelley [Calif.]), and to amend the Act of September 3, 1954 (68 Stat. 1145) to authorize the admission of an additional 350 skilled alien sheepherders.[55]

Several bills related to aliens and the Armed Forces. Two were to permit enlistment of aliens in the regular Army (S. 2420, Saltonstall [Mass.]; H.R. 8122, Vinson [Ga.]). After being quickly reported out and passed in both Senate and House (S. Rept. 541, H. Rept. 689), the Senate bill was signed into law as the Act of July 24, 1957 (71 Stat. 311). Intro-

[53] S. 561, O'Mahoney (Wyo.); S. 1222, Potter (Mich.); H.R. 4273, Ford (Mich.).

[54] S. 1715, Beall (Md.), Goldwater (Ariz.), and Capehart (Ind.); H.R. 3642, Nimtz (Ind.).

[55] S. 129, Dirksen (Ill.). The bill included a number of other provisions, in particular to define petty offenses not constituting grounds for exclusion, to limit deportation in case of misrepresentation by aliens in fear of repatriation, to authorize the reassignment of unused quota numbers, to allow the admission of not more than 1,200 aliens with tuberculosis, and other purposes.

duced but not acted on was a bill for the deportation of aliens for failure to register as required under the Universal Military Training and Service Act (S. 1493, Potter [Mich.]).

Also related to aliens was a bill to exempt the survivors of certain deceased members of the Armed Forces from the provision of the Social Security Act preventing the payment of benefits to aliens outside the United States (H.R. 1944, Kean [N.J.]). It was reported out by the House committee with amendment to exclude cases of dishonorable discharge from the benefits of the bill (H. Rept. 818, July 16, 1957). Passed then by the House and reported out in the Senate (S. Rept. 869), it was debated in the Senate on August 20, 1957, amended to clarify the eligibility of widows, and passed to become the Act of August 30, 1957 (71 Stat. 518). Another bill to be enacted during the session was to amend the Act of August 28, 1935 to permit the disposal of lands and interests in lands to aliens (H.R. 8929, Kilgore [Tex.]). Reported out and passed by both House and Senate (H. Rept. 945; S. Rept. 862), it became the Act of August 28, 1957 (71 Stat. 475).

Among miscellaneous other bills during the session was one to increase the limit for quota immigration by not more than 350, available to immigrants at ports of the Commonwealth of Puerto Rico (H.R. 4509, Fernós-Isern [P.R.]), the allotment according to quota area to be made by the Commonwealth. And finally there were two Senate bills, both from Eastland of Mississippi, to guard against subversive aliens coming as members of the diplomatic service of foreign governments (S. 2896 and 2897). One of these bills was to require any alien entering under diplomatic passport to declare any past connection with the espionage service of a Communist country, the other to make it a criminal offense for an alien to enter by diplomatic passport under an assumed name. No action was taken on these bills other than the usual referral to committee.

The second session of the 85th Congress opened on January 7, 1958 and continued to August 24 of that year. After the activity of the preceding session, relatively few immigration bills were introduced. Several progressed to enactment, although none made major revisions of immigration law and policy.

Special emergency legislation was proposed to alleviate certain cases of distress. There were four bills[56] for relief of the Hungarian refugees or escapees paroled into the United States following the 1956 uprising, a group not cared for under the Kennedy bill enacted in the preceding session. Of the four similar bills, the House bill by Feighan of Ohio for

[56]S. 3635, Aiken (Vt.); H.R. 10639, Reuss (Wis.); H.R. 11033, Feighan (Ohio); H.R. 11858, Fulton (Pa.).

the purpose of authorizing retroactive adjustment of status for paroled Hungarian refugees was reported out with only minor clarifying amendments (H. Rept. 1661, April 28, 1958). Passed as amended by the House, it was reported out by the Senate committee without amendment (S. Rept. 1817, July 10, 1958) and passed to become the Act of July 25, 1958 (72 Stat. 419). As enacted, the bill granted admission for permanent residence to Hungarian parolees of at least two years' residence in the United States, on condition of a finding upon inspection that the alien in question was admissible at time of entry and still admissible.

Another emergency relief bill was for the aid of persons displaced as a result of the recent earthquake in the Azores (S. 3942, Pastore [R.I.]). It authorized a maximum of 1,500 special nonquota immigrant visas for that purpose. Amended by the Senate committee to set a cutoff date of December 31, 1959 (S. Rept. 1875, July 22, 1958), the bill as so amended was passed by the Senate. The House committee amended the bill further (H. Rept. 2558) to include citizens and nationals of the Netherlands displaced from Indonesia subsequent to January 1, 1949 and living in continental Netherlands on the enactment date of the act. Special nonquota immigrant visas not to exceed the annual quota of the Netherlands (3,136) were provided for them, and the cutoff date for visas to be issued under the bill was advanced to June 30, 1960. The amended bill was passed by the House, accepted by the Senate, and became the Act of September 2, 1958 (72 Stat. 1712). A more general refugee bill, for the admission of 50,000 aliens of that class (H.R. 13691, Celler [N.Y.]), remained in committee.

Several bills were to authorize the adjustment of the status of various classes of nonrefugee residents of the United States to that of immigrant, admitted for permanent residence. One such bill would extend to any parolees the same privilege of adjustment of status accorded to the Hungarian parolees by the Feighan bill described above, provided they had two years' residence, good moral character, and their entrance was not contrary to the national welfare or security (S. 3391, Dirksen [Ill.]). A bill introduced by Walter of Pennsylvania (H.R. 13451) was to amend section 245 of the 1952 Act to authorize the Attorney General to adjust the status of any alien who was admitted as a bona fide nonimmigrant (i.e., a temporary admission) and is eligible for admission for permanent residence. Such adjustment was to be conditional on the availability of an immigrant visa for the alien's quota area, and the adjustment was to be charged to the appropriate quota. The House committee reported out the bill (H. Rept. 2258, July 23, 1958) with amended title and with addition of a new section, section 2, to amend the Act of September 11, 1957 (71 Stat. 639) with a new section 12A extending from July 1, 1957 to July 1, 1958 the authority of the Attorney General to grant nonquota status to aliens approved for first preference under the 1952 Act but denied visas because of oversubscription of the first preference portion of the quota for their area of origin.[57] Passed by the House as amended, the bill was then reported out in the Senate (S. Rept. 2133, Aug. 4, 1958) without amendment, passed, and became the Act of August 21, 1958 (72 Stat. 699).

Adjustment of a different sort was provided by another bill from Walter of Pennsylvania (H.R. 11874) to give the Attorney General discretionary power to create a record of lawful entry in the case of an alien who entered prior to June 28, 1940 and who satisfies the Attorney General he has lived here continuously, is of good moral character, and is not ineligible to citizenship.[58] Reported out with only a technical change by the House committee (H. Rept. 1727, May 20, 1958), the bill was passed and sent to the Senate where it was amended without substantive change (S. Rept. 1905, July 23, 1958), passed, and became the Act of August 8, 1958 (72 Stat. 546).

The only other noteworthy bill to be passed during the second session provided for the cancellation of departure bonds required under the 1924 and 1952 Acts, in the case of refugees admitted as nonimmigrants between May 6, 1945 and July 1, 1953 and subsequently had their status adjusted to that of admission for permanent residence (H.R. 8439, Celler [N.Y.]). Amended in wording and reported out by the House committee (H. Rept. 1320, Jan. 30, 1958), it was passed by the House. The Senate committee reported out the bill (S. Rept. 1624, May 21, 1958), amended to transfer responsibility for the refund from the Treasury Department to the Attorney General. The Senate gave approval but added the further proviso of a cutoff date for applications for refund at five years from passage of the act. With House acceptance of the Senate amendments the bill was enacted as the Act of July 18, 1958 (72 Stat. 375).

Amendment of the 1952 Act was proposed, unsuccessfully, in several additional bills,[59] some of which called for major revision of the Act. The Keating bill was a lengthy bill in thirty-nine sections and incorporated a number of the provisions of the bill sponsored in earlier sessions by the group of Senators opposed to the McCarran-Walter Act.[60]

[57]This was in effect to add on the provisions contained in another Walter bill, H.R. 13481, that remained in committee.

[58]This was an amendment of section 249 of the 1952 Act, and changed only the cutoff date, previously July 1, 1924.

[59]H.R. 11167, Keating (N.Y.); H.R. 12043, Libonati (Ill.); H.R. 13642, Barrett (Pa.); H.R. 13796, Bow (Ohio).

[60]These provisions included a different quota formula, formation of a supplementary quota pool for distribution to quota areas in proportion to actual immigration and separate pooling within four world areas, revised preference structure, etc.

Amendment of the Act of September 11, 1957, also referred to above as the Kennedy measure, was the objective of at least three additional bills during the session (H.R. 9625, 13726, Barrett [Pa.]; H.R. 10465, Walter [Pa.]), none of which was reported out of committee. Of these the Walter bill was to amend section 7, clause A, of the 1957 Act to require that certain aliens in order to be eligible for the relief from deportation provided in section 7 must show to the satisfaction of the Attorney General that their misrepresentation in acquiring a visa or in other documentation was not committed for the purpose of evading inspection or examination for admission. The Barrett bills were to give Italy an additional quota of 25,000 per annum and to extend the cutoff date in section 12 of the Act by one year to July 1, 1958.[61]

Finally there were scattered immigration bills on various other topics but none was approved by both houses of Congress. A bill from the chairman of the House subcommittee (H.R. 13311, Walter [Pa.]) concerned judicial review of deportation orders. It provided that, with limited exceptions, an alien under deportation order may seek judicial review only by filing a petition with the United States circuit court of appeals and that the writ of *habeas corpus* is reserved for an alien held in custody pending deportation. A further provision was that review of exclusion orders may be secured only by means of *habeas corpus* writs. Amended in committee without substantive change other than in a procedural matter, the bill was reported out[62] and passed by the House late in the session. Referred to the Senate committee only a few days before the end of the session and of the 85th Congress, it went no further.

Other bills, introduced but not acted on, were to give nonquota status to the alien children and spouses of lawfully admitted immigrants (H.R. 13409 by Teller of New York), and to facilitate the entry of adopted children and certain other relatives of citizens (H.R. 12037 by Libonati of Illinois). And Judd of Minnesota renewed earlier attempts to have the portion of the Ryukyu Islands under American jurisdiction treated as a separate quota area (H.R. 10161). There were in addition Senate resolutions for study by the Judiciary Committee or a subcommittee of problems created by the flow of "refugees from Communist tyranny" into

[61]Section 12 granted nonquota status to aliens in the three preference classes, given approval of their petitions by the Attorney General prior to the specified date.

[62]H. Rept. 2478, August 6, 1958. During consideration of the bill by the House on August 12, 1958 (*Congressional Record,* 104:17172), Walter (Pa.) stated the purpose of the bill to be "to provide a method of judicial review of deportation orders and to spell out the procedure so that aliens who are under deportation orders and who can afford it, cannot find access to the courts by some subterfuge or other, interminably."

western European and Asian nations,[63] and for official action through the Intergovernmental Committee for European Migration (ICEM) in favor of an "international conference of nations of the Free World" to formulate programs for the solution of refugee problems (S. Res. 357).

86th Congress (1959, 1960)

The first session of the 86th Congress convened on January 7, 1959 and adjourned some eight months later on September 14. Like its predecessor it was a Democratic Congress and there was little or no change in the composition of the Senate and House subcommittees under the conservative chairmanships of Eastland of Mississippi and Walter of Pennsylvania. No major legislation regarding immigration was passed during the session, which was, however, one of moderate activity in the number of bills introduced. Most numerous were those for the regulation of immigration, for amendment of the 1952 and 1957 Acts, and for the admission of refugees and of relatives of citizens or resident aliens.

There were fourteen or more bills with the stated purpose to amend and revise the laws relating to immigration, nationality, naturalization, and citizenship—lengthy bills designed not so much to amend as to repeal the 1952 Act and to provide a new code of immigration law in its place. Included among them was one Senate bill sponsored by Humphrey of Minnesota and ten other Senators (S. 2358), along the lines of previous bills introduced by members of the sponsoring group. Representative of the House bills was the one introduced by Celler of New York,[64] which differed little if at all from his corresponding bill of the preceding Congress (H.R. 3364 [85-I]). Following the pattern set by predecessor bills, it began with the now familiar statement of purpose, set an annual immigration quota of 250,000 to be allocated by the President within the prescribed preference limits, designated five preference classes of which the "Family Unification class" could receive up to half of the entire quota of a country, provided for a downward adjustment of immigration in times of national emergency, and went on to cover the whole additional range of immigration and nationality law. None of these bills came out of committee.

Another group of approximately twenty bills, of which nearly half were in the Senate, dealt with amendment of one or another section of

[63]S. Res. 239, Kefauver (Tenn.); same as S. Res. 53 (85-I), agreed to on January 30, 1957, except for extension of dates by one year and reduction of appropriation for committee expenses.

[64]H.R. 16; in most respects the same as the Humphrey bill.

the 1952 Act. Especially noteworthy were four Senate bills, introduced by Humphrey of Minnesota, Javits of New York, Kennedy of Massachusetts, and Dirksen of Illinois, and thus represented both Republican and Democratic thinking on immigration policy. The Humphrey bill (S. 952) provided for the granting of nonquota status to professors in educational institutions and their immediate dependents as well as to ministers of religion, the determination and allocation of quotas as in his earlier bills, the pooling of unused quotas, elimination of the Asia-Pacific triangle, and a board to review the cases of aliens denied visas. Provisions of the Javits bill[65] included change of the base year for computation of national origins quotas from 1920 to 1950, pooling of unused quotas and their allocation in the following fiscal year to persons on the waiting lists of countries whose quotas do not exceed 12,000, authorization for the admission on parole of approximately 60,000 refugees annually and for the adjustment of their status after two years of residence in the United States, and authorization for the nonquota admission of 40,000 refugee-escapees in support of the World Refugee Year program. The bill also included repeal of the Asia-Pacific triangle provision in the 1952 Act and put colonial peoples under the quota of the governing nation.

Features of the Kennedy bill (S. 1996), which contained elements that reappeared several years later in the immigration bill sponsored by the Kennedy administration, included an increase in allowable quota immigration to 250,000 from the current level of approximately 154,000, authority for admission under parole of approximately 60,000 refugees annually with right of adjustment of status at the end of one year, a new system of national origins quota allocation based on the population of the quota area,[66] alternative charging of immigrant aliens to their country of citizenship instead of country of birth, elimination of the Asia-Pacific triangle by the foregoing provisions, a new preference structure consisting of 60 percent for designated relatives to the third degree of relation (i.e., including nephews, nieces, and their dependents) and the remaining quota divided equally between aliens with special skills or qualifications and so-called "new seed immigration."

The Dirksen (Ill.) bill (S. 2178) embodied the administration program and resembled a bill by two Republican Senators, Watkins of Utah and Keating of New York, in the preceding Congress. Also similar in

[65]S. 1919; also sponsored by other Republican Senators Case (N.J.), Keating (N.Y.), and Saltonstall (Mass.).

[66]A minimum quota of 200, a maximum quota of 25,000 for countries of 50 million population or more, a maximum for smaller countries of one-twentieth of 1 percent of their population, and a setting of each national quota annually between these limits by the Secretary of State, the Secretary of Commerce, and the Attorney General.

certain of its provisions to contemporary bills just described, it did away with the Asia-Pacific triangle, used the 1950 census as the basis of quota allocation, increased allowable quota immigration by a formula of one-seventh of 1 percent of the 1950 census population of the United States, allocated the additional quota numbers so provided in proportion to immigration from each quota area during the fiscal years 1925 through 1955, authorized the annual admission on parole of not more than 10,000 refugees, and made them eligible for adjustment of status after two years of residence. Like the other Senate bills described above, the Dirksen bill remained in committee; nor were any of the other bills for basic revision of the 1952 Act approved by either Senate or House committees during the session.

A number of bills, ten in all, were for amendment of the Act of September 11, 1957 (71 Stat. 639), to extend by one or in most cases by two years the cutoff date given in section 12 of the act for eligibility for nonquota status made available to certain aliens.[67] No action was taken on these bills during the session beyond referral to committee. Other bills for amendment of the 1957 Act with regard to the admission of orphans and aliens afflicted with tuberculosis are noted below.

Refugee problems, which had been prominent among congressional concerns during the postwar years, received added attention during the 86th Congress. The United Nations had recently taken the initiative of calling for a World Refugee Year during which extra effort would be made for the alleviation of the continuing problem of the refugees, and thirty-one nations had offered their support. A conference to discuss American participation in the UN program was called by President Eisenhower for May 21 and 22, 1959, and shortly before the conference a presidential proclamation designated the period of July 1, 1959 to June 30, 1960 as Refugee Year for the United States. Many of the bills introduced for revision of the immigration laws and amendment of the 1952 Act proposed more liberal admissions of refugees, as already noted. Resolutions were introduced for inquiry into refugee problems and for aid in the resettlement of refugees;[68] and there were five or more bills to authorize additional refugee admissions.[69] None came out of committee.

Relatives of residents and citizens of the United States were the specified beneficiaries of a dozen or so bills to facilitate the entry of

[67]Section 12 gave nonquota status to aliens eligible for first, second, or third preference if their petitions had been approved by the Attorney General prior to July 1, 1957.

[68]H. J. Res. 397, Walter (Pa.), May 21, 1959; S. J. Res. 110, Kennedy (Mass.), June 17, 1959.

[69]Certain of the refugee bills had a "Cold War" tone, being specifically for aid of persons having fled from Communist countries.

fiancés, brothers and sisters, children, and spouses of citizens and resident aliens, in some instances with nonquota status. Only one was reported out, a House bill by Walter of Pennsylvania (H.R. 5896; with H. Rept. 582, June 26, 1959). As reported out with several committee amendments, section 1 of the bill would move unmarried children, over twenty-one years of age, of citizens from the fourth to the second preference category, a preference then available only to parents of citizens and not generally utilized fully. Section 2 would give third preference to the unmarried children over twenty-one years of age of lawfully resident aliens, whose spouses and minor children were already in that preference category. Section 3 was to increase the fourth preference allocation from 25 to 50 percent of the visas not taken by the first three preferences, and expanded the fourth to include accompanying spouses and children of fourth preference aliens (i.e., brothers and sisters and married children of citizens). Passed by the House, the bill was amended and passed by the Senate, amendment concerned principally with procedural matters. With House acceptance the bill became the Act of September 22, 1959 (73 Stat. 644).

Ten or so bills were to facilitate the continued entry under nonquota status of alien orphans adopted or to be adopted by American citizens, in view of the approaching expiration on June 30, 1959 of the provision in the Act of September 11, 1957 (71 Stat. 639) granting nonquota status to such orphans. The administration bill (S. 2004) for this purpose, introduced by Senator Wiley of Wisconsin on May 20, would establish such granting of nonquota status on a permanent basis and require assurance of proper care for the child after adoption. Similar bills came from Senators Javits and Keating of New York, from Senator Kennedy of Massachusetts with Neuberger and Morse of Oregon, and from several other members of Congress. None of these bills progressed during the session.

Smaller numbers of bills were offered on a wide range of other matters. Four would have made quota numbers unused in one year available to oversubscribed areas in the following year.[70] Judd of Minnesota persisted with his many-times proposed bill to make any territory over which the United States has treaty jurisdiction a separate quota area (H.R. 110), and a companion bill of the same purpose (H.R. 5426) was also introduced by Miller of California. Multer of New York continued his effort to prevent loss of priority to aliens transferred from a former to a current quota waiting list.[71]

[70]H.R. 613, Philbin (Mass.); H.R. 2529, Donohue (Mass.); H.R. 3344, O'Neill (Mass.); H.R. 5497, Glenn (N.J.).

[71]H.R. 595; offered again in the next session: H.R. 785 (87-I).

Veterans legislation was represented by only three bills during the session, two of which were to accord equal naturalization privileges to Korean War veterans and to admit for permanent residence certain aliens with five years of service in the Armed Forces.[72] The third of the group was to grant nonquota status to the unmarried children of certain former members of the Armed Forces or Philippine Scouts, H.R. 1962 by Shelley (Calif.).

Two bills introduced by Powell of New York related to British possessions or former possessions in the Western Hemisphere, these being British Guiana, British Honduras, the British Virgin Islands, and the newly formed West Indies Federation (H.R. 6589 and 6609). One of the bills was to give natives of these areas unlimited access to the British quota, the other to give them nonquota status. Not acted on at this session, the bills were to be introduced again in the 87th Congress.

Several other bills were designed to facilitate immigration from other areas. One was to amend the Refugee Relief Act of 1953 to provide additional visas for aliens of Armenian ethnic origin (S. 1441, Saltonstall and Kennedy [Mass.]). Others were to admit 50,000 from Italy (H.R. 3343, O'Neill [Mass.]) and 5,000 Assyrian [*sic*] immigrants (H.R. 6177, McFall [Calif.]). All of the bills of this group remained in committee.

There were a few bills to relax the excludability of aliens for certain medical and mental ailments. Senate and House bills[73] were to eliminate tuberculosis as grounds for exclusion in the case of "the spouse or child, including the minor unmarried adopted child" and the parents of citizens or lawfully admitted aliens, at the discretion of the Attorney General after consultation with the Surgeon General of the United States Public Health Service. Another House bill (H.R. 7280, Wilson [Calif.]) was to exempt the natural-born child of a citizen, or lawfully admitted resident alien, or quota or nonquota immigrant from the excluding provisions of paragraphs (1), (4), and (7) of section 212(a) of the 1952 Act, which provided for the exclusion of aliens who are feebleminded, afflicted with "psychopathic personality, epilepsy, or a mental defect," or having a physical defect that may affect the ability of the alien to earn a living if in need of doing so.

None of the above bills for relaxing the exclusion provisions received committee approval, but action was taken on another bill introduced by Walter of Pennsylvania, chairman of the House subcommittee (H.R. 6118). This called for amendment of section 6 of the Act of September 11, 1957 (71 Stat. 639), which gave admissibility to the alien spouse,

[72] S. 1196, Neuberger (Oreg.) and Engle (Calif.); H.R. 7209, Shelley (Calif.).

[73] S. 1523, Kennedy (Mass.), Neuberger (Oreg.); H.R. 3089, Walter (Pa.).

child, or parent of a citizen or lawfully admitted resident alien even though afflicted with tuberculosis, under certain conditions, but with a cutoff date of June 30, 1959. The Walter bill was to extend the provision by one year. It was reported out (H. Rept. 291, April 23, 1959) favorably by the House committee, but amended to prolong the life of the provision by two years and to expand its coverage to include the specified relatives of aliens who have been issued an immigration visa. So amended it was passed by the House. Reported with amendment in the Senate, it was passed there, the amendment was approved by the House, and became the Act of September 9, 1959 (73 Stat. 490). In its final form (referred to as "the T.B.-Orphan bill") after Senate amendment, it included a second section to further amend the 1957 Act to extend by one year, to June 30, 1960, the granting of special nonquota immigrant visas to certain orphans as provided in subsections 4(a) and 4(b) of the 1957 Act.

Relating to aliens within the country were three bills on deportation and two concerned with the employment of aliens. The former three were from the chairmen of the Senate and House subcommittees, Eastland of Mississippi and Walter of Pennsylvania. The Eastland bill (S. 1302) was to make certain clarifying changes of wording in sections of the 1952 Act defining the deportable classes of aliens and prescribing procedures for their apprehension and deportation (sec. 241 and 242). One of the two Walter bills dealt with the supervision of deportable aliens (H.R. 5136); the other was to consolidate and provide a single statutory authority for the judicial review of orders of deportation (H.R. 2807). It was reported out by Walter's committee in the House (H. Rept. 423, June 2, 1959), accompanied by dissenting minority views from Representatives Celler and Lindsay of New York and Libonati of Illinois, who argued in part that the bill if enacted would restrict an alien's ability to win a stay of deportation, and that even though some aliens have been able to fend off deportation by resort to the courts, a few such abuses do not justify legislation harmful to all aliens facing deportation. The Senate took no affirmative action on the bill after its passage by the House, and the bill repeated the fate of a Walter bill in the preceding session (H.R. 13311 [85-II]).

Regarding the employment of aliens, a Senate bill proposed a consolidation and revision of laws relating to the employment of aliens by the states, the District of Columbia, the Post Office Department, and the Civil Service (S. 1495, Johnston [S.C.]). Reported out with only "perfecting" amendments (S. Rept. 437, June 29, 1959), the bill was passed by the Senate but did not advance in the House. And a House bill to extend authorization for the enlistment of aliens in the regular army was introduced but not reported out (H.R. 6761, Vinson [Ga.]).

The first session of the 86th Congress thus ended with the passage of only two amending acts related to immigration, in spite of the growing effort for major change of immigration policy and in spite of the number of bills introduced. Both of the bills enacted were sponsored by Walter of Pennsylvania, one of them to alter and somewhat liberalize the allocation of quota preference in favor of certain classes of relatives, the other to extend provisions in the 1957 Act facilitating the entry of orphans and of aliens with tuberculosis. Despite the efforts of a number of members of both houses of Congress, the Immigration and Nationality Act of 1952 had been defended against any basic change.

The second session of the 86th Congress ran from January 6 to September 1, 1960. Pressures from within and without Congress for revision of the 1952 Act and for a less restrictive immigration policy continued and received administrative endorsement in a special message to Congress from President Eisenhower on March 17 (H. Doc. 360). With the statement that "I again urge the liberalization of some of our existing restrictions upon immigration," the message recommended two principal steps: a doubling of the present immigration quota of 154,000 per annum and special provision to admit considerable numbers of refugees resulting from political upheavals and persecution. In more detail with regard to the quotas were the recommendations that the ceiling of 2,000 on quotas in the Asia-Pacific triangle be removed, that the base year for the computation of quotas be changed from 1920 to 1960, that the overall annual quota be one-sixth of 1 percent of the population of the United States, that national quotas be based on a percentage of actual immigration from the given nation between 1924 and 1959 rather than on race or ethnic classification, and that unused quotas be allocated to oversubscribed nations.

Congress already had before it the numerous bills from the first session incorporating many if not all of the presidential recommendations and going beyond them in some respects. There were, therefore, ample proposals already in the hands of the immigration subcommittees if they chose to act on them, and only a few new bills along these lines were introduced during the second session. A lengthy codification of immigration and nationality law was introduced by Roosevelt of California (H.R. 10069) and another bill for amendment and revision of the laws came from Gilbert of New York (H.R. 11082). Other bills from New York Representatives called for amendment of several sections of the 1952 Act.[74] None of the above new bills nor those carried over from the first session came out of committee.

[74]H.R. 11570, Halpern, to extend nonquota status to the child, spouse, and parent of lawfully admitted aliens and to the parent of citizens, to revise the preference classes under quota, and to revise procedures for the granting of nonquota or immigrant status on the basis of relationship; and H.R. 13175, Santangelo, to expand the second preference quota class and to redefine procedure for the granting of nonquota or preference status on the basis of relationship.

The principal legislative concern of the session in the field of immigration, to judge from the number of new bills, was with regard to refugees. There were four identical House bills to provide 5,000 special nonquota immigrant visas for citizens or nationals of Italy displaced from Tunisia and temporarily residing in Italy, together with accompanying spouse and unmarried children under twenty-one years of age, including children adopted prior to July 1, 1959.[75] There were, in addition, three identical bills[76] to amend the Act of September 2, 1958 (72 Stat. 1712), a refugee relief act that provided 1,500 nonquota immigrant visas for aliens from the Azores and 3,136 such visas for Dutch refugees from Indonesia and residing in the Netherlands. The proposed amendment of the 1958 Act was to extend it by two years to June 30, 1962, increase the visa allocation for the Azores refugees to 2,000, and double the visas allocated to the refugees from the Netherlands with an additional 3,136. Of the three bills, the Walter bill was reported out with amendment (H. Rept. 1306), to add a third section extending by one year, to June 30, 1961, the provision in the Act of September 11, 1957 (71 Stat. 639)[77] for the issuance of special nonquota immigrant visas to orphans under fourteen years of age and adopted or to be adopted by a citizen. Passed by the House as so amended, the bill was not reported out in the Senate.

There was in addition a House bill for the relief of certain refugees from Indonesia living in the Netherlands (H.R. 9455, Ford [Mich.]), and a Senate bill for national participation in the resettlement of so-called refugee-escapees (S. 3513, Dodd [Conn.]). Neither bill was acted on, but the House committee reported out a Walter resolution from the first session (H. J. Res. 397, with H. Rept. 1433) of the same title as the Senate bill above.

The resolution authorized the Attorney General to parole alien refugee-escapees, subject to conditions of eligibility for admission, and made them eligible for admission for permanent residence after two years if found admissible upon inspection by an immigration officer. After hearings the resolution was amended and reported out by the House committee (H. Rept. 1433, March 29, 1960); the principal amendments being to direct the Attorney General to make semiannual reports to Congress of the number of refugee-escapees admitted by other nations during the preceding six months and to set one-fourth of that number as the upper limit of the number of such aliens to be admitted into the

[75]H.R. 12029, Celler (N.Y.); H.R. 12071, Rodino (N.J.); H.R. 12321, Rodino (N.J.); H.R. 12367, Addonizio (N.J.).

[76]S. 3028, Pastore (R.I.); H.R. 10419, Walter (Pa.); H.R. 10439, Fogarty (R.I.).

[77]Sec. 4(a) of the 1957 Act, originally to June 30, 1959, extended by one year to June 30, 1960 by the Act of September 9, 1959 (73 Stat. 490).

United States during the following six months. A terminal date for the program of July 1, 1962 was also added. Passed by the House as amended in committee, the resolution was then extensively amended in the Senate committee. The 25 percent limit was eventually retained, but provision was made for the admission of up to 500 refugee-escapees classified by the United Nations High Commissioner for Refugees as "difficult to resettle," provided that they were not in need of institutionalization. The Senate committee also proceeded to add onto the resolution the substance of two Walter bills previously passed by the House (H.R. 9385, see below; H.R. 10419), to increase from 1,500 to 2,000 the special nonquota immigrant visas allocated for refugees from the Azores, double the visa allocation for Indonesian refugees from the Netherlands, to extend the Act of September 2, 1958 (72 Stat. 1712) that made the original provision for these two categories of refugees by two years to June 30, 1962, and to extend the Act of September 11, 1957 (71 Stat. 639) providing special nonquota immigrant visas for adopted or to-be-adopted orphans under fourteen years of age by an additional year to June 30, 1961. The 1952 Act was also amended to add specific mention of marihuana in the sections concerning exclusion and deportation for offenses. And a final amendment inserted by the Senate committee was to make alien seamen ineligible for adjustment of status from that of temporary admission or parole to that of admission for permanent residence. The reason given was that there had been frequent abuses by such aliens. The Senate accepted the resolution as amended by its committee but added a further amendment proposed by Fong of Hawaii, to authorize the Attorney General to parole in an additional 4,500, or 2,250 per year from July 1, 1960 to June 30, 1962, of refugees from areas not under the authority of the United Nations High Commissioner for Refugees. The House-Senate conference committee presented a revised draft (H. Rept. 2088, July 2, 1960) that dropped the Fong amendment but otherwise substantially followed the Senate version and became the Act of July 14, 1960 (74 Stat. 504).

The presidential message that had stimulated Congress to consider refugee legislation had also called for revision of the quota system. Four identical bills for that purpose were introduced immediately after the presidential message and embodied the Eisenhower recommendations.[78]

Other than these, only a sprinkling of new bills appeared during the second session of the 86th Congress. Several dealt with the admission of

[78]S. 3225, Dirksen (Ill.) and nine others; H.R. 11234, Miller (N.Y.); H.R. 11235, Lindsay (N.Y.); H.R. 11287, Macdonald (Mass.). All but the last of the four came from Republican members of Congress.

alien relatives, two of which bills were to extend by one year the provision in the Act of September 22, 1959 (73 Stat. 644) for the granting of nonquota status to certain aliens on a consular waiting list prior to December 31, 1953 (S. 3011, Moss [Utah]; H.R. 11819, Brademas [Ind.]) and one was to authorize the Attorney General to deny nonquota status or quota preference on the basis of marriage to a citizen or lawfully resident alien if the marriage is determined to have been contracted for the purpose of evading the immigration laws (H.R. 12786, Henderson [Ohio]). Another bill proposed amending section 9 of the Act of September 11, 1957 (71 Stat. 639) to extend by two and one-half years, to December 31, 1959, the time limit for approval of an alien's petition for adjustment of status to that of lawfully admitted for permanent residence under the terms of the act (S. 3695, Proxmire [Wis.]). And reintroduced from the preceding Congress was a bill to grant natives of Malta unlimited access to the British quota (H.R. 11771, Mrs. St. George [N.Y.]).

Finally, there was the Walter bill to provide for the exclusion or deportation of any alien convicted of violation of "any law relating to illicit possession of marihuana" (H.R. 9385, Walter [Pa.]), which carried additionally a statement of conditions under which the Attorney General was authorized to adjust the status of an alien previously given temporary admission or paroled into the United States, and specifically excluded alien seamen from the privilege of such adjustment. In reporting the bill favorably, the House committee added two new sections. One provided nonquota status for spouses and children of beneficiaries of approved first preference visa petitions, if accompanying or following the admitted alien. The other section provided for the temporary admission of fiancés or fiancées of citizens for the purpose of marriage, and for their departure or deportation if the marriage does not take place. Passed by the House, the bill went to the Senate committee, which later consolidated it with the Walter resolution for the admission of certain refugees, as described above.

87th Congress (1961, 1962)

The 87th Congress convened on January 3, 1961 for a first session that was to end on September 27. With a Democratic majority as in the preceding Congress, it now had a Democratic President and one who had been active in Senate efforts for liberalization of the immigration laws. The immigration subcommittees in Senate and House continued unchanged or substantially unchanged in membership under their conservative chairmen, Eastland of Mississippi in the Senate and Walter of Pennsylvania in the House.

The principal legislative effort of the session as far as immigration was concerned was still for amendment or replacement of the McCarran-Walter Act of 1952; and as in the preceding Congresses this effort was effectively resisted by the leaders of the two crucial committees. Numbers of bills were introduced, but little new legislation came out. Three bills were for the broadly stated purpose of amending and revising the whole body of immigration, naturalization, nationality, and citizenship law.[79] Approximately fifteen others were more specifically designated for amendment of the 1952 Act and dealt piecemeal with revision of certain sections of the act rather than presenting a new code of immigration law. Among the provisions contained in one or another of the bills was the setting of the overall annual quota at one-sixth or one-seventh of 1 percent of the 1950 population, revised preference classes, granting of visa petitions in the order in which received, exclusion for adherence to totalitarian forms of government, creation and reallocation of a "quota reserve" from unused quota numbers, waiver of certain inspection and examination requirements for aliens in transit through the United States, formation of a Skilled Specialists Selection Board, elimination of the designation of race and ethnic classification on visa applications and alien registration, and much else.

Representative of this group was a bill introduced by Walter of Pennsylvania on April 13, 1961.[80] Principal purposes of the bill, duplicated in many of the others, were stated by its author as follows:

1. reuniting of families to be facilitated by means of a quota reserve of unused quota numbers from the preceding year, available to relatives of citizens and resident aliens from countries having quotas of less than 7,000 annually;

2. permanent codification of laws relating to admission of adopted alien children;

3. waiver of inadmissibility because of tuberculosis for relatives of citizens and resident aliens;

4. establishment of an interdepartmental Skilled Specialists Selection Board to facilitate the entry of highly skilled immigrants;

5. improved procedures and amended laws to facilitate the deportation of racketeers, subversives, and aliens who have evaded the immigration laws by fraud.

Neither this nor the other similar bills were acted on during the session.

Several of the bills noted above included sections on revision of the

[79]H.R. 428, Keogh (N.Y.); H.R. 607, Anfuso (N.Y.); H.R. 662, Gilbert (N.Y.).

[80]H.R. 6300; its Senate counterpart was S. 1809, Dirksen (Ill.).

quota formula and the allocation of visas under the quota. There were in addition a number of other bills, a dozen or so in number, primarily concerned with revision of the quota system. Among them were five bills[81] whose purpose was quite fully set forth in the long title "To amend the Immigration and Nationality Act so as to provide that the base year for determining any quota shall be 1950, to provide that the unused annual quota of any quota area be made available for use in quota areas where the annual quota is oversubscribed. . . ." These duplicate bills also provided for the paroling in annually of no more than 60,000 aliens from Communist countries or the Middle East if refugees because of race, religion, or political opinion; the granting of nonquota status to eligible aliens on consular waiting lists since December 31, 1955; the transfer of unmarried brothers and sisters of citizens from the fourth to the second preference category; and their replacement by married brothers and sisters in the fourth preference category.

Two bills were identified as being "To amend the Immigration and Nationality Act so as to modernize and liberalize the quota system and provide for the admission of persecuted peoples."[82] Another pair of bills (H.R. 117, O'Neill [Mass.]; H.R. 1160, Glenn [N.J.]) was limited to setting up a quota pool from unused quota numbers for allocation to countries with quotas of less than 7,000 and oversubscribed, but with certain limitations, including a ceiling of 7,000 on the total of the national quota plus the allocation from the pool. And reintroduced from preceding Congresses were bills to preserve the priority of aliens on quota application lists and to assign a separate quota to any territory over which the United States has jurisdiction by treaty.[83]

Another group of bills, half a dozen in number, were to extend the terminal date or make permanent the adopted orphan legislation.[84] And

[81]H.R. 37, Santangelo (N.Y.); H.R. 5201, Giaimo (Conn.); H.R. 5514, Addonizio (N.J.); H.R. 5759, Libonati (Ill.); H.R. 5779, Fulton (Pa.).

[82]H.R. 7987, Lindsay (N.Y.); H.R. 8397, Conte (Mass.). These identical bills called for a total quota of one-sixth of 1 percent of the population of 1960, that aliens of the refugee class admitted under several acts no longer be charged to quotas, that unused quota numbers be put into a quota pool for reallocation, that the Attorney General be authorized to parole in not more than 10,000 members of designated classes of refugees annually with the privilege for them of adjustment of status at the end of two years under certain conditions of good behavior and official approval, that provision of 20,000 nonquota visas be made annually for certain other classes of refugees, and that information on race and ethnic classification be eliminated from the visa application and alien registration forms.

[83]H.R. 785, Multer (N.Y.); S. 1157, Long (Hawaii), Gruening (Alaska).

[84]S. 583, Wiley (Wis.), Javits (N.Y.), Keating (N.Y.); S. 1766, Neuberger (Oreg.); S. 2168, Keating (N.Y.); S. 2237, Pastore (R.I.), Dirksen (Ill.), Keating (N.Y.), Javits (N.Y.); H.R. 561, Rodino (N.J.); H.R. 7910, Conte (Mass.).

on July 12, 1961 the Senate attached an amendment to the unrelated Cultural Exchange bill (S. 1154, Fulbright [Ark.]) to extend the orphan legislation for two years. Of this group, the one to receive active legislative attention was the Pastore bill to provide nonquota immigrant visas for eligible orphans under fourteen years of age, with a limit of two such adoptions per family "unless necessary to prevent the separation of brothers or sisters."[85] Reported out in the Senate (S. Rept. 646), amended, and passed, the bill went to the House committee, which struck out the whole bill and inserted a lengthy new draft in twenty-five sections that included the orphans provision but also a number of other matters on the docket of the House committee. The multiple purposes of the bill, as stated in the committee report (H. Rept. 1086, Aug. 30, 1961), were to codify and make permanent the law for the admission of adopted children, to provide a single statutory form of judicial review of orders of deportation, to omit information on race and ethnic origin from the visa application, to ensure a minimum quota of 100 for newly independent nations, to strengthen existing law against the fraudulent gaining of nonquota status by marriage, to leave to the Public Health Service the determination of what diseases are dangerous and contagious to constitute grounds for exclusion, and various additional provisions concerned with nationality and naturalization. Passed by the House, the bill went to a conference committee which rewrote the bill (H. Rept. 1172, Sept. 12, 1961), keeping the main substance of the House draft. Accepted by Senate and House, this became the Act of September 26, 1961 (75 Stat. 650).

Another area of active interest during the first session of the 87th Congress was refugee legislation, especially stimulated by a letter of July 21, 1961 from President Kennedy to Speaker of the House Rayburn; and the letter accompanied the draft of a bill submitted to Congress. This administration bill was introduced at the same time by Walter of Pennsylvania (H.R. 8291). The purpose of the bill as stated in the presidential letter was to authorize continued support for international organizations and efforts for the aid of refugees and for assisting the refugees coming from Cuba. The House committee received the bill and reported it out with amendment (H. Rept. 1066, Aug. 29, 1961). The amendment consisted of the substitution of a completely new draft, which nevertheless kept to the original purposes of authorizing cooperation in existing programs for the aid of refugees and also authorizing the appropriation of funds for the above purpose and for the aid of Western Hemisphere

[85]In a separate action the Senate on July 12 attached an amendment proposed by Keating (N.Y.) and Neuberger (Oreg.), on extension of the adopted orphan legislation by two years, to the unrelated Fulbright Cultural Exchange bill (S. 1154). After lengthy debate the Senate passed the similar House bill, H.R. 8666, in lieu of its own bill.

refugees. As so amended the bill was passed by the House on September 6 and was later reported out with amendment by the Senate committee (S. Rept. 989, Sept. 12, 1961). The principal Senate committee amendments consisted of authorizing aid to Cuban refugees rather than more broadly to Western Hemisphere refugees, authorizing aid to Cuban refugees already admitted for permanent residence, broadening the definition of escapee and the types of aid available to them, and making certain other changes concerning the administration of the act. Passed by the Senate on September 15, the bill as amended was not accepted by the House, nor did the House appoint conferees. Therefore, the bill carried over to the next session.

Several other refugee bills appeared during the session. Ford of Michigan reoffered his bill for the relief of distressed Indonesian refugees in the Netherlands (H.R. 3978; see also his H.R. 9455 [86-II]). Fulbright of Arkansas was author of a bill to make funds available for the aid of refugees, including the support of work of the United Nations High Commissioner for Refugees (S. 2351). Other bills were to make Cuban refugees eligible for adjustment of status and to make nonquota immigrant visas available to certain refugees (S. 552, Keating [N.Y.] and five others; S. 2637, Javits [N.Y.]).

Another perennial subject of new bills was the reuniting of families by means of facilitated entry of certain relatives; and a few such bills appeared during the session. One such was to give nonquota status to immediate relatives of citizens.[86] Another was to make the unused quota numbers of one year available for the preference classes within the same broad geographical area in the following year.[87] A third was to grant nonquota status to aliens in one of the preference classes by reason of relationship and having been on a consular waiting list prior to December 31, 1954, with the same status to apply to spouse and children of the qualifying aliens (H.R. 8736, Pirnie [N.Y.]). Of another sort was a bill against the acquisition of nonquota status by reason of a fraudulent marriage (H.R. 5097, Moorehead [Ohio]; similar to H.R. 12786, Henderson [Ohio] [86-II]).

Other bills dealt with the admission of certain special classes of aliens. Several concerned the waiver of tuberculosis as reason for exclusion in the case of close relatives.[88] Attached to the Cultural Exchange bill (H.R. 8666, Hays [Ohio]) that was enacted as the Act of September

[86]H.R. 520, Osmers (N.J.). The relatives concerned were mothers, fathers, brothers, sisters, sons, and daughters.

[87]H.R. 5705, Fogarty (R.I.). The areas were Europe, Africa, Asia, and Oceania.

[88]S. 2437, Long (Hawaii) and two others; S.J. Res. 103, Dirksen (Ill.); H.R. 192, Walter (Pa.). Note the related provision in the Act of September 26, 1961, passed later in the session.

21, 1961 (75 Stat. 527) was a provision, contained in both House and Senate drafts of the bill, for creation of a new nonimmigrant class for aliens, together with their spouses and children, who are admitted temporarily as participants in a cultural program within the terms of the act. Powell of New York reintroduced bills to give natives of certain British possessions in the Caribbean area unlimited access to the British quota and, separately, to give them nonquota status.[89] Two bills were to provide nonquota status during a two-year period for the unmarried children of certain former members of the Armed Forces or of the Philippine Scouts (H.R. 2069, 2293, Shelley [Calif.]). And to facilitate immigration from Italy were bills to admit 50,000 and to increase the Italian quota (H.R. 118, O'Neill [Mass.]; H.R. 3426, Barrett [Pa.]).

Finally, there were a few bills concerning aliens within the United States. House and Senate bills continued the effort to secure new legislation on the judicial review of orders of deportation (S. 2212, Ervin [N.C.]; H.R. 187, Walter [Pa.]), a matter taken care of late in the session with passage of the above-mentioned Act of September 26, 1961 (75 Stat. 650). There was a proposal for exclusion or deportation of any alien convicted of violation of any law relating to illicit possession of marihuana (H.R. 2787, Poff [Va.]). A Senate bill was to authorize the Secretary of Commerce to employ aliens in scientific or technical capacities (S. 2236, Magnuson [Wash.]), and another Senate bill proposed to authorize the Federal Communications Commission to issue to aliens licenses for the operation of amateur radio stations, good for a period not to exceed three years, on finding by the commission that the national security would not be endangered (S. 2361, Goldwater [Ariz.]; Schoeppel [Kans.]). And a bill, introduced by Walter of Pennsylvania (H.R. 181), provided that in peacetime no volunteer is to be accepted in the army or air force unless a citizen or an alien admitted for permanent residence. It was approved by both House and Senate committees (H. Rept. 582; S. Rept. 657), and became the Act of August 17, 1961 (75 Stat. 364).

The principal legislative product of the session was thus the Act of September 26, 1961 (75 Stat. 650), the omnibus product of the House committee, which dealt with a number of specific points of immigration law that had come to the attention of the committee. It was, however, far from satisfying to those who had long urged basic revision of immigration law and policy as set by the 1952 Act.

The second session of the 87th Congress, from January 10 to October 13, 1962, saw continued efforts for amendment of the McCarran-Walter Act and for liberalization of immigration policy, especially for change in

[89]H.R. 543, 549; see his H.R. 6589, 6609 (86-I).

the quota system of regulating immigration. In spite of the large number of bills carried over from the first session, a number of new bills for amendment of the 1952 Act were introduced. Prominent among them was a Senate bill from Hart of Michigan,[90] one of the Senate leaders in the effort for amendment of the 1952 Act; and a dozen or more counterparts of his bill were introduced in the House. The principal features of the Hart bill were the provision of 250,000 quota visas each year, of which 50,000 were designated for refugees; allocation of 80,000 of the other visas to countries in proportion to their population size but with a limit of 3,000 each; allocation of the remaining 120,000 visas to countries in proportion to the average quota and nonquota immigration from them over the past fifteen years; a maximum total national quota of 25,000 but otherwise no smaller national quotas than prevailed before; aliens eligible to visas either on the basis of country of birth or country of citizenship if of ten years' residence or more; and unused quota numbers of one year, up to a maximum of 100,000 annually, to be assigned in the following year to countries of oversubscribed quotas, not to exceed the annual quota of each such country. The bill also provided that national quotas were to be revised every five years, that 60 percent of the quota go to relatives, that the remaining 40 percent be for "new seed" immigrants, and that immigrants from the Western Hemisphere and immigrants with special skills be free of quota limitation. The bill without explicitly doing so also eliminated the Asia-Pacific triangle limitation of immigration. It was not brought to a vote in the Senate, nor were any of its counterparts in the House, but it received sufficient support within Congress and from outside for its chief sponsor to promise to reenter it in the next Congress.

Introduced a few days before the Hart bill was another Senate bill (S. 3028, Pell [R.I.], March 19, 1962) similar in many of its provisions. It differed principally in that persons with special skills, instead of being quota-free, were assigned 10,000 visa numbers, and the allocation to refugees was reduced by that amount.

Other bills deal with amendment of designated sections of the 1952 Act. A Senate bill (S. 3002, Dodd [Conn.]) was for the computation of quotas on the basis of the 1960 population instead of that for 1920 and to reassign unused quota numbers. A House bill (H.R. 11219, Geo. Miller [Calif.]) was to omit epilepsy from the grounds for exclusion, and another was to increase the fees charged for certain applications and petitions.[91] Walter of Pennsylvania introduced several bills concerned largely with

[90]S. 3043, March 21, 1962. It was sponsored by ten Democrat and three Republican senators, and the support later grew to twenty-five senators.

[91]H.R. 12304, Celler (N.Y.). The fee for filing an application for suspension of deportation, for example, was to be increased from $25 to $34.

administration of certain sections of the 1952 Act. One of these dealt with procedures in deportation cases (H.R. 12829), and two sought to abolish the Bureau of Security and Consular Affairs in the Department of State and to distribute its units including the visa office elsewhere within the Department (H.R. 9904, 10079). The second of these two bills was reported out (H. Rept. 1369, Feb. 20, 1962) by Walter's committee; and in addition to reorganization within the Department of State it provided for financial aid to Cuban refugees and for continued support of certain other refugee activities. Passed by the House, the bill did not progress in the Senate.

Active interest in refugee legislation continued, with support from the administration. Five Senators entered a resolution to express concern over the Chinese refugee problem and made specific proposals for a conference to seek collective action, the admission of up to 5,000 Chinese refugees, and other forms of aid.[92] And two resolutions calling for studies of certain problems were introduced by Eastland of Mississippi, chairman of the Senate Judiciary Committee (S. Res. 263, 293). One was for a general study of matters pertaining to immigration and naturalization, the other to investigate problems resulting from the "flow of escapees and refugees from communistic tyranny." Both were reported out (S. Rept. 1144, 1216) and passed by the Senate.[93]

In more positive action a conference committee on the Walter bill passed by both House and Senate in the preceding session (H.R. 8291 [87-I]) was at last convened, and issued its report on June 26, 1962 (H. Rept. 1293, June 26, 1962). Adopted by both House and Senate on the following day, it received presidential signature to become the Act of June 28, 1962 (76 Stat. 121). Entitled the Migration and Refugee Assistance Act of 1962, it provided for continued support for various international programs in aid of refugees, as in the original Walter bill. With regard to the Bureau of Security and Consular Affairs, which Walter's bills had sought to abolish, it merely stipulated that the Administrator of the Bureau be a presidential appointee with the advice and consent of the Senate.

One other refugee bill, introduced early in the session, was to make Cuban refugees eligible for adjustment of status (H.R. 9639, Barry [N.Y.]). It remained in committee to the end of the session and the Congress.

[92]S. Res. 346, Dodd (Conn.), Humphrey (Minn.), Douglas (Ill.), Engle (Calif.), Mundt (S.D.).

[93]Whatever the eventual findings, the immediate effect of such investigations presumably would be to delay legislative action.

Other efforts for change in the immigration laws were directed toward the quota system and the admission of relatives. Family reunion was to be facilitated by several bills, of which three would give nonquota status to aliens eligible for certain quota preferences.[94] Additional bills were to give nonquota status to certain alien relatives entitled to fourth preference and whose visa petitions were prior to a specified date.[95] And two bills (H.R. 12013, Shelley [Calif.]; H.R. 12172, Farbstein [N.Y.]) provided for the issuance of nonquota visas to aliens residing in Hong Kong, on a consular waiting list and eligible for second, third, or fourth preference. Limits of 25,000 and 50,000 were put on the number of such visas to be issued, and a time limit of two years. Two other bills proposed that unused quota numbers be made available to oversubscribed areas for the admission of brothers, sisters, and married children of citizens (H.R. 11571, Lane [Mass.]; H.R. 12028, Farbstein [N.Y.]).

There were also bills for revision of the quota system without reference to relatives. An attempt was made to increase the minimum quota for any area from 200 to 250 annually (S. 3104, Dodd [Conn.]); and Judd of Minnesota tried again to have areas under the jurisdiction of the United States by treaty dealt with as separate quota areas (H.R. 11473).

A movement to encourage the immigration of aliens with special skills developed quite suddenly during the second session of the 87th Congress. Approximately sixteen bills to facilitate the entry of "alien skilled specialists" were introduced at the time, regularly carrying additional provision for the admission of relatives of citizens. Of these, the ones to receive particular attention were a Senate bill from Pastore of Rhode Island and an identical bill from Walter of Pennsylvania (S. 3361, May 29, 1962; H.R. 11911, May 24, 1962). Short bills in four sections, they provided (1) nonquota immigrant visas for aliens eligible for fourth preference (i.e., brothers, sisters, children of citizens), registered on a consular waiting list prior to December 31, 1954, and with a visa petition approved by the Attorney General prior to January 1, 1962, and also for spouses and children of such aliens; (2) nonquota status accorded to first preference aliens (i.e., aliens with special skills), together with their spouses and children, if in possession of a petition approved prior to

[94]H.R. 9493, Barrett (Pa.); H.R. 10093, Glenn (N.Y.); H.R. 11570, Lane (Mass.). The bills applied to the second, third, and fourth preference classes, of which the second and fourth were for relatives.

[95]S. 3150, Dodd (Conn.); H.R. 11756, Lindsay (N.Y.); H.R. 11885, Monagan (Conn.). The Dodd and Monagan bills concerned brothers, sisters, and married children of citizens; the Lindsay bill covered all fourth preference cases on a consular waiting list prior to December 31, 1955 and eligible for fourth preference status under a petition approved prior to January 1, 1962.

April 1, 1962; (3) semimonthly report to Congress from the Attorney General of first preference petitions approved; and (4) a record of lawful entry available to aliens who entered prior to December 24, 1952.[96] The Pastore bill was reported out by the Senate committee (S. Rept. 2276, Oct. 4, 1962), unchanged except for amendment of the cutoff dates for the fourth preference cases that was estimated to reduce the number of eligible aliens from 65,000 to 16,000.[97] As so amended, the bill was passed by the Senate on the next day, October 5; and with unusually prompt action the House considered the bill, amended it, and passed it on the same day. The House amendments were to eliminate the advanced date for creation of a record of lawful entry and to add a new section to create a new Bureau of Consular Affairs in the Department of State. The conference report (H. Rept. 2552, Oct. 11, 1962) left the first three sections and provisions of the bill intact, eliminated the House provision for the Bureau, and in a rewritten and enlarged fourth section dropped the new cutoff date for eligibility for creation of a record of lawful entry and substituted provision for suspension of deportation with approval by the Attorney General and Congress in the case of aliens who have been physically present for at least seven years in some cases, ten years in others. With acceptance by Congress and presidential signature, the conference draft became the Act of October 24, 1962 (76 Stat. 1247).

Two bills (S. 2956, Javits [N.Y.]; H.R. 10711, Lindsay [N.Y.]), one each in Senate and House, had sought to facilitate the entry of aliens with special skills by granting nonquota status to those in the first preference class, as in the Pastore bill, but without accompanying provision for relatives. No action was taken on them, since the Pastore bill dealt with the matter. Concerned with the utilization of the skills of aliens already in the United States was a bill, like others in earlier sessions, to authorize the Secretary of the Interior to employ aliens in scientific and technical capacities (S. 3344, Anderson [N.Mex.]).

The only other immigration bill of the session to be noted was to prohibit the deportation of any alien who entered the United States, lawfully admitted for permanent residence, before the age of fourteen and has had a continuous residence of at least ten years thereafter (H.R. 12421, Santangelo [N.Y.]). It was not acted on by the House committee. The second session and the 87th Congress thus ended, having accomplished only several amendments of the McCarran-Walter Act, in spite of the considerable pressures for fundamental changes in the act. In what

[96]Amending section 249 of the 1952 Act, to change the date from June 28, 1940.

[97]Greeks, Italians, and Portuguese were expected to be the principal beneficiaries.

was perhaps a concession to the forces for change, Chairman Walter of the House subcommittee had announced in the House on June 27, 1962, the tenth anniversary of the McCarran-Walter Act, that the staff of the subcommittee would undertake a study "in depth" of the problems of immigration and refugees. It remained to be seen, however, whether this action was in fact a concession or a delaying tactic.

88th Congress (1963, 1964)

The 88th Congress convened on January 9, 1963, for a first session that was to last until December 30; like its predecessor it was a Democratic Congress with a Democratic President. And as in the preceding Congress the major order of business regarding immigration was for major change of policy as represented by the McCarran-Walter Act of 1952. Strong support came from the administration, for President Kennedy when in the Senate had been active in efforts to change the 1952 Act. Early in the session at a press conference on January 24, 1963 Kennedy stated that the administration was giving attention to immigration questions and would present proposals for the redistribution of unused quotas.

Beginning early in the session there came a flood of bills for amendment of the 1952 Act, of which the prototypes were counterpart bills in House and Senate introduced by Multer of New York and Hart of Michigan.[98] During the next several months the number of such bills grew to at least thirty-one, twenty-nine of which were in the House and duplicates of or close to the prototypes.

The Hart bill, introduced on February 7, had the bipartisan sponsorship of thirty-four other Senators, of whom six were Republicans, and can be taken as representative of the whole group of bills. Very little different from the Hart bill of the preceding Congress, supported by twenty-four members of the Senate (S. 3043 [87-II]), it was described by its introducer as a

> reform bill . . . not a radical proposal designed to flood this country with immigration or an irresponsible measure to negate the gains achieved under the Act of 1952. It replaces only the quota provisions of the Act of 1952.

Its principal provisions were the following:

1. to give nonquota status to alien parents of citizens, to natives of newly independent islands adjoining Central or South America, and to

[98]H.R. 552, Multer (N.Y.), Jan. 9, 1963; S. 747, Hart (Mich.), Feb. 7, 1963.

immigrants whose services are determined by the Secretary of Labor to be needed because of "high education, technical training, specialized experience, or exceptional ability";

2. to set an annual limit of 250,000 quota immigrant visas, of which 50,000 are to be available without regard to quota area to designated categories of refugees together with their spouse and children; 80,000 are to be allocated among quota areas in proportion to their fraction of the world population, exclusive of that of the Western Hemisphere, but with a maximum such quota of 3,000 for each area; and the remaining 120,000 visas are to be divided among the separate quota areas in proportion to their quota and nonquota immigration to the United States during the preceding fifteen years but with maximum and minimum quotas for each area of 25,000 and 200, respectively;

3. to assign unused visas not in excess of 100,000 per annum available in the following year to oversubscribed quota areas, the distribution to be in proportion to the size of the waiting lists of the various such areas;

4. to charge an immigrant to the quota of his area of birth or his area of citizenship, if domiciled there for at least ten years immediately preceding his application, or to the quota of the governing country in the case of a dependent area;

5. to review and, if necessary, revise area quotas after each period of five years;

6. to allot the first 60 percent of any area's quota, plus any unused quota numbers, to the spouse, child, or parent of aliens lawfully admitted for permanent residence, with any unused portion of the above to go to qualified immigrants who are blood relatives of citizens and lawfully admitted aliens within the third degree of consanguinity, together with spouses and children;

7. to make available to any other qualified immigrants the remaining 40 percent plus any unused portion;

8. to issue quota immigrant visas strictly in chronological order of the registration of applicants for admission.

The Multer bill and other House bills followed the same pattern,[99] but there was some diversity among the Senate bills for amendment of the 1952 Act. A Senate bill (S. 751, Feb. 7, 1963) introduced by Pell of Rhode Island was the same as his bill of the preceding Congress (S. 3028 [87-II]; see previous description); it provided for the same amount of

[99]The Celler bill (H.R. 3926) and its counterparts adopted the four preference classes, entitled Family Unification, Occupational, Refugee Asylum, and Resettlement, contained in earlier bills from the "liberal" group in Congress.

immigration under numerical limitation but differed in the details of allocation of quota and nonquota status, national quotas, and quota preference. Also different was the Senate bill introduced by Javits of New York on behalf of himself and five cosponsors.[100] In addition to a number of specific changes in the form of rewording of sections of the 1952 Act dealing with exclusion, deportation, and administrative procedure under the act, the bill provided for shifting the base year for the computation of quotas from 1920 to 1960, reallocation of unused quota numbers, giving of nonquota status to fourth preference classes (alien brothers, sisters, sons, and daughters of citizens) if in possession of a petition for admission approved prior to January 1, 1963, elimination of certain charges of admissions against national quotas, a time limit of ten years on deportability for offenses, and the establishment of a Board of Visa Appeals in the Department of State.

Senate hearings on the Hart bill were expected, and meanwhile the House subcommittee continued to hold hearings and assemble testimony in its wide-ranging inquiry into "population and immigration." No further action was taken, however, and none of the above-mentioned bills for amendment of the 1952 Act was reported out.

Later events combined to accelerate progress toward the long-delayed and long-urged revision of immigration policy. Walter of Pennsylvania, coauthor of the 1952 Act, chairman of the House subcommittee, and long-time defender of the status quo, died on May 31, only a few days after his sixty-ninth birthday.[101] And on July 23 President Kennedy sent a message[102] to Congress on immigration, a message that had been under preparation for some time and that recommended far-reaching revision of the quota system. Stating that the national origins quota system was in most urgent need of reform, the message recommended that quotas be based not on birthplace but on (1) the skills of immigrants and the relation of these skills to national needs; (2) family relationships; and (3) priority of registration for the immigrant visa. More specific proposals were for the gradual elimination of the old national quotas over a five-year period, a limit of not more than 10 percent of the quota total to any one country, authority for the President under advisement to have a reserve of one-half of the total quota for issuance to aliens disadvantaged by the change, plus up to 20 percent of the unallocated quota for emer-

[100]S. 1823, July 2, 1963. All sponsors were Republicans except Morse of Oregon.

[101]He was succeeded as chairman of the subcommitee by Feighan of Ohio, whose views on immigration may not have been greatly different but who was not as able to exercise the de facto veto power over new legislation possessed by his predecessor.

[102]The message was in the form of a letter to the President of the Senate and the Speaker of the House. It accompanied and explained the administration's immigration bill.

gency cases such as refugees. The Asia-Pacific triangle, consisting of "all countries from Pakistan to Japan and the Pacific islands north of Australia and New Zealand," should no longer be discriminated against by quota allocation on the basis of ancestry, but be treated like other countries. Modification of the preference structure was also recommended with change of alien parents of citizens from a preference class to nonquota status and the parents of resident aliens changed from nonpreference to a preference class to be set up after other relatives and skilled immigrants; the granting of preference to skilled immigrants without requirement that they have assurance of employment as a condition for admission; and also the creation of a preference class for immigrants of lesser skills "who can fill specific needs in short supply in this country." Another needed change enumerated in the message was nonquota status for natives of newly independent Jamaica, Trinidad, and Tobago to conform with the treatment of other Western Hemisphere nations. And it was urged that aliens with mental problems be made admissible if certain standards can be met rather than having to seek admission by private bill even though there is a family waiting to receive and care for them.

On the day of the presidential message Celler of New York, chairman of the House Judiciary Committee, introduced a bill (H.R. 7700, July 23, 1963) embodying the administration proposals. A counterpart bill (S. 1932, July 24, 1963) was introduced in the Senate on the following day by Hart of Michigan with twenty-six other sponsors, including members of both political parties. Fifty-one counterpart bills soon appeared in the House. The principal features of the Hart and Celler bills followed the guidelines set by the presidential recommendations, as follows:

1. a five-year period of transition from the national origins quotas to the new system of quota allocation, with the numbers progressively deducted from the former national origins quotas to go into a quota reserve for allocation without regard for national origin to aliens from oversubscribed areas and to other admissible aliens, but with the proviso that no quota area shall receive more than 10 percent of the total available in any one year;

2. allocation of the quota reserve and unused quota numbers from the preceding year according to the preference classes set by the 1952 Act and within preference class according to chronological order of registration;

3. authorization for the President after consultation with the Immigration Board established under the act to reserve up to one-half of the quota reserve for admissible aliens who suffer hardship by reason of the reduction of the old quotas or whose admission is in the interest of the national security; and similar authorization for the allocation of up to

20 percent of the quota reserve to admissible aliens in the refugee category;

4. charging of immigrants born in a colony or dependency to the quota of the governing country, under certain numerical limits;

5. improvement of quota and preference status for certain relatives and for "qualified quota immigrants capable of performing specified functions for which a shortage of employable and willing persons exists";

6. elimination of epilepsy as ground for exclusion, and also tuberculosis and mental ailments in the case of certain relatives and under appropriate controls;

7. establishment of an Immigration Board for promulgation of regulations, continuous study of immigration, and advice to the President and members of the administration;

8. elimination of the Asia-Pacific triangle provisions of the 1952 Act;

9. accordance of nonquota status to natives of newly independent nations of the Western Hemisphere;

10. elimination of requirement of aliens with special skills to have assurance of employment as a condition for admission.

Additional sponsors came forward to endorse the administration bill, and support came from many sources outside Congress. Hearings were in prospect, but then the assassination of President Kennedy late in the session removed one of the strongest supporters of the new legislation and led to a period of legislative uncertainty. President Johnson, who succeeded to the office, declared his intention of carrying on the policies of the Kennedy administration; but none of the bills that would have given a new direction to American immigration policy came out of committee during the first session. They carried over to the second session of the 88th Congress.

Various bills for amendment of one or another section of the 1952 Act were introduced but made no progress. The old liberal bill from previous Congresses reappeared with new proposers.[103] There were two bills to eliminate epilepsy as a cause for exclusion (S. 2001, McCarthy [Minn.]; H.R. 2896, Miller [Calif.]), one to give nonquota status to aliens who have been members of a religious order for at least two years and who seek entry to teach in a school of the order (H.R. 2602, Joelson [N.J.]), and others to broaden the terms under which the Attorney General is authorized to permit certain nonimmigrants to remain (S. 1887, Allott [Colo.]; H.R. 7919, Anderson [Ill.]). Two bills were to authorize and encourage the admission as immigrants of defecting members of the

[103] H.R. 4159, Derwinski (Ill.); H.R. 7941, Barry (N.Y.); H.R. 188, Gilbert (N.Y.).

Soviet armed forces serving in Cuba (H.R. 3966, Marsh [Va.]; H.R. 4435, Derwinski [Ill.]), and there were three to further define the special powers of the President by proclamation to restrict or prohibit departure and entry.[104]

There was also the usual distribution of bills dealing with one or another point of immigration law. Most numerous of these were bills concerned with some particular aspect of the quota system. Three were to carry over unused quota numbers to the next fiscal year,[105] and two were to move forward the base year for the computation of quotas from 1920 to 1960 (H.R. 44, Boland [Mass.]; H.R. 3402, Mrs. Kelly [N.Y.]). Other familiar topics were proposals to preserve priority of place for aliens on quota waiting lists (H.R. 540 by Multer of New York), and to make every area over which the United States has treaty jurisdiction a separate quota area (S. 612 by Inouye of Hawaii). Related to the latter were bills to treat the Ryukyu Islands and the Tonga Islands as separate quota areas, S. 588 and 589 by Fong of Hawaii.

Many of the earlier-mentioned bills for the extensive revision of the 1952 Act provided quota preference or nonquota status for relatives of citizens and resident aliens. Other bills dealt only with this facilitation of the uniting of families, the relationships concerned being as a rule parents, brothers and sisters, children, and the spouses and children of such relatives.[106] There were in addition two bills to provide up to 1,500 nonquota immigrant visas per annum over a five-year period for alien children of World War I veterans of the United States Armed Forces, H.R. 6507 and 6931 by Libonati (Ill.).

Another small group of bills resumed the effort to secure a statute of limitations on deportation. Three bills were to set a time limit of five years, after the commission of a deportable act, for the initiation of deportation proceedings or the revocation of citizenship.[107] Approximately the same group of Congressmen introduced bills to prohibit deportation of any alien admitted for permanent residence prior to his fourteenth birthday or of any alien who has resided in the United States continuously for ten years or more following his admission.[108]

Only a few other bills on scattered topics remain to be noted for the

[104]H.R. 5320, Cramer (Fla.); H.R. 9045, Willis (La.); H.R. 9441, Johansen (Mich.).

[105]H.R. 1106, Philbin (Mass.); H.R. 2129, Glenn (N.J.); H.R. 3403, Mrs. Kelly (N.Y.).

[106]H.R. 1103, Osmers (N.J.); H.R. 2130, Glenn (N.J.); H.R. 3763, 5767, Barrett (Pa.); H.R. 8005, Reid (N.Y.).

[107]S. 1500, Morse (Oreg.); H.R. 6831, Matsunaga (Hawaii); H.R. 6832, Gill (Hawaii). See also S. 1641, Pell (R.I.) and Hart (Mich.).

[108]S. 1501, Morse (Oreg.) and Hart (Mich.); H.R. 6833, Matsunaga (Hawaii); H.R. 6834, Gill (Hawaii); H.R. 6859, Brown (Calif.).

session. A bill to grant nonquota status to any immigrant born in an independent country of the Western Hemisphere was designed by Celler (N.Y.) to include the recently independent nations of the West Indies (H.R. 6238). Bills by Cederberg (Mich.) and Brown (Calif.) related to the licensing and employment of aliens were to permit certain aliens to operate amateur radio stations (H.R. 750 and H.R. 9035) and to be employed in a scientific or technical capacity by the Secretary of Commerce.[109] Reaching back to nineteenth-century legislation still on the statute books, five bills called for repeal of the "cooly trade" laws.[110]

A Senate bill was designed to provide a statute of limitations with regard to the period of time after admission for deportation of aliens lawfully admitted for permanent residence and to eliminate certain distinctions made in the 1952 Act between native-born and naturalized citizens (S. 1641, Pell [R.I.], and Hart [Mich.]). And an effort was made to put pressure on foreign governments in two bills to stop the issuance of immigration visas in any country that refuses to accept back a deported alien or to allow extradition of an alien criminal.[111]

The drive for revision of the McCarran-Walter Act and in particular for doing away with the national origins quota system continued and intensified in the second session of the 88th Congress. Congress reconvened on January 7, 1964 for a session that was to last until early October, and the following day it received from President Johnson a state of the union message that included the following reference to immigration policy:

> We must also lift by legislation the bars of discrimination against those who seek entry into our country, particularly those with much-needed skills and those joining their families. In establishing preferences, a nation that was built by the immigrants of all lands can ask those who now seek admission: "What can you do for our country?" But we should not be asking: "In what country were you born?"

The latter sentence clearly follows a turn of phrase used by the late President Kennedy in his inaugural address of just three years before.

The presidential initiative continued in a January 13–14 White House conference on immigration, a two-day meeting that brought together members of the related Senate and House subcommittees, several

[109] S. 1291, Magnuson (Wash.); H.R. 5029, Harris (Ark.). The former was reported out (S. Rept. 335) and passed by the Senate.

[110] S. 1871, Engle (Calif.); H.R. 7557, Corman (Calif.); H.R. 7562, McFall (Calif.); H.R. 7564, Matsunaga (Hawaii); H.R. 7565, Moss (Calif.).

[111] H.R. 962, Walter (Pa.); H.R. 1654, Johansen (Mich.). The Walter bill was introduced Jan. 9, 1963.

officials from the State Department and the Department of Justice, and representatives of a number of private organizations concerned with immigration policy. In his opening statement to the conference President Johnson spoke of the need for "a fair immigration law," endorsed the administration bill before Congress, and stressed the desirability of changing the basis of admission from national origin to the training and qualifications of the immigrant. Subsequently, the President found repeated opportunities to reaffirm his support of new legislation, as at an April 22 conference of editors and broadcasters, where he stated that "The immigration bill is very high on our priority list" and expressed the hope that it would be passed during the present session of Congress, and again at a White House meeting of representatives of the Italian-American community on September 18.

Revision of the immigration laws was high on the agenda of the new session of Congress. In addition to the large number carried over from the first session, seventeen or more bills for amendment of the 1952 Act were introduced during the second session. Several were to amend specific sections and provisions of the act, but the majority were for more drastic revision and for elimination of the national origin basis for the selection of immigrants after the pattern of the first session bills incorporating the Kennedy proposals.[112] With these additions the number of such bills before Congress approached sixty.

In spite of the pressures for action, the legislative machinery continued to move exceedingly slowly. The Senate and House subcommittees, under the chairmanship of Eastland[113] of Mississippi and Feighan of Ohio, continued to conduct public hearings on the bills before them, which went on and on without visible end to the number of witnesses called to testify. The legislative picture was further complicated when on August 10, 1964 Feighan of the House subcommittee introduced a bill (H.R. 12305) entitled "To create a selective immigration board and to provide for the allocation of authorized but unused quota numbers . . . ," an additional measure for his subcommittee to consider and one that would set up a temporary advisory group to make recommendations to Congress up to three years later. Principal features of the bill were continuation of the national origins quota system and the present national quotas for the next two years, creation of a temporary Selective Immigration Board to end on October 1, 1967, preparation by the Board for congressional approval of a plan for reallocation of authorized but

[112] Especially S. 1932 and H.R. 7700, and their counterparts.

[113] Senator Edward Kennedy of Massachusetts often chaired the subcommittee.

unused quota numbers for the fiscal years ending June 30, 1964 and 1965, and preference in the allocation of such quota numbers to certain alien relatives of citizens of the United States, aliens whose services are considered to be needed, and certain refugees from Communist oppression.[114]

In a statement to the House two days after the introduction of his new bill,[115] Feighan explained the purpose and terms of the bill and assured the House that "we will continue those hearings until we have heard as many witnesses as time will permit." He also reiterated his plea for funding of the Joint Committee on Immigration Policy, for the reason that "Congress will require studies, investigations, and public hearings in depth to weld an immigration policy." Later, on the final day of the 88th Congress, Feighan reported on the work of his subcommittee, with regret that his immigration bill had not been reported out for House action, and went on to imply that his efforts as subcommittee chairman had been impeded by Chairman Celler of the parent committee, the Judiciary Committee.[116] There were, however, those impatient to get on with what they considered needed reform of the 1952 Act, who felt sure the continued hearings were a delaying tactic, and who suspected the immigration subcommittees were being used deliberately to block new legislation. In any event, no bill for amendment of the 1952 Act came out of either Senate or House committee. A few days after the adjournment of the 88th Congress, President Johnson in Feighan's home town of Cleveland and in his presence was moved, while expressing his regard for the Congressman, to complain that Feighan's committee had done nothing on the administration's immigration bill, and he vowed that the bill would be resubmitted in the new Congress.

There was only a sprinkling of new immigration bills on other topics during the second session of the 88th Congress. In addition to the Feighan bill were three specifically for the reassignment of unused quota numbers.[117] Two Senate bills were to facilitate the entry of skilled

[114]Other provisions were activation of the Senate and House Joint Committee on Immigration and Nationality Policy which Congress had authorized in 1952 but never adequately funded, termination of occupational preference for any occupational category in which over 20 percent of the aliens admitted under that preference had failed to remain in that occupation for at least one year following admission, and termination of the paroling in of Hong Kong refugees from Communist China and refugee-escapees under authority of the Act of July 14, 1960 (74 Stat. 504).

[115]*Congressional Record,* 110:19250–51, August 12, 1964.

[116]Ibid., pp. 24303–4, October 3, 1964.

[117]H.R. 10093, O'Neill (Mass.); H.R. 12576, Derwinski (Ill.); H.R. 12792, Moore (W.Va.).

aliens;[118] and a House bill on a familiar topic was to authorize the Secretary of the Interior to employ aliens in a scientific or technical capacity (H.R. 11203, Aspinall [Colo.]). Another was to grant nonquota status to certain aliens eligible for preference under the 1952 Act (H.R. 10893, Derounian [N.Y.]). Two were for the aid of refugees from Indonesia (S. 3183, Hart [Mich.]; H.R. 12191 Celler [N.Y.], and another was to grant nonquota status to any immigrant from an independent country of the Western Hemisphere (H.R. 9987, Mrs. Kelly [N.Y.]). Like the other immigration bills, none of these was reported out of committee during the final session of the 88th Congress.

89th Congress, First Session (1965)

The 89th Congress convened for its first session on January 4, 1965, in a session that was to continue until October 22 and was at last to bring success in the long-continued struggle to give a new direction to American immigration policy.

Very early in the session, on January 13, Congress received a presidential message on immigration (H. Doc. 52). It expressed the conviction that a change of policy was needed and pointed out that four Presidents in succession had called attention to that need. The message set forth the administration's views on needed amendments to the 1952 Act and described a forthcoming administration bill that would contain the recommended amendments.[119] On the same day Celler of New York introduced the administration bill in the House (H.R. 2580), and two days later Hart of Michigan introduced an identical bill in the Senate for himself and thirty-two other sponsors (S. 500). During the later course of the session no less than seventy bills, whose stated purpose was "to amend the Immigration and Nationality Act," were introduced, all but two in the House and mostly counterparts of the Celler and Hart bills.[120] In addition to the above were a dozen bills for the limited purpose of amending designated sections of the 1952 Act.

Another group of bills involved limited amendment of the 1952 Act by proposing adjustments of the existing quota system. Four of them

[118]S. 3102, Javits (N.Y.); S. 3228, Humphrey (Minn.). The Javits bill also carried provision for reassignment of unused quotas.

[119]For a summary of the presidential recommendations, see below under the account of the administration bill in Congress.

[120]The distribution of the introducers of the seventy bills by state was New York, 16; New Jersey, 13; California, 7; Michigan, 6; Illinois, Massachusetts, and Pennsylvania, 5 each; Connecticut, 3; Maryland and Rhode Island, 2 each; and one each from Arizona, Colorado, Hawaii, Ohio, Oregon, and West Virginia.

provided for the reallocation of unused quota numbers;[121] others proposed preserving the priority of aliens on former waiting lists,[122] giving a separate quota to any country over which the United States has treaty jurisdiction (S. 162 by Inouye of Hawaii), and computing the quotas on the basis of the 1960 census population (H.R. 1049 by Mrs. Kelly of New York).

Another small group of bills concerned alien labor and labor policy. Of a type introduced in earlier Congresses, two bills introduced by Jackson (Wash.) and Aspinall (Colo.) were to authorize the Secretary of the Interior to employ aliens in a scientific or technical capacity (S. 1243, H.R. 5638); two others were to give like authority to the Secretary of Commerce (S. 905, Magnuson [Wash.]; H.R. 4779, Harris [Ark.]). The former was reported out by the Senate committee (S. Rept. 163) and passed the Senate, but it did not receive House action during the session. Three bills provided variously for the temporary admission of agricultural laborers,[123] but another was to prohibit the importation of aliens to perform agricultural labor (H.R. 8313 by Gilbert of New York). And a final bill of this group was to facilitate the entry of alien skilled specialists and their families, S. 894 introduced by Mondale (Minn.).

Another effort continued from previous Congresses was to give designated aliens the protection of a statute of limitation. There was a Senate bill to provide that no alien lawfully admitted for permanent residence shall be deported "by reason of any conduct occurring more than ten years prior to the institution of deportation proceedings against him";[124] and two other bills of similar purpose were introduced (S. 2364, Pell [R.I.]; H.R. 502, Matsunaga [Hawaii]). Still another was to prohibit deportation of any alien admitted for permanent residence prior to his fourteenth birthday or any alien who has a continuous residence of ten years immediately following admission (H.R. 7911, Matsunaga [Hawaii]). Miscellaneous other bills were to repeal the "cooly trade" laws,[125] and make any alien of five years' continuous residence eligible for health insurance benefits for the aged under Title XVIII of the Social Security Act (H.R. 10807, Roybal [Calif.]).

None of these various bills progressed during the session, for the urgent business of both the Senate and House subcommittees on immigration was the administration bill. Both subcommittees began public

[121]H.R. 1048, Mrs. Kelly (N.Y.); H.R. 2078, Philbin (Mass.); H.R. 5793, Moore (W.Va.); H.R. 8339, Derwinski (Ill.).

[122]H.R. 845, Multer (N.Y.); same as his H.R. 540 (88-I).

[123]H.R. 8156, Gubser (Calif.); H.R. 10982, Rogers (Tex.); H.R. 11282, Tupper (Me.).

[124]S. 2546, Morse (Oreg.), Kennedy (Mass.), Long (Mo.), Pell (R.I.).

[125]H.R. 6175, Moss (Calif.); see his H.R. 7565 (88-I) and others in that session.

hearings on the bill, the Senate committee on February 10 under Senator Edward Kennedy[126] as acting chairman, and the House committee on March 3; the hearings continued on through the greater part of the session.

The administration bill, as represented by the Celler and Hart bills in House and Senate, was in twenty sections and consisted entirely of amendments of the 1952 Act. In its major provisions it was essentially the same as its predecessor bill in the 88th Congress; these provisions were change of the basis of admission from the national origin to the personal qualifications of the immigrant according to the preference classes; elimination of the Asia-Pacific triangle provisions of the 1952 Act; a five-year period of transition from the old to the new basis of admission; a limit of 10 percent of the total quota number to any one quota area; a presidential reserve made up of quota numbers deducted progressively from the old quotas and of unused numbers to be reallocated to hardship cases in the transition period; continued nonquota status for persons born in the Western Hemisphere; a 10 percent reserve for refugees from oppression; and establishment of an Immigration Board to advise the President, promulgate regulations, and make studies. Differences from the administration bill of the preceding Congress were principally in designation of the composition of the Immigration Board, reduction of the presidential reserve from 50 to 30 percent, a halving of the presidential reserve limit for refugees, and rewording of an exclusion provision on mental grounds from *feebleminded* to *mentally retarded.*

Circumstances at the time appeared more favorable for passage than ever before for the administration bill and elimination of the almost forty-year-old national origins quota system. President Johnson strongly supported the bill, and as already noted, in part, he took various opportunities to express his convictions on the subject. Another favorable factor was that in the 89th Congress the Democratic party had a two-to-one majority in both Senate and House, and it was the members of that party who had led the attack on the 1952 Act and the national origins quota system in Congress. Testimony received in the public hearings ran strongly in favor of the bill, and in these hearings and by direct communication to the President and members of Congress many religious, ethnic, and labor organizations expressed their support. Lobbying for and against the bill was intensive, but the greater political weight was in its

[126]For an authoritative and eyewitness account of legislative action on the bill, see Edward M. Kennedy, "The Immigration Act of 1965," *Annals of the American Academy of Political and Social Science,* Sept. 1966, 367:137–49.

favor. And Feighan of Ohio, in the strategic position of chairman of the House subcommittee, rightly or wrongly regarded as being a chief stumbling block to the new legislation, had in fact indicated he was willing to eliminate the national origins quota system.[127] Meanwhile, Feighan's committee had been enlarged from five to nine members, the four new members ensuring a firm majority in favor of the administration bill whenever it was brought to a vote in the committee. Altogether, there appeared to be a well-organized campaign for passage of the bill, aided by a favorable majority opinion both within and without Congress. What opposition was voiced came largely from the traditionally anti-immigration groups. It centered on the old and persistent fears that revision and relaxation of control measures would let in much larger numbers of immigrants and that immigrant workers would be harmful to American labor. This opposition was less active, however, than heretofore. The major labor organizations were on record as favoring the bill, and Secretary Wirtz of the Labor Department loyally supported it in his testimony at the hearings; but concern over the effects of the bill may have lingered at lower labor union levels.

The seemingly favorable legislative outlook for the administration bill suddenly became more clouded and confused when on June 1 Chairman Feighan introduced his own substitute immigration bill.[128] In his accompanying statement to the House he stated that his committee's hearings had shown the need for a truly selective system of immigrant admissions with both numerical and qualitative controls, and that the national origin system had failed to provide such selectivity. His bill, he stated, was designed to provide the needed selective system, by implication an improvement on the administration bill in this respect. The principal provisions of the Feighan bill were:

1. an annual limit of 225,000 quota admissions for permanent residence exclusive of the nonquota admissions of natives of independent countries of the Western Hemisphere and returning resident aliens;
2. no preference or priority to be granted on the basis of race, sex, or national origin;

[127]Pressure was doubtless brought to bear on Feighan, as by the President in a remark quoted earlier and also by ethnic groups among his constituents in Cleveland, where his congressional seat was not altogether secure in spite of his long tenure. And by coincidence or not, the Joint Committee on Immigration Policy, established by the 1952 Act but never able to function because of limited funds, and which Feighan had made repeated but fruitless efforts to activate, was suddenly voted a greatly enlarged appropriation of $120,000 by the House on June 8. Senate appropriation of its share was not immediately forthcoming.

[128]H.R. 8662, "To establish a selective immigration system, and for other purposes." Introduced soon after was another bill of the same title, H.R. 8679, Dent (Pa.).

3. a limit of 20,000 immigrant visas annually for any one foreign state;

4. allotment of visas according to seven preference classes;

5. visas to be awarded "strictly in the chronological order" of registration on waiting lists or of filing of a petition for preference.

The seven preference classes were a distinctive feature of the Feighan bill, and were as follows:

1. first preference without numerical or percentage limitation to spouses, unmarried children, or parents of citizens;

2. 10 percent of the remaining number of visas to members of the professions;

3. the next 20 percent to spouses, unmarried children, and parents of aliens lawfully admitted for permanent residence;

4. the next 20 percent to married children of citizens;

5. the next 20 percent to brothers or sisters of citizens;

6. the next 20 percent to immigrants "capable of performing specified skilled or unskilled labor, not of a temporary or seasonal nature, for which a shortage of employable and willing persons exists;"

7. the next 10 percent to refugees from Communist or Communist-dominated countries.

It was further provided that in the fourth quarter of a fiscal year visas not needed for preference classes two to five inclusive may be made available cumulatively to qualified immigrants in the succeeding preference classes, three through six; also that on advice the President may reserve up to one-half of the nonpreference visas for aliens suffering hardship because of change in the quota system, for refugees beyond the seventh preference class, and for aliens unable to return to their homes because of natural calamity or military operations.

In its sevenfold preference structure, the Feighan bill differed widely from the Celler-Hart administration bill, which for the allocation of visas retained the three preference classes and one residual class of the 1952 Act as amended.[129]

After extensive hearings and many days of executive sessions spent

[129]The administration bill did make several changes in eligibility for preference: a shift of parents of citizens from second preference to nonquota status; the addition to the fourth or residual class of the parents of aliens lawfully admitted for permanent residence; and also in this fourth class giving to immigrants capable of performing work for which a shortage of labor exists a preference of not over one-half of the visa numbers remaining after satisfaction of the requirements of eligible relatives of citizens and resident aliens.

in working on the bill, the House committee reported out the Celler bill, H.R. 2580, with amendment on August 6, 1965. The committee had been thorough in its amending. In the formal wording of the committee report (H. Rept. 745 [89-I]),

> The Committee on the Judiciary . . . having considered the same (H.R. 2580), report favorably thereon with an amendment and recommend that the bill do pass.
> The amendment is as follows:
> Strike out all after the enacting clause. . . .

In its place the committee inserted a new draft; and the new draft clearly bore much more resemblance to Feighan's substitute bill than to the Celler original.

The purpose of the bill was stated in one brief sentence: "the elimination of the national origins system as the basis for the selection of immigrants to the United States."[130] Actually it went considerably further, for it amended many sections of the 1952 Act and introduced a number of new provisions. The following are to be noted in particular:

1. An annual limit of 170,000 aliens who may enter as immigrants, have their status changed to that of permanent resident, or enter conditionally as refugees. Not to be counted in the total were natives of independent countries of the Western Hemisphere and their immediate families and parents of citizens.

2. Continuation of the national quotas for three fiscal years to June 30, 1968, quota numbers unused in one year to be put in a presidential pool the following year and made available to immigrants unable to obtain visas because of oversubscribed quotas.

3. Repeal of the Asia-Pacific triangle provisions contained in section 202(b) of the 1952 Act.

4. Immigrant visas from the presidential pool and all 170,000 visas after June 30, 1968 to be issued in the following order of preference:

(a) unmarried sons and daughters of citizens—first 20 percent.

(b) spouses and unmarried sons and daughters of resident aliens —next 20 percent plus any unused portion of (a).[131]

(c) members of professions, scientists, and artists—next 10 percent.

(d) married sons and daughters of citizens—next 10 percent plus any unused portion of (a) through (c).

[130]H. Rept. 745 (89-I), p. 8.

[131]The former second preference category, parents of citizens aged twenty-one and over, was now given nonquota status.

(e) brothers or sisters of citizens—24 percent plus any unused portion of the preceding classes.

(f) skilled or unskilled persons capable of filling labor shortages —next 10 percent.

(g) refugees from persecution by Communist governments or from certain Middle Eastern countries—next 6 percent, of which one-half may be used for adjustment of status of such refugees with two years of residence in the United States.

Any remainder of the 170,000 total was to be available to otherwise qualified immigrants "in the order of their qualification" (i.e., not in the order of their application).

5. Prerequisite for the issuance of a visa of an affirmative finding by the Secretary of Labor that an alien seeking to enter as a worker, skilled or not, will not replace a worker in the United States nor adversely affect the wages and working conditions of similarly employed individuals in the United States. Exempted from the above condition are parents, spouses, and minor children of citizens and resident aliens.

6. Requirement that the President notify Congress if in any year immigrants from the Western Hemisphere exceed the annual average of the preceding five years by 10 percent or more.

7. Denial of adjustment of status to natives of the Western Hemisphere.

8. Inclusion of "sexual deviation," deletion of epilepsy, and substitution of "mentally retarded" in place of "feebleminded" as grounds for exclusion.

Numerous other amendments of the 1952 Act were included in the committee bill, but they dealt for the most part with procedural matters and adjustments of wording in the act.

The elimination of the national origin system and the Asia-Pacific triangle provisions was a common feature of the administration and Feighan bills, but several additional features of the new House committee draft are to be noted. The complex sevenfold preference structure resembles the Feighan system of selective admissions but with some modification of the proportions, with a clear emphasis on the admission of relatives, and with comparatively small and noncumulative allocations to the two occupational preference classes. Further and striking evidence of the sensitiveness of the labor issue is the new provision requiring approval from the Secretary of Labor for the granting of visas to immigrant workers.[132] This requirement, furthermore, applied to both preference

[132]Under section 212(a)(14) of the 1952 Act, an alien seeking to enter for the purpose of performing skilled or unskilled labor was excludable if the Secretary of Labor certified

and nonpreference immigrants and to the nonquota Western Hemisphere immigration. Another sensitive issue, that of the number of immigrants to be admitted, was met by the setting of a ceiling of 170,000 per annum, considerably reduced from the Feighan bill's figure of 225,000; only natives of the Western Hemisphere and parents of citizens were exempted.

A third new issue that appears in the bill is Western Hemisphere immigration. Appended to the committee report was what was in effect a dissenting opinion signed by seven Republican members of the House Judiciary Committee, led by MacGregor of Minnesota. They argued that the bill as reported out, in eliminating the national origin system, went only half the way toward establishing a fully nondiscriminatory immigration policy, for the retention of nonquota status for the twenty-four nations of the Western Hemisphere was in effect a discrimination against the hundred or so other nations of the world. It was also revealed that a MacGregor amendment to put a ceiling of 115,000 per annum on Western Hemisphere immigration had been adopted in the subcommittee on July 22 but was later rejected on reconsideration just before the bill was reported out.[133] The Western Hemisphere issue did leave its mark on the bill as reported out, however. Contained in it was the denial of adjustment of status to natives of the Western Hemisphere, for which the explanation given in the committee report was abuses of the privilege by persons admitted on a temporary basis who immediately applied for permanent residence. And there was the watchdog provision that Congress be alerted whenever there is a considerable increase in Western Hemisphere immigration.

The House began consideration of the bill on August 24, with Feighan as floor manager. He reported that the committee had conducted thirty-nine public hearings, heard from ninety-four members of Congress, and then met in eighteen executive sessions to produce the final draft. It had been approved unanimously by the subcommittee with one abstention, and approved without amendment by the Judiciary Committee, 27 to 4. He then gave an analysis of the bill, and was followed by

---

that sufficient able, willing, and qualified workers were available to perform such work or that the employment of such aliens would adversely affect wage and working conditions for such work. The proposed amendment shifted responsibility for taking action from the Secretary of Labor to the immigrant. Or, differently stated, under the 1952 Act an immigrant worker was admissible unless the Secretary of Labor took adverse action; under the amendment an immigrant worker was excludable unless he obtained affirmative action from the Secretary of Labor.

[133]It is known that the administration made a strong effort to defeat the amendment, citing possible harmful effect on hemisphere relations.

Chairman Celler of the Judiciary Committee who stated his support. Numerous other members of the House rose to speak at length in favor of the bill.[134] Amendments were then proposed. MacGregor of Minnesota reoffered the amendment, newly defeated in committee, to set a quota limit of 115,000 per annum on Western Hemisphere immigration, beginning after June 30, 1968, visas to be issued in the chronological order of application, and adjustment of status cases to be deducted from the quota. The amendment was opposed by Feighan, Celler, and others, with the arguments that it would endanger Latin American relations and that such immigration had averaged less than 115,000 over the past decade; but the amendment was accepted by the close vote of 156 to 154. Brought up again with a rollcall vote, however, it was defeated 189 to 218, with 25 not voting.[135]

Various other amendments were proposed. One by Gilbert of New York, to empower the Secretary of Labor to exercise the same control over the admission of nonimmigrants coming for temporary labor as over immigrant labor, was rejected. But the House accepted an amendment by Fogarty of Rhode Island to allow the Surgeon General and the Attorney General to admit mentally retarded children for the purpose of family unification, under due safeguards as already provided for in the case of tuberculosis. As amended, the bill was passed by the House, 318 to 95, with 19 not voting.[136]

The Senate committee reported out the House bill (S. Rept. 748) with amendment on September 15, and the Senate began its consideration one day later. As stated in the report, the Senate committee had struck out the House bill and inserted a new draft. Many of the principal features of the House bill had been retained, however, in particular the quota limit of 170,000 immigrants per annum, a transition period from the old to the new basis of admission of three rather than the five years of the administration bill, and the accumulation of unused quota numbers during the three years to form a presidential pool for allocation to persons from oversubscribed areas and to persons with certain specified

[134]The speeches extend over 45 pages of the *Congressional Record.*

[135]*Congressional Record,* 111:21807, 21819, Aug. 25, 1965.

[136]*Congressional Record,* 111:21821, Aug. 25, 1965. Passage of the bill was followed by a partisan statement from Moore of West Virginia, member of the subcommittee, according to whom the bill just passed was "almost wholly a Republican bill" and contained many features from his own H.R. 9136. Among such points he enumerated was the phasing out of the national origin system in three rather than five years, reallocation of unused quotas, emphasis on family reunification, stricter controls on immigration for employment, and provision for reporting to Congress of a 10 percent or greater increase of Western Hemisphere immigration.

priorities. And after June 30, 1968, visas were to be apportioned according to a sevenfold preference system, the same as that of the House bill and with the same percentage distribution. Also duplicated from the House bill was the provision for labor certification by the Secretary of Labor.

The Senate committee had also inserted some provisions not contained in the bill as received from the House. Chief among them was the Ervin amendment, proposed by Ervin of North Carolina and strongly supported by Dirksen of Illinois, both members of the subcommittee. Like the twice-defeated MacGregor amendment in the House, it put an annual quota limit on Western Hemisphere immigration, in this case 120,000 per annum; and although still opposed by the administration it was adopted, five to three, by the subcommittee and approved by the Senate Judiciary Committee as a whole. As set forth in the Ervin amendment, the limitation on the Western Hemisphere was to take effect beginning after June 30, 1968 unless otherwise provided by Congress before that time; meanwhile, the subject was to be studied by a Select Commission on Western Hemisphere Immigration established by the same amendment.

Other additions made by the Senate committee were:

1. broadening of the definition of refugee to include persons "uprooted by catastrophic natural calamity";
2. making alien crewmen eligible for suspension of deportation and adjustment of status;
3. exemption of Western Hemisphere refugees from the House provision denying adjustment of status to natives of the Western Hemisphere;
4. authorization for the admission under suitable safeguards of certain close relatives of citizens, although technically excludable because of mental retardation or history of mental illness.

The purposes of the bill, more broadly stated by the Senate committee than in the House report, were to end the national origin system, to substitute a new form of selection based on family relations and skill or ability, to end the Asia-Pacific triangle provisions of the 1952 Act, and to grant quota-free immigration to the newly independent countries of Jamaica and Trinidad and Tobago. The report was approved by vote of 14 to 2 in the Senate Judiciary Committee, but the addenda to the report revealed divergent opinions among members of the subcommittee. Appended to the report were a dissenting minority report by Chairman Eastland of Mississippi and McClellan of Arkansas, supplementary views by Ervin of North Carolina, and a statement of opposition to the limitation of Western Hemisphere immigration signed by Kennedy of

Massachusetts, Hart of Michigan, and Javits of New York. The principal arguments presented with some fervor in the dissenting opinion were that the McCarran-Walter system of immigration controls should not be abandoned, that American citizens may be adversely affected by the proposed changes, that immigration is a privilege to be granted rather than owed to other peoples, and that the underdeveloped nations may be harmed by loss of trained citizens.

Senate debate on the bill began September 17 and continued with interruptions for four days, to end on September 22 after filling more than 130 pages of the *Congressional Record.* Kennedy of Massachusetts, the floor manager, began the debate with a long statement of the purposes of the bill and analysis of its contents. Extended debate then followed, during which the opposition was stronger or at least more vocal than in the House. Ervin of North Carolina, although registering his general support for the bill, took the occasion to protest against what he called the "mischievous nonsense and sanctimonious propaganda" in the "constant and consistent harangues from lobbyists and well-meaning humanitarian organizations" against the national origin system and the McCarran-Walter Act. His annoyance, however, was directed against the lobbying methods rather than the bill itself, which he regarded as a compromise between opposing views within the Senate subcommittee and which he characterized as "the best immigration law obtainable at present."

Most outspoken in opposition was a group of conservative southern Senators, the first of whom was Thurmond of South Carolina who approved the labor certification and Western Hemisphere features of the bill but remained loyal to the national origin system and stated that his opposition to immigration even of the restricted amount proposed led him to reject the bill. Eastland of Mississippi, chairman of the Senate Judiciary Committee, condemned the bill as an "assault on our immigration laws by those . . . who appeal to organized minority blocs in the great urban areas," and in a long speech he charged that the purpose of the bill was to increase immigration and change its composition. He was seconded by McClellan of Arkansas, who with Eastland had cast the two negative votes in the Judiciary Committee. Ellender of Louisiana pointed out that there were presently 4 million unemployed and urged that all immigration be stopped for a period of five years. These opponents, however, were much outnumbered by those who recorded their favorable views during debate, led by Hart of Michigan. Among the points made in favor of the bill were its elimination of racial discrimination, its prospective aid to the national economy, and the value of skills and training brought in by immigrants.

Although the bill was the occasion for many and long speeches, for or against, only a few amendments were offered. Javits of New York and Morse of Oregon spoke in favor of a ten-year limit on deportability but did not formally present such as an amendment. Miller of Iowa offered an amendment to reduce the quota total by one for each special (that is, nonquota) immigrant admitted except for close relatives of citizens. The amendment was opposed by Kennedy and was rejected. The mood of the Senate and its leaders seemed to be to press forward for passage of the bill, after due opportunity for everyone who wished to put his views on the record; and so without amendment of the committee draft the bill was brought to vote on September 22 and passed by the ample margin of 76 to 18, with 6 abstaining.

A conference committee was appointed to work out an acceptable compromise between the House and Senate versions of the bill, not a difficult assignment because of the agreement in substance between the two. The conference report (H. Rept. 1101) was presented on September 29; it accepted Senate amendments of what was basically the House bill, including the Select Commission on Western Hemisphere Immigration, the ceiling of 120,000 on immigration from the Western Hemisphere, and the broadened definition of refugees to include victims of natural calamity. Changes in the Senate modifications of the bill included striking out the provision for adjustment of status by Western Hemisphere refugees and change in the mode of appointment of members of the Select Commission to reduce the number of presidential appointees to only one-third of the total.[137] The conference draft was accepted by both House and Senate. On signature by President Johnson it became the Act of October 3, 1965 (79 Stat. 911).

The 1965 Act was, obviously, a turning point in American immigration policy—a turning point, that is, in the system of selection of immigrants for admission. It brought to an end the selection of immigrants on the basis of their national origin, a basis of selection introduced by the 1924 Act and actually becoming effective at midyear of 1929. And along with national origins it did away with any selection, more often called discrimination, on the basis of race or ancestry. It did not do away with selectivity in admission, however; it only substituted new and less invidious criteria for admission. The new criteria were, first and principally, relationship to a citizen or lawfully resident alien; second and less heavily

[137]Other changes made by the conference committee in Senate additions to the bill were limitation of the eligibility of alien crewmen to suspension of deportation and adjustment of status to those who entered by June 30, 1964 and changing of the limiting date for creation of a record of lawful entry. The 1952 Act limited such action to aliens who entered prior to June 28, 1940. The Senate approved change of the date to June 28, 1958; the conference report moved it back to June 30, 1948.

weighted, personal qualifications of ability and training;[138] and finally chronological order of application for admission. The latter, although not a selective factor in a strict sense, had a considerable effect on the distribution of admissions, especially in the first years of the new act.

Other principal elements of American immigration policy, however, remained largely unchanged. The 1965 Act was an amending act, and the 1952 Act remained the basic law governing immigration and naturalization, its structure little changed. There was little if any relaxation in the criteria for exclusion or the grounds for deportation of aliens, and the principle of numerical limitation or quota limits on immigration remained and was expanded to world coverage by the setting of a quota limit on Western Hemisphere immigration.

This points to the observation that the 1965 Act did more than replace certain disfavored features of the 1952 Act. It went further by adding several new components to the structure of immigration law and policy. The original administration proposals had contemplated merely doing away with the national origins and the Asia-Pacific triangle provisions and providing a more acceptable replacement. At the hands of Congress and its committees, however, several new elements were added, notably the ceiling on Western Hemisphere immigration and the labor certification requirement. Neither had been contemplated by the original designers of the bill, and the former if not both were opposed by the administration.

This raises the questions of how these amendments to the original bill arose and what motivated the subsequent handling of the bill by the administration and leaders in Congress. Without information on what went on within the legislative committees or what pressures may have been brought to bear on individual members of Congress, it can only be inferred that the amendments in question were to reassure those concerned at the possibility of large immigration from Latin America or fearful of ill effects on the labor market or to provide a *quid pro quo* to influential members of Congress or interest groups in return for their support of the bill. Various reasons can be seen why the leadership, after some resistance to the Western Hemisphere limitation, chose to go along with the changes made at the hands of Congress. The choice may have been as simple as this bill or no bill. The legislative process tends to be one of compromise, not compromise in an invidious sense but in a sense of reconciling divergent interests; and with general acceptance of its top

[138]Selection of immigrants on the basis of individual quality had been recommended sixty years earlier by President Roosevelt in his message on the opening of the 59th Congress (see p. 136).

priorities of doing away with national origins quotas and the Asia-Pacific triangle, the leadership was probably willing to accept some less palatable additions in order to avoid conflict in the committees or on the House or Senate floor that might have jeopardized the whole bill. Another consideration to be noted is that although the administration had overwhelming majorities in both houses of Congress, immigration bills notoriously raise divisive issues that do not follow party lines. So there may well have been reluctance to put party loyalty to the test, a reluctance underlined by the conspicuous defection of conservative Democrats in the Senate. As a whole, the long campaign for repeal of the national origins provisions, especially in the last Congresses, appears to have been skillfully conducted from President Johnson on down; in the final stages it was marked by political compromise in order to achieve the main purpose, a redemonstration that politics is the art of the possible.[139]

[139]A *Wall Street Journal* account of the bill shrewdly attributed its passage to "committee-packing, Presidential flattery, and abject compromise." *Wall Street Journal,* Oct. 4, 1965.

II

Elements of Policy

9 Introduction: Immigration Law and Policy

Part I gave an account of congressional action on immigration and immigration-related bills, including those affecting immigrants after arrival, from the first such action in the late 1790s to the passage of the Act of October 3, 1965 by the 89th Congress. Included in this account were the relevant bills introduced in Congress, whether acted on or not, all but a small proportion of which died in committee, and of those reported out only a small number were enacted. Part II, by contrast, looks at the immigration acts actually passed by Congress, to see what continuing lines of policy appear to run through the body of immigration legislation.

The immigration laws are a formidable body of legislation in themselves,[1] but they form only part of the total structure for the regulation of immigration. Executive and departmental orders, presidential proclamations, and treaties also affect international migration. Moreover, when a law concerning immigration and aliens is passed by Congress, it is typically the Immigration and Naturalization Service (referred to hereafter as the Service or the INS) of the Department of Justice that has the responsibility of administration and enforcement, and it issues or modifies its regulations to translate the terms of the act into operations instructions. These regulations are published as required under the Administrative Procedure Act of June 11, 1946, and they constitute Title 8 of the U.S. Code of Federal Regulations. Particularly where a law includes phrasing in broad and general terms,[2] as is sometimes the case, the regulations in effect spell out or define the provisions of the act in terms more directly applicable to specific cases or detail a procedure to be followed.

Further, there are cases not clearly covered by existing law and

[1]The 1953 edition of *Laws Applicable to Immigration and Nationality* (Washington, D.C.: U.S. Government Printing Office) ran to 1,345 pages of text and 208 pages of index. Supplements covering legislation subsequent to 1953 up to December 31, 1962 add almost four hundred more pages of text.

[2]For example, the excludable classes of aliens with "a loathsome or dangerous contagious disease," "liable to become a public charge," or of "constitutional psychopathic inferiority."

regulations, or where the interpretation of law and regulation is contested, on which a special inquiry and determination has to be made. Within the Service, cases appealed or referred from the immigrant inspector at the port of entry or from a local board of special inquiry may go to the Board of Immigration Appeals (BIA) in the Department of Justice, or to the Attorney General. Precedent-setting decisions made in such cases, and in some instances decisions made within the Service itself, are published in a series of volumes, *Administrative Decisions under Immigration and Nationality Law,* as again required by the Administrative Procedure Act.[3] In the aggregate the administrative decisions constitute an accumulating body of precedent that supplements the statutory law.

Judicial decisions also contribute precedent-setting interpretations of the laws on immigration. Appeal to the courts is limited for the immigrant, and decisions of the BIA and the Attorney General are final as a rule; but a resident alien, for example in a deportation case, may appeal to the courts if there are sufficient grounds for such appeal. The judicial decisions constitute precedent-setting interpretations of immigration law, as do the administrative decisions, and both are incorporated into revisions of the regulations.

All three branches of government—the legislative, executive, and judicial—thus contribute to determining the regulation of immigration, from enactment of laws to regulations for operating procedures and on to administrative and judicial interpretation. The setting of policy in a strict sense, however, is the exclusive function of the legislative branch, and both administrative and judicial action remains within the framework of the law. Consequently, although actual practice regarding immigration is determined at several levels, immigration policy formation and statement is regarded as contained within the immigration acts.[4] The following chapters that trace out the development of the principal elements of American immigration policy do so within the context of the legislation passed by Congress.

At this point the relation between immigration legislation and immigration policy needs to be considered before going further. Simply stated, immigration policy is seen as an objective sought by Congress and legislation as the means used by Congress to attain the objective. Policy is therefore a matter of intent or purpose, a reason for the legislation

[3]A first volume of decisions covering the period from Aug. 1940 through Dec. 1943 was published in 1947. At this time of writing, thirteen volumes of the series have been published, the individual volumes averaging nearly 900 pages and containing upwards of 150 cases each.

[4]Executive and departmental orders, presidential proclamations, and treaties are not as a rule policy-forming and are not dealt with here.

whether or not it is well designed or appropriate for the purpose. As a rule the intent of Congress in a particular measure is well and clearly stated. The title of a bill often states its purpose, which is also set forth more fully by the committee reporting out a bill; and debate in House and Senate provides a forum for the reasoning pro and con. Some reservations are needed here, of course. There may be some speciousness in the stated views and objectives; and immigration bills often tend to involve emotion-charged issues that stimulate long and impassioned debate in which the real issues may become clouded. Sensitivity on such matters as race and ethnicity may lead to some suppression of prejudiced remarks and concealment of true intent; but at the same time one finds much earnest and outspoken statement of views in the proceedings of Congress, and not so many years ago there seem to have been few inhibitions in expressing opinions derogatory to minority racial, ethnic, and alien groups. And whatever has been said for public consumption, the nature of legislative provisions is an indication of the underlying intent, and the members of Congress were presumably well aware of the implications of a provision whether or not they were openly stated in debate.

The history of congressional action on immigration in Part I showed there have been a multitude of congressional concerns regarding immigrants and aliens over the years. The nature of these concerns has varied from period to period, and the concerns find expression in the bills presented to Congress. The direction of congressional thinking is shown in a negative way by the proposals Congress rejected as well as in a positive way by those that were approved. On the positive side, however, not all new legislation fits into any continuing pattern of policy, for some of it is ad hoc legislation designed to meet a specific need at the time or to accomplish a specific but limited purpose. Examples in point are the measures to divert passenger travel to American-owned vessels, to provide labor for the sheep-raising industry, or to deal with problems of enemy aliens in wartime. But the piecemeal character of such legislation should not obscure the cumulative character of American immigration law, which has grown gradually through a continuing process of addition and amendment from session to session of Congress. Certain basic objectives have persisted and been developed over the years, and it is these that constitute the elements of American immigration policy treated in the chapters that follow.

Included among the elements of policy to be considered are both the publicly stated policies and the unstated but evident policies that run through the immigration laws. The former are the well-known policies that have been explicitly affirmed and long followed by Congress, the oldest of which is the selection of those immigrants to be admitted and the exclusion of those regarded as undesirable. Of more recent origin are the policies of limitation of the number admitted and facilitation of the entry of close relatives of citizens and alien residents of the United States. Less publicized and less numerous, but also significant, are certain unemphasized or unstated policies that have nevertheless been pursued with some consistency by Congress over a number of years. One such is the preference of Congress that it keep the regulation of immigration quite closely within its own hands, to legislate in detail, and to give only limited discretionary powers in immigration matters to administrative officials. At the same time there has been a de facto policy, perhaps in recognition of the danger of excessive rigidity in a system of regulation by law, to build in some elements of flexibility to deal with deserving and hardship cases not eligible for relief by other sections of immigration law. Certain such de facto policies have been treated in later chapters, in addition to the better-known immigration policies.

There is also the question of what treatment to give to another type of policy, those that now are of only historical significance. Over the long span of years covered here, from 1798 to 1965, immigration problems and policies have arisen and then declined or disappeared. Examples of such are the so-called passenger acts for the protection of persons arriving by vessel and the contract labor laws, which were important in their day but are no longer so. Furthermore, they are already well covered in various older works. Note has been made of them in the appropriate sections of Part I, but only brief attention is given to them in the account of immigration policies that follows.

Another question of treatment concerns measures that can have served and may have been intended to serve more than one purpose. For example, the head taxes provided revenue to meet expenses of immigrant inspection, but there is good reason to suspect that head taxes were raised higher and higher in order to reduce the number of aliens seeking admission, and especially the number belonging to the poorest classes. That is to say, the intent may have been both restrictive and selective, as well as revenue-raising. Similar is the case of the literacy test, long proposed and finally adopted in the 1917 Act, which clearly served the double purpose of restricting numbers and selecting those admitted. Such multipurpose provisions are not infrequent in the immigration bills, and Congress certainly was well aware of the various possible effects of both head tax and literacy test. With this in view, it has seemed most appropriate, to take the example of the literacy test again, to treat it as representing a double policy measure, both quantitative and qualitative in its intended effect.

One final note concerns the next chapter. Congress was not without precedents in facing the problem of regulating immigration and developing immigration policies. Before federal legislation on immigration, certain of the Atlantic Coast states and cities had adopted laws and regulations regarding immigration and aliens, and before them some of the American colonies had faced similar problems and adopted similar measures to meet them. A brief account of the colonial and state action is given in the next chapter to show the antecedents of federal action on immigration.

10 Colonial and State Policies

The history of American immigration policy does not begin with the first federal legislation, but goes back a century and a half earlier to the founding of the first permanent European settlements in North America. Almost from the first the early settlers began to look with mixed feelings at those who followed them, became concerned at what they considered to be problems of immigration, and formulated measures and policies to meet those problems. Later on, after independence, it was the states that took the place of the colonies and inherited the problems and responsibilities related to immigration. When the federal government in turn took over the responsibility for dealing with immigration, therefore, it was not venturing into an altogether new and unexplored area of national policy formation, but rather entering on an already trodden path. The problems and concerns of the colonies from their pioneer beginnings on to the coming of independence were in many respects the same but in some respects different from those of the successor states; and the problems and interests of the federal government when it preempted authority over immigration were not in all respects identical with those of the East Coast states that had been the recipients of European migration. But in the main there were basic similarities in the impact of immigration and the reaction to it in colony, state, and nation. Correspondingly, there are numerous parallels between the national policies and those adopted earlier by colony and state. And even some of the instruments of policy employed in federal legislation, such as the head tax and the attempt to force the transporters of migrants to exercise selection at the port of departure, already had been devised and applied by the colonial and state authorities.

Colonial Policies

Attitudes toward new arrivals were more conflicting in the colonial days than in later years. Still in the pioneer stage, with at first only a fringe of settlement on the coast of a largely unexplored continent, the colonists inevitably looked on newcomers as a recruitment of numbers that gave greater strength and security. Some remnants of this attitude lingered on even after the need for reinforcements became less urgent. But quite soon, and sooner in some colonies than in others, the older settlers began to look at the later arrivals with a more critical eye and to seek means of fending off those judged to be undesirable. Whether or not such means could be and were adopted depended on various factors, including the form of charter or government of a colony, the circumstances of its founding, and the number and type of migrants seeking entry; but several lines of policy on immigration appear in certain of the colonies most active in dealing with immigration.[1]

Encouragement of Immigration. The original founders and proprietors of the colonies pursued their own policies for the recruitment of settlers in the light of their own interests, but once some form of local government was established, the colonial authorities were in a position to deal with matters of immigration, subject to the limitations of their charter in some colonies, to approval by the Crown or the Proprietor in others. Official encouragement took the form of various inducements to the prospective immigrant, including land grants as in a number of colonies, religious toleration, especially in Maryland and Pennsylvania, tax exemption for a term of years as in North Carolina,[2] and various forms of financial assistance or travel grants to immigrants or to those recruiting them. Easy terms of naturalization were also provided as another form of attraction. These and other forms of inducement, incidentally, were not entirely directed at migrants from Europe, for one gets the impression of competition between the colonies to attract each other's settlers.

Exclusion for Religion. The encouragement of immigration was more a policy of the early days of settlement than of later times, much more rare for the states than for the colonies, and still more rare on the part of the federal government. Much more common were the policies for the selection of immigrants through exclusion of those regarded as undesirable. Among the grounds for exclusion established at one time or another there was one that was unique to the colonies. That was the exclusion of

[1]The most useful work on the subject is E. E. Proper, *Colonial Immigration Laws.* vol. 13, no. 2, Studies in History, Economics and Public Law (New York: Columbia University Press, 1900). R. E. Albright, "Colonial Immigration Legislation," *Sociology and Social Research* 12:443–48 (May 1928), is a brief article on the subject but it gives little beyond what can be found in Proper, and the same can be said of the sections on the colonial period in the various works on American immigration policy. The present section is based on Proper, supplemented by the text of such colonial acts as have been located, but there is no assurance that all relevant acts have been found.

[2]Proper, *Colonial Immigration Laws,* p. 12.

persons because of their religion. Confined to the earliest days of settlement, it was a byproduct of the European religious rivalries of the time. Religious intolerance was prevalent, religious minorities and dissenters from the established church were subject to discrimination and persecution, and religious refugees who had fled from the continent to Britain and then went on to the New World were numerous among the settlers. In the spirit of the time, colonial charters frequently denied admission to Catholics,[3] and various disabilities were placed on members of that religion in some colonies. According to Proper,

> The colonial archives of the period are filled with laws placing restrictions in the way of Catholic settlers. These took the form of a duty on Irish Catholic servants; a positive prohibition of the Roman worship; a double tax on their lands; and the "Abjuration Oath" which practically excluded members of this faith, unless they chose to break their vows.[4]

Quakers were also excluded by law and were subject to persecution and banishment in some of the colonies; and other dissenting sects were regarded with disfavor. It was especially in Massachusetts that the leadership sought to establish and maintain religious homogeneity, even at the expense of population growth. In Maryland a Toleration Act was adopted in 1649, but disabilities began to be placed on Catholics within a few years thereafter.

Protection against Public Charges. Early in their history the colonies sought to protect themselves from the immigration of persons who might become public charges. Like religious intolerance, this was in the spirit of the time, for England then had the Settlement Acts that strictly defined who might and who might not claim relief in a community by reason of legal settlement; and similar laws appeared in the English colonies in North America. To ensure that immigrants would not be added to the relief rolls, the colonies adopted a variety of protective measures, of which the principal one was the exclusion of potential public charges, or paupers in the then-current term. Laws to prohibit the admission of poor and indigent immigrants are reported to have been passed by the Massachusetts colony as early as 1645 and 1655.[5] An act of 1700 in the same colony excluded the infirm unless security was given that they would not become public charges, and this was reaffirmed in later acts. In the wording of a 1756 act, "An Act to Prevent Charges Arising by Sick, Lame or

[3] Ibid., p. 18. [4] Ibid.

[5] Albright, "Colonial Immigration Legislation," p. 445.

Otherwise Infirm Persons, not belonging to this Province, Being Landed and Left Within the Same,"

> no master or commander of any ship or vessel whatsoever, coming into, abiding in or going forth of any port, harbour or place within this province, shall cause or suffer to be landed or put on shoar within the same, any sick or otherwise impotent and infirm person, not being an inhabitant of this province . . . unless the consent of the selectmen of the town where such sick or infirm person shall be landed be first had and obtained therefor, the same to be signified in writing, under their hands; nor unless security be first given, if demanded, to the satisfaction of such selectmen, for indemnifying and keeping such town free from any charge that may arise for the support or relief of the persons so landed.[6]

Another protective measure, included in the Massachusetts 1756 act quoted above, was to require security or bond that would be forfeited if the immigrant in question became a public charge. Such a bonding requirement was set in Massachusetts as early as 1722, and was reaffirmed in a later act in 1724–1725.[7] The latter act called for a bond not to exceed £100 per passenger and to have a term of five years. Of earlier date was a New York act of May 13, 1691, which read in part as follows:

> all persons that shall come to Inhabit within this Province, or any part or place thereof and hath not a visible Estate, or hath not a manual occupation shall before he be admitted an Inhabitant give sufficient surety, that he shall not be a burden or charge to the respective places, he shall come to Inhabit, which security shall continue for two years provided always that all those that have Manual Crafts or occupations may at all times come and inhabit in any place within the Province and be always admitted.[8]

The device of bonding or giving security against eventual relief costs was adopted by the later state legislation. Another provision found in some colonial laws and also carried over to the later legislation was designed to put responsibility on the master of a vessel if he brought an immigrant who might become a burden to the receiving community. The bonding requirement did not really do that, for although responsibility

[6] *Acts and Resolves of the Province of Massachusetts Bay,* vol. 3 (Boston: Albert Wright, 1878), chap. 4, p. 982.

[7] *Acts and Resolves of Massachusetts Bay,* vol. 2 (Boston: Wright and Potter, 1874), pp. 244–45, 336–37.

[8] "An Act for the defraying of the Public and necessary charge throughout this Province and maintaining the poor and preventing Vagabonds," *Laws of the Colony of New York from the Year 1664 to the Revolution,* vol. 1 (Albany: James Lyon, 1894), pp. 237–38.

for securing the bond fell on the owner or master, the cost presumably was passed on to the immigrant in the form of a higher fare. Some colonial laws required that an inadmissible and unbonded passenger must be taken back to his place of departure. Not only was this a means of getting rid of an unwanted immigrant, but in effect it put pressure on the transportation agency to screen applicants for passage and reject those who might be inadmissible at destination. Such a provision was contained in the New York act of 1691, previously referred to, as follows:

> if any vessell bring in any person as aforesaid not able to give suerty for their well demeanour That then and in such case, that the master of such vessell or vessells shall be oblidged to transport all such to the place from whence they came or at least out of this Province.[9]

Proper cites a 1700 Massachusetts act that contained the same requirement in the case of "lame, impotent, or infirm persons, incapable of maintaining themselves."[10] More comprehensive in its terms and not limited to new arrivals but applicable to undesirables who had already gained admission was a 1740 Delaware act, "An Act Imposing a Duty on Persons Convicted of Heinous Crimes and to Prevent Poor and Impotent Persons being Imported." According to its indignant preamble,

> WHEREAS Many persons trading into this government, have, for lucre and private gain, imported, sold, or disposed of, and daily do import passengers and servants into this government, who, by reason of age, impotence or indigence, have become a heavy burthen and charge upon the inhabitants thereof; and likewise, do frequently import divers persons convicted of heinous crimes, who soon after their coming into this government, do often commit many felonies, robberies, thefts and burglaries, to the great hurt of his Majesty's subjects . . .

Dealing in part with criminals as the title indicates, the act further provided in section 5 that

> upon information given to any two Justices of the Peace within this government, that any old persons, infants, maimed, lunatick, or any vagabond or vagrant persons are imported, come or brought into this government . . . it shall and may be lawful for the said justices . . . [to] compel said master, merchant, or other person who imported any such infant, lunatick, aged, maimed, impotent or vagrant person or persons, to give sufficient security to carry and transport such . . . person or persons to the place or places from whence such person

[9]Ibid.

[10]Proper, *Colonial Immigration Laws,* p. 29.

> or persons were imported, or otherwise to indemnify the inhabitants of this government from any charge that may come or be brought upon them by such infant, lunatick, maimed, aged, impotent or vagrant person coming into or living within this government.[11]

Similar provisions were probably contained in other colonial acts, and as noted above the requirement that unwanted immigrants be returned "whence they came" was carried forward in postcolonial legislation.

Resistance to the Coming of Criminals. A policy of penal transportation to the colonies appears to have been adopted by the British government quite early in the colonial period, a policy that promised the double advantages of ridding the home country of undesirables and providing a much-needed labor force for the colonies. The colonists were not altogether able to defend themselves against this official practice, but there is record of a Virginia Assembly order of 1671 against the bringing in of "jail-birds,"[12] a resolution of the Pennsylvania Council in 1683 against the sending of "fellons," and an act of similar effect in that colony in 1722.[13] There is also the previously cited Delaware act of 1740. Section 2 of the latter act provided that anyone bringing into the colony

> any person in the condition of a servant, or otherwise within the intent and meaning of this act, who hath been convicted of any murder, burglary, rape, sodomy, forgery, perjury, or any other felony, at any time before such importation or coming into this government, shall, before the said convicts be landed or put on shore, pay the sum of Five Pounds for every such convict so imported or otherwise brought in . . . and further, shall become bound . . . in the sum of Fifty Pounds, for the good behaviour of such convict person, for the space of one year next after his or her importation or coming into this government.[14]

Section 4 provided further that if such a convict or other person within the meaning of the act was discovered in the colony within one year after arrival a fine of twenty pounds was to be levied against the master or merchant responsible for bringing him.

The number of criminal immigrants, and certainly the legislative reaction to them, varied considerably from one colony to another. New England as a whole appears not to have been troubled by penal transpor-

[11] *Laws of the State of Delaware, 1700–1797,* 1:166–70.

[12] Proper, *Colonial Immigration Laws,* p. 65.

[13] *Minutes of the Provincial Council of Pennsylvania* (Philadelphia: Severns, 1852), 1:72; 3:166.

[14] *Laws of the State of Delaware.*

tation, which was directed more toward the plantation economics further south.

Reporting of Arrivals. Another prominent feature of the colonial legislation was the requirement that all persons entering a colony be reported. The responsibility was especially laid on the masters of incoming vessels to deliver passenger lists or manifests to the appropriate authorities, but arrivals by land were also made reportable. In some cases not only a list of names but further information about each person arriving was called for. This reporting requirement was a logical supplement to the checks on the coming of paupers, criminals, and other unwanted classes, for it gave closer control on who entered and it aided enforcement of the checks to undesirable immigration.

This interpretation of the purpose of the reporting requirement is supported by its usual association with a bonding requirement and by an explanation contained in the Delaware act cited below. New York and Massachusetts were especially active in such legislation, which they both carried on after statehood. A New York act of 1691 directed masters of vessels arriving with passengers to deliver a list of such passengers to the chief magistrate of the place of arrival within twenty-four hours of landing, the list to report the "qualities and conditions" of each passenger under penalty of "ten pounds current money of this province."[15] Massachusetts acts of 1722 and 1724–1725 set bonding and reporting requirements, the former of which acts read in part:

> upon the arrival of any ship or vessel in any port or harbor within this province, transporting any passengers . . . and before bulk be broken, or such passengers . . . be suffered to land . . . , the master of such ship or vessel shall repair to the selectmen . . . and give in a list or certificate of all the passengers . . . he has brought in his ship . . . from beyond the sea, with their circumstances.[16]

In the case of the Delaware act, the reason for calling for the passenger lists was explained in section 7 as follows:

> And for the better discovery of such convicts, and poor and impotent, or idle, or vagrant persons, who shall hereafter be imported into, and shall be likely to become chargeable to the inhabitants of this government, *Be it further enacted* . . . That all masters of vessels, merchants and others, who shall hereafter bring into any port or place belonging to this government, by land or water, any men or

[15]*Laws of the Colony of New York,* p. 238.

[16]*Acts and Resolves of Massachusetts Bay,* 2:244–45.

> women passengers or servants, shall . . . cause to be given, upon oath or affirmation, to the Collector of the said duties where such importation is made, a true and just account of all the names of the servants and passengers so imported or brought in. . . .[17]

One wonders if there was not also a further reason, conscious or unconscious, for the insistence on reporting newcomers—an underlying distrust of strangers and foreigners in the still very new society. An indication of this distrust is found, for example, in the preamble of a proclamation against riots that was adopted by the Pennsylvania Council on March 31, 1729:

> Whereas, several dissolute & disorderly Persons, press'd by their necessitous Circumstances, do daily crowd into this Province, as well as from Parts beyond the Sea, as from our neighboring Colonies, & bringing with them Dispositions incompatible with . . . good Order, Peace and Unanimity.[18]

Taxes on Immigrants. The device of a general head tax on immigrants, whether for revenue or for restraint on immigration, was a later development in the period of state legislation. The closest approximation found in the colonial legislation is in the form of special duties or admission taxes levied for the purpose of checking the immigration of certain classes of immigrant. An example is the fee of five pounds for each convict admitted under the 1740 Delaware act, noted above. There is also report of a short-lived duty imposed on foreigners, Irish servants, and "Negroes imported into this Province" by two Pennsylvania acts of May 10, 1729.[19]

Comment on Colonial Policy. The above review has covered the main elements in colonial immigration policy, but with focus on the several colonies that received the bulk of the immigration and that reacted most strongly through legislation. A more searching examination of colonial records would no doubt demonstrate considerable differences from one colony to another in the nature of their immigration policies, and whether or not they were impelled to deal with immigration at all. The immigrant flow varied in amount and composition from colony to colony; the New England colonies took the most vigorous action, and the colonial charters gave less independence of local authority to some than to others. To the colonies as a whole, immigration brought solid

[17]*Laws of the State of Delaware,* pp. 170–71.
[18]*Provincial Council of Pennsylvania,* 3:351–52.
[19]Ibid., p. 359.

benefits, and without it they could not have been established and expanded as they were; but it also brought some associated difficulties. The problem was to devise a system of control or regulation that would keep the benefits and reduce the difficulties. In this as in many other matters, the colonies faced what for them were new problems and were without precedents for guidance. They were forced to experiment with various measures for dealing with immigration, and during the colonial period accumulated experience that could be transmitted to the states that came after.

State Policies

The only direct reference in the Constitution to the control of immigration is in Article I, section 9, clause 1:

> The migration or importation of such persons as any of the States now existing shall think proper to admit shall not be prohibited by the Congress prior to the year one thousand and eight hundred and eight, but a tax or duty may be imposed on such importation, not exceeding ten dollars for each person.

This was interpreted to give control over both the slave trade and immigration to the federal government on and after 1808, but Congress at first was in no hurry to exercise its perhaps still uncertain authority over immigration, except for the brief episode of the Alien and Sedition Acts. Congress even gave some encouragement to the states to deal with immigration. Not surprisingly, state action continued in the pattern of the colonial legislation, the same states as colonies were most active, and the same basic policies were pursued although with some change of relative emphasis as time went on.[20] Direct legislative encouragement of immigration had disappeared long before the end of the colonial period, and was not resumed by any states until much later and under different circumstances.[21] Exclusion on religious grounds, which also was predominantly an enactment of the early rather than the late colonial years, did not reappear in state legislation although anti-Catholicism and antialien sentiment had by no means disappeared.

[20]An authoritative but brief account of state legislation on immigration is contained in the 1911 Immigration Commission Report, *Immigration Legislation,* vol. 39, chaps. 1–3. Pt. 4, pp. 505–956 of the same volume is a compilation of state laws on immigration and aliens, but is not complete, especially for the earliest years of statehood.

[21]Some of the southern states adopted measures for the encouragement of immigration during the Reconstruction period of the late 1860s, and various inland states also sought to attract migrants in the later decades of heavy immigration from Europe.

Protection against Public Charges. For the principal receiving states, the problem of destitute immigrants and those with poor prospects of self-support was the same as it had been for the colonies, and it became more acute as the number of arrivals increased. The protective measures adopted by the states were much the same as before: compulsory reporting of arrivals, screening of the immigrants and exclusion of those in the barred classes, and bonding of those admitted against eventual dependency on public support.

It is not clear if colonial regulations automatically continued in force after statehood. Presumably they did and new legislation was not immediately needed, but New York did reaffirm the manifesting requirement as early as 1788 and Massachusetts in 1789 (see below). The New York act of March 7, 1788, a settlement act, provided further

> That if any master of any ship or other vessel shall bring or land within this State, any person who cannot give a good account of himself or herself to the mayor or the recorder of the said city . . . or who is like to be a charge to the said city, such master shall within one month, carry or send the person so imported by him, back again to the place from whence he or she came, and shall for that purpose, enter into bond to the mayor, alderman and commonality of the city of New York . . . in the sum of one hundred pounds, conditioned that the person so imported shall not be or become a charge to the said city as aforesaid or any other city or town in this State; and in case such master . . . shall refuse to become bound as aforesaid, it shall and may be lawful . . . to cause such person so refusing, to be committed to the common gaol . . . there to remain until he shall consent to become bound as aforesaid.[22]

How rigorous the enforcement was is not known, but the law itself was stern and uncompromising. Equally firm was the Massachusetts act of February 14, 1789, also a settlement act, which included a manifesting requirement and further provided with respect to the destitute, immigrant or not, that

> Overseers or Selectmen, or the major part of them, are hereby further authorized and empowered, by and with the assent of two Justices of the Peace, to set to work, or bind out to service for the space of one whole year, at any time . . . all such persons, married or unmarried, upwards of twenty years of age, able of body, who have no visible means of support.[23]

[22]An Act for the Better Settlement and Relief of the Poor, *Laws of the State of New York, 1785 to 1788,* pp. 742–43.

[23]An Act providing for the Support of the Poor, *The Perpetual Laws of the Commonwealth of Massachusetts, 1780 to 1789* (Boston: Adams and Nourse, 1789), pp. 468 and 469.

The bonding requirement was repeated in a New York act of April 3, 1797, which set a $500 fine on the master of a vessel for each immigrant alien allowed to land unbonded. A later act of February 11, 1824 set a time limit of two years on the bond, stipulated that it also cover the support of children born to immigrants after arrival, and set the same penalty of $500 for refusal to provide bond. This was followed by an act of April 14, 1827 providing a fine of fifty dollars on anyone bringing into New York State a "poor or indigent person, not having a legal settlement therein." Twenty years later on May 5, 1847, the state passed a comprehensive "Act concerning passengers in vessels coming to the city of New York," which provided an alternative to bonding in the form of a commutation payment of one dollar for each alien.[24] The act also called for the examination of the passengers by the commissioners of emigration of the port of New York, a bond in place of the commutation payment to be given for such passengers as were found to be

> lunatic, idiot, deaf and dumb, blind or infirm . . . not members of emigrating families, and who, from attending circumstances, are likely to become permanently a public charge.[25]

The bond for each was to be $300 and for a term now extended to five years.[26] The penalty for neglect or refusal to provide such bond was set at $300 per case and constituted a lien on the vessel of the offending master.

Massachusetts was also active in legislation to protect itself from the financial burden of indigent immigrants. Following the 1789 act mentioned above, another settlement act was passed on February 26, 1794. It repeated the requirement that arrivals be reported, excluded criminals (see further below), but otherwise did not refer directly to alien immigrants. It was followed a few years later by "An Act to prevent the introduction of Paupers from foreign ports or places," adopted on February 25, 1810. It had the usual provisions of a report of arriving passengers by the master of the vessel, plus a bond in the amount of $500 for each passenger thought "liable to become chargeable," the bond to run for three years, and a penalty of $200 against the master for each such passenger for whom he fails to provide the required

[24]The wording of the act indicates that commutation money was taken in place of bonding under the earlier act of February 11, 1824.

[25]*Laws of the State of New York,* First Meeting of the Seventieth Session, 1847, vol. 1, chap. 195, pp. 182 ff. Printed by Charles Van Benthnysen, 1847.

[26]That is, public expenses for the migrant were recoverable up to five years after his arrival.

bond.[27] The same provisions were reenacted in an 1830 act, but with the additional proviso that local officials may dispense with the bond for any alien passenger considered unlikely to become a public charge, on condition of payment by the ship's master of five dollars for each such unbonded immigrant allowed to land.[28]

In 1835 the Massachusetts House received a "Report on Foreign Paupers"[29] and in the same year passed "An Act to prevent the Introduction of foreign Paupers into this Commonwealth," of nearly identical title to the 1820 act. A much more lengthy and detailed act in ten or more sections, the new act forbade the master of any vessel to land any alien passengers unless given a license to do so by the local authorities, and to make report of the passengers to the same authorities. A local official, inspector of alien passengers, was to board the vessel, obtain certain information from all alien passengers, including whether they had "in whole or in part been supported as paupers any time within the next preceding three years," the information to be collected under penalty of fine or imprisonment for false answers. A bond of $200 for each alien passenger was required of the master or agent of the vessel, the bond to be for two years, but it was waived for passengers who were to be removed beyond the limits of the Commonwealth. Each bonded immigrant was to receive a certificate on payment of a fee of one dollar, landing without the certificate being a misdemeanor punishable by fine not to exceed $100 or imprisonment in the common jail or house of correction for a period not exceeding six months. Further, no alien passenger found on inspection to have been a pauper within the preceding three years or to be "evidently impotent in mind and body" was to be allowed to land unless the master was found to have had no prior knowledge, in which case the immigrant in question may be landed on giving a bond of $500 by the master to guarantee removal of the immigrant within one month to the port from whence he came or "to any port beyond the limits of the United States."

A later Massachusetts act of 1837,[30] "An Act Relating to Alien Passengers," reaffirmed and built on earlier legislation. Permission to land was to be denied to any alien passengers found on inspection by an authorized official to be

[27] *Laws of the Commonwealth of Massachusetts passed by the General Court . . . 1820* (Boston: Russell & Gardner, 1820), chap. 290, pp. 428–29.

[28] *Laws of Massachusetts,* 1830, chap. 150.

[29] Mass. H. Doc. for 1835, No. 60.

[30] *Laws of the Commonwealth of Massachusetts, Passed . . . 1837* (Boston: Dutton and Wentworth, 1837), chap. 238, p. 270. The text of this act is also given in vol. 39 of the 1911 Immigration Commission Report, pp. 692–93.

> lunatic, idiot, maimed, aged or infirm persons incompetent in the opinion of the officer so examining, to maintain themselves, or who have been paupers in any other country . . .

unless the master, owner, consignee, or agent of the vessel give a bond, the amount of which was now increased to $1,000 and for a term of ten years. For all other alien passengers, a payment of two dollars each was to be made and to be used "for the support of foreign paupers." Another Massachusetts act of importance for the treatment of alien passengers followed in 1848.[31] For the most part it repeated the language of earlier laws, continued the ten-year bond of $1,000 for alien passengers considered potential public charges and the fee of two dollars for all other alien passengers. The latter portion of the act was repealed the following year, after the Supreme Court had held the fee or head tax to be unconstitutional.

Other states passed laws to protect themselves against the burden of the immigrant poor, but it was New York and Massachusetts that took the lead in this form of legislation. The seriousness with which they regarded the problem is testified to by the severity of the measures they passed and the penalties attached to evasion. And it was the attempts of these two states to obtain revenue from immigration in order to defray the costs of poor relief and administration that led to the challenge of the constitutionality of the states' action. Meanwhile, although the dominant problem and policy related to this economic aspect of immigration, there were several other elements in the state legislation regarding immigration.

Exclusion of Criminals. The colonies, as noted earlier, did not as a rule have sufficient independence of action to defend themselves against the British policy of penal transportation, but the states were not so restricted. Congress itself had encouraged them to take measures against the coming of criminals, in the form of a resolution adopted on September 16, 1788:

> Resolved, that it be, and it is hereby recommended to the several states, to pass proper laws for preventing the transportation of convicted malefactors from foreign countries into the United States.[32]

It is said that such laws were adopted by Georgia, Massachusetts, New York, Pennsylvania, South Carolina, and Virginia[33] but copies of these

[31] Ibid., pp. 695–97.

[32] *Journal of the American Congress,* vol. 4 (Washington, D.C.: Way & Gideon, 1823), p. 867. The resolution was moved by Baldwin of Georgia, seconded by Williamson of North Carolina.

[33] Marion T. Bennett, *American Immigration Policies* (Washington, D.C.: Public Affairs Press, 1963), p. 7.

acts were not included in the 1911 Immigration Commission Report compilation of state laws, nor have they been located elsewhere. Of not much later date is the Massachusetts settlement act of February 26, 1794, which was mentioned previously. Section 16 of that act read in part:

> be it further enacted, that if any master or other person, having charge of any vessel, shall therein bring into, and land, or suffer to be landed in any place within this Commonwealth, any person, before that time convicted in any other State, or in any foreign country, of any infamous crime, or any for which he hath been sentenced to transportation, knowing of such conviction, or having reason to suspect it, or any person of a notoriously dissolute, infamous and abandoned life and character, knowing him or her to be such, shall, for every such offense, forfeit the sum of One hundred pounds.[34]

This portion of the act was not reaffirmed in later Massachusetts legislation. Examination of the later laws relative to immigration in this and other states gives the impression of great preoccupation with pauper immigration but no concern with the coming of criminals. The same appears to be true from an examination of the contemporary activity in Congress, except for occasional agitation by supporters of nativist movements. After the colonies became independent, penal transportation had shifted to Australia, and if occasional criminals still entered it was the more visible economic problem of destitute immigrants that preempted attention.

Reporting of Arrivals. The requirement of passenger lists or manifests was part of the system of controls on immigrants who might become public charges, regularly included along with bonding. Without going into the specific terms in which the requirement was stated, the various acts are noted below, together with what detail of information was called for beyond the mere listing of names.

Manifesting of passengers had been called for by various colonies, New York and Massachusetts included, and the practice continued. The State of Massachusetts is represented by a series of enactments that carried on the colonial period laws of 1722 and 1724 on manifesting. The previously mentioned law of 1794 called for the names of all passengers together with their "character and condition." The 1794 act specified a report in writing to be made by the master within forty-eight hours of arrival, with the "names, age, character and condition" of the passengers. According to an act of 1820 it was to be a list of the names and places of residence of passengers without legal settlement within the Common-

[34] *Laws of Massachusetts, 1830,* 2:628.

wealth. This act was supplemented by another in 1830 that specified "a full and complete list" of the names of alien passengers, and the ports or places at which they had been taken on board. The comprehensive act of 1835 for preventing the introduction of foreign paupers designated an inspector of alien passengers who was to record for all persons

> their age, name, calling, trade or employment; their prospects and intentions within this Commonwealth, and intended place of future residence, and . . . the circumstances under which such passenger departed from any foreign port or place . . . (Mass., 1835 act, sec. 3)

with particular inquiry into whether they had been supported as paupers within the past three years. And the detailed 1848 act "concerning alien passengers" made mandatory the recording of a slightly changed list of items of information: "name, age, sex, occupation, place of birth, last place of residence, and condition" of every alien passenger.[35] Later Massachusetts acts included in volume 39 of the 1911 Immigration Commission Report do not mention the listing of passengers, alien or not, but that may have been considered unnecessary because such listing had been required by federal law since 1819.

The New York State series of acts incorporating provisions for manifesting passengers begins with the previously mentioned 1788 act requiring reporting of the names and occupations of every person brought into the port of New York, the reporting to be within twenty-four hours of arrival and under penalty of twenty pounds for each person not reported. This was repeated in the 1797 act, except the fine was changed to fifty dollars. In 1824 the necessary information was expanded to "the name, place of birth, and last legal settlement, age and occupation," and the penalty for nonreporting was raised to seventy-five dollars for each person falsely reported or unreported. This was repeated in substantially the same language in the Act of May 5, 1847 but with the following addition:

> The said report shall further specify whether any of said passengers so reported are lunatic, idiot, deaf and dumb, blind or infirm, and if so, whether they are accompanied by relatives likely to be able to support them; and shall further specify particularly the names, last place of residence, and ages of all passengers who may have died during said last voyage of such vessel. (N.Y. Act of May 5, 1847, sec. 1)

Manifesting requirements are not found in the dozens of later New York laws related to immigration,[36] but of course the subject was already covered by federal legislation.

[35] 1911 Immigration Commission Report, 39:695.

[36] See 1911 Immigration Commission Report, 39:759–838.

Other coastal states passed manifesting laws, for example Maryland in 1833 and California in 1852,[37] but none approached the legislative effort made by New York and Massachusetts, which have been described here in sufficient detail for comparison with the federal legislation to be described later.

Taxes on Immigrants. The one distinctive development by the states in dealing with immigration was the commutation payment for all immigrants. As described in a preceding section this levy on immigrants, popularly referred to as a head tax, was adopted by Massachusetts and New York in place of a bond for persons not deemed likely to become public charges; and the funds so obtained were to be used to meet the costs of public relief for indigent immigrants. This was declared unconstitutional by a much divided Supreme Court decision in 1849 that interpreted Article I, section 9 of the Constitution to give Congress power over all immigration. The States attempted to devise laws acceptable under the decision, but a last attempt by New York in 1881 to find a means of collecting "head money" was again struck down by a 1883 decision, which established in effect that a state may not raise money for poor relief by a levy on immigration, and that the regulation of immigration is the prerogative of the federal government.[38]

Final Comment on State Policies. The state policies on immigration are seen to follow mainly in the pattern of the preceding colonial measures, with some selection and a small amount of innovation. The problems were, after all, basically much the same for colony and state, and not surprisingly the policies of one profited by the experience and followed in the steps of the other. Similarly, it will be found that there was a basic similarity between the state policies and action of the federal government when it at last came to exercise its authority over immigration. The state treatment of immigration, therefore, is intermediate in content as well as in time between colonial and federal action.

The above review of state legislation concentrates largely on the two states of New York and Massachusetts. It was the former that bore the brunt of the rising tide of immigration during the nineteenth century, and Massachusetts that had reacted with special vigor since colonial times. Other states of the eastern seaboard also dealt with immigration, to some

[37]Ibid., pp. 681, 533.

[38]For a detailed history of events leading up to the Supreme Court decisions, see Roy L. Garis, *Immigration Restriction* (New York: Macmillan, 1928), or 1911 Immigration Commission Report, 39:24–27.

extent following the model of New York or Massachusetts, but without corresponding legislative effort.

It is evident that the dominant concern of the legislators was that immigrants would add to the burden of poor relief, and there was strong suspicion at the time that Europe was deliberately exporting its human liabilities. That the legislators took the matter very seriously, at least in two states, is shown by the number of immigration bills enacted and their growing length and detail. A more and more elaborate control system was developed in the effort to detect all suspect cases, with compulsory reporting of all arrivals, with more and more information about them, bonding or exclusion of persons thought to be likely to become public charges for any reason, making the master or owner of a vessel incur considerable liabilities for bringing a migrant of an undesirable class, requirement of a longer and longer term of years of coverage under the bonds, the meeting of certain conditions before a migrant is allowed to land, appointment of an official to board ships and inspect alien passengers, and severe penalties of fine or imprisonment for noncompliance or false information.

The escalating requirements may have been counterproductive beyond a point, for especially in the days of the smaller sailing vessel of shallower draft unknown numbers of passengers were landed at out-of-the-way places along the coast, such as eastern Long Island, and made their way on foot to New York City or whatever their destination, having thus escaped head taxes, bonding, and the attentions of the immigration authorities. And such evasive practices did not end with the end of state controls over immigration. Enforcement, however, is another matter: the policies and the instruments of policy developed by the principal states of immigration formed a pattern of rigorous control over immigration as a whole, admission under financial safeguards, or exclusion for those considered less desirable.

11 Selection by Exclusion

An early and principal objective of American immigration policy, like that of other receiving nations, has been to select those aliens permitted to enter. From colonial times, immigrants were judged on various criteria —religious, economic, moral, and others—and the relative weight of the various criteria varied with circumstances and over time; but whatever the criteria of judgment were, they served to identify some newcomers as desirable and others as undesirable. Selective immigration policy, accordingly, developed in two directions: a negative selection through exclusion and deportation of those defined as undesirable, and a positive selection by means of facilitated entry for those regarded as desirable. It is the former of these, selective exclusion, that has predominated in American immigration policy. It is dealt with in this chapter. Later chapters deal with elements of positive selection in American immigration law.[1]

The first federal act to provide for the exclusion of certain classes of aliens was the Act of 1875, which designated two classes of excludables. Since that time the number of excludable classes has grown through a process of gradual accumulation as subsequent acts have reaffirmed the earlier provisions and added new grounds for exclusion. Only rarely have previously established grounds for exclusion been repealed. Altogether there are now thirty or more separate grounds for exclusion (sec. 212[a] of the 1952 Act). These may be conveniently grouped into several broad categories, such as the immoral classes, the politically undesirable or subversive classes, criminal classes, and others. In order to trace the development of exclusion policy more clearly, the growth of these broad categories of excludables is traced below, rather than the many separate excludable classes. For a final overview and summary, a listing of the exclusion provisions by date of enactment is given at the end of this chapter.

[1]See chapters 16, 17, and chapter 22, sect. 2, Preferred Immigrants.

The Criminal Classes

As noted in the preceding chapter, the coming of criminals gave continuing concern to both colonies and states of the Atlantic seaboard. Congress, however, was slow and seemingly hesitant to engage in the regulation of immigration. With regard to the exclusion of criminals in particular, Congress in a resolution of September 16, 1788[2] recommended that the states "pass proper laws for preventing the transportation of convicted malefactors from foreign countries into the United States." The problem remained unsolved, however, and was exploited by nativist efforts in Congress many years later. The Senate on July 4, 1836 adopted a resolution for the Secretary of the Treasury to make an inquiry into the immigration of criminals and paupers.[3] A House resolution adopted two years later, on February 19, 1838, set up a congressional investigating commission that introduced a drastic bill calling for a fine of $1,000 or imprisonment for one to three years for the master of a vessel bringing in "anyone convicted of an infamous crime" or certain other undesirable aliens. The bill was not acted on.[4]

As reported in Part I, the subject of immigrant criminals came up again and again in Congress during the following years. To review briefly: House and Senate resolutions in the second session of the 28th Congress (1844–1845) called for information; and an extensive report based on inquiries in principal seaports of the United States was presented to Congress at the close of the session. A bill to prevent the immigration of paupers and criminals was introduced during the following session, but without further action being taken.[5] A decade later, early in 1855, the Senate debated a resolution calling for information from the Secretaries of State and Treasury and for consideration of legislation to exclude paupers and criminals. Soon after a bill to prohibit the entry of such undesirables passed the Senate but was tabled in the House.[6] A House bill for the same purpose was introduced in the next Congress, the 34th (1855–1857), accompanied by a lengthy report on the immigration of criminals and other undesirable classes of aliens, but again without success.[7] No further action was taken in Congress until after the Civil War, when in 1866 the Senate Committee on Foreign Relations presented a joint resolution that protested the alleged practice of several foreign governments of pardoning persons convicted of "infamous offenses" if they would emigrate to the United States. The resolution was passed by

[2]Quoted in full on p. 400.

[3]1911 Immigration Commission Report, 39:10.

[4]See further, pp. 28–29 above.

[5]See pp. 33, 34, 36.

[6]See pp. 40–41.

[7]See p. 92.

both Senate and House, and was signed by President Johnson. A bill for the exclusion of convicts was introduced later but made no progress.[8]

The subject of immigrant criminals reappeared in 1874, during the first session of the 43rd Congress (1873–1874), when the House adopted a resolution of inquiry calling on the President for information on the landing of foreign convicts and for his advice on what legislation if any was needed to prevent "such outrages." Consular reports and official correspondence on the subject were transmitted to Congress, and a Senate bill including a provision to forbid the immigration of foreign criminals was introduced soon after but remained in committee.[9] In its second session, however, the 43rd Congress passed the first federal law for the regulation of immigration, the Act of March 3, 1875 (18 Stat. 477).[10] This act, which prohibited the importation of prostitutes, coolie labor, and criminals, defined the latter excludable class as "persons who are undergoing a sentence for conviction in their own country of felonious crimes . . . or whose sentence has been remitted on condition of their emigration." To this was attached a significant qualification that set a precedent followed in later legislation—the exemption of crimes of a political character from the excluding provision.

The 1875 Act did not put an end to congressional concern over the entrance of alien criminals. The next session of Congress saw the reintroduction of an earlier House bill to provide, among other things, for the exclusion of criminals, and a Senate resolution instructing one of its committees to consider legislation to forbid the entry of certain undesirable aliens, criminals included.[11] No action was taken on either measure at the time. The same bill reappeared two years later in the next Congress, the 45th, but it was again unsuccessful. Some reassurance was given a few years later, in President Hayes's message opening the second session of the 46th Congress, on December 1, 1879, that discussions about pauper and convict immigration had been held with the Swiss government.

The number of classes of aliens who "shall not be permitted to land" was increased in the second act regulating immigration, the Act of August 3, 1882 (22 Stat. 214). Section 4 read in part as follows:

> That all foreign convicts except those convicted of political offenses, upon arrival, shall be sent back to the nations to which they belong and from whence they came. The Secretary of the Treasury may designate the State board of charities of any State in which such board shall exist by law, or any commission in any State, or any

[8]See p. 51.

[9]See p. 64.

[10]See pp. 65–66.

[11]See p. 67.

> person or persons in any State whose duty it shall be to execute the provisions of this section without compensation. The Secretary of the Treasury shall prescribe regulations for the return of the aforesaid persons to the countries from whence they came. . . . The expense of such return of the aforesaid persons not permitted to land shall be borne by the owners of the vessels in which they came.

And the next section stated concisely, "That this act shall take effect immediately."

The Act of 1882 was followed after an interval of less than nine years by the next regulatory act, the Act of March 3, 1891, a general immigration act that considerably expanded the grounds for exclusion. The criminal class to be excluded was redefined in section 1 of the act as "persons who have been convicted of a felony or other infamous crime or misdemeanor involving moral turpitude," but with the following proviso attached:

> That nothing in this act shall be construed to apply to or exclude persons convicted of a political offense, notwithstanding said political offense may be designated as a "felony, crime, infamous crime, or misdemeanor, involving moral turpitude" by the laws of the land whence he came or by the court convicting. (Sect. 1, Act of March 3, 1891 [26 Stat. 1084])

Essentially the same provisions for the exclusion of alien criminals and for the exemption of political offenders, with some rephrasing and amplification, were continued in the immigration acts immediately following, the Acts of March 3, 1903 (32 Stat. 1213), February 20, 1907 (34 Stat. 898), March 26, 1910 (36 Stat. 263), and February 5, 1917 (39 Stat. 874).[12]

During this period an attempt had been made in the 63rd Congress (1913–1915) to expand the excludable class to include aliens "who at the time of seeking admission to the United States are legally charged with a felony," in addition to the already excludable class of those convicted of designated types of crime. The change was proposed by the Senate

[12]Changes in the excluding phrase after 1891 were omission of the adjective "infamous" in the 1903 Act, and the addition of persons who "admit having committed" a felony, etc., in 1907. The wording then remained unchanged in 1910 and 1917. The proviso exempting political offenders was abbreviated in 1903 to "Provided, That nothing in this Act shall exclude persons convicted of an offense purely political, not involving moral turpitude." In 1907 the condition that the political offenders be otherwise admissible was added. The second proviso of section 3 of the 1917 Act expanded the definition of the admissible political offenders to read: "if otherwise admissible, persons convicted, or who admit the commission, or who teach or advocate the commission, of an offense purely political," and "moral turpitude" was omitted.

committee in the form of an amendment to the Burnett bill, a bill that incorporated recommendations of the 1911 Immigration Commission Report, but the amendment was rejected by the Senate during consideration of the bill in December 1914 to early January 1915.[13] Substantially the same bill was eventually passed over presidential veto as the Act of February 5, 1917 (39 Stat. 874). This restrictive act introduced the literacy test.

The exclusion of alien criminals as provided in the 1917 Act remained in effect until reaffirmed in much amplified form by the McCarran-Walter Act, the Act of June 27, 1952 (66 Stat. 163), which became the basic immigration and nationality law. As stated in section 212(a)(9) and (10), the following are "ineligible to receive visas and shall be excluded."

> (9) Aliens who have been convicted of a crime involving moral turpitude (other than a purely political offense), or aliens who admit having committed such a crime, or aliens who admit committing acts which constitute the essential elements of such a crime; except that aliens who have committed only one such crime while under the age of eighteen years may be granted a visa and admitted if the crime was committed more than five years prior to the date of the application for a visa or other documentation, and more than five years prior to date of application for admission to the United States, unless the crime resulted in confinement in a prison or correctional institution, in which case such alien must have been released from such confinement more than five years prior to the date of the application for a visa or other documentation, and for admission, to the United States; (10) Aliens who have been convicted of two or more offenses (other than purely political offenses), regardless of whether the conviction was in a single trial or whether the offenses arose from a single scheme of misconduct and regardless of whether the offenses involved moral turpitude, for which the aggregate sentences to confinement actually imposed were five years or more.

Other evidence of the congressional attitude toward criminality of potential immigrants is given by the willingness or unwillingness to waive excludability in hardship or other deserving cases. An example is the Act of May 26, 1926 (44 Stat. 654) for the purpose of facilitating the entry of aliens who had served in the armed forces of the United States during World War I. For such veterans all grounds for exclusion were waived except six, of which conviction of crime was one; and the same provision was incorporated in the Act of June 28, 1932 (47 Stat. 336) to facilitate

[13]See p. 162 above.

the immigration of natives of the Virgin Islands residing in foreign countries. A reversal of attitude appears in more recent legislation. The Act of September 11, 1957 (71 Stat. 639) provided in section 5 that certain alien relatives of citizens or resident aliens who are excludable under paragraphs (9), (10), and (12) (concerning certain immoral classes) of section 212a of the 1952 Act may nevertheless be admitted if the Attorney General is satisfied that their exclusion would result in "extreme hardship" to the relatives in question, if admission of the aliens "would not be contrary to the national welfare, safety, or security," and if the Attorney General gives approval under whatever regulations he may prescribe. The same provision was reenacted in section 14 of the Act of September 26, 1961 (75 Stat. 650); section 13 of the same act also amended paragraph (9) to add the stipulation that aliens excludable because of conviction and punishment for a petty offense or admission of having committed a misdemeanor may nevertheless be granted a visa and admitted if there has been only one such offense. Thus the recent tendency appears to be toward some relaxation of excludability for lesser offenses.[14]

Public Charges

The other long-standing concern from the time of provincial and state regulation of immigration was with the coming of persons who might become a burden to the community; as was seen earlier, both colonies and states sought to protect themselves by exclusion of potential public charges, as well as by other means. Federal legislation for the exclusion of potential public charges was delayed until 1882, but the question had appeared many times before in Congress. A first active consideration of the subject occurred in the first session of the 24th Congress (1835–1836) when a resolution from the Massachusetts legislature called for protective legislation. Near the end of the session on July 4, 1836 the Senate called on the Secretary of the Treasury to make inquiry into the practice of Great Britain and other countries of sending paupers. His presentation of consular reports and other information in the next session gave no firm evidence of assisted emigration of paupers from Europe.[15] The same question came up again in the 25th Congress in the form of a petition from a nativist organization, and a House resolution in March 1838 requested the Secretary of State and the President to provide information on "the introduction of foreign paupers." The presidential report con-

[14]Concerning violators of narcotic drug acts see p. 434 of this chapter.
[15]See p. 26 above.

sisted for the most part of already transmitted material but also included some new material that raised suspicion of some systematic sending of undesirables.[16]

Other evidence was obtained nearer at hand. An extensive House inquiry of the following year, 1839, collected information on the extent of alien poor relief in major cities of the country, sufficient to convince the congressional committee of inquiry that certain nations were sending their paupers to the United States. A bill was introduced at the time to impose a heavy fine on the master of any vessel bringing in certain undesirable aliens, but no action was taken on it. Some years after, in 1845 during the second session of the 28th Congress, the subject of criminal and pauper immigration came up again, with resolutions of inquiry and a lengthy presentation of testimony concerning the problem of alien paupers and criminals in several large cities.[17] No further legislative action was taken at the time, however. Two years later, in the second session of the 29th Congress, a House bill for the exclusion of such aliens made no progress; and the second session of the 30th Congress saw rejection of a resolution that certain alien passengers be required to give security against becoming public charges.[18]

More determined efforts to enact legislation to exclude undesirable aliens were made in 1855 during the second session of the 33rd Congress. A resolution had called on the House Committee on Commerce to consider legislation for the exclusion of certain unwanted types of aliens, and early in the year the committee reported out a bill to prevent the introduction of foreign criminals, paupers, the blind, and mental defectives. The Senate Committee on the Judiciary was likewise petitioned to consider such legislation, and a bill for the exclusion of alien paupers and others was presented and passed by the Senate, but was rejected by the House. Reintroduced in the next Congress with a lengthy report on crime and poverty attached, the bill again failed of enactment.[19] The state rights issue was becoming more prominent, and it may have led to resistance to national legislation on matters of concern to the separate states.

During the wartime years of the early 1860s immigration was looked upon with more favor, and it was not until well into the postwar decade that congressional attention returned to the regulation and control of immigration. The 1875 Act, passed near the close of the 43rd Congress, did not include foreign paupers among the several classes of aliens to be excluded, but this omission was pointed out in the next Congress. A

[16]See pp. 27–28.

[17]See p. 34 above.

[18]See p. 37.

[19]See p. 40–42.

resolution proposed but not adopted in the Senate called on the Committee on Commerce to consider legislation for protection against "the evils of pauperism, crime, and other injuries to the morals and good order of society." The problem of Chinese immigration on the West Coast took precedence over other immigration matters for a time, and it was not until early in the next decade that Congress undertook further legislation for the regulation and control of immigration. The product was the Act of August 3, 1882 (22 Stat. 214), which built on and greatly expanded the regulatory provisions of the 1875 Act. The immediate occasion for the new act was that the Supreme Court had recently and conclusively struck down the states' efforts to control immigration. This action brought forth a number of petitions to Congress for protective legislation, and members of Congress from the most concerned states, especially New York, were active in promoting action by Congress.

The central problem, from the viewpoint of the states concerned, was that of destitute immigrants and the burden of providing for them, but the various petitions also pointed out other problems arising from immigration. The 1882 Act, a broad regulatory act, quite closely followed the example of the earlier provincial and state laws dealing with the alien poor. Added to the excludable classes was "any persons unable to take care of himself or herself without becoming a public charge." Like other excludables, they were to be returned in the vessel of arrival "to the countries from whence they came," at the expense of the vessel's owners. Also as in the preceding state laws, a head tax was imposed to meet the expenses of regulating immigration and caring for needy immigrants on arrival.

Evidently the 1882 Act did not put an end to the problem, for in his annual message to Congress on December 4, 1883, President Arthur noted the need for further legislation. Paupers were still coming from Great Britain, and although numbers of them had been sent back, the movement should be checked at the source rather than at the port of arrival. And paupers were also coming by way of Canada, presumably without inspection on arrival in the United States.[20] The message brought no action from Congress.

The next step toward tighter controls on immigration was the report in early 1889 of the House Select Committee on Investigation of Foreign Immigration, better known as the Ford Committee. Among the conclusions drawn by the Committee after lengthy study was that facilities were not adequate for the proper inspection of arriving passengers, that there was evidence of assisted immigration of paupers, and that the Canadian

[20]See p. 85 above.

border was a wide-open route for uninspected immigration. In spite of the evidence presented in the report, the Committee's bill incorporating its recommendations was not acted on by the House.[21]

Two years later, the regulatory Act of March 3, 1891 was passed (26 Stat. 1084). More concisely than the 1882 Act, it excluded "paupers or persons likely to become a public charge" and inadmissible aliens were to be returned immediately if practicable, maintained while on land and returned by vessel at the expense of the vessel's owner or agent. The 1891 Act was eventually superseded by the Act of March 3, 1903 (32 Stat. 1213), which raised the head tax on alien passengers, continued the exclusion of paupers and persons likely to become public charges, and added "professional beggars" as a new excludable class.

A financial test for likelihood of becoming a public charge was proposed several years later, in 1906, in an omnibus immigration bill sponsored by the House Committee on Immigration and Naturalization. A male alien over sixteen years of age not in possession of twenty-five dollars was to be considered likely to become a public charge, unless he was the member of a family whose head was in possession of fifty dollars. For females over sixteen years of age the required minimum was fifteen dollars. Exemption from the financial requirement was granted to refugees from religious and political persecution. As finally passed, the bill combined House and Senate provisions as the Act of February 20, 1907 (34 Stat. 898). The language for the exclusion of aliens of the public charge class remained as in the 1903 Act, without the committee's financial test. And the head tax was doubled. A new provision was the added excludability of

> persons not comprehended within any of the foregoing excluded classes who are found to be and are certified by the examining surgeon as being mentally or physically defective, such mental or physical defect being of a nature which may affect the ability of such alien to earn a living. (Sect. 2, Act of February 20, 1907 [34 Stat. 898])

The language of the 1907 Act concerning the exclusion of aliens of the public charge class was repeated unchanged in the Act of 1910. The 1917 Act somewhat altered the statement to "paupers; professional beggars; vagrants" and "persons likely to become a public charge," but it repeated the exclusion of the 1907 Act concerning mental or physical defect that may affect ability to earn a living (sect. 3, Act of February 5, 1917 [39 Stat. 874]). It also provided, in the case of the general exclusion

[21]See p. 97.

of children under sixteen years of age unaccompanied by a parent or not coming to join one or both parents, that exception might be made at the discretion of the Secretary of Labor if in his opinion the child in question is not likely to become a public charge and is otherwise admissible.

The excludability of aliens falling in the public charge class as defined in the 1917 Act remained unchanged for thirty-five years, although as previously noted the phrase "likely to become a public charge" was more strictly interpreted during the Depression years.[22] The 1952 Act, which took the place of the 1917 Act as the basic law of immigration and naturalization, followed the pattern of the earlier act in the designation of three classes of excludables of the public charge group:

> (7) Aliens . . . who are certified by the examining surgeon as having a physical defect, disease, or disability, when determined by the consular or immigration officer to be of such a nature that it may affect the ability of the alien to earn a living, unless the alien affirmatively establishes that he will not have to earn a living
> (8) Aliens who are paupers, professional beggars, or vagrants
> (15) Aliens who, in the opinion of the consular officer at the time of application for a visa, or in the opinion of the Attorney General at the time of application for admission, are likely at any time to become public charges. (Sect. 212 (a)(7), (8), and (15) of the 1952 Act)

In this form there is not a great change in substance from the immediately preceding acts, but the last paragraph explicitly gives a large measure of discretion to the administrative officers. And the intention of Congress here as in the corresponding portion of the 1917 Act was to authorize exclusion on economic as well as other considerations.

Mental Defectives

Mental defect has been ground for exclusion ever since it was first included in the 1882 Act. In contrast to the previously described cases of alien criminals and public charges, there appears to have been little vocal

[22]See p. 219 above. According to instructions to immigrant inspectors in the 1940s, an alien excludable as likely to become a public charge "is one who by reason of poverty, insanity, or disease or disability will probably become a charge upon the public" (*Immigration Manual,* Washington, D.C.: U.S. Government Printing Office, 1946). Supported by legal decisions, the following conditions were to be taken as evidence that an alien belongs in this excludable class: insufficient funds for support to destination or until work is found, advanced age and lack of friends or relatives responsible for support, crippled, low earning power and burdened with dependents, addiction to drinking or gambling, and deaf-mutism if accompanied by poverty and ignorance. On the other hand, an offer of assistance from someone not under legal obligation to do so or an offer of employment did not necessarily remove an alien from the excludable class.

concern over the possible entry of alien mental defectives, and their eventual addition to the list of excludables was seemingly by common consent and without debate. As early as 1838 a bill was introduced in the House to impose a heavy fine on any ship's master bringing in "an idiot, lunatic, maniac," or certain other undesirable aliens, but no action was taken.[23]

Once instituted in 1882 the exclusion of mental defectives was continued by act after act with only limited change of terminology. Excluded by the 1882 Act were lunatics and idiots. This became idiots and insane persons in the 1891 Act, and was then expanded in the 1903 Act to

> All idiots, insane persons, epileptics, and persons who have been insane within five years previous; persons who have had two or more attacks of insanity at any time previously.

The same wording was used in the 1907 Act except for the addition of imbeciles and feebleminded persons to the list of excludable mental defectives; and as described in the preceding section there was the addition of the new excludable class of those with mental or physical defects that might affect ability to earn a living. This was followed within a few years by the renewed and revised statement of exclusions in the 1910 Act, which repeated the wording of the 1907 Act regarding the mental defect classes.

Soon after came the 1911 Immigration Commission Report that strongly argued the need for a much more selective and restrictive immigration policy. The drive in Congress centered on the so-called Burnett bill reintroduced in the immediately following Congresses and eventually leading to the 1917 Act. In December 1914 the Senate committee proposed, among other amendments to the bill, that a new class of exclusion for mental defect be added: "persons of constitutional psychopathic inferiority." The new term was discussed in the course of the Senate debate and was defended as based on good authority, but it was referred back to committee for further consideration. The bill itself was defeated by veto but reappeared in the next Congress, the 64th (1915–1917). The accompanying report stated that the term "constitutional psychopathic inferiority" was well understood by alienists, and was defined as "a congenital defect in the emotional or volitional fields of mental activity which results in inability to make proper adjustment to the environment."[24] This was sufficiently convincing to the members of Congress, for the new excludable class was included in the bill that eventually became the 1917 Act over President Wilson's veto.

There is finally the 1952 Act, which retained the substance of the

[23]See p. 29.

[24]H. Rept. 95 (64-I), p. 2.

preceding act concerning mental defect, although with some change of form in the first four paragraphs of its section 212a:

(1) aliens who are feebleminded;
(2) aliens who are insane;
(3) aliens who have had one or more attacks of insanity;
(4) aliens afflicted with psychopathic personality,[25] epilepsy, or a mental defect.

In paragraph (7) which followed, exclusion for a defect that may affect the ability to earn a living is now limited to physical defects, rather than both mental and physical defects as formerly.

There was a reversal after 1952 in the trend to more and more excludable classes. It came to be held that with modern knowledge and methods of treatment of the ailment, epilepsy was no longer sufficient cause for exclusion. Bills introduced by the "liberal" group in Congress in 1962 and 1963[26] called for elimination of epilepsy as ground for exclusion, and it was finally eliminated by the Act of October 3, 1965 (79 Stat. 911). The same act amended section 212(a)(1) of the 1952 Act to read "mentally retarded" instead of "feeble-minded."

Health and Physical Defect

Included within this group of excludable classes are two types of cases: certain communicable diseases, and physical defects considered serious enough to warrant denial of entry. The presumable policy or purpose is therefore for quarantine or public health protection in one case, and protection against present or future dependency in the other case. In fact, however, economic considerations may enter in both types of cases, in view of ailments requiring hospitalization or long, continued care.

Congress at first preferred to leave such matters to the states and port authorities, but in midyear of 1838 the House received a bill and an accompanying committee report proposing a heavy fine on a ship's master who brings in an alien passenger afflicted with "any incurable disease," mental defect, or a criminal record. The specification of incurability suggests that economic as well as health considerations were involved; but in any event the bill did not progress in Congress.[27] Eleven years later Congress received a bill for bonding of certain foreign passen-

[25]The new term "psychopathic personality" replaced "constitutional psychopathic inferiority" and was not further defined but left to be determined by the examining medical officer at the port of entry. On May 22, 1967 the Supreme Court ruled that the term is not unconstitutional because of vagueness (*Boutilier* v. *I & NS*).

[26]See pp. 353, 361. [27]See p. 29.

gers, including those "who are diseased," lest they become public charges,[28] emphasizing economic rather than health considerations. Again there was no action on the bill.

The emphasis changed when the threat of an epidemic arose. Thus a number of petitions for sanitary inspection of immigration reached Congress in 1882–1883, and bills were introduced for that purpose but not passed.[29] Ten years later there was fear that the epidemic of cholera prevailing in Europe would cross the Atlantic; vessels from abroad were put under quarantine, and a presidential message to Congress stressed the need for strict controls on immigration for health as well as other reasons. Suspension of all immigration while the danger lasted was proposed but not adopted; but Congress did adopt the Act of February 15, 1893 (27 Stat. 449) to give the President power to prohibit "the introduction of persons and property" if a serious threat of disease arises.[30] The power so granted was never exercised and was eventually repealed a half-century later by the Act of July 1, 1944 (58 Stat. 682).

Meanwhile, Congress had established a new excludable class in the 1891 Act, consisting of "persons suffering from a loathsome or a dangerous contagious disease," a rather comprehensive but imprecise term that left considerable margin of discretion to the examining surgeon at the port of entry. This exclusion was reaffirmed in the 1903 Act, strengthened in section 9 of the Act with the provision that it is unlawful for any person or company to transport to the United States an alien so afflicted, subject to a fine of $100 for every alien so transported if it is shown that "such disease might have been detected by means of a competent medical examination."[31] This was, again, the familiar device of shifting responsibility for examination and selection—in fact of enforcement of the immigration laws— to the transporter of alien passengers to the United States.

An exception to the exclusion of cases of disease was made in section 37 of the 1903 Act. There it was provided that if a resident alien has filed his first papers or declaration of intention to become a citizen, has sent for his wife or minor children to join him, and any of such relatives are found on arrival to have a contagious disease, they are not to be excluded and deported if it can be proved the disease was contracted on shipboard, but instead are to be held until it is determined if the disease is easily curable or that they can be allowed to land without danger to others.

[28]See p. 37.

[29]See p. 83.

[30]See pp. 106–7 above.

[31]Such a penalty for bringing an alien with a loathsome or contagious disease had been recommended by the Industrial Commission in its report to Congress of two years before (see p. 128 above).

A constructive suggestion was made in the session following passage of the 1903 Act. A bill introduced by Dillingham of Vermont, who was later to become a Senate leader in immigration legislation, proposed that the medical examination of passengers be made before departure rather than on arrival. An argument in favor of the bill was that this measure would help protect the health of passengers on shipboard. The bill was not approved by Congress, and preinspection did not appear until a number of years later.

Exclusions for disease and defect were expanded somewhat further in later acts. The 1907 Act enlarged the excluding phrase to "persons afflicted with tuberculosis or with a loathsome or dangerous contagious disease," continued the fine for bringing in this or other excludable classes of aliens, and continued the exclusion of aliens with mental or physical defects that might interfere with self-support. The provision in section 37 of the 1903 Act for the reuniting of families in spite of a finding of disease was changed in section 37 of the 1907 Act to remove the limitation to cases of disease proved to have been contracted in transit.

The classes excludable by reason of disease and physical defect remained unchanged in the 1910 Act. In the 1917 Act the exclusion of tuberculosis was expanded to "tuberculosis in any form," thus making clear the inclusion of nonpulmonary forms of the disease. Section 22 of the act continued the provision for the reuniting of families, under certain conditions, in spite of "contagious disorder," but broadened its applicability to include the families of both naturalized and permanently resident aliens.

Finally, excludability for disease and defect under the 1952 Act was, first, for tuberculosis in any form, leprosy, or "any dangerous contagious disease"; it was, second, for physical defect, disease, or disability that may interfere with ability to earn a living "unless the alien affirmatively establishes that he will not have to earn a living." Admission under bond was permitted for aliens excludable because likely to become a public charge or because of physical disability, except those with tuberculosis in any form, leprosy, or a dangerous contagious disease (sect. 213 of the 1952 Act). And as in preceding acts, exclusion was reinforced by a penalty against anyone bringing in aliens excludable because of mental defect, chronic alcoholism, tuberculosis in any form, leprosy, any dangerous contagious disease, or drug addiction. The penalty was now increased to $1,000 for each such alien brought in (sect. 272a of the 1952 Act).

After 1952 opinion gradually shifted in favor of a more lenient immigration policy, and one manifestation of this trend was a disposition on the part of Congress to grant exceptions to the strict exclusion requirements in some hardship and especially deserving cases. And with regard to certain diseases, it was felt that recent progress in control measures and treatment had ended the need to exclude them. In 1956, for example, the second session of the 84th Congress received four refugee bills that included authorization for the admission of as many as a thousand refugees with tuberculosis, subject to adequate assurance that they would not become public charges or a danger to the health of others.[32] None of the bills was adopted at the time, but the following year Congress passed the Act of September 11, 1957 (71 Stat. 639), section 6 of which authorized the admission of aliens with tuberculosis provided they were the spouse, child, or parent of a citizen or of an alien lawfully admitted for permanent residence. Report of each such admission was to be made to Congress, and no visas under this section of the act were to be issued after June 30, 1959. This termination date was extended two years to June 30, 1961 by the Act of September 9, 1959 (73 Stat. 490), which also expanded the coverage of the provision to include the specified relatives of aliens who have been issued an immigration visa. The termination date was later removed, to make the provision regarding tuberculous relatives permanent, by the Act of September 26, 1961 (75 Stat. 650). As first introduced, the bill that eventually became this act contained authorization for the Public Health Service to determine what diseases would justify denial of entry. As passed, the act amended the list of excludable classes in the 1952 Act to make the excluding paragraph for diseases read: "Aliens who are afflicted with any dangerous contagious disease," omitting specific mention of tuberculosis in any form and leprosy (sect. 212[a][6] of the 1952 Act). The omission was recognition that the diseases were no longer the public health menace they had once been.

The Immoral Classes

From its first selective immigration law in 1875, Congress took a moralistic position and forbade the entry of those who might corrupt the morals of the American people. From this beginning Congress labored to devise more and more comprehensive measures, free of legal loopholes, for the exclusion of all aliens regarded as immoral.

Three of the five sections of the 1875 Act related wholly or partly to the exclusion of prostitutes. The first section made it the duty of consular officials at any port from which subjects of China, Japan, or any other Oriental nation were to depart for the United States to determine whether such travel was "free and voluntary," to ascertain whether any such travelers were under contract or agreement to serve for "lewd and immoral purposes" in the United States, and in the latter case to refuse

[32]See p. 327 above.

to grant the required permit for the travel. The third section of the act forbade the importation of women for prostitution, outlawed all contracts and agreements for such importation, and made illegal importation a felony subject to imprisonment of up to five years and a fine of up to $5,000. The fifth section included "women imported for the purposes of prostitution" as one of the excluded classes. Especially noteworthy here is the first provision for consular inspection at the point of departure, a strengthening of the exclusion provision.

The 1903 Act made excludable "prostitutes, and persons who procure or attempt to bring in prostitutes or women for the purpose of prostitution." This phrasing was in accordance with the recommendation of the Industrial Commission in 1901. And section 3 of the act repeated the prohibition of importation of females for prostitution, under the same penalties as provided in the 1875 Act.

A bill from the House committee in 1906 recommended among other things a further strengthening and revision of the laws against the admission of aliens classified as immoral.[33] In the expanded wording of the act of the following year, exclusion was stipulated for

> prostitutes, or women or girls coming into the United States for the purpose of prostitution or for any other immoral purpose; persons who procure or attempt to bring in prostitutes or women or girls for the purpose of prostitution or for any other immoral purpose. (Sect. 2, Act of 1907)

Three years later the Act of March 26, 1910 added the phrase "persons who are supported by or receive in whole or in part the proceeds of prostitution (sect. 1). Soon after Congress passed the White Slave Traffic Act of June 25, 1910 (36 Stat. 825), better known as the Mann Act, which prohibited the importation and the interstate transportation of women for immoral purposes.

Following the 1911 Immigration Commission Report there was a long-continued drive in Congress to secure more stringent immigration legislation. One proposal that failed of enactment at the time was to deny citizenship through marriage with an American citizen to certain "sexually immoral females."[34] The 1917 Act, which marked the eventual triumph of restrictionist efforts, retained the earlier definition of the immoral classes to be excluded. Exclusion was reinforced, however, by severe penalties of fine and imprisonment for anyone found guilty of importing, attempting to import, or employing an alien for the purpose of prostitution; and further penalty was provided for any alien, previously

[33]See p. 138 above.

[34]See p. 162 above.

excluded and deported under the act as it related to the immoral classes, who seeks again to enter the United States (sect. 4, 1917 Act). A later section incorporated the proposal of several years earlier by providing that "a female of the sexually immoral classes" who has been excluded and deported under the terms of the act cannot acquire citizenship through marriage to an American citizen if the marriage occurred after her arrest or after commission of the immoral acts in question (first proviso, sect. 19[a] of the 1917 Act).

Although it excluded what were basically the same immoral classes as the preceding act, the 1952 Act sought through more elaborate statement to give an inclusive definition of such classes, which included prostitutes, procurers, those receiving proceeds of prostitution, aliens engaged in other forms of vice, and those coming to "engage in any immoral sexual act."[35] The act also designated as a felony and provided penalties for bringing in or maintaining an alien for the purpose of prostitution (sect. 278).

More recently there has been a tendency to relax the mandatory exclusion of the immoral classes in a few special cases. The Act of September 11, 1957 (71 Stat. 639) permitted the admission under certain conditions of several classes of technically excludable aliens, including the immoral classes designated in section 212(a)(12) of the 1952 Act,[36] provided the alien in question is the spouse, child, or parent of a citizen or lawfully resident alien, and exclusion would be an extreme hardship to the relatives in the United States (sect. 5, 1957 Act). This provision was restated and somewhat broadened by the Act of September 26, 1961 (75 Stat. 650) in section 14. Sexual deviation was added as a ground for exclusion by the 1965 Act (sect. 15[b]).

Another class of excludables appearing quite early in the development of federal immigration legislation is that of polygamists. It is not clear whether their exclusion was more on moral or religious grounds, or a combination of both, but it occurred at a time of public outcry over

[35]Excluded by section 212(a)(12) and (13) are:

(12) Aliens who are prostitutes or who have engaged in prostitution, or aliens coming to the United States solely, principally, or incidentally to engage in prostitution; aliens who directly or indirectly procure or attempt to procure, or who have procured or attempted to procure or to import, prostitutes or persons for the purpose of prostitution or for any other immoral purpose; and aliens who are or have been supported by, or receive or have received, in whole or in part, the proceeds of prostitution or aliens coming to the United States to engage in any other unlawful commercialized vice, whether or not related to prostitution;

(13) Aliens coming to the United States to engage in any immoral sexual act.

[36]See footnote 35.

the reported practice of polygamy among the followers of Brigham Young in Utah. It was the 1891 Act that first made polygamists excludable, to be followed unchanged by the 1903 Act. The 1907 Act, however, expanded the exclusion to include "polygamists, or persons who admit their belief in the practice of polygamy"; and the same wording was used in the 1910 Act. Several years later an attempt was made in the Senate to substitute the phrase excluding those who "believe in, advocate, or practice polygamy," but this wording was not adopted.[37] The 1917 Act, however, adopted similar wording, the formulation there being "polygamists, or persons who practice polygamy or believe in or advocate the practice of polygamy." This phrase was carried in the 1952 Act except for omission of belief in polygamy.

Other indications of congressional concern with the moral character of newcomers to the United States are to be found in addition to those noted above. In the exclusion of criminals, as already seen in an earlier section, Congress laid much stress on crimes defined as involving "moral turpitude." And it will be seen in later chapters that a condition for favorable treatment of an alien, such as for suspension of deportation, is that the alien be shown to be "of good moral character." To make clear the intention of Congress, the 1952 Act set forth at some length what is to be taken as evidence of a lack of good moral character.[38] Much more than sexual immorality alone was included.

[37]See p. 163 above.

[38]Section 101(f) of the 1952 Act reads:

(f) For the purposes of this Act—

No person shall be regarded as, or found to be, a person of good moral character who, during the period for which good moral character is required to be established, is, or was—

(1) a habitual drunkard;

(2) one who during such period has committed adultery;

(3) a member of one or more of the classes of persons, whether excludable or not . . . [criminal, polygamist, immoral, drug law violator, or who has aided an alien to enter illegally] . . . if the offense described . . . for which such person was convicted or of which he admits the commission, was committed during such period;

(4) one whose income is derived principally from illegal gambling activities;

(5) one who has been convicted of two or more gambling offenses committed during such period;

(6) one who has given false testimony for the purpose of obtaining any benefits under this Act;

(7) one who during such period has been confined, as a result of conviction, to a penal institution for an aggregate period of one hundred and eighty days or more, regardless of whether the offense, or offenses, for which he has been confined were committed within or without such period;

(8) one who at any time has been convicted of the crime of murder.

The fact that any person is not within any of the foregoing classes shall not preclude a finding that for other reasons such person is or was not of good moral character.

Subversives

It was not until relatively late and after repeated attempts at new legislation that Congress embarked on a policy of excluding aliens for their political beliefs. Once embarked Congress labored in act after act to produce all-inclusive and unevadable definitions of the subversive classes to be excluded. The product was a lengthy, labored, and tortuous chapter of immigration law that was fundamentally unenforceable or only partially enforceable at the level of exclusions.

A fear of alien subversion, it will be recalled, appeared early in the history of the new republic and found expression at that time in the short-lived Alien and Sedition Acts.[39] Some ninety years later a new fear of alien ideologies took form, directed now against what was considered to be a sinister group, the anarchists. The Ford Committee report of early 1889 noted that anarchists were being driven out of European countries and recommended that they be "rigidly excluded."[40] Bills for their exclusion were introduced in 1893 and 1894 but not approved.[41]

Pressure for action against anarchists increased with the assassination of President McKinley on September 6, 1901. Three months later his successor, Theodore Roosevelt, included in his message on the opening of the 57th Congress a strong plea for the exclusion of "anarchists or persons professing principles hostile to all government."[42] Two days later the Industrial Commission in its report on immigration recommended the exclusion and deportation of anarchists.[43] It was not until the 1903 Act, however, that

> anarchists, or persons who believe in or advocate the overthrow by force or violence of the Government of the United States or of all government or of all forms of law, or the assassination of public officials

were made excludable. As if this listing of anarchists among the other excludable classes in section 2 of the act was not enough to satisfy congressional concern, the final two sections of the act, sections 38 and 39, were devoted to a detailed outlawing of anarchists[44] that called for

[39]See pp. 12–16 above.
[40]See p. 97 above.
[41]See pp. 108, 111–13.
[42]See p. 127 above.
[43]See p. 128 above.
[44]In the language of the sections, an anarchist was a "person who disbelieves in or is opposed to all organized government, or who is a member of or affiliated with any organization entertaining and teaching such disbelief in or opposition to all organized government, or who advocates or teaches the duty, necessity, or propriety of the unlawful assaulting or killing of any officer or officers, either of specific individuals or of officers generally, of the Government of the United States or of any other organized government, because of his or their official character. . . ."

(1) denial of entry to such aliens;
(2) fine or imprisonment for anyone who aids them in any way to enter;
(3) denial of naturalization;
(4) fine or imprisonment for those who secure naturalization illegally;
(5) and similar punishment for anyone who knowingly aids their naturalization.

The 1907 Act retained the exclusion of anarchists, repeated the exclusion in a later section, and continued the penalty for anyone who aids the entry of an anarchist (sect. 38). The brief exclusion Act of 1910 amended the 1907 Act but left its treatment of anarchists unchanged. The 1917 Act consolidated, in one lengthy statement of the subversive classes to be excluded, much of the substance of the several sections of the immediately preceding acts that dealt with subversives,[45] but reserved for a later section the penalty for those who knowingly aid an anarchist to enter (sect. 28).

Under wartime conditions the terms of the 1917 Act came to seem inadequate not long after its passage, and it was soon followed by the so-called Anarchists Act of October 16, 1918 (40 Stat. 1012). In more explicit and greater detail than its predecessors, the new act excluded aliens of the anarchist and related classes, ordered their deportation if within the United States, and made it a felony punishable by not over five years imprisonment for those previously excluded or deported to reenter or try to reenter.

Two years later the 1918 Act, apparently being considered insufficient safeguard against the anarchist menace, was amended and rewritten by the Act of June 5, 1920 (41 Stat. 1008). Included more specifically in the anarchist class were aliens who advocate or are members of organizations advocating "the unlawful damage, injury or destruction of property, or sabotage." And added to the excludable anarchist class

[45]The subversive classes in section 3 of the 1917 Act were given as "anarchists, or persons who believe in or advocate the overthrow by force or violence of the Government of the United States, or of all forms of law, or who disbelieve in or are opposed to organized government, or who advocate the assassination of public officials, or who advocate or teach the unlawful destruction of property; persons who are members of or affiliated with any organization entertaining and teaching disbelief in or opposition to organized government, or who advocate or teach the duty, necessity, or propriety of the unlawful assaulting or killing of any officer or officers, either of specific individuals or of officers generally, of the Government of the United States or of any other organized government, because of his or their official character, or who advocate or teach the unlawful destruction of property. . . ."

were aliens who themselves or who are affiliated with organizations that

> write, publish, or cause to be written or published, or who knowingly circulate, distribute, print, or display, or knowingly cause to be circulated, distributed, printed, published, or displayed, or who knowingly have in their possession for the purpose of circulation, distribution, publication or display . . .

any material advocating any of the anarchist principles or purposes as set forth earlier in the act. To make clear the full intention of the act, the final section defined advocacy to include "the giving, loaning or promising of money or any thing of value" to be used for the promotion of anarchist principles; and "affiliation," according to the act, meant similar support of any organization engaged in any way in the promotion of those principles.

Fear of alien subversion revived during the Depression years of the 1930s, but now with Communists replacing anarchists as the target of legislation and with Dies of Texas the most active proponent of strong measures. Eight bills for the addition of Communists to the excludable classes were introduced during the session of 1931 to 1932 but none was passed.[46] Two Congresses later, in 1935 to 1936, exclusion and expulsion of alien Communists and Fascists were proposed, but again not approved by Congress.[47]

Later bills and legislation concerned themselves more particularly with the deportation of subversive aliens who had gained entry,[48] but a new excludable class of subversives was added by the Act of May 25, 1948 (62 Stat. 268). The new class was

> . . . aliens who the Attorney General knows or has reason to believe seek to enter the United States for the purpose of engaging in activities which will endanger the public safety of the United States.

Although it refrained from stating so, the act was presumably directed against Communist espionage and related activities. Presumably for the same purpose, although again not so stated, was a provision in an act passed one month later, the Displaced Persons Act of June 25, 1948. According to section 13 of that act (62 Stat. 1009),

> No visas shall be issued under the provisions of this Act to any person who is or has been a member of, or participated in, any movement

[46]See p. 224 above. [47]See p. 237 above.

[48]See pp. 246–47, 252–53, 260; also the following chapter on deportation.

> which is or has been hostile to the United States or the form of government of the United States.

Two years later this section was amended to explicitly deny entry to any displaced persons of Communist persuasion,[49] together with those who had engaged in the persecution of others because of race, religion, or national origin, and those who had borne arms against the United States. For good measure each applicant for a visa under the act was required to make oath or affirmation that he had never been a member of any organization or movement of the proscribed type.

The 81st Congress (1949–1951) continued the effort to write legislation denying entry to all alien Communists, Communist sympathizers, and allied classes,[50] and for this purpose included in the Internal Security Act of 1950 (64 Stat. 987) a section (sect. 22) rewriting the anarchist exclusion and expulsion act of 1918. As rewritten, the first section of the 1918 Act excluded the following classes of subversives:

1. aliens who seek to enter for harmful or subversive purposes;
2. aliens who are or have been
   - A. anarchists
   - B. advocates or members of organizations that advocate opposition to organized government
   - C. members or affiliates of a communist or totalitarian party or organization
   - D. advocates or members of any organization that advocates communist or totalitarian doctrines
   - E. members or affiliates of organizations listed under the Subversive Activities Control Act of 1950, unless shown to be unaware it was a communist organization
   - F. advocates or members of an organization that advocates violence directed against any organized government, or sabotage
   - G. associated in any way with the publication or circulation of subversive material

[49]As amended by the Act of June 16, 1950 (64 Stat. 219), the section came to read in part: "No visas shall be issued under the provisions of this Act . . . to any person who is or has been a member of the Communist Party, or to any person who adheres to, advocates, or follows, or who has adhered to, advocated, or followed, the principles of any political or economic system or philosophy directed toward the destruction of free competitive enterprise and the revolutionary overthrow of representative governments, or to any person who is or has been a member of any organization which has been designated by the Attorney General . . . as a Communist organization, or to any person who is or has been a member of or participated in any movement which is or has been hostile to the United States or the form of government of the United States. . . ."

[50]See pp. 292–94 above.

H. members or affiliates of organizations concerned with such subversive material;

3. aliens believed likely to engage in subversive activities after entry.

Realizing that there might be innocent members of Communist organizations and that the amended 1918 Act would apply to them with equal severity, Congress moved in the following year to instruct the Attorney General that the terms "members of" and "affiliated with" as used in the act should be interpreted to include only

> membership or affiliation which is or was voluntary, and shall not include membership or affiliation which is or was solely (a) when under sixteen years of age, (b) by operation of law, or (c) for purposes of obtaining employment, food rations, or other essentials of living, and where necessary for such purposes.

These instructions were contained in the Act of March 28, 1951 (65 Stat. 28).

In the next year the McCarran-Walter Act of 1952 incorporated the exclusion provisions of the amended 1918 Act without substantive change, together with the interpretation of membership and affiliation added in 1951;[51] but to the latter it added the further qualification that an alien who has given up his membership or affiliation with a subversive organization in the terms of the act may be admitted if

> (a) since the termination of such membership or affiliation, such alien is and has been, for at least five years prior to the date of the application for a visa, actively opposed to the doctrine, program, principles, and ideology of such party or organization or the section, subsidiary, branch, or affiliate or subdivision thereof, and (b) the admission of such alien into the United States would be in the public interest.

Later antisubversive acts[52] dealt with internal security and did not revise the exclusion of subversives as contained in the 1952 Act.

Labor Classes

The close connection between immigration policy and labor policy is evident, and Congress has been well aware of this politically sensitive aspect of immigration. On the one hand, Congress has recognized the

[51] Paragraphs 27, 28, and 29 of sect. 212a of the 1952 Act.

[52] Such as the Communist Control Act of August 24, 1954 (68 Stat. 775) and the August 1, 1956 Act (70 Stat. 899) for the registration of persons trained in sabotage, espionage, etc.

economic advantages of an ample labor supply and has sought to facilitate the entry of aliens with needed skills and abilities; on the other hand, Congress has acted to protect the domestic labor force from undue immigrant competition and has excluded certain classes of workers. Chapter 15 deals with labor policy elements in immigration legislation as a whole, but exclusions based on labor market considerations are summarized here.[53]

The first federal attempts to keep out unwanted labor were the so-called contract labor laws, the earliest of which was the Act of February 26, 1885. Among the provisions of that act designed to suppress the recruitment of labor abroad was a provision to make it unlawful to prepay the transportation or otherwise encourage the immigration of laborers under contract, to declare such contracts void, and to levy a fine for knowingly transporting a contract laborer to the United States. Specifically exempted were skilled laborers brought to establish a new industry, skilled laborers not obtainable in the United States, professional actors, artists, lecturers, singers, personal or domestic servants, and relatives or personal friends coming for the purpose of settlement (sect. 5, 1885 Act [23 Stat. 332]). The amending Act of February 23, 1887 provided that all prohibited contract laborers "be sent back to the nations to which they belong and from whence they came" (sect. 8 [24 Stat. 414]). The exclusion of contract laborers was reaffirmed by the Act of October 19, 1888.

The first section of the Immigration Act of March 3, 1891 listed the classes of aliens to be excluded, including contract laborers as defined by the 1885 Act. Also excluded was "any person whose ticket or passage is paid for with the money of another or who is assisted by others to come," with the exception of those sent for by a friend or relative. Exemption was expanded to include "ministers of any religious denomination, . . . persons belonging to any recognized profession, [and] professors for colleges and seminaries" (sect. 5, 1891 Act [26 Stat. 1084]). The Act of April 30, 1900 (31 Stat. 141) extended the laws respecting contract laborers to Hawaii. The wording of the 1891 Act was carried over to the Act of March 3, 1903 (32 Stat. 1213), which also excluded those who within one year before their application for admission have been deported as contract laborers.

In the 1907 Immigration Act Congress, aware of loopholes in and evasions of the contract labor laws, sought to write exclusion provisions

[53]The Chinese coolie and Chinese exclusion laws may not have been entirely for the purpose of preventing the introduction of a new form of servitude and of keeping out an alien race, for they may have contained labor market considerations as well; but treatment of these laws is postponed to a later chapter on racial and ethnic group policy.

that would deny entry to all possible cases of recruited labor. To be excluded in the words of the act were

> persons hereinafter called contract laborers, who have been induced or solicited to migrate to this country by offers or promises of employment or in consequence of agreements, oral, written or printed, express or implied, to perform labor in this country of any kind, skilled or unskilled; those who have been, within one year from the date of application for admission to the United States, deported as having been induced or solicited to migrate as above described; any person whose ticket or passage is paid for with the money of another, or who is assisted by others to come, unless it is affirmatively and satisfactorily shown that such person does not belong to one of the foregoing excluded classes, and that said ticket or passage was not paid for by any corporation, association, society, municipality, or foreign government, either directly or indirectly.

But provisos attached to section 2 of the act exempted several occupational groups from the above exclusions, which included

> skilled labor . . . if labor of like kind unemployed can not be found in this country, . . . professional actors, artists, lecturers, singers, ministers of any religious denomination, professors for colleges or seminaries, persons belonging to any recognized learned profession, or persons employed strictly as personal or domestic servants.

These exclusions and exceptions were reaffirmed by the Act of March 26, 1910 (36 Stat. 263) with only minor change except for a new proviso to exempt aliens in transit through the United States from exclusion if their ticket or passage was paid by another.

The Immigration Act of 1917 somewhat expanded the definition of the excludable classes of contract laborers, presumably in response to problems that had arisen in interpretation and enforcement of the laws. The additions to the excludable classes were (1) persons assisted or encouraged to come, (2) those induced to come by false offers or promises of employment, and (3) "persons who have come in consequence of advertisements for laborers printed, published, or distributed in a foreign country." Provisos for exemption from the contract labor laws remained as in 1907 except for the addition of nurses to the exempt occupations.

The 1917 Act remained the basic immigration and nationality act until repealed and replaced by the 1952 Act, and during the intervening years the contract labor exclusion remained unchanged, with only a clarifying act during the Depression years. The Act of March 17, 1932 (47 Stat. 67) affirmed the application of the contract labor provisions of the 1917 Act to instrumental musicians by declaring such a musician not to be considered an "artist" or "professional actor" within the meaning of the act unless "of distinguished merit and ability" and coming for professional engagements "of a character requiring superior talent." Two years later bills were introduced to apply the same standard to professional actors, singers, and choristers, but failed of passage.[54]

The 1952 Act repealed the 1917 Act, as noted above, and substituted for the now obsolete contract labor provisions[55] an entirely new basis for the control of worker immigration. This was the establishment of a new excludable class consisting of aliens entering to perform skilled or unskilled labor if the Secretary of Labor has certified that

> (A) sufficient workers in the United States who are able, willing, and qualified are available at the time (of application for a visa and for admission to the United States) and place (to which the alien is destined) to perform such skilled or unskilled labor, or (B) the employment of such aliens will adversely affect the wages and working conditions of the workers in the United States similarly employed. (Sect. 212[a][14] of the 1952 Act)

Such excludability, however, was limited to aliens in the nonpreference class, to Western Hemisphere immigrants, and to certain limited cases of reacquisition of citizenship.[56]

Racial or Ethnic Classes

Chapter 14 deals with the elements of immigration law designed to control or maintain the racial and ethnic composition of the American population; and the present section therefore is limited to a brief summary of exclusions based on racial and related criteria.

The first exclusion on a racial basis was by the Act of May 6, 1882 (22 Stat. 58) and was for a limited duration of ten years only. It applied to "Chinese laborers," but these were broadly defined "to mean both skilled and unskilled laborers and Chinese employed in mining." The only Chinese specifically exempt were officials of the Chinese government together with "their body and household servants."

[54]See p. 234 above.

[55]The contract labor laws had lost their relevance during the Depression years in particular, for at that time an alien arriving without some assurance of employment could be denied entry as "likely to become a public charge."

[56]This labor certification procedure was reversed in the 1965 Act to make aliens coming for employment excludable unless there is affirmative finding by the Secretary of Labor that the alien in question will not displace a worker in the United States or adversely affect wages and working conditions. See pp. 372–73 above.

This first Chinese exclusion act was followed by a succession of supplementary acts as Congress sought to legislate means to check the continuing inflow of the Chinese and to satisfy the demands of the Pacific Coast states for protection from the inflow. The amending act of July 5, 1884 (23 Stat. 115) continued the exclusion provisions of the preceding act but made clear that they applied to all Chinese, whether subjects of China or not. It further provided that every Chinese person other than a laborer must be supplied with an identification certificate issued by the Chinese government and that the class of admissible merchants did not include hucksters, peddlers, fishermen, or gatherers of shellfish. Four years later, pending ratification of a treaty, the Act of September 13, 1888 (25 Stat. 476) made it unlawful for any Chinese person, whether a citizen of China or not, to enter the United States unless he was a Chinese official or his attendant, a teacher, student, merchant, or traveler for pleasure or curiosity. And a Chinese laborer having left the country was to be denied reentry unless he had a wife, child, parent, property to the value of $1,000, or debts of that amount due him in the United States (sects. 5 and 6). This law was followed very soon after by the Act of October 1, 1888 (25 Stat. 504) that denied reentry to all Chinese laborers who had not returned by the date of the act.

Chinese exclusion, due to end ten years after the effective date of the May 6, 1882 Act (which became effective ninety days after passage), was continued by the Act of May 5, 1892 (27 Stat. 25). This act extended all the previous Chinese exclusion laws by ten years from the date of passage of the 1892 Act. A further extension was set by the Act of April 29, 1902 (32 Stat. 176). Meanwhile the amending Act of November 3, 1893 (28 Stat. 7) had further defined the terms "laborer" and "merchant" as used in the Chinese exclusion laws; and the Hawaii Annexation Act of July 7, 1898 (30 Stat. 750) had extended those laws to the new island territory. Finally, the Act of April 27, 1904 (33 Stat. 428) put an end to the periodic extension of Chinese exclusion by reenacting and extending all the previous such legislation without limitation. The same act further prohibited the entry of alien Chinese laborers from the island territories to mainland United States.

The permanent exclusion of Chinese laborers was followed by de facto exclusion of Japanese labor, but without formal enactments. The so-called Gentlemen's Agreement of 1907 included an understanding that the Japanese government would not issue passports to laborers for travel to the United States unless coming to resume an established residence or to join resident parents, wives, or children.

The policy of excluding Asiatics was greatly extended by the Act of 1917 (39 Stat. 874), which added natives of the so-called Barred Zone to the excludable classes. The Zone, defined in terms of latitude and longitude, covered South Asia from Arabia to Indo-China and the islands adjacent to Asia and not possessed by the United States. It thus omitted the Philippines and Guam, and it was so drawn as to omit China and Japan, whose citizens already were largely excluded. Certain occupational classes were not subject to the Barred Zone provisions, however, these being

> Government officers, ministers, or religious teachers, missionaries, lawyers, physicians, chemists, civil engineers, teachers, students, authors, artists, merchants, and travellers for curiosity or pleasure, nor . . . their legal wives or their children under sixteen years of age who shall accompany them or who subsequently may apply for admission. (Sect. 3 of the 1917 Act)

The Barred Zone exclusion of Asiatics was supplemented and reinforced by a new exclusion formula introduced in the Immigration Act of 1924, a formula designed to stop the continuing influx of Japanese in spite of the Gentlemen's Agreement. Contained in section 13c of the act was the requirement that "no alien ineligible to citizenship shall be admitted," unless belonging to a nonquota class, the wife or unmarried child under eighteen of an admissible alien, or not coming as an immigrant. Eligibility to naturalization was at the time limited on a racial basis to white persons, persons of African nativity or descent, and persons of races indigenous to the Western Hemisphere.[57] The only exceptions allowed to the exclusion of such ineligibles were for returning resident aliens, ministers and professors with their wives and children, students, and temporary admissions of the nonimmigrant class (sect. 13c of the act).

The trend thereafter was toward a gradual relaxation on the racial restrictions on admission. The Act of June 13, 1930 (46 Stat. 581) waived exclusion for racial ineligibility in the case of Chinese wives of American citizens if the marriage was prior to the May 26, 1924 Immigration Act. And the Chinese exclusion laws were finally repealed by the wartime measure, the Act of December 17, 1943 (57 Stat. 600). Eligibility to naturalization was extended to persons of races indigenous to India and the Philippines by the Act of July 2, 1946 (60 Stat. 416). The racial barrier to admission was waived for the spouses of American citizens by the Act of July 22, 1947 (61 Stat. 401), and the same was done for persons of Guamanian origin or descent by the Act of August 1, 1950 (64 Stat. 384). And, finally, race as a barrier to naturalization and admission for perma-

[57]Also ineligible were certain limited classes, such as resident aliens who had refused military service in wartime.

nent residence was ended by the Immigration Act of 1952 (sect. 311). The act did restrict the immigration of the formerly barred racial and ethnic groups by means of small quotas (concerning selective restriction on the basis of race or ethnic group, see chapter 14), until such restriction was ended by the 1965 Act.

Educational Defect

Perhaps most controversial of all criteria for exclusion of would-be immigrants was the literacy test, first proposed as early as 1891,[58] reintroduced in bill after bill which were vetoed by three Presidents,[59] and finally passed over President Wilson's veto in 1917. Because the policy objectives underlying the literacy test were restriction of the number of admissions and selection with respect to ethnic or national origin more than the exclusion of illiterates per se, the legislative history of the test will be dealt with in later chapters on those elements of policy (chapters 13 and 14), and only the exclusion provisions are noted briefly at this point.

The new excludable class as defined in the Immigration Act of 1917 (sect. 3) consisted of

> All aliens over sixteen years of age, physically capable of reading, who can not read the English language, or some other language or dialect, including Hebrew or Yiddish.

The test itself was to consist of reading a passage of thirty to forty words clearly printed in any language chosen by the immigrant. An attached proviso permitted any admissible alien or an already admitted alien to bring in "his father or grandfather over fifty-five years of age, his wife, his mother, his grandmother, or his unmarried or widowed daughter" if otherwise admissible, whether literate or not. Exemption from the literacy test was also given to refugees from religious persecution, to returning resident aliens of five years' continuous residence who return within six months, and to certain other classes of aliens.

The literacy test has remained with few amendments since 1917. The postwar Act of June 5, 1920 (41 Stat. 981) added a further proviso to exempt an alien coming to marry a citizen veteran of the recent war, but limited the duration of the proviso to five years following approval of the act and required marriage at an immigration station. The Immigration Act of 1952 (sect. 212[a][25]) retained the test but with some change of wording and emphasis as noted by italics in the following definition of the excludable class:

[58]See p. 102 above.

[59]Presidents Cleveland, Taft, and Wilson; see pp. 121, 154, 163 above.

> Aliens (other than aliens who have been lawfully admitted for permanent residence and who are returning from a temporary visit abroad) over sixteen years of age, physically capable of reading, who cannot read *and understand* some language or dialect. (Italics added)

The original requirement of five years' continuous residence and return within six months for the exemption of returning resident aliens was omitted.

Narcotics Violators

As early as 1919 or 1920 Congress entertained proposals for use of the immigration laws as weapons against the traffic in narcotics.[60] The first such measures were for the deportation of distributors of narcotics (see chapter 12, Narcotics Law Violators), but the 1952 Act excluded alien "narcotic drug addicts" along with chronic alcoholics (sect. 212[a][5]). It also provided, in very comprehensive terms, for the exclusion of aliens connected in any way with "illicit traffic in narcotic drugs," the latter defined to include any "addiction-forming or addiction-sustaining opiate."[61] Amendment of the 1952 Act by the Act of July 18, 1956 (70 Stat. 567), known as the Narcotic Control Act of 1956, further broadened the terms of exclusion of traffickers in narcotics to include aliens convicted of a conspiracy to violate an antinarcotic law, and among such laws it specifically included those banning possession of as well as traffic in narcotics.[62]

[60]See p. 173 above.

[61]Section 212(a)(23) of the 1952 Act read

> Any alien who has been convicted of a violation of any law or regulation relating to the illicit traffic in narcotic drugs, or who has been convicted of a violation of any law or regulation governing or controlling the taxing, manufacture, production, compounding, transportation, sale, exchange, dispensing, giving away, importation, exportation, or the possession for the purpose of the manufacture, production, compounding, transportation, sale, exchange, dispensing, giving away, importation or exportation of opium, coca leaves, heroin, marihuana, or any salt derivative or preparation of opium or coca leaves, or isonipecaine or any addiction-forming or addiction-sustaining opiate; or any alien who the consular officer or immigration officers know or have reason to believe is or has been an illicit trafficker in any of the aforementioned drugs . . .

[62]As amended, the excluding paragraph (footnote 61) read as follows (additions in italics):

> Any alien who has been convicted of a violation of, *or a conspiracy to violate,* any law or regulation relating to the illicit *possession of or* traffic in narcotic drugs, or who has been convicted of a violation of, *or a conspiracy to violate,* any law or regulation governing or controlling the taxing, manufacture . . . etc. (amendment by section 301a of the 1956 Act).

Violators of Admission Regulations

A type of exclusion that arose with the restriction of immigration and the requirement of an immigration visa was that of aliens who had violated admission procedures or whose documents were not in order. The several such classes of excludable aliens are described below.

Stowaways. The 1917 Act introduced the new excludable class of stowaways, but with the proviso that if otherwise admissible the stowaway may be admitted at the discretion of the Secretary of Labor (sect. 3). In the following year such excludability was waived in the case of aliens who had enlisted or been conscripted into the armed forces of the United States or one of its allies in the recent war, if formerly a lawful resident of the United States and returning within a year of the termination of the war (Act of October 19, 1918 [40 Stat. 1014]). Stowing away on a vessel arriving in or departing from the United States was later made a misdemeanor punishable by fine or imprisonment.[63] The exclusion of stowaways was continued by the 1952 Act, without provision of discretionary action on the part of the Attorney General, except as the Attorney General had discretionary power in the case of certain returning resident aliens.

Without Proper Documents. The Quota Act of 1924 denied admission to immigrants unless in possession of an unexpired immigration visa with correct designation of nationality and quota status (sect. 13a). A later act added the further requirement of correct designation of preference class under the quota (Act of May 14, 1937 [50 Stat. 164]). The requirement of proper papers and appropriate visa was continued in restated form by the 1952 Act (sects. 212[a][20] and [21]).

False Statements. Excluded by the 1952 Act were aliens who seek to gain entry by means of false statements. As defined, the excluded class consisted of

> Any alien who seeks to procure, or has sought to procure, or has procured a visa or other documentation, or seeks to enter the United States, by fraud, or by willfully misrepresenting a material fact. (Sect. 212[a][19])

Misrepresentation of a material fact has been held to include concealment of identity or of grounds for exclusion, such as a criminal record, history of mental disease, or subversive associations.

[63]Act of June 11, 1940 (54 Stat. 306), amended by the Act of April 4, 1944 (58 Stat. 188).

Aid to Illegal Immigration. To reinforce the provisions against illegal immigration, Congress directed the exclusion of aliens who assist others to enter illegally. Excluded under the 1952 Act is

> Any alien who at any time shall have, knowingly and for gain, encouraged, induced, assisted, abetted, or aided any other alien to enter or to try to enter the United States in violation of law. (Sect. 212[a][31])[64]

Miscellaneous Other Classes

In addition to those already mentioned are a few other grounds for exclusion that do not fall within any clearly defined group or line of policy except as they may contribute to the enforcement of the immigration laws or support other legislation. They are noted briefly below in approximately chronological order of introduction.

Accompanying Alien. Under the 1903 Act if an arriving alien is certified as helpless because of sickness, physical disability, or infancy, and is therefore excluded, an accompanying alien required for the care and protection of the helpless alien is also to be excluded, with both being returned on the vessel on which they came (sect. 11). The excluding section was repeated in the 1907 and 1917 Acts (sect. 11, 1907 Act; last proviso of sect. 18, 1917 Act), and it reappears slightly reworded in the 1952 Act, section 212(a)(30).

Previously Excluded and Deported Aliens. A new excludable class under the 1917 Act consisted of aliens "who have been deported under any of the provisions of this Act, and who may again seek admission within one year of the date of such deportation," unless permission to reapply for admission had been given by the Secretary of Labor. The Act of March 4, 1929 (45 Stat. 1551) amended the clause to apply to those "who have been excluded from admission and deported in pursuance of law" unless prior permission had been received. This excludable class was retained in the 1952 Act (sect. 212[a][16]) with little or no change of wording; and the following new excludable class was added:

> Aliens who have been arrested and deported, or who have fallen into distress and have been removed pursuant to this or any prior act, or who have been removed as alien enemies, or who have been removed at Government expense. . . . (Sect. 212[a][17])

But again there is the opportunity for admission if permission is granted prior to arrival.

[64]Concerning deportability on the same grounds, see p. 448 below.

Travel by Nonsignatory Line. At the time of the second quota act of 1924, transportation lines bringing aliens to the United States were subject to regulations and agreements concerning the entry and inspection of immigrants. It was a concern of Congress at the time to have similar arrangements with transportation lines bringing aliens to foreign contiguous territory but destined for the United States; and written into the 1924 Act was a section prohibiting the entry of such aliens if they came on a so-called nonsignatory line. The section read in part as follows:

> After this section takes effect no alien applying for admission from or through foreign contiguous territory (except an alien previously lawfully admitted to the United States who is returning from a temporary visit to such territory) shall be permitted to enter the United States unless upon proving that he was brought to such territory by a transportation company which had submitted to and complied with all the requirements of this Act, or that he entered, or has resided in, such territory more than two years prior to the time of his application for admission. . . . (Sect. 17)

The 1952 Act continued the same exclusion with slight modification.[65]

Draft Evaders. The wartime Act of September 27, 1944 (58 Stat. 746) created a new excludable class of aliens who had departed previously for the purpose of evading service or training in the armed forces during wartime or a time of national emergency according to presidential proclamation. The exclusion was restated in the 1952 Act to apply to "persons who have departed from or who have remained outside the United States to avoid or evade training or service . . . etc." (sect. 212[a][22]). Exception was made, reasonably enough, for aliens who were nonimmigrants at the time of departure and who seek to reenter again as nonimmigrants.

Former Exchange Visitors. A class of temporarily excludable aliens was created by the Act of June 4, 1956 (70 Stat. 241), which amended the Information and Educational Exchange Act of 1948[66] (62 Stat. 6) to require that no person admitted after June 4, 1956 as, or acquiring the status of, an exchange visitor[67] under the 1948 Act shall be eligible to

[65]Section 212(a)(24) of the Act defined the excludable class as those aliens, other than natives of the Western Hemisphere and returning resident aliens, "who seek admission from foreign contiguous territory or adjacent islands, having arrived there on a vessel or aircraft of a nonsignatory line, or if signatory, a noncomplying transportation line . . ." and of less than two years' residence in the territory or islands.

[66]Entitled "An Act to promote the better understanding of the United States among the peoples of the world and to strengthen cooperative international relations."

[67]Exchange visitors include those admitted temporarily as students, trainees, teachers, etc.

receive an immigrant or nonimmigrant visa or an adjustment of status to that of immigrant within two years after departure from the United States, except on a finding by the Attorney General that such action is in the public interest.

Formerly Excludable Classes

As seen, the tendency has been to accumulate more and more excludable classes over the years, for once established exclusions have been carried forward from act to act. There have been a few reversals of this tendency, however, in the form of admissibility granted to formerly excluded classes. Although noted in earlier sections of this chapter, the few eliminations of excludability are listed below in summary.

Contract Labor. The original and basic law for the exclusion of contract labor, the Act of February 26, 1885, together with the acts designating related classes, was repealed by the 1952 Act.[68]

Asiatics. The exclusion of Chinese ended in 1943, and that of Indians in 1946; the Asiatic Barred Zone as a whole was eliminated by the 1952 Act.[69]

Unaccompanied Children. The 1907 Act created a new excludable class, "all children under sixteen years of age, unaccompanied by one or both of their parents," subject to discretionary action by the appropriate authority. The same provision was contained in the 1910 Act. In 1917 the excludable class was somewhat revised to consist of

> all children under sixteen years of age, unaccompanied by or not coming to one or both of their parents, except that any such children may, in the discretion of the Secretary of Labor, be admitted if in his opinion they are not likely to become a public charge and are otherwise eligible. . . .

Thereafter the exclusion remained unchanged until it was dropped by the 1952 Act.

Certain Ailments. Advances in medical knowledge and effectiveness of treatment have led to the elimination of a few diseases and ailments as grounds for exclusion. As previously described,[70] certain relatives of citizens and resident aliens were made admissible in spite of tuberculosis

[68]See further on pp. 427–30.

[69]See further on pp. 430–33.

[70]See pp. 414–19.

by the Act of September 11, 1957 (sect. 6); and tuberculosis, leprosy, and epilepsy as designated grounds for exclusion were eliminated in 1961 and 1965.[71]

Final Comment on Exclusion

Exclusion of aliens is not a policy in itself. It is rather an instrument of policy, but selective exclusion is a first component of what throughout has been a foundation stone of American immigration policy: a choosing of which aliens are to be permitted to become residents of the United States. The other components of selective policy, selection through deportation after arrival and selection by means of facilitated entry, will be dealt with later, but before proceeding to these topics some evaluation of the practice of excluding aliens classified as undesirable because of personal characteristics or for administrative considerations is in order.

Exclusion was a long-established procedure for the regulation of immigration well before it was first adopted by Congress in 1875, but at best it probably has been of limited effectiveness and enforceability. In this and other areas, Congress seems to have acted in the belief or at least the hope that a problem can be solved by passing a law against it; but not all laws are enforceable in practice, and legislation does not necessarily solve problems. The contract labor laws, for instance, were an example of legislative futility, for however Congress amended and elaborated them, they were not really enforceable against those who chose to violate them. Their greatest effectiveness was perhaps as a deterrent, but they were all too easily evaded. A laborer coming with promise of employment was not visibly different from another laborer; he could not be identified at the port of entry and excluded except on his own admission of guilt, and therefore evasion was easy.[72]

Similarly, an arriving alien is not visibly different from a native or naturalized citizen except as he may differ in dress and language; aliens with records of crime, poverty, or immorality cannot be identified by inspection; and there are similar difficulties in the case of other excludable classes. Or if aliens feared they might be excluded on arrival, it was possible for many years to avoid inspection by coming in first or cabin class on transatlantic vessels, or by way of Canada and across the land border. Only the literacy test, finally introduced in 1917, provided a readily determined basis for admission or exclusion, and this was no doubt a recommendation for the test.

[71]See pp. 416, 419 above.

[72]See reference to "coaching," p. 101 above.

Faced with the difficulty of identifying excludables, Congress adopted a practice from the time of colonial and state regulation, which was to impose on the transportation agency the responsibility of identifying and weeding out the excludables by penalizing the transporter or active agent for bringing such aliens to the United States. The penalty took the form of a heavy fine or at least the cost of transportation back for the rejected alien. In other cases a bond was required of the transporter, to be forfeited if the bonded alien became a public charge within a specified time after entry.[73]

As early as 1838, long before federal exclusion legislation, a congressional commission investigating immigration problems recommended a fine of $1,000 or imprisonment for one to three years of the master of a vessel bringing in an alien convicted of an "infamous crime."[74] The pattern of penalizing those responsible for bringing an excludable alien was followed in the 1875 Act, which marked the entry of the federal government into the field of immigration regulation. Section 2 of the act set a fine of not over $2,000 and imprisonment of not more than one year for any person, citizen or not, who brought any subject of an Oriental country against their will for a term of service. Section 3 provided imprisonment not exceeding five years and a fine not exceeding $5,000 for bringing in a prostitute. Section 4 outlawed contracts to supply "cooly" labor, declared such action a felony, with fine of up to $500 and imprisonment for a term of up to one year. Section 5 required the master or owner of a vessel bringing a criminal or prostitute to provide a bond of $500 for the return of such "obnoxious persons" within six months, and subject to forfeiture of the vessel for violation of the act. Similar penalties were provided against the transporter for the bringing in of Chinese laborers by the acts of 1882 and 1884, and for the bringing in of contract laborers by the acts of 1885, 1887, and 1888. The 1891 Act provided fine and imprisonment for anyone bringing in any excludable alien, the cost of maintenance on land and of return by sea to be levied on the owner of the vessel on which the aliens arrived, and clearance of the vessel to be denied until payment of any fines levied because of violation of the terms of the act. Such penalties were reaffirmed in acts of 1903, 1907, 1917, 1922, 1924, and March 1952.[75] The McCarran-Walter Act of several months later in 1952 declared it unlawful to bring an alien without a valid visa, and set a fine on the transporter of $1,000 per

[73]See chapter 10 on colonial and state immigration policies.

[74]See p. 406 above.

[75]The last is the Act of March 20, 1952 (66 Stat. 26), "An Act to assist in preventing aliens from entering or remaining in the United States illegally."

alien plus the amount paid for his transportation to the United States.[76]

With the requirement that aliens be provided with an entry permit or visa[77] came consular inspection of aliens abroad, a procedure that had been long recommended as the best means of screening aliens for admissibility. By means of application forms and the submission of documents from the applying aliens, the selective process could become much more effective in terms of identification of excludable cases as well as more efficient in that rejection could take place before departure rather than on arrival.

There was an earlier and additional reinforcement of the exclusion requirements in immigration law, and that was the deportability of those aliens found to have been improperly admitted or to have entered illegally. As is described in the chapter that follows, deportability could arise from causes subsequent to entry; but a number of the deportable classes paralleled the excludable classes, and violation of the requirements for admission made an alien liable to deportation. The screening process thus came to operate at three levels, first through consular inquiry at place of origin, second through immigrant inspection at the port of entry, and finally through liability to deportation after entry if an excludable alien had not been detected in the two preceding stages.

Synopsis

For summary, the present excludable classes of aliens are listed below, numbered as in section 212a of the 1952 Act as amended. The date following each class is the year in which the class or its equivalent first became excludable.

1. mentally retarded (1882)[78]
2. insane (1891)
3. with one or more attacks of insanity (1903)[79]
4. with psychotic personality or a mental defect (1917)[80]

[76]Section 273 of the Act. The fine was refundable on showing that the transporter "did not know, and could not have ascertained by the exercise of reasonable diligence," of the lack of the necessary visa.

[77]The wartime Act of May 22, 1918 (40 Stat. 559) required that aliens come provided with a passport and visa. This requirement was extended by the Act of March 2, 1921 (41 Stat. 1217) and continued under the quota acts.

[78]Lunatics and idiots in 1882; idiots and insane persons in 1891; imbeciles and feebleminded added in 1907; feebleminded changed to mentally retarded in 1965.

[79]Two or more attacks of insanity at any time previously, or an attack within five years of application in 1903 and after; one or more attack in 1952.

[80]Constitutional psychopathic inferiority in 1917; psychopathic personality, epilepsy,

5. narcotic drug addicts (1952), chronic alcoholics (1917)

6. with any dangerous contagious disease (1891)[81]

7. with physical defect, disease, or disability that may affect ability to earn a living (1907)[82]

8. paupers, professional beggars, or vagrants (1891)[83]

9. convicted of crime involving moral turpitude (1875)[84]

10. convicted of two or more offenses, with aggregate sentence of five years or more (1952)

11. polygamists and related classes (1891)

12. prostitutes and related classes (1875)

13. coming to engage in any immoral sexual act (1952)[85]

14. skilled or unskilled laborers, if sufficient workers already available or if would adversely affect wages and working conditions (1952)

15. likely to become a public charge (1882)

16. previously excluded and deported within one year (1917)

17. previously deported for any of various reasons (1952)

18. stowaways (1917)

19. entry by means of false statements (1952)

20. without proper documents (1924)

21. without proper preference classification (1937)

22. ineligible to citizenship (1924)

23. narcotics law violators (1952)

24. arrival by nonsignatory line (1924)

25. illiterates over sixteen years of age (1917)

26. (certain nonimmigrants without proper documents) (1924)

27. admission prejudicial to public interest or safety (1948)

28. subversive classes (1903)[86]

29. suspected of subversive intent (1950)

30. accompanying excluded alien (1903)

31. aid to illegal immigration (1952)

---

or a mental defect in 1952; epilepsy, excludable since 1903, was deleted and sexual deviation added in 1965.

[81]Loathsome or dangerous contagious disease in 1891; tuberculosis added in 1907, changed to tuberculosis in any form in 1917, dropped in 1961; leprosy added in 1952, dropped in 1961.

[82]Mental and physical defect that may affect ability to earn a living in 1907; present wording adopted in 1952.

[83]Paupers in 1891; professional beggars added in 1903; vagrants added in 1907.

[84]Convicted of felonious crime, 1875; convicts in 1882; felony or crime involving moral turpitude in 1891; present wording from 1952.

[85]Sexual deviation added, section 15(b) of the 1965 Act.

[86]Anarchists and related classes, 1903; Communists added, 1948, 1950.

12 Selection by Deportation

Deportation, like exclusion, is an instrument of immigration policy, not a policy in itself; but also like exclusion it is a means of implementing a policy of selecting those allowed to become and remain residents of the United States. The development of the deportable classes has been broadly parallel to that of the excludable classes. Many of the grounds for deportation are similar to those for exclusion, and they have increased in number in a parallel way over the years.

Congress has prescribed deportation for two broad types of cases. One is that of the alien who has gained entry through some error in the admission process of screening or through some evasion of that process on his part. The other is that of the alien who, through his own behavior or other circumstances subsequent to entry, has fallen within one of the deportable classes. In the former case deportation functions as a second line of defense against the entry of aliens defined as excludable; in the second case deportation may be a penalty for misdeeds on the part of the alien,[1] or in other circumstances is imposed as a consequence of misfortunes that may befall the alien (such as poverty, mental ailment, etc.). In either case deportation is a threat or jeopardy that overhangs the alien after entry.

The following account of the deportable classes and their development is parallel to the preceding chapter on the excludable classes. The grounds for deportation are grouped as far as possible into a few broad categories that correspond to those used in the preceding description of exclusion.

Subversives

The first class of aliens declared deportable by Congress were those who might endanger the new Republic. In 1798, as previously described,[2] at

[1]Deportation functions in such cases as a part of the larger body of law against the narcotics traffic, organized prostitution, etc.

[2]See pp. 13, 14 above.

a time of heightened suspicion of subversive activities, it was proposed in the Senate that the President be given the power to expel dangerous aliens. The draft of the Aliens Act subsequently presented to Congress was more drastic in that it empowered the President to expel any alien who is or may be imprisoned for seditious speaking, writing, or printing prohibited by the act. As later passed, however, the Aliens Act of June 25, 1798 (1 Stat. 570) stated more mildly that

> it shall be lawful for the President of the United States at any time during the continuance of this act, to order all such aliens as he shall judge dangerous to the peace and safety of the United States, or shall have reasonable grounds to suspect are concerned in any treasonable or secret machinations against the government thereof, to depart out of the territory of the United States. . . . (Sect. 1)

The same section also provided opportunity for the accused alien to present evidence in his own defense to the President, who might then grant a license to remain, with or without a bond for good conduct. The act was passed for a term of two years only, and was not reenacted. During the term of the act, President Adams appears to have made very limited if any use of the power granted to him.

As recounted in the preceding chapter,[3] congressional attention did not return to the question of subversive activities until late in the nineteenth century when it was feared that European anarchists were coming to the United States. The first response took the form of the exclusion of anarchists, but deportation was a logical corollary and was to come later. As early as 1901 the Industrial Commission report on immigration recommended both the exclusion and deportation of anarchists, of which only the former recommendation was incorporated in the 1903 Act. Deportation of alien anarchists was finally included in the Burnett bill of 1914–1915,[4] defeated by presidential veto. Reintroduced, accepted by Congress, and then passed over another veto, substantially the same bill became the 1917 Act. Among other things it made aliens of the anarchist and related classes doubly deportable. They were deportable up to five years after entry if at the time of entry they were excludable by reason of being in one of the subversive classes. And they were deportable without time limit after entry if

[3]See chapter 11, pp. 423–27.

[4]See p. 161 above. An earlier proposal that failed of passage in 1912 would have deported any alien who while resident in the United States conspired for the overthrow of a government recognized by the United States (p. 152 above).

> found advocating or teaching the unlawful destruction of property, or advocating or teaching anarchy, or the overthrow by force or violence of the Government of the United States or of all forms of law or the assassination of public officials. . . . (Sect. 19)

Although more concisely defined, the deportable classes of subversives corresponded to the excludable classes.[5] The five-year time limit on deportation was subsequently removed by the Act of October 16, 1918 (40 Stat. 1012).

The 1918 Act was followed by the Act of May 10, 1920 (41 Stat. 593), which established additional deportable classes of aliens. Giving evidence of the persistence of wartime feeling toward aliens, it called on the Secretary of Labor to hold hearings concerning certain classes of aliens who had come to governmental attention during the war years, and to order their deportation if they were found undesirable as residents of the United States. The classes of aliens in question were those under internment at the time of the act and aliens convicted since August 1, 1914 of violation of certain wartime laws.[6]

A number of bills for the exclusion and deportation of alien subversives were presented to Congress during the 1930s; and more drastic was a bill to revoke the naturalization and to deport naturalized citizens found guilty of subversive activities.[7] Although not accepted by Congress at the time, these bills may have borne later fruit in the form of the Alien Registration Act of 1940, which established several new deportable classes of aliens, including those who within five years of entry have been convicted of subversive activity within the armed forces or against any government in the United States, or who without time limit after entry have been so convicted more than once.[8]

The deportation provisions of the 1918 Act were amended and reinforced by the Internal Security Act of 1950 (sect. 22); and the deportability of subversives was dealt with in still further detail by the 1952 Act. In addition to the general deportability of any alien who belonged to an excludable class at time of entry, section 241(a)(6) of the act enumerated some eight classes of subversives to be deported, corresponding to those

[5]For the statement of the excludable classes of subversives under the 1917 Act, see footnote 45, p. 424.

[6]The acts dealt with espionage, manufacture and possession of explosives, unauthorized departure and entry in wartime, destruction of war materials, military service, trading with the enemy, etc.

[7]See pp. 224–25, 237, 246–47, 252–53 above.

[8]Sect. 23 of the 1940 Act restated the deportability without time limit of aliens who at time of entry or thereafter are members of the proscribed classes.

declared excludable by the same act.[9] Later paragraphs (paragraphs 15, 16, and 17 of sect. 241a) of the same section made aliens deportable for violation of certain acts, for the most part wartime and war-related acts, including the Alien Registration Act of 1940[10] and the several acts given similar significance for deportability by the Act of May 10, 1920.[11] The deportation provisions of the 1952 Act remained on the statute books up to and including the 1965 Act.

Illegal Immigrants

Except for subversive aliens who might endanger the national security, the subject of deportation did not arise until certain classes of aliens came to be denied entry; but once they were made excludable it logically followed that they should be deported if they gained entry. As described in the preceding chapter, excludable classes were not established until the immigration acts of 1875 and the 1880s. In 1882 Congress received and considered a bill, one section of which required that

> all foreign paupers, convicts, or accused persons of other than political offenses, or persons suffering from mental alienation . . . who are a public charge on their arrival . . . shall be sent back.

From the above sentence and the fact that a preceding section of the bill specified that such aliens "shall not be permitted to land," it appears that the intention of Congress was deportation in case the alien had already landed, although the phrase "on their arrival" indicates immediate rather than later deportability. As finally reworded and included in the Immigration Act of 1882, the section in question merely provided that "all foreign convicts, except . . . political . . . , upon arrival shall be sent back,"[12] and does not make clear for what time period, if any, deportability continued after arrival.

The wording of the Chinese Exclusion Act of the same year was quite clear on this point, for it required the deportation of "any Chinese person found unlawfully within the United States"[13] and no time limit was set on deportability in this case. Equally clear was the provision of deportation by the Contract Labor Act of 1888, which empowered the Secretary of the Treasury, if satisfied that an immigrant who had entered was in fact

[9]For a condensed listing of the excludable classes, see p. 426–27.

[10]Deportability was for violation of the Alien Registration Act within five years of entry, or for more than one violation of the act without time limit after entry.

[11]The Act of May 10, 1920 was repealed by the 1952 Act, which incorporated the substance of the earlier act.

[12]See pp. 79–80 above.

[13]See p. 82 above.

a contract laborer, to take in custody and deport the immigrant; but in this case deportability was limited to within one year of arrival.[14] In the same year, 1888, Congress received but did not act on a bill that included deportation within two years of arrival of aliens who had entered illegally.[15] A five-year period of deportability for contract laborers was later sponsored by a Senate committee but not accepted by Congress.[16]

The Immigration Act of 1891 set a general principle of deportation for aliens who enter illegally. As stated in the act,

> any alien who shall come into the United States in violation of law may be returned as by law provided, at any time within one year thereafter, at the expense of the person or persons, vessel, transportation company, or corporation bringing such alien into the United States, and if that can not be done, then at the expense of the United States. (Sect. 11)

A decade later the one-year time limit on deportability was being reconsidered. In 1901 a House bill would have raised the period of deportability to two years. In the same year the Industrial Commission recommended that the period be increased to five years;[17] that recommendation was accepted in a House bill of the following year. The bill also made it illegal and grounds for deportation for an alien to enter except at a designated port or place of entry.[18] The eventual legislation that came out of Congress, the Immigration Act of 1903, increased deportability to the lesser period of three years, but that was still a threefold increase over the 1891 Act. No change in this respect was made by the next major immigration act, that of 1907.

Thereafter the trend of congressional thought as indicated by proposed measures was toward lengthening the period of deportability after arrival, and consistent with its restrictive character, the 1917 Act in section 19 extended the time limit on deportability to five years after arrival for illegal immigrants and certain other deportable classes of aliens (sect. 19a as amended in 1940). The act also directed that a deportation order approved by the Secretary of Labor shall be final and that seamen who land illegally are subject to arrest and examination within three years thereafter, and if they are found unqualified for admission shall be deported (sect. 34, 1917 Act).

The final step in lengthening the period of liability to deportation for the illegal immigrant was taken in the Immigration Act of 1924, which directed deportation for

[14]See p. 96 above.
[15]See p. 97 above.
[16]See p. 101 above.
[17]See p. 128 above.
[18]See p. 132 above.

> Any alien who *at any time after entering* the United States is found to have been at the time of entry not entitled under this Act to enter the United States, or to have remained therein for a longer time than permitted under this Act or regulations made thereunder. (Sect. 14, italics added)

Two steps are taken in this passage: the removal of the time limit on deportability of the illegal immigrant and treatment of the alien who violates the terms of a temporary admission as an illegal immigrant.

The years immediately preceding and during the Depression saw a number of deportation bills introduced in Congress. The principal legislative product related to illegal immigrants during this period was the Act of March 4, 1929 (45 Stat. 1551) on the reentry of deported aliens. Evidently recognizing such reentry as a problem, and that punishment beyond deportation or redeportation was called for, Congress acted to make reentry by a previously deported alien a felony punishable by imprisonment of up to two years, a fine of up to $1,000, or both fine and imprisonment.[19] An equal fine or imprisonment of up to one year was set for

> Any alien who hereafter enters the United States at any time or place other than as designated by immigration officials or eludes examination or inspection by immigration officials, or obtains entry to the United States by a willfully false or misleading representation or the willful concealment of a material fact. . . . (Sect. 2)

Such entry was declared a misdemeanor. The act provided further that an alien sentenced to imprisonment shall not be deported until he has served his sentence.

The Alien Registration Act of 1940 created several new deportable classes, including

> Any alien who, at any time within five years after entry, shall have, knowingly and for gain, encouraged, induced, assisted, abetted, or aided any other alien to enter or to try to enter the United States in violation of law. (Sect. 20[b][1])

The following paragraph prescribed deportation without time limit for the second such offense.

The section of the 1952 Act defining deportability (sect. 241a) underwent only minor amendment up to and including the 1965 Act. Regarding illegal immigrants, it reaffirmed the existing deportation requirements by providing deportability without time limit for aliens who

[19] Admission if prior permission was obtained from the Secretary of Labor was provided for by the Act of June 24, 1929 (46 Stat. 41).

were excludable at time of entry or who entered without inspection at other than a designated place, or who were admitted temporarily as nonimmigrants and failed to maintain that status. Deportation was also prescribed for aliens who, prior to or at the time of entry or within five years after entry, aid others to enter illegally (sect. 241[a][13]).

Public Charges

The first federal act to deal with public charges, the Immigration Act of 1882, excluded "any person unable to take care of himself or herself without becoming a public charge." It was left to later legislation to deal with those who were found to be public charges subsequent to admission. The draft of the act, as approved by the House, had in fact directed, in addition to the above exclusion that "all foreign paupers . . . in the United States who are a public charge on their arrival in this country shall be sent back," but this provision did not meet with Senate approval and was omitted from the act as it was finally passed.[20]

It was the next major immigration act, that of March 3, 1891, that established the principle that aliens who enter unlawfully are to be sent back. Unlawful entry included the entry of those such as public charges who were excluded by law. As described in the preceding section, the period of deportability after arrival of such illegal immigrant aliens was progressively lengthened, from one year after arrival in the 1891 Act, to three years in 1903, to five years in 1917, and without time limit in 1924 and thereafter.

The other direction of development in the deportability of alien public charges concerned those lawfully admitted who required public aid at some time after their arrival. The 1891 Act took the first step in this direction by providing that

> any alien who becomes a public charge within one year after his arrival in the United States from causes existing prior to his landing therein shall be deemed to have come in violation of law and shall be returned as aforesaid. (Sect. 11)

This established a one-year period of deportability after arrival, but with the attached condition that the dependency constituting grounds for deportation be the result of a cause that existed prior to entry—presumably a cause that if recognized at the time of entry would have made the alien "likely to become a public charge" and thus excludable.

[20]See p. 80 above.

The next immigration act, in 1903, extended deportability to aliens who become public charges within two years after entry, but continued the condition that it be for causes existing prior to landing (sect. 20). The 1907 Act increased the period of deportability to three years after landing, with the same condition that the cause of the dependency precede arrival (sects. 20 and 21).

The disposition of Congress to impose longer and longer periods of deportability for aliens of the public charge class did not end with the three years set by the 1907 Act. Proposals to lengthen the period of deportability appeared from time to time in the following years, and in 1917 the immigration act of that year increased deportability to five years after entry for many classes of aliens, including those who became public charges within that interval after arrival "from causes not affirmatively shown to have arisen subsequent to landing." The intention and the effect of this altered wording was to put on the alien the burden of proving that his dependency had arisen after immigration and was not cause for deportation.

In spite of numerous proposals, especially during the Depression years, Congress did not act to facilitate the deportation of public charges until the Act of May 14, 1937 (50 Stat. 164), which proposed the removal of alien public charges at public expense. This act provided that aliens who "fall into distress or need public aid from causes arising subsequent to their entry and are desirous of being so removed," may be sent back at government expense to their native country. An attached stipulation was that aliens so removed "shall forever be ineligible for readmission" except with approval by the Secretary of State and the Secretary of Labor.

Finally, the 1952 Act in its enumeration of the deportable classes of aliens continued the terms of the 1917 Act with respect to aliens who have become public charges after entry, that is, a five-year period of deportability unless the alien is able to show that the causes of his dependency arose after entry (sect. 241[a][8]).

Criminals

Alien criminals, like the public charges of the preceding section, were excludable on arrival, and therefore were deportable as illegal immigrants if they gained entry into the United States.[21] To be considered in the present section is the development of deportability of aliens who become deportable by reason of conviction of crime after entry,

[21]See pp. 446–49.

for the most part crimes defined as involving "moral turpitude."[22]

The long effort by Congress to keep out alien criminals, supplemented by deportation of those who gained entry, has been described above. It was not until 1917 that the exclusion and deportation of aliens coming with a criminal record was supplemented by legislation for the deportation of aliens convicted of certain crimes committed after entry. The new deportable class as defined by the 1917 Act consisted of

> any alien who is hereafter sentenced to imprisonment for a term of one year or more because of conviction in this country of a crime involving moral turpitude, committed within five years after the entry of the alien to the United States, or who is hereafter sentenced more than once to such a term of imprisonment because of conviction in this country of any crime involving moral turpitude, committed at any time after entry. (Sect. 19)

Following provisos in the same section of the act directed that the deportability of an alien convicted of a crime involving moral turpitude shall not apply if the alien has been pardoned or if the court or judge that imposed the sentence recommends to the Secretary of Labor within thirty days that the alien not be deported; also, an alien sentenced to imprisonment shall not be deported until after serving the term of imprisonment (sect. 19). The 1952 Act retained the same terms for the deportation of aliens convicted of crimes after entry, with only a minor change of wording.[23]

[22]The definition given by Frank L. Auerbach, *Immigration Laws of the United States*, 2d ed. (Indianapolis: Bobbs-Merrill, 1955), p. 277, is "Any crime involving an act intrinsically and morally wrong, or an act done contrary to justice, honesty, principle, or good morals, is a crime involving moral turpitude. . . . It is to be distinguished from an act which is not inherently immoral, but becomes an offense only because its commission is expressly forbidden by law." For contrasting definition of good moral character, see p. 422 above.

[23]Section 241(a)(4) of the 1952 Act directed deportation upon the order of the Attorney General for any alien who "is convicted of a crime involving moral turpitude committed within five years after entry and either sentenced to confinement or confined therefor in a prison or corrective institution, for a year or more, or who at any time after entry is convicted of two crimes involving moral turpitude, not arising out of a single scheme of criminal misconduct, regardless of whether confined therefor and regardless of whether the convictions were in a single trial."

According to section 241b of the same act, "The provisions of subsection (a)(4) respecting the deportation of an alien convicted of a crime or crimes shall not apply (1) in the case of any alien who has subsequent to such conviction been granted a full and unconditional pardon by the President of the United States or by the Governor of any of the several States, or (2) if the court sentencing such alien for such crime shall make, at the time of first imposing judgment or passing sentence, or within thirty days thereafter, a recommendation to the Attorney General that such alien not be deported. . . ."

Immoral Classes

The strong feeling on the part of Congress over the years that good moral character is a prime requisite for acceptance of an alien for residence in the United States expressed itself in lengthy and detailed legislation for the deportation as well as for the exclusion of aliens who had transgressed. As already described, aliens of the immoral classes were among the first to be excluded, in 1875, and to be deportable if found to have entered, in 1891. The Act of 1907 extended deportability to aliens guilty of immorality subsequent to arrival in the United States. Section 3 of the act, after making it a felony to import or to maintain any alien woman or girl "for the purpose of prostitution, or for any other immoral purpose," declared that

> any alien woman or girl who shall be found an inmate of a house of prostitution or practicing prostitution, at any time within three years after she shall have entered the United States, shall be deemed to be unlawfully within the United States and shall be deported. . . .

This statement of the deportable class was amended and the three-year time limit was removed by the Act of March 26, 1910 (36 Stat. 263), to read that

> Any alien who shall be found an inmate of or connected with the management of a house of prostitution or practicing prostitution after such alien shall have entered the United States, or who shall receive, share in, or derive benefit from any part of the earnings of any prostitute; or who is employed by, in, or in connection with any house of prostitution or music or dance hall or other place of amusement or resort habitually frequented by prostitutes, or where prostitutes gather, or who in any way assists, protects, or promises to protect from arrest any prostitute, shall be deemed to be unlawfully within the United States and shall be deported. . . .

The amended section further provided that an alien so deported who attempts to return shall be deemed guilty of a misdemeanor and imprisoned for not more than two years and then deported; also that in prosecutions under the section "the testimony of a husband or wife shall be admissible and competent evidence against a wife or husband." The same terms of deportability were incorporated in the Immigration Act of 1917 but with the added proviso:

> That the marriage to an American citizen of a female of the sexually immoral classes the exclusion or deportation of which is prescribed by this Act shall not invest such female with United States citizenship if the marriage of such alien female shall be solemnized after her arrest or after the commission of acts which make her liable to deportation. . . . (First proviso, sect. 19)

The Immigration Act of 1952, which superseded the 1917 Act, designated the deportable aliens of the immoral classes as consisting of any aliens who through "conduct, behavior or activity at any time after entry" become members of any of the excludable immoral classes,[24] together with any alien who

> is or at any time after entry has been the manager, or is or at any time after entry has been connected with the management, of a house of prostitution or any other immoral place. (Sect. 241[a][12])

This portion of the 1952 Act was unamended through 1965.

Deportation was also prescribed for any alien who imports another alien for an immoral purpose. Such importation was declared a felony punishable by fine and imprisonment by section 4 of the Immigration Act of 1917 and section 278 of the Immigration Act of 1952. The latter act made deportable any alien convicted under the above sections of either act (sect. 241[a][18] of the 1952 Act).

Narcotics Law Violators

Aliens connected with traffic in narcotic drugs became subject to deportation at an earlier date than their excludability, which did not come until 1952.[25] Dealing in narcotics and the importation of the drugs was perhaps regarded as un-American, controlled and carried on by aliens, for aliens were a particular target of legislation to suppress the traffic. Several bills for the deportation of aliens convicted of importing or dealing in narcotics appeared in the first session of the 66th Congress (1919–1920).[26] The later Act of May 26, 1922 (42 Stat. 596), to prohibit the importation and use of opium for other than medicinal purposes, set both fine and imprisonment for the importation of or dealing in the specified narcotic drugs,[27] and added deportation at the termination of imprisonment for any alien convicted under the act.

This legislation was followed by the Act of February 18, 1931 (46 Stat. 1171), specifically for the deportation of aliens convicted of violating any antinarcotic law of the United States. To be deported was

> any alien (except an addict who is not a dealer in, or peddler of, any of the narcotic drugs mentioned in this Act) who, after the enactment of this Act, shall be convicted and sentenced for violation of or conspiracy to violate any statute of the United States taxing, prohibit-

[24]See list of excludables, p. 421 above, paragraph (12).

[25]See the preceding chapter, p. 434. [26]See p. 173 above.

[27]"Opium, coca leaves, cocaine, or any salt, derivative, or preparation of opium, coca leaves, or cocaine."

> ing, or regulating the manufacture, production, compounding, transportation, sale, exchange, dispensing, giving away, importation, or exportation of opium, coca leaves, heroin, or any salt, derivative, or preparation of opium or coca leaves.

The terms of the act were broadened in 1940 (Act of June 28, 1940, 54 Stat. 673) to omit the words "and sentenced" from the phrase "any alien . . . who . . . shall be convicted and sentenced," to add marihuana to the list of prohibited narcotics, and to extend the laws violation of which brought deportability from "any statute of the United States" to "any statute of the United States or of any State, Territory, possession, or of the District of Columbia."

The 1931 Act as so amended was repealed by the 1952 Act, section 241 (a)(11) of which directed the deportation of any alien who

> is, or hereafter at any time after entry has been, a narcotic drug addict, or who at any time has been convicted of a violation of any law or regulation relating to the illicit traffic in narcotic drugs, or who has been convicted of a violation of any law or regulation governing or controlling the taxing, manufacture, production, compounding, transportation, sale, exchange, dispensing, giving away, importation, exportation, or the possession for the purpose of the manufacture, production, compounding, transportation, sale, exchange, dispensing, giving away, importation or exportation of opium, coca leaves, heroin, marihuana, any salt derivative or preparation of opium or coca leaves or isonipecaine or any addiction-forming or addiction sustaining opiate.

The first lines of the above paragraph were amended by the Narcotic Control Act of July 18, 1956 (70 Stat. 567) to read as follows (additions in italics):

> is, or hereafter at any time after entry has been, a narcotic drug addict, or who at any time has been convicted of a violation of, *or a conspiracy to violate,* any law or regulation relating to the illicit *possession of or* traffic in narcotic drugs, or who has been convicted of a violation of, *or a conspiracy to violate,* any law or regulation. . . .

Finally, the Act of July 14, 1960 (74 Stat. 504) amended the above section of the 1952 Act to change the phrase "traffic in narcotic drugs" to "traffic in narcotic drugs or marihuana" (sect. 9).

Inmates of Public Institutions

Parallel to that of public charges was a new deportable class instituted by the 1952 Act, consisting of any alien who

> within five years after entry, becomes institutionalized at public expense because of mental disease, defect, or deficiency, unless the alien can show that such disease, defect, or deficiency did not exist prior to his admission to the United States. (Sect. 241[a][3])

Supplemental to the public charge class of deportables, this paragraph gave deportability of aliens who avoided falling into the public charge class technically by paying the low fees of public institutions largely supported by public funds.

Fraudulent Marriage

From time to time Congress has shown concern lest aliens obtain ready entry by means of marriage to a citizen of the United States. A bill for the deportation of aliens who enter into a collusive marriage for the purpose of gaining entry appeared in the first session of the 72nd Congress (1931–1932) but was not acted on at the time.[28] Two later bills for the same purpose were introduced in 1936, again without approval by Congress.[29] In the following year, however, section 3 of the Act of May 14, 1937 (50 Stat. 164), the so-called Gigolo Act, provided that

> any alien who at any time after entering the United States is found to have secured either non-quota or preference-quota visa through fraud, by contracting a marriage which, subsequent to entry into the United States, has been judicially annulled retroactively to date of marriage, shall be taken into custody and deported. . . . This section shall be effective whether entry was made before or after the enactment of this Act.

Of similar effect was the postwar Act of June 29, 1946 (60 Stat. 339) for the admission of alien fiancées and fiancés of members of the armed forces. Section 2 of the act stipulated that

> In the event the marriage does not occur within the period for which the alien was admitted, the alien shall be required to depart from the United States and upon failure to do so shall be deported at any time after entry.

The 1937 Act was repealed by the 1952 Act, which reformulated the terms of deportation for fraudulent marriage as follows:

> An alien shall be deported as having procured a visa or other documentation by fraud . . . if (1) hereafter he or she obtains any entry into the United States with an immigrant visa or other documenta-

[28]See p. 225 above.

[29]See p. 240 above.

> tion procured on the basis of a marriage entered into less than two years prior to such entry of the alien and which, within two years subsequent to any entry of the alien into the United States, shall be judicially annulled or terminated, unless such alien shall establish to the satisfaction of the Attorney General that such marriage was not contracted for the purpose of evading any provisions of the immigration laws; or (2) it appears to the satisfaction of the Attorney General that he or she has failed or refused to fulfill his or her marital agreement which in the opinion of the Attorney General was hereafter made for the purpose of procuring his or her entry as an immigrant. (Sect. 241c)

This provision remained unamended up to 1965.

Gun Law Violators

Among the new deportable classes established by the Alien Registration Act of 1940, in amendment of section 19 of the 1917 Act, was

> Any alien who, at any time after entry, shall have been convicted of possessing or carrying in violation of any law any weapon which shoots or is designed to shoot automatically or semiautomatically more than one shot without manual reloading, by a single function of the trigger, or a weapon commonly called a sawed-off shotgun. (Sect. 20)

This statement of deportability was incorporated without change in the 1952 Act, section 241(a)(14).

Violators of Registration Laws

Deportation was a threat held over the heads of aliens guilty of a considerable variety of offenses in addition to those involving moral turpitude. Already noted in preceding sections as being deportable are violators of laws related to national security, narcotics, and gun control. Laws concerning required registration of aliens also carried the penalty of deportability on violation. The registration requirements under the Alien Registration Act of 1940 and Chapter 7 of the 1952 Act are, for aliens remaining within the United States for thirty days or longer, an annual report of address within thirty days of January 1 each year, a report of change of address within ten days of the change, and for aliens temporarily present (i.e., nonimmigrants) an address report at the end of each three-month period. The Act of June 8, 1938 (52 Stat. 631), amended by the Act of April 29, 1942 (56 Stat. 248), required the registration of agents of foreign governments with special reference to propagandists and with deportation for failure to register. This action was reaffirmed by the 1952 Act in section 241(a)(5).

Nonsignatory Line Arrivals

Under the 1952 Act aliens arriving from foreign contiguous territory or adjacent islands by a vessel or airplane operated by a nonsignatory transportation company were excludable unless they were natives of these countries, had resided there for at least two years, or were nonquota immigrants.[30] Any such aliens who entered were therefore deportable as illegal immigrants; but their deportability was specifically stated in the 1952 Act, in section 241(a)(10).

Final Comment on Deportation

Deportation has been a legislative weapon quite freely aimed at aliens who have gained entry through some error or evasion of the admission process, who have transgressed in some manner after entry, or who for these or other reasons have been judged undesirable as residents of the United States. Members of Congress have been inventive in the various and innumerable grounds for deportation they have proposed over the years, from such diverse grounds as conspiring against a foreign government, participating in riots, failure to support dependents in their home country, manufacture and sale of intoxicants, and failure to become naturalized within a specified time, to wholesale deportations during periods of unemployment.

That Congress has paid little or no attention to the extreme and antialien measures for deportation submitted to it, even in times of some popular emotional excitement over subversion on the part of radicals, threats to national security from enemy aliens, or prevalent unemployment, is testimony to considerable stability of judgment on the part of Congress and its immigration committees. But if the most extreme measures have been avoided, Congress has nevertheless been ready to use deportation and the threat of deportation for various purposes.

A first purpose, already noted, has been to use deportation as a second line of defense against the entry of unwanted classes of aliens, the "illegal immigrants," who should have been excluded but for some reason were not. Allied to the above is the deportability of aliens who become public charges or institutionalized at public expense from causes presumably existing prior to arrival. A second general purpose that can

[30]See p. 437 above for terms of exclusion.

be inferred is the removal of aliens who prove by their conduct after admission that they are not of good moral character, evidenced by conviction of crimes involving "moral turpitude." Third, Congress has made deportable the alien violators of a wide variety of laws relating to sabotage and internal security, certain proscribed wartime activities, narcotics, gun control, and the registration of aliens and foreign agents; and here the intention evidently has been to provide an additional deterrent and penalty for aliens who might engage in activities contrary to the national security and interest.

Although Congress has rejected the great majority of bills to add more and more new deportable classes, the grounds for deportation have in fact become more numerous over the years, much as the number of excludable classes has increased. Entry for the alien has thus tended to become increasingly selective, while at the same time the number of ways of incurring deportation after entry has increased. Meanwhile, another development is that the period of liability to deportation after entry has been lengthened for the alien. Originally deportation was intended to be effected as promptly as feasible after erroneous or unlawful entry, but since 1891 and with new deportable classes the period of deportability after entry has been progressively lengthened, from one year to three years and then to five years; and now many of the deportable classes are subject to deportation without time limit after arrival. The alien is thus liable indefinitely to deportation for certain causes, as long as he remains an alien.

The terms of deportation law appear severe, directed in a punitive manner against the offending alien; but in practice deportability is not equivalent to mandatory deportation, and the alien is not without defenses against the full rigor of the law. As indicated earlier, the alien may become a naturalized citizen and thereby very nearly eliminate the possibility of deportation.[31] Also, as described more fully in a later chapter, Congress has set various checks and relief measures on the power of deportation. The sections of law providing for deportation as a rule direct that deportation shall be on the warrant or order of the Attorney General, and this action is taken only after investigation and hearings. The alien under order of deportation also has a right of appeal to the courts, a right not available in the case of exclusion. The Attorney General is also given

[31] Revocation of citizenship and subsequent deportation can follow certain offenses, but it is relatively rare. Most revocations of citizenship, which have averaged somewhat under 2,000 annually during the past decade, are because of affirmative action by the individual, such as voting or serving in the armed forces of another country, renunciation of citizenship, and naturalization abroad.

discretionary power to grant relief from deportation in certain deserving and hardship cases by means of procedures provided by Congress, suspension of deportation, and adjustment of status. In consequence, deportation is not necessarily mandatory, nor does it necessarily take place in cases where deportability exists under the letter of the law.[32]

After growing cumulatively over a number of years, deportation law appears to have reached a state of relative maturity where it provides adequate legal authority to deal with the cases that may arise. The tendency in recent decades, except under wartime and "Cold War" stresses, has not been toward the addition of new deportable classes but rather toward the development of elements of administrative discretion and flexibility within the system, to give consideration to special cases and hardship situations. A further reasonable step toward the limitation of deportability that has been advanced in several bills before Congress but not yet acted on is to have a statute of limitations on deportation so that an alien is no longer subject to deportation after some period such as ten years of continuous residence. There appears to be progress in this direction of liberalizing deportation law.

Synopsis

For summary, the present deportable classes of aliens under the 1952 Act are listed below. The numbering is that of section 241a of the act. The present time limit on deportability after arrival and the year in which the present class or its equivalent first became deportable are also given.

1. excludable at time of entry, no limit (1891)
2. entered illegally, no limit (1903?)
3. institutionalized at public expense, 5 years (1952)
4. convicted of crime involving moral turpitude, 5 years (1917); second such offense, no limit (1917)
5. failure to register as required, no limit (1938, 1940)
6. member of subversive class, no limit (1917)
7. considered threat to national security, no limit (1950?)
8. public charge due to preexisting causes, 5 years (1891)
9. (nonimmigrant who failed to maintain that status), no limit (1924)
10. nonsignatory arrival, no limit (1952)
11. drug addict or violator of narcotics law, no limit (1922)
12. immoral classes, no limit (1891)

[32]For elements of flexibility and methods of relief, see chapter 20.

13. aided alien to enter illegally, 5 years (1940); second such offense, no limit (1940)

14. violation of gun control law, no limit (1940)

15. violation of national security laws, under Title I, 1940 Act, 5 years (1940)

16. second such violation, no limit (1940)

17. violation of certain wartime acts, no limit (1920)

18. importation of alien for immoral purposes, no limit (1917). Also: fraudulent marriage, no limit (1937)

13 Restriction of Admissions

In addition to the selection of immigrants, a long-term objective of American immigration law and policy has been to restrict the number of admissions. Actually, the two processes of selection and restriction go hand in hand, and the one merges almost indistinguishably with the other. That is to say, selection as it becomes more and more rigorous reduces the number admitted; and, on the other hand, formulas for restriction of the number of immigrants inevitably bear more heavily on some would-be migrants than on others. In fact, as will be described below, the various formulas or systems used for the restriction of immigration undoubtedly have been chosen quite purposefully for their expected differential effect of repressing the immigration of some classes of aliens and permitting the unobstructed immigration of others. It is only in the abstract, therefore, that selection and restriction can be regarded as separate and distinct policies, for in practice they may be only different aspects of a given measure, such as the literacy test.

Described below is a succession of immigration measures regarded as restrictive in effect, and in all or almost all cases restrictive in intention as well. Clearly, however, they were not exclusively restrictive, for as just noted they also had selective aspects. And they may have had still other purposes, for typically they appear to have been double-purpose or multipurpose measures. But their common element and the reason for their being included here is that each was of a nature to reduce immigration and presumably was so intended. In some cases the restrictive nature of a given measure was clearly stated by its supporters in congressional debate or by the committee report on the original bill. In other cases the restrictive intention is more implied than explicit; but if the presumable effect of a given measure such as a higher head tax was to make it possible for fewer aliens to immigrate, it is most unlikely that Congress was unaware of such an effect whether or not it was mentioned in discussion of the measure.

Head Tax

Head taxes were levied on immigrants by a few colonies and later by several states, until the practice was ended by Supreme Court decision in 1883.[1] Many years before then, as early as 1850 after a first Supreme Court decision against the state head taxes, a federal tax on immigrants was proposed in Congress but not adopted.[2] Again in the early 1870s there was a bill to outlaw state head taxes and to substitute a federal tax of a dollar and a half on each immigrant, but as before it was not adopted. The same amount of tax was proposed in a later session of the same Congress, the 42nd (1871–1872), again without success.[3]

It was the Immigration Act of 1882 that imposed the first federal head tax, at the modest rate of fifty cents for each alien "who shall come by steam or sail vessel from a foreign port." The funds so collected were to go into an immigrant fund for defraying expenses incurred in the administration of the act, "for the care of immigrants arriving in the United States," and "for the relief of such as are in distress." The tax was to be paid by a representative of the transporting agency, but presumably came to be included in the cost of passage. Several years later (Act of June 26, 1884 [23 Stat. 53]), to correct an inequity that became apparent in the 1882 Act, aliens coming by coastwise vessels from Canada and Mexico were exempted from the head tax until such time as it was made applicable "to passengers coming . . . by land carriage."

Public sentiment in favor of reducing immigration was evident during the second session of the 53rd Congress (1893–1894), and one manifestation of this sentiment was a proposed amendment, to a bill then being considered by Congress, that the head tax be raised to ten dollars. The amendment was rejected and the bill, later passed as the Act of August 18, 1894 (28 Stat. 390) and concerned chiefly with enforcement of Chinese exclusion and establishment of a Bureau of Immigration, raised the head tax to the still moderate amount of one dollar.[4]

The head tax continued to be thought of from time to time as an instrument useful for other purposes than the raising of revenue. In 1896, for example, there was a motion in the Senate to set the tax at ten dollars on immigrants who do not come in an American vessel.[5] Five years later the Industrial Commission presented the results of its extensive inquiry into immigration;[6] and among its recommendations was an

[1]See chapter 10, pp. 395, 403, above.

[2]See p. 38 above.

[3]See p. 63 above.

[4]See pp. 112–13 above.

[5]See p. 120 above.

[6]For further reference to the Report, see p. 128 above.

advance of the head tax from one to three dollars.[7] The Commission's thinking on the subject was contained in a section entitled "Restrictive Head Tax,"[8] in which it was made clear that the objective of the proposed tax increase was to reduce immigration. An increase from only one to two dollars, it was said, "would be simply a fiscal tax . . . and would not be considered restrictive." The higher tax proposed by the Commission, however, was regarded as "an additional means of reducing the flood of immigration" and "a means of reducing the volume of immigration as a whole by a test which leaves as little discrimination as possible to the inspectors of immigration."[9] Similar administrative advantage was seen in the educational or literacy test, supported by some members of the Commission but not by the Commission as a whole.

Increase of the head tax from one to one and a half dollars or to three dollars was considered at that time by the 57th Congress (1901–1903), which was working on a new immigration act.[10] As finally passed, the 1903 Act doubled the head tax to two dollars and exempted citizens of Canada, Cuba, and Mexico. The exemption was extended to Newfoundland the following year (Act of March 22, 1904 [33 Stat. 144]), as well as to aliens in transit and returning resident aliens. The tax money was to go as before to an immigrant fund used to meet expenses incurred under the act, and the purpose of the tax increase does not appear to have gone beyond this use of the proceeds, in spite of the restrictive leanings of the Commission.

Members of Congress continued to favor further increase of the head tax, in spite of its doubling by the 1903 Act, and one may well suspect that their intention was restrictive. A 1906 bill would have raised the tax to five dollars, and both majority and dissenting minority reports that accompanied the bill reveal that the tax was now seen as an instrument of policy and not just a source of revenue. The majority report recommended the higher tax because it would reduce immigration and have the selective effect of keeping out certain undesirable but unspecified classes of aliens. The minority objected that the higher tax was unjustified and furthermore was really designed to discriminate against migrants from the poorer countries of southern and eastern Europe.[11] The bill as finally passed to become the Immigration Act of 1907 set a somewhat lower tax of four dollars, but this was still twice the amount set only four years

[7] *Commission Reports,* vol. 19, p. 1010, published as H. Doc. 380, 57th Congress, 1st sess., 1902.

[8] Ibid., p. 1003.

[9] Ibid.

[10] See especially pp. 131, 132, 133 above.

[11] See further, pp. 138–40 above.

before. Exemptions from the head tax were as before, with the addition of aliens arriving in outlying possessions.

Pressure for higher and higher head taxes did not stop with the new doubling. Two years later, in 1909, anti-immigration views were strongly presented to Congress, with particular reference to immigration from southern Europe; sharp increases of the head tax to ten and twelve dollars were recommended.[12] Congressional investigation of the whole subject of immigration was then underway through the Dillingham Commission that produced the multivolume 1911 Immigration Commission Report. As the final product of its labors, the Commission made a series of recommendations; the eighth and last of these was that, having found an oversupply of unskilled labor in basic industries and presumably in the industries of the country as a whole, the situation "demands legislation restricting the further admission of such unskilled labor."[13] Having arrived at this conclusion, the Commission accepted the condition that an acceptable method of restriction should meet the criteria of being strong enough to have a significant effect on the supply of unskilled labor, act most strongly against those having no intention of becoming permanent residents and citizens, and tend to exclude those least readily assimilated and least desirable as fellow citizens. Alternative methods of restriction were then listed as follows:

a. exclusion of those unable to read or write in any language;
b. racial group restriction in proportion to earlier immigration;
c. exclusion of unskilled workers unaccompanied by families;
d. limitation of admissions by port of entry;
e. increase of minimum financial resources per migrant;
f. material increase of the head tax;
g. head tax adjusted to favor migrants with families.[14]

It was the first alternative that the Commission favored, although recognizing that each had its own range of effectiveness.

A year later Congress labored on a bill embodying the Commission recommendations. Different amendments to the committee draft proposed setting the head tax at ten and twenty-four dollars but these were finally rejected in favor of five dollars.[15] Bills in later Congresses set the tax variously at five, six, and eight dollars, and the 1917 Act, passed over a veto, carried a head tax of eight dollars,[16] with new exemptions for children under sixteen years of age accompanied by a parent (sect. 2).

[12]See p. 145 above.

[13]S. Doc. 747 (61-III), Dec. 5, 1910; 1911 Commission Report, 1:47–48.

[14]Ibid.

[15]See p. 152 above.

[16]See pp. 160, 162, 164, 167 above.

The Quota Act of 1924 added an additional fee of nine dollars for an immigrant visa. Exemption from the head tax and visa fee was later granted to eligible displaced persons and orphans by the Displaced Persons Act of June 25, 1948 (62 Stat. 1009);[17] and the 1952 Act repealed the earlier laws and set a new schedule of immigrant fees including one of twenty dollars for the immigrant visa. Although at a considerably higher level, this fee presumably had little if any restrictive effect compared to the former head taxes; but Congress had long since turned to other and more effective methods of restriction.

Literacy Test

As mentioned in the preceding section, the literacy test was considered but not adopted by the Industrial Commission in its 1901 report and was advocated by the Dillingham Commission in 1911. By the latter date it had been before Congress for at least twenty years, for in 1891 the recently elected Congressman from Massachusetts, Henry Cabot Lodge, expressed his conviction that the coming of unskilled immigrants should be checked and the best means to that end was a literacy test, for such a test would be both selective and restrictive. In his words,

> We have the right to exclude illiterate persons from our immigration, and this test, combined with the others of a more general character, would in all probability shut out a large part of the undesirable portion of the present immigration. It would reduce in a discriminating manner the total number of immigrants, and would thereby greatly benefit the labor market and help to maintain the rate of American wages.[18]

From then on Lodge made himself the leading advocate of the literacy test. Two years later the House committee, of which he was a member, reported out a bill for the better enforcement of the immigration laws that added several new excludable classes of aliens, one consisting of "All persons physically capable and over sixteen years of age who can not read and write with reasonable facility their own language." Exemption from the test was granted to certain elderly relatives of admissible immigrants.[19] Deleted from the bill before its eventual passage, the liter-

[17]Section 5 of the 1948 Act. Exemption for certain other orphans was added by the Act of June 28, 1951 (65 Stat. 96).

[18]Henry Cabot Lodge, "The restriction of immigration," *North American Review* (January 1891); reprinted in the *Congressional Record,* 22:2956–58, Feb. 19, 1891. He also favored consular inspection for the weeding out of excludable aliens.

[19]See p. 108 above.

acy test provision reappeared in House and Senate bills presented in the 54th Congress (1895–1897). Two of the bills dropped the literacy test minimum age down to fourteen and prescribed that the test passage be from the Constitution. The test was recommended for its selective and "discriminatory" ability to favor northern and western Europeans and to repress the immigration of the most delinquent and pauper elements from abroad. A bill including the test provision was passed by the House, revised and passed by the Senate, and after a troubled course and much amending was finally vetoed by President Cleveland on March 2, 1897.[20]

Lodge, now in the Senate, was ready with a new literacy test bill on the opening day of the 55th Congress, two weeks after the defeat by veto of the earlier bill. In spite of seemingly favorable disposition in Congress and White House with a new administration, the literacy test did not progress during the session. Later it was favored by only a minority of the Industrial Commission that reported at the opening of the 57th Congress (1901–1903). During the session a literacy test amendment was inserted in and then removed from the bill that became the 1903 Act.[21] The test next reappeared in a new immigration bill considered by House and Senate in the 59th Congress (1905–1907), at which time it was strongly advocated for its ability to "separate the ignorant, vicious, and the lazy from the intelligent and industrious,"[22] and for various other selective qualities; but though adopted by the House it was eliminated in the conference draft of the 1907 Act.[23]

The literacy test does not reappear on the record of congressional deliberations until it was revived by the Dillingham Commission as its preferred means of restricting immigration.[24] The Burnett bill of the 62nd Congress (1911–1913) incorporated many of the Commission's recommendations, including a literacy test of the same specifications as in earlier bills, was passed after some amendment, and was finally vetoed on February 14, 1913 by President Taft, who refused to accept the literacy test.[25]

The same story was repeated in the 63rd Congress (1913–1915). Disappointed but not discouraged after the succession of defeats, the restrictionists in Congress rallied for another effort. The Burnett bill was reintroduced with an accompanying committee statement that it represented a new development in the regulation of immigration, for whereas

[20]For further detail see pp. 115–21 above.
[21]See pp. 131–32, 133 above.
[22]Senator Underwood (Ala.), *Congressional Record,* 40:9155, June 25, 1906.
[23]See pp. 138, 139, 140, 141 above. [24]See p. 466 above.
[25]For further account see above, pp. 150–51, 153–54.

"all laws heretofore enacted on this subject have been of a selective rather than restrictive character," the bill contained "one provision intended directly to restrict immigration." This provision was, of course, the literacy test, which was said to have incidental selective effects as well.[26] After House and Senate labors to amend and perfect the bill, it was finally passed, only to meet a veto from President Wilson that could not be overridden. As before, the literacy test was the principal reason for the veto.[27]

The congressional forces that had supported the Burnett bill and its literacy test provision rallied from this latest defeat, confident that they represented a majority in both houses of Congress and had the support of public opinion in the nation at large. Behind the drive for more effective restriction was also a sense of urgency, for the higher and higher head taxes had not perceptibly checked the rising tide of immigration up to the outbreak of war in Europe in 1914; and there was reason to expect an even greater influx of immigrants once the war was over. New bills for the regulation and restriction of immigration were introduced in the next Congress, the 64th (1915–1917); among them was a Burnett bill essentially the same as the one recently vetoed. After lengthy consideration in both House and Senate, the bill was finally passed in the second session of the 64th Congress, vetoed by President Wilson, and passed over his veto to become the Immigration Act of February 5, 1917 (39 Stat. 874).[28] The most strongly restrictive immigration act yet passed, its literacy test provision excluded "all aliens over sixteen years of age, physically capable of reading, who can not read the English language, or some other language or dialect, including Hebrew or Yiddish" (sect. 3). To take effect three months from the passage of the Act, the exclusion of illiterates was modified by a provision that exempted from the test the father or grandfather over fifty-five years of age, the wife, mother, grandmother, and unmarried or widowed daughter of a legally admitted alien or citizen. Also exempt were refugees from religious persecution, returning resident aliens of five years' continuous residence who had been absent for less than six months, and aliens in transit through the United States (first proviso, sect. 3). The text to be used in the test was to contain from thirty to forty words "in ordinary use," in any language designated by the immigrant.

Once established in immigration law, the exclusion of illiterates and the exemptions from the test underwent little subsequent change. A proviso was added by the Act of June 5, 1920 (41 Stat. 981) to allow any

[26]See p. 161 above.
[27]See p. 248 above.
[28]See pp. 165–67 above.

citizen who had served in the armed forces of the United States during the recent war to obtain the admission of an illiterate but otherwise admissible alien fiancé or fiancée, on condition of marriage to the so-admitted alien at an immigration station on arrival.[29] The literacy test provision was continued in the 1952 Act with one small but significant addition: to expand the definition of the excludable class from those who cannot read to those "who cannot read and understand" some language or dialect (sect. 212[a][25]). Exemption from the test was given to an alien who has been lawfully admitted for permanent residence and who is returning from a temporary visit abroad; to the parent, grandparent, spouse, daughter, or son of an admissible alien or lawfully resident alien or citizen; and to one who is able to prove he is seeking admission to avoid religious persecution (sects. 212[a][25] and 212b).

In its early years the literacy test was the target of repeated attempts at repeal on the part of the opponents of restriction, but all such attempts died in the immigration committees of Congress; later the attacks shifted to the succeeding and more effective restriction, the quota system.

The Quota System

By the close of the war in 1918, it became apparent from consular reports and other sources that a new and greater wave of immigration from Europe was in prospect, limited only by the carrying capacity of trans-atlantic shipping once peacetime travel facilities were restored. It was also foreseen that the literacy test would not be an effective barrier against the postwar immigrants, possessed of higher educational qualifications than the prewar immigrants. Faced with what it believed was an urgent need for protection against excessive immigration, Congress turned to a method of restriction that had been previously considered but not adopted—to set a numerical ceiling or quota on immigration.

The idea of numerical limitation was not new. The Dillingham Commission in its 1911 report and recommendations had listed among alternative modes of restriction a numerical limit by "race,"[30] according to the number admitted in preceding years, or a restriction of admissions by port of entry.[31] Dillingham of Vermont, chairman of the Commission, did in fact introduce a bill to give each country a fixed immigration quota, computed as a fixed percent of the number of resident foreign-born from

[29]See pp. 173–74 above. The act was for a term of five years only.

[30]The term "race" was used in the report but may have corresponded to what now would be called a national or ethnic group.

[31]1911 Commission Report, 1:47–48.

each country according to the most recent census;[32] but at the same time he declared his preference for the literacy test, which he considered a more feasible means of restriction.

In December 1920 the House, told that immigration could rise to ten million a year if transportation were available, considered a bill to suspend immigration for two years and passed it after reducing the period of suspension to fourteen months. The less restrictionist Senate substituted a quota limitation of immigration from each country to 5 percent of the number of natives of that country recorded in the United States census, a formula that would give a ceiling of approximately 592,000 immigrants per annum. During the course of debate, an attempt was made to reduce the quota percentage to one percent, but the Senate settled on a quota formula of 3 percent of the foreign-born population as given in the 1910 census, this quota to apply for the period April 1, 1921 to June 30, 1922. Accepted by the House, the bill received a pocket veto from President Wilson.[33]

The new 67th Congress (1921–1923) set to work immediately with the restriction of immigration a first order of business. Complete suspension of immigration for a time was again proposed and rejected, and a bill similar to the one just vetoed was passed and signed into law by the new President, Harding, to become the first quota act of May 19, 1921 (42 Stat. 5). It granted exemption from the quota, among others, to aliens who have resided continuously for at least one year in a Western Hemisphere country.[34]

The quota act, due to expire on June 30, 1922, was extended for two years by the Act of May 11, 1922 (42 Stat. 540), which also raised the Western Hemisphere residence requirement for quota exemption to five years.[35] Late in the same session, shortly before the end of the 67th Congress, the House committee reported out a new immigration bill that revealed a desire for further restriction. The bill was to change the quota formula from the existing 3 percent of the 1910 base population to 2 percent of an 1890 census base, a change that would have dropped the quota total from the prevailing figure of 387,803 per annum under the 1921 Act as amended down to 186,437 per annum. The bill, also providing a number of nonquota (i.e., quota-free) classes, was not taken up by the House in the little remaining time before the end of the 67th Congress.[36]

The regulation and restriction of immigration was given high prior-

[32]See p. 166 above. [33]See pp. 174–76 above.
[34]For a full list of quota exemptions, see pp. 178–80 above.
[35]See pp. 182–83 above. [36]See pp. 184–85 above.

ity by the 68th Congress, which convened on December 3, 1923. The 1921 Quota Act as extended was due to expire on June 30, 1924, and it was feared that immigration would rise to new heights unless restrictive measures were continued. Although not acted on at the time, the quota formula proposed by the House committee in the preceding Congress apparently met with congressional favor, for a bill embodying the same formula of 2 percent of the 1890 base reappeared and was considered by the House. During House debate a new quota formula was proposed in the form of an amendment to the committee bill, being to set an immigration limit of 200,000 per annum and to allocate that number of immigrant visas according to the estimated national origin composition of the American population in 1920, exclusive of those referred to euphemistically as descendants of "involuntary immigrants." The amendment was not accepted by the House, which did approve the 2 percent of 1890 formula. Meanwhile the Senate was working on its own bill and adopted a national origin provision, the same as that just rejected by the House except for a lower ceiling of 150,000. As finally passed in the form of the second quota act of May 26, 1924 (43 Stat. 153), the Senate-House conference draft set quotas at the House figure of 2 percent of 1890 for the period up to June 30, 1927, after which quotas were to change to the Senate's formula of 150,000 per annum distributed according to the estimated national origin composition of the 1920 population.[37]

The effective date of the national origin system of quota determination was postponed for one year, to July 1, 1928, by the Act of March 4, 1927 (44 Stat. 1455), and to July 1, 1929 by the Act of March 31, 1928 (45 Stat. 400), at which time it became operative. Thereafter the quota formula remained unchanged until revised by the 1952 Act, which set the annual quota of any quota area at "one-sixth of 1 per centum of the number of inhabitants in the continental United States in 1920" except for the differently treated Asia-Pacific triangle area (sect. 201[a]). The revision made only a slight increase in the allowable immigration under quota. The quota ceiling on immigration remained unchanged thereafter until the national origin system of quota determination was abolished by the 1965 Act that set a limit on the number of quota visas issued to 170,000 per annum for non-Western Hemisphere immigrants and, effective July 1, 1968, a limit of 120,000 per annum for Western Hemisphere immigration.

[37]See pp. 188–94 above. Excluded in the computation from the 1920 base population were (1) natives of the Western Hemisphere and their descendants, "(2) aliens ineligible to citizenship and their descendants, (3) the descendants of slave immigrants, and (4) the descendants of American aborigines" (sect. 11d of the Act).

Quota Exemptions and Admissions

The quota acts were in some respects less restrictive, in some respects more restrictive, than appeared at first glance—less restrictive because each act from the first quota act of 1921 on provided exemption from quota limitation for certain classes of immigrants; more restrictive because some areas received larger quotas than their normal demand and the unused quota numbers could not be reallocated.

Certain of the nonquota classes have been noted in the preceding account of the quota acts, but the full list of such classes is more extensive. Under the first quota act of 1921, nonquota status was given to "aliens who have resided continuously for at least one year immediately preceding the time of their admission" in the Western Hemisphere, and the alien children under eighteen years of age of citizens of the United States.[38] The required Western Hemisphere residence was raised to five years by the later act of May 11, 1922. The 1924 quota act provided a greater number of nonquota classes, consisting of (1) the unmarried child under eighteen years of age, or the wife, of a resident citizen, (2) a lawfully admitted alien returning from a temporary visit abroad, (3) a native of the Western Hemisphere, his wife, and unmarried children under eighteen,[39] (4) a minister of any religious denomination or a professor, with his wife and unmarried children under eighteen,[40] and (5) bona fide students. Other nonquota classes, for the most part numerically small, were added by later acts.[41]

[38]Sect. 2(a) of the 1921 Act, which also exempted certain nonimmigrant classes such as officials of foreign governments and their families, aliens in transit, etc.

[39]With the exception of natives of colonial possessions in the Caribbean and Central and South America.

[40]Limited to those who have carried on the vocation for two years continuously prior to seeking admission and who seek admission solely to continue their vocation. See also the Act of July 3, 1926 (44 Stat. 812).

[41]Act of May 26, 1926 (44 Stat. 654): alien veterans; also their spouses and unmarried children under eighteen years of age if accompanying or coming to join, within six months of parental arrival (sects. 2 and 3 of the act).

Act of July 3, 1926 (44 Stat. 812): the wife or unmarried child, arriving before July 1, 1927, of certain ministers and professors who arrived prior to July 1, 1924.

Act of May 29, 1928 (45 Stat. 1009) as amended by the Act of July 3, 1930 (46 Stat. 854): a woman former citizen who lost her citizenship by marriage to an alien, but is no longer so married; also the wife or unmarried child under twenty-one of a citizen, and the husband of a citizen by marriage prior to June 1, 1928.

Act of June 28, 1932 (47 Stat. 336): a native of the Virgin Islands residing in a foreign country.

Act of July 11, 1932 (47 Stat. 656): husbands of citizens by marriage prior to July 1, 1932, and parents of citizens over twenty-one years of age.

The 1952 Act, repealing earlier provisions, gave nonquota status to (1) the child and spouse of a citizen, (2) Western Hemisphere natives, with spouse and children, (3) certain former citizens who apply for reacquisition of citizenship, (4) certain ministers with spouse and children, and (5) employees with fifteen or more years of service with the United States government abroad (sect. 101[a][27]). Later acts added several more nonquota classes prior to passage of the 1965 Act.[42]

The cumulative effect of the additions to the nonquota classes, although many of them were small in themselves, was to give an upward trend of the ratio of nonquota to quota immigration. During the five years following the 1924 Act, for instance, nonquota immigrants were on the average nearly equal in numbers to the immigrants coming in under quota. During the decade preceding the 1965 Act, in contrast, the nonquota immigrants outnumbered the quota immigrants by about two to one. In both periods Western Hemisphere immigration made up the greater part of the nonquota immigration, but in the more recent period the nonquota total was also swelled by various classes of refugees who came in free of quota under special postwar legislation. The limits set by the quota acts were thus not absolute upper limits on all immigration, and over the years they became

---

Act of August 9, 1946 (60 Stat. 975): the Chinese wife of an American citizen by marriage prior to May 26, 1924.

Act of May 19, 1948 (62 Stat. 241): the unmarried child under twenty-one or the spouse of a citizen, provided the marriage was before issuance of the visa and, in the case of husbands, prior to January 1, 1948.

Act of June 25, 1948 (62 Stat. 1009): eligible displaced persons up to the number of 202,000, also eligible displaced orphans up to the number of 3,000. (Sects. 3[a] and 3[b] of the Displaced Persons Act. Technically the displaced persons, admitted "without regard to quota limitations" up to 202,000, later increased to 341,000, were to be charged to their national quota up to one-half of the quota, including the quotas of future years as needed.)

Act of June 16, 1950 (64 Stat. 219): certain eligible orphans under ten years of age, coming with assurance of adoption or permanent residence (sect. 3 of the act).

[42]Act of September 11, 1957 (71 Stat. 639): aliens eligible for first, second, or third preference under sect. 203(a) of the 1952 Act whose visa petitions were approved by the Attorney General prior to July 1, 1957 (i.e., aliens whose services were needed, plus certain relatives of citizens and lawfully admitted aliens).

Act of September 26, 1961 (75 Stat. 650): an eligible orphan child adopted abroad or coming to be adopted by a citizen (sect. 2); also aliens eligible for second or third preference status on the basis of a petition filed with the Attorney General prior to July 1, 1961 (sect. 25a).

Act of October 24, 1962 (76 Stat. 1247): aliens on a consular waiting list under priority date earlier than March 31, 1954 and eligible for fourth preference on the basis of a petition filed with the Attorney General prior to January 1, 1962, together with spouse and children; also aliens eligible for first preference on the basis of a petition filed with the Attorney General prior to April 1, 1962 (sects. 1 and 2 of the act).

less and less limiting as Congress created more and more nonquota classes.

In another respect, the quota acts were somewhat less restrictive than may appear, for they set a minimum quota for each quota area. Thus the 1924 and 1952 Acts set a minimum quota of 100, so that the actual number of immigrant visas issuable under the acts was approximately 154,000 rather than precisely 150,000 prior to the 1952 Act, and somewhat more than 154,600 thereafter.

The 1965 Act further liberalized the provision of nonquota status to relatives by enlarging the nonquota class from spouse and children of citizens to include the parents of citizens at least twenty-one years of age and over.[43] On the other hand, the act removed the nonquota status of natives of the Western Hemisphere and gave them an annual quota of 120,000 effective for the fiscal year beginning July 1, 1968. Since that time the immigration not subject to numerical limitation has dropped to somewhat less than one-fourth of the total.

In another respect the quota acts were more restrictive than appeared from the allowable total of quota immigration, for by the quota allocation formula some nations received larger quotas than they regularly filled, and unused quota numbers could not be reallocated. The demand for immigrant visas has of course fluctuated with economic and political conditions on both sides of the Atlantic, but in the decade preceding the 1965 Act quota immigration averaged somewhat under 100,000 per annum or only about two-thirds of the allowable amount. From at least 1947 onward there was a continuing campaign in Congress for legislation to provide for the reallocation of unused quotas, a campaign that was finally successful in the 1965 Act.

On balance, then, the quota acts were considerably less restrictive than appears on the surface, for although they limited broad classes of immigration, they established certain quota-free classes that permitted large numbers of immigrants to enter. Congress was indeed of a restrictive disposition when the first of the acts was passed but made concessions to facilitate the entry of alien relatives of citizens, and gradually became more lenient in granting quota exemptions to further classes of relatives, refugees, and other hardship or deserving classes of aliens.

Quota Allocation and Preference

The quota system established and rounded out by the Acts of 1921, 1924, and 1952, together with the amending acts, had several objectives or

[43]Sect. 201(b) of the 1952 Act as amended by sect. 1 of the 1965 Act.

distinct policy elements, of which the setting of an upper limit on the principal sources of immigration was only one. The other elements of policy built into the quota system were, first, to achieve a desired racial-ethnic composition of immigration by means of a formula for the allocation of national quotas, and, second, to facilitate the entry of certain favored types of aliens by means of quota-free classes as described above and by the setting of preferences under quota. Although integral parts of the quota system as a whole, these aspects of the quota system will be dealt with in later chapters in the wider context of both quota and other provisions designed to regulate the composition of immigration (see chapter 14) and to facilitate the entry of desired classes, such as family members of citizens and persons with needed skills.[44]

Suspension of Immigration

The development of restrictive legislation is only the most visible part of the long struggle over immigration policy. There has always been some latent anti-immigration sentiment in Congress, and from time to time that body has been under strong outside pressure to reduce immigration, most notably during the 1890s.[45] Individual members have introduced countless bills to limit immigration in various ways; and the most drastic have called for complete suspension of immigration for a time. It is true that discretionary authority to suspend immigration has in fact been granted on occasion, but for other purposes. Thus at a time of a pandemic of cholera the President was given authority to suspend immigration by the Act of February 15, 1893 (27 Stat. 452); and the Public Health Service Act of July 1, 1944 (58 Stat. 682) conferred the same authority on the Surgeon General if a threat of epidemic disease existed (sect. 362). Under the 1952 Act (sect. 212e) the President has the broad power to "suspend the entry of all aliens or any class of aliens as immigrants or nonimmigrants" whenever he finds such entry would be "detrimental to the interests of the United States." Such special powers have not been exercised, however, and are held in reserve if emergency arises. Of quite different purpose are the suspension bills introduced from time to time, and the supporting reasons reveal some of the thinking and purpose behind them.

Early, if not the earliest, examples of such bills in the present century were a half-dozen bills in the third session (1918–1919) of the 65th

[44]For the preference classes established by the Acts of 1924, 1952, and 1965 for the allocation of visas, see pp. 176, 308–9, and 371–72.

[45]See pp. 110, 122 above.

Congress that would have prohibited immigration for as much as four years.[46] A number of similar bills in the first session of the next Congress (1919–1920) provided suspension of immigration for periods of three to five years. More extreme was a bill to suspend immigration from the former enemy countries for fifty years, and for twenty years from other nations.[47] Other bills providing suspensions of from two to five years were introduced in the final session of the same Congress (1920–1921). In support of the one such bill reported out, the House committee noted the rising volume of immigration, the undesirable composition of the immigrant stream, and the threat of excessive immigration in the future.[48] New bills for suspension of immigration for up to eight years appeared in the first session of the 67th Congress (1921), to be followed by other similar bills later in the same Congress.[49] In the first session of the next Congress (1923–1924) a half-dozen bills raised the proposed period of suspension to five, six, and ten years.[50] Although single bills were reported out in several sessions of Congress, none progressed further.

The impetus for suspension up to this point had come from wartime and postwar concerns, but economic and labor force reasons became more prominent with the coming of the Depression years. Restriction and suspension bills appeared early in the 70th Congress (1927–1929) but without success, and they were followed by other bills in later sessions of the same Congress.[51] One was specifically entitled "In aid of the unemployed," and others were presumably for the same purpose. More suspension bills appeared in the first session (1931–1932) of the 72nd Congress and again in the 74th Congress (1935–1937),[52] but they do not appear to have received serious consideration.

The Depression's influence on attitudes toward immigration faded in the late 1930s, but the outbreak of war in Europe and its spread to a world conflict stirred up new and reinforced opposition to immigration and to aliens in general. From this period was a bill in the first session (1939) of the 76th Congress to exclude all immigrants and to deport all aliens,[53] but this was only the most extreme of a number of bills to limit immigration. It was reintroduced in the next Congress, where it was accompanied by others to stop immigration during the existing wartime emergency or whenever the number of unemployed exceeds one million.[54] Two years later the new 78th Congress (1943–1944) received at

[46]See p. 170 above.

[47]See pp. 171–72 above.

[48]See p. 175 above.

[49]See pp. 171, 181, 183 above.

[50]See p. 186 above.

[51]See pp. 205, 215, 220 above.

[52]See pp. 221, 236 above.

[53]See pp. 254–55 above.

[54]See p. 261 above.

least six bills to suspend immigration either for the duration of the war or until such time after the war as unemployment had fallen below one million.[55] Again in the 79th Congress (1945–1946) there were bills to prohibit immigration whenever unemployment exceeds a given level, set at one million or as low as 100,000, or for a fixed period of five years after the end of the war.[56] Suspension for periods of five and ten years after the war were proposed in the 80th Congress (1947–1948).[57]

The bills for suspension so persistently introduced in session after session died uniformly without committee approval. At this distance in time it cannot be said whether the sponsors of the bills were genuinely concerned with the present or prospective problems of unemployment and postwar readjustment, were seeking to gain political advantage with their constituents by introducing bills they knew could not be passed, or were convinced restrictionists grasping at current issues in order to persuade Congress to check immigration. Perhaps something of all these positions was to be found; but the setting of a low unemployment limit[58] was certainly a very thinly disguised attempt to stop immigration permanently. The bills for suspension as a group are in some measure an indication of a continuing minority effort to restrict and even suspend immigration; but perhaps more notable is the firmness with which the leadership in Congress as represented by the immigration committees resisted the politically attractive and, to some extent, demagogic appeal for a suspension of immigration.

Final Comment on Restriction

Restriction has long been a tenet of our immigration policy, first instituted indirectly and gradually through increasing selectivity of admissions and then more directly through measures against contract laborers and Oriental peoples, higher and higher head taxes, the educational test, and setting a quota ceiling. The real policy debate over restriction in Congress, therefore, has not been whether or not to restrict but how much to restrict immigration. In this debate Congress has been pulled in opposite directions. On the one hand, there has been a persistent body of restrictionist sentiment derived from diverse sources; this has been compounded perhaps by a common-sense view that the entry of aliens

[55]See pp. 266–67 above. [56]See p. 271 above.

[57]See p. 276 above.

[58]The 80th and 81st Congresses (1947–1950) saw bills to stop immigration whenever unemployment exceeds 100 (p. 289). Many years later the argument that immigration should be linked with unemployment came up again during debate on the 1965 Act (p. 376).

should be kept within some bounds, concern lest a large influx would harm the American institutions and way of life, fear of pauper and criminal or subversive elements from abroad, nonspecific antialien prejudice, regional interests, a strong infusion of nativist political activity especially during the nineteenth century, a later and politically persuasive argument that American workers and their standard of living should be protected from the competition of immigrant labor, and no doubt other sources of restrictionist sentiment as well. On the other hand, Congress has been quite consistently sympathetic toward specific hardship and deserving classes of aliens, such as refugees and victims of religious and political oppression, relatives of citizens and resident aliens, and other special classes. The overall effect has been to close the door partially with one hand and open it selectively with the other.

Although these two opposite elements have run through at least the past century of American immigration policy and are still with us, the balance between them has shifted over time. Restriction had its greatest successes in the Act of 1917 and the quota acts which closely followed; it was increasingly on the defensive after World War II and especially after the 1952 Act. The disposition to relax or waive restrictions for selected classes of aliens has grown since then; but such leniency toward special classes should not conceal the fact that the literacy test and the quota limitation of immigration set by the Acts of 1917, 1921, and 1924 still exist virtually intact. The 1965 Act was regarded as a triumph by those in favor of a more "liberal" immigration policy, but it was also an example of the duality of the congressional thinking on admissions. That is, the act did add to the quota-free classes, but in the same act Congress asserted its independence of the administration's wishes by putting a quota ceiling on what had been the largest class of nonquota immigration, that from the Western Hemisphere.

To judge from past behavior, Congress will continue an overall and perhaps somewhat increasing restriction of immigration, while allowing special exemptions as emergencies arise. The actual trend of policy, of course, will continue to be affected in the future as in the past by changing definitions of national interest during periods of high unemployment, or labor shortages, or disturbed international relations. Changed social, economic, and political conditions, however, will not necessarily call for new immigration legislation, for the present regulatory system possesses considerable flexibility at the administrative or enforcement level, as will be described later, especially if greater restriction is wanted.

14 Race and Ethnic Composition

In the long process of enactment and amendment through which immigration law has developed, what was in effect a policy toward the racial and ethnic composition of immigration emerged out of the complicated structure of exclusions, restrictions, quota formulas, and preferences under quota. Strictly speaking, it was more an implicit than an explicit policy in its earliest development, for although individual members of Congress were outspoken on matters of race and national preferences, diplomatic considerations if no other generally prevented the singling out of specific peoples for adverse discrimination.[1] Later, with the quota acts, policy toward the composition of immigration became more evident and continued to be so until the end of the national origin basis of admissions in 1965.

Rather slow to assume responsibility for the regulation of immigration, as has been seen above, Congress did give attention to the composition of immigration quite soon after it embarked on immigration legislation. In this policy area Congress had lagged considerably behind public opinion, for whatever indiscriminate antialien sentiment may have existed earlier, the electorate as a whole soon came to differentiate between preferred and disfavored sources of immigration; and although Congress was able to resist nativist and antialien pressures for some time, its first discriminatory act was in response to strong political pressures. That was, of course, the Chinese Exclusion Act of 1882.

Oriental Exclusion and Restriction

The peoples most explicitly rejected or restricted as immigrants were those from southern and eastern Asia and the adjacent islands, of which the Chinese were the first to be so treated. The body of excluding legislation was described in an earlier chapter:[2] the Chinese Exclusion Acts of

[1]Notable exceptions are, of course, the Chinese exclusion laws and the abrogation of the understanding with Japan in 1924.

[2]See chapter 11, pp. 430–33 above.

1882 and onward, the attempt to check Japanese laborer immigration by the Gentlemen's Agreement of 1907, the exclusion of all but certain professional classes of natives of the so-called Asiatic Barred Zone in 1917, and, last, the abrogation of the agreement with Japan and the imposition of racial eligibility for citizenship as a condition for admission for permanent residence in 1924. Also described was the termination of the racial barrier to naturalization and admission for permanent residence for selected peoples from 1943 onward and the complete removal of such barriers in 1952.

This repeal of racial bases for exclusion was indeed a victory for the "liberal" forces in Congress, but it was a limited victory, more of principle than substance—that is, the repeal did open the door to immigrants from China, Japan, and the Asiatic Barred Zone, but it opened the door only slightly, for only token quotas were granted; and these quotas were allocated on the basis of racial origin rather than national origin. The change for the peoples concerned was from complete exclusion to severe restriction.

The pattern was set by the first of the new acts, the Act of December 17, 1943 (57 Stat. 600) that repealed the Chinese Exclusion Acts.[3] This act directed that a quota be computed under the provisions of the 1924 Act, section 11, for "all Chinese persons," and as more fully defined by a later act[4] a "Chinese person" was "any person who is as much as one-half Chinese blood." The quota was thus a global quota for persons of as much as half Chinese ancestry, regardless of place of birth. The quota so assigned was 105 per annum, with a preference of 75 percent of the number given to "Chinese persons born and resident in China."[5] Two and a half years later the Act of July 2, 1946 (60 Stat. 416) made "Filipino persons or persons of Filipino descent" and "persons of races indigenous to India" eligible for naturalization and therefore for admission for permanent residence. The admissibility of the Indians was on the same terms as were applied earlier to the Chinese. That is, they were classified on the basis of racial origin rather than national origin as "any person who is as much as one-half of the blood of a race indigenous to India." India received the minimum quota of 100 per annum, and again

[3]China already had a quota of 100 per annum under the 1924 Act, but the quota was available only to those persons born in China who were racially eligible to naturalization, not to persons of Chinese blood.

[4]Sect. 5(b) of the Act of July 2, 1946 (60 Stat. 416).

[5]Nonquota status was given to a lawfully resident Chinese returning from a temporary visit abroad, to certain ministers and professors, to bona fide students, and to certain women who were former citizens. The Act of August 9, 1946 (60 Stat. 975) gave nonquota status to Chinese alien wives of American citizens.

a 75 percent preference was given to those born and resident in that country.[6]

The Immigration and Nationality Act of 1952, as already noted, continued the national origin formula for the assignment of national quotas but made changes in the admissibility of Asiatic and Pacific peoples. It did away with racial criteria for naturalization and admissibility, it abolished the Asiatic Barred Zone, and it set up a newly defined area for separate treatment in admission by quota. The new area, known as the Asia-Pacific triangle, consisted approximately of "all Asian countries from India to Japan and all Pacific Islands north of Australia and New Zealand."[7] Independent nations, self-governing dominions, and United Nations trust territories within the area already had their own quotas,[8] but as in the case of China prior to the 1943 Act the quotas had been available only to natives of these areas who were racially eligible for naturalization. The 1952 Act removed such racial restriction for the quota areas in the triangle and in addition gave a quota of 100 to the triangle as a whole available to immigrants attributable to (1) a colony or dependent area or (2) a combination of separate quota areas or (3) a combination of a separate quota area and a colony or dependency, within the Asia-Pacific triangle. As in the earlier Act of 1943, however, the 1952 Act did not entirely do away with racial selectivity in quota immigration, for the quotas of the separate areas within the triangle and of the triangle as a whole applied not on the basis of birthplace but to "an immigrant who is attributable by as much as one-half of his ancestry to a people or peoples indigenous to the Asia-Pacific triangle" (sect. 202b of the 1952 Act). The Asia-Pacific triangle provisions of the 1952 Act thus continued the race or ancestry basis of quota allocation of the immediately preceding acts, and it continued in force until it was repealed by the 1965 Act that did away with any discrimination between racial or ethnic groups in admissions.

[6]In the case of those of half Indian and half Chinese blood, the act directed that they be charged to the quota for India if born there, to the Chinese quota if born in China. If they were born in neither country, then they were to be charged to whichever of the two countries had the fewer applicants for visas.

[7]Frank L. Auerbach, *Immigration Laws* (Indianapolis: Bobbs-Merrill, 1955), p. 94. As defined in sect. 202b of the act, the area comprised "all quota areas and all colonies and other dependent areas situate wholly east of the meridian sixty degrees east of Greenwich, wholly west of the medidian one hundred and sixty-five degrees west, and wholly north of the parallel twenty-five degrees south latitude. . . ."

[8]Separate quota areas within the triangle were Afghanistan, Bhutan, Burma, Cambodia, Ceylon, China, India, Indonesia, Japan, Korea, Laos, Nauru, Nepal, New Guinea, Pacific Islands, Pakistan, the Philippines, Thailand, West Samoa, and Vietnam. There was also the quota for Chinese persons, separate from the area quota for China.

Literacy Test

As previously mentioned, any formula or procedure for the restriction of immigration is apt to bear more heavily on some groups than on others, and it may be preferred precisely because of that effect. The head tax, for example, was originally a revenue-producing device but in time began to take on the further function of a restrictive measure;[9] there is also evidence that its supporters came to see in it the further advantage of bearing most heavily on immigrants from the poorer countries of southern and eastern Europe.[10] It is even clearer in the case of the literacy test that it was proposed and eventually adopted not just to exclude illiterates as such, but because in so doing it would act most strongly against certain types and sources of immigration regarded as undesirable for reasons other than educational level.

The selective quality of the literacy test was clearly described in the Senate committee report accompanying the first literacy test bill to be brought before Congress.[11] Voicing its concern that immigration threatens the "quality of our race and citizenship" as well as the level of wages, the committee explained its preference for the literacy test over restriction by means of a capitation tax or consular certificates, stating that evidence before the committee indicated that

> The illiteracy test will affect almost entirely those races whose immigration to the United States has begun within recent times and which are most alien in language and origin to the people who founded the 13 colonies and have built up the United States; that it would tell most heavily against those classes of immigrants which now furnish paupers, diseased and criminal, excluded by existing law . . . ; that the immigrants who would be excluded by the illiteracy test do not go out into the Western and Southern States, where immigration is needed, and become an agricultural population, but remain almost entirely in the Atlantic States and in the great centers of population, where the labor market is already overcrowded; that the illiterate immigrants . . . furnish a large proportion of the slum population; that the illiteracy test would shut out those classes of immigrants which statistics show contribute most heavily to pauperism and crime and juvenile delinquents. . . . In one word, it may be said that this measure will exclude a larger number of undesirable immigrants, so far as statistics can be relied upon, than any restriction which could be devised.[12]

[9]See pp. 462–65 above. [10]See p. 465 above in particular.

[11]S. 2147 (54-I), accompanied by S. Rept. 290, February 18, 1896. For a history of the bill and its counterpart in the House, see pp. 115–18, 119–21 above.

[12]From S. Rept. 290 (54-I); also quoted in 1911 Immigration Commission Report 39:47.

Similar testimony in favor of the Senate bill was given by the author of the bill, Lodge of Massachusetts, who spoke on behalf of the committee when the bill was brought up for consideration by the Senate on March 16, 1896. With regard to its selectivity according to nationality, he testified further that

> the illiteracy test will bear most heavily upon the Italians, Russians, Poles, Hungarians, Greeks, and Asiatics, and very lightly, or not at all, upon English-speaking emigrants or Germans, Scandinavians, and French. In other words, the races most affected by the illiteracy test are those whose emigration to this country has begun within the last twenty years and swelled rapidly to enormous proportions, races with which the English-speaking people have never hitherto assimilated, and who are most alien to the great body of the people of the United States. On the other hand, immigrants from the United Kingdom and of those races which are most closely related to the English-speaking people, and who with the English-speaking people themselves founded the American colonies and built up the United States, are affected but little by the proposed test.[13]

To this Lodge added sober remarks about the danger of "changing the quality of our race and citizenship through the wholesale infusion of races whose traditions and inheritances, whose thoughts and whose beliefs are wholly alien to ours. . . ."[14] At the same time the House committee reported out its own literacy test bill, with the assurance that it would not greatly affect immigration from Great Britain, Germany, Scandinavia, and other nations of western Europe but would "considerably restrict" immigration from southern Europe.[15]

In the eyes of its sponsors, it would seem the literacy test was the panacea to solve all the problems of immigration, and it continued to be so regarded long after the 1896 bill was defeated by presidential veto. For the next twenty years, in spite of veto after veto, literacy test bills were reported out by the Senate and House committees, until one was finally passed over a fourth veto to become the 1917 Act.[16] It is ironic to note from a later perspective, however, that in spite of the high and long-

[13]*Congressional Record,* 28:2817, March 16, 1896.

[14]Ibid., p. 2820.

[15]H. Rept. 1079, April 12, 1896; to accompany H.R. 7864 (54-I), substituted for H.R. 9.

[16]For a summary of the legislative history of the literacy test, see chapter 13, pp. 465–68 above. The House report on the bill that became the 1917 Act referred to the literacy test as a means of excluding the unskilled classes that produced the problems of overcrowding and poverty, but as regards national selection noted only that it would check immigration from southern and eastern Europe. H. Rept. 95 (64-I).

deferred hopes entertained for the literacy test as both a restrictive and a selective measure, only a few years after its adoption the test together with the other restrictive features of the 1917 Act were seen to be inadequate to check the influx of immigrants impending after the First World War. It was then, as was previously described, that Congress turned to the quota system as a surer means of controlling immigration. Although most directly designed for the numerical limitation of immigration, the new system was also devised to exercise a racial and ethnic selection, as described in the following section.

The Quota Formulas

The legislative history and restrictive aspect of the quota acts have been dealt with previously,[17] but their selectivity in the allocation of national quotas remains to be noted. The first quota act, the Act of May 19, 1921 (42 Stat. 5) directed that

> the number of aliens of any nationality who may be admitted . . . in any fiscal year shall be limited to 3 per centum of the number of foreign-born persons of such nationality resident in the United States as determined by the United States census of 1910.[18]

Not to be counted in the total of quota admissions were various classes of temporary arrivals, aliens from the Asiatic Barred Zone, who were not admissible for permanent residence in any case, aliens who for one year[19] prior to arrival have resided in a Western Hemisphere nation, and alien children under age eighteen of citizen parents.

The 1921 formula thus set the annual quota of a nation to be proportional to the number of resident immigrants from that nation as enumerated in 1910. The intention was evidently to give to new immigration the same distribution by place of origin as the resident foreign-born white population in 1910; the effect was to give ample quotas to certain of the nations of old immigration such as the United Kingdom, Germany, Norway, and Sweden, whose migrants to the United States had accumulated over a number of years, but also to the nations of more recent and heavy immigration such as Italy, Russia, Poland, and Czechoslovakia.[20]

[17]See especially chapter 13, pp. 468–78 above.

[18]Section 2a of the 1921 Act. The wording was perhaps clear at the time, but in terms of modern usage the census figure used for the determination of a nation's quota was not on the basis of nationality in the sense of citizenship but on the basis of birthplace.

[19]Increased to five years by the Act of May 11, 1922 (42 Stat. 540).

[20]Out of a total quota of 355,825 for the year ending June 30, 1922, the United Kingdom had an annual quota of 77,206, Germany 68,039, Italy 42,021, Russia 34,247, Poland 20,019, Sweden 19,956, Czechoslovakia 14,269, and Norway 12,116.

The quota formula was changed drastically by the Act of May 26, 1924, the second quota act, whose stated purpose was "to limit the immigration of aliens into the United States." It provided an interim quota formula based as in the 1921 Act on the foreign-born population of the United States, to be superseded later by a new system of so-called national origins quotas. In the interim,

> The annual quota of any nationality shall be 2 per centum of the number of foreign-born individuals of such nationality resident in continental United States as determined by the United States census of 1890, but the minimum quota of any nationality shall be 100. (Sect. 11a of the 1924 Act)

The smaller percentage and the change of the base year from 1910 to 1890 reduced the total allowable annual quota immigration from nearly 356,000 to under 165,000. The changed formula also had the effect of allocating the greater part of the total quota to the nations of older immigration, the nations of northern and western Europe, and of giving small quotas to the nations of newer immigration that were predominantly in southern and eastern Europe.[21] Quite clearly the 1890 base was chosen for precisely that effect. In explanation of its adoption of the 1890 base the House committee wrote in part as follows:

> If . . . the principle of individual liberty . . . is to endure, the basic strain of our population must be maintained and our economic standards preserved.
>
> With full recognition of the material progress which we owe to the races from southern and eastern Europe, we are conscious that the continued arrival of great numbers tends to upset our balance of population, to depress our standard of living, and to unduly charge our institutions for the care of the socially inadequate.
>
> If immigration from southern and eastern Europe may enter the United States on a basis of substantial equality with that admitted from the older sources of supply, it is clear that if any appreciable number of immigrants are to be allowed to land upon our shores the balance of racial preponderance must in time pass to those elements of the population who reproduce more rapidly on a lower standard of living than those possessing other ideals.[22]

[21]Out of a total quota of 164,667 per annum, the 1924 Act allocated quotas as follows: Great Britain and Northern Ireland 34,007, Irish Free State 28,567, Germany 51,227, Italy 3,845, Russia 2,248, Poland 5,982, Sweden 9,561, Czechoslovakia 3,073, and Norway 6,453. For comparison see footnote 20 above.

[22]H. Rept. 350 (68-I), pp. 13–14.

The report continued

> The present quota law gives 44.6 per cent of our total quota immigration to the countries of southern and eastern Europe, including Asiatic Turkey and Palestine—an amount vastly in excess of what they could claim on any theory of proportional representation. . . . The use of the 1890 census is not discriminatory. It is used in an effort to preserve, as nearly as possible, the racial status quo in the United States. It is hoped to guarantee, as best we can at this late date, racial homogeneity in the United States.[23]

The same point of view with its emphasis on "the basic strain of our population" and "racial status quo" lay behind the national origins quota formula, stated as follows by the 1924 Act:

> The annual quota of any nationality . . . shall be a number which bears the same ratio to 150,000 as the number of inhabitants in continental United States in 1920 having that national origin . . . bears to the number of inhabitants in continental United States in 1920. . . .[24]

In other words, "racial homogeneity" was to be maintained by allocating national quotas to conform to the estimated composition by national origin of the population of the United States in 1920; but actually only the population of directly European origin was to be considered in the computation. Excluded from the 1920 base population were immigrants from the Western Hemisphere and their descendants, "aliens ineligible to citizenship or their descendants, the descendants of slave immigrants, or the descendants of American aborigines" (sect. 11d of the 1924 Act).

The national origin basis for the allocation of national quotas as set by the 1924 Act and effective in 1929 was continued by the 1952 Act, and remained in force until repealed by the 1965 Act. Although the latter act brought success to the long campaign to do away with the national origin system, it should be noted that the preference structure of the new act allocated up to 74 percent of the quota plus unused portions of the other preference classes to certain relatives of the resident foreign-born population of the United States. To this extent the ethnic origin distribution of new immigration would tend to conform to that of the surviving immigrants admitted under the old act.[25]

[23]Ibid., p. 16.

[24]Sect. 11b of the 1924 Act. The quotas so determined were, for the fiscal year 1930 and for the same nations as in the preceding footnotes, Great Britain and Northern Ireland 65,721, Irish Free State 17,853, Germany 25,957, Italy 5,802, Russia 2,784, Poland 6,524, Sweden 3,314, Czechoslovakia 2,874, Norway 2,377.

[25]For description of the preference structure of the 1965 Act, see pp. 371–72 above.

Western Hemisphere Immigration

The quota formulas that repressed the immigration of certain disfavored ethnic or national origin groups by granting them low quotas as described above, at the same time facilitated the immigration of certain more favored groups that received larger quotas, as is illustrated by the differential treatment of "new" immigration from southern and eastern Europe and "old" immigration from elsewhere in that continent. In addition the immigration of certain other classes and groups was still further facilitated by the granting to them of nonquota status, an exemption from quota limits on the number admitted. Included among the several nonquota classes established by the first and later quota acts was one class defined on the basis of place of origin, which consisted of migrants from the Western Hemisphere.

This particular element of immigration law, whose rationale does not appear to have gone beyond a simple "good neighbor" policy, began with the first quota act in 1921. That act, as previously described, gave nonquota status to

> aliens who have resided continuously for at least one year immediately preceding the time of their admission to the United States in the Dominion of Canada, Newfoundland, the Republic of Cuba, the Republic of Mexico, countries of Central or South America, or adjacent islands.[26]

In the next year the above subsection was amended to change the required period of residence in the Western Hemisphere from one to five years.[27] Two years later, on suspicion that the provision was being used by immigrants to bypass the national origin controls on immigration, the 1924 Act redefined the nonquota class to consist of

> An immigrant who was born in the Dominion of Canada, Newfoundland, the Republic of Mexico, the Republic of Cuba, the Republic of Haiti, the Dominican Republic, the Canal Zone, or an independent country of Central or South America, and his wife, and his unmarried children under 18 years of age, if accompanying or following to join him. (Sect. 4c of the 1924 Act)

Birthplace was thus made the basis for Western Hemisphere nonquota status, as it was already for allocation of the national quotas.

The actual proportion of quota immigration coming under family preference during the five fiscal years 1969 to 1973 inclusive (preference classes 1, 2, 4, and 5) was 442,300 out of 818,962, or about 54 percent.

[26]Section 2(a)(7) of the Act of May 19, 1921 (42 Stat. 5).

[27]Section 2, Act of May 11, 1922 (42 Stat. 540).

A further step regarding Western Hemisphere immigration was taken in the 1965 Act. With the exception of certain classes of immigrants not subject to numerical limitation, the new act set a limit of 120,000 per annum on Western Hemisphere immigration, along with the limit of 170,000 per annum on immigration from other parts of the world.[28] As is described more fully in an earlier chapter, the administration and individual members of Congress opposed the limitation of Western Hemisphere immigration, but a congressional majority, which had heard much about the obligation to end discrimination in the immigration laws, was not disposed to permit unlimited immigration from one favored area while imposing a quota ceiling on other parts of the world.

The congressional problem of what policy to adopt toward Western Hemisphere immigration was much more complex and controversial than appears from the quite simple legislation itself. One troublesome fact was that diplomatic considerations called for treating all Western Hemisphere nations alike, but actually the immigrants from some areas had a long history of ready acceptance whereas immigrants from elsewhere had a record of illegal entry and other problems. And there was always the lingering concern that the nonquota status of the Western Hemisphere gave a vulnerability to any future rising tide of immigration or to sudden waves of immigrants caused by political or economic distress. As early as the first quota act in 1921, differing views were expressed in Congress about the regulation of Western Hemisphere immigration, and the proposals for change took two principal forms. One was a limitation of the number of immigrants from the hemisphere to be admitted and the other was some kind of formula that appeared nondiscriminatory but in fact favored certain sources of immigration over others.

The various bills and sections of bills dealing with Western Hemisphere immigration were noted in Part I, chapters 5 to 8, but the direction of policy expressed in them is best seen by looking at the group of bills as a whole. Proposals to impose a quota limit on Western Hemisphere immigration began to appear in Congress within a year or two after the 1924 Act made birth in the Western Hemisphere rather than five years of residence confer nonquota status. A quota bill was introduced in the first session (1925–1926) of the 69th Congress,[29] and several more were offered in the first session (1927–1928) of the next Congress.[30] One of the latter was reported out by the Senate committee in the second session, after being rewritten in committee to deny nonquota status to immi-

[28]See further concerning the 1965 Act, especially pp. 373, 374, and 375 above.
[29]See p. 200 above. [30]See p. 204.

grants from Mexico.[31] Another Western Hemisphere quota bill appeared in the next Congress.[32]

A number of such quota bills appeared early in the Depression period, during the second session (1929–1930) of the 71st Congress. A bill reported out by the House committee was to set quotas for Canada, Newfoundland, Mexico, and Cuba at four times the number of American citizens who migrated to those countries during a given fiscal year. This device gave a large quota to Canada and small quotas to Cuba and Mexico. Other Western Hemisphere nations were to receive quotas equal to the number of immigrant visas granted to their citizens during the same base period. Meanwhile, the Senate committee reported out a bill to retain nonquota status for Canada and Newfoundland but to apply quotas to all other Western Hemisphere areas. Amended to apply a quota only to Mexico, the bill passed the Senate but died in the House.[33] Later in the same session was a proposal to subject Western Hemisphere nations to a quota computed at one tenth of the number of nonquota visas issued to them during the fiscal year ending June 30, 1930.[34] A later bill in the next Congress was directed especially at restriction of immigration from Central and South America.[35] Whether specifically mentioned or not, Mexican immigration was the major target of the proposals for restriction, but several bills during the next years singled out Mexico to be brought under quota.[36]

Efforts to restrict Western Hemisphere immigration died out with the easing of the economic depression and unemployment after the middle 1930s; and labor was even recruited from Mexico and other countries during the war years. Another consideration that argued against new restrictive legislation was that experience had shown during the Depression years that immigration could be effectively restricted with the already available laws. Western Hemisphere immigrants, although quota-free, were fully subject to the same criteria of admissibility and exclusion as other immigrants and could be excluded for any one of many reasons on the judgment of the immigrant inspector. It can be assumed, therefore, that such powers were used as they were thought needful to restrict the number of Western Hemisphere immigrants as was done for European immigrants. Furthermore, the same powers could very well be used selectively as between different countries of Western Hemisphere origin; for example the public charge provision could be applied with different force to immigrants from Canada and Mexico.

[31]See p. 207.
[32]See p. 215.
[33]See p. 217.
[34]See p. 220.
[35]See p. 226 above.
[36]See pp. 234, 236 above.

Final Comment

In addition to the measures and legislative proposals described above there have been occasional bills to single out one or another national or ethnic group for different treatment under the immigration laws. In some cases the purpose has been to further limit immigration, as in bills to reduce the number of Filipinos admitted; other bills have been to facilitate immigration, as for example by increasing the Italian or Greek quota. The congressional committees, however, regularly ignored such bills. This negative action could have been expected, for the bills may not have been serious legislative proposals but rather designed to win minority or special interest group votes for the bills' sponsors.

Viewed as a whole, congressional action to regulate the national or ethnic composition of immigration is one part of the broader policy of selective immigration. Selection of the immigrants permitted to enter and allowed to remain has always been one of the fundamentals of American immigration policy,[37] and race, national origin, or ethnicity are among the sometimes acknowledged and sometimes unacknowledged criteria of selection. In this respect Congress has more or less reflected the prejudices and preferences of the national population, but often with considerable lag, for the legislative process does not lend itself to quick action, and Congress has shown independence of judgment in resisting popular clamor and emotional appeals regarding immigration.

Congress cannot be said to have established any continuing and formal policy with regard to the racial and ethnic composition of immigration over the years from the 1880s up to 1965. Legislation consisted of ad hoc legislation to meet the problems and political pressures of the time; but insofar as there was an underlying policy objective running through legislative action, it was to maintain the ethnic composition of the national population undisturbed or minimally disturbed by immigration. Probably without any conscious effort to do so, Congress moved toward that objective from the 1880s onward until it found its fullest expression in the national origin system for the allocation of immigration quotas. Thereafter the system was to remain on the statute books until repealed by the 1965 Act, but actually the system was being progressively weakened long before then. The system itself was not able to set the composition of immigration in the desired pattern because some of the large national quotas were not filled and immigration from the Western Hemisphere was quota-free, and, as is described in later chapters, Congress in the World War II period and after enacted many departures from

[37]See especially chapters 11 and 12.

the national origin system, in the form of nonquota status for various classes of relatives and refugees, and authorized other admissions out of quota.

Included in this chapter's account of legislation are both measures that directly regulated the ethnic composition of immigration and other measures that had an indirect but presumably intended effect. The material can be summarized conveniently in terms of the instruments of policy devised and utilized by Congress over the years. The first and also most direct action was against Oriental immigration, beginning with the Chinese in 1882. The instrument used then was exclusion for all but limited classes of Chinese, set for a term of ten years but renewed at the end of each ten-year period so that it amounted to permanent exclusion. A more diplomatic method was adopted later for the Japanese, in the form of an agreement with the Japanese government to keep out laborers. This was followed in 1917 by exclusion of natives of the so-called Asiatic Barred Zone, certain professional classes excepted; and then, when dissatisfaction with the Japanese agreement arose, the 1924 Act denied admission for permanent residence to persons racially ineligible to naturalization, a measure that excluded the Japanese as well as other Asiatics. Such exclusion was ended by the 1952 Act, which granted quotas to the formerly excluded peoples, but unlike other quotas these were allocated on the basis of a person's race or ancestry instead of birthplace.

Less drastic and more selective policy instruments were employed for European immigration. The head tax was described earlier as a restrictive measure,[38] but its doubling and redoubling in the first decades of the present century was presumably in part at least to discourage immigration from the poorer nations of southern and eastern Europe.[39] Another instrument of policy long considered by Congress and finally adopted in 1917 was the literacy test. This again was a restrictive measure but also selective in intention, for it was well understood that it would bear most heavily on immigration from the less desired classes and national origins.

When it became evident that the literacy test would not serve the restrictive and selective purposes for which it was designed, Congress labored again and brought forth a succession of new instruments of policy, the quota formulas. As described in a preceding section, the progression through the 1921, the 1924, and the national origins quota formulas for the allocation of national quotas was toward the double objective of reduction of immigration and an immigration approximating the composition of the American population.

[38]Chapter 13, pp. 462–65.

[39]On this point see especially pp. 465–66 above.

In the main the instruments of policy developed by Congress were for what may be called a selective restriction of immigration; but there were in fact some provisions for the encouragement or at least facilitation of immigration. The overly large quotas granted to some nations may be thought of in this sense,[40] but more positive in its action on the distribution of immigration by origin was the provision of quota-free immigration for natives of Western Hemisphere nations. The Western Hemisphere migrants, however, were still subject to all the grounds for exclusion under the immigration laws, and these provided ample means for selection and limitation.

After many years of effort both within and outside Congress for revision of the quota system, the 1965 Act at last made several major changes. One change was to do away with the national origin system of visa allocation, to substitute a new allocation system while retaining an overall quota ceiling, and, last, to put a quota ceiling on Western Hemisphere immigration. It is noted, however, that the preference system of visa allocation under the new act was heavily weighted in favor of relatives of residents of the United States and thus influenced by earlier immigration.

A final point to be made is that the story of legislation affecting the racial and ethnic make-up of immigration is not quite the whole story. There are also the many bills introduced in Congress but not enacted; and the action taken by Congress can be seen in somewhat fuller perspective in comparison to what Congress chose not to do. Earlier chapters in Part I include mention of bills that did not come to enactment, and the section on Western Hemisphere immigration immediately above includes note of unsuccessful proposals. Except in the matter of Oriental exclusion, the general impression is that Congress brought itself to deal with immigration only with some difficulty and that when it did so it tended to follow a middle course between the extremes of anti-immigration and proimmigration urgings. Especially it paid little or no attention to the most extreme restrictionist and discriminatory proposals. One may infer that these qualities in legislative action on racial and ethnic issues are not so much due to any guiding policy or philosophy as to the averaging out of divergent views within the Congress, a considerable degree of inertia in the legislative process, a usually firm control by old and experienced members of the immigration committees, and in the background the presidential veto power.

[40]But since unused quotas could not be reassigned prior to 1965, the surplus quota numbers granted to some nations meant that the actual amount of quota immigration was reduced by that amount.

15 Labor Market Policy

An element that runs through congressional debate and action on immigration is that of labor market considerations. It would in fact be difficult to determine where immigration policy ends and labor policy begins, the two are so closely interrelated. One may indeed suspect that some ostensibly immigration bills and some provisions in immigration law are actually designed with labor market objectives and that immigration legislation in such cases is being used as an instrument of labor market policy.

Although not particularly emphasized, it can be observed in preceding chapters that labor considerations were frequently raised in the discussion of immigration measures. Protection of the American working man and maintenance of the American wage level or standard of living were prominently mentioned in support of proposals to regulate and restrict immigration, but what was genuine and what was specious cannot be determined with any assurance. Proponents of restriction may have grasped the labor protection argument for its plausibility, friends of native labor may have argued for restriction to serve their own purposes, and others without convictions either way may have had an eye on the labor vote in their constituency. But in any case labor considerations have been quite prominent in congressional debate on immigration policy, and immigration laws show numerous provisions related to the admission of workers.

The labor clauses in immigration bills fall into two broad and opposite groups: one to restrict or even exclude unwanted types or classes, the other to facilitate or encourage the immigration of desirable and needed workers. The underlying difference between the two types of provision is not precisely that between interests of the employee on the one hand and the employer on the other, or between the restriction of unskilled and encouragement of skilled labor immigration, although these aspects are prominent. Rather, labor provisions can be regarded as congressional responses to various and diverse labor market needs and pressures that call in some instances for restriction of the labor supply and in others for selective recruitment or encouragement.

Protection by Restriction

Immigration restriction has been for American labor what the protective tariff was for the manufacturer: protection against foreign competition. Restriction of immigration, as already noted, has been a feature of American immigration policy since the earliest days of federal regulation, and although restriction drew support from various sources, labor protection was prominent among them. In its most drastic form, protection took the form of exclusion of certain classes of aliens. As described in chapter 11 on exclusions, the Chinese Exclusion Acts of 1882 and onward were directed against "Chinese laborers," and the Gentlemen's Agreement of 1907 was for the purpose of excluding Japanese laborers.[1] In the same chapter is an account of the body of legislation known as the Contract Labor Laws, designed to exclude laborers brought in under contract or agreement with employers in the United States.[2]

There is also reason to believe, as noted above, that the less drastic action of restricting rather than prohibiting immigration was adopted, among other reasons, to protect the domestic labor market from excessive immigration of alien labor. On this point we have the testimony of its sponsors, if taken at face value. For example, the literacy test, the first of the avowedly restrictionist measures, was recommended by its congressional father, Senator Lodge, because it would reduce immigration

> and would thereby greatly benefit the labor market and help to maintain the rate of American wages.[3]

This theme was repeated over and over during the years that followed, until adoption of the literacy test in the 1917 Act. Bills for the protection of American labor, including one to prohibit the immigration of both skilled and unskilled foreign manual labor, appeared in the first session (1895–1896) of the 54th Congress.[4] Another bill to exclude foreign-born laborers was introduced late in the same session.[5] There was also congressional sentiment for excluding workers who leave their families behind and those who come repeatedly.[6] Protection of native labor was urged by President Roosevelt in at least two messages to Congress, one in 1901, which stated that the "influx of cheap labor" should be stopped, and another in 1904 that urged Congress to deny admission to

[1]Chapter 11, pp. 430–33. [2]Chapter 11, pp. 427–30.

[3]For more extended quotation and reference, see p. 465 above.

[4]See p. 114 above.

[5]See p. 118 above. See also p. 118 concerning the Republican party platform of that year.

[6]See pp. 118 and 121.

> masses of men whose standards of living and whose personal customs and habits are such that they tend to lower the level of the American wage-worker.[7]

Some years later, in 1911, the Dillingham Commission report spoke of the need to protect the wage level and the conditions of employment.[8]

There was much legislative activity in favor of restriction during the 1920s when the quota acts were under active development. While the quota formulas were being devised, attention focused on the distribution of quota numbers according to country of origin, however, and the labor protection issue receded into the background. It is true that the countries from which immigration was most reduced by the final quota formula were primarily those from which large numbers and proportions of unskilled laborers had come recently, but the labor issue as such did not appear prominently in congressional deliberations at the time. The issue did reappear in the following decade when depression and unemployment were the great national problems. As described in an earlier chapter, numerous bills were introduced in Congress at that time to suspend immigration whenever the national unemployment figure exceeded a certain amount;[9] similar bills are found on into the 1940s. Since then the issue of labor market protection has been in abeyance, although by no means forgotten, under the conditions of limited immigration, and altered composition of immigration because of the preference structure, and unemployment rates generally within acceptable limits; but the issue inevitably would become active again in case of high unemployment rates.

Occupational Preference Classes

The opposite aspect of labor policy in immigration law is represented by the various exemptions from alien labor restrictions and exclusions that have been granted to certain occupational classes regarded as desirable. The original Chinese Exclusion Act of 1882, for example, was careful to state it did not apply to a "Chinese person other than a laborer who may be entitled by . . . treaty and this act to come within the United States."[10] Similarly the first Contract Labor Act of February 26, 1885 (23 Stat. 332)

[7]See pp. 127–28, 135 above. [8]See p. 148 above.

[9]See chapter 13, especially pp. 475–76.

[10]Sect. 6, Act of May 6, 1882 (22 Stat. 58). The exemption applied chiefly to so-called treaty merchants. But an act of two years later (Act of July 5, 1884) took care to specify that the term "merchant" did not include "hucksters, peddlers, or those engaged in taking, drying, or otherwise preserving shell or other fish for home consumption or exportation."

was designed not to apply to (1) private secretaries, servants, or domestics employed by foreigners temporarily residing in the United States, (2) skilled laborers brought in to work in "any new industry not at present established in the United States," provided that skilled labor for that purpose cannot be otherwise obtained, or

> (3) professional actors, artists, lecturers, or singers, nor to persons employed strictly as personal or domestic servants. (Sect. 5 of the 1885 Act)

That is, the exemptions were principally for aliens with special training or ability and workers in short supply. A later act[11] amended the 1885 Act by adding ministers of any religious denomination, persons belonging to any recognized profession, and professors for colleges and seminaries to the occupational classes exempt from the contract labor law.

Later immigration acts followed a pattern of occupational exemption from the contract labor laws similar to that already set by the 1882 and 1885 acts. A proviso in the Immigration Act of 1903 was that "skilled labor may be imported, if labor of like kind unemployed can not be found in this country." And a following proviso contained the previous occupational exemptions from the contract labor laws.[12] Of these provisos the former broadened the corresponding exemption contained in the 1885 Act and established a principle that was to persist in later immigration legislation.

The same provisos are found in the immigration acts of 1907 and 1910. The 1917 Act amplified the proviso on skilled labor to read

> skilled labor, if otherwise admissible, may be imported if labor of like kind unemployed can not be found in this country, and the question of the necessity of importing such skilled labor in any particular instance may be determined by the Secretary of Labor . . . after a full hearing and an investigation into the facts of the case.[13]

Another proviso added nurses to the list of occupations exempt from the contract labor laws, and the exempt servant class was redefined more briefly as "persons employed as domestic servants."

The quota acts, which limited the number of immigrants to be admitted, created a new situation with regard to the entry of persons with desirable occupational qualifications, and Congress took care to facilitate the entry of such persons in spite of quota limitations. The first quota act contained a proviso that

[11]Act of March 3, 1891 (26 Stat. 1084), sect. 5.

[12]Second and third provisos, sect. 2 of the Act of March 3, 1903 (32 Stat. 1213). The occupational classes exempt were the same as established by the 1885 and 1891 acts.

[13]Fourth proviso, sect. 3, Act of February 5, 1917 (39 Stat. 874).

> aliens who are professional actors, artists, lecturers, singers, nurses, ministers of any religious denomination, professors for colleges or seminaries, aliens belonging to any recognized learned profession, or aliens employed as domestic servants

may be admitted even if in excess of the quota for their nationality but are to be charged to the appropriate quota if the quota is not yet filled and they do not belong to one of the nonquota classes.[14] This was a continuation of the preferential treatment of these same occupational classes under the preceding act into the terms of the new quota act.

As the June 30, 1924 expiration date of the 1921 Quota Act approached, the congressional committees worked on the drafts of new bills to take the place of the old. House bills in 1923 and 1924 would have given nonquota status, among other classes, to "a skilled laborer, if labor of like kind unemployed cannot be found in the United States," and to

> an immigrant who for at least two years has been and seeks admission to carry on his vocation of ministry, professor of a college or seminary, or member of any recognized learned profession.[15]

The 1924 Act as finally passed, however, gave nonquota status on occupational grounds to only two professions and further limited them to

> An immigrant who continuously for at least two years immediately preceding the time of his application for admission to the United States has been, and who seeks to enter the United States solely for the purpose of, carrying on the vocation of minister of any religious denomination, or professor of a college, academy, seminary, or university; and his wife, and his unmarried children under eighteen years of age, if accompanying or following to join him.[16]

Another provision of the 1924 Act relating to the occupations of immigrants employed a newly invented device from the Quota Act of 1921—to give preference in granting immigration visas under quota as a means of facilitating the admission of a favored group. The 1924 Act created a preference class based on occupation, in the form of a first preference of up to half of each national quota for (1) certain relatives of American citizens, and

> (2) a quota immigrant who is skilled in agriculture, and his wife, and his dependent children under the age of 16 years, if accompanying

[14]Second proviso, sect. 2d of the 1921 Act.

[15]See pp. 185, 188 above.

[16]Sect. 4d of the Act of May 26, 1924 (43 Stat. 153).

> or following to join him. The preference provided in this paragraph shall not apply to immigrants of any nationality the annual quota for which is less than 300.[17]

Once invented as a means of promoting the immigration of a particular class of aliens, quota preference was used again and again. After occupational preference was first used in the 1924 Act, it reappeared in the Displaced Persons Act of 1948. In place of the 1924 Act preferences, the new act set up its own preference structure. This consisted of a first preference of not less than 30 percent of all visas issued under the act to go to

> eligible displaced persons who have been previously engaged in agricultural pursuits and who will be employed in the United States in agricultural pursuits.

A second occupational preference went to

> eligible displaced persons who are household, construction, clothing, and garment workers, and other workers needed in the locality in the United States in which such persons propose to reside; or eligible displaced persons possessing special educational, scientific, technological or professional qualifications.[18]

An amending act on June 16, 1950 (64 Stat. 219) combined the first and second preferences of the 1948 Act into a new first preference, and created a new second preference class consisting of blood relatives of citizens or lawfully admitted alien residents of the United States formerly given third preference under the 1948 Act.

The Immigration Act of 1952 gave a very heavily weighted occupational preference in the form of a first preference of 50 percent of each national quota plus any unused portions of the other preference classes to

> qualified quota immigrants whose services are determined by the Attorney General to be needed urgently in the United States because of the high education, technical training, specialized experience, or exceptional ability of such immigrants and to be substantially beneficial prospectively to the national economy, cultural interests, or welfare of the United States

[17]Sect. 6a of the 1924 Act. This paragraph was amended by the Act of May 29, 1928 (45 Stat. 1009) to read "in the case of any nationality the quota for which is three hundred or more, quota immigrants who are skilled in agriculture, and the wives, and the dependent children under the age of eighteen years, of such immigrants skilled in agriculture" (sect. 6[a][1] of the 1924 Act as amended).

[18]Sect. 6a and 6b, Act of June 25, 1948 (62 Stat. 1009).

together with the spouse and children of such immigrants.[19] This facilitation of entry based on occupational and other qualifications was balanced by the explicit exclusion on occupational grounds of the following:

> aliens seeking to enter the United States for the purpose of performing skilled or unskilled labor, if the Secretary of Labor has determined and certified to the Secretary of State and to the Attorney General that (A) sufficient workers in the United States who are able, willing, and qualified are available at the time (of application for a visa and for admission to the United States) and place (to which the alien is destined) to perform such skilled or unskilled labor, or (B) the employment of such aliens will adversely affect the wages and working conditions of the workers in the United States similarly employed. (Sect. 212[a][14] of 1952 Act)

The above exclusion was limited to aliens in the nonpreference class, as defined by the act, and to certain nonquota classes of which Western Hemisphere immigration was the largest.

The Refugee Relief Act of the following year provided a first priority in the consideration of visa applications under the act similar to the first preference class of the 1952 Act. Priority, as it was called in the 1953 Act, was to be given to

> persons whose services or skills are needed in the United States, if such need has been certified to the Administrator, . . . and who are to be employed in a capacity calling for such services or such skills.[20]

Finally, the 1965 Act made two principal changes in the labor-related provisions of the 1952 Act. One change was a new preference structure that contained two occupational classes: a third preference, not to exceed 10 percent of the total quota,

> to qualified immigrants who are members of the professions, or who because of their exceptional ability in the sciences or the arts will substantially benefit prospectively the national economy, cultural interests, or welfare of the United States.

A sixth preference of the same amount was given

> to qualified immigrants who are capable of performing specified skilled or unskilled labor, not of a temporary or seasonal nature, for which a shortage of employable and willing persons exists in the United States.[21]

[19]Sect. 203(a)(1) of the 1952 Act. Aliens eligible for first preference under this section and who had applied for admission prior to April 1, 1962 were given nonquota status by the Act of October 24, 1962 (76 Stat. 1247).

[20]Sect. 12(1) of the Act of August 7, 1953 (67 Stat. 400).

[21]Sect. 3, Act of October 3, 1965 (79 Stat. 911).

The second change was by amendment of the 1952 Act's paragraph excluding skilled and unskilled alien workers; the amended paragraph, with changes noted, read

> Aliens seeking to enter the United States for the purpose of performing skilled or unskilled labor, *unless* [*if,* in the 1952 Act] the Secretary of Labor has determined and certified to the Secretary of State and to the Attorney General that (A) there are *not* sufficient workers in the United States who are able, willing, qualified, and available at the time of application for a visa and admission to the United States and at the place to which the alien is destined to perform such skilled or unskilled labor, and (B) the employment of such aliens will *not* adversely affect the wages and working conditions of the workers in the United States similarly employed.[22] (Italics indicate words inserted by the 1965 Act.)

Both before and after amendment, the paragraph tied the exclusion of skilled and unskilled workers to the state of the labor supply and to the predicted effect of the immigration on wages and working conditions; but exclusion under the 1952 Act was only on action by the Secretary of Labor. In the 1965 Act, however, exclusion was automatic unless the Secretary of Labor took favorable action. The effect was to reaffirm and strengthen the power of the Secretary over the admission of aliens coming to seek employment.[23]

Aid to Occupations

In addition to the occupational preferences and occupational exclusions incorporated in the basic immigration laws, special immigration legislation was occasionally designed for the aid of specific occupations or industries. Pleas for special legislation to meet problems in certain occupations were most numerous during the Depression years, when it was felt that foreigners were overcrowding the occupations and taking employment away from natives. Quite early in the Depression, in the second session of the 71st Congress (1929–1930), a bill was introduced in the House to protect American instrumental musicians from the competition of foreigners who came as professional artists (H.R. 10816 [71-II]). The bill was to construe the application of the contract labor laws to such musicians, but with the stipulation that musicians of recognized reputation were not to be affected. Reported out by the House committee, the bill was not acted on. Reintroduced in the first session of the next Con-

[22]Sect. 10 of the 1965 Act. See footnote 56, p. 430.

[23]And there may have been a political purpose to assure organized labor that their interests would not be endangered by the act.

gress, it was passed by both houses of Congress and became the Act of March 17, 1932 (47 Stat. 67). It was the only such act to be passed. In brief, it declared the contract labor laws applicable to all instrumental musicians except those of distinguished ability and whose professional engagements are "of a character requiring superior talent." Similar bills were introduced concerning alien actors (H.R. 8877[72-I]), singers, and choristers (H.R. 7613, 8978 [72-I]), but these were not adopted by Congress.

Most notable of the special legislation is that for the admission of Basque sheepherders from Spain, in aid of the Western sheep-raising industry which had become dependent on immigrant workers. Having an effective spokesman in Congress, the industry was able to obtain the enactment of a series of bills over the years from 1950 to 1954. The first of these (Act of June 30, 1950 [64 Stat. 306]) provided for the admission of 250 otherwise admissible and skilled sheepherders, provided that the employment offered to them is permanent and there is no available quota number left for them. Another act two years later (Act of April 9, 1952 [66 Stat. 50]) provided for the admission of an additional 500 skilled sheepherders on the same terms but directed that the admissions be charged to the appropriate quotas of future years if the quota for the current year is exhausted. A third similar act was passed on September 3, 1954 (68 Stat. 1145) to authorize the admission of not more than 385 skilled sheepherders on the same conditions except that the admissions were to be nonquota. A bill two years later to admit up to 350 additional sheepherders, and for other purposes, passed the Senate but too late for House action to be taken.[24]

Other industries were less active or less successful in pressuring Congress for new legislation to admit needed workers. The only other bill of the same type as the sheepherders measures was a bill for the relief of the spongefishing industry, to provide nonquota visas for skilled spongedivers; however, no action was taken on this bill.[25]

Some Rejected Bills

As in other areas of legislation, congressional thinking on the subject of immigrant labor and the American labor market is shown not only by the bills that are enacted but also by the nature of the bills introduced by individual members of Congress from session to session and those that fail to be adopted. Worth noting here are several recurrent topics of legislative proposals.

[24]See p. 328 above.

[25]See p. 328 above.

During the final decades of the nineteenth century, when it had become accepted that Congress had the authority and responsibility for regulating immigration and numerous petitions were being sent to Congress, the so-called bird of passage was in much disfavor. In its report to Congress on January 19, 1889 (H. Rept. 3792 [50-II]), the select committee known as the Ford Committee acknowledged that immigrants had been of great aid to the United States in the past, but it was doubtful whether present-day immigrants were of the same quality. The time had come, the committee concluded, to select out the desirable from the undesirable, and one of the undesirable classes of aliens consisted of those coming only for temporary employment, the birds of passage. Their very low standard of living was noted, and the committee held further that

> persons who immigrate to the United States should at least be composed of those who in good faith desire to become its citizens and are worthy to be such.

Later congressional committees reaffirmed the undesirability of the bird of passage, this in reports on bills in the middle of the next decade.[26]

Toward the end of the Depression period in the middle to late 1930s, similar disfavor was directed against what then were called habitual commuters. Two bills to restrict habitual commuting by aliens were introduced in the first session of the 74th Congress in 1935, three more appeared two years later, and there were two such bills in the 76th Congress in 1939. Two were reported out (H.R. 4340 [74-I], H.R. 3679 [75-I]) but were not enacted.

Another recurrent idea was to direct immigration to the benefit of American shipping. Of such purpose was a bill in the first session of the 54th Congress (1895–1896) to impose a tax on all immigrants not coming in an American vessel (S. 2574 [54-I]). Approximately fifteen years later a bill was proposed to require all immigrants to come in vessels of American registry (S. 1378 [62-I]), but like the preceding bill it was not reported out of committee. The only requirement concerning the use of American transportation facilities was taken many years later and then only if travel was at the expense of the American government. The Act of June 16, 1950 (64 Stat. 219) added a final section to the Displaced Persons Act of 1948 to provide that

[26]S. Rept. 290, February 18, 1896, to accompany S. 2147 (54-I); H. Rept. 1597, May 4, 1896, to accompany H.R. 7415 (54-I). The Senate report was presented by Lodge of Massachusetts for the committee.

> All transportation by ships or planes of aliens under this Act, to the United States, the cost of which is defrayed in whole or in part by the Government of the United States, shall be by ships or planes registered under the United States flag, or by ships owned by the United States. (Sect. 17 of the 1948 Act as amended)

Various bills concerning particular classes of alien workers can also be noted, some containing ideas that found a place in later legislation. The exclusion of manual workers, skilled or unskilled, was proposed by several bills as early as the mid-1890s. Other bills of later date were for the admission of agricultural workers and aliens with special skills. There were also numerous bills to limit the rights of aliens in economic respects, such as to own land or engage in certain occupations, which will be summarized in a later section.[27]

Summary and Comment

This chapter has dealt with the labor-related provisions found in immigration legislation. The provisions are numerous, for immigration so directly affects labor supply that immigration policy and labor policy are closely interrelated. Provisions of immigration law concerning the admission of alien workers have formed a prominent part of the total body of immigration law, for Congress in designing immigration legislation has been responsive to considerations of the labor supply and the labor market. This responsiveness on the part of Congress no doubt reflects the political sensitivity of the subject, but whatever the reasons Congress has tended to use immigration legislation as an instrument of labor policy.

Congress can be seen to have pursued two different and in fact opposite objectives in this area of legislative action. The first objective, and one of high political priority, has been to protect the American worker from undue immigrant competition for jobs and from the supposedly harmful effects of immigrant labor on the American wage level and standard of living. The second objective has been to permit and even facilitate the admission of aliens with high qualifications or workers in occupations where there are labor shortages.

In furtherance of the former policy objective Congress has resorted to both the general restriction of immigration by one means or another, and exclusion of specific classes of aliens. Earlier excluded classes were contract laborers and Chinese and Japanese laborers. In recent acts, those of 1952 and 1965, Congress has directed the exclusion of skilled

[27]See chapter 21, Disabilities of Resident Aliens, pp. 590–92.

and unskilled alien workers coming without preference status to seek employment, if there are already sufficient such workers in the United States and if the employment of the immigrant workers would adversely affect the wages and working conditions of American workers. As a declaration of policy and principle, this directive is no doubt defensible from the viewpoints of conventional labor economics or practical politics, but there is ground for skepticism about the administrative feasibility of making such determinations of admissibility or excludability with any accuracy. Whether or not it was intended, the terms of the labor exclusion provision have the effect of giving a large measure of administrative discretion in its application.

The opposite direction of policy has been to facilitate the entry of aliens with occupational qualifications defined as desirable. In practice this has meant exemption of such classes of aliens from the restrictive or excluding measures by one means or another. Several classes of aliens have been accorded such preferential treatment, consisting principally of persons in the learned or artistic professions, persons with skills needed and not available in the United States, and persons needed to fill labor shortages. The first contract labor law of 1885, for example, exempted members of professions and domestic servants. Later acts extended exemption to skilled workers with the formula "if labor of like kind unemployed can not be found in this country." After the quota laws were adopted, the same favored classes of immigrants were enabled to bypass the quota restrictions by being given nonquota status or preference in the allocation of visas. In the terms of the 1952 Act, preference in the granting of immigration visas was to be given to aliens found to be urgently needed in the United States "because of the high education, technical training, specialized experience, or exceptional ability." This basis for preference was continued, though the language was somewhat reworded in the amendment by the 1965 Act.

Much less common than legislation concerning broad classes of workers is specific legislation for the aid of a particular occupation or industry. The few examples of such measures were the application of the contract labor laws to instrumental musicians early in the Depression and the sheepherder acts of the 1950s.

Viewed as a whole, the sections of immigration law dealing with the admission of alien workers illustrate the selectivity that characterizes American immigration policy. The basis of selection is the occupational qualifications of the aliens, and depending on the nature of those qualifications there is a negative or positive procedure of selection—negative through exclusion or limitation of the number admitted, positive through free entry as nonquota immigrants or facilitated entry by means of preference in the granting of immigrant visas. Underlying the terms of selection are evident considerations of both quantity and quality; restrictive measures are applied to limit the number of alien workers admitted especially in the less skilled classes, and favorable conditions are provided for the entry of those with needed skills and demonstrated high ability. In this area of immigration legislation Congress has shown awareness of political and economic realities on the one hand and the national interest on the other; it has been responsive to pressures to protect the labor force from large-scale immigrant competition and at the same time aware of the large contributions that selected immigrants can make to the national welfare.[28]

[28]An early expression of such awareness was a congressional committee recommendation in 1868 that "persons of capital, industry, or skill" be induced to immigrate (p. 54 above).

16 Family Unification

Another element of policy that, like labor policy, runs throughout immigration legislation is family unification. As immigration came to be more and more regulated, with numerous grounds for exclusion and especially with the imposition of quota limits on the number who could be admitted, there was greater risk that family members might be separated from one another by strict application of the law. Families coming together might include excludable members, and an already resident immigrant might be unable to bring other members of his family to join him later. From the beginning of federal regulation of immigration, however, Congress consistently followed a policy of facilitating the coming of families as a unit and the reuniting of families whose members did not all immigrate at the same time.

The reasons for this consistent policy have to be largely inferred, for family unification has never been a controversial or debatable issue in Congress, but rather has been considered obviously desirable. Probably there has been a mixture of altruism and calculation, based on the assumption that family unification contributes to both immigrant welfare and the national welfare. It is, however, clear from the early discussion of immigration problems and policies in and out of Congress that the most highly approved immigrant was one who came with the intention of remaining permanently, becoming a citizen, and bringing his family or establishing it after arrival. Conversely, as shown in the preceding chapter, there was long-standing prejudice against the "bird of passage" who came alone and with the intention of staying only long enough to accumulate savings, and against the "habitual commuter" who came and went without putting down roots. Such aliens, it was felt, were of doubtful value and even did real harm to the nation, for they competed with native workers, were thought to live at the lowest possible level in order to save money, sent or carried their savings back home, and took no part in the national life. As seen above, efforts were made in Congress from time to time to devise legislation that would repress such undesired temporary immigration and keep the doors open for the permanent immigrant, but these efforts were unsuccessful. Temporary immigration was a matter of intention, not observable fact, and the immigrant himself was not always sure of what he would do later.

If Congress was not successful in devising means of selective control of temporary immigration, it did devise a variety of positive measures to facilitate the admission of immigrant families and family members coming to join earlier immigrants. The various such measures are described below, arranged according to type rather than by chronological order.

Reduced Excludability

As described in chapter 11, the first provision of excludability in federal law was in 1875, and more excludable classes were added in the next decade. The Contract Labor Act of 1885, however, was the first to establish the excludability of a presumably numerous but not personally objectionable class of aliens, and Congress in writing the act made clear that

> nothing in this act shall be construed as prohibiting any individual from assisting any member of his family or any relative or personal friend, to migrate from any foreign country to the United States for the purpose of settlement here. (Second proviso, sect. 5 of the 1885 Act)

Later this came to be regarded as too liberal, and the words "or any relative or personal friend" were deleted by the Act of March 3, 1891 (sect. 5). The same act, however, did provide that a relative or friend sent for by a person living in the United States is exempt from the excludable class defined as "any person whose ticket or passage money is paid for with the money of another or who is assisted by others to come."[1]

The literacy test for admission also carried a threat of family disruption, but care was taken in the first literacy test bill to be passed by both House and Senate to soften its effect. The 1896 bill provided that the test applied only to males between sixteen and sixty years of age, and it exempted from the test the alien parents of present or future residents of the United States.[2] A 1906 bill increased the family exemption from the literacy test to include the wife, mother, fiancée, or a father over fifty-five years of age of a resident alien.[3] Later literacy test bills carried similar provisions, and the literacy test that finally became law in 1917 permitted any admissible alien to bring in or send for

> his father or grandfather over fifty-five years of age, his wife, his mother, his grandmother, or his unmarried or widowed daughter, if otherwise admissible, whether such relative can read or not.[4]

[1]Sect. 1; restated in the Act of March 3, 1903.

[2]See p. 118 above.

[3]See p. 138 above.

[4]First proviso, sect. 3 of the 1917 Act; continued by section 212b of the 1952 Act.

Exemption from other grounds for exclusion was also granted to certain relatives under certain conditions. The Act of March 3, 1903, for example, provided that if an alien who has taken up permanent residence and filed his first papers for naturalization sends for his wife or children to join him, and they are found on arrival to have a contagious disorder that was contracted on shipboard, they are not to be deported if the disorder is found to be easily curable and if they can be permitted to land without danger to others (sect. 37). The same provision, more fully stated, was repeated in the Act of February 20, 1907. Many years later the Act of September 11, 1957 permitted an alien with tuberculosis to be admitted under safeguards if he or she was the spouse, child, or parent of an American citizen or lawfully admitted alien.[5]

Certain other grounds for exclusion have been waived conditionally for alien relatives of citizens and residents of the United States. The racially ineligible spouse and child of a veteran of service in the Armed Forces were made admissible by the Act of August 19, 1950 (64 Stat. 464), provided the marriage takes place before six months after enactment.[6] The Act of September 11, 1957 (71 Stat. 639) permitted the admission under due conditions of aliens technically excludable as criminals or prostitutes if they are the spouse, child, or parent of a citizen or an alien lawfully admitted for permanent residence, provided it is established to the satisfaction of the Attorney General that exclusion would be an extreme hardship to the relative or relatives in the United States and that admission is "not . . . contrary to the national welfare, safety, or security."[7]

Reduced Deportability

Deportation is another possible source of family disruption, and the possession of close relatives and especially of dependents in the United States confers on the alien some defense against deportation. The procedure that has been used is that of suspension of deportation at the discretion of the appropriate administrative official, formerly the Secretary of Labor but more recently the Attorney General.

The Immigration Act of 1924 conferred on the Secretary of Labor the power to suspend the deportation of an alien child under sixteen

[5]Sect. 6 of the 1957 Act; restated without change of the above terms by the Acts of September 9, 1959 and September 26, 1961.

[6]Changed to twelve months by the amending Act of March 19, 1951 (65 Stat. 5).

[7]Sect. 5 of the 1957 Act. Slightly revised by sect. 14 of the Act of September 26, 1961 (76 Stat. 650).

years of age who had been temporarily admitted and overstayed the term of admission, provided that either of the parents is a citizen of the United States (sect. 14).

Suspension of deportation for alien relatives appears again in the Alien Registration Act of 1940, but now with a new emphasis. In the case of a deportable alien "who has proved good moral character for the preceding five years," the Attorney General is empowered to permit voluntary departure at the alien's own expense, or to

> suspend deportation of such alien if not racially inadmissible or ineligible to naturalization in the United States if he finds that such deportation would result in serious economic detriment to a citizen or legally resident alien who is the spouse, parent, or minor child of such deportable alien. (Sect. 20)

These terms were restated by the Act of July 1, 1948 (62 Stat. 1206), which also authorized suspension of deportation at the discretion of the Attorney General for a deportable alien who has resided continuously in the United States for seven years and is still a resident on the effective date of the act.

The 1952 Act greatly expanded the eligibility of deportable aliens for suspension of deportation. Enumerated in the act were five classes of deportable aliens, defined in terms of period of residence and grounds for deportation, but with the necessary condition in each class that the alien in question

> is a person whose deportation would, in the opinion of the Attorney General, result in exceptional and extremely unusual hardship to the alien or to his spouse, parent, or child, who is a citizen or an alien lawfully admitted for permanent residence.[8]

The basis for leniency was thus changed from economic detriment to extreme hardship.

Later acts revised the provisions for the relief of deportable aliens through suspension of deportation. The Act of September 11, 1957 (71 Stat. 639) gave such eligibility to aliens deportable because of incorrect or fraudulent entry documents, provided that they are the spouse, parent, or child of a citizen or resident alien (sect. 7). This was followed by the Act of October 24, 1962 (76 Stat. 1247) that amended the section of the 1952 Act dealing with suspension of deportation. Two classes of deportable aliens were made eligible for suspension of deportation at the discretion of the Attorney General. One class consists of aliens deportable for

[8]Paragraphs (1), (2), (3), (4), and (5), sect. 244a of the 1952 Act.

any one of eleven causes,[9] in which case a continuous residence of ten years is required during which there is a record of good moral character. The other class includes those aliens deportable for other reasons, and a continuous residence of seven years and good moral character for that time is required. In both cases, suspension of deportation is conditional as it was in the 1952 Act upon a finding by the Attorney General that deportation would result in extreme hardship to the alien or to his immediate relatives who are citizens or lawfully resident aliens (sect. 4 of the 1962 Act).

Nonquota Status

Several means were adopted by Congress to make sure the quota laws did not bring an enforced separation of family members and to reduce the effect of the quota limitations on certain other degrees of kinship. The provisions that facilitated family unification were the granting of nonquota status to certain relatives, and preference in the allocation of quota visas to certain other relatives of citizens and lawfully resident aliens; and as a rule the nonquota or preference status granted to the immigrant head of a family was also extended to the members of the immediate family.

The only relatives given nonquota status under the first quota act in 1921 were "aliens under the age of eighteen who are children of citizens of the United States" (sect. 2a). Expansion of the number of nonquota classes was foreshadowed by a House bill in 1923 that would have given such status to the husband, wife, parents, unmarried minor children, unmarried minor brother or sister, and the unmarried minor niece or nephew of a citizen; also to the spouse and minor child of an immigrant of two or more years of residence and who has filed his first papers for naturalization at least one year before. And the bill extended the nonquota status of ministers, professors, and certain skilled laborers to their wives and minor children.[10]

The 1924 Act, the second quota act, granted nonquota status on the basis of relationship somewhat less freely than the 1923 bill had; it granted such status to the unmarried child under eighteen and the wife of a resident citizen and to qualifying ministers and professors with their families.[11]

[9]The eleven deportable classes are numbers 4, 5, 6, 7, 11, 12, 14, 15, 16, 17, and 18 on pp. 459–60 above; numbering as in section 241a of the 1952 Act.

[10]See p. 185 above.

[11]Sect. 4a and 4d of the 1924 Act. Sect. 4a was amended by the Act of May 29, 1928 (45 Stat. 1009) to change the limiting age of an unmarried child from eighteen to twenty-

Numerous bills were introduced to extend nonquota status to additional classes of relatives.[12] An alien veterans Act of May 26, 1926 (44 Stat. 654) conferred nonquota status on the unmarried child under eighteen and the spouse of such a veteran if accompanying or following to join him within six months. A later act of July 3, 1926 (44 Stat. 812) concerned the admission free of quota of the wife or unmarried child under eighteen of certain ministers and professors. Various bills to extend the nonquota privilege to more classes of alien relatives continued to appear in the Depression period, but they were not adopted.[13] During this period a bill was proposed that took another but unadopted approach to the goal of keeping families together, or perhaps discouraging the temporary migrant; it excluded aliens who leave dependents behind them on coming to the United States.[14]

The postwar years brought some further extension of nonquota status to selected relatives. The Act of August 9, 1946 (60 Stat. 975) gave such status to Chinese wives of American citizens if the marriage was before May 26, 1924; and thus it applied only to marriages of long standing. The Immigration Act of 1952 gave nonquota status to "an immigrant who is the child or the spouse of a citizen of the United States." A child was defined as unmarried and under twenty-one years of age, but there was no condition as to date of marriage (sect. 101[a][27][A]). The act also continued the provision that eligible nonquota ministers could bring a spouse or child under the same status (paragraph F).

The Act of September 22, 1959 (73 Stat. 644) amended the 1952 Act to provide for the entry of certain relatives of citizens and resident aliens. For the most part it was concerned with change of the preference classes of relatives. In addition, however, it sought to clear up a backlog of relatives waiting for an immigration visa by giving nonquota status to any alien who had been registered on a waiting list since before December 31, 1953 and who is eligible for a second, third, or fourth preference under the 1952 Act,[15] on the basis of a petition approved by the Attorney General prior to January 1, 1959. Two years later the amending Act of September 26, 1961 (75 Stat. 650) made a similar grant of nonquota

---

one and to grant nonquota status to the husband as well as the wife of a citizen, but with the proviso in the case of a husband that the marriage was prior to June 1, 1928. The latter date was changed to July 1, 1932 by the Act of July 11, 1932 (47 Stat. 656) and to January 1, 1948 by the Act of May 19, 1948 (62 Stat. 241).

[12]See for example pp. 197–98.

[13]See pp. 216, 225–26 above.

[14]See p. 240 above.

[15]That is, (2) parents of citizens at least twenty-one years of age, (3) spouses and children of resident aliens, and (4) the siblings and not quota-free sons and daughters of citizens.

status to second and third preference cases on the basis of a petition filed with the Attorney General prior to July 1, 1961 (sect. 25a).

Finally, the 1965 Act admitted quota-free "immediate relatives," defined as "the children, spouses, and parents of a citizen," but with the proviso that only the parents of citizens at least twenty-one years of age are included.[16] Also admitted without quota limit were aliens referred to in the act as "special immigrants." These included eligible ministers, alien employees or honorably retired former employees of the United States government abroad with fifteen or more years of service, together with their spouses and unmarried children under twenty-one years of age.[17]

Quota Preference

The preference classes established by the quota acts from the Act of 1921 onward were a device for giving certain favored alien applicants for admission a less assured entry than by means of nonquota status but first claim on a designated percent of each nation's quota of immigration visas. As noted earlier, certain of the preference classes were defined in terms of occupational and other qualifications. Others were assigned on the basis of relationship to American citizens or resident aliens. The 1921 Act, after exempting certain classes of aliens from quota limitation, provided

> That in the enforcement of this Act preference shall be given so far as possible to the wives, parents, brothers, sisters, children under eighteen years of age, and fiancées, (1) of citizens of the United States, (2) of aliens now in the United States who have applied for citizenship in the manner provided by law, or (3) of persons eligible to United States citizenship who served in the military or naval forces of the United States at any time between April 6, 1917, and November 11, 1918, both dates inclusive, and have been separated from such forces under honorable conditions. (Third proviso of sect. 2d of the 1921 Act)

The next quota act in 1924 gave equal preference to aliens skilled in agriculture with their immediate families, and to

> a quota immigrant who is the unmarried child under 21 years of age, the father, the mother, the husband, or the wife, of a citizen of the United States who is 21 years or over. (Sect. 6[a][1] of the 1924 Act)

[16]Sect. 201b of the 1952 Act, as amended by sect. 1 of the 1965 Act.

[17]Sect. 101(a)(27)(D) and (E) of the 1952 Act, as amended by sect. 8 of the 1965 Act.

The two preference classes combined were allowed not over one-half of the quota of each nationality. The above quoted definition of the relatives given preference was amended by the Act of May 29, 1928 (45 Stat. 1009) to become

> Quota immigrants who are the fathers or the mothers, or the husbands by marriage occurring after May 31, 1928, of citizens of the United States who are twenty-one years of age or over.

It was again amended by the Act of July 11, 1932 (47 Stat. 656) to read

> Quota immigrants who are the fathers or the mothers of citizens of the United States who are twenty-one years of age or over or who are the husbands of citizens of the United States by marriages occurring on or after July 1, 1932.

The Act of May 19, 1948 (62 Stat. 241) changed the required marriage date from July 1, 1932 to January 1, 1948.

The Displaced Persons Act of 1948 gave preference to certain relatives. After first and second preferences on the basis of occupation, a third preference went to

> Eligible displaced persons who are the blood relatives of citizens or lawfully admitted alien residents of the United States, such relationship in either case being within the third degree of consanguinity computed according to the rules of the common law. (Sect. 6)

This third preference class was changed to second preference by the amending Act of June 16, 1950 (64 Stat. 219).

The 1952 Act established a more developed preference structure than had existed previously. After a first preference class based on occupational qualifications and entitled to up to 50 percent of the quota of each quota area, a second preference class received the next 30 percent plus any unused portions of other preference class allocations; this class was designated for the parents of citizens who are at least twenty-one years of age. Third preference of 20 percent plus any unused portions of other classes went to spouses and children of lawfully resident aliens. Finally, brothers, sisters, sons, and daughters of citizens were to have preference for up to one-fourth of any unused quota numbers in each quota area.

Priority in the consideration of visa applications under the Refugee Relief Act of 1953, corresponding to preference, was given first to persons with needed skills and second to

> Persons who are (A) the parents of citizens of the United States, such citizens being at least twenty-one years of age, or (B) spouses or unmarried sons or daughters under twenty-one years of age, includ-

ing stepsons or stepdaughters and sons or daughters adopted prior to July 1, 1953, of aliens lawfully admitted for permanent residence, or (C) brothers, sisters, sons or daughters of citizens of the United States. (Sect. 12)

The preference structure remained unchanged until the Act of September 22, 1959 (73 Stat. 644) to provide for the entry of certain classes of alien relatives by means of amendment of the 1952 Act. Included were the following changes in preference:

1. Unmarried sons or daughters of citizens were added to the second preference class.

2. The third preference category, children of lawfully resident aliens, was changed to unmarried sons and daughters of such aliens.[18]

3. The statement of the fourth preference was changed to read in part:

> Qualified quota immigrants of each quota area who are the brothers, sisters, married sons or married daughters of citizens of the United States shall be entitled to a preference of not exceeding 50 per centum of the immigrant visas available for issuance for each quota area under this paragraph, and such preference shall be available to the spouses and children of such qualified quota immigrants if accompanying them. (Sect. 3)

Finally, the 1965 Act introduced a much expanded preference structure consisting of seven classes, of which four included relatives of citizens or resident aliens. These were the first, second, fourth, and fifth preferences, with a total allocation of 74 percent of the quota of each quota area, plus any unused portion of other preference classes.[19]

Adopted Children and Others

Special provision for the admission of adopted children or children coming for adoption was especially a development of the postwar period following World War II. Although such legislation fitted into the pattern of concern for family unification, it was also a part of the postwar attention to the problems of victims of the war, the refu-

[18]Note that under the 1952 Act children were defined as unmarried and under twenty-one years of age.

[19]The preference classes of the 1965 Act are the same as those of the House committee bill listed on pp. 371–72 above. The four classes of relatives are, briefly, as follows: first, unmarried sons and daughters of citizens, 20 percent; second, spouses and unmarried sons and daughters of resident aliens, 20 percent; fourth, married sons and daughters of citizens, 10 percent; fifth, brothers and sisters of citizens, 24 percent.

gees and displaced persons, for many of the children were war orphans.

The question of whether provision concerning the admission of children accompanying or joining parents applied equally to adopted children presumably did not arise until there were quota limits on immigration; and the 1921 Act did not deal with this point. The second quota act in 1924, however, was explicit in ruling that

> The terms "child," "father," and "mother," do not include a child or parent by adoption unless the adoption took place before January 1, 1924. (Sect. 28m of the 1924 Act)

This interpretation of terms may have been included in the act in order to rule out a possible means of evasion of the quota limit on immigration, just as the same act closed another loophole by ending the acquisition of nonquota status through a term of residence in the Western Hemisphere. In any event this interpretation stood until opinion began to shift in the postwar period in response to problems of the time. In 1950 the Displaced Persons Act was amended to specify that children to be admitted with an eligible displaced person included adopted children and stepchildren;[20] and this position was maintained in other amendments of the act.[21]

The Act of July 29, 1953 (67 Stat. 229) was for the purpose of admitting orphans adopted by citizens of the United States, and provided up to 500 special nonquota immigrant visas for that purpose. Conditions for eligibility included that the orphan is under ten years of age at the time of visa application, that the orphan was lawfully adopted abroad or coming with assurance of adoption after arrival, and that the adoptive parents have served abroad as members of the armed forces or employees of the United States government. Of the same year was the Refugee Relief Act of August 7, 1953 (67 Stat. 400), which followed the pattern of the preceding acts in making clear that the children to be admitted as members of refugee families included adopted children and stepchildren and in providing up to 4,000 special nonquota immigrant visas for admission of orphans adopted or to be adopted by citizens (sect. 3 and 5).

Similar provisions were contained in the Act of September 11, 1957 (71 Stat. 639). The definition of the term "child" as used in the 1952 Act was amended by adding

[20]Sect. 2c of the 1948 Act, as amended by sect. 1 of the Act of June 16, 1950 (64 Stat. 219).

[21]See for example sections 2, 3g, and 12a of the Act of June 16, 1950.

> a child adopted while under the age of fourteen years if the child has thereafter been in the legal custody of, and has resided with, the adopting parent or parents for at least two years.[22]

To be consistent, the age of the adopted orphans eligible for a nonquota visa was raised to the upper limit of fourteen years (sect. 4a of the 1957 Act). Finally, the 1965 Act revised but essentially continued the definition of "child" used in the 1952 Act as amended, to include adopted or to be adopted orphans (sect. 8c).

Other types of child members of families were also noted in the immigration laws. The inclusion specifically of stepchildren among those to be admitted as family members has been mentioned above. The 1952 Act defined the term "child" to include

> an unmarried person under twenty-one years of age who is . . . (B) a stepchild, provided the child had not reached the age of eighteen years at the time the marriage creating the status of stepchild occurred. (Sect. 101[b][1][B] of 1952 Act)

This definition was amended by the Act of September 11, 1957 (71 Stat. 639) by insertion after the word "stepchild" in the first line of the phrase "whether or not born out of wedlock."

The matter of legitimacy had been dealt with in the 1952 Act, which defined a child, and thereby determined eligibility for the provisions concerning the admission of children in the status of family members, as an unmarried person under twenty-one years of age who is (A) a legitimate child, or (B) a stepchild meeting the age condition noted above, or

> (C) a child legitimated under the law of the child's residence or domicile, or under the law of the father's residence or domicile, whether in or outside the United States, if such legitimation takes place before the child reaches the age of eighteen years and the child is in the legal custody of the legitimating parent or parents at the time of such legitimation. (Sect. 101[b][1][C] of 1952 Act)

The Act of September 11, 1957 added a fourth paragraph to the definition:

> (D) an illegitimate child, by, through whom, or on whose behalf a status, privilege, or benefit is sought by virtue of the relationship of the child to its natural mother. (Sect. 101[b][1][D] of 1952 Act as amended)

[22]Sect. 2 of the 1957 Act, amending sect. 101(b)(1) of the 1952 Act.

Thus by 1965 the children whose admission was facilitated as being family members included adopted, illegitimate, and stepchildren under given conditions.

Fiancées

Fiancées were mentioned in the first quota act among those to be given preference in the allocation of immigration visas,[23] but they were not given preference by the subsequent Quota Act of 1924. There was no special provision for fiancées thereafter until the postwar period, when several acts provided for the entry of the so-called war brides, the fiancées of members or former members of the armed forces who had served overseas. The first war brides act was the Act of June 29, 1946 (60 Stat. 339) that provided for the temporary admission on or before July 1, 1947 for a period of three months pending marriage, of

> the alien fiancée or fiancé of a citizen of the United States who is serving in or who has been honorably discharged from, the armed forces . . . during World War II.

This provision was extended by six months, to December 31, 1947, by the Act of June 28, 1947 (61 Stat. 190), and for an additional year to December 31, 1948 by the Act of March 24, 1948 (62 Stat. 84).

On expiration of the 1946 Act as amended at the end of 1948, there were still several hundred cases of alien fiancées and fiancés pending at consular offices. In view of this situation and the fact that the corresponding quotas were oversubscribed in most cases by several years, Congress passed a resolution[24] on April 21, 1949 (63 Stat. 56) authorizing consular officials to finish processing all such cases pending as if the 1946 Act were still in effect, but with several conditions attached. One was that processing of the cases be completed and the aliens concerned arrive within five months of the effective date of the act. Another was the interesting condition that "the American citizen concerned in each case has personally met his or her fiancé or fiancée." Congressional memory was sufficiently long or congressional suspicions of alien attempts to evade the immigration laws were sufficiently high that Congress was determined to leave no loophole for "picture brides" to enter.

Further evidence that Congress was on guard to prevent any abuse of the war bride act was the inclusion in that act of the stipulation that

[23]See quotation from the 1921 Act, p. 511 above.

[24]H. J. Res. 160 (81-I). At least eight or nine fiancée bills were also introduced in that session of Congress.

> In the event the marriage does not occur within the period for which the alien was admitted, the alien shall be required to depart from the United States and upon failure to do so shall be deported at any time after entry. (Sect. 2, Act of June 29, 1946 [60 Stat. 339])

Summary and Comment

Family unification has been one of the consistent elements of policy running through American immigration legislation, almost since the beginning of federal regulation. Each new measure for the regulation and control of immigration—the contract labor laws, the literacy test and other grounds for exclusion, the quota limits on immigration—has brought with it new possibilities for the separation of family members through the denial of entry to some members of a family group on arrival or prevention of alien relatives from joining an immigrant in the United States.

But as the structure of immigration law became more and more complex through the addition of new measures to select and restrict immigration, Congress has gone to some pains to provide special consideration for the near relatives of citizens and alien residents of the United States. As described in preceding sections of this chapter, the special consideration has taken the form of (1) more limited excludability, (2) more limited deportability, (3) nonquota status for certain relatives, and (4) preference in the granting of immigration visas under quota. As a rule special consideration has been given if enforced separation of family members would result in "economic detriment" or, in more recent law, "extreme hardship" to one or another member of the family resident in the United States.

As one would expect, the degree of special consideration has varied with closeness of relationship. In general the trend over the years has been toward granting special consideration to a wider and wider range of relatives. The First Quota Act of 1921, for example, granted quota-free (that is, nonquota) immigration only to alien children under eighteen years of age of a citizen parent. By 1965 nonquota status was granted to the unmarried children under twenty-one years of age, the spouses, and the parents of citizens, but with the condition that the citizens must be at least twenty-one years of age to confer nonquota status on parents. Similarly, the definition of a child to be admitted quota-free has expanded over the years to include, with certain conditions, adopted children, illegitimate children, and stepchildren. Family unity has also been protected by the general practice of according to the immediate family as a whole the immigration status of the head of the family. And special provision was made during the recent postwar period for the admission of orphans coming with the prospect of adoption, and alien fiancées or fiancés coming with the prospect of marriage to a veteran of the armed forces.

The impression is of a continuing and kindly concern on the part of Congress for the unity and the happiness of the immigrant family, but there is another and less apparent side of the family-related provisions in immigration law. Congress has not been unaware that every waiver of the immigration laws opens a door for possible fraudulent entry. On close reading of the provisions for special consideration of relatives, one finds in fact that Congress has generally written in careful checks and qualifications. Waiver of the grounds for exclusion and deportation, for example, is made conditional upon investigation and approval by the Attorney General, with a finding on his part that the waiver would not be contrary to the best interests of the nation and that denial of the waiver would cause detriment or hardship for a citizen. Suspension of deportation is made conditional upon demonstration that the alien in question has a record of "good moral character" for the preceding seven or ten years. And waiver of a ground for exclusion may be with the requirement that the alien in question is "otherwise admissible."

In the case of special consideration on the basis of marriage or adoption, a common practice has been to set a date prior to which the marriage or adoption must have taken place, the date so chosen that only bona fide and nonfraudulent cases would qualify. And an adoption to qualify for nonquota admission must have been of a child under fourteen years of age.

Although well-disposed to facilitate the entry of genuine family members, Congress has shown suspicion that attempts may be made to gain entry by fraud. In 1936 one of the most consistent friends of the immigrant in Congress introduced bills to deport aliens who gain entry by means of fraudulent marriage.[25] The bills did not progress, but many years later the 1952 Act gave attention to the matter. The first section of the act contained the sharply pointed definition:

> The terms "spouse," "wife," or "husband" do not include a spouse, wife, or husband by reason of any marriage ceremony where the contracting parties thereto are not physically present in the presence of each other, unless the marriage shall have been consummated. (Sect. 101[a][35] of 1952 Act)

[25]See p. 240 above.

Elsewhere in the same act it was directed that

> An alien shall be deported as having procured a visa or other documentation by fraud . . . if (1) hereafter he or she obtains any entry into the United States with an immigrant visa or other documentation procured on the basis of a marriage entered into less than two years prior to such entry of the alien and which, within two years subsequent to any entry of the alien into the United States, shall be judicially annulled or terminated, unless such alien shall establish to the satisfaction of the Attorney General that such marriage was not contracted for the purpose of evading any provisions of the immigration laws; or (2) it appears to the satisfaction of the Attorney General that he or she has failed or refused to fulfill his or her marital agreement which in the opinion of the Attorney General was hereafter made for the purpose of procuring his or her entry as an immigrant.[26]

A later amendment of the 1952 Act directed that nonquota or preference status is not to be granted to an alien whom the Attorney General has previously found to have entered into a marriage for the purpose of evading the immigration laws.[27] In the same spirit, as described in the preceding section, Congress directed that fiancées or fiancés were not to be admitted for the purpose of marrying a citizen unless they had met previously and that an alien so admitted was to be deported if the marriage did not take place within the time for which the fiancée or fiancé was temporarily admitted. So far as it has been able to do so by legislation, Congress has evidently been determined to prevent aliens from gaining entry fraudulently through loopholes made available to family members.

There were other problems of policy connected with the facilitated entry of relatives, even if not prominently discussed. The nonquota admission of relatives, like nonquota admissions as a whole, was in conflict with the policy of restricted immigration, for it opened the door to as many qualified aliens as chose to apply and were found to be admissible. During the fiscal years 1969 to 1973 inclusive, for example, approximately one out of every four aliens admitted for permanent residence were nonquota immigrants, and nearly 90 percent of the nonquota cases were immediate relatives.

The other quota concession given to alien relatives, the preference

[26]Sect. 241(a)(18)(c) of the 1952 Act. Quoted at length to show the detailed attention given to this provision.

[27]Sect. 10 of the Act of September 26, 1961 (75 Stat. 650), amending sect. 205c of the 1952 Act.

under quota, meant preempting a portion of each area's quota for certain relatives; and the disposition of Congress has been to increase that reserved portion of the quotas. The 1921 Act gave preference to certain relatives without indicating an upper limit. Under the 1924 Act certain relatives shared up to one-half of each area's quota with immigrants skilled in agriculture, but the 1952 Act gave preference of one-half or more. And finally the 1965 Act raised the portion designated for relatives to 74 percent plus any unused portion of other preference classes.[28]

Congress does not appear to have raised serious question about the policy of giving nonquota status or preference to the alien relatives of American citizens and resident aliens; it has, in fact, shown a disposition to deal more and more generously with them. Some voices have been raised outside of Congress about the desirability of "new seed" immigration, but that immigration can come in under the third and sixth preferences given to aliens with professional or occupational qualifications, under the seventh preference for refugees, or as nonpreference immigrants if the preference classes are not filled.[29]

Another and undebated aspect of favoring the entry of relatives is that the admission of one immigrant can lead to the subsequent admission of a whole sequence of family members. According to a Canadian estimate, the admission there of one Italian immigrant in the 1950s meant the eventual coming of forty-nine relatives; but the Canadian system of sponsorship contributes heavily to this total.[30] The corresponding figure for the United States would doubtless be much lower, but in any event there is a multiplier effect consequent upon the special consideration given to relatives. Such concerns, however, if they have occurred to members of Congress, have been entirely outweighed by the human consideration that families should not be separated by immigration barriers; and to apply the immigration laws without regard for family ties would be unthinkable.

[28]For the fiscal years 1969 through 1973 the preference classes of relatives constituted about 54 percent of immigrant admissions exclusive of Western Hemisphere immigrants.

[29]Nonpreference immigrants for the fiscal years 1969 through 1973 constituted a little more than 20 percent of immigrant admissions exclusive of Western Hemisphere immigrants.

[30]Freda Hawkins, *Canada and Immigration: Public Policy and Public Concern* (Montreal: McGill Press, 1972), p. 51.

17 Refugee Asylum

Congressional action on immigration has seldom fallen into an entirely consistent pattern. More often there has been a combination of differing and sometimes seemingly inconsistent elements, a combination of rigorous and even antialien elements on the one hand with considerate and almost sentimental action on the other.[1] The family-related legislation, described in the preceding chapter, falls for the most part in the latter category of sympathetic treatment of the alien and the immigrant; and this softer side of congressional action is fully as evident in refugee legislation.

President Jefferson, as quoted earlier,[2] spoke feelingly in favor of asylum for oppressed humanity. Congressmen in later years, ready in moments of oratory to quote the Emma Lazarus lines on the base of the Statue of Liberty, have no doubt been moved by various considerations, political and national as well as humanitarian, but have consistently shown sympathy for the unfortunate and a sense of obligation to preserve the national image and provide a haven of refuge for the oppressed. Although part of the whole pattern of refugee legislation, the various principal aspects of that legislation are described separately below.

Sympathy for Independence Movements

A precedent of refugee migration to the New World was established well before the founding of the United States, which included among its citizens the descendants of the Huguenots, the Palatines, and other refugees from Europe. In view of its own revolutionary origin, the new nation had a natural sympathy for independence movements and was disposed to welcome the members of such movements who had to flee

[1]The two aspects of congressional approach to immigration and the alien perhaps represent not an inconsistency of attitude but a political compromise between the two opposite schools of thought often evident in Congress, one doubtful or negative toward immigration, the other seeing immigration in positive and humanitarian terms.

[2]See p. 17 above.

their homelands. The German liberals of 1832 and 1848 were received without special legislative action, but efforts were made in Congress to help the Polish exiles of the earlier period. As described in Part I, grants of land were made to the Poles on easy terms, and the subject came up again from time to time in Congress, but the results appear to have been disappointing.[3]

Similar sentiments were aroused by the Hungarian refugees of 1956 and after, but the legislation passed to aid them was part of the group of refugee measures adopted following World War II and will be described below in that connection.

Admission of Political Offenders

A logical extension of the sympathy with independence movements was to regard those who protested against governmental oppression and were penalized under the laws of their homeland as political refugees rather than as criminals. Accordingly it was carefully stated in the laws excluding criminals that political offenders were to be admitted. Thus the first act to exclude criminals defined the excludable class as

> persons who are undergoing a sentence for conviction in their own country of felonious crimes other than political or growing out of or the result of such political offenses. (Sect. 5 of the Act of March 3, 1875)

Similarly the next immigration act, that of August 3, 1882, stated that

> all foreign convicts except those convicted of political offenses, upon arrival, shall be sent back. (Sect. 4 of 1882 Act)

The following immigration act of March 3, 1891 was even more explicit on the subject, for the first section contained the proviso

> That nothing in this act shall be construed to apply to or exclude persons convicted of a political offense, notwithstanding said political offense may be designated as a "felony, crime, infamous crime, or misdemeanor, involving moral turpitude" by the laws of the land whence he came or by the court convicting. (Sect. 1 of 1891 Act)

A decade later the Industrial Commission in its report presented to Congress in December 1901 recommended continuation of the admission of aliens whose offenses were political and not involving moral turpitude.

The Immigration Act of March 3, 1903 incorporated the recommendation of the Industrial Commission by inclusion of the proviso that

[3]See pp. 24–25, 26, 29 above.

> nothing in this Act shall exclude persons convicted of an offense purely political, not involving moral turpitude. (First proviso, sect. 2 of 1903 Act)

This proviso was repeated in the Immigration Act of 1907 except for the qualification that the alien in question be otherwise admissible (first proviso, sect. 2); similarly, it was repeated in the Immigration Act of 1910. Finally the 1952 Act (sect. 212[a][9]) briefly stated that exemption from exclusion was to be given to aliens whose crimes were "purely political."

Victims of Persecution

Many types of migrants are included under the broad term "refugee," but historically and legislatively Congress has dealt separately with the refugees leaving their homelands or unable to return because of discrimination and persecution and the wartime and postwar refugees of the recent decades. Measures concerning the former are dealt with in this section and the latter in the next section.

American sentiments for the provision of a haven of refuge for the oppressed were directly touched by the victims of persecution and oppression; and psychologically the coming of such refugees may have served to reinforce the American sense of the superiority of their own government and political institutions. With the essentially unrestricted immigration that obtained during the greater part of the nineteenth century, the question of differential treatment for refugees did not really arise except when public opinion and sympathy were aroused as in the case of the Polish exiles in the 1830s. As more and more restrictions were applied to immigration, however, a need to waive certain of the restrictions on immigration for the benefit of refugees came to be felt. This was especially true since the circumstances causing and attending the refugee movement were such as to put the refugees in one or another of the excludable classes in many cases.

Waiver to the excludability of a person convicted of a crime if the offense was purely political has already been noted. Other exceptions for the benefit of refugees came to be proposed. A 1906 bill, for example, would have allowed an alien to enter and remain, even if destitute or probably unable to earn a living, if he was fleeing for his life or trying to avoid persecution on religious or political grounds.[4] Later, when attempts were made to pass a literacy test, it was proposed to exempt refugees fleeing from religious persecution.[5] By 1914, with literacy test bills in Congress, waiver of the test for refugees from religious persecu-

[4] See p. 141 above.

[5] See pp. 151, 152 above.

tion was accepted, but denied to political and racial refugees; however, the bill as à whole was not passed.[6]

When the test was finally enacted in 1917, the first of those to be "exempt from the operation of the illiteracy test" were

> All aliens who shall prove . . . that they are seeking admission to the United States to avoid religious persecution in the country of their last permanent residence, whether such persecution be evidenced by overt acts or by laws or governmental regulations that discriminate against the alien or the race to which he belongs because of his religious faith. (Sect. 3)

This act remained the basic immigration law until superseded by the Act of 1952. The latter act repeated the above exemption from the literacy test but substituted the phrase, "any group to which he belongs" in place of "the race to which he belongs" (sect. 212[b][2]). The same act authorized the Attorney General to suspend the deportation of any alien

> to any country in which in his opinion the alien would be subject to physical persecution and for such period of time as he deems to be necessary for such reason. (Sect. 243H)

Other acts of the period included persons forced to flee from or unable to return to their homes for fear of persecution, sometimes referred to as "escapees" or "persecutees," within the terms of legislation for the relief of refugees and displaced persons.[7]

A further relaxation of the immigration laws was made by the Act of September 11, 1957 (71 Stat. 639) for the benefit of victims of persecution. A provision of that act was that an alien deportable on the ground of having procured or sought to procure an immigration visa by fraud or misrepresentation, or on the ground of having misrepresented his nationality or other personal information in applying for a visa, may nevertheless remain if able to establish that

> the misrepresentation was predicated upon the alien's fear of persecution because of race, religion, or political opinion if repatriated to his former home or residence, and was not committed for the purpose of evading the quota restrictions . . . or an investigation of the alien at the place of his former home, or residence, or elsewhere. (Sect. 7)

Later the 1965 Act established a seventh preference class of not over 6 percent of the quota total for aliens of the refugee category, including those who

[6]See pp. 162–63 above.

[7]See, for example, sect. 2c of the Displaced Persons Act of 1948; sect. 2 of the Act of June 16, 1950; and sect. 2a and 2b of the Refugee Relief Act of August 7, 1953.

> because of persecution or fear of persecution on account of race, religion, or political opinion . . . have fled from any Communist or Communist-dominated country or area, or from any country within the general area of the Middle East, and are unable or unwilling to return to such country or area on account of race, religion, or political opinion.[8]

The 6 percent corresponded to an allocation of up to 10,200 visas per annum for refugees, and by establishing a permanent provision might obviate the need for emergency legislation if new refugee problems arose in the future.

Displaced Persons and Related Classes

The most considerable body of refugee legislation dates from the World War II period and its immediate aftermath. Essentially the legal problem was to provide special exceptions to the immigration laws for the benefit of the refugees, many of whom were technically excludable because of lack of proper documents or because of destitution or other reasons, and to waive the quota limits if necessary.

The first wave of refugees consisted of persons fleeing from Central Europe in the latter part of the 1930s. Bills to assure them of asylum were introduced in Congress in 1937 and again in 1939,[9] but no new legislation resulted at the time, for the new arrivals could be dealt with in the framework of the existing immigration laws. With the end of the war, however, the dimensions and the changed character of the refugee problem led to new efforts to deal with it. Numerous bills for the aid of the so-called displaced persons and for the special admission of Poles, who had suffered heavily during the war and in the postwar relocation of frontiers, were introduced during the immediate postwar years, 1946 through 1948.[10] Incorporating elements from the various earlier bills was the Displaced Persons Act of June 25, 1948. Having been described earlier,[11] its principal provisions are noted only briefly below:

[8]Sect. 3 of the 1965 Act. Included under the seventh proviso were also victims of natural calamity.

[9]See pp. 246, 256 above.

[10]For account of these bills see pp. 271, 274, 278–80 above. Prior to legislation on the D.P. problem, the President's directive of December 22, 1945 authorized the use of 90 percent of the quotas of central and eastern European countries for persons in the American occupied zone of Europe who could not or would not return to their prewar homes, with special attention to orphaned children. Over 40,000 had been so admitted by June 30, 1948 (INS *Annual Report,* 1948).

[11]See pp. 280–81 above concerning the Displaced Persons Act.

1. Not more than 220,000 visas to be issued to eligible displaced persons, without regard to quota, during the two fiscal years following the passage of the act, but charged to the appropriate quota for the current year or up to one-half of the quotas of future years (sect. 3).
2. Special nonquota immigrant visas to be granted to eligible displaced orphans, but not to exceed 3,000 (sect. 3b).
3. Authority to the Attorney General, with the approval of Congress, to adjust the status to that of admission for permanent residence for any eligible displaced persons who have been admitted temporarily to the United States and who entered prior to April 1, 1948, the number not to exceed 15,000 and to be charged to quotas as in (1) above (sect. 4a).

The amending Act of June 16, 1950 changed item 1 to provide not more than 341,000 immigrant visas to be issued during the three fiscal years beginning July 1, 1948 and to be charged as needed to future quotas at the maximum rate of one-fourth of quotas for the fiscal years 1951 through 1954 and thereafter as needed at the rate of one-half of the quotas of later years. The number of special nonquota immigrant visas for eligible displaced orphans was increased to 5,000 but to be within the above limit of 341,000. The same act changed the authorization for adjustment of status (item 3 above) to include eligible aliens who enter the United States prior to April 30, 1949, but it retained the limit of 15,000 and the charge to present or future quotas. Finally, it added a new section (sect. 2f of 1948 Act as amended) to the 1948 Act to provide an additional 5,000 special nonquota immigrant visas for orphans under the age of ten, coming for adoption or for permanent residence with a near relative or to a public or private agency. Further amendment of the Displaced Persons Act by the Act of June 28, 1951 extended the time for the issuance of the 341,000 visas to three and one-half years, from July 1, 1948 to December 31, 1951, for eligible displaced persons and to a full four years for the eligible displaced orphans.

The refugee problem persisted, and further congressional action was urged by President Truman in a message to Congress early in 1952. His recommendation was for the admission of an additional 300,000 over a three-year period, and bills for that purpose and for the admission of more orphans were introduced then and in the following year.[12] The outcome of this legislative activity was the Refugee Relief Act of August 7, 1953. It designated three classes to be aided: (1) refugees, defined as persons not in a Communist or Communist-dominated country who are

[12]See pp. 310, 318, 319 above.

unable to return to their homes "because of persecution, fear of persecution, natural calamity or military operations"; (2) escapees, defined as refugees who had fled from a Communist area "because of persecution or fear of persecution on account of race, religion, or political opinion" and are unable to return for the same reason; (3) German expellees, defined as refugees of German ethnic origin, presently in West Germany, West Berlin, or Austria, who were expelled or forced to flee from certain countries (sect. 2).

The bill authorized the issuance of 205,000 special nonquota immigrant visas to aliens of the above classes, together with the members of their immediate family if accompanying them, and the apportionment of visas by class or national origin of the refugees was prescribed.[13]

The years that followed saw many bills introduced for the aid of refugees, but few were adopted.[14] Apart from the measures for the relief of particular classes of aliens (see next section), more general provision for the aid of refugees was contained in the Act of September 11, 1957. This was authorization for the reassignment of any unused visas remaining from the 205,000 special nonquota immigrant visas provided by the Refugee Relief Act of 1953; the visas so available were to go in designated numbers to German expellees, Dutch refugees, and certain refugee-escapees (sect. 15 of 1957 Act). The later Act of July 14, 1960 (74 Stat. 504) authorized the Attorney General to admit not over 500 refugee-escapees listed by the United Nations High Commissioner for Refugees as "difficult to resettle," and it also gave the Attorney General the important further authorization to parole certain refugee-escapees.[15] Parole was a special procedure for the conditional admission of otherwise inadmissible aliens that was to be most heavily used for Cuban refugees.

[13]Sect. 4a of the act set the following upper limits and allocation: (1) 55,000 to German expellees residing in West Germany, West Berlin, and Austria; (2) 35,000 to escapees in the above areas; (3) 10,000 to escapees residing in NATO countries or in Turkey, Sweden, Iran, or Trieste; (4) 2,000 to certain members of the Polish armed forces; (5) 45,000 to refugees of Italian ethnic origin in Italy or Trieste; (6) 15,000 as in (5) but qualified for second, third, or fourth preference; (7) 15,000 to refugees of Greek ethnic origin residing in Greece; (8) 2,000 as in (7) who qualify for second, third, or fourth preference; (9) 15,000 to refugees of Dutch ethnic origin residing in the Netherlands; (10) 2,000 as in (9) who qualify for the second, third, or fourth preference; (11) 2,000 to refugees residing within the district of an American consular office in the Far East and not indigenous to the area; (12) 3,000 as in (11) but indigenous to the area; (13) 2,000 to certain refugees of Chinese ethnic origin; and (14) 2,000 to refugees eligible for assistance from the United Nations Relief and Works Agency for Palestine Refugees in the Near East.

[14]See pp. 321, 327, 332, 334–35, 339, 340, 345–46 above.

[15]The parole procedure, as will be explained more fully later, is a de facto and conditional admission, presumably temporary in duration unless later adjusted to another status.

Finally, the 1965 Act as previously described established a seventh preference class that provided up to 10,200 visas available annually for certain classes of refugees. Whereas the earlier refugee legislation was typically of a special and temporary nature, the 1965 provision was permanent and available for future needs as they might arise.

Special Emergency Legislation

In addition to legislation providing for refugees in general or various classes of refugees in one measure, there have been special ad hoc measures to meet emergency situations not fully covered or provided for by existing immigration laws. Such an emergency arose in 1922 to 1923 with the plight of the Armenian refugees from Turkey. Public sympathy was aroused at the time, and several proposals to aid the immigration of the Armenian refugees were presented to Congress, but the only bill to be acted on was eventually blocked by House and Senate disagreement.[16] Thirty-five years later there was the emergency of the Hungarian refugees from the 1956 uprising, and bills specifically for their aid were introduced in 1957 and 1958.[17] The legislative product was the Act of July 25, 1958 (72 Stat. 419) to authorize the adjustment of the status of Hungarian refugees who had been paroled in after October 23, 1956 to that of admission for permanent residence, provided that they had been in the United States for at least two years, had not yet acquired permanent residence, and were found on examination to be admissible as immigrants except for the lack of proper documents.

Several months later Congress passed another emergency act, to provide 1,500 nonquota immigrant visas for Portuguese citizens

> who, because of natural calamity in the Azores Islands subsequent to September 1, 1957, are out of their usual place of abode in such islands and unable to return thereto, and who are in urgent need of assistance for the essentials of life. (Sect. 2 of the Act of September 2, 1958 [72 Stat. 1712])

Attached to the bill was a provision of additional nonquota visas for nationals or citizens of the Netherlands residing in that country after displacement from their former homes in Indonesia. The number of additional visas to be so issued was not to exceed the annual quota of the Netherlands.

The Azores refugees were of a distinctive type, the victims of a

[16]See p. 184 above.

[17]See pp. 332, 334 above.

natural calamity rather than of discrimination or warfare, and other acts were to make general provision for such cases of need. The Refugee Relief Act of 1953 broadly defined a refugee to be

> any person in a country or area which is neither Communist nor Communist-dominated, who because of persecution, fear of persecution, natural calamity or military operations is out of his usual place of abode and unable to return thereto, who has not been firmly resettled, and who is in urgent need of assistance for the essentials of life or for transportation. (Sect. 2)

The 1965 Act also included "persons uprooted by catastrophic natural calamity" among the refugees eligible for the seventh preference.

The Cuban refugees constituted one of the largest if not the largest of the single nationality emergency groups, but they could be accommodated under existing immigration laws. Although most of them were technically excludable because of lack of documents or for economic reasons, the majority were given de facto admission under parole, with opportunity for later adjustment of status.

Safeguards and Controls

Congress was characteristically careful to write numerous checks and safeguards into the refugee legislation, so that even at the most generous the door was not opened wide to unscreened and unselected immigration. This characteristic of the refugee legislation is illustrated by the two principal acts, the Displaced Persons Act of 1948 and the Refugee Relief Act of five years later.

The 1948 Act carefully defined those eligible for admission under the act, referred to as "eligible displaced persons," and among the conditions for eligibility were that the alien be "qualified under the immigration laws of the United States for admission into the United States for permanent residence," and that

> assurances . . . have been given [by a citizen or citizens of the United States] that such person . . . will be suitably employed without displacing some other person from employment and that such person, and the members of such person's family . . . shall not become public charges and will have safe and sanitary housing without displacing some other person from such housing.[18]

[18]Sect. 2c and 2d of the 1948 Act; words "safe and sanitary" were omitted in amendment by the Act of June 16, 1950, which added a new sect. 2g containing similar wording to sect. 2c and 2d. Bracketed phrase added by the Act of June 16, 1950 (64 Stat. 219).

The act further required that

> No eligible displaced person shall be admitted into the United States unless there shall have first been a thorough investigation and written report . . . regarding such person's character, history, and eligibility under this Act. (Sect. 10)

A later section of the act was designed for the screening out of any subversives by directing that

> No visas shall be issued under the provisions of this Act to any person who is or has been a member of, or participated in, any movement which is or has been hostile to the United States or the form of government of the United States. (Sect. 13)

The above section was amended and expanded by the Act of June 16, 1950 to read in part as follows:

> No visas shall be issued under the provisions of this Act, as amended, to any person who is or has been a member of the Communist Party, or to any person who adheres to, advocates, or follows, or who has adhered to, advocated, or followed, the principles of any political or economic system or philosophy directed toward the destruction of free competitive enterprise and the revolutionary overthrow of representative governments, or to any person who is or has been a member of any organization which has been designated . . . as a Communist organization, or to any person who is or has been a member of or participated in any movement which is or has been hostile to the United States or the form of government of the United States, or to any person who advocated or assisted in the persecution of any person because of race, religion, or national origin, or to any person who has voluntarily borne arms against the United States during World War II. Upon arrival at the port of entry in the United States, every person eighteen years of age or older authorized to be admitted under this Act, shall take and subscribe an oath or affirmation that he is not and has never been a member of any organization or movement named in this section, and shall be liable to prosecution for perjury if such oath or affirmation is willfully false.[19]

And in the latter case, deportation was also prescribed. Clearly, the above amendment was in the contemporary Cold War spirit, which was still further expressed several months later in the Internal Security Act of September 22, 1950 (64 Stat. 987).

The Refugee Relief Act of 1953 likewise made the admission of refugees under the act contingent upon various safeguards and assur-

[19]Sect. 13 of the 1948 Act as amended by sect. 11 of the 1950 Act.

ances, even though the extreme fear of subversive infiltration had waned by that time. As in the earlier act, assurance prior to admission was required concerning suitable employment without displacement of other workers, a similar assurance concerning housing accommodations, and assurance that the alien would not become a public charge. The required assurances were to come from a responsible citizen and constituted a "personal obligation" on the part of the assurer (sect. 7a). Furthermore, no alien was to be admitted under the act without thorough investigation into his "character, reputation, mental and physical health, history and eligibility," nor without complete information on the alien's history during the preceding two years (sect. 11a, 11d).

A final point to be noted is that both of the above refugee acts were term legislation. The Displaced Persons Act provided for the issuance of the designated number of visas within a period of two years, later extended to three and a half years ending December 31, 1951.[20] The Refugee Relief Act directed in its final section that "no immigrant visas shall be issued under this Act after December 31, 1956" (sect. 20 of 1953 Act).

Summary and Comment

It has been a long-standing element of American immigration policy to provide a place of refuge and a haven for the oppressed of all nations. Various components have no doubt entered into shaping this policy, including a tradition of accepting refugees since early colonial days, a heritage from the nation's revolutionary origin of sympathy for political dissenters, a national self-concept of being an asylum for the poor and oppressed, and direct humanitarian considerations. But whatever the reasons, Congress has been disposed to facilitate the entry of refugees, and to do so even if wide exceptions to the immigration laws are required.

Congressional sympathy has extended to various types of persons broadly classifiable as refugees, including not only those fleeing from military operations or unable to return home in a postwar period, but also the voluntary or enforced exiles following unsuccessful political movements, victims of persecution or those in fear of persecution because of race or religion or political opinion, and, last, the victims of natural disasters. Such persons could be and were admitted originally without special legislation, but with the development of measures for the selection and restriction of immigration, refugee immigration would have been greatly impeded. That is, the circumstances creating refugees are such that many of the migrants are without the required documents, are

[20]Four years, to June 30, 1952, in the case of eligible orphans.

destitute or likely to become public charges, are in excess of quota numbers, or are excludable for other reasons. Aid to the admission of refugees has thus taken two principal forms: the waiver of certain grounds for exclusion or deportation in the case of refugees, and the setting aside or avoidance of quota limits on the number of aliens admitted. There has also been, most recently, the creation of a preference class for refugees that provides up to 10,200 visas for them annually.

The exemptions of refugees from the terms of immigration law have been several. Oldest, and still maintained, is the stipulation that they are not to be excluded for crimes that are purely political. And refugees from religious persecution have not been subject to the literacy test of admissibility since it was first introduced in 1917. With regard to deportability, a deportable alien refugee has been made eligible for suspension of deportation if there is fear of his persecution on return to his homeland, nor is an alien deportable on grounds of fraud or misrepresentation on seeking admission, provided that such action on his part was because of fear of persecution on account of his race, religion, or political opinion.

Avoidance of the quota limits on admissions took several forms. A first form, represented in the Displaced Persons Act of 1948, was to charge admissions as needed to the quota of the refugee's area of origin for future years, with no stated limit on the number of years in advance the area quota might be charged. The number of visas issuable under the act, however, was limited to 220,000, later increased to 341,000. In addition the act authorized 3,000 nonquota visas for orphans, later increased to 5,000, and 15,000 suspensions of deportation and adjustments of status for displaced persons who had been admitted temporarily. An act in 1950 provided 5,000 additional nonquota visas for orphans under ten years of age.

A second means of avoiding the quota limits was to authorize nonquota visas. The Displaced Persons Act, as noted above, provided such visas for certain orphans. Later the Refugee Relief Act of 1953 authorized 205,000 nonquota immigrant visas for certain classes of refugees; and in 1960 nonquota immigrant visas for 500 "difficult to resettle" cases from the refugee camps were provided.

Similar means were used to allow the admission for permanent residence of several emergency groups of refugees, under legislation passed in 1958. Included here was authorization for the adjustment of status for Hungarian refugees previously paroled into the United States, 1,500 nonquota immigrant visas for refugees from earthquake and flood in the Azores, and nonquota visas for residents of the Netherlands displaced from Indonesia.

The third means of admitting refugees outside the quota limits was that of paroling in technically inadmissible aliens. This was a temporary entry at the discretion of the Attorney General but with the possibility of adjustment of status, as in the case of the Hungarian refugees mentioned earlier, to that of immigrants admitted for permanent residence. A 1960 act gave the Attorney General authority to adjust the status of certain refugee-escapees; and the parole procedure, which had been designed to permit the temporary and conditional admission of a few special cases, was further used for the admission of several hundred thousand refugees from Cuba.

A note from the immediately preceding section of this chapter is that congressional benevolence toward refugees was tempered with some caution. The principal refugee legislation was term legislation, and admission under that legislation was only after investigation of each alien and was hedged with due precautions and safeguards against the entry of subversives and other undesirables. Each of the refugee relief acts set a numerical limit as well as a time limit on admissions under the terms of the act.

A final and general observation is that Congress, in its sympathy for refugees and in its concern for family unification, had adopted a great many exceptions to and departures from the old structure of immigration selection and restriction. The 1965 Act when it finally came was thus only a further and decisive step in a direction of immigration policy that Congress had been gradually adopting over the preceding years.

18 Information on Immigration

A requirement that runs through the major immigration acts is that a count be made and personal information be collected for each person, and particularly each alien, who enters the United States. Unlike the elements of immigration policy dealt with in preceding chapters, this policy of record-keeping is an administrative and procedural matter rather than a matter of the regulation of immigration. Nevertheless it has been considered of sufficient importance for Congress to give detailed directives for the collection of the required information and to establish the collection of immigration data long before federal regulation of immigration.

The reasons for Congress's action have to be largely inferred, for the matter was not a subject of congressional debate nor of detailed justification in committee reports on immigration bills. Presumably it was thought self-evident that the information to be collected was intrinsically important and was needed by Congress to follow the trend and composition of immigration in order to direct immigration policy; and evidence of congressional interest is that the acts required that the information be reported to Congress.

There was precedent for the collection of the information, and the material served various purposes. The requirement that passenger lists or ship manifests be delivered to the appropriate port official, originally the collector of customs, was parallel to the procedure for cargo manifests, and was part of routine port procedure for the control of vessel arrivals and departures. Later the procedure was extended with due modifications to the land borders and airports. Precedent for the collection of the manifests came from the colonies and later the seaboard states; and also in the pattern established by state legislation was the putting of responsibility for preparing and submitting the manifests on the master of the passenger vessel. In the case of those states that levied head taxes or required bonding of immigrants, the record-keeping was an essential part of the control procedure. Another purpose later served by the manifests was to provide the necessary proof of lawful admission for permanent residence in naturalization proceedings.

Another aspect to note concerning the requirements for the collection of data on immigration is the great detail in which Congress wrote the sections in question. As will be discussed in a later chapter, immigration legislation as a rule has been written in explicit detail, but this characteristic is especially evident in the portions dealing with the collection of information.

The Act of June 25, 1798

The 1798 Aliens Act, as previously described,[1] was enacted at a time of antialien feeling and was designed to give the President power to order the deportation of aliens judged "dangerous to the peace and safety of the United States." Also included in the act was the requirement that the master of every vessel arriving at a port of the United States make report to the local collector of customs or other customs official of all aliens on board, under penalty of a $300 fine for failure to do so. The act further prescribed the information to be reported for each alien to consist of

> their names, age, the place of nativity, the country from which they shall have come, the nation to which they belong and owe allegiance, their occupation and a description of their persons. . . . (Sect. 3, Act of June 25, 1798 [1 Stat. 570])

True copies of the reports were to be sent "forthwith" to the Department of State, but the series of data so collected was short, for the act expired in two years and was not renewed.

Passenger Acts of 1819 and 1855

The next act to contain a manifesting requirement was the Act of March 2, 1819, with which the continuous collection of immigration statistics began. Prepared for a very different purpose from the 1798 Act, it was to protect passengers through regulation of conditions on vessels.[2] Its terms for manifesting were like those of the earlier act, for the responsibility for delivery of a passenger list to the local collector of customs at the port of arrival was placed upon the captain or master of an arriving vessel, under penalty for failure to do so. The amount of information to be collected, however, was somewhat increased, to give for every passenger embarked at a foreign port

> the age, sex, and occupation, of the said passengers, respectively, the country to which they severally belong, and that of which it is their

[1]For account of the act, see pp. 13–15 above.
[2]See account of the 1819 Act, pp. 21–22 above.

> intention to become inhabitants; . . . and what number have died on the voyage. (Sect. 4 of the 1819 Act [3 Stat. 488])

Since embarcations were to be listed on the manifest, the reporting of deaths allowed actual arrivals to be computed; but actually the official reports do not begin to show deaths until 1856 or after.

The act further directed that quarterly reports consisting of copies of the manifests be sent to the Secretary of State, "by whom statements of the same shall be laid before Congress at each and every session" (sect. 5 of 1819 Act).

The Act of March 3, 1855 was also a passenger act, and it restated the earlier manifesting requirement with little change except for the addition of one new item of information to be collected, "the part of the vessel occupied by each during the voyage" (sect. 12 of the 1855 Act [10 Stat. 715]). As before, the collectors of customs were to send copies of the lists quarterly to the Secretary of State for presentation to Congress.

Chinese Exclusion Acts of 1882 and 1888

Separate lists or manifests of all Chinese passengers on board were required by the Exclusion Acts of 1882 and 1888. The earlier of the two acts called for "the names and other particulars, as shown by their respective certificates," with accredited officers of the Chinese government traveling on official business noted separately. No Chinese passengers were to be allowed to land until after delivery of the required list to the collector of customs.[3]

The 1888 Act repeated the requirement of a separate list of Chinese passengers, without significant change from the terms of the 1882 Act.[4]

Immigration Acts of 1882 to 1893

The Passenger Act of August 2, 1882 included a section that set terms for the reporting of passenger arrivals similar to those of the 1855 Act, but with some additional information required. Cabin passengers were to be listed separately, with report of their names, sex, calling, country of citizenship, and number of pieces of baggage belonging to each. The same information was to be supplied for each "emigrant passenger, or passengers other than cabin passengers,"[5] plus their intended destina-

[3]Sect. 8 of the Act of May 6, 1882 (22 Stat. 58); wording amended slightly by the Act of July 5, 1884 (23 Stat. 115).

[4]Sect. 4 of the Act of September 13, 1888 (25 Stat. 476).

[5]The wording indicates that cabin or first-class passengers were not included as immigrants, and the same practice seems to have been followed in the official statistics.

tion and "the location of the compartment or space occupied by each of such passengers." Deaths on the voyage were also to be listed by name, age, and cause of death.[6]

The Immigration Acts of 1891 and 1893 reaffirmed the manifesting requirement. The 1891 Act gave only the brief directive that the arrival by water of an alien immigrant at any place within the United States be reported, together with "the name, nationality, last residence, and destination" (sect. 8 of the Act of March 3, 1891 [26 Stat. 1084]).

The 1893 Act went to the opposite extreme of requiring much additional information and setting forth in detail the procedure to be followed. The required information was for alien immigrants arriving by water, and the reports were to state for each such immigrant

> the full name, age, and sex, whether married or single; the calling or occupation; whether able to read or write; the nationality; the last residence; the seaport of landing . . . ; the final destination, if any, beyond the seaport of landing; whether having a ticket through to such final destination; whether the immigrant has paid his own passage or whether it has been paid by other persons or by any corporation, society, municipality, or government; whether in possession of money, and if so, whether upwards of thirty dollars and how much if thirty dollars or less; whether going to join a relative, and if so, what relative and his name and address; whether ever before in the United States, and if so, when and where; whether ever in prison or almshouse or supported by charity; whether a polygamist; whether under contract, express or implied, to perform labor in the United States; and what is the immigrant's condition of health, mentally and physically, and whether deformed or crippled, and if so, from what cause. (Sect. 1, Act of March 3, 1893 [27 Stat. 569])

Beyond all of the above the act went on to direct that the manifests were not to exceed thirty names per page, that the head of each family was to be given a ticket identifying his page and line number on the manifest, and that the ship's master was to attest on the basis of his own inspection and physical and oral examination by the ship's surgeon that

> no one of said passengers is an idiot or insane person, or a pauper or likely to become a public charge, or suffering from a loathsome or dangerous contagious disease, or a person who has been convicted of a felony or other infamous crime or misdemeanor involving

[6]Sect. 9 of the Act of August 2, 1882 (22 Stat. 186). Amendment by the Act of February 9, 1905 (33 Stat. 711) omitted the separate specifications for cabin passengers but called for the location of the compartment or space occupied by the passenger if other than a cabin passenger and added two new items, marital status (married or single) and whether a citizen or not.

> moral turpitude, or a polygamist, or under a contract or agreement, express or implied, to perform labor in the United States. (Sect. 2)

The act also gave detailed directions on the procedures to be followed, and as a whole gave evidence of the determination of Congress to prescribe the manifesting in minute detail. A probable reason for this close attention on the part of Congress is that by 1893 immigration had become a subject of very considerable congressional and public concern; also there were then a number of excludable classes and Congress was at some pains to strengthen the controls on immigration and prevent the entry of excludable aliens. Certain of the new items of information asked for on the manifest were aimed directly at the excludable or prospectively excludable classes, such as aliens who had not paid for their own passage, criminals, paupers, polygamists, illiterates, contract laborers, and others. More clearly than the earlier acts, the 1893 Act showed that the manifesting procedure had become an integral part of the system of immigration regulation and control being developed by Congress.

Immigration Acts of 1903 and 1907

The statement of manifesting requirements in the Immigration Act of 1903 closely followed that of the 1893 Act but added several items of new information to be collected. The new items on the manifest were the race of the alien, the amount of money in his possession if less than fifty dollars, whether he was ever in "an institution or hospital for the care and treatment of the insane," whether he was an anarchist, and the duration of his handicap if he was deformed or crippled. And to the certification required of the ship's master was added that to the best of his knowledge no alien passenger was a prostitute.[7]

The Immigration Act of 1907 dealt with manifesting in four sections as had the 1903 Act, but it treated the subject at even greater length. The most important innovation was to require lists of alien passengers on vessels departing from the United States, thus beginning the collection of departure statistics for aliens. The information called for in such cases was more limited than for arrivals—the alien's name, sex, age, nationality, residence in the United States, occupation, and time of last arrival in the United States; no vessel was to be granted clearance papers unless the required list had been delivered.[8] The terms of the section calling for

[7]Sect. 12–15, Act of March 3, 1903 (32 Stat. 1213).

[8]Sect. 12–15, Act of February 20, 1907 (34 Stat. 898). A proviso in sect. 12 of the act permitted later delivery of the list of alien passengers in the case of vessels making regular trips to ports of the United States, on official approval.

testimony from the ship's master that no excludable aliens were on board to the best of his knowledge were also expanded and made more inclusive. He was called on to state that no imbecile or feebleminded persons, in addition to idiots and insane persons, were among the passengers. The class of polygamists was expanded to include "one admitting belief in the practice of polygamy," and the class of prostitutes was enlarged by addition of "a woman or girl coming to the United States for the purpose of prostitution, or for any other immoral purpose" (sect. 13). The evident attempt was, as in the definitions of the excludable classes, to make the terminology broad enough to incorporate all cases within the general area of intention of Congress.

Immigration Act of 1917

The elaboration of the directions for manifesting was carried still further in the three sections of the 1917 Act devoted to the subject. The requirement of manifesting was extended to include arriving citizens of the United States,[9] to all alien passengers and all citizens of the United States or of an insular possession departing by vessel with the stated intention of residing permanently abroad,[10] to departing citizens who do not intend to reside permanently abroad,[11] and to resident aliens and citizens leaving by way of the Canadian or Mexican borders for permanent residence in a foreign country.[12] New items added to the manifest specifications were country of birth, name and address of the nearest relative in the country from which the alien came, whether he was ever supported by charity, a greatly expanded definition of anarchists and related classes,

[9]The information to be obtained for arriving citizens was limited to their sex, age, class of travel, and the foreign port of embarcation (presumably name also, but not so stated in the act).

[10]The information to be recorded for such departures was "Name, age, and sex; whether married or single; calling or occupation; whether able to read or write; nationality; country of birth; country of which citizen or subject; race; last permanent residence in the United States or insular possession thereof; if a citizen of the United States or of the insular possession thereof, whether native born or naturalized; if native born, the place and date of birth, or if naturalized the city or town in which naturalization has been had; intended future permanent residence; and time and port of last arrival in the United States, or insular possessions thereof."

[11]For such citizens the manifest was to show sex, age, class of travel, and port of debarcation.

[12]For such border crossers the required information was "Name, age, and sex; whether married or single; calling or occupation; whether able to read or write; nationality; country of birth; country of which citizen or subject; race; last permanent residence in the United States; intended future permanent residence; and time and port of last arrival in the United States; and if a United States citizen, whether native born or naturalized."

"whether coming with the intent to return to the country whence such alien comes after temporarily engaging in laboring pursuits in the United States," and "such other items of information as will aid in determining whether any such alien belongs to any of the excluded classes." These new items can be seen as reflecting new excludable classes, current concerns about subversive aliens and "birds of passage," and the use of the manifesting inquiry as part of the screening process applied to arriving aliens.[13]

Thirty years later the section of the 1917 Act stating the requirements for manifesting was amended, in the case of aliens, citizens, or nationals arriving by water at any port of continental United States or an insular possession, to require the reporting of such arrivals in lists or manifests that are

> in such form and contain such information as the Commissioner of Immigration and Naturalization, with the approval of the Attorney General, shall by regulation prescribe as necessary for the identification of the persons transported and for the enforcement of the immigration laws. (Act of July 30, 1947 [61 Stat. 630])

The same authority was given to the Commissioner with regard to the manifesting of departures by vessel. For departures over the land borders of aliens, citizens, and nationals for permanent residence in a foreign country, however, the required items of information were substantially unchanged from the 1917 Act. For other departures and all arrivals the change to administrative regulation of manifesting did not alter the collection of information, but it did give opportunity for more flexibility. Thereafter, the law with respect to manifesting remained essentially unchanged by the Act of 1952.[14]

Alien Registration

Although a quite different matter from the manifesting of arrivals, alien registration can be thought of as an extension of the record of who and what manner of aliens enter to a follow-up of them after arrival. It arises, presumably, from a certain attitude of suspicion or uncertainty toward aliens; and call for the registration of aliens historically has come at times of war or fears of war and heightened antialien feeling.

There is a long history of congressional proposals that all resident aliens be required to register. The first such proposal was in 1798, at a

[13]Sect. 12–14 of the Act of February 5, 1917 (39 Stat. 874).

[14]Manifesting is dealt with in sect. 231 of the Act of June 27, 1952 (66 Stat. 163).

time of fears of alien subversion, when a congressional committee recommended an alien register; but Congress did not then adopt the recommendation.[15] The idea did not again appear in Congress until the winter of 1844 to 1845, when a resolution and a bill advanced such a means of preventing naturalization frauds.[16]

Thereafter, attempts to establish an alien register did not appear again until World War I and after. Among a number of antialien bills introduced in the spring of 1917 was one for the registration of all aliens, which was followed by another such bill in the next Congress.[17] Immediately after the close of the war there were other bills for compulsory registration, as well as various antialien and anti-immigration measures.[18] A few years later there were other registration bills in the middle 1920s.[19]

The Depression period saw new attempts to restrict immigration and to take various measures against resident aliens. From this period came several bills to require resident aliens to register, but like the earlier bills none appears to have been seriously considered by Congress.[20] It was the approach of World War II that gave the strongest impetus to attempts to establish a system of alien registration, for then even more than at the time of the preceding war there were fears of alien disloyalty, saboteurs, espionage, and "fifth columnists." Seven or more registration bills appeared in Congress in 1939, one at least to require the fingerprinting of all aliens. Carried over to the next session of Congress, one of the bills became the Alien Registration Act of 1940.[21] A multipurpose act dealing with subversion and providing deportation for various offenses as well as with registration, its registration requirements included the registration and fingerprinting of an alien in advance of issuance of a visa for admission to the United States and registration and fingerprinting of every alien then or thereafter in the United States who is fourteen years of age or older and who remains for thirty days or longer. Parents or guardians had the duty of registering aliens under fourteen years of age who were to remain for thirty days or longer. Every alien required to be registered was further required to report in writing to the Commissioner of Immigration and Naturalization every change of address within five days of the

[15]See p. 12 above.

[16]See pp. 32, 33 above; the bill would have included a personal description as well as other information about each alien.

[17]See pp. 168, 170 above.

[18]See pp. 171–172, 177–78, 184 above.

[19]See pp. 197, 202 above.

[20]See pp. 219, 227 above.

[21]Act of June 28, 1940 (54 Stat. 670). Title III of the Act contains the registration requirements.

change (sect. 35). Amendment in 1950 changed the above requirement to reregistration within ten days following the first of January of each year (Act of September 23, 1950 [64 Stat. 987]). Penalties of fine and imprisonment were provided for failure or refusal to comply with the terms of the act.

The Alien Registration Act was repealed in part by the 1952 Act, which, however, reenacted the registration provisions.[22] The new act further provided that on registration every alien be provided with a registration certificate or card that must be carried on his person at all times by every alien aged eighteen or over (sect. 264d and 264e).

Comment

The collection of information on arrivals, and later on departures, is rather a matter of administrative or operations procedure than of immigration policy in a strict sense.[23] But Congress had given attention to the matter long before the beginning of federal regulation of immigration. The manifesting of aliens was first adopted in 1798, to last for only two years, but it was resumed twenty years later in 1819 and has continued to the present time. And Congress has not only enacted and reenacted the manifesting requirement but has written the requirement in quite minute detail by prescribing the procedure and forms to be used, has specified at length just what items of information are to be collected, and has set penalties for noncompliance.

If not a policy toward immigration in itself, the collecting of information has several purposes as an adjunct or reinforcement to major elements of policy. The 1798 provision was presumably intended as an aid to the surveillance of aliens at a time of fear that they might be a threat to the young Republic. Later we may infer that Congress saw manifesting as serving the purpose in the Passenger Acts of providing an accounting from a ship's master of the passengers who had been in his charge; and then or later the passenger lists may have been seen as a source of information on the number and kind of passengers and immigrants on which information immigration policy could be judged and based by Congress. Still later, after the 1880s, the collection and reporting of

[22]Chap. 7, sect. 261–266 of the 1952 Act.

[23]For a collection of the full texts of the sections of immigration law dealing with manifesting, see Appendix C, pp. 1016–1025 of E. P. Hutchinson, "Notes on Immigration Statistics of the United States," *Journal of the American Statistical Association* 53 (Dec. 1958): 963–1025.

information about arriving aliens formed a part of the procedure for the control of immigration and especially for the detection and exclusion of certain classes of aliens.

The manifest record also served or came to serve certain purposes after the admission of an alien. It provided a record of lawful admission for permanent residence, a record (or some valid substitute for it) required for naturalization. It was also available if needed later as evidence bearing on whether an alien had overstayed or violated the terms of a temporary admission or had been admitted for permanent residence through fraud or misrepresentation and therefore was deportable.

Also mentioned in the preceding section was registration of the resident alien population, a wartime measure that has continued in force since 1940.

An important step with regard to manifesting was taken in 1947. After more than a century of congressional specification of each item of information to be included on the manifest, a new act authorized the Commissioner of Immigration and Naturalization to determine what information should be collected "as necessary . . . for the enforcement of the immigration laws." This provision made clear the congressional conception of the manifesting procedure's role in law enforcement, but it also gave a flexibility through administrative regulation that could not be had through the cumbersome process of legislation. Such flexibility of arrival and departure procedures had become increasingly needed. The greatly increased volume of travel, principally by automobile, over the land borders, and the expansion of air travel created pressure for streamlining and expediting of border clearance even at the expense of detail of information and closeness of inspection.[24] As long ago as 1891 the immigration act of that year (26 Stat. 1084) authorized the Secretary of the Treasury to prescribe rules for inspection along the land borders "so as not to obstruct or unnecessarily delay, impede, or annoy passengers in ordinary travel" (sect. 8); and the trend in recent years has been toward more and more simplification of procedures and information collection at ports of entry and departure. Something is no doubt lost thereby in the amount and detail of immigration statistics, and illegal entry may be made easier; but rigorous inspection of each arrival such as was possible in the days of transatlantic voyages is clearly no longer feasible.[25]

[24]The recent effort to attract foreign tourists has also generated pressure for rapid clearance by immigrant inspectors at ports of entry.

[25]Concerning congressional attention to problems of illegal immigration, see chapter 21, pp. 604–11 below.

19 Legislative and Administrative Roles

In addition to the fully debated and formal policies developed and enacted by Congress are certain unstated but continuing patterns in congressional action on immigration. These latter are what might be called de facto or tacit policies, evidently not the product of deliberate planning but rather indicative of some uniformity from Congress to Congress in attitudes toward immigration or in thinking about how to deal with it. The present chapter concerns one such area of de facto policy: the role Congress has chosen for itself in the regulation of immigration and the residual latitude left to administrative discretion within the guidelines of policy set by Congress.

The regulation of immigration involves both legislative and administrative functions: the setting of policy is the legislative function, and the carrying out of that policy on a day-to-day basis is the administrative function. But between these poles there may be considerable differences from one country to another in the extent of the role assumed by the legislative and that assigned to the administrative branch of government. At one extreme the legislative branch may dictate in detail the regulation of immigration and leave little room for administrative discretion; at the other extreme the immigration officials may have very wide discretionary powers within the broad framework of policy set by immigration law.

Australia and Canada, the two countries most comparable to the United States in regard to immigration, provide examples of wide discretionary powers possessed by the immigration officials. Writers on Australian immigration policy record that "the Minister for Immigration has enormous latitude in administrative matters,"[1] and that discretionary powers are wide and may be exercised "away from public scrutiny."[2] Similarly a recent work on Canadian immigration policy refers to "the considerable degree of administrative discretion permitted under the

[1]H. I. London, *Non-white Immigrants and the "White Australia" Policy* (Sydney: Sydney University Press, 1970), p. 99.

[2]A. C. Palfreeman, *The Administration of the White Australia Policy* (Melbourne: Melbourne University Press, 1967), pp. 4, 59.

1952 Immigration Act," and "the degree of uncontrolled discretionary power vested by the Act in the Minister of Citizenship and Immigration and his officials."[3] The opposite extreme of tight legislative control over immigration is found in the United States, as described below.

The Early Pattern

The early legislative ventures undertaken by Congress in relation to immigration, such as the Passenger Acts to regulate conditions on shipboard, the manifesting of passengers, and Chinese exclusion, were made without any staff of immigration officials, and enforcement of these early acts devolved on various already available governmental agents such as consular officials, port officers, and collectors of customs. It was thus natural under the circumstances that the new rules and requirements should be set forth in full detail for the benefit of the inexperienced officials.

The items of information about each passenger to be recorded on the ship manifests were listed in each of the acts from 1819 onward, together with directions to whom the manifests were to be delivered at the port and how they should be transmitted and eventually reported to Congress.[4] By late in the nineteenth century the sections of law dealing with manifesting had expanded greatly to increase the items of information to be recorded, to give some directions for the form of the manifest sheets, and to direct how the correctness of the information was to be attested.

The Passenger Acts, or Steerage Laws as they were formerly called, were quite as explicit and detailed concerning shipboard provisions and accommodations. The 1819 Act set a limit of two passengers for every five tons of vessel and stipulated the minimum of food stores per passenger.[5] Later acts dictated the minimum size of berths,[6] provision for ventilation, a more diversified stock of provisions,[7] and much else. En-

[3]Freda Hawkins, *Canada and Immigration: Public Policy and Public Concern* (Montreal: McGill Press, 1972), pp. 73, 102.

[4]See further on manifesting in chapter 18.

[5]". . . at least sixty gallons of water, one hundred pounds of salted provisions, one gallon of vinegar, and one hundred pounds of wholesome ship bread." Sect. 3 of the Act of March 2, 1819.

[6]If in tiers of more than two berths, "at least six feet in length, and at least eighteen inches in width," and raised not less than six inches above the deck. Sect. 3 of the Act of February 22, 1847.

[7]For each passenger, "at least fifteen pounds of good navy bread, ten pounds of rice, ten pounds of oatmeal, ten pounds of wheat flour, ten pounds of peas and beans, thirty-five pounds of potatoes, one pint of vinegar, sixty gallons of fresh water, ten pounds of salted pork, free of bone, all to be of good quality." Act of May 17, 1848.

forcement, so far as specified by the Passenger Acts, was in the hands of the collector of customs at the port of arrival, who was authorized to direct inspectors to examine each incoming passenger vessel,[8] and any circuit or district court.[9]

New duties were created by the Acts of March 3, 1875 and August 3, 1882, which were the first to provide for the exclusion of certain classes of aliens. Inspection of passengers was therefore called for, and the first of the acts directed that "Every vessel arriving in the United States may be inspected under the direction of the collector of the port at which it arrives" (sect. 5 of the Act of March 3, 1875 [18 Stat. 477]). The duties of the inspecting official were also set forth. The 1882 Act made a different assignment of responsibility for enforcement by providing that

> the Secretary of the Treasury is hereby charged with the duty of executing the provisions of this act and with supervision over the business of immigration to the United States, and for that purpose he shall have power to enter into contracts with such State commission, board, or officers as may be designated for that purpose by the governor of any State to take charge of the local affairs of immigration in the ports within said State, and to provide for the support and relief of such immigrants therein landing as may fall into distress or need public aid, under the rules and regulations to be prescribed by said Secretary; and it shall be the duty of such State commission, board, or officers so designated to examine into the condition of passengers arriving at the ports within such State in any ship or vessel, and for that purpose all or any of such commissioners or officers, or such other person or persons as they shall appoint, shall be authorized to go on board of and through any such ship or vessel.[10]

In the section quoted above Congress took an important new step in the regulation of immigration, the delegation of powers to an administrative officer in the form of discretionary authority to the Secretary of the Treasury to enter into certain contracts and to prescribe rules and regulations under the act. The same act granted further power to the Secretary to

> establish such regulations and rules and issue from time to time such instructions not inconsistent with law as he shall deem best calculated to protect the United States and immigrants into the United

[8]Sect. 7 of the Act of May 17, 1848; sect. 9 and 17 of the Act of March 3, 1855.

[9]Sect. 1 of the Act of February 22, 1847; sect. 1 and 6 of the Act of March 3, 1855.

[10]Sect. 2 of the Act of August 3, 1882 (22 Stat. 214). Sect. 8 of the Act of March 3, 1891 directed that "all duties imposed and powers conferred" on state officials acting under contract by the 1882 Act were to be performed thereafter "as occasion may arise, by the inspection officers of the United States."

> States from fraud and loss, and for carrying out the provisions of this act, and the immigration laws of the United States; and he shall prescribe all forms of bonds, entries, and other papers to be used under and in the enforcement of the various provisions of this act. (Sect. 3)

Also granted to the Secretary of the Treasury was certain authority in the sending back of foreign convicts to the country "from whence they came" (sect. 4). Several years later the Secretary was also charged with the duty of executing the provisions of the Contract Labor Act of 1885 and given the authority to establish rules and regulations, issue instructions, and prescribe the form of bond and other papers under the terms of the act.[11]

The first step toward the creation of a separate governmental agency and officials to administer the immigration laws was taken by Congress in the Immigration Act of March 3, 1891, which included provision for an office of superintendent of immigration within the Treasury Department. The superintendent was to be a presidential appointee, under the control and supervision of the Secretary of the Treasury, and provided with three clerks. The duties of the superintendent were not specified beyond the reporting in writing periodically or on demand to the Secretary and the hearing of appeals from aliens excluded by inspecting officers; but the duties presumably included some supervision of those officers. Four years later a Bureau of Immigration within the Treasury Department and headed by a Commissioner-General of Immigration was established by the Act of March 2, 1895 (28 Stat. 780).[12] The wording of the act indicates that the new official had the duty of "regulating immigration" and was also directed to administer the contract labor laws. No discretionary powers separate from those already possessed by the Secretary of the Treasury were accorded by the act.

The Immigration Act of 1903 set forth the powers and duties of the Commissioner-General, who was to act under the direction of the Secretary of Commerce and Labor to

> have charge of the administration of all laws relating to the immigration of aliens into the United States, and shall have the control, direction, and supervision of all officers, clerks, and employees appointed thereunder. He shall establish such rules and regulations, prescribe such forms of bonds, reports, entries, and other papers,

[11]Sect. 6, 7, and 8 of the Act of February 26, 1885 as added by the Act of February 23, 1887 (24 Stat. 414).

[12]Jurisdiction over immigration was transferred to the Department of Commerce and Labor by the Act of February 14, 1903 (32 Stat. 825), to the Department of Labor by the Act of March 4, 1913 (37 Stat. 737), and to the Department of Justice in 1940 (54 Stat. 1238).

> and shall issue from time to time such instructions, not inconsistent with law, as he shall deem best calculated for carrying out the provisions of this Act. . . . (Sect. 22 of 1903 Act)

The Commissioner-General or the Secretary were also empowered under the act to direct the "immigrant fund" obtained from the head tax, to assess penalties against a transporter of an alien with a dangerous contagious disease, to prescribe conditions for suspension of deportation of a contract laborer whose testimony is needed in the prosecution of offenders, to fix the rate of compensation of immigration officers, to prescribe rules for the inspection of aliens at the land borders, and to deal with various other matters, but all within the limits set by law. The defined powers of the office were strictly administrative, with little or no range of discretion outside of administrative matters.

The next general immigration act, that of 1907, closely followed the pattern and language of the 1903 Act. The recital of powers and duties of the Commissioner-General was as before (sect. 22 of 1907 Act), but two new responsibilities were added. One was to issue regulations concerning lists of passengers departing by vessel from the United States and the other to establish an information division within what had by then become the Bureau of Immigration and Naturalization (sect. 12 and 40, 1907 Act). But also contained within the act was one limited grant of discretion. The last of the enumerated classes of excludable aliens was "all children under sixteen years of age, unaccompanied by one or both of their parents," but this exclusion was qualified by the attached clause, "at the discretion of the Secretary of Commerce and Labor or under such regulations as he may from time to time prescribe."[13]

The Immigration Act of 1917, a much longer and more detailed act than its predecessors, went much further in the granting of powers and discretion to the immigration officers and the Secretary of Labor, who had then become the responsible cabinet officer. In addition to having authority to issue various rules and regulations, the Secretary was specifically given discretion to admit unaccompanied children if otherwise eligible and considered not likely to become public charges (sect. 3); to admit otherwise admissible stowaways (sect. 3); to admit under bond or on other terms such aliens as are liable to be excluded because they are likely to become public charges or because they have a physical disability other than tuberculosis or contagious disease (sect. 21); and to take certain other actions. Important powers were also granted to the Secretary to

[13]Sect. 2 of the 1907 Act, continued by Act of March 26, 1910.

give discretionary relief to certain classes of excludable aliens, under the terms of two provisos attached to the section of the act dealing with exclusions (sect. 3). The seventh proviso gave the Secretary discretion for the admission of "aliens returning after a temporary absence to an unrelinquished United States domicile of seven consecutive years." And the ninth proviso gave the Commissioner of Immigration and Naturalization, as he was now entitled, authority with the approval of the Secretary to issue rules and prescribe conditions for the admission of otherwise inadmissible aliens applying for temporary admission.[14]

Later Extent of Administrative Powers

The 1917 Act remained the basic immigration law until superseded and repealed by the 1952 Act. During the interval of thirty-five years new duties and responsibilities came to the immigration authorities under the quota acts and several wartime measures, and in addition there were several extensions of discretionary powers to the Commissioner of Immigration and Naturalization or his superior, now the Attorney General. The Alien Registration Act of 1940 authorized the Attorney General to permit a deportable alien to depart voluntarily at his own expense[15] to any country of his choice, or to grant a suspension of deportation if the alien had proved to be of good moral character during the preceding five years and if deportation would result in "serious economic detriment" to a close relative who was a citizen or a legally resident alien.[16] In 1947 an amendment to the 1917 Act did away with the detailed statement of the information to be recorded on passenger manifests, and simply authorized the Commissioner, with the approval of the Attorney General, to prescribe the form and information content of manifests "as necessary for the identification of the persons transported and for the enforcement of the immigration laws" (Act of July 30, 1947 [61 Stat. 630]).

Certain special powers were also conferred in the case of displaced persons and refugees. The Displaced Persons Act of 1948 authorized the Attorney General, with the approval of Congress, to adjust the status of certain displaced persons resident in the United States to that of admission for permanent residence, subject to admissibility and certain other

[14]Concerning administrative authority to suspend deportation or to admit certain classes of excludable aliens, see further in the next chapter on elements of flexibility in immigration law.

[15]Thereby being eligible to apply later for readmission.

[16]Sect. 20 of the 1940 Act, amending sect. 19 of the 1917 Act; reamended by the Act of July 1, 1948 (62 Stat. 1206).

conditions.[17] And the Internal Security Act of 1950 forbade the deportation of any alien to any country if the Attorney General found that the alien would be subject to physical persecution on arrival.[18]

The 1952 Act generally continued and somewhat expanded the previously granted statutory authority of administrative officers in matters related to immigration, including discretion in the temporary admission of technically excludable aliens, the suspension of deportation in certain cases, and the adjustment of status. An important new power granted to the Attorney General was that of paroling in aliens on a temporary basis.[19] As stated in the act:

> The Attorney General may in his discretion parole into the United States temporarily under such conditions as he may prescribe for emergent reasons or for reasons deemed strictly in the public interest any alien applying for admission to the United States, but such parole of such alien shall not be regarded as an admission of the alien and when the purposes of such parole shall, in the opinion of the Attorney General, have been served the alien shall forthwith return or be returned to the custody from which he was paroled and thereafter his case shall continue to be dealt with in the same manner as that of any other applicant for admission. . . . (Sect. 212[d][5] of the 1952 Act)

Congress presumably contemplated a limited use of the parole power for temporary admission of aliens in special cases not provided for under existing law, but the power came to be used later for the emergency admission of refugees strictly excludable under immigration law.

Additional discretionary powers were conferred on the Attorney General by later law. A 1957 act gave authority for the admission under certain conditions of eligibility those aliens excludable because of criminality or tuberculosis, of which the latter cases were to be reported to Congress.[20] In 1960 authority was given to parole in certain refugee-escapees.[21] In 1961 the Attorney General was authorized to admit certain aliens with tuberculosis, no longer with report to Congress necessary; and the 1952 Act was amended by the addition of subsections incorporat-

[17]Sect. 4a of the Act of June 25, 1948 (62 Stat. 1009); the terms of eligibility amended later by the Act of June 16, 1950 (64 Stat. 219).

[18]Sect. 23 of the Act of September 23, 1950 (64 Stat. 987).

[19]A different kind of parole authority had existed previously in the case of aliens awaiting deportation or final decision on deportation proceedings. Sect. 20 of the 1917 Act, as amended by sect. 23 of the Act of September 23, 1950 (64 Stat. 987).

[20]Sect. 5 and 6 of the Act of September 11, 1957 (71 Stat. 639); applicable to aliens excludable under paragraphs 212(a)(6), (9),(10), and (12) of the 1952 Act.

[21]Sect. 1 of the Act of July 14, 1960 (74 Stat. 504).

ing the provisions of the 1957 Act noted just above.[22] In 1962 the Attorney General was given discretionary authority to suspend the deportation and to adjust the status of additional classes of aliens, under certain conditions of eligibility and with required report to Congress of the pertinent provisions of law and reasons for suspension in each case (sect. 4 of the Act of October 24, 1962 [76 Stat. 1247]).

The 1965 Act assigned certain new duties to the Attorney General and immigration officials, especially for the determination of eligibility for preference status, but the new duties were administrative, within the confines of the act, and there was no extension of discretionary powers beyond those confines.

Congressional Control

The preceding section is by no means a complete account of all the specific powers assigned by law to the immigration officials in addition to their responsibilities for the routine operations under the immigration acts, but it records the principal statutory powers and areas of administrative discretion and is sufficient to indicate the extent to which Congress has delegated decision making to administrative officers. It is clear, especially in comparison with other countries, that Congress has kept a firm grip on immigration matters and that administrative discretion has been granted by Congress only in designated types of cases and within specified guidelines.[23] The special powers delegated by Congress to the Attorney General or the Commissioner, it may be noted, are predominantly for making decisions in individual cases, such as determining which excludable aliens may be admitted without detriment to the public interest or which technically deportable aliens merit suspension of deportation. Providing such means of relief from the strict terms of the law allows for a tempering of the law on humanitarian and hardship grounds and gives a needed element of flexibility to the system.[24] But if individual

[22]Sect. 12, 14, and 15 of the Act of September 26, 1961 (75 Stat. 650).

[23]Thus, for example, the conditions of eligibility for the admission of certain classes of excludable aliens at the discretion of the Attorney General under authority given by sect. 5 of the Act of September 11, 1957 (71 Stat. 639) were (1) being the spouse or child, including a minor unmarried adopted child, of a citizen or of an alien lawfully admitted for permanent residence, or the parent of a citizen or lawfully admitted alien, (2) being otherwise admissible, (3) determination by the Attorney General that the alien's exclusion would cause extreme hardship to a citizen or lawfully resident alien who is the spouse, parent, or child of the alien, (4) determination by the Attorney General that admission would not be contrary to the national welfare, safety, or security, and (5) consent by the Attorney General for the alien to apply or reapply for a visa and admission.

[24]See further on the subject of flexibility in the next chapter.

cases are indeed to be considered on their separate merits, it becomes almost necessary to delegate such responsibility, for neither Congress nor its immigration committees are in a good position to deal with the numbers of cases that arise.[25]

Further evidence of the firm grip that Congress has retained is the fact that some of the more important delegated powers of decision are not fully delegated. That is, Congress has retained for itself the right to review certain administrative decisions or has made those decisions final only on congressional approval. Such is the case with regard to temporary or conditional admission, suspension of deportation, and adjustment of status, all of which involve the granting of exceptions to the immigration laws. For example, the 1917 Act, as previously described, conferred on the Secretary of Labor authority to suspend the deportation of aliens under certain conditions but with the 1940 reservation that

> If the deportation of any alien is suspended under the provisions of this subsection for more than six months, all of the facts and pertinent provisions of law in the case shall be reported to the Congress with the reasons for such suspension. . . . If . . . the two Houses pass a concurrent resolution stating in substance that the Congress does not favor the suspension of such deportation, the Secretary of Labor shall thereupon deport such alien in the manner provided by law. (Sect. 20c of the 1940 Act)

Deportation proceedings were to be cancelled if no such resolution was passed within a specified time. The same provision was reaffirmed with a slight change of the reporting terms by the Act of July 1, 1948 (62 Stat. 1206). The 1952 Act expanded the discretionary powers of the Attorney General to grant both suspension of deportation and adjustment of status to a number of classes of aliens who met certain conditions of eligibility, but it continued the requirement that all such cases be reported as before to Congress, which could then disapprove the suspension (sect. 244a).

Adjustment of status from temporary admission to that of immigrant was provided for certain displaced persons by the Displaced Persons Act of 1948, up to a maximum of 15,000, subject to recommendation to Congress by the Attorney General and passage of a concurrent resolution.[26] The 1952 Act gave the Attorney General the discretionary power to adjust the status of aliens who had been admitted on a bona fide temporary basis (i.e., as nonimmigrants), subject to admissibility for per-

[25] See account of private bills in the next chapter, p. 573.

[26] Sect. 4a of the Act of June 25, 1948; terms of eligibility amended to be somewhat more restrictive by the Act of June 16, 1950.

manent residence and availability of a quota number, but without requirement of report to Congress or congressional approval.

While making provision for the temporary or conditional admission of certain special classes of technically excludable aliens, Congress was careful to retain for itself some measure of control over such admissions. The ninth proviso of the 1917 Act[27] had authorized the temporary admission of certain classes of otherwise inadmissible aliens. Later the Internal Security Act of 1950 imposed some limitations on the proviso, forbidding its use for the admission of certain classes of aliens who might endanger the public safety, and requiring report to Congress of other classes of subversives admitted temporarily under authority of the proviso.[28] Reporting by the Attorney General to Congress was required under the 1952 Act on admissions of certain former Communists (sect. 212[a][28][I] of the 1952 Act) and the temporary admission of certain otherwise inadmissible aliens (sect. 212[d][6]).

Subsequently the 1965 Act made new provision for keeping Congress closely informed on matters of immigration. The Attorney General was instructed to provide Congress with a "complete and detailed statement of facts" on the case of each alien of refugee status conditionally admitted under the seventh preference of the new act and also a statement of "the basis for his approval and such facts as were by him deemed to be pertinent in establishing the beneficiary's qualifications" for third and sixth preference, the occupational preferences.[29]

These numerous provisions for reporting and review of administrative action are evidence that Congress, while willing to delegate many decision-making functions to the immigration authorities, nevertheless makes clear to those authorities that they act under the eye of Congress and in some measure subject to congressional approval.

The reasons for this close control have not been stated by Congress, and can only be inferred. In part it is a continuation of a close control pattern established much earlier, with some carryover of attitude from the time when the constitutional issue was decided and the federal government took over immigration control from the states. There may be also an element of possessiveness in immigration matters on the part of the immigration committees and especially their strong chairmen who have been in a position to build power and influence in Congress. An-

[27]See p. 549 above and p. 560 below.

[28]Sect. 22 of the Act of September 23, 1950 (64 Stat. 987), amending sect. 6b of the Act of October 16, 1918 (40 Stat. 1012).

[29]Sect. 3 of the 1965 Act, adding new subsect. 203f and 204d to the 1952 Act.

other consideration is that immigration is or has been at times a politically sensitive issue, and Congress may not feel complete confidence that the administration of the immigration laws will always be fully in tune with congressional thinking. For whatever reasons, Congress has continued to write immigration law with detailed specification of terms, has granted only limited discretionary powers to immigration officials, and has kept a comparatively close control over immigration.

Legislation in General Terms

As described earlier, Congress has often shown a preference for writing the immigration laws in such specific detail of terms that relatively little latitude has been left for administrative interpretation and discretion. There are exceptions, however, for now and then Congress has chosen to state some provisions in quite general language. Examples of such general terminology include several of the grounds for exclusion, stated as "crime involving moral turpitude," "dangerous contagious disease," "likely to become a public charge," and "constitutional psychopathic inferiority." In such cases responsibility is in effect delegated to administrative officials to prepare regulations that interpret and spell out the intent of Congress within the broad guidelines set by law.

The Immigration Act of 1891 introduced two of the above terms in providing for the exclusion of aliens who had been convicted of felonies or crimes involving moral turpitude and those having a "loathsome or a dangerous contagious disease." The term "moral turpitude" was then in current usage and has continued to be used in law, and although it does not lend itself to precise definition, through acceptance and testing in the courts it has come to be applied to certain types of crimes and not to others. In general it has been held to include various offenses against morality, robbery, and fraudulent practices.[30] What constituted a loathsome or dangerous contagious disease, later shortened to dangerous contagious disease, was likewise left to be defined, with the exception of two diseases Congress later designated as grounds for exclusion: tuberculosis in 1907 and leprosy in 1952. The Public Health Service has ruled that nearly a score of diseases, for the most part venereal diseases and fungus or parasitic infections, are excludable.[31]

[30]For discussion of the definition of moral turpitude, see Charles Gordon and Harry Rosenfield, *Immigration Law and Procedure* (1959), pp. 466–468. A list of the principal crimes that have been held to involve moral turpitude is given by Frank Auerbach, *Immigration Laws of the United States,* 2d ed. (Indianapolis: Bobbs-Merrill, 1961), p. 279.

[31]For a list of the diseases in question, see Auerbach, *Immigration Laws,* p. 276, or Gordon and Rosenfield, *Immigration Law and Procedure,* p. 237.

Persons considered likely to become public charges form one of the oldest excludable classes, for their excludability dates from the Immigration Act of 1882. Obviously the likelihood cannot be precisely measured or determined, involving as it does a judgment as to the probability of some future event; and the wording of the provision in the 1952 Act makes clear that exclusion for this reason depends on administrative judgment, the excludable class being defined as

> Aliens who, in the opinion of the consular officer at the time of application for a visa, or in the opinion of the Attorney General at the time of application for admission, are likely at any time to become public charges. (Sect. 212[a][15] of the 1952 Act)

The excluding decision, however, is to be based on such relevant factors and considerations as are appropriate to each case. According to a statement of the procedure,

> The evaluation usually will take into account, among other things, the alien's age, mental and physical condition, the presence of friends or relatives in this country, and his willingness to find useful employment.[32]

The weight given to these and other factors necessarily varies with employment and economic conditions at the time.

To consider one other general provision, there is the 1917 Act's exclusion of aliens with "constitutional psychopathic inferiority." When first proposed to Congress in a bill for the regulation of immigration, the phrase was said by the House committee to have a well-defined meaning among alienists,[33] and to apply to "a congenital defect . . . which results in inability to make proper adjustment to the environments." In 1952 it was replaced by the briefer but not necessarily more readily definable "psychopathic personality." The latter has been described as "inherent personality derangements, rather than mental or emotional symptoms," and as "developmental defects or pathological trends in the personality structure manifest by life-long patterns of action or behavior."[34] Diagnosis of such a condition obviously would have to be made professionally rather than by a consular or immigration official. And in practice the phrase has been interpreted to include sexual deviation.

Other examples of the use of broad and general terms in immigra-

[32]Gordon and Rosenfield, *Immigration Law and Procedure*, pp. 241–42; see further pp. 238–45 for their treatment of the public charge provision.

[33]See pp. 162, 164 above.

[34]Gordon and Rosenfield, *Immigration Law and Procedure*, p. 233; Auerbach, *Immigration Laws*, p. 274.

tion law could be found, but these four serve to illustrate this type of phraseology. With the use of such terms by Congress, responsibility devolves on administrative personnel to interpret and define the terms, and further defining may follow in the form of court decisions that seek to clarify the intention of Congress. The question that arises is what purpose is served by such broad directives in immigration law? It may be, in the case of the excluding provisions dealt with above, that Congress merely envisaged the excluding of certain broad classes or types of aliens, did not wish to try to define them more closely, and left it to the discretion of the immigration authorities to translate the general directive into operational terms. Also, other and longer-range purposes may be served by the broad terms of certain provisions, for the wording allows the interpretation to vary as conditions change. Likelihood of becoming a public charge is a very different thing during a period of economic difficulty and in times of prosperity. In fact, this provision was more strictly interpreted during the Depression years than it had been previously. Also, what was a dangerous disease at one time may cease to be so if there are advances in prevention, diagnosis, and treatment. Thus the nonspecific language used in the above instances gives a degree of flexibility to immigration law.[35] The response to changing conditions can be much more prompt, in the form of revised regulations or administrative procedures, than by the lengthy and uncertain process of getting an amending bill through Congress.

Policy of Public Record

Another unstated but fully developed and implemented policy of Congress is that decisions with respect to immigration and aliens shall not be made "away from public scrutiny," but rather that the rules governing admissions, exclusions, and related matters shall be a matter of public record.[36] Much of immigration law, as described in a preceding section, is specific and detailed, and beyond the wording of the statutes is the thinking of Congress as published in the *Congressional Record* of debates and in committee reports. Judicial decisions in clarification or interpretation of the law are likewise published and matters of record, as are precedent-setting decisions by the Board of Immigration Appeals and, on occasion, boards of special inquiry. Administrative regulations, dealing for the most part with procedural matters, are on record in the *Code of Federal Regulations,* with revisions reported on a current basis in the *Federal*

[35]See further on the subject of flexibility of immigration law in the next chapter.

[36]For reference to the Administrative Procedure Act of June 11, 1946, see p. 383 above.

Register. And decisions on individual cases that are not consistent with law and regulation can be challenged in the courts.

The policy of having publicly stated rules governing admissions, exclusions, deportations, and other related matters is altogether desirable, making as it does the regulation of immigration as nearly as possible an open and impartial process. But at the same time it incurs the risk of undue rigidity and inflexibility in the treatment of individual aliens if all are treated by formula according to the strict letter of the law. Individual cases occur in endless diversity, as one can see by looking at some of the hundreds of cases reported by the Board of Immigration Appeals, and so strict uniformity of treatment could cause much greater hardship in one case than in another. From humanitarian considerations as well as consideration of hardship to the alien and his relatives, there is need for some degree of flexibility regarding the exclusion, deportation, or other treatment of aliens. The impossibility of writing legislation that anticipates all types of cases, and the need for some degree of flexibility in the application of immigration law, has indeed been recognized by Congress. Some provisions for discretion and flexibility have been noted in the present chapter, and additional elements of flexibility devised by Congress are described in the chapter that follows.

20 Elements of Flexibility

As the preceding chapter has described, Congress long ago adopted and maintained a de facto policy of immigration controlled through legislation and has given only limited discretionary authority to the immigration officials. Whatever the advantages of this from a congressional viewpoint, such as making explicit the will of Congress in an important area of policy and correspondingly limiting bureaucratic authority, there is on the other hand a certain inherent danger of undue inflexibility. If policy is set by enactment, its change is through the cumbersome, usually slow, and uncertain legislative process; and there is also the danger that the treatment of the individual alien may be legalistic and formal, without sufficient responsiveness to exceptional circumstances and special considerations.

The full rigor of the law is mitigated for the alien in two general ways. As has been seen, a measure of discretionary power in the treatment of individual cases is given to the immigration officials. And although there is no formal policy for such action, in actual practice a number of provisions and opportunities for flexibility have been introduced into immigration law and procedures. Certain of these elements of flexibility have been noted in other connections. Decisions made by consular officers, the Attorney General, or his representatives on questions of admissibility, good moral character, whether "beneficial to the national welfare," "prejudicial to the public interest," of adverse effect on wages and working conditions, and so on, are made with due consideration and investigation of each case at hand. Adverse decisions can be appealed, as from the immigrant inspector at a port of entry to a local board of special inquiry. And as previously noted, the phrasing of certain exclusion provisions in very general terms permits some latitude of interpretation at any given time and revised interpretation in the course of time as changed conditions dictate.

Beyond such latitude of judgment and interpretation within the terms of the immigration law are certain specific provisions written into the law. It would appear that Congress has been aware that strict application of the law could work undue hardship in some cases, and thus has inserted certain provisions that can be used to soften the rigor of the law in deserving cases. Such provisions concern the admission of certain aliens who are technically excludable and suspension of the deportation of certain aliens who are technically deportable.

Admission under Bond

A first procedure for permitting the admission of technically excludable aliens or those of doubtful admissibility has been that of admission under bond. Two types of bond can be recognized: an indemnity bond in the case of aliens considered likely to become public charges and a departure bond to ensure the due departure of aliens admitted temporarily.

It was seen in an earlier chapter that bonding against eventual dependency was established in certain state legislation on immigration. In federal legislation the Immigration Act of 1907 provided for the admission under bond of

> any alien liable to be excluded because likely to become a public charge or because of physical disability other than tuberculosis or a loathsome or dangerous contagious disease . . . if otherwise admissible. (Sect. 26, 1907 Act [34 Stat. 898])

Such admission was to be at the discretion of the Secretary of Commerce and Labor, who was to set the amount of the bond. The purpose of the bond, as in earlier practice, was to indemnify the public authority concerned if the alien in question became a public charge. The same provision was repeated in the Immigration Act of 1917, with the alternatives of substituting an "undertaking" or cash deposit in place of a bond, and "tuberculosis in any form" was now specified (sect. 21). Except for the addition of leprosy as a disqualifying disease, the provision was continued by the 1952 Act (sect. 213).

As regards the bonding of aliens temporarily admitted, such provision for "otherwise inadmissible aliens" to ensure their later departure was contained in the Immigration Act of 1917 (ninth proviso, sect. 3). A 1932 act authorized the Secretary of Labor to require bond when deemed necessary in the case of instrumental musicians who were coming for a temporary period and were exempt from the contract labor laws.[1] And the power of the Attorney General "to control and regulate the admission and return of excludable aliens applying for temporary admission," including the exaction of bonds if necessary, was affirmed in the 1952 Act (sect. 212[d][6]).

[1]Sect. 3 of the Act of March 17, 1932 (47 Stat. 67).

Seventh and Ninth Provisos

The two provisos,[2] contained in section 3 of the Immigration Act of 1917, provided relief in the form of admissibility for two classes of aliens, at the discretion of the Secretary of Labor (the Attorney General from June 14, 1940). The seventh proviso stated that

> aliens returning after a temporary absence to an unrelinquished United States domicile of seven consecutive years may be admitted in the discretion of the Secretary of Labor, and under such conditions as he may prescribe.

Such admission was later denied to aliens regarded as subversive, under the terms of the Internal Security Act of September 23, 1950 (sect. 6a). The 1952 Act reaffirmed the power of the Attorney General to admit returning aliens as under the seventh proviso, except for those excludable as members of one of the subversive classes (sect. 212c).

The ninth proviso concerned aliens applying for temporary admission. It directed that the Commissioner of Immigration and Naturalization, with the approval of the cabinet officer his superior,

> shall issue rules and prescribe conditions, including exaction of such bonds as may be necessary, to control and regulate the admission and return of otherwise inadmissible aliens applying for temporary admission. (Sect. 3 of 1917 Act)

Like the seventh proviso, this was amended by the Internal Security Act of 1950 to exclude certain subversive classes of aliens from temporary admission under the proviso (sect. 22). The terms of the proviso as so amended were continued by the 1952 Act.[3]

The effect of the 1917 provisos and of the corresponding provisions of the 1952 Act is thus to waive many of the grounds for exclusion, with the exception of certain subversive classes, at the discretion of the Attorney General in the case of aliens applying for temporary admission and aliens who have had an unrelinquished domicile of seven consecutive years in the United States and are returning after a temporary visit abroad. The effect, it should be emphasized, is not to vitiate the excluding

[2]See also p. 549 above on the provisos.

[3]Sect. 212(d)(3) of the 1952 Act, which provides that with the exception of certain subversive classes, "an alien (A) who is applying for a nonimmigrant visa and is known or believed by the consular officer to be ineligible for such visa . . . may, after approval by the Attorney General of a recommendation by the Secretary of State or by the consular officer that the alien be admitted temporarily despite his inadmissibility, be granted such a visa . . . or (B) who is inadmissible . . . but who is in possession of appropriate documents or is granted a waiver thereof and is seeking admission, may be admitted (temporarily)."

provisions of the law but rather to prevent their being absolute barriers to admission and to provide a mechanism for their waiver in the case of aliens judged to be worthy of admission.

Entry under Parole

The authority to parole in[4] aliens temporarily, given to the Attorney General by the 1952 Act, was mentioned in the preceding chapter as a grant by Congress of discretionary power.[5] Actually the parole procedure was not new, for limited numbers of technically inadmissible aliens had been paroled in many years previously by immigration officials and the Board of Immigration Appeals. Without specific authorization for such action in immigration law, paroling in had been used in cases of particular necessity such as when an alien was in need of medical treatment. Aliens so allowed to enter were technically not admitted, they were not included in the immigration statistics, and the presumption was that they would depart as soon as the purpose of their entry was accomplished.

Statutory authority to parole in aliens where such action was deemed in the public interest or called for in an emergency was given to the Attorney General by the 1952 Act.[6] It was made clear by the terms of the act that the paroled alien is to be allowed to stay only temporarily, is not admitted either as an immigrant or nonimmigrant, and must depart when the purpose of the parole has been served.

Once established by law, the parole power was recognized to be a flexible means of allowing the entry of necessitous and deserving aliens who sought admission but were barred by existing law. Beyond the previous parole practice and perhaps beyond the original intent of Congress, parole came to be used extensively for the admission of certain classes of refugees; and Congress eventually accepted such use of the parole power.[7]

A first such use of the parole power was in aid of certain alien orphans. The Refugee Relief Act of August 7, 1953 as previously described provided for the issuance of not more than 4,000 special non-quota immigrant visas to orphans under ten years of age adopted or to be adopted by American citizens, with the terminal date for the issuance of these and other visas under authority of the act on December 31, 1956

[4]The term "parole" is also used in the usual sense in the case of an alien who is arrested or under order of deportation, who may be kept in custody, released under bond, or released on parole.

[5]See p. 550 above.

[6]Sect. 212(d)(5) of the Act; quoted on p. 550 above.

[7]Some alien temporary laborers are also admitted under parole.

(sect. 5a and 20). The allocation of the 4,000 visas was exhausted several months before expiration of the act, and there remained many additional eligible orphans who were inadmissible because the quotas to which they would have to be charged were already filled. In this emergency the service paroled 923 orphans into the custody of their adoptive parents in the United States.[8] The later adjustment of the status of these parolees to that of admission for permanent residence was authorized by the Act of September 11, 1957 (sect. 4d).

A second refugee group to be paroled into the United States under authorization granted to the Attorney General by section 212(d)(5) of the 1952 Act was that of Hungarians who had fled from their country following the uprising in the fall of 1956.[9] Parole of the Hungarian refugees terminated on December 31, 1957. A total of 31,915 were paroled in between November 1956 and June 30, 1958, and during the same period an additional 6,130 Hungarian refugees were admitted under section 4(a)(2) of the Refugee Relief Act of 1953.[10]

By far the greatest use of the parole procedure has been in the case of Cuban refugees. Statistics of the number of such parolees have not been routinely tabulated in the reports of the Immigration and Naturalization Service, but the Service does give a total of 621,403 Cuban nationals coming to the United States between January 1, 1959 and June 30, 1972.[11] It can be assumed that parolees made up the great majority.

Further use of the parole procedure was authorized by the Act of July 14, 1960 (74 Stat. 504), which empowered the Attorney General to parole in alien refugee-escapees,[12] on the condition that the aliens (1) apply for parole while physically present in a country neither Communist, Communist dominated, or Communist occupied, (2) are not nationals of the country where the parole application is made, and (3) are within the mandate of the United Nations High Commissioner for Refugees (sect. 1). The number paroled in during any six-month period was not to exceed one-fourth of the total number of refugee-escapees resettled in other countries during the preceding six months, and the program was

[8]INS, *Annual Report,* 1957, p. 6.

[9]Concerning the circumstances of the paroling in of the Hungarian refugees, see Frank Auerbach, *Immigration Laws of the United States* (Indianapolis: Bobbs-Merrill, 1961), p. 373–74.

[10]INS *Annual Report*, 1958, table 10B.

[11]INS, *Annual Report,* 1972, p. 3.

[12]Defined by sect. 15(c)(1) of the Act of September 11, 1957 (71 Stat. 639) as "any alien who, because of persecution or fear of persecution on account of race, religion, or political opinion has fled or shall flee (A) from any Communist, Communist-dominated, or Communist-occupied area, or (B) from any country within the general area of the Middle East and who cannot return to such area, on account of race, religion, or political opinion.

to end on July 1, 1962.[13] In addition, permission was given for the paroling in of 500 refugee-escapees classified as "difficult to resettle" by the High Commissioner for Refugees, subject to the provision that a recognized organization found that the alien in question could become self-supporting with due assistance, or that he was "a member of a family unit capable of becoming self-supporting" (sect. 2b). The number of refugee-escapees paroled in under the 1960 Act, between July 14, 1960 and June 30, 1962 was 8,260.[14]

Change of Status after Entry

Congressional and administrative action has made it possible for an alien to acquire the status of lawful admission for permanent residence after his entry into the United States. Relief is thereby provided for two quite different types of case. One is the alien who has been admitted for a temporary stay only, but later seeks to become a permanent resident. The other is the alien who lacks a record of lawful admission for permanent residence, whether because of illegal entry or because unidentifiable in the immigration records, and who therefore cannot be naturalized. Over the years several procedures have been developed to aid deserving aliens in these circumstances.

The first step was taken in the Registry Act of March 2, 1929 (45 Stat. 1512), which provided for the creation of a record of admission for permanent residence (i.e., registry) where none existed in the case of aliens not ineligible to citizenship who met the following conditions:

1. entry prior to June 3, 1921;
2. continuous residence in the United States thereafter;
3. good moral character; and
4. not subject to deportation.

Admittedly, the effect of the act was to legitimate the entry of certain illegal aliens, but it was felt to be justified under the conditions set of at least eight years of continuous residence and a record of good character during that time.

Five years later the Act of June 8, 1934 (48 Stat. 926) extended the registry privilege to certain bona fide political and religious refugees who entered prior to July 1, 1933 and were without record of admission for permanent residence. The later Act of August 7, 1939 (53 Stat. 1243) amended the 1929 Act to advance the limiting date of entry from June

[13] Act of 1960, sect. 2a; time limit removed by the Act of June 18, 1962 (76 Stat. 124).
[14] INS, *Annual Report*, 1962, table 14A.

3, 1921 to July 1, 1924, corresponding then to a continuous residence of fifteen years or more. The latter date was reaffirmed by the Nationality Act of 1940 (sect. 328b [54 Stat. 1152]). The registry provision to create a record of lawful admission for permanent residence for those lacking such a record was continued unchanged by the 1952 Act (sect. 249), including the July 1, 1924 date which, by 1952, corresponded to twenty-eight or more years of residence.

More liberal terms of eligibility for the creation of a record of lawful admission were provided by the Act of August 8, 1958 (72 Stat. 546), in two respects. The limiting date for entry was advanced to June 28, 1940, the time at which the Alien Registration Act of 1940 took effect. And if the other conditions for eligibility were met, deportability under the 1952 Act was no longer a barrier to registry except in the case of "criminals, procurers and other immoral persons, subversives, violators of the narcotic laws or smugglers of aliens." Some years later the Act of October 3, 1965 extended the limiting date to June 30, 1948 (sect. 19).

Aliens for whom a record of lawful entry is created are now added to the total of nonquota immigrants for the year in which the action is taken, although actually they must have entered many years before. The number of such aliens was included in the reported immigration total (classified as "Aliens adjusted under Sec. 249, Immigration and Nationality Act"), beginning with the fiscal year ending June 30, 1959. The number averaged somewhat above 4,000 per annum for the five-year period 1959–1963, and ten years later dropped to an annual average of a little over 1,400 for the years 1969 through 1973.

A second procedure to accomplish the same purpose—to change status from temporary to permanent admission or for regularization of the status of aliens without record of lawful admission—was provided by administrative regulation in 1935. That was by means of so-called preexamination to determine admissibility, departure to Canada, securing of an immigration visa from an American consular official there, and then readmission to the United States.[15] Previously, such change of status had been legally obtainable by return of the alien to his country of origin and application there for an immigrant visa, without assurance that he would be found admissible. The preexamination procedure was devised to spare the alien that trouble and uncertainty, but it was conditional upon a finding that the alien was in fact admissible and that a quota number if needed was available for him.

The granting of preexamination was suspended for a time on the

[15]For detailed account of the preexamination procedure, see Charles Gordon and Harry Rosenfield, *Immigration Law and Procedure* (1959), sect. 7.3, pp. 711–21.

provision in the 1952 Act (sect. 245) of adjustment of status without departure and reentry; but when the terms of eligibility for such adjustment of status under the 1952 Act were found to be more restrictive than those under the earlier procedure, preexamination was resumed in 1955 and continued until June 30, 1959,[16] by which time the relevant section of the 1952 Act had been amended as described more fully below.

In the fiscal year 1959, 2,241 aliens were admitted under the preexamination procedure.[17] During the immediately preceding years, annual admissions under preexamination had ranged from approximately 3,000 to nearly 5,000. Such admissions were included in the immigration total for the year, classified as quota or nonquota admissions according to the alien's status.

The 1952 Act, as noted above, provided statutory authorization for the adjustment of status to that of admission for permanent residence without the necessity of departure and return. The adjustment was available only to "aliens who entered the United States in good faith as nonimmigrants" (that is, were lawfully admitted on a temporary basis, and had not entered illegally), who were found to qualify for permanent residence, and for whom a quota or nonquota visa was available both at the time of application for adjustment and at the time of approval of the application. The act was also interpreted to deny adjustment of status to aliens who were natives of the nonquota countries of the Western Hemisphere.[18] Furthermore, those claiming nonquota status as a child or spouse of a citizen of the United States must have been in the United States for at least one year prior to acquisition of that status (sect. 245 of the 1952 Act [66 Stat. 163]).

These limitations on eligibility made the adjustment procedure more restrictive than preexamination had been, and, as previously noted, the latter procedure was reestablished until the 1952 Act could be modified. Amendment was made by the Act of August 21, 1958 (72 Stat. 699), which eliminated the one-year residence requirement for certain nonquota classes and made adjustment available to natives of Western Hemisphere countries except for contiguous countries and adjacent islands.[19] In 1960 the terms for adjustment were further liberalized to include aliens other than crewmen who had been inspected and admitted or paroled in, regardless of status at the time of application for adjustment

[16]INS, *Annual Report*, 1959, p. 4.

[17]Ibid.

[18]"Generally speaking, aliens who entered the United States as nonimmigrants are not eligible for adjustment under Sec. 245 if at the time of such entry they were entitled to nonquota visas by reason of birth in a nonquota country." INS, *Annual Report*, 1954, p. 29.

[19]Saint Pierre, Miquelon, Bermuda, the Bahamas, and the Caribbean islands (sect. 101[b][5] of the 1952 Act).

(sect. 10, Act of July 14, 1960 [74 Stat. 504]). In 1965, however, the provisions of the section of law dealing with adjustment of status were made inapplicable to "any alien who is a native of any country of the Western Hemisphere or of any adjacent island."[20]

Increasing use was made of the adjustment of status procedure since passage of the 1952 Act and later broadening of the terms of eligibility. In the fiscal year ending June 30, 1953, one year after passage of the 1952 Act, only 54 aliens adjusted their status from nonimmigrant to immigrant.[21] The number grew to 1,461 in the following year; and with continued growth attained an average of around 60,000 per annum in the fiscal years 1972 and 1973. Such adjustments are added to the immigration total for the year in which the adjustments are made and have come to contribute as much as one-sixth of all reported immigration.

In addition to the general provisions for adjustment of status noted above, Congress from time to time attached terms for eventual adjustment in legislation for the admission of certain special groups. The Displaced Persons Act of June 25, 1948 provided that an alien might apply to the Attorney General within two years after the effective date of the act for adjustment of status if he met the following conditions:

1. entry prior to April 1, 1948;
2. admissible under the immigration laws;
3. a displaced person residing in the United States.

Upon consideration of "all the facts and circumstances of the case" and determination that the alien had met the above conditions, the Attorney General was then to report the cases of qualified aliens to Congress. If within a specified period Congress passed a concurrent resolution of approval, the aliens were to be recorded as admitted for permanent residence; but if no such resolution was passed, the aliens were to be deported forthwith. The number of such adjustments was limited to 15,000, and those of aliens who were members of a quota class at time of entry were to be charged to the quota of the current year or a succeeding year for which quota numbers were available (sect. 4a of the 1948 Act [62 Stat. 1009]). Amendment in 1950 (sect. 5, Act of June 16, 1950 [64 Stat. 219]) extended the life of the adjustment provision to two years after the effective date of the act as amended, but the number of admissions allowed was not increased.

Further provision of adjustment of status was contained in the Refu-

[20]Section 13b of the Act of October 3, 1965 (79 Stat. 911).
[21]INS, *Annual Report*, 1953, p. 38.

gee Relief Act of 1953, under terms similar to those of the Displaced Persons Act of 1948. The conditions of eligibility were

1. lawful admission into the United States as a bona fide nonimmigrant prior to July 1, 1953;
2. inability to return to country of birth, nationality, or last residence "because of persecution or fear of persecution on account of race, religion, or political opinion";
3. determination by the Attorney General that the alien has been of good moral character for the preceding five years;
4. physical presence in the United States on the date of enactment of the act (August 7, 1953); and
5. qualified for admission except that no quota number is available.

Application to the Attorney General was to be made within one year of the effective date of the act; eligible cases were to be reported to Congress and were to be given permanent admission status if Congress gave approval in the form of a concurrent resolution. Deportation was to take place if the approval of Congress was not forthcoming (sect. 6 of the Act of August 7, 1953 [67 Stat. 400]).

The next special provision for adjustment was contained in an amending act in 1957, one section of which authorized the Attorney General to adjust the status of certain orphans paroled into the United States, provided that the orphans in question were adopted then or later by a citizen of the United States.[22] Another section of the act authorized the Attorney General to adjust the status of an alien and his spouse and children if they were physically present in the United States and he had been admitted as a highly qualified immigrant in the first preference category under the 1952 Act.[23] A third section of the act provided for the same action with respect to certain foreign government representatives and officials who had failed to maintain such official status, on condition of a finding of good moral character and admissibility for permanent residence. Report of each case was to be made to Congress, with admission for permanent residence to be granted unless a resolution of disapproval was passed by Congress within a specified time. Each such adjust-

[22]Sect. 4d of the Act of September 11, 1957 (71 Stat. 639). The orphans concerned were those admitted under sect. 212(d)(5) of the 1952 Act, and at entry they were "eligible orphans" as defined by sect. 5 of the Refugee Relief Act of 1953.

[23]Sect. 9 of the 1957 Act. The eligible aliens were those admitted under sect. 203(a)(1)(A) of the 1952 Act, defined there as aliens "whose services are determined by the Attorney General to be needed urgently in the United States because of the high education, technical training, specialized experience, or exceptional ability of such immigrants and to be substantially beneficial prospectively to the national economy, cultural interests, or welfare of the United States."

ment was to be charged to the appropriate quota if the alien in question belonged to a quota class; such admissions were limited to fifty in any fiscal year (sect. 13 of the 1957 Act).

In 1960 a further act granted the status of lawful admission for permanent residence to refugee-escapees whose parole had not been terminated, who had not yet acquired permanent residence, and who on inspection were found to be admissible under the 1952 Act except for lack of the required documents (sect. 3 and 4, Act of July 14, 1960 [74 Stat. 504]).[24]

Suspension of Deportation

The preceding section dealt with means whereby aliens can have their status adjusted to that of lawfully admitted for permanent residence if they meet certain conditions of eligibility. That form of relief from the strict terms of the law has not been available generally to aliens found to be deportable; but for such deportable aliens Congress has provided a measure of flexibility and relief in the form of provision for the suspension of deportation as a step toward the granting of permanent status, under certain safeguards and provided certain conditions of eligibility are met.

The present provision for suspension of deportation leading to adjustment of status is of fairly recent origin, established by the Alien Registration Act of 1940. Authorization for the suspension of deportation was indeed available earlier but in the form of a temporary suspension or stay of deportation. The earliest such authorization was contained in the early Act of June 25, 1798 (1 Stat. 570), which gave to the President the authority to order the departure of any alien judged dangerous to the peace and safety of the nation; but contained in the same section of the act was the proviso that if any alien under order to depart satisfies the President that he is not in fact a danger to the United States, the President "may grant a license to such alien to remain . . . for such time as he shall judge proper." The act expired at the end of its two-year term, and provision for suspension of deportation was not to reappear for many years. It was not until the Act of March 3, 1903 (32 Stat. 1213) that a section dealing with the return of illegally landed aliens (sect. 19) con-

[24]One year after the cut-off date of this account, the Act of November 2, 1966 (80 Stat. 1161) granted adjustment of status to "any alien who is a native or citizen of Cuba and who has been inspected and admitted or paroled into the United States subsequent to January 1, 1959, and has been physically present . . . for at least two years." Spouses and children residing with such aliens were also included.

tained the cautious proviso that the Commissioner-General of Immigration, with the direction or approval of the Secretary of Commerce and Labor and upon conditions prescribed by the Commissioner-General and the act, may suspend the deportation of an alien found to have violated the sections of the act dealing with contract labor if the testimony of the alien is judged to be necessary for the prosecution of any person or organization accused of violation of the contract labor laws. A similar proviso was included in section 19 of the later Act of February 20, 1907 (34 Stat. 898), but it was now broadened to include aliens whose testimony was necessary in the prosecution of offenders against any part of the act. The suspension of deportation so provided for in these acts was in fact temporary rather than a cancellation of deportation proceedings, and the alien in question was presumably to be deported after testifying.

Suspension of deportation was given a new meaning by the Alien Registration Act of 1940, which made the suspension a step toward adjustment of status to that of permanent resident. The act provided that deportable aliens who could prove good moral character during the preceding five years were to be allowed to depart voluntarily at their own expense[25] or alternatively could be granted suspension of deportation if admissible and eligible to naturalization; but such relief was denied to deportable aliens of the subversive, narcotic, criminal, immoral, mental defective, anarchist, and similar classes; it was also denied to aliens made deportable by the 1940 Act because of aiding other aliens to enter illegally, violation of a firearms control law, or found guilty of certain subversive acts enumerated in Title I of the 1940 Act. A condition for the suspension was proof that deportation would result in "serious economic detriment to a citizen or legally resident alien who is the spouse, parent, or minor child of such deportable alien" (sect. 20). Suspensions of more than six months by the Attorney General were to be reported by him to Congress, with deportation to follow if Congress passed a concurrent resolution disapproving of the suspension. If Congress did not disapprove, the alien's admission for permanent residence was to be recorded as of the date of last entry into the United States and charged to the appropriate quota.[26] A later act in 1948 made suspension available to aliens who could prove seven years of continuous residence up to the effective date of the act, whether or not deportation might be to the detriment of family members (Act of July 1, 1948 [62 Stat. 1206]).

In response to objections to what were considered the lenient terms

[25]See next section, pp. 571–72.

[26]The Act of December 8, 1942 (56 Stat. 1044) amended the time period within which Congress might take action.

of the 1940 Act as amended, the Immigration and Nationality Act of 1952 redefined the terms of eligibility for suspension of deportation. Required of applicants for suspension were proof of good moral character for a specified period during which the alien must have been resident in the United States and evidence that deportation would cause extreme hardship; but now such hardship to the alien himself and not only to immediate relatives was to be taken into consideration. Such eligible aliens were further divided into five classes according to several criteria and with the conditions for suspension set separately for each class. Members of the first three classes, who must have had at least five or seven years of continuous residence in the United States and generally whose cause for deportability would not have made them ineligible for suspension under the 1940 Act, might have their deportation suspended by the Attorney General unless Congress passed a resolution of disapproval within an appointed time. Members of the two other classes were generally those deportable for causes that would have disqualified them for suspension under the 1940 Act; and to be eligible under the 1952 Act must have had not less than ten years of continuous residence. Unlike the preceding classes, their deportation could be suspended only on the recommendation of the Attorney General and affirmative action in the form of a concurrent resolution passed by Congress.[27]

[27]Sect. 244(a), (b), and (c) of the 1952 Act. For further treatment of suspension see Auerbach, *Immigration Laws,* chap. 47; Gordon and Rosenfield, *Immigration Law and Procedure,* sect. 7.9, pp. 758–93. The definitions of the five classes, in abbreviated form and in addition to the conditions already noted, were as follows:

1. Last entered the United States prior to June 27, 1950; continuous residence in the United States for at least seven years prior to application for suspension of deportation; and deportable on grounds other than those included under (4) below.

2. Last entered at any time after June 26, 1950; deportable solely for an act committed or status existing prior to or at time of entry, and not of a deportable class included under (4) below; continuous residence of at least five years prior to application for suspension; and has not been served with a final order of deportation up to time of application.

3. Last entered at any time after June 26, 1950; deportable for an act committed or status acquired subsequent to entry; and not belonging to class (4) or (5) below; continuous residence of at least five years since incurring deportability; and has not been served with a final order of deportation prior to application.

4. Last entered at any time after June 26, 1950; deportable on grounds of criminality, immorality, subversion, narcotic violation, or illegal entry without inspection or without proper documents; continuous residence of at least ten years after such entry; and has not been served with a final order of deportation prior to application.

5. Deportable on certain specified grounds including crime involving moral turpitude, subversion, narcotic violation, and firearms violation arising subsequent to entry, or has overstayed period for which admitted; continuous residence of at least ten years since incurring deportability; and has not been served with a final order of deportation prior to application.

The number of aliens availing themselves of the opportunity for suspension of deportation rose rapidly after passage of the 1940 Act. Between the June 28, 1940 date of the act and the end of the 76th Congress on the following January 3, a total of 120 cases were submitted for congressional action. Approximately 700 more cases were reported to the next Congress up to the end of the fiscal year on June 30, 1942. By that time a backlog of several thousand applications for suspension of deportation had accumulated for consideration in the next fiscal year.[28] Suspensions granted to aliens averaged nearly 3,000 a year through the fiscal year 1948. Following the liberalizing amendment made by the Act of July 1, 1948, the number of cases submitted to Congress averaged in excess of 4,300 per annum in the immediately following years.[29] For the four fiscal years 1950 through 1953, 21,097 suspension cases were submitted to Congress, of which 14,071 or two-thirds were approved.[30] Since then the number of suspensions has diminished, however, to average only a few hundred cases a year in the early 1970s.

Voluntary Departure

As stated in the preceding section,[31] the Alien Registration Act of 1940 provided two alternative forms of relief for certain aliens who were deportable: suspension of deportation as just described and voluntary departure at their own expense.[32] Eligibility for voluntary departure at the discretion of the Attorney General was the same as for suspension of deportation: good moral character for the preceding five years, and deportability on other than subversive, narcotic, criminal, immoral, mental, anarchist, or related grounds, or on grounds for deportation added by the 1940 Act.[33] Twelve years later the 1952 Act continued the provision for voluntary departure.

Voluntary departure of deportable aliens at their own expense presented advantages for all concerned. From the administrative viewpoint it saved the trouble and expense of deportation proceedings; for the alien

[28]*Annual Report* of Lemuel B. Schofield, Special Assistant to the Attorney General in charge of the INS, year ending June 30, 1942, p. 17.

[29]INS, *Annual Reports,* 1949 and 1950.

[30]INS, *Annual Report,* 1953, p. 35.

[31]See p. 569 above.

[32]Sect. 20 of the 1940 Act (54 Stat. 670), which amended the 1917 Act by addition of three new subsections to sect. 19 of the latter. Concerning administrative procedures for voluntary departure, see Gordon and Rosenfield, *Immigration Law and Procedure,* pp. 703–11; Auerbach, *Immigration Laws,* chap. 46, sect. 13, pp. 442–44.

[33]The deportable classes added by Title I of the 1940 Act were aliens who aid other aliens to enter illegally, who are convicted of violation of a firearms control law, or convicted of certain subversive acts.

it offered the advantages of avoiding a record of deportation, gave opportunity for later readmission, and allowed choice of the manner and destination of departure. The procedure had in fact been instituted on an informal basis by immigration officials as early as 1925 or soon after, long before formal provision was made by Congress.[34] By the 1970s the terminology of the INS as used in the *Annual Reports* distinguished between two classes of aliens apprehended and expelled—those deported and those "required to depart," of which the latter corresponds to the earlier category of voluntary departure.

Serving a useful purpose, voluntary departure has been a much used procedure since its inception. As reported by the INS the number of cases per decade has been as follows:[35]

1921–1930	72,233
1931–1940	93,330
1941–1950	1,470,925
1951–1960	3,883,660
1961–1970	1,334,528

The above total for the first decade presumably covers only the last four years, 1927 to 1930 inclusive. The number of cases rose rapidly during the 1940s, by which time up to 98 percent of the departures were from the Mexican border districts. Such departures thereafter have fluctuated with wage differentials between Mexico and the United States and with border crossing control. A maximum of over one million such departures was recorded in the fiscal year 1954; and since 1970 the number has averaged 450,000 or more per annum.[36]

[34]Chart G, p. 115 of INS, *Annual Report,* 1945, indicates the first voluntary departures in 1925 or 1926, but no totals are given. Recent *Annual Reports* state that such departures were first recorded in 1927.

[35]INS, *Annual Report,* 1973, p. 78.

[36]In addition to the voluntary departure of deportable aliens at their own expense, there has been provision for the removal at government expense of certain aliens who "fall into distress or need public aid from causes arising subsequent to their entry and are desirous of being so removed." This provision was made in sect. 23 of the 1917 Act for removal to the alien's native country within three years after entry. Amendment by the Act of May 14, 1937 (50 Stat. 164) extended the removal to any time after entry and to include "the country from whence they came, or . . . the country of which they are citizens or subjects." But any alien so removed "shall forever be ineligible for readmission except upon the approval of the Secretary of State and the Attorney General."

Private Bill

A final measure of flexibility is provided by the private bill, the last recourse of the alien who is unable to gain admission, to escape deportation through regularization of his status, or to qualify for naturalization through any of the available forms of administrative relief. For a private bill to be introduced in Congress, a member of that body must first be convinced that an alien's case has merit and be persuaded to introduce a bill for relief of the alien. To achieve enactment the private bill must then follow the same difficult course as a public bill: referred to the House or Senate Judiciary Committee and then to its immigration subcommittee, reported out if approved in the subcommittee and then in the full committee, voted on and passed in the house of Congress where introduced, then through the same steps in the other house of Congress, and finally presidential approval.

In practice the House and Senate subcommittees do not consider a private bill unless the alien concerned has tried and failed to obtain relief through the other means available. Before consideration of a private bill, a report on the case is routinely sought from the administrative agency concerned: the State Department if an admissions case and the INS if a deportation or naturalization case.

A private bill if passed is final, in that it overrules any administrative action. Thus, in a deportation case it automatically confers suspension of deportation and adjustment of status; and the alien given permanent status is charged to the admission total for the appropriate class. On the other hand, the private bill offers very slender hope to the alien, for the proportion enacted is small. According to a recent report from the INS,[37] the number of private bills introduced in Congress from 1937 to 1973 has been nearly 55,000, of which approximately 6,300 were approved. During that period the number of private bills introduced rose to a maximum of over 7,000 in the 90th Congress (1967 and 1968) but fell to less than half that number in the 92nd Congress. The proportion approved, which ran as high as one-fourth or more in some sessions, has also declined to only about two percent of the bills introduced. Thus the private bill offers a last but only limited means of relief for the alien; but to the alien threatened with deportation it may nevertheless give substantial benefit through postponement of deportation proceedings pending action on the bill.[38]

[37]INS, *Annual Report,* 1973, table 56, p. 126.

[38]It is reported that the INS routinely defer deportation proceedings for a year if a private bill is introduced; and the year of grace so obtained may serve the alien's purpose even if the bill is not acted on favorably. Since 1969, however, the one-year deferral is no longer automatic.

Summary and Comment

As described in this chapter, Congress has gradually built certain elements of flexibility into the body of immigration and alien law. Such provisions are designed or can be used to meet emergencies that may arise from time to time, to deal with the great diversity of individual cases that may in part fall outside the specific terms of the law, to grant more lenient treatment to especially deserving aliens, and to prevent undue hardship that might be inflicted through strict application of the law.

One means of providing a measure of flexibility in the treatment of individual cases is the granting by Congress of discretionary authority to administrative officers, but that authority has typically been granted with clearly stated limits and with specification of the conditions of alien eligibility or ineligibility for such use of discretion. A second means of providing flexibility is through certain formal provisions, as described in this chapter.

These provisions, enacted by Congress, are in effect special exceptions to the immigration and alien laws, available to aliens who meet the stipulated conditions and are considered worthy of relief; and each is designed to meet a particular need on the part of aliens. One group of such provisions concerns the alien seeking admission and who is technically excludable. A first provision in such cases is admission under bond, either for indemnity if the alien becomes a public charge or as a guarantee of eventual departure of those aliens admitted only temporarily. Another provision is the seventh proviso for the readmission of aliens of seven or more years of residence in the United States. The ninth proviso permits the admission of certain otherwise inadmissible aliens on a temporary basis. And the parole power is available in still other cases to allow a de facto entry without formal admission, presumably for a temporary stay only but often in fact with the possibility of eventual admission on a permanent basis.

Other provisions provide relief for certain problems of aliens already in the United States. One problem is the lack of a record of lawful admission, either because of illegal entry, violation of the terms of admission, or some defect of the records. Available relief in such case, for those who qualify, is in the form of registry, the creation of a record of lawful admission that is a prerequisite for naturalization. Another procedure is adjustment of status from temporary admission, such as under a visitor's or student visa, to admission for permanent residence. For aliens actually under threat of deportation, recourse may be had to what is known as voluntary departure, which avoids the actual deportation that would constitute an impediment to subsequent application for admission. Or the deportable alien may apply for suspension of deportation, which if granted brings with it adjustment of status to that of permanent residence. Finally, if all else fails, there is the possibility of relief through a private bill introduced in Congress.

All these possible exceptions to the terms of the immigration and alien laws are of course limited by numerous conditions, available only to what are judged to be deserving aliens. Certain classes of aliens are generally excluded from such relief, particularly aliens of the subversive classes. But with such exceptions, the various provisions give a degree of flexibility in that the personal qualifications and record of an alien can be taken into consideration, not just the letter of the law. In favorable cases neither exclusion nor deportation are completely mandatory and beyond appeal.

Apart from the immediate purpose of these various provisions, there is an additional dimension of flexibility beyond the elements of flexibility in who is allowed to enter and who is allowed to stay. That further flexibility is in the number of aliens that can be admitted. It is true that Congress quite regularly stipulated that aliens who are admitted and aliens whose status is adjusted be charged to the appropriate quota if of a quota class. But the parole procedure is in at least temporary disregard of any quota limit, as in the case of the hundreds of thousands of Cuban refugees who were so permitted to enter. On eventual adjustment of status, however, the parolees may be charged to quota unless their numbers are such that an exception has to be made.

This body of exceptions to the immigration and alien laws can be variously appraised depending on one's point of view. From a restrictionist viewpoint it would doubtless be seen as providing loopholes in the law. One could also argue that the varied provisions of immigration law and the many means of relief that are available invite some abuses and make it possible for some aliens to delay or defeat the purpose of the law by lengthy appeals and legal proceedings. But on the other hand, if immigration and alien affairs are to be controlled largely by law rather than by more readily adjustable administrative regulations, some means need to be found to soften the application of the law, to make it responsive in individual cases to human considerations, and to make it sufficiently elastic to meet emergency situations as they arise.

21 The Instruments of Policy

Preceding chapters traced the development of some principal elements of immigration policy at the hands of Congress. Before concluding, however, there is another aspect of this congressional action that deserves separate mention. That is the measures or instruments of policy devised by Congress as legislative answers to problems that arise in the regulation of immigration.

The explicit objectives of immigration policy have been quite few and simple, such as to keep out undesirables, to limit the number of admissions, and to expel aliens found to be undesirable after entry. Some of the measures adopted to accomplish these objectives also have been quite direct and simple, such as the exclusion and deportation of designated classes of aliens. But other policy objectives and certain problems encountered in the regulation of immigration have not had simple or ready-made solutions, and therefore Congress has labored over the years to find effective but at the same time acceptable answers. The product of these labors is worth looking at, not only as evidence of the creative efforts of Congress, but also because immigration-related problems of the past are recurrent or are still with us today; and the record of past attempts can give some guidance for the present.

The chapter just preceding noted the apparent if unstated concern of Congress to provide some flexibility in the application of immigration law and described the various measures or instruments that do in fact give a degree of discretional flexibility. The present chapter presents other instances in which Congress, faced with problems related to immigration, has devised new measures or instruments of policy to deal with them. In the first instance, once Congress had accepted the principle of limiting the number of immigrants, it then had to devise a system for allocating the limited number of admissions in a manner consistent with its prevailing policy objectives and at the same time ensure that in the national interest aliens with desirable personal characteristics were not excluded. The congressional solution to this double problem is summarized in the following sections on Selectivity and Facilitated Entry.

But perhaps the immigration problem that has been most troublesome over the years has been that of enforcement, for some portions of the immigration laws have created difficulties of compliance, notably the contract labor laws of the 1880s and later, the Chinese exclusion laws of approximately the same period, the more recent legislation on subversives, and the efforts to prevent illegal immigration in general. The usual pattern of congressional reaction to the enforcement problem has been to amend and expand the laws in question, to make them more explicit and comprehensive, and to provide the immigration authorities with stronger and stronger powers. Additionally, Congress has sought to reinforce and strengthen portions of the regulatory system by means of new control measures or administrative procedures, as described below in the sections on personal identification of immigrants, advance (that is, consular) inspection, and imposition of liability on those who contribute to or facilitate an alien's violation of the immigration laws. On a different topic, a section on Disabilities of Resident Aliens is included to illustrate the great diversity and innovation of proposals introduced in bills in Congress, which with very few exceptions die in committee. As said before, what does not pass is part of the story of congressional action and the judgment exercised in formulating immigration policy.

Selectivity

The desire to pick and choose between the applicants for admission has pervaded the thinking of the immigration policy makers. The designation of certain classes of aliens as excludable is a form of selection, a negative sort of selection levied against those with specifiable defects of mind, health, ideology, or behavior; and such selectivity runs through much of admissions policy. But more broadly if less overtly, the policy makers have sought a mode of selection, not obviously invidious or discriminatory, that would sift out and admit the newcomers thought most likely to assimilate well and blend into the native population, while repressing the migration of those not possessing those desirable attributes. By the 1890s, when the volume and composition of immigration were such as to move Congress to action, the literacy test was seen as the answer to the problem of separating the desirables from the undesirables. Its anticipated virtues were several, for the test could be administered readily, and it would exclude the educationally deficient, who were thought to be deficient in certain other respects as well. It also possessed the advantage, according to its sponsors, of bearing most heavily on migration from southern and eastern Europe, regarded as generally less desirable than that from other parts of Europe; moreover, this admissions test was on the basis of a defensible criterion rather than being overtly discriminatory in national terms. The alternative device of an increased head tax was considered by the Dillingham Commission, which recognized some selective and limiting action of the tax but gave preference to the literacy test.

Only a few years after its adoption in 1917 the literacy test was found inadequate under postwar conditions to select and restrict as desired. Congress then quickly devised and adopted a new means of selective restriction, the quota formula of the 1921 Act, that allocated to each nation an annual immigration quota of 3 percent of the number of immigrants from that nation in the United States at the 1910 census. This formula, too, served the selective purpose of giving ample quotas to favored nations and minimal quotas to others; that purpose was even clearer in the 1924 revision of the quotas to 2 percent of the smaller and differently constituted foreign-born population of 1890. The latter was an interim formula, however, for the 1924 Act provided for an approximately equal amount of quota immigration to be allocated later according to the estimated national origin composition of the 1920 white population of the United States. Here again, with a plausible and apparently nondiscriminatory basis of allocation, the national origin system achieved a distribution very heavily weighted toward the most favored nations of origin.[1]

The continuing search by members of Congress for an admissions test or formula that would act selectively to favor certain classes of aliens and restrict others is indicated by some of the other measures proposed but not adopted. Thus amendment was offered to a literacy test bill in 1912 that the test be given only in a European language.[2] Later when the 1921 Quota Act was being considered, an alternative proposal was to base national quotas on the number of naturalized aliens from a country rather than on the total foreign-born population.[3] Many years after, during the Depression period, a bill was introduced to restrict immigration to those able to speak, read, and write the English language.[4] A few years thereafter an intelligence test for admission was proposed.[5] Of quite different effect would have been a 1959 bill to base quotas on a nation's population size.[6] And a later proposal was to base national quotas on actual immigration, again a formula to preserve the status quo.[7]

Selection, of course, did not end with the repeal of the national origins quota system in 1965. Only the basis of selection was changed, within the limits of a ceiling on quota immigration; and although the basis may be revised from time to time, selectivity may be regarded as a permanent element of immigration policy.

[1]No such care was taken of the sensibilities of Asiatics, who were totally excluded as immigrants by the Asiatic Barred Zone and later the Asia-Pacific triangle provisions.

[2]See p. 153 above.

[3]See p. 176 above.

[4]See p. 233 above.

[5]See p. 255 above.

[6]See p. 339 above.

[7]See p. 344 above.

Facilitated Entry

Selection is exercised not only by the exclusions and restrictions imposed on certain classes of aliens but also, on the positive side, by facilitated entry for other classes. As early as restrictions were put on admissions, Congress took care to provide exemptions for certain cases. Thus the contract labor laws from the beginning specifically exempted skilled workers of kinds not found in the United States, domestic servants, professional actors, artists, lecturers, and singers. A later amendment extended the exemption to ministers of any religious denomination, members of any recognized profession, and professors for colleges and seminaries (sect. 5, Act of March 3, 1891 [26 Stat. 1084]). At the same time political offenders were also given exemption from the contract labor laws. Years later the 1917 Act brought further restrictions in the form of the literacy test and the Asiatic Barred Zone but provided certain exemptions from each. And since that time immigration law has continued to give exemption or partial exemption from restrictive provisions to certain classes of aliens, especially religious and political refugees, persons with needed skills or professional qualifications, and close relatives of citizens or legally resident aliens.

The quota acts from 1921 onward brought a new form of restriction, but Congress again softened the impact on immigration by means of new exemptions and qualifications. Two principal instruments were employed by Congress to reduce the effect of the quota system: first, the granting of nonquota status to certain classes of aliens; second, the establishment of preference in the granting of immigration visas to certain other classes. Nonquota status, to summarize briefly, was given under the original Quota Act of 1921 to aliens under eighteen years who were the children of citizens and to aliens who had resided continuously in an independent Western Hemisphere country for at least one year[8] immediately preceding admission to the United States.[9] The next quota act in 1924 changed the principal nonquota classes of immigrants to aliens born in an independent country of the Western Hemisphere, together with unmarried children under eighteen years of age[10] and the spouse of a citizen, and aliens who had served as ministers or professors for two years preceding application for admission and who sought admission in order to continue practice of their profession. Spouses and unmarried children under eighteen years of age of such professors, ministers,

[8]Changed to five years of residence by the Act of May 11, 1922 (42 Stat. 540).

[9]Sect. 2(d) of the 1921 Quota Act allowed members of certain professions and domestic servants to be admitted even if their national quota was exhausted.

[10]Changed to twenty-one years by the Act of May 29, 1928 (45 Stat. 1009).

and natives of the Western Hemisphere were also to come in quota-free.

Thereafter bills were introduced from time to time to terminate the nonquota status of Mexicans or of all Latin Americans, but these were denied approval by Congress in the interests of "good neighbor" policy.[11] It was not to be until the 1965 Act that an overall ceiling of 120,000 per annum was put on Western Hemisphere immigration. Before then, however, some revision of the nonquota categories was made by the 1952 Act, which removed the twenty-one-year age limit on the quota-free admission of children of citizens, denied nonquota status to the professor class, and gave nonquota status to certain alien employees of the government abroad with fifteen or more years of service (sect. 10[a] [27] of the 1952 Act). The 1965 Act extended nonquota status to parents of citizens aged twenty-one or over (sect. 1). Those parents had constituted the second preference class under the 1952 Act.

The other means adopted by Congress to favor selected classes of aliens was to grant them preference, a prior claim in the issuance of quota visas. Very early in its work on the bill that became the first quota act in 1921,[12] Congress considered the device of preference in the issuance of visas as a means of giving favored treatment to certain aliens. As finally passed, the act directed that preference in the granting of visas under the act be given "so far as possible" to wives, parents, brothers, sisters, children under eighteen, and fiancées of citizens, lawfully admitted resident aliens, and aliens eligible to citizenship because of service in the armed forces during the period of United States engagement in World War I (last proviso, sect. 2d).

From this beginning, quota preference became more structured in later acts. The 1924 Quota Act directed that not more than one-half of each national quota was to be provided for a preference class made up of immigrants skilled in agriculture and of certain close relatives of citizens aged twenty-one or over.[13] The amending Act of May 29, 1928 set up two preference classes. The first, which received one-half of each national quota, incorporated part of the preference group established under the 1924 Act;[14] and the second, which received any remaining unused visas after the first preference classes, went to unmarried children under twenty-one years of age and wives of lawfully admitted alien resi-

[11]See for example pp. 204, 217, 236 above.

[12]See pp. 176, 179, 180 above.

[13]See p. 194 above.

[14]It consisted of the parents of citizens aged twenty-one or over, husbands of such citizens provided the marriage occurred after May 31, 1928, and quota immigrants skilled in agriculture together with their wives and dependent children under age eighteen. Later amendments changed the above marriage date to July 1, 1932, and then to January 1, 1948 (Acts of July 11, 1932, May 19, 1948).

dents. Any unused portion of a national quota after satisfaction of the first and second preferences was to be available to other eligible immigrants.

Some years later the Displaced Persons Act of June 25, 1948 provided that the quota preference in the 1924 Act as amended should not apply to displaced persons admitted under the new act and instead established three preference classes. First preference of at least 30 percent of visas provided by the act went to displaced persons previously engaged in agriculture, second preference to those with certain occupational qualifications, and third preference to certain blood relatives of citizens or lawfully resident aliens.[15]

The preference structure was elaborated further in the 1952 and 1965 Acts, for Congress had found preference to be a useful means of quota allocation that differentiated between one class of immigrant and another. The 1952 Act set up four preference classes and assigned 50 percent of the visas available under each national quota, plus any unused portion from other preferences, to a new preference class of immigrants considered to be "needed urgently in the United States" by reason of personal qualifications. Second and third preferences of 30 and 20 percent, respectively, went to certain close relatives of citizens and resident aliens; and one-fourth of any unused quota numbers was to be reserved for certain other relatives of citizens.[16] The 1965 Act introduced a still more complex preference structure consisting of seven classes. Two of them were on an occupational basis, for members of the professions and persons of "exceptional ability" in one class (10 percent) and skilled or unskilled workers of whom there is a shortage in the United States in the other (10 percent). Four preference classes were for certain relatives of citizens and resident aliens, assigned a total of 74 percent plus any unused portion of the occupational preferences; and a new seventh preference (6 percent) was for immigrants who qualified as refugees.[17]

Viewed together, nonquota status and quota preference can be seen as means chosen by Congress to modify the effect of the quota laws, to give selectivity within the framework of quota restriction of the number admitted, and to facilitate the entry of certain classes of immigrants. So favored have been aliens within certain degrees of relationship to citizens and to alien residents of the United States, aliens with occupational or

[15]For more detailed description of the three preference classes see sect. 6 of the 1948 Act or pp. 280–81 above. Amendment by the Act of June 16, 1950 reduced the preference classes to two in number by dropping the old first preference class and moving the former second to a new first preference class with the addition of farm workers to the list of occupations given preference.

[16]Sect. 203a of the 1952 Act. Or for description see pp. 308–9 above.

[17]Sect. 3 of the 1965 Act. Or for description see pp. 371–72 above.

other qualifications that make them especially desirable immigrants, and refugees. These are, in effect, the ones "whom we shall welcome," to use a phrase from the Truman Commission on Immigration and Naturalization. Criticism has at times been directed especially at nonquota status as undermining the principle of restriction of the number of aliens to be admitted; but imposition of an annual quota limit on Western Hemisphere immigration by the Act of 1965 has closed the widest door, and political or humanitarian considerations will no doubt continue to support facilitated entry of relatives and refugees.

Identification of Immigrants

It is in the area of enforcement of the immigration laws that some of the most pressing and persistent demands have been made on Congress; and although Congress has labored long with the problem and has considered and adopted many measures, enforcement has proved difficult and results disappointing. Of several approaches to the enforcement problem, personal identification of the immigrant is dealt with here and others in the several sections that follow.

The very first steps toward regulation and control of immigration created a need for recording and identification of the immigrants, to record who had been lawfully admitted, posted bond, or paid a head tax. Very early in the history of transatlantic immigration, some coastal states and port cities had kept lists of arrivals, and the early federal Act of March 2, 1819 had included a manifesting requirement that called only for the identifying items of name, sex, age, and occupation of passengers. In 1845 a bill to check naturalization frauds by means of a registry of aliens and description of each was proposed but not adopted.[18] Later acts[19] added to the information to be recorded. The Act of 1917 included on the manifest each alien's "personal description (including height, complexion, color of hair and eyes, and marks of identification)" (sect. 12). More recent acts have directed the collection of "such information . . . as necessary for the identification of the persons transported and for the enforcement of the immigration laws."[20]

The outstanding example of effort to obtain firm identification of each immigrant—and of failure of such effort—is provided by the legislation attempting to enforce Chinese exclusion. The first of the acts ex-

[18]See p. 33 above.

[19]See above, chapter 18, Information on Immigration.

[20]Act of July 30, 1947 (61 Stat. 630) amending sect. 12 of the 1917 Act; reaffirmed by sect. 231a of the 1952 Act (66 Stat. 163).

cluding Chinese laborers, in 1882, dealt with the identification of those already in the United States who might depart temporarily and then return,

> in order to furnish them with the proper evidence of their right to go from and come to the United States of their free will and accord, as provided by the treaty between the United States and China. . . . (Sect. 4, Act of May 6, 1882 [22 Stat. 58])

The collector of customs was charged with the duty of boarding ships about to depart with such Chinese laborers on board, to record in a registry book

> the name, age, occupation, last place of residence, physical marks or peculiarities, and all facts necessary for the identification of each of such Chinese laborers. . . .

On request they were to provide each Chinese laborer with a certificate bearing the above information. The certificate was to be surrendered on reentry as proof of right to be admitted (sect. 4). A similar certificate was to be issued to those departing by land (sect. 5). Chinese persons of the nonexcluded classes (not laborers) were to be provided by the Chinese government with a certificate of identification attesting to their right to come to the United States, and giving their name, title or rank, age, height, "all physical peculiarities," former and present occupation or profession, and place of residence in China (sect. 6). Penalties were provided for substituting names or otherwise altering or forging any identification certificates. A later section of the act required the master of any vessel arriving in the United States with Chinese passengers aboard to provide, in addition to the usual passenger list, a separate list or manifest of all the Chinese passengers, giving their names and other information obtained from their identification certificates (sect. 8).

The requirement of identification certificates was reaffirmed two years later with the addition, among other things, of a requirement in the case of the certificate of admissibility issued by the Chinese government for a nonlaborer Chinese, of an endorsement by a diplomatic representative of the United States, whose duty before making the endorsement was to satisfy himself as to the truth of the identifying information on the certificate.[21]

Acting on reports of continuing and large-scale evasion of the excluding provisions of the 1882 and 1884 Acts, Congress attempted to check the illegal flow with more stringent identification and other re-

[21]Act of July 5, 1884 (23 Stat. 115), amending sect. 6 of the 1882 Act.

quirements in an 1888 act. With regard to the certificate of identity for officials, students, and others entitled to enter temporarily, it was now to be made out by a consular representative of the United States rather than obtained from the Chinese government. The required personal description was much as before, but the certificate was to be made out in duplicate, one copy retained by the passenger, the other copy sealed and delivered to the captain of the transporting vessel for delivery by him to the collector of customs at the port of landing in the United States. The intention of the new procedure presumably was to prevent substitutions or other misuse of the certificates.[22] Conditions for the issuance of certificates to Chinese persons departing temporarily from the United States were also elaborated and made more stringent. The applicant for such a certificate, really a reentry permit, was to give under oath to a collector of customs a description of his family, property, or debts, with such proofs as might be called for, together with a "full description" of himself, the record no longer to be put on the certificate; rather the record of information was to be given a number and retained by the collector, and the same number was to be placed on the certificate issued to the applicant. Validity of the certificate for reentry was limited to one year except for illness or other delays beyond the individual's control and attested to by a consular officer abroad; included among other detailed terms was that reentry must be at the port of departure, which was restricted to seven designated ports unless by special action of the Secretary of the Treasury (sect. 7). High penalties were provided for any alteration or misuse of the certificates of identity.

Only a few weeks after adoption of the above severe requirements, Congress in annoyance at evasions of the law and in quick reaction to a reported refusal of the Chinese government to sign a treaty draft, passed an act to prohibit the return of any Chinese person who departs from the United States and to declare void any certificates of identity that might be used for reentry under the preceding acts (Act of October 1, 1888 [25 Stat. 504]). This law remained in force until repealed by the Chinese treaty of 1894.

A next step, taken in 1892, was to pass a law requiring all Chinese persons resident within the United States to obtain a certificate of residence from the local collector of internal revenue, and those without such a certificate after the expiration of one year[23] were declared deportable. The certificate of residence was to carry a personal description of the holder, provision was made for replacement of lost or destroyed certifi-

[22]Sect. 2 and 4, Act of September 13, 1888 (25 Stat. 476).

[23]Amended to six months by the Act of November 3, 1893 (28 Stat. 7).

cates,[24] and there were severe penalties for forging or altering the certificates.[25] The Chinese community, however, strongly resisted the new law, and it could not be effectively enforced.[26] Later acts continued to reaffirm the anti-Chinese legislation, which was not repealed until 1943. It is generally agreed that the attempts to secure identification of the Chinese were never really successful and that a large amount of illegal Chinese immigration occurred in spite of all efforts of Congress and the enforcement authorities.

The Chinese may have presented a particularly difficult and baffling problem of identification and immigration control in Western eyes, but federal legislation had in fact called for identifying information on all arriving aliens ever since the manifesting requirement in the 1819 Act.[27] And even more detailed personal information came to be required additionally on the visa application form to be submitted by every would-be immigrant under the Quota Act of 1924. The required information as set forth by the act was:

> (1) the immigrant's full and true name; age, sex, and race; the date and place of birth; places of residence for the five years immediately preceding his application; whether married or single, and the names and places of residence of wife or husband and minor children, if any; calling or occupation; personal description (including height, complexion, color of hair and eyes, and marks of identification); ability to speak, read, and write; names and addresses of parents, and if neither parent living, then the name and address of his nearest relative in the country from which he comes; port of entry into the United States; final destination, if any, beyond the port of entry; whether he has a ticket through to such final destination; whether going to join a relative or friend, and, if so, what relative or friend and his name and complete address; the purpose for which he is going to the United States; the length of time he intends to remain in the United States; whether or not he intends to abide in the United States permanently; whether ever in prison or almshouse; whether he or either of his parents has ever been in an institution or hospital for the care and treatment of the insane; (2) if he claims to be a non-quota immigrant, the facts on which he bases such claim; and (3) such additional information necessary to the proper enforcement of the immigration laws and the naturalization laws, as may be by regulations prescribed. (Sect. 7b of the 1924 Act [43 Stat. 153])

[24]With the requirement of "at least one credible witness other than Chinese."

[25]Act of May 5, 1892 (27 Stat. 25); amended and restated by the Act of November 3, 1893 (28 Stat. 7).

[26]See p. 109 above.

[27]See chapter 18, Information on Immigration, pp. 534–43 above.

The immediately following subsections of the act also required that the alien furnish, if available,

> two copies of his "dossier" and prison record and military record, two certified copies of his birth certificate, and two copies of all other available public records concerning him kept by the Government to which he owes allegiance.

The alien was also to state

> whether or not he is a member of each class of individuals excluded from admission to the United States under the immigration laws, and such classes shall be stated on the blank. (Sects. 7c and 7d)

With some rephrasing, the same information requirements were contained in the 1952 Act (sect. 222a and 222b). The question on race ("race and ethnic classification" in the 1952 Act) was deleted in 1961.[28]

Quite apart from the special case of the Chinese, there has been strong sentiment in favor of registration[29] and identification of aliens in the United States, variously motivated by concern over fraudulent naturalizations, alien job-holding when unemployment is high, illegal immigration, or enemy alien minorities in times of war. The 1845 bill to create an alien register with personal identification of the aliens has been mentioned. Such proposals became more frequent as immigration policy became more and more selective and restrictive. An act in 1906 established a Bureau of Immigration and Naturalization and, among other duties, directed it to establish "books of record," registers of every alien admitted at each port. To be recorded therein was the "name, age, occupation, personal description (including height, complexion, color of hair and eyes), the place of birth," and certain other information about the alien. And each alien was to be provided with "a certificate of such registry, with the particulars thereof."[30]

A number of years later the 67th Congress, which had passed the first Quota Act in its first session in 1921, received in one of its later sessions several bills for registration of aliens but did not act on them.[31] Two bills for the registration of alien nonresidents at their port of entry and for issuance of certificates of immigration, essentially for evidence of lawful entry, appeared in the first session of the next Congress.[32] Although none

[28]Section 6, Act of September 26, 1961 (75 Stat. 650).

[29]Registration of aliens is to be distinguished from the so-called registry proceeding, which is for the purpose of creating the record of lawful admission that is a prerequisite for naturalization. For an early registration proposal see p. 12.

[30]Sect. 1, Act of June 29, 1906 (34 Stat. 596); repealed by the Act of October 14, 1940 (54 Stat. 1137), but for the most part reenacted there.

[31]See p. 184 above.

[32]See pp. 186, 187 above.

of the above bills was passed, Congress did incorporate in the 1924 Act a requirement that applicants for an immigrant visa supply two copies of their photograph (sect. 2b).

The indication is that the above-cited provisions of the 1906 Act were not adequate, for bills for the issuance of certificates of admission or arrival and for a registry of immigrants continued to appear in later Congresses, in the 70th Congress (1927–1929),[33] in the 71st Congress (1929–1931),[34] and in the 72nd Congress (1931–1933).[35] Included in the latter Congress were also bills for certificates of identity and for the registration of resident aliens. Some attention was given to certain of the bills but none was enacted. Wartime conditions later in the decade, however, brought up the matter of alien identification or surveillance with more urgency. Bills calling for the registration and fingerprinting of aliens were introduced in the first session of the 76th Congress (1939–1940).[36] One of these bills was enacted as the Alien Registration Act of 1940.[37] Reregistration of aliens was to take place annually thereafter, and changes of address by aliens were to be reported by registrants within five days after the date of change. This requirement was changed to ten days by the 1952 Act.[38] Although passed as a wartime act, alien registration is now a permanent requirement. With the alien registration card and the penalties attached to nonregistration, it provides a partial if by no means fully effective measure against the illegal immigrant.

Advance Inspection of Immigrants

Denial of entry to certain classes of aliens by the 1875 Act and later acts made advance inspection of would-be immigrants desirable. Not only might excludable aliens be stopped before departure; there was also the prospect of more accurate determination of admissibility or excludability under circumstances more favorable for careful examination than on debarcation of passengers at the port of arrival. The 1875 Act merely provided for inspection of each vessel on arrival by the collector of the port, to determine if any "obnoxious persons"[39] were on board and, if so, to forbid their landing.

The next acts to contain exclusion provisions were the Chinese Ex-

[33]See pp. 204, 208 above.

[34]See p. 218 above.

[35]See p. 227 above.

[36]See pp. 252–53, 254, 257 above.

[37]Act of June 28, 1940 (54 Stat. 670). See especially Title III, sect. 30–39, inclusive.

[38]Chap. 7, sect. 261–266, inclusive, of the 1952 Act.

[39]Defined by the act as "persons who are undergoing a sentence for conviction in their own country of felonious crimes other than political or growing out of or the result of such political offenses, or whose sentence has been remitted on condition of their emigration," and women "imported for the purposes of prostitution."

clusion Act of May 6, 1882 and the general immigration act of several months later. The former of these two acts did not provide for any advance inspection of the Chinese entitled to proceed to the United States except for whatever inquiry the Chinese authorities may have made before issuing the identity certificate required for admission. This omission of verification was rectified by the amending act of two years later, which provided that admissibility be verified by a diplomatic representative of the United States. Later amendments provided that the identity certificate required of every Chinese person proceeding to the United States be issued by a consular representative of the United States rather than by Chinese authorities.[40] The immigration act of the same year increased the number of excludable classes over those designated in the 1875 Act, but again it carried no provision for advance inspection. Administration of the act was in the hands of the several states with ports of arrival, and the number of aliens refused entry was reportedly "not large."[41]

Even if the number of exclusions was small, the fact of excludability made advance inspection a logical step to the advantage of all concerned. A recommendation that exclusion be by examination of aliens abroad was made in the first session of the 50th Congress (1887–1888), but without congressional acceptance.[42] Four years later the first session of the 52nd Congress (1891–1892) received petitions calling for consular inspection of immigrants abroad, and bills including such a provision were introduced.[43] It was uncertain how foreign governments would regard such inspection of their citizens, and no legislation ensued. The same proposal reappeared in the second session of the following Congress in 1894, in the form of a bill to establish consular inspection. Reported out and passed by the House, the bill went to the Senate, where the immigration committee rejected the principle of consular inspection for a variety of reasons.[44] The alternative of stationing immigrant inspectors at ports of immigrant embarcation was incorporated in the bill as rewritten by the Senate committee, but the House did not like the revision, and no legislation for advance inspection came out of the 53rd Congress in spite of petitions in its favor.[45]

A new initiative for inspection abroad was taken by President Roosevelt in his message of December 3, 1901 on the opening of the 57th Congress, but again with no result. Many years later the Immigration Act

[40]See preceding section, pp. 582–87 above.

[41]1911 Immigration Commission Report, 3: 366.

[42]See p. 95 above.

[43]See p. 105 above.

[44]See pp. 111–12 above.

[45]See pp. 112, 113, 114 above.

of 1917 gave the Commissioner of Immigration and Naturalization authority to detail immigration officers for service in foreign countries and further to request that the Public Health Service assign medical officers for service abroad for the purpose of enforcement of the act. It is not known what use was made of this authority. The subject of inspection abroad reappeared in 1921 with a bill for inspection at the port of embarcation of aliens desiring to emigrate to the United States. The first quota act of that year set limits on the number of immigrant aliens to be admitted from each quota country and provided for frequent reporting to transportation companies of the remaining number of immigrants admissible under the national quotas, but it included no provision for the stationing of American representatives abroad to aid in the administration of the act.

Inspection abroad was incorporated into the second quota act, that of 1924. Under the terms of the act, a visa issued by an American consular officer was required for admission, and an alien applying for the visa was required to submit evidence of his admissibility in the form of detailed personal information, as described in the preceding section of this chapter.[46] This requirement was continued by the Immigration Act of 1952 (sect. 222).

The foregoing account concerns inspection abroad. Of earlier origin was provision in immigration law for examination of passengers on shipboard and proceeding to the United States. Although such inspection in transit could not serve to prevent the coming of aliens who might be turned back on arrival, it did possess the advantage of providing better and more leisurely opportunity during the voyage for the observation of excludable cases than might exist at the port of arrival. As early as 1882 the so-called passenger or steerage acts had required that vessels bringing more than fifty steerage passengers have a medical officer on board.[47] No immediate advantage was taken of the opportunity so created, but two decades later the Immigration Act of 1903 added to the manifesting requirement the further stipulation that

> the surgeon of said vessel sailing therewith shall also sign each of said lists or manifests and make oath or affirmation . . . that he has made a personal examination of each of the said aliens named therein, and that the said list or manifest . . . is full, correct, and true in all particulars relative to the mental and physical condition of said aliens. (Act of March 3, 1903, sect. 14 [32 Stat. 1213])

[46]See pp. 585–86 above.

[47]Act of August 2, 1882 (22 Stat. 186), sect. 5.

The same provision is repeated in the Immigration Act of February 20, 1907 (sect. 14).

The Immigration Act of 1917 reaffirmed the requirement concerning inspection of alien passengers by a ship's surgeon, but added to it the obligation placed on the ship's master or the first or second officer below him in command to verify that

> he has caused the surgeon of said vessel sailing therewith to make a physical and mental examination of each of said aliens, and that from the report of said surgeon and from his own investigation he believes that no one of said aliens is of any of the classes excluded from admission into the United States. . . . (Sect. 13)

With what appears to be a lack of full confidence in such examination by ship's personnel, the act provided further

> That the Secretary of Labor is hereby authorized and directed to enter into negotiations, through the Department of State, with countries vessels of which bring aliens to the United States, with a view to detailing inspectors and matrons of the United States Immigration Service for duty on vessels carrying immigrant or emigrant passengers between foreign ports and ports of the United States. When such inspectors and matrons are detailed for said duty they shall remain in that part of the vessel where immigrant passengers are carried; and it shall be their duty to observe such passengers during the voyage and report to the immigration authorities in charge at the port of landing any information of value in determining the admissibility of such passengers that may have become known to them during the voyage. (Sect. 11a)

The 1917 Act remained in force, with amendment, until repealed by the 1952 Act; but the latter did not contain the earlier provisions for verification of the admissibility of aliens by the ship's surgeon and by a representative of the Service on board.

Disabilities of Resident Aliens

Congress appears generally to have viewed the alien who seeks admission with a rather critical eye and to have persisted in that view of the alien if and when he is admitted to the United States. That is to say, Congress has given evidence of some continuing doubts or reservations about the alien who is allowed to take up residence, for in effect his admission has been on a somewhat conditional and trial basis. Long after he takes up residence, the alien is still subject to deportation for any one of a number of causes, as described in an earlier chapter; and beyond that Congress has often considered imposing certain disabilities or limitations of the rights and privileges of aliens. The history of congressional attention to immigration matters, given in Part I, has included mention of a number of initiatives taken by individual members of Congress to impose certain limitations on aliens or to deny them certain activities or opportunities that would thus be reserved for citizens only. Summarized below are the principal types of such antialien proposals that have appeared in Congress since 1798. Omitted from this summary are the various anti-Chinese measures of the late nineteenth century, special wartime restrictions on aliens,[48] and the antisubversive proposals of the Cold War period in order to focus more clearly on action aimed against aliens as aliens, as distinct from aliens as members of an Oriental race, enemy aliens, or suspected subversives. The principal directions taken by the legislative proposals have been as follows:

1. denial of federal or public works employment to aliens, first recommended as early as 1798,[49] again in 1824,[50] and then frequently from the 1890s onward;[51]
2. denial of certain other employments, including enlistment in the navy[52] and marines[53] or the armed forces in general,[54] engaging in business in specified areas,[55] fishing in the waters of Alaska;[56] and Depression period bills of the 1930s would have denied employment to aliens while citizens able and willing to work were unemployed;[57]
3. restriction or denial of right to purchase or own land, from the 1880s onward,[58] with particular reference to the sale of public lands and to benefits under the homestead acts, and with concern over the evils of absentee ownership.

Miscellaneous other proposals over the years were to prohibit alien franchise or suffrage,[59] to deny social security benefits,[60] to forbid aliens to draw pensions,[61] to forbid the purchase and possession of firearms by aliens,[62] to deny aliens the right to vote or hold office in labor unions,[63] to refuse government contracts to business organizations having any

[48]But it should be noted that the requirements of fingerprinting and registration instituted by the 1940 Act remained on the law books.

[49]See p. 13 above.

[50]See p. 23 above.

[51]See pp. 106, 114, 119, 132, 160, 164 above.

[52]See p. 98 above.

[53]See p. 113 above.

[54]See pp. 122, 352 above.

[55]See p. 173 above.

[56]See pp. 245, 248 above.

[57]See pp. 236, 241 above.

[58]See pp. 88, 90, 91, 94, 98–99, 103, 113, 172 above.

[59]See pp. 113, 114 above.

[60]See p. 241 above.

[61]See p. 133 above.

[62]See pp. 160, 244, 255 above.

[63]See pp. 262, 266, 267–68, 269 above.

alien officers,[64] and to bar aliens from holding office in any business organization engaged in interstate commerce.[65]

Although some individual congressmen sponsored such antialien measures, the congressional committees and Congress as a whole gave them very little support. Almost all of the bills died in committee; only a few went on to enactment. Sufficient concern at the alleged dangers of alien landholding was generated to pass the Act of March 3, 1887 (24 Stat. 476) that forbade the subsequent acquisition of land in the United States by any nondeclarant[66] alien or foreign corporation, except as acquired by inheritance, in settlement of debt, or under existing treaty.[67] Not long after its passage, however, the act was found to create difficulties, as in the acquisition of residences in the District of Columbia by foreign governments, and in the attracting of foreign capital for the development of mineral resources. Efforts were soon made, therefore, to soften the impact of the act.[68] In the next decade a prohibition of employment of nondeclarant male aliens on public works was included in the first literacy test bill, passed by Congress but vetoed by President Cleveland.[69] More successful was the effort in the next decade to bar aliens from fishing in Alaskan waters, which led to the Act of June 14, 1906 (34 Stat. 263).[70] As passed, the act did not entirely bar aliens, for declarant aliens retained fishing rights and aliens were allowed to work as employees in the Alaskan fishing industry. The terms of the act applied more to commercial than individual fishing. Some thirty years later the act was further moderated to permit fishing by Filipinos and by certain aliens who were bona fide residents of Alaska.[71]

As might have been noted in other connections above, what Congress does not do is in some ways as significant as what it chooses to do. In the present connection we can observe that many forms of discrimination against the alien have been brought forward for approval but that, with the exception of wartime and the earlier anti-Chinese legislation, Congress has been notably disinclined to impose limitations or disabilities on the alien who is a resident of the United States.[72]

[64]See pp. 268, 269 above. [65]Ibid.

[66]That is, not having declared intention of becoming naturalized.

[67]For further terms of the act, see p. 91 above.

[68]See p. 44 above. [69]See p. 121 above.

[70]See p. 137 above. [71]See pp. 245, 248 above.

[72]The same does not apply at the state or local level. Concerning citizenship requirements for certain occupations, for example, see Herman I. Branse, "State Laws Barring Aliens from Professions and Occupations," *INS Monthly Review* 3, no. 9 (March 1946): 281–84; and Grover H. Sanders, "Aliens in Professions and Occupations—State Laws Restricting Participation," *I & N Reporter* 16, no. 3 (January 1968): 37–40.

Imposed Liability

In its long and still continuing search for effective means of enforcement of the immigration laws, Congress has not limited itself to legislation directed against the alien alone. From time to time Congress has used the device of reaching beyond the alien to impose liability on those dealing with the alien, to require them to aid in observance of the immigration laws or to penalize them for contributing to the violation of those laws by an alien. Historically there have been two principal examples of this type of enforcement effort. One has been to hold the transportation agencies responsible for bringing in excludable aliens for immigration to the United States. The other has been to impose severe penalties on anyone, alien or not, who aids an alien to enter illegally.

A preceding section dealt with the advance inspection of immigrants. In effect, the imposition of liability for bringing in certain classes of aliens was a means of forcing the transporter to perform a first screening of the alien passengers. To make the transporter liable for bringing in an alien who became a public charge was an old device, found in colonial period laws that required the master of a vessel to post bond, or, perhaps more effective, to carry back the undesirable alien.[73] This colonial practice was continued later by the principal states receiving immigrants,[74] and congressional thinking eventually began to move in the same direction. As early as 1838 Congress received a petition for legislation to make masters and owners of vessels responsible for the relief of aliens who were destitute on landing.[75] A House bill introduced later in the same year provided the heavy fine of $1,000 or one to three years of imprisonment for the master of a vessel who took on board certain prohibited classes of aliens with the intention of transporting them to the United States.[76] This legislative area was still regarded as a matter for the states and cities to handle, however, and no action was taken at the national level.

Years later the first session of the 34th Congress (1855–1856) received a bill requiring a ship owner or master to certify that each alien landed from the vessel was of good character and without record of criminality or pauperism;[77] but again Congress did not give its approval. Twenty years later the 1875 Act established the first excludable classes under federal law. The act provided for the inspection of the arriving passengers, and that if any "obnoxious person or persons" were found, they

[73]See section on Protection against Public Charges, under colonial policies, pp. 390–93 above.

[74]See similarly under state policies, pp. 397–400.

[75]See p. 27 above. [76]See p. 29 above.

[77]See p. 41 above.

> shall be returned on board of said vessel, and shall not thereafter be permitted to land, unless the master, owner, or consignee of the vessel shall give bond and security . . . in the sum of five hundred dollars for each such person permitted to land, conditioned for the return of such person, within six months from the date thereof, to the country whence his or her emigration shall have taken place, or unless the vessel bringing such obnoxious person or persons shall be forfeited, in which event the proceeds of such forfeiture shall be paid over to the collector of the port of arrival, and applied by him, as far as necessary, to the return of such person or persons to his or her own country within the said period of six months. And for all violations of this act, the vessel, by the acts, omissions, or connivance of the owners, master, or other custodian, or the consignees of which the same are committed, shall be liable to forfeiture, and may be proceeded against as in cases of frauds against the revenue laws, for which forfeiture is prescribed by existing law.[78]

In 1880 Congress considered but did not adopt a bill requiring that certain prohibited classes of arriving aliens be returned to their port of embarcation at the expense of the owners of the vessel that brought them to the United States.[79] Again, in 1882 this provision was included in an immigration bill. Adopted by the House, the provision was dropped after Senate action; and when enacted as the Act of August 3, 1882 (22 Stat. 214) the return of excluded aliens at the expense of the owners of the vessel on which they arrived was limited to foreign convicts (sect. 4).

The contract labor and Chinese exclusion acts of the 1880s created new excludable classes, and in both cases Congress tried to strengthen enforcement measures by requiring that such excludables on arrival at a port of the United States be sent back at the expense of the ship owner. Thus the first Chinese Exclusion Act in 1882 directed in its second section that

> the master of any vessel who shall knowingly bring within the United States on such vessel, and land or permit to be landed, any Chinese laborer, from any foreign port or place, shall be deemed guilty of a misdemeanor, and on conviction thereof shall be punished by a fine of not more than five hundred dollars for each and every such Chinese laborer so brought, and may be also imprisoned for a term not exceeding one year. (Sect. 2 of the Act of May 6, 1882 [22 Stat. 58])

As if this were not enough, later sections made "every vessel whose master shall knowingly violate any of the provisions of this act" liable to seizure and condemnation, and further that

[78]Sect. 5, Act of March 3, 1875 (18 Stat. 477).

[79]See p. 75 above.

> any person who shall knowingly bring into or cause to be brought into the United States by land, or who shall knowingly aid or abet the same, or aid or abet the landing in the United States from any vessel of any Chinese person not lawfully entitled to enter the United States, shall be deemed guilty of a misdemeanor, and shall, on conviction thereof, be fined in a sum not exceeding one thousand dollars, and imprisoned for a term not exceeding one year. (Sect. 10 and 11)

These were indeed strong measures that sought to effect the exclusion of Chinese under the threat of severe penalties against anyone knowingly aiding them to come to the United States.

These provisions of the 1882 Act were reenacted in reworded but not substantially changed form in 1884.[80] The Chinese Exclusion Act of 1888 repealed the Acts of 1882 and 1884, but reenacted the penalties against the master of any vessel who knowingly brought Chinese to the United States in violation of the act.[81] The indicated term of imprisonment was changed, however, to not less than one year nor more than five years at the discretion of the court.

A similar pattern is found in the contract labor legislation of the same period. A fine of $1,000 was levied

> for every violation of any of the provisions of section one of this act the person, partnership, company, or corporation violating the same, by knowingly assisting, encouraging or soliciting the migration or importation of any alien or aliens . . . to perform labor or service of any kind under contract or agreement, express or implied . . . shall forfeit and pay for every such offense the sum of one thousand dollars.[82]

Additionally, as in the Chinese legislation,

> the master of any vessel who shall knowingly bring within the United States on any such vessel, and land, or permit to be landed, from any foreign port or place, any alien laborer, mechanic, or artisan who, previous to embarkation on such vessel, had entered into contract or agreement . . . to perform labor or service in the United States, shall be deemed guilty of a misdemeanor, and on conviction thereof, shall be punished by a fine of not more than five hundred dollars for each and every such alien laborer, mechanic or artisan so brought as aforesaid, and may also be imprisoned for a term not exceeding six months. (Sect. 4)

[80]Sect. 2, 10, and 11 of the Act of July 5, 1884 (23 Stat. 115).
[81]Sect. 9 of the Act of September 13, 1888 (25 Stat. 476).
[82]Sect. 3 of the Act of February 26, 1885 (23 Stat. 332).

Any contract laborers discovered on inspection at arrival were to be sent back at the expense of the owners of the vessel bringing them, under the Contract Labor Act of February 23, 1887 (sect. 8). It was broadened in an act of the following year to provide for return of a detected contract laborer up to one year after entry at the expense of the owner of the vessel as before or, in the case of such unlawful entry from an adjoining country, at the expense of whoever contracted for the illegal services.[83]

Despite all this legislation on the statute books, it is evident that Congress did not regard the problem of illegal immigration as solved, for it continued to consider further penalties against those who might aid the illegal immigrant. Early in 1889 the Ford Commission's bill in the second session of the 50th Congress reaffirmed the contract labor laws and provided for deportation of illegal aliens up to two years after entry at the expense of the transporter.[84] No action on this proposal was taken at the time, but two years later the Immigration Act of March 3, 1891 (26 Stat. 1084) dealt very explicitly with the matter, as follows:

> any person who shall bring into or land in the United States by vessel or otherwise, or who shall aid to bring into or land in the United States by vessel or otherwise, any alien not lawfully entitled to enter the United States shall be deemed guilty of a misdemeanor, and shall, on conviction, be punished by a fine not exceeding one thousand dollars, or by imprisonment for a term not exceeding one year, or by both such fine and imprisonment. (Sect. 6)

A later section of the same act made it a responsibility of the transporter to land aliens only at designated ports of entry for inspection by the immigration authorities:

> It shall be the duty of the . . . officers and agents of such vessel to adopt due precautions to prevent the landing of any alien immigrant at any place or time other than that designated by the inspection officers, and any such officer or agent or person in charge of such vessel who shall either knowingly or negligently land or permit to land any alien immigrant at any place or time other than that designated by the inspection officers, shall be deemed guilty of a misdemeanor and punished by a fine not exceeding one thousand dollars, or by imprisonment for a term not exceeding one year, or by both such fine and imprisonment. (Sect. 8)

Perhaps aimed most directly at evasions of the head tax, a not uncommon practice at the time, this provision may have been adopted with the

[83]Act of October 19, 1888 (25 Stat. 566); and p. 96 above.
[84]See p. 97 above.

further thought that if the masters of vessels were responsible for the bringing of excludable aliens they might be tempted to land aliens of doubtful admissibility at out-of-the way places where they would escape inspection. But whatever the intended target, the provision did follow the principle of extending liability for the coming of an excludable alien beyond the alien himself. And in 1894 a Senate committee rejected a bill for consular inspection with the explanation that it was more feasible to make the transportation companies responsible for rejecting excludable aliens.[85]

Several years later the Industrial Commission, established by act of Congress on June 18, 1898, presented the results of its hearings on immigration to Congress on December 5, 1901 in the form of volume 15 of its full report (H. Doc. 184 [57-I]). Included in the digest of testimony was a summary of statements from a number of witnesses regarding the inspection by the steamship companies before embarcation.[86] Although some suspected abuses on the part of the companies were reported,[87] the testimony was generally favorable to the procedure, and in its final proposals for new legislation the Commission recommended the transportation companies' liability for the return of deportable aliens up to one year after arrival and special penalties for the bringing of aliens with loathsome or contagious diseases.[88]

New legislation did not follow immediately on the Industrial Commission's report, but the next general immigration act on March 3, 1903 (32 Stat. 1213) outdid preceding acts in renewing and adding to the requirements and liabilities it imposed on transportation companies and persons bringing immigrants to the United States:

1. Transportation companies were forbidden to "solicit, invite, or encourage" immigration except through the customary announcements of sailings and terms of travel (sect. 7).
2. They were not to bring in or land any alien "not duly admitted by an immigrant inspector," under penalty of up to $1,000 fine for each such alien, imprisonment for not less than three months or more than two years, or both fine and imprisonment (sect. 8).
3. Whoever brought in any alien suffering from a loathsome or dangerous contagious disease was subject to a fine of $100 for

[85]See p. 112 above. [86]H. Doc. 184, pp. ciii–cv.

[87]Abuses such as the charging of double passage money in the case of doubtful admissibility, or the putting of such aliens in first or cabin class where they would not be inspected by the immigration authorities on arrival.

[88]Commission report, vol. XIX, H. Doc. 380 (57-I), recommendations 10 and 18, pp. 1010–12.

each such alien provided the disease was present and detectable at time of embarcation (sect. 9).[89]

4. Owners of vessels and their representatives were liable for the cost of maintenance on land and for the return passage of aliens brought in violation of law, and with a fine of not less than $300 for each such alien (sect. 19).
5. Any person bringing an alien into the United States was liable for the cost of return transportation, including one-half of the inland transportation cost, of aliens subsequently deported at any time within two years after arrival because of illegal entry or because of their becoming public charges from causes existing prior to landing in the United States (sect. 20).
6. Such persons were similarly liable for the cost of return transportation of aliens found in the United States in violation of the 1903 Act, within a period of three years after entry (sect. 21).

Incorporating provisions from earlier legislation and adding new ones, this portion of the 1903 Act represented a much expanded effort to control immigration through the transporting agencies. With the addition of mental ailments to the list of conditions for which aliens were to be denied transportation to the United States, essentially the same provisions were reenacted in the next Immigration Act of 1907.[90]

The Immigration Act of 1917 that established the literacy test marked the triumph of long-frustrated restrictionist sentiment. It was passed in a climate of opinion favorable to strict control of immigration, and toward that end it continued and extended the practice of putting responsibilities on transportation companies and others concerned with the movement of aliens. Such provisions in earlier acts were reenacted and new provisions were added to meet new concerns of the period. Continued from earlier acts, often with some rewording or change in the penalty terms were the provision which made it unlawful for any person or organization to encourage immigration;[91] a similar prohibition on the bringing of aliens with certain diseases or defects but now with a longer list of such excludables (sect. 9);[92] the duty placed on persons and on representatives of transportation companies except railways to prevent the entry of aliens at an undesignated time or place

[89]But "railway lines entering the United States from foreign contiguous territory" were exempted.

[90]See sect. 7, 8, 9, 18, 19, 20, and 21 of the Act of February 20, 1907 (34 Stat. 898).

[91]Act of February 5, 1917 (39 Stat. 874), section 7.

[92]Concerning "any alien afflicted with idiocy, insanity, imbecility, feeble-mindedness, epilepsy, constitutional psychopathic inferiority, chronic alcoholism, tuberculosis in any form, or a loathsome or dangerous contagious disease."

(sect. 10); the liability of ship owners for the free return passage plus cost of maintenance while on land of aliens brought in violation of law together with a fine for knowingly bringing back an alien within one year of deportation (sect. 18); and the cost of deportation within five years after entry including half the cost of transportation to the port of deportation at the expense of whoever induced the alien to enter illegally or at the expense of the transportation line by which the alien came (sect. 20).

The above provisions were not essentially different from those in preceding acts, but the designers of the 1917 Act devised additional deterrents for those who might give aid to the illegal alien and additional requirements for cooperation from others in the prevention of illegal entry. Particular attention was given to the problem of alien seamen. One section of the new act directed that

> any person . . . who shall knowingly sign on the ship's articles, or bring to the United States as one of the crew of such vessel, any alien, with intent to permit such alien to land . . . in violation of the laws . . . or who shall falsely and knowingly represent to the immigration authorities at the port of arrival that any such alien is a bona fide member of the crew, shall be liable to a penalty not exceeding $5,000. . . . (Sect. 31)

Further,

> no alien excluded from admission . . . and employed on board any vessel arriving in the United States from any foreign port or place, shall be permitted to land . . . except temporarily for medical treatment, or pursuant to regulations . . . providing for the ultimate removal or deportation of such alien. . . . (Sect. 32)[93]

Additionally,

> it shall be unlawful . . . to pay off or discharge any alien employed on board any vessel arriving in the United States from any foreign port or place, unless duly admitted pursuant to the laws and treaties . . . regulating the immigration of aliens. . . . (Sect. 33)

The act also required lists of all alien seamen on arriving vessels and for departing vessels a report of seamen paid off or discharged and those who had deserted or landed (sect. 36).

Another problem class of aliens given separate attention was that of anarchists and related persons. Under the 1917 Act,

[93]A penalty of not exceeding $1,000 was attached. This section was repealed by sect. 20(d) of the Act of May 26, 1924 (43 Stat. 168).

> any person who knowingly aids or assists any anarchist . . . or who connives or conspires with any person or persons to allow, procure, or permit any such anarchist or person aforesaid to enter . . . shall be deemed guilty of a felony, and on conviction thereof shall be punished by a fine of not more than $5,000 or by imprisonment for not more than five years, or both.
>
> Any person who knowingly aids or assists any alien who advocates or teaches the unlawful destruction of property to enter the United States shall be deemed guilty of a misdemeanor and on conviction thereof shall be punished by a fine of not more than $1,000, or by imprisonment for not more than six months, or by both such fine and imprisonment. (Sect. 28)

Previously mentioned was the provision making it unlawful to bring in an alien suffering from certain specified mental defects and diseases, an expansion of such provisions in the 1903 and 1907 Acts.[94] Additionally, the 1917 Act made it similarly unlawful to bring in any alien with other mental defects than those already prohibited or with "physical defect of a nature which may affect his ability to earn a living," subject to a penalty of twenty-five dollars plus passage money if the mental or physical defect could have been detected by competent medical examination at the time of entry; to bring in an alien excludable under the literacy test or as a native of the Asiatic Barred Zone was subject to penalty of $200 plus passage money if excludability was detectable under reasonable examination at the time of entry.[95]

A new direction of attack on those who might assist the illegal alien was taken in another section of the 1917 Act, which read as follows:

> any person . . . who shall bring into or land in the United States, by vessel or otherwise, or shall attempt, by himself or through another, to bring into or land in the United States, by vessel or otherwise, or shall conceal or harbor, or attempt to conceal or harbor, or assist or abet another to conceal or harbor in any place, including any building, vessel, railway car, conveyance, or vehicle, any alien not duly admitted by an immigrant inspector or not lawfully entitled to enter or to reside within the United States under the terms of this Act, shall be deemed guilty of a misdemeanor, and upon conviction thereof shall be punished by a fine not exceeding $2,000 and by imprisonment for a term not exceeding five years, for each and every alien so landed or brought in or attempted to be landed or brought in. (Sect. 8)[96]

[94]See footnote 92, p. 598.

[95]Sect. 9 of the 1917 Act; changed to $250 and $1,000 by the 1924 Act.

[96]The word "misdemeanor" was changed to "felony" by the Act of June 25, 1948 (62 Stat. 683).

The departure from previous law was to go beyond the act of bringing in an alien illegally and to set heavy penalties against whoever knowingly conceals or shields from detection an illegal alien *within* the United States.

The body of legislation directed at those who bring aliens to the United States at first dealt only with arrival by vessel, and although broadened in application over the years it continued to be concerned principally with such arrivals. The Immigration Act of 1924, the second of the quota acts, however, included a section directly aimed at transportation of aliens from foreign contiguous territory and by way of such territory. The Commissioner of Immigration and Naturalization, with the approval of his superior[97] was given the power to enter into contracts with transportation lines "for the entry and inspection of aliens coming to the United States from or through foreign contiguous territory" and to prescribe rules and regulations for the entry and inspection of such aliens. To give force to this provision it was further directed that an alien coming from or through foreign contiguous territory shall not be admitted unless he can prove he was "brought to such territory by a transportation company which had submitted to and complied with" all the requirements of the 1924 Act or that he had been in the contiguous territory for more than two years prior to coming to the United States.[98] Alien passengers on noncooperating transportation lines were made excludable—a means of exerting pressure on immigrant traffic coming by way of Canada or Mexico rather than directly to the United States.

The Immigration Acts of 1917 and 1924 remained in effect until repealed in 1952, but the supplementing and amending of the immigration laws that continued over the intervening years included proposals directed against those who give aid to the illegal immigrant. One such proposal was presented at the opening of the first session of the 70th Congress in December 1927, to authorize the seizure and forfeiture of vehicles used in violation of the immigration laws.[99] Such authority had been included in special wartime powers,[100] but in peacetime the House committee did not endorse the bill.

A different approach to the problem of illegal immigration was taken by other bills some years later, one in the second session of the 71st

[97]The Secretary of Labor until June 14, 1940, thereafter the Attorney General.

[98]Immigration Act of May 26, 1924 (43 Stat. 153), sect. 17.

[99]See p. 105 above.

[100]Such authority was contained in sect. 3 of the Act of May 22, 1918 (40 Stat. 559), entitled "Prevention in Time of War of Departure from or Entry into the United States Contrary to the Public Safety"; reaffirmed by the amending act of the same title of June 21, 1941 (55 Stat. 252); reenacted by the 1952 Act, sect. 215(c) on travel control in time of war or national emergency.

Congress (1929–1930) to prohibit the giving of employment to illegal aliens, another in the second session of the 74th Congress (1936) to prohibit the employment, the making of loans to, or the giving of relief to aliens who had entered unlawfully.[101] The bills did not come out of committee. It was not until 1940 that the legal defenses against illegal immigration were reinforced by an amendment to the 1917 Act to make deportable an alien who aids another alien to enter illegally. Two new deportable classes were created for that purpose, consisting of

> (1) Any alien who, at any time within five years after entry, shall have, knowingly and for gain, encouraged, induced, assisted, abetted, or aided any other alien to enter or to try to enter the United States in violation of law.
> (2) Any alien who, at any time after entry, shall have on more than one occasion, knowingly and for gain, encouraged, induced, assisted, abetted, or aided any other alien or aliens to enter or to try to enter the United States in violation of law. (Sect. 20, Act of June 28, 1940 [54 Stat. 670])

Deportability of an offending alien, in other words, was for a first offense committed within five years after entry of the alien, but without time limit for a second or later offense.

Congressional attention returned to the problem of illegal immigration and especially that from Mexico during the early 1950s. Bills against the bringing in and harboring of such aliens appeared in the first session of the 82nd Congress (1951), and one of them was finally passed after considerable legislative struggle and disagreement between House and Senate as the Act of March 20, 1952, entitled "To Assist in Preventing Aliens from Entering or Remaining in the United States Illegally."[102] The act amended section 8 of the 1917 Act to reaffirm the previous prohibition against bringing in, harboring, or concealing an illegal alien and declared such action a felony punishable by fine or imprisonment or both. To this was added the new provision that it is similarly a felony and similarly punishable if anyone knowing that an alien is in the United States in violation of law,

> and knowing or having reasonable grounds to believe that his last entry into the United States occurred less than three years prior thereto, transports, or moves, or attempts to transport or move [an alien] within the United States by means of transportation or otherwise, in furtherance of such violation of law. . . . (Sect. 1, Act of March 20, 1952 [66 Stat. 26])

[101]See pp. 218 and 240 above, and p. 608 et seq. below.
[102]See pp. 300–301, 302–3 above.

At the same time that the act added this significant new measure against the transportation of illegal aliens within the country, it somewhat weakened the law against the harboring of such aliens with the proviso

> That for the purposes of this section, employment (including the usual and normal practices incident to employment) shall not be deemed to constitute harboring. (Sect. 1)

This addition to the original bill was presumably for the reassurance in particular of the employers of Mexican farm workers.

Congress had been working meanwhile on the bill that became the Immigration and Nationality Act of June 27, 1952, commonly known as the McCarran-Walter Act, which repealed the 1917 Act and replaced it as the basic immigration law. As regards the provisions directed against those who might aid or contribute to the entry of illegal aliens, the new act for the most part continued the previous provisions that have been described above, but did add several new liabilities and penalties to those already available as weapons against illegal immigration. As stated earlier, the 1924 Act had excluded an alien coming by way of foreign contiguous territory if brought to such territory by a nonsignatory transportation line and had not lived for at least two years in such territory prior to seeking admission to the United States. As reformulated by the 1952 Act the exclusion applied to aliens seeking admission from adjacent islands as well as foreign contiguous territory, exemption was given to aliens born in Western Hemisphere countries and to returning alien residents of the United States, and exclusion was extended to aliens who came by a signatory but noncomplying transportation line (sect. 212[a][24], Act of June 27, 1952 [66 Stat. 163]). A new provision was that such aliens were made deportable without time limit (sect. 241[a][10]). The act also rounded out the penalties for aliens who aid others to enter illegally. Such aliens had been made deportable in 1940; in 1952 a new excludable class was created to consist of

> Any alien who at any time shall have, knowingly and for gain, encouraged, induced, assisted, abetted, or aided any other alien to enter or to try to enter the United States in violation of law. (Sect. 212[a][31])

Excludability was thus without time limit, whereas deportability without time limit was only on a second offense. With this, the 1952 Act rounded out what was in toto a formidable array of legal weapons available to the immigration authorities for use against illegal immigration.[103] These

[103]Since 1952 Congress has continued to receive occasional bills to forbid the employment of known illegal aliens and for confiscation of vehicles used in their transportation. See, for example, pp. 322–23 above.

weapons, in addition to the direct penalties of exclusion and deportation for the illegal alien, included return travel costs, fines, and the liability to imprisonment placed on whoever brings in certain excludable aliens or enables them to escape inspection, special requirements with respect to alien crewmen placed on transportation companies, penalities for the harboring or concealment or transportation of a known illegal alien within the United States, and both exclusion and deportation penalties provided for the alien who aids another alien to enter illegally.

Congress and the Illegal Alien

The preceding sections of this chapter have described certain of the procedures or instruments of policy Congress has adopted to facilitate the administration and especially the enforcement of the immigration laws. To conclude, the present section traces the development of congressional efforts to deal with an especially difficult problem of enforcement and describes how Congress has tried to solve the problem. The problem in question is that of the alien who is present in the United States in violation of the immigration laws, commonly referred to as an illegal alien or more technically as an out-of-status alien. During the past century, ever since the first designation of excludable classes of aliens, Congress has been confronted with a succession of enforcement problems in its efforts to exclude certain aliens: Chinese laborers and contract laborers in the nineteenth century, and subversives and illegal aliens generally in the twentieth. Each has presented its own particular difficulties for the enforcement officials, and each has stimulated Congress to special efforts and new control measures. Thus the history of congressional response to the illegal alien problem shows a cumulative series of legislative steps, with new measures added as earlier measures were found inadequate to cope with the problem that defied and still defies solution.

The measures for the control of illegal immigration can best be described in relation to the several different types of illegal or out-of-status alien, which are as follows:

1. the alien who evades inspection by the immigration authorities on entering the United States;
2. the alien who gains admission by fraud or misrepresentation, such as by concealment of facts that if known would make him excludable, or by claim of citizenship as with a false Puerto Rican birth certificate, by fraudulent marriage or claim of marriage to an American citizen, by claim of American citizen parentage, or by forged documents of identity;
3. the alien who is properly admitted as a nonimmigrant for a tem-

porary stay but who stays on in the United States or takes employment forbidden under the terms of admission.

Aware of this diversity of illegal immigration and the related enforcement problems, Congress has provided the immigration authorities with an ever-increasing range of enforcement measures. Two general classes of such measures can be distinguished, those primarily for the prevention of illegal immigration, and those for dealing with the aliens who succeed in entering illegally, or violate their terms of admission.

Very early Congress discovered it was not enough to forbid the entry of certain classes of aliens. Means of enforcement of the exclusion were needed as well, and the first and apparently most feasible line of defense against an illegal inflow was at the borders. With this in view, Congress came to designate certain ports of entry and border crossing stations, forbade aliens to enter at other than designated points, established the Border Patrol, and set severe penalties against persons and transportation lines that enable or aid aliens to enter uninspected. Individual congressmen have suggested even more extreme measures, such as the building of a fence along the Mexican border,[104] use of the Army, Navy, and militia to prevent the smuggling in of aliens,[105] and the giving of rewards to informers who report illegal aliens.[106]

Prevention of the second type of illegal immigration, entry by fraud or misstatement, is a quite different matter. As described earlier in this chapter,[107] the procedure finally adopted after considerable discussion and hesitation on the part of Congress, seeking to prevent the admission of aliens who were in fact excludable, was the advance examination of prospective immigrants by American consular officers abroad and the requirement that documentary evidence be submitted with the visa application. The third type of illegal alien, the nonimmigrant who violates the terms of admission, does not lend itself to preventive measures except for whatever the deterrent effect of the penalties attached and the insecurity of the illegal status after entry.

The question is how effective the deterrent and preventive measures have been in keeping aliens from entering and taking up unlawful residence in the United States. The past and present evidence is that it has not been possible to prevent illegal immigration, in spite of all the legislation and the efforts of the enforcement authorities. Numbers of Chinese came in despite the rigorous exclusion laws, the contract labor laws were

[104]See p. 278 above.

[105]See pp. 200, 204 and elsewhere above.

[106]See p. 96 above, with reference to contract laborers.

[107]See pp. 587–90 above.

not really enforceable, and at the present time the illegal population is known to be large. Recent estimates run as high as twelve million, and the number is semiofficially put at around eight million.[108] Even if the latter figure is much too high, as some believe, it is evident that preventive measures alone have not kept the illegal inflow within acceptable limits.

The relative frequency of the three modes of unlawful entry, by avoidance of inspection, by fraud, and by nonimmigrant status, being unknown, the effectiveness of the measures against them can only be inferred. Illegal entry by means of forged documents or other fraudulent devices cannot be prevented entirely, but the screening of immigrant visa applicants and the alerting of consular officials to common subterfuges are probably as effective procedures as can be devised for preventing this type of illegal entry. Much the same is true in the case of nonimmigrant visas, where actual violations of status cannot be detected until after admission. It is, however, the surreptitious entry that is thought to be the principal source of illegal immigration.[109] The Border Patrol apprehends and expels hundreds of thousands of illegals every year, but it does not cover all avenues of entry nor does it have the manpower to cope fully with the massive inflow of aliens. To seal off the land borders is obviously impossible, and it is still less possible to prevent entry along the coastline or by air. As experience with the Chinese and Mexican cases shows clearly, ways to get in legally or illegally will be found by those determined to enter the country.

Recognizing that excluding measures alone are not enough, Congress has established a second line of defense against illegal immigration in the form of measures directed against the aliens who are illegally present in the country. One response to the problem has been to make each of the three types of illegal aliens deportable without time limit after date of entry.[110] Deportability, however, does not get at the heart of the problem, which is to detect the alien violator of the immigration laws. But detection is difficult, for the illegal alien is not readily distinguishable from the lawfully resident alien, nor for that matter is the alien readily distinguishable from the native-born or the naturalized citizen.

The obvious response to the problem of detecting illegal aliens within the country is to establish an identification system for aliens; and this is what Congress has done on two separate occasions. The first was

[108]Leonard F. Chapman, Jr., Commissioner of Immigration and Naturalization, *I and N Reporter* 24, no. 2 (Fall 1975):15.

[109]This is undoubtedly true for the Mexican illegals, who make up the greater part of the illegal inflow, but it may not be true for those coming from other sources.

[110]See deportable classes 1, 2, and 9, p. 459 above.

when illegal Chinese immigration was perceived as a major problem in the 1880s, at which time Congress required detailed personal identification for each Chinese person, first for new arrivals, and then for the resident Chinese community as a whole.[111] Again, when the number of excludable classes increased and illegal immigration from Europe became a matter of concern, proposals for registration or identification of all aliens began to appear in Congress.[112] It was not until 1940, however, that a national alien registration system was adopted, a system that remains in force up to the present time.

Thus there have been two major experiments with identification or registration systems for aliens. In theory and in actual intention they were to provide an inventory of the resident alien population, and especially in the Chinese case, to help in combatting illegal immigration. The immediate question is how effective they have been for such a purpose. The Chinese legislation was described in some detail earlier in this chapter[113] to show the length to which Congress then went to secure personal identification of the Chinese. But even though the laws for the Chinese went far beyond anything that conceivably could be directed against immigrants and immigrant communities today, they must be regarded as much less than successful in the face of resistance on the part of the Chinese community and large-scale evasion by illegal immigrants.

As regards the current alien registration requirement, it was strongly designed by Congress to provide a continuous listing and identification of the alien population of the United States. The registration requirement was instituted by the Alien Registration Act of 1940[114] and continued by the 1952 Act. Registration and fingerprinting with some exceptions[115] were required of all aliens present in the United States at the time of the 1940 Act or entering subsequently who are fourteen years of age or over and who are to remain for thirty days or longer. And the 1952 Act further requires that

> Every alien, eighteen years of age and over, shall at all times carry with him and have in his personal possession any certificate of alien registration or alien registration receipt card issued to him. . . . Any alien who fails to comply with the provisions of this subsection shall be guilty of a misdemeanor and shall upon conviction for each

[111]See pp. 582–85 above.

[112]For the history of proposals for alien identification or registration see chapter 18, pp. 540–42; also pp. 582–87 of this chapter.

[113]See pp. 582–85 above.

[114]See chapter 17, pp. 540–42 above.

[115]Fingerprinting of nonimmigrant aliens may be waived at the discretion of the Secretary of State and the Attorney General and on a basis of reciprocity. Sect. 8, Act of September 11, 1957 (71 Stat. 639).

> offense be fined not to exceed $100 or be imprisoned not more than thirty days, or both. (Sect. 264e)

The same act, as previously described, also requires reregistration of every alien, subject to the terms of the act, each year during the month of January and reporting in writing each change of address within ten days of the change, under penalty of deportation.[116]

With these stringent provisions, Congress appears to have done what it could legislatively to establish a complete register of the alien population. Actually, however, the registration law and identity card have not provided the full listing of the resident alien population that was contemplated, nor have they proved an effective tool for detecting the illegal alien. Compliance with the registration requirement appears to be far from complete, and the illegal alien may well prefer to take his chances with being apprehended for nonregistration rather than report his name and address to the authorities. From the point of view of the authorities, violation of the registration act does provide a more readily established ground for deportation than proving that a person is an illegal alien; but from the point of view of the illegal alien he is already subject to deportation if detected, and he may feel more secure from detection by not reporting his presence.

From the above considerations and from the more detailed review of congressional attempts to establish a system of identification of individual aliens in the United States that was given in an earlier section of this chapter,[117] the conclusion is that feasible control of illegal immigration has not been found in that direction. The experience of the United States and other countries suggests in fact that an alien identification system cannot be reasonably effective unless it is part of a broader registration system for the total population, alien and citizen alike, with civil registers and identity cards for all as found in certain European countries. For the United States at the present time, such a system is judged to be both politically and practically out of the question.

Faced with the fact that forbidding and penalization do not deter illegal immigration entirely, that border controls cannot be more than partially effective, and that registration of aliens does not point out who is and who is not entitled to be in the country, Congress began to look in another direction for an answer to the illegal immigration problem. Some congressmen reasoned that illegal immigration might be checked by reducing or removing the economic attraction that drew such immigration to the United States, and they accordingly introduced bills forbid-

[116]Ibid., sect. 265 and 241(a)(5); see 1952 Act, deportable class 5, p. 459.

[117]See pp. 582–87 above.

ding the employment of aliens not properly admitted as lawful residents. Such a bill was introduced in the second session of the 71st Congress (1930),[118] early in the Depression period. More sweeping was a bill of about six years later to prohibit the making of loans, the granting of relief, or the giving of employment to aliens who have entered illegally.[119] Neither of the above bills came out of committee. Many years later two identical bills entitled "Illegal Employment of Aliens Act of 1954" were introduced in House and Senate during the second session of the 83rd Congress.[120] They were to make it illegal for any person or organization to employ any alien whom they knew or had reasonable grounds to suspect of having entered illegally within the past three years. Again the bills failed of enactment. More recently a renewed concern over the illegal alien problem has led to the introduction of bills establishing penalties for employers who knowingly hire illegal aliens.

Only time will tell how effective this attack on the illegal alien problem will prove to be. The approach to the problem through denial of employment appears strategic, but the procedure of placing responsibility on the employer of the illegal alien, though attractive in theory, may be vulnerable in practice. A preceding section of this chapter[121] reviewed the long experience with congressional attempts to secure enforcement of the immigration laws by means of imposing responsibility on persons or organizations aiding or dealing with alien violators of those laws. The record of such attempts is not encouraging, from the time of the contract labor laws of the 1880s and the laws making transportation companies liable for bringing in excludable aliens, down to the present time. Ways of evasion have been devised,[122] enforcement has been difficult, and a weakness of such laws as generally and perhaps necessarily written is that a person or organization cannot be held responsible unless shown to have dealt with an alien violator in full knowledge of the alien's status or through negligence. In the case of the recent bills directed against the illegal alien's employer, it could be difficult to prove that the latter knew his employee was both an alien and out-of-status.

The problem thus comes back to one of identification, for unless the employer has an adequate means of finding the status of employees he cannot be expected in reason to know who is ineligible to employment. It was asserted earlier that for a registration or identification system to be effective it should cover both aliens and citizens. But even if such a

[118]See p. 218 above.

[119]See p. 240 above.

[120]See p. 322 above.

[121]See Imposed Liability, pp. 593–604 above.

[122]See footnote 87, p. 597 above.

system is not acceptable for the total population, it could nevertheless be applied to the employed portion of the population; and in fact it already exists in substance for workers covered by social security. The one further step would be to record immigration status on the social security card of aliens so that the card serves as evidence of whether an alien is eligible for employment.[123]

In view of the long history of past efforts and failures to solve the illegal immigration problem, no simple or immediate answer to the problem can be expected. The attack on the problem through denial of employment is promising, but modes of evasion[124] and difficulties of enforcement are to be anticipated, especially in what are already the trouble spots of alien employment such as agriculture, small ethnic enterprises that may not be under social security, self-employment, and employers who exploit deportable workers. But an even partially effective program may be most productive as a deterrent to illegal immigration and an incentive to voluntary departure of aliens living under the risk of detection and deportation who might hope to return lawfully at some later time.

To conclude: at this time of writing the illegal alien problem is still unsolved, and it remains to be seen what course will be taken by further measures for control, or what the effectiveness of such measures will be. Some conclusions, however, can be drawn from the experience provided by congressional attempts to deal with the problem over the past century or more. Congressional action to meet the problem has taken two general directions, one to prevent illegal entry, the other to apprehend and expel the illegals who gain entry. Experience has shown that measures for prevention of illegal entry, although partially successful, are not sufficient in themselves, and need to be reinforced by other measures for the apprehension of those who take up residence illegally. Here the problem becomes one of identification;[125] and American experience as well as the example of other countries indicates that an identification system to be effective must cover the entire resident population, citizen and alien alike. Requirement of a European type of identity card for every resident of the United States probably would not be acceptable at the present time, but inasmuch as the principal motive for illegal entry is to obtain employment

[123]See Appendix B, Linkage of Social Security and Immigration Records.

[124]As regards fraudulent documents, the Immigration and Naturalization Service is reported to be trying to develop an alien registration card that cannot be counterfeited, and the State Department has a similar project for passports.

[125]Measures adopted in the past to combat various types of illegal immigration by the imposition of liability on those who transport, employ, or aid illegals have also encountered the difficulty of identifying the excludable and illegal aliens.

it would be sufficient to have an identification system for the employed population only; also, the foundation for such a means of identification already exists in the social security system. Probably no identification system can be expected to discover all out-of-status aliens. The ultimate method of personal identification, fingerprinting, can be required for certain aliens,[126] not more widely within the general population; but reasonably effective, even if not completely effective, measures for the identification of illegals could have a significant deterrent effect. From both human and administrative considerations, an illegal entry deterred is far better than an alien stopped at the border or apprehended and deported after illegal entry.

Finally, there are, of course, other considerations in dealing with the illegal alien problem, beyond control measures such as deterrence, identification, and enforcement. Many of the aliens of doubtful status within the United States must be of established residence, and a program of enforcement would need to proceed carefully to allow time for documentation of status where possible, in other cases to facilitate voluntary departure with the hope of lawful admission at some later time, and to act with flexibility and consideration in hardship and deserving cases.

[126]Fingerprinting was required for immigrant and resident aliens aged fourteen and over by sect. 30 and 31 of the Alien Registration Act of 1940 (54 Stat. 670) and for immigrant visa applicants under sect. 221(b) of the 1952 Act (66 Stat. 163).

22 Conclusion: Some Remaining Issues

This survey of congressional action on immigration has ended with the 1965 Act and with the preceding chapter, but in conclusion it is appropriate to look forward to consider issues that may lie ahead and directions that may be taken by future developments in immigration policy. We have seen that over their long history American immigration law and policy have grown into certain well-established patterns but at the same time have continued to evolve through additions and amendments. We therefore can expect the main lines of policy and practice to continue, in the form of numerical limitation of admissions, selectivity in admissions and exclusions, and expulsion of aliens who enter unlawfully or who become liable to deportation after entry. At the same time, however, policy decisions are always subject to reconsideration, and at any given time there are always some specific issues that remain to be resolved. At this time of writing the immediate concern of Congress is with illegal immigration, a subject already dealt with in the final section of the preceding chapter[1] and more strictly a matter of enforcement than of policy per se. Lying ahead for future consideration, however, are certain other questions of immigration regulation and long-range policy, which in conclusion are commented on below.

How Many to Admit

A recurrent question of immigration policy is the rate of admission. Since passage of the 1965 Act, immigration, which is to say, admission for permanent residence, has averaged about 400,000[2] per annum, consisting for the most part of near relatives of citizens and resident aliens; and this rate of admissions appears to be now acceptable both in its total amount and in its composition. From past experience, however, it seems likely that sooner or later a more restrictive immigration policy will be

[1]See pp. 604–11 above.

[2]Composed of Western Hemisphere limited to 120,000 per annum, 170,000 quota immigration from the rest of the world, and the balance made up of the nonquota classes.

considered by Congress. Especially if the nation continues to move toward the zero population growth urged by various concerned groups, through a balancing of births and deaths, the logical corollary of zero immigration would certainly suggest itself. And if not because of population trends, other conditions might well lead to a reconsideration of the number of aliens being admitted.

If Congress at some future time should consider a more restrictive policy, the nonquota provisions would come in for review, for they are the obvious large "loophole" in the limitation of immigration. The principal source of nonquota immigration was cut off by the 1965 Act that terminated the nonquota status of natives of the Western Hemisphere and imposed a quota ceiling on the numbers admitted. Further tightening of the limits on immigration, if it should come, might well include reduction or elimination of at least the larger nonquota classes (that is, certain relatives) and a shifting of them to the high preference classes within the total quota. Such a move would be all the more likely if nonquota immigration should follow a steadily rising trend in the years ahead as Western Hemisphere nonquota immigration had done prior to 1965. Family unification has long been a principle[3] of American immigration policy and is not apt to be abandoned in the near future; but the fact remains that under the system of nonquota status and preferences each immigrant who is admitted is the potential head of a whole chain of relatives who may follow after,[4] and if future concern should arise over the numerical extent of such chains of migration, such family admissions might well be put partly or more fully under quota.

Preferred Immigrants

Preceding chapters have dealt with the provisions of facilitated entry for certain favored classes of immigrants, the principal criteria for such favored treatment being personal qualifications, relationship to a lawful resident of the United States, or refugee status.[5] In principle, these provisions for facilitated entry appear to be firmly established, although, of course, subject to readjustment in accordance with any future changes in policy. As suggested in the preceding section, for example, a more restrictive admissions policy might bring with it a charge to quota of certain classes now entering free of quota limitation.

What has come most into question is the attraction to the United

[3]See chapter 16, Family Unification, pp. 505–20 above.

[4]Although scarcely the forty-nine relatives reported for Canada (p. 520 above).

[5]See especially pp. 492–504, 505–20, and 521–33 above.

States of immigrants with skills and abilities needed in their home countries, the so-called "brain drain"; and it has been suggested that there should be some restraint on the admission of such highly qualified migrants rather than granting them easy entry. As American immigration law is now constituted, there is no basis for denial of the immigration visa or admission because of the needs of the country of origin. The American position appears to be one of sympathetic understanding of the problem but belief that it is up to the country of emigration to restrain unwanted departures. Barring some form of treaty or international agreement, it does not appear likely that the United States will depart from this position by putting restraints on the international movement of highly qualified persons.

Labor Admissions Policy

International migration is to an important degree a movement of labor, and immigration policy correspondingly contains elements of labor policy.[6] The labor issue, also, is one of the most politically sensitive aspects of immigration; and concern over the volume of immigration, legal or illegal, predictably rises and falls with the amount of unemployment. Reasonable assurance that immigrant admissions will not be so large or so composed as to affect the labor market adversely or depress wages is provided by the overall quota limits, the composition of the nonquota classes, and the preference structure that gives strong priority to various classes of relatives and allocates only 20 percent of the quota to aliens who come in under the third and sixth occupational preferences. As regards these latter, further assurance is given by the 1965 Act's amendment of section 212(a) of the 1952 Act to confer a stronger power of labor certification on the Department of Labor. The power so conferred, whereby given occupations can be added to or removed from the list of certified occupations, gives the Department a high degree of flexibility in reacting to labor surplus or shortage in specific occupations.

Illegal immigration is another matter. Here the labor aspect is much more acute because the inflow is large, perhaps several times the legal immigration, and typically comes in search of employment. To take the Mexican case as an illustration: the illegal movement is powered by a wide wage differential, a labor surplus south of the border, and available jobs to the north. It is safe to say the northward flow will continue as long as these economic forces operate and will continue in spite of governmental efforts to stop it. In effect, the immigration laws in this case impose an artificial barrier on a powerful natural stream of population and labor;

[6] On this point, see chapter 15, Labor Market Policy.

and some part of the stream will find its way through and around the barrier if the pressure is sufficient.

If we accept the view that the barrier cannot be made watertight and that the migrant Mexican labor will make its way to the United States either legally or illegally, then it would appear far better to have a program of regulated and controlled admissions. Admission could be for temporary employment only, with safeguards for departure in due season and with sufficient personal description, including photograph and fingerprints if thought necessary, to permit later identification of those who might violate their terms of admission. The model here is obviously the earlier Mexican agricultural labor or *bracero* program, which was terminated at the end of 1964, but the admission of foreign workers on a temporary basis has been a common practice in Europe as well.

Apart from certain special exceptions, only aliens admitted for permanent residence under an immigrant visa may lawfully take employment. The temporary admission of aliens for a specified term of employment, however, would offer both theoretical and practical advantages: a tangible program of intergovernmental cooperation to alleviate a common problem, a draining off of surplus labor abroad that might otherwise seek illegal entry, admission of labor when and as in demand, provision of a more elastic labor supply, regulation of wages and conditions of employment for the temporarily admitted workers to protect current standards, prevention of immigrant labor exploitation, and provision for eventual departure. In opposition would be the protests and political pressures that forced the termination of the *bracero* program in 1964. But if the problem of illegal immigration becomes sufficiently acute, the temporary admission of alien labor would become correspondingly more attractive. There is a persuasive argument here that the attack on the problem of illegal immigration from Mexico could be broadened, no longer limited to the defensive measures of guarding the borders and attempting to apprehend and deport those who gain entry, but directed constructively toward reducing some of the immediate causes that are present in the form of labor surplus below the border and unfilled job opportunities waiting on the other side. The logic of the matter would seem to point toward such a new approach to the problem.

Legislative Versus Administrative Regulation

As described in chapter 19, Legislative and Administrative Roles,[7] Congress has traditionally exercised tight control over immigration and immigration policy. Compared with Canada and Australia, for example,

[7]See pp. 544–57 above.

American policy determination has been kept closely in the hands of Congress, and only limited powers of administrative discretion have been granted.

Further evidence of the unwillingness of Congress to delegate any of its powers over immigration policy is its repeated rejection of proposals for the establishment of a permanent official advisory body on immigration policy. Most recent were the proposals for an advisory Immigration Board contained in the administration bills of the 88th Congress (H.R. 7700, Celler [N.Y.]; S. 1932, Hart [Mich.]) and the 89th Congress (H.R. 2580, Celler [N.Y.]; S. 500, Hart [Mich.]), which were eliminated from the bill finally passed by Congress. One may infer that the congressional committees on immigration had no enthusiasm for the Board.

The reasons for the close congressional control of immigration, largely by law and only secondarily by regulation, can only be conjectured: perhaps a compound of long precedent, retention of what has been construed to be a constitutional power of Congress, a concern that administrative officers if given more independent authority might not conform to the wishes of Congress, a clutching of the reins of power by congressional specialists on immigration, or whatever other reasons there may be.

Given the long and uncertain course an immigration bill must travel from introduction to enactment,[8] it would be more efficient to allow wider administrative authority and discretionary powers in the regulation of immigration. Some movement in that direction can in fact be seen in recent years, for example, in the 1947 substitution of Department of Justice regulations for legislation to specify the personal information required of each immigrant[9] and in the greatly expanded labor certification power given to the Department of Labor in 1965.[10] It is reasonable to expect further such movement in the future. The congressional committees on immigration have been overburdened with the writing of minutely detailed legislation as well as with the thousands of private immigration bills that were introduced in every Congress. Greater latitude of administrative discretion would leave Congress correspondingly more free to deal with broad issues of policy, and at the same time give promise of greater flexibility in dealing with out-of-the-ordinary cases on their individual merits and prompter response to the new emergencies in international migration that arise from time to time.

Although such a change toward greater administrative responsibility

[8]For description of the legislative process see pp. 4–6 above.

[9]See p. 540 above.

[10]See p. 614 above; also in chapter 19, Later Extent of Administrative Powers, pp. 549–51.

in the regulation of immigration offers certain advantages, it is most unlikely that the setting of basic policy would come into administrative hands to the extent that it has in some other countries, if for no other reason than the American preference that policy be made by elective rather than appointive officials.

To conclude, the preceding chapters have followed the development of immigration law and policy since the early days of independence (Part I), and then traced the course of the separate elements into which immigration policy as a whole can be analyzed (Part II). During the century and more of its history, American immigration policy has continued to change and evolve. Like other areas of policy, it probably will never be completed but will continue to evolve as it has in the past. If so, it remains to be seen what directions will be taken in the future, whether some of the alternatives outlined in the preceding sections of this chapter are in fact adopted by Congress, or whether new and now unanticipated directions will emerge. Much will depend on future domestic and world developments that touch on international migration and on future currents of opinion in and out of Congress.

From the account of legislative history, we can see that many influences and considerations come to bear on immigration policy formation; the policy formation is a complex process whereby many legislative proposals are presented in the form of House and Senate bills but only a chosen few go on to enactment. For one thing, immigration policy does not stand independently, but rather is a component of national policy as a whole; and it is influenced by the prevailing direction of that national policy or orientation, whether isolationist or internationalist, whether colored by the optimism of good times or by the pessimism of bad, whether directed by immediate national self-interest or by a sense of humanitarian obligation. Thus both immigration policy and the spirit with which it is enforced are formed and conditioned by the prevailing national climate of opinion.

Other considerations that enter into immigration policy formation are revealed by the lengthy congressional debates on the major immigration bills and by the reports that set forth the thinking of the immigration committees of Congress. These sources reveal the many conflicting concerns—the political, economic, regional, cultural, ethnic, xenophobic, international, humanitarian, and others—that influence members of Congress and their voting behavior. The debate also demonstrates that the subject of immigration, unfortunately, arouses strong feelings and emotions, both for and against immigration in general and immigrants in particular; and such sentiments can be powerful enough to becloud the real issues and policy objectives.

All of these influences, at their different levels, vary with time and create pressures for change in immigration law and policy. From the nature of the legislative process, however, and perhaps also from the nature of the subject itself, there has also been marked resistance to change, a tendency for immigration policy to persist in its old established patterns. The massive body of immigration law has an inertia of its own, there are always ardent defenders of the status quo, and Congress as a whole may be reluctant to engage in an always bitterly fought and divisive battle over immigration policy. It is therefore all the more the task, the responsibility even, of Congress and its immigration committees to maintain an immigration policy responsive to the changing national needs and the changing international and humanitarian responsibilities of the years ahead.

Bibliographical Notes and References

Principal Sources

1. *Congressional Record,* vols. 1– , Special session and 43rd Congress– , 1873 to date. Preceded by *Annals of Congress,* vols. 1–41, 1st to 18th Congress, first session, 1789 to 1824; *Register of Debates in Congress,* vols. 1–13, 18th Congress, second session to 24th Congress, 1824 to 1837; *Congressional Globe,* vols. 1–46, 23rd to 42nd Congress, 1833 to 1873.
2. *U. S. Statutes at Large,* vols. 1– , 1789 to date. Footnote reference to acts by volume number and first page of the act, as Act of June 27, 1952 (66 Stat. 163).
3. House and Senate committee reports on immigration bills, in congressional document series. Where not clear from the context, footnote references to congressional committee reports give the number and session of Congress, as H. Rept. 350 (68-I).
4. Copies of House and Senate immigration bills. Identification of number and session of Congress as above.

Compilations of Immigration Law

1. U.S. Department of Justice, Immigration and Naturalization Service, *Laws Applicable to Immigration and Nationality.* Washington, D.C.: U.S. Government Printing Office, 1953. An indispensable compendium of immigration and nationality laws, from 1798 through 1952. Gives text of laws *as amended* up to and including amendment by the Act of June 27, 1952, but fully footnoted to give wording as it was before amendment. Part II, pp. 1035–1258, contains the text of constitutional provisions, executive and departmental orders, presidential proclamations, and treaties concerned with immigration and nationality.

   Supplements I, II, III, and IV (Washington, D.C.: U.S. Government Printing Office, 1954, 1955, 1960, 1963) extend through December 31, 1962. For later years see below.
2. *Immigration and Nationality Act with Amendments and Notes on Related Laws and Summaries of Pertinent Judicial Decisions.* Committee print for the use of the Committee on the Judiciary, House of Representatives. 6th ed., rev. through May 1, 1969. Washington, D.C.: U.S. Government Printing Office, 1969.

3. U.S. Department of Justice, Immigration and Naturalization Service. *Immigration and Nationality Laws and Regulations as of March 1, 1944.* Washington, D.C.: U.S. Government Printing Office, 1944. Supersedes all previous editions, and itself is superseded by the 1953 edition of different title above. For immigration and nationality law not as useful or detailed as the 1953 edition, but does contain Title 8—Aliens and Nationality, of the Code of Federal Regulations. Supplements I, II, and III (Washington, D.C.: U.S. Government Printing Office, 1945, 1946, 1947) extend through December 31, 1946.
4. Reports of the Immigration Commission, vol. 39. *Immigration Legislation.* Senate Document No. 758, 61st Congress, 3rd session, Washington, D.C.: U.S. Government Printing Office, 1911. Contains U.S. Immigration Laws, 1844–1910, Appendix B, pp. 95–123; U.S. Contract-labor Laws, 1885–1887, Appendix C, pp. 125–126; Treaties and Laws respecting Chinese Immigration, 1881–1904, Appendix E, pp. 131–144; Steerage Legislation, 1819–1908, pp. 339–485; State Immigration and Alien Laws, pp. 505–956.

Surveys of Immigration Legislation

1. *Reports of the Immigration Commission.* Vol. 39 (see above), pp. 5–81. An account of federal legislation on immigration, 1798–1910, with a final chapter on Chinese exclusion (pp. 67–81).
2. U.S. Congress, Senate. *The Immigration and Naturalization Systems of the United States.* Senate Report No. 1515, 81st Congress, second session. Report of the Committee on the Judiciary pursuant to Senate Resolution No. 137, 80th Congress, first session. April 20, 1950.

Other Sources

Useful secondary sources of current information on congressional activities related to immigration are the legislative notes included in the following two serial publications: *News,* issued by the American Immigration and Citizenship Conference, and *Interpreter Releases,* American Council for Nationalities Service.

Note: for guides to current immigration law and practice (Auerbach, Gordon and Rosenfield, Wasserman), see footnote 4, chapter 1.

Appendix A
Immigration Policy in Party Platforms and Composition of Congress, 1848–1964

The first platform issued by a political party prior to a presidential election is attributed to the National Republican party meeting in convention in Baltimore in December of 1831.[1] The practice was gradually adopted thereafter by other parties and conventions, but no reference to immigration or immigrants appeared until the election of 1848. In that year the antislavery Free Soil Party Convention, meeting in Buffalo, N.Y., included in one of its resolutions against the establishment of more slave states or territories the plea that

> the soil of our extensive domain be kept free for the hardy pioneers of our own land and the oppressed and banished of other lands seeking homes of comfort and fields of enterprise in the new world.[2]

1848 Election
President: Zachary Taylor (Whig)

31st Congress (December 3, 1849–March 3, 1851)
Senate: 35 Democrats, 25 Whigs, 2 Free Soil
House: 116 Democrats, 111 Whigs
32nd Congress (December 1, 1851–March 3, 1853)
Senate: 36 Democrats, 23 Whigs, 3 Free Soil
House: 140 Democrats, 88 Whigs, 5 Free Soil

[1]Sources for this appendix: Thomas H. McKee, *The National Conventions and Platforms of All Political Parties, 1789 to 1905*, 6th ed. (Baltimore: Friedenwald, 1906); Kirk H. Porter and Donald Johnson, *National Party Platforms, 1840–1968* (Urbana: University of Illinois, 1970); and *Congressional Directory*.
[2]McKee, *National Conventions*, p. 68.

1852 Election

Free Soil Democratic platform, section 15: "That emigrants and exiles from the Old World should find a cordial welcome to homes of comfort and fields of enterprise in the New; and every attempt to abridge their privilege of becoming citizens and owners of soil among us ought to be resisted with inflexible determination."[3]

President: Franklin Pierce (Democrat)

33rd Congress (December 5, 1853–March 3, 1855)
    Senate: 38 Democrats, 22 Whigs, 2 Free Soil
    House: 159 Democrats, 71 Whigs, 4 Free Soil
34th Congress (December 3, 1855–March 3, 1857)
    Senate: 42 Democrats, 15 Republicans, 5 Americans (Know-Nothing)
    House: 83 Democrats, 108 Republicans, 43 Americans

1856 Election

Democratic platform, section 10: reference is made to "asylum of the oppressed of every nation," as being a cardinal principle of the Democratic party, together with resistance to "every attempt to abridge the privilege of becoming citizens and the owners of soil among us."[4]

American (Know-Nothing) platform: includes denial of voting rights and holding of public office to aliens; twenty-one-year residence requirement for naturalization.[5]

President: James Buchanan (Democrat)

35th Congress (December 7, 1857–March 10, 1859)
    Senate: 39 Democrats, 20 Republicans, 5 Americans
    House: 131 Democrats, 92 Republicans, 14 Americans
36th Congress (December 5, 1859–March 28, 1861)
    Senate: 38 Democrats, 26 Republicans, 2 Americans
    House: 101 Democrats, 113 Republicans, 23 Americans

1860 Election

Republican platform, section 14: states opposition to "any change in our naturalization laws, or any state legislation by which the rights of citizens hitherto accorded to immigrants from foreign lands shall be abridged or impaired."[6]

[3]Ibid., p. 82.
[4]Ibid., p. 90.
[5]Ibid., pp. 101–2.
[6]Ibid., p. 115.

President: Abraham Lincoln (Republican)

37th Congress (July 4, 1861–March 9, 1863)
Senate: 11 Democrats, 31 Republicans, 7 Americans
House: 42 Democrats, 106 Republicans, 28 Americans
38th Congress (December 7, 1863–March 11, 1865)
Senate: 12 Democrats, 39 Republicans
House: 80 Democrats, 103 Republicans

1864 Election

Republican platform, section 8: "That foreign immigration, which in the past has added so much to the wealth, development of resources, and increase of power to the nation—the asylum of the oppressed of all nations—should be fostered and encouraged by a liberal and just policy."[7]

President: Abraham Lincoln (Republican)

39th Congress (December 4, 1865–March 2, 1867)
Senate: 10 Democrats, 42 Republicans
House: 46 Democrats, 145 Republicans
40th Congress (March 4, 1867–March 3, 1869)
Senate: 11 Democrats, 42 Republicans
House: 49 Democrats, 143 Republicans

1868 Election

Democratic platform, section 8: calls for equal rights and protection for both naturalized and native-born citizens at home and abroad.[8]

Republican platform: section 11 same as section 8 of 1864.[9]

President: Ulysses Grant (Republican)

41st Congress (March 4, 1869–March 3, 1871)
Senate: 11 Democrats, 61 Republicans
House: 73 Democrats, 170 Republicans
42nd Congress (March 4, 1871–March 3, 1873)
Senate: 17 Democrats, 57 Republicans
House: 104 Democrats, 139 Republicans

[7]Ibid., p. 126.
[8]Ibid., p. 133.
[9]Ibid., p. 139.

1872 Election

No reference to immigration in the party platforms of the major parties; following statement in the Labor Reform platform, section 6: "That the presence in our country of Chinese labor, imported by capitalists in large numbers, for servile use, is an evil, entailing want and its attendant train of misery and crime on all classes of the American people, and should be prohibited by legislation."[10]

President: Ulysses Grant (Republican)

43rd Congress (December 1, 1873–March 3, 1875)
  Senate: 19 Democrats, 54 Republicans
  House: 88 Democrats 203 Republicans
44th Congress (December 6, 1875–March 3, 1877)
  Senate: 29 Democrats, 46 Republicans
  House: 181 Democrats, 107 Republicans, 3 Independents

1876 Election

Democratic platform: deplores the errors and omissions of the government that

> have exposed our brethren of the Pacific Coast to the incursions of a race not sprung from the same great parent stock, and in fact now by law denied citizenship through naturalization, as being neither accustomed to the traditions of a progressive civilization nor exercised in liberty under equal laws. We denounce the policy which thus discards the liberty-loving Germans and tolerates a revival of the coolie-trade in Mongolian women imported for immoral purposes, and Mongolian men held to perform servile labor contracts, and demand such modification of the treaty with the Chinese Empire, or such legislation within Constitutional limitations, as shall prevent further importation or immigration of the Mongolian race.[11]

Republican platform, section 11:

> It is the immediate duty of Congress to fully investigate the effect of the immigration and importation of Mongolians upon the moral and material interests of the country.[12]

Prohibition platform, section 13:

[10]Ibid., p. 155.
[11]Ibid., p. 166.
[12]Ibid., p. 172.

> The practice of a friendly and liberal policy to immigrants from all nations, the guarantee to them of ample protection and of equal rights and privileges.[13]

President: Rutherford B. Hayes (Republican)

45th Congress (March 5, 1877–March 3, 1879)
Senate: 36 Democrats, 39 Republicans, 1 Independent
House: 156 Democrats, 137 Republicans

46th Congress (March 18, 1879–March 3, 1881)
Senate: 43 Democrats, 33 Republicans
House: 150 Democrats, 128 Republicans, 14 others

1880 Election

Democratic platform, section 11: amendment of the Burlingame Treaty. No more Chinese immigration, except for travel, education, and foreign commerce.[14]

Republican platform, section 6:

> Since the authority to regulate immigration and intercourse between the United States and foreign nations rests with the Congress of the United States and the treaty-making power, the Republican party, regarding the unrestricted immigration of Chinese as a matter of grave concernment under the exercise of both these powers, would limit and restrict that immigration by the enactment of such just, humane, and reasonable laws and treaties as will produce that result.[15]

Greenback Convention platform, section 4:

> Slavery being simply cheap labor, and cheap labor being simply slavery, the importation and presence of Chinese serfs necessarily tends to brutalize and degrade American labor; therefore immediate steps should be taken to abrogate the Burlingame Treaty.[16]

President: James A. Garfield (Republican)

47th Congress (December 5, 1881–March 3, 1883)
Senate: 37 Democrats, 37 Republicans, 2 others
House: 130 Democrats, 152 Republicans, 11 others

48th Congress (December 3, 1883–March 3, 1885)
Senate: 36 Democrats, 40 Republicans
House: 200 Democrats, 119 Republicans, 6 others

[13]Ibid., p. 177.
[14]Ibid., pp. 184–85.
[15]Ibid., p. 189.
[16]Ibid., p. 192.

1884 Election

Democratic platform: states belief in the principle of asylum for the oppressed of every nation, but opposed to

> the importation of foreign labor or the admission of servile races, unfitted by habits, training, religion, or kindred, for absorption into the great body of our people, or for the citizenship which our laws confer. American civilization demands that against the immigration or importation of Mongolians to these shores our gates be closed.[17]

Republican platform:

> we denounce the importation of contract labor, whether from Europe or Asia, as an offense against the spirit of American institutions; and we pledge ourselves to sustain the present law restricting Chinese immigration, and to provide such further legislation as is necessary to carry out its purposes.[18]

Greenback Convention platform, section 7:

> We condemn all importations of contract labor, made with a view of reducing to starvation wages the workingmen of this country, and demand laws for its prevention.[19]

President: Grover Cleveland (Democrat)

49th Congress (December 7, 1885–March 3, 1887)
Senate: 34 Democrats, 41 Republicans
House: 182 Democrats, 140 Republicans, 2 others
50th Congress (December 5, 1887–March 2, 1889)
Senate: 37 Democrats, 39 Republicans
House: 170 Democrats, 151 Republicans, 4 others

1888 Election

Democratic platform:

> The exclusion from our shores of Chinese laborers has been effectually secured under the provisions of a treaty, the operation of which has been postponed by the action of a Republican majority in the Senate.[20]

Republican platform:

> We declare our hostility to the introduction into this country of foreign contract labor and of Chinese labor, alien to our civilization and our Constitution, and we demand the rigid enforcement of the

[17]Ibid., p. 207.
[18]Ibid., p. 212.
[19]Ibid., p. 216.
[20]Ibid. p. 234.

existing laws against it, and favor such immediate legislation as will exclude such labor from our shores.[21]

Prohibition platform, section 12:

> That our immigration laws should be so enforced as to prevent the introduction into our country of all convicts, inmates of other dependent institutions, and all others physically incapacitated for self-support; and that no person should have the ballot in any state who is not a citizen of the United States.[22]

American Convention platform:

> Whereas, One of the greatest evils of unrestricted foreign immigration is the reduction of the wages of the American working-man and working-woman to the level of the underfed and underpaid labor of foreign countries; therefore
>
> Resolved, That we demand that no immigrant shall be admitted into the United States without a passport obtained from the American consul at the port from which he sails; that no passport shall be issued to any pauper, criminal, or insane person, or to any person who, in the judgment of the consul, is not likely to become a desirable citizen of the United States; and that for each immigrant passport there shall be collected by the consul issuing the same the sum of one hundred dollars. . . .
>
> Resolved, That the present naturalization laws of the United States shall be unconditionally repealed.[23]

President: Benjamin Harrison (Republican)

51st Congress (December 2, 1889–March 3, 1891)
Senate: 37 Democrats, 47 Republicans
House: 156 Democrats, 173 Republicans, 1 Independent

52nd Congress (December 7, 1891–March 4, 1893)
Senate: 39 Democrats, 47 Republicans, 2 others
House: 231 Democrats, 88 Republicans, 14 others

1892 Election

Democratic platform, section 12:

> We heartily approve all legitimate efforts to prevent the United States from being used as the dumping ground for the known criminals and professional paupers of Europe, and we demand the rigid enforcement of the laws against Chinese immigration, or the importation of foreign labor, to degrade American labor and lessen its

[21]Ibid., p. 240.
[22]Ibid., p. 248.
[23]Ibid., pp. 255–256.

wages; but we condemn and denounce any and all attempts to restrict the immigration of the industrious and worthy of foreign lands.[24]

Republican platform:

We favor the enactment of more stringent laws and regulations for the restriction of criminal, pauper, and contract immigration.[25]

Prohibition platform, sections 6 and 7 (in part):

Foreign immigration has become a burden upon industry, one of the factors in depressing wages and causing discontent; therefore our immigration laws should be revised and strictly enforced. The time of residence for naturalization should be extended, and no naturalized person should be allowed to vote until one year after he becomes a citizen. Non-resident aliens should not be allowed to acquire land in this country. . . .[26]

Farmers' Alliance platform, section 4 (in part):

We demand the passage of laws prohibiting the alien ownership of land, and that Congress take early steps to devise some plan to obtain all lands now owned by aliens and foreign syndicates. . . .[27]

National People's platform, 4th resolution:

That we condemn the fallacy of protecting American labor under the present system, which opens our ports to the pauper and criminal classes of the world and crowds out our wage-earners, and we denounce the present ineffective law against contract labor, and demand the further restriction of undesirable immigration.[28]

President: Grover Cleveland (Democrat)

53rd Congress (August 7, 1893–March 2, 1895)
Senate: 44 Democrats, 38 Republicans, 3 others
House: 220 Democrats, 128 Republicans, 8 others
54th Congress (December 2, 1895–March 3, 1897)
Senate: 39 Democrats, 44 Republicans, 6 others
House: 104 Democrats, 245 Republicans, 8 others

[24]Ibid., p. 266; correction from Porter and Johnson, *National Party Platforms*, p. 88.
[25]Ibid., p. 271.
[26]Ibid., p. 276.
[27]Ibid, p. 279.
[28]Ibid., p. 284.

1896 Election

Democratic platform:

> We hold that the most efficient way of protecting American labor is to prevent the importation of foreign pauper labor to compete with it in the home market. . . .[29]

Republican platform:

> For the protection of the quality of our American citizenship and of the wages of our workingmen against the fatal competition of low-priced labor, we demand that the immigration laws be thoroughly enforced, and so extended as to exclude from entrance to the United States those who can neither read nor write.[30]

National party platform, section 12:

> Our immigration laws should be so revised as to exclude paupers and criminals. None but citizens of the United States should be allowed to vote in any state, and naturalized citizens should not vote until one year after naturalization papers have been issued.[31]

President: William McKinley (Republican)

55th Congress (March 15, 1897–March 3, 1899)
  Senate: 34 Democrats, 44 Republicans, 12 others
  House: 121 Democrats, 203 Republicans, 28 others
56th Congress (December 4, 1899–March 2, 1901)
  Senate: 26 Democrats, 51 Republicans, 9 others
  House: 161 Democrats, 185 Republicans, 8 others

1900 Election

Democratic platform:

> We favor the continuance and strict enforcement of the Chinese Exclusion Law, and its application to the same classes of all Asiatic races.[32]

Republican platform:

> In the further interest of American workmen we favor a more effective restriction of the immigration of cheap labor from foreign lands. . . .[33]

[29]Ibid., p. 295.
[30]Ibid., p. 303.
[31]Ibid., p. 322.
[32]Ibid., p. 338.
[33]Ibid., p. 343.

People's party platform:

> The importation of Japanese and other laborers under contract to serve monopolistic corporations is a notorious and flagrant violation of the immigration laws. We demand that the federal government take cognizance of this menacing evil and repress it under existing laws. We further pledge ourselves to strive for the enactment of more stringent laws for the exclusion of Mongolian and Malayan immigration.[34]

Silver Republican platform:

> We observe with anxiety and regard with disapproval the increasing ownership of American lands by aliens, and their growing control over international transportation, natural resources, and public utilities.
>
> We are opposed to the importation of Asiatic laborers in competition with American labor, and advocate a more rigid enforcement of the laws relating thereto.[35]

President: William McKinley (Republican)

57th Congress (December 2, 1901–March 4, 1903)
Senate: 27 Democrats, 54 Republicans, 7 others
House: 149 Democrats, 195 Republicans, 8 others
58th Congress (November 9, 1903–March 4, 1905)
Senate: 33 Democrats, 57 Republicans
House: 178 Democrats, 208 Republicans

1904 Election

Republican platform:

> We cordially approve the attitude of President Roosevelt and Congress in regard to the exclusion of Chinese labor, and promise a continuance of the Republican policy in that direction.[36]

President: Theodore Roosevelt (Republican)

59th Congress (December 4, 1905–March 4, 1907)
Senate: 32 Democrats, 58 Republicans
House: 136 Democrats, 250 Republicans
60th Congress (December 2, 1907–March 4, 1909)
Senate: 30 Democrats, 60 Republicans
House: 164 Democrats, 222 Republicans

[34]Ibid., p. 352.
[35]Ibid., pp. 359, 362.
[36]Ibid., p. 398.

1908 Election

Democratic platform:

> We favor full protection, by both National and State governments within their respective spheres, of all foreigners residing in the United States under treaty, but we are opposed to the admission of Asiatic immigrants who can not be amalgamated with our population, or whose presence among us would raise a race issue and involve us in diplomatic controversies with Oriental powers.[37]

Independence platform:

> We oppose Asiatic immigration which does not amalgamate with our population, creates race issues and un-American conditions, and which reduces wages and tends to lower the high standard of living and the high standard of morality which American civilization has established.
>
> We demand the passage of an exclusion act which shall protect American workingmen from competition with Asiatic cheap labor and which shall protect American civilization from the contamination of Asiatic conditions.[38]

People's party platform:

> We demand the exclusion from American shores of foreign pauper labor, imported to beat down the wages of intelligent American workingmen.[39]

President: William Taft (Republican)

61st Congress (March 15, 1909–March 4, 1911)
Senate: 33 Democrats, 59 Republicans (second session)
House: 170 Democrats, 219 Republicans (second session)

62nd Congress (April 4, 1911–March 4, 1913)
Senate: 40 Democrats, 51 Republicans
House: 228 Democrats, 160 Republicans, 1 other

1912 Election

Progressive platform:

> Through the establishment of industrial standards we propose to secure to the able-bodied immigrant and to his native fellow workers a larger share of American opportunity.
>
> We denounce the fatal policy of indifference and neglect which has

[37]Porter and Johnson, *National Party Platforms*, p. 150.
[38]Ibid., p. 154.
[39]Ibid., p. 156.

left our enormous immigrant population to become the prey of chance and cupidity.

We favor Governmental action to encourage the distribution of immigrants away from the congested cities, to rigidly supervise all private agencies dealing with them and to promote their assimilation, education and advancement.[40]

Republican platform:

> We pledge the Republican party to the enactment of appropriate laws to give relief from the constantly growing evil of induced or undesirable immigration, which is inimical to the progress and welfare of the people of the United States.[41]

President: Woodrow Wilson (Democrat)

63rd Congress (April 7, 1913–March 4, 1915)
  Senate: 51 Democrats, 44 Republicans, 1 other
  House: 290 Democrats, 127 Republicans, 9 Progressives, 8 others
64th Congress (December 6, 1915–March 4, 1917)
  Senate: 56 Democrats, 40 Republicans
  House: 228 Democrats, 197 Republicans, 9 others

1916 Election

Republican platform:

> We reiterate the unqualified approval of the action taken in December, 1911, by the President and Congress to secure with Russia, as with other countries, a treaty that will recognize the absolute right of expatriation and prevent all discrimination of whatever kind between American citizens whether native-born or alien, and regardless of race, religion or previous political allegiance. We renew the pledge to observe this principle and to maintain the right of asylum. . . .[42]

President: Woodrow Wilson (Democrat)

65th Congress (April 2, 1917–March 4, 1919)
  Senate: 54 Democrats, 41 Republicans, 1 other
  House: 212 Democrats, 213 Republicans, 7 others
66th Congress (May 19, 1919–March 4, 1921)
  Senate: 47 Democrats, 48 Republicans, 1 other
  House: 191 Democrats, 237 Republicans, 3 others

[40]Ibid., p. 181.
[41]Ibid., p. 187.
[42]Ibid., p. 205.

1920 Election

Democratic platform:

> The policy of the United States with reference to the non-admission of Asiatic immigrants is a true expression of the judgment of our people, and to the several states, whose geographical situation or internal conditions make this policy, and the enforcement of the laws enacted pursuant thereto, of particular concern, we pledge our support.[43]

Republican platform:

> The standard of living and the standard of citizenship of a nation are its most precious possessions, and the preservation and the elevation of those standards is the first duty of our government. The immigration policy of the U.S. should be such as to insure that the number of foreigners in the country at any one time shall not exceed that which can be assimilated with reasonable rapidity, and to favor immigrants whose standards are similar to ours.
>
> The selective tests that are at present applied should be improved by requiring a higher physical standard, a more complete exclusion of mental defectives and of criminals, and a more effective inspection applied as near the source of immigration as possible, as well as at the port of entry. Justice to the foreigner and to ourselves demands provision for the guidance, protection and better economic distribution of our alien population. To facilitate government supervision, all aliens should be required to register annually until they become naturalized.
>
> The existing policy of the United States for the practical exclusion of Asiatic immigrants is sound, and should be maintained.[44]

Socialist platform:

> No alien should be deported from the United States on account of his political views or participation in labor struggles, not in any event without proper trial on specific charges. The arbitrary power to deport aliens by administrative order should be repealed.[45]

President: Warren Harding (Republican)

67th Congress (March 4, 1921–March 4, 1923)
    Senate: 36 Democrats, 59 Republicans, 1 other (second session)
    House: 132 Democrats, 301 Republicans, 1 other (second session)
68th Congress (December 3, 1923–March 4, 1925)
    Senate: 43 Democrats, 51 Republicans, 2 others
    House: 205 Democrats, 225 Republicans, 3 others

[43]Ibid., p. 223.
[44]Ibid., p. 235–36.
[45]Ibid., p. 240.

1924 Election

Democratic platform:

> We pledge ourselves to maintain our established position in favor of the exclusion of Asiatic immigration.[46]

Prohibition platform:

> Recognizing the fact that there are large numbers of unassimilated aliens now in this country who, in their present condition and environment, are incapable of assimilation, and are therefore a menace to our institutions, we declare for an immediate, scientific investigation, looking forward to a constructive program for Americanizing these aliens.[47]

Republican platform:

> The unprecedented living conditions in Europe following the world war created a condition by which we were threatened with mass immigration that would have seriously disturbed our economic life. The law recently enacted is designed to protect the inhabitants of our country, not only the American citizen, but also the alien already with us who is seeking to secure an economic foothold for himself and family from the competition that would come from unrestricted immigration. The administrative features of the law represent a great constructive advance, and eliminate the hardships suffered by immigrants under emergency statute.
>
> We favor the adoption of methods which will exercise a helpful influence among the foreign born population and provide for the education of the alien in our language, customs, ideals and standards of life. We favor the improvement of naturalization laws.[48]

President: Calvin Coolidge (Republican)

69th Congress (December 7, 1925–March 4, 1927)
Senate: 39 Democrats, 56 Republicans, 1 other
House: 183 Democrats, 247 Republicans, 5 others
70th Congress (December 5, 1927–March 4, 1929)
Senate: 47 Democrats, 48 Republicans, 1 other
House: 195 Democrats, 237 Republicans, 3 others

[46]Ibid., p. 249.
[47]Ibid., p. 257.
[48]Ibid., p. 265.

1928 Election

Democratic platform:

> Laws which limit immigration must be preserved in full force and effect, but the provisions contained in these laws that separate husbands from wives and parents from infant children are inhuman and not essential to the purpose or the efficacy of such laws.[49]

Republican platform:

> The Republican Party believes that in the interest of both native and foreign-born wage-earners, it is necessary to restrict immigration. Unrestricted immigration would result in widespread unemployment and in the breakdown of the American standard of living. Where, however, the law works undue hardships by depriving the immigrant of the comfort and society of those bound by close family ties, such modification should be adopted as will afford relief.
>
> We commend Congress for correcting defects for humanitarian reasons and for providing an effective system of examining prospective immigrants in their home countries.[50]

President: Herbert Hoover (Republican)

71st Congress (April 15, 1929–March 4, 1931)
Senate: 39 Democrats, 56 Republicans, 1 other
House: 163 Democrats, 267 Republicans, 1 other

72nd Congress (December 7, 1931–March 4, 1933)
Senate: 47 Democrats, 47 Republicans, 1 other
House: 218 Democrats, 214 Republicans, 1 other

1932 Election

Farmer-Labor platform:

> Total exclusion of all immigrants until the period of unemployment has terminated.[51]

Republican platform:

> The restriction of immigration is a Republican policy. Our party formulated and enacted into law the quota system, which for the first time has made possible an adequate control of foreign immigration.
>
> Rigid examination of applicants in foreign countries prevented the coming of criminals and other undesirable classes, while other provisions of the law have enabled the President to suspend immi-

[49]Ibid., p. 276.
[50]Ibid., p. 289.
[51]Ibid., p. 335.

gration of foreign wage-earners who otherwise, directly or indirectly, would have increased unemployment among native-born and legally resident foreign-born wage-earners in this country. As a result, immigration is now less than at any time during the past one hundred years.

We favor the continuance and strict enforcement of our present laws upon this subject.[52]

President: Franklin Roosevelt (Democrat)

73rd Congress (March 4, 1933–June 18, 1934)
Senate: 60 Democrats, 35 Republicans, 1 other
House: 310 Democrats, 117 Republicans, 5 others
74th Congress (January 3, 1935–June 20, 1936)
Senate: 69 Democrats, 25 Republicans, 2 others
House: 322 Democrats, 102 Republicans, 10 others

1936 Election

No immigration sections in the major party platforms.

President: Franklin Roosevelt (Democrat)

75th Congress (January 5, 1937–June 16, 1938)
Senate: 75 Democrats, 16 Republicans, 4 others
House: 333 Democrats, 88 Republicans, 13 others
76th Congress (January 3, 1939–January 3, 1941)
Senate: 69 Democrats, 23 Republicans, 4 others
House: 260 Democrats, 169 Republicans, 4 others

1940 Election

Republican platform:

> We favor the strict enforcement of all laws controlling the entry of aliens. The activities of undesirable aliens should be investigated and those who seek to change by force and violence the American form of government should be deported.[53]

Socialist platform:

> We oppose alien and sedition legislation as directed toward the abridgment of civil liberty.
>
> We condemn the use of immigration laws to return, directly or

[52] Ibid., p. 346.

[53] Ibid., p. 393.

indirectly, refugees to the tyranny of totalitarian states and favor a more generous treatment of them. America must be kept the land of political asylum.[54]

President: Franklin Roosevelt (Democrat)

77th Congress (January 3, 1941–December 16, 1942)
Senate: 66 Democrats, 28 Republicans, 2 others
House: 268 Democrats, 162 Republicans, 5 others

78th Congress (January 6, 1943–December 19, 1944)
Senate: 57 Democrats, 38 Republicans, 1 other
House: 222 Democrats, 208 Republicans, 4 others

1944 Election

Socialist platform:

we pledge ourselves to work for American hospitality to war refugees and the end of the exclusion of Asiatic peoples. The law applying to the Chinese the general provisions concerning immigration and admitting them to citizenship, should be extended to all Asiatic countries.[55]

President: Franklin Roosevelt (Democrat)

79th Congress (January 3, 1945–August 2, 1946)
Senate: 56 Democrats, 38 Republicans, 1 other
House: 242 Democrats, 190 Republicans, 2 others

80th Congress (January 3, 1947–December 3, 1948)
Senate: 45 Democrats, 51 Republicans
House: 188 Democrats, 245 Republicans, 1 other

1948 Election

Democratic platform:

We pledge ourselves to legislation to admit a minimum of 400,000 displaced persons found eligible for United States citizenship without discrimination as to race or religion. We condemn the undemocratic action of the Republican 80th Congress in passing an inadequate and bigoted bill for this purpose, which law imposes un-American restrictions based on race and religion upon such admissions.[56]

[54]Ibid., p. 398.

[55]Ibid., p. 416.

[56]Ibid., p. 435.

Progressive platform:

> The Progressive Party calls for the repeal of the anti-Catholic anti-semitic Displaced Persons Act of 1948 which permits the entry into the United States of fascists and collaborators. We call for the enactment of legislation to open our doors in the true American tradition to the victims of fascist persecution.
>
> We advocate the repeal of discriminatory immigration laws based upon race, national origin, religion, or political belief.[57]

Socialist platform:

> The United States, whose greatness has been built by the creativity of generations of immigrants from all parts of the world, must open its doors to those displaced persons who have no home. At the very least, 400,000 such persons can be admitted under unused immigration quotas from the war years. Full support for the International Refugee Organization is essential as long as the present emergency exists, but the goal must be the free and unrestricted movement of peoples, according to their own choice, throughout the world.
>
> All forms of discriminating barriers against immigration on grounds of race, color or national origin must be abolished.[58]

President: Harry Truman (Democrat)

81st Congress (January 3, 1949–January 2, 1951)
Senate: 54 Democrats, 42 Republicans
House: 263 Democrats, 171 Republicans, 1 other

82nd Congress (January 3, 1951–July 7, 1952)
Senate: 49 Democrats, 47 Republicans
House: 234 Democrats, 199 Republicans, 1 other

1952 Election

Democratic platform:

> Solution of the problem of refugees from communism and over-population has become a permanent part of the foreign policy program of the Democratic Party. We pledge continued cooperation with other free nations to solve it.
>
> We pledge continued aid to refugees from communism and the enactment of President Truman's proposals for legislation in this field. In this way we can give hope and courage to the victims of Soviet brutality and can carry on the humanitarian tradition of the Displaced Persons Act.

[57]Ibid., pp. 441, 442.

[58]Ibid., pp. 460, 457.

Subversive elements must be screened out and prevented from entering our land, but the gates must be left open for practical numbers of desirable persons from abroad whose immigration to this country provides an invigorating infusion into the stream of American life, as well as a significant contribution to the solution of the world refugee and over-population problems.

We pledge continuing revision of our immigration and naturalization laws to do away with any unjust and unfair practices against national groups which have contributed some of our best citizens. We will eliminate distinctions between nativeborn and naturalized citizens. We want no "second-class" citizens in free America.[59]

President: Dwight Eisenhower (Republican)

83rd Congress (January 3, 1953–December 2, 1954)
Senate: 47 Democrats, 48 Republicans, 1 other
House: 210 Democrats, 221 Republicans, 1 other

84th Congress (January 5, 1955–July 27, 1956)
Senate: 48 Democrats, 47 Republicans, 1 other
House: 232 Democrats, 203 Republicans

1956 Election

Democratic platform:

America's long tradition of hospitality and asylum for those seeking freedom, opportunity, and escape from oppression, has been besmirched by the delays, failures and broken promises of the Republican Administration. The Democratic Party favors prompt revision of the immigration and nationality laws to eliminate unfair provisions under which admissions to this country depend upon quotas based upon the accident of national origin. Proper safeguards against subversive elements should be provided. Our immigration procedures must reflect the principles of our Bill of Rights.

We favor eliminating the provisions of law which charge displaced persons admitted to our shores against quotas for future years. Through such "mortgages" of future quotas, thousands of qualified persons are being forced to wait long years before they can hope for admission.

We also favor more liberal admission of relatives to eliminate the unnecessary tragedies of broken families.

We favor elimination of unnecessary distinctions between native-born and naturalized citizens. There should be no "second class" citizenship in the United States.

[59]Ibid., p. 477.

> The administration of the Refugee Relief Act of 1953 has been a disgrace to our country. Rescue has been denied to innocent, defenseless and suffering people, the victims of war and the aftermath of wars. The purpose of the Act has been defeated by Republican mismanagement.[60]

Republican platform:

> The Republican Party supports an immigration policy which is in keeping with the traditions of America in providing a haven for oppressed peoples, and which is based on equality of treatment, freedom from implications of discrimination between racial, nationality and religious groups, and flexible enough to conform to changing needs and conditions.
>
> We believe that such a policy serves our self-interest, reflects our responsibility for world leadership and develops maximum cooperation with other nations in resolving problems in this area.
>
> We support the President's program submitted to the 84th Congress to carry out needed modifications in existing law and to take such further steps as may be necessary to carry out our traditional policy.
>
> In that concept, this Republican Administration sponsored the Refugee Relief Act to provide asylum for thousands of refugees, expellees and displaced persons, and undertook in the face of Democrat opposition to correct the inequities in existing law and to bring our immigration policies in line with the dynamic needs of the country and principles of equity and justice.
>
> We believe also that the Congress should consider the extension of the Refugee Relief Act of 1953 in resolving this difficult refugee problem which resulted from world conflict. To all this we give our wholehearted support.[61]

President: Dwight Eisenhower (Republican)

85th Congress (January 3, 1957–August 24, 1958)
  Senate: 49 Democrats, 47 Republicans
  House: 233 Democrats, 200 Republicans

86th Congress (January 7, 1959–September 1, 1960)
  Senate: 64 Democrats, 34 Republicans
  House: 282 Democrats, 152 Republicans

[60] Ibid., p. 528.

[61] Ibid., p. 555.

1960 Election

Democratic platform:

> We shall adjust our immigration, nationality and refugee policies to eliminate discrimination and to enable members of scattered families abroad to be united with relatives already in our midst.
>
> The national-origins quota system of limiting immigration contradicts the founding principles of this nation. It is inconsistent with our belief in the rights of man. The system was instituted after World War I as a policy of deliberate discrimination by a Republican Administration and Congress.
>
> The revision of immigration and nationality laws we seek will implement our belief that enlightened immigration, naturalization and refugee policies and humane administration of them are important aspects of our foreign policy.
>
> These laws will bring greater skills to our land, reunite families, permit the United States to meet its fair share of world programs of rescue and rehabilitation, and take advantage of immigration as an important factor in the growth of the American economy.
>
> In this World Refugee Year it is our hope to achieve admission of our fair share of refugees. We will institute policies to alleviate suffering among the homeless wherever we are able to extend our aid.
>
> We must remove the distinctions between native-born and naturalized citizens to assure full protection of our laws to all. There is no place in the United States for "second-class citizenship."
>
> The protections provided by due process, right of appeal, and statutes of limitation, can be extended to non-citizens without hampering the security of our nation.
>
> We commend the Democratic Congress for the initial steps that have recently been taken toward liberalizing changes in immigration law. However, this should not be a piecemeal project and we are confident that a Democratic President in cooperation with Democratic Congresses will again implant a humanitarian and liberal spirit in our nation's immigration and citizenship policies.[62]

Republican platform:

> Immigration has historically been a great factor in the growth of the United States, not only in numbers but in the enrichment of ideas that immigrants have brought with them. This Republican Administration has given refuge to over 32,000 victims of Communist tyranny from Hungary, ended needless delay in processing applications for naturalization, and has urged other enlightened legislation to liberalize existing restrictions.

[62]Ibid., pp. 577–78.

Immigration has been reduced to the point where it does not provide the stimulus to growth that it should, nor are we fulfilling our obligation as a haven for the oppressed. Republican conscience and Republican policy require that:

The annual number of immigrants we accept be at least doubled.

Obsolete immigration laws be amended by abandoning the outdated 1920 census data as a base and substituting the 1960 census.

The guidelines of our immigration policy be based upon judgment of the individual merit of each applicant for admission and citizenship.[63]

President: John Kennedy (Democrat)

87th Congress (January 3, 1961–October 13, 1962)
Senate: 65 Democrats, 35 Republicans
House: 260 Democrats, 172 Republicans

88th Congress (January 9, 1963–October 3, 1964)
Senate: 67 Democrats, 33 Republicans
House: 258 Democrats, 177 Republicans

1964 Election

Democratic platform:

In 1960 we proposed to—

"Adjust our immigration, nationality and refugee policies to eliminate discrimination and to enable members of scattered families abroad to be united with relatives already in our midst.

"The national-origins quota system of limiting immigration contradicts the founding principles of this nation. It is inconsistent with our belief in the rights of men."

The immigration law amendments proposed by the Administration, and now before Congress, by abolishing the national-origin quota system, will eliminate discrimination based upon race and place of birth and will facilitate the reunion of families.

The Cuban Refugee Program begun in 1961 has resettled over 81,000 refugees, who are now self-supporting members of 1,800 American communities. The Chinese Refugee Program, begun in 1962, provides for the admission to the United States of 12,000 Hong Kong refugees from Red China.[64]

Republican platform: pledge of—

immigration legislation seeking to re-unite families and continuation of the "Fair Share" Refugee Program.[65]

[63]Ibid., p. 620.
[64]Ibid., p. 652.
[65]Ibid., p. 683.

President: Lyndon Johnson (Democrat)

89th Congress (January 4, 1965–October 22, 1965: first session)
Senate: 68 Democrats, 32 Republicans
House: 294 Democrats, 140 Republicans

Appendix B
Linkage of Social Security and Immigration Records

Although the action described in this appendix comes after the period ending in 1965, it is worth noting that steps have in fact been taken to link social security and immigration records. In 1972 an act for amendment of the Social Security Act dealt in one section with the method of issuance of social security numbers.[1] It added a new subsection to provide for the issuance of such numbers to several additional classes of individuals, including:

(I) "to aliens at the time of their lawful admission . . . either for permanent residence or under other authority of law permitting them to engage in employment . . . and to other aliens at such time as their status is so changed as to make it lawful for them to engage in such employment."

(II) "to any individual who is an applicant for or recipient of benefits under any program financed in whole or in part from Federal funds. . . ."

(III) "to other individuals not in possession of a social security number, "but only after such investigation as is necessary to establish . . . the identity of such individual . . . and the fact that such individual is a citizen or a noncitizen who is not, because of his alien status, prohibited from engaging in employment."

Also added by amendment was another subsection stating that:

> The Secretary shall require of applicants for social security account numbers such evidence as may be necessary to establish the age, citizenship, or alien status, and true identity of such applicants. . . .

In compliance with the above provisions, the Social Security Administration moved to require proof of citizenship, or, in the case of aliens, proof of admission under terms that allow employment before issuance of a

[1]Section 137 of the Act of October 30, 1972 (86 Stat. 1329), amending sect. 205(c)(2) of the Social Security Act.

social security number. Notice was published on August 7, 1973 of an amendment to the social security regulations proposed by the then Acting Commissioner of Social Security, with the approval of the Secretary of Health, Education, and Welfare. The proposed rule was for (1) assignment of social security numbers to aliens at the time of lawful admission for permanent residence or otherwise on receiving permission to engage in employment, and (2) to direct the Secretary "to require applicants for social security numbers to furnish evidence to establish their age, citizenship, or alien status, and true identity," and to give evidence if an earlier number had been issued to them. The proposed amendment would also authorize the issuance of social security numbers to aliens "for a nonwork purpose but without authority to engage in employment." A significant added provision was for notification to be sent to the Immigration and Naturalization Service if an alien applicant refuses to provide the information.[2] The earlier practice had been to give such information to the Service only in response to a specific request.

Implementation of the proposed rule was announced, effective March 13, 1974.[3] Several months later notice was given of a proposed further amendment of the social security regulations:

> The proposed amendment authorizes the Social Security Administration to notify the Immigration and Naturalization Service when an alien fails, after a reasonable period of time, to produce appropriate Immigration and Naturalization Service documents or produces invalid or expired documents to establish his alien status in applying for a social security number for any purpose, when an alien applies for a social security number to be used for employment purposes and cannot or does not establish that he is permitted to work in the United States, and when earnings are reported to the record of an alien who has been assigned a social security number to be used only for nonwork purposes.[4]

The control system proposed here, in short, included an identification requirement for applicants for social security numbers, identifying numbers for aliens not entitled to take employment, and reporting to the immigration authorities of aliens who do not or cannot establish their lawful admission for permanent residence or who take employment without the authorization to do so. It thus promised a more effective identification of alien status and control of alien employment than had been possible before within the limits of social security coverage. Uncovered

[2] *Federal Register*, 38 (151):21271–72, August 7, 1973.
[3] Ibid., 39 (54):10238–40, March 19, 1974.
[4] Ibid., 39 (122):22428, June 24, 1974.

employment would still remain a problem until more of the labor force was brought under social security, or until workers in uncovered employment were required to show proof of identity by means of birth certificate, alien registration card, or other identification.[5]

[5]For further discussion see the section, "On SSA/INS Cooperation," pp. 89–95 of *Preliminary Report*, Washington, D.C.: Domestic Council Committee on Illegal Aliens, December 1976.

Index of Names

Political Party Notation*

Major Parties

D–Democrat
F–Federalist
R–Republican
W–Whig

Other Parties

AL–American Labor
AP–American Party
Co–Coalition candidate
Cons–Conservative
FL–Farm Labor
FS–Free Soil
Ind–Independent
L–Liberal
NR–National Republican
NS–not stated
PD–Popular Democrat
Peo–People's Party
Pop–Populist
PR–Progressive Republican
Pro–Progressive
S–Socialist
UD–Union Democrat
UL–Union Labor
Un–Unionist
UR–Union Republican

*Party affiliation from *Biographical Directory of the American Congress, 1774–1971,* 91st Congress, 1st session, S. Doc. No. 92–8, U.S. Government Printing Office, Washington, D.C., 1971.

Index of Subjects